# THE ESSENTIAL PSYCHO-CYBERNETICS

# THE ESSENTIAL PSYCHO-CYBERNETICS

## THE SCIENCE OF SUCCESS

CONTAINS COMPLETE AND
ORIGINAL EDITIONS
OF 4 CLASSIC BESTSELLERS,
PLUS BONUS MATERIAL

**MAXWELL MALTZ**, MD, FICS

ST. MARTIN'S
ESSENTIALS
NEW YORK

Published in the United States by St. Martin's Essentials,
an imprint of St. Martin's Publishing Group

www.stmartins.com

The Library of Congress Cataloging-in-Publication Data is available upon request.

ISBN 978-1-250-33508-1 (trade paperback)
ISBN 978-1-250-33507-4 (ebook)

Our books may be purchased in bulk for promotional, educational, or
business use. Please contact your local bookseller or the Macmillan Corporate
and Premium Sales Department at 1-800-221-7945, extension 5442, or by email at
MacmillanSpecialMarkets@macmillan.com.

*The Conquest of Frustration* was first published in 1965

*The Search for Self-Respect* was first published in 1964

*Live and Be Free Thru Psycho-Cybernetics* was first published in 1969

*The Magic Power of Self-Image Psychology* was first published in 1964

*Thoughts to Live By* was first published in 1975

First St. Martin's Essentials Edition: 2024

10  9  8  7  6  5  4  3  2  1

# CONTENTS

# PREFACE

I WAS FIRST INTRODUCED TO THE TEACHINGS OF DR. MAXWELL MALTZ IN MAY of 1987. At the time I was just starting out in business as a fitness trainer, and one of my first clients, Jack, a successful real estate broker, asked me if I had read *Psycho-Cybernetics*.

After telling Jack I hadn't read it, I asked for more information. He told me that *Psycho-Cybernetics* was "the bible of self-development."

As soon as our session ended, I drove to the bookstore, picked up a copy, and began reading. I was enthralled with the book's timeless message and couldn't stop thinking about how it applied to my life.

Upon finishing the book, I looked for everything I could find that was written by Dr. Maltz. Over the next month, I bought every book I could find that had Dr. Maltz' name on it, and I spent every spare moment studying his teachings and applying them to my life.

Little did I know or imagine at the time, that I would eventually become the heir to the Maltz library and business, that I would be involved in an updated and expanded version of *Psycho-Cybernetics*, that I would be coaching and consulting with business executives, salespeople, doctors, lawyers, teachers, coaches and world-class athletes, passing on the amazing and life-transforming teachings of self-image psychology.

As one thought and action lead to another, my fascination with Dr. Maltz' teachings took another turn for the better when I began a co-venture with Deborah Herman of Thought Works Books, a division of Micro Publishing Media. With her help, we are keeping the Maltz legacy alive by bringing the good doctor's books that have inexplicably fallen out of the public eye, or that needed a slight refreshing, together in this new single volume with our new publishing partner, St. Martin's Press.

If you loved *Psycho-Cybernetics*, I am certain you will adore the other books that Dr. Maltz wrote and that Thought Works Books rediscovered and encouraged. When you apply Dr. Maltz' words of wisdom, you will discover, as I did, that they are timeless because they are true. You can apply his principles at any age and for virtually any endeavor. I began benefitting from his advice straight out of college, and I'm still doing so today.

Enjoy this book, which brings together the best Maltz classics into one single library, and watch as your life continues to grow and expand in any and all areas that are important to you.

—Matt Furey
President of *The Psycho-Cybernetics Foundation*
Psycho-Cybernetics.com

# ABOUT THE AUTHOR

DR. MAXWELL MALTZ (MARCH 10, 1889–APRIL 7, 1975) WAS AN AMERICAN cosmetic surgeon who created his self-improvement phenomenon, *Psycho-Cybernetics*, at age 61, after an already varied, colorful, and exceptionally successful career as a surgeon, writer, and speaker. Published in 1960, *Psycho-Cybernetics* has sold over 30 million copies since its original printing and remains a classic of self-help, self-improvement, and personal development.

According to Dr. Maltz, Psycho-Cybernetics involves steering your mind to a productive, useful goal *to* reach peace of mind. It is the roadmap to improve self-image and create a better quality of life. This theme permeates his flagship book and all the classic books that followed. Dr. Maltz expanded his application of the principles in his additional volumes and added practical examples for applying them in daily life.

In *Psycho-Cybernetics* and all the following books, Dr. Maxwell Maltz leveraged his background as a plastic surgeon to boldly assert that how we see ourselves changes everything. He believed that all aspects of our lives will align if we see ourselves as the Creator sees us.

This spiritual revelation led him down the path of human psychology and studying the value and importance of a healthy self-image.

Dr. Maltz was inspired to move from treating "outer scars" to "inner scars" after seeing some patients continuing to have feelings of unhappiness, unworthiness as well as personal insecurities that were not cured through cosmetic surgery, even though they and Dr. Maltz believed they would feel happy after he gave them the perfect new faces they desired.

Dr. Maltz first wrote of this discovery in his book *New Faces, New Futures.* In this groundbreaking book, Dr. Maltz suggested that many people "see themselves" inaccurately, their perceptions distorted by unchallenged and often erroneous beliefs embedded in their subconscious minds. After a decade of counseling hundreds of patients with his evolving "success conditioning techniques," Dr. Maltz published his findings in 1960 in the original *Psycho-Cybernetics*.

*Psycho-Cybernetics* became an instant bestseller, making Dr. Maltz one of the most in-demand motivational speakers in the 1960s and early 1970s. He went on to amass a wealth of "case history" material. He produced numerous seminars, workshops, radio broadcasts, and more than a dozen books, all applying Psycho-Cybernetics to different purposes, from business success to athletic achievement to sex life improvement.

We continue to make Dr. Maltz's timeless work available to a new generation.

# BOOK ONE

# THE CONQUEST OF
# FRUSTRATION

# CONTENTS

# SUMMARY

The Conquest of Frustration is the action program by the renowned author of *Psycho-Cybernetics* that points you away from disappointment and despair toward a happy and zestful life. It shows the reader how to implement the principles of the most life-changing self-help discovery as relevant today as when Dr. Maltz wrote his flagship book *Psycho-Cybernetics* in the early 1960s.

Psycho-Cybernetics means steering your mind to a productive, useful goal. Dr. Maltz wrote this subsequent book to reinforce his belief that when we are overcome with frustration, we steer our minds to unproductive, useless, destructive, annihilating goals. He recommends setting positive goals every day.

As "it is the person who finds no purpose, no meaning in life who feels failure so intensely. You must make your own purpose . . . you must make your own meaning. No one else can do this for you."

# 1

# THE ART OF OVERCOMING FRUSTRATION

PAX VOBISCUM. PEACE BE WITH YOU. BUT HOW DO YOU ACHIEVE THIS PEACE, this peace of mind which takes you away from your negative feelings, which helps you conquer frustration?

We will study this all-important question, and we will analyze the forces you must harness. We will also study the components of frustration and discuss the art of overcoming these negative forces.

Not too long ago, I gave a three-day seminar in Salinas, California, and after that, another seminar in San Luis Obispo, a lovely little town. At this latter meeting, I was quite surprised to see the warden of the local men's colony—a penitentiary accommodating over 2,000 people. He was there with his educational staff. We became friends, and I visited the colony—a beautiful place. The men serving time there were learning various trades. We talked about setting up a self-fulfillment program in *Psycho-Cybernetics: The Conquest of Frustration*. I thought it was a wonderful idea, and we arranged to start it soon.

Two days later, I left California and returned home to New York. When I got to my office, there was a large envelope addressed to me from the Department of Justice, Bureau of Prisons. I thought, "Now what have I done wrong?" I opened the envelope. Inside were two letters and a pamphlet. One letter was from the Director of Education of one of the largest federal penitentiaries in our country, requesting that I come to the graduating exercises of a course in Psycho-Cybernetics they had just completed in the penitentiary. I was amazed, for I didn't even know it existed. There was also a letter from the main teacher, a man who was serving over fifteen years, who has been a marvelous teacher in Psycho-Cybernetics over a period of three years—and I was overwhelmed. He hoped and prayed that I would appear. I immediately wired them that I would be there, and so I participated in the graduation exercises of men who were serving sentences for a long period of time.

And this reminded me of another story; you can find it in greater detail in my book *Creative Living for Today*. It was about a woman named Anna, whose three-month-old infant was torn from her and trampled to death during the Nazi occupation of Poland in 1942. She was thrown into a concentration camp, her husband in another. She thought him dead. Although heartbroken, she refused to let her spirit be crushed. She refused to admit defeat when she worked in a slave labor factory.

Nothing could destroy her self-respect. The German guards beat her and scarred her face, but she refused to yield to frustration and despair. Eventually, she was freed when the Nazis were defeated. Her husband, too, was freed. They found each other again. Her son, born in America, is now studying to be a doctor.

She came to see me at my office, hoping I could remove the scar from her face so that her son could see her as she really was. The operation was successful, but the beauty of her face could never match the beauty of her self-image—an image that refused to be buried under the heavy weight of terrifying persecution.

These problems of overcoming frustrations are arresting since the frustrations involved imprisonment. I mention them because they are so illustrative of an imprisonment that is real and physical.

But you are outside of prison—aren't you? Or are you? Is your prison better or worse than an actual prison? Truly, this is debatable. For it is a torturous prison, an antisocial prison, the prison without, the prison you create inside yourself through frustration, hiding behind locked doors and walking away from the realities of life, making your image of yourself shrink to the size of a small potato. Who are you? Are you in prison, or can you be free from the dead weight of negative feelings? This is what the problem is all about, as I see it.

Recently, I spoke in Washington to an assemblage of insurance people— and I saw Washington burn. *Pax vobiscum*! Peace be with you! Where is this Peace with our country burning? Which is the worse conflagration, the outside one or the fires within us—the hatred, the bigotry, the resentment within us? We hear talk of better policing, but there are not enough policemen to police this world; there are not enough UNs to police this world. This business of creative Psycho-Cybernetics is self-fulfillment—peace of mind—and it starts with knowing how to police yourself first. You can't be a friend to others unless you are a friend to yourself. You can't be a success with others unless you are a success with yourself. You can't have the love of others unless you have the love of yourself as SOMEBODY! Somebody capable of blunders, but someone capable of rising above them. The mistake-maker but, thank God, the mistake-breaker. Someone overcome by frustration, yet someone able to rise above—to conquer it.

You wake up in the morning, and your day is reality—but what are you preparing to do with this reality?

Oh, how vital are these first few minutes of your day! You look in the mirror. What kind of day is it going to be, Betsy, baby? What kind of day is it going to be, Charlie, old boy? You have to make a decision.

You see two people in the mirror. You see the person of frustration, and you see the person of confidence. Who will win out—inside of you?

Who are you going to be those first few minutes of your day? If you permit some frustration of the past to insinuate itself into your day, you have lost. Your day will be fruitless, self-destructive. On the other hand, suppose you look in the mirror and say: "Betsy, baby, Charlie, my boy, this is my day. Today I fulfill myself, and even if I fall flat on my face, I'm going to stand up and keep punching until I reach my goal." Well! You are reaching out toward utility, toward dynamic living, toward your goals. You are planning success—and even if you don't reach your goals that day, chances are you will reach them another time. The baby who reaches out with open arms to his mother feels a faith that she will answer his need for affection. You, at a later age, must re-awaken in yourself this same kind of deep faith.

In the final analysis, the conquest of frustration depends on you and no one else. No one can make you unhappy without your consent. No one can make you lonely without your consent. No one can fill you with frustration without your consent.

## THE DISPLACED PERSON

Are you a displaced person? Ask yourself—are you? Think about it. Just the other day, I looked in the papers and saw some pictures of the harrowing situation in Vietnam—mothers and children displaced, tragedy written on their faces. Displaced people—almost as bad as during the Nazi occupation. Are you, despite your sense of freedom, a displaced person? Ask yourself that. You are displaced if you live in your own prison. You are displaced if you are filled with frustration.

Now, by frustration, I don't mean the daily complaints we all have—the normal frustrations we experience during twenty-four hours of living. I'm talking about chronic frustration, piling on your mental back fifty pounds of extra mental and spiritual weight—the old heartaches, the old tragedies, the old guilt, the old misfortunes, the old loneliness of a yesterday which should remain a yesterday.

The conquest of frustration, the quest for happiness, the business of creative living to achieve peace of mind starts with living now. You've got to live now—n-o-w. Forget yesterday, lost in the vacuum of time, buried deep, deep in the tomb of time. The conquest of frustration starts now! You must realize this.

Still, it isn't worth anything if you don't turn these thoughts into golden opportunities, if you don't transform them into creative performance. In creative performance, you've got to be your own plastic surgeon. You have to be your own creative sculptor. Take these thoughts and mold them and shape them into things of beauty. Use the principles of Psycho-Cybernetics— which means living in the present and steering your mind to productive, useful goals.

Let us hear from some people who have used Psycho-Cybernetics as a springboard to better living. Here is one comment from a man serving a sentence in Leavenworth Penitentiary:

To say that the use and practice of the principles of Psycho-Cybernetics, as laid out by Dr. Maxwell Maltz, have been beneficial to me would be a gross understatement. Learning to control my emotions and not feel anger at all, real or imagined wrong, has been the principal achievement I have made by studying and using the principles of Psycho-Cybernetics.

Here is another one:

In preparing myself to re-enter society as a productive and useful member, I have in these past four years given considerable thought along the lines of reestablishing my values and attitudes. Although I have learned a beneficial and worthwhile trade to support my family, there was still something lacking. Not being able to put my finger on it, I enlisted in various courses of self-help programs to try to fill that empty something within me . . . I enrolled in a Psycho-Cybernetics class. As the weeks of instruction and study passed, I was pleasantly surprised to find that I had developed an Inner Peace within myself. Re-evaluating my self-image through conscientious practice of Psycho-Cybernetics exercises of a positive mental attitude has filled the void in my life. I am now prepared to return to society and my family, thanks to Psycho-Cybernetics.

Are you prepared to return to society? Are you even part of society? If you are a displaced person through negative feelings, resentment, frustration, you don't belong to society yet. You will build your concentration camp a hundred feet tall unless you learn to tear the wall of Jericho down, down, down, so that you can see your image, a true image, an image in God's image. The whole business of living is to fulfill yourself, to enhance your sense of self-respect. When you do this, you express the God-like quality within you. Are you prepared to stop being a displaced person? Are you prepared to stand on your mental and spiritual feet, opening the doors of the jail into which you put yourself?

Here's another comment:

Since enrolling in the Psycho-Cybernetics workshops, I can honestly and truthfully say there has been a definite change in my mental outlook towards many things. Where I would look on the darker or negative side of things and find only darkness, now I am slowly but surely seeing the brighter side of my everyday life. Use of the principles of Psycho-Cybernetics has helped me in many ways to a better life and a brighter future.

Could you write this—now? Maybe not? Still, let's see how you feel after reading these chapters and then re-reading them.

Now let us consider five roadblocks that lead to frustration:

1. *You worry after you have made a decision.* Worry, at times, has validity. If you have five ways of reaching your goal and you can't reach the goal taking the five ways, you are anxious. Which road should you take? You must make up your mind. But once you have made your decision, reach out for the goal and fight for it. Then stop worrying about your decision!

2. *You worry about today, yesterday, and tomorrow.* How many of us would like to escape to that lovely island in the sun, forgetting everything, all our tensions, where we could sit under a coconut tree eating luscious coconuts? The opposite of this is constant worry—about today, yesterday, tomorrow—and it leads only to frustration.

3. *You try to do too many things at one time.* You must carefully select your goals and accept your limitations. Set goals you can achieve, goals you're equipped to achieve. Set reasonable time limits. And you can do many things at *different times.* Julius Caesar couldn't do two things at one time—he did two things at two different times.

4. *You wrestle with problems all day.* If something defies solution, you sleep with it, not on it. You forget that there are three eight-hour periods to a day: eight hours for work, eight hours for rest, and eight hours for sleep. Who asked you to bring the troubles of your office to your home? Who asked you to bring the troubles of your home to your office? You refuse to realize that those middle eight hours are yours, and in these hours, you are a king or a queen who can develop pursuits or hobbies to give you pleasure.

5. *You refuse to relax.* You toss and turn on your pillow, trying to count sheep jumping through a window. You stay up all night, wondering if you gave yourself the right count. Stop counting. Get your sleep and attack your new day in the morning.

These are your five roadblocks—emotional dead ends that will lead you only to despair.

Now, here is the other side of the coin—four steps on the road to relaxation:

1. *You forgive others.* Oh, how difficult that is! Forgiveness with no strings attached; a clean, clean slate. No forgiveness on the install-ment plan—the kind that says I love you today, I hate you tomorrow.

2. *You forgive yourself.* This is a human achievement. Alexander Pope said, "To forgive is Divine." We all want to be human, not divine, of course, so let's just try to be human, realizing our capacity for error but also our capacity for rising above it through forgiveness. Forgive others. Forgive yourself.

3. *You see yourself at your best,* as a person of confidence, not as a person of frustration. You must make the decision. No one can make it for you.

4. *You keep up with yourself.* If you try to carry someone else's image, you are beginning to practice frustration. You are beginning to walk into your own concentration camp. You are worse off than many inmates of our penitentiaries.

Five roadblocks to frustration, four principles of relaxation. Stop being a displaced person and start walking out of the jail you have created for yourself.

## THE ART OF COMMUNICATION

Now—how do you do this? Through the art of communication. How do you communicate? Let me tell you a story.

About a year ago, I went to Atlanta, Georgia, to address eight hundred people of the Sales and Executive Marketing Group, celebrating their 25th Anniversary. In honor of the occasion for me, a Yankee from New York coming down to At-lanta, Georgia, there was a young boy named Ray who was fourteen years old. He had a horn, and he was going to blow his horn and play "Yankee Doodle" for me. Behind him was a boy, two years older, taller, with a drum. When Ray blew his horn, the other boy would beat the drum. Ray took the horn and put it to his lips. Nothing came out—not a sound. I looked at him, standing there so de-jected. It didn't occur to me that the boy had come unprepared to play that song to eight hundred people. I was sure he had practiced for weeks—at least—but he couldn't blow his horn. He couldn't communicate.

He stood there for a while, wondering what had happened. Then he took the mouthpiece off, put a new mouthpiece on, put the horn to his lips. Again, nothing came out. My heart went out to this boy in his utter dejection. Defeated, he moved listlessly to a huge round table at the rear of the room where a huge piece of apple pie and cheese and a glass of milk had been set out for him, but he didn't see them. He sat, head bowed in shame. And so I got up, and I said: "Ladies and gentlemen, the topic of my talk tonight is: 'Ray, who couldn't blow his horn.'"

And I told them about the Ray within every one of us who, because of some fear, panic, or frustration, cannot communicate—cannot blow his horn.

And I also told them the story of another Ray, an eighteen-year-old second-year medical student who wanted to be a doctor and could not recite in class, could not communicate, could not blow his horn.

I was this Ray. When the professor of pathology called on me to quiz me orally, I was in a panic even though I knew my subject. I could not communicate. I thought that the eighty fellow students who looked at me were angry at me, wanted me to fail. And so I did. I sat down defeated. Time after time, the same thing happened to me in these oral quizzes.

But I had such a great desire to be a doctor that I refused to let this fear overcome me. I remembered that when I took written examinations, that when I looked through a microscope at a specimen slide I had to identify, when I didn't see the faces of the professor and the students, I was completely relaxed. I wrote down what I saw and got an "A" for my efforts.

I suddenly resolved that the next time the professor gave me an oral quiz, I would make believe I was looking at a slide through a huge microscope, and I would pay no attention to my audience. And, sure enough, the next time it happened, I was relaxed, I was confident, I answered properly without hesitation. I canceled out my fears. I overcame that terrifying feeling of frustration and passed the course with honors.

What am I trying to say? That, like Ray, I, at the age of eighteen, couldn't blow my horn—from panic, from frustration. But I overcame my fears. And if I can do it, you can do it. It doesn't matter where you come from. When we are afraid we all come from the same place.

Communicate? How do you communicate? Once, before a lecture, a man came over to me and said, "Dr. Maltz, you wrote a terrific book. The men of our insurance agency study a chapter a week, and we get a great bang out of it. Thank you for writing this wonderful book, *Psycho-Ceramics.*"

Well, I don't know what Psycho-Ceramics is, but I do know what Psycho-Cybernetics is. Psycho-Cybernetics is the conquest of frustration. Psycho-Cybernetics comes from a Greek word, kybernetes, or helmsman, referring to the man who steers a ship to port. And Psycho-Cybernetics means steering your mind to a productive, useful goal. I say that advisedly because, far too often, when we are overcome with frustration, we steer our minds to unproductive, useless, destructive, annihilating goals. Psycho-Cybernetics: steering your mind to a productive, useful goal. When you do that, you can't be frustrated even if you don't reach your goal. For, once you try to reach your goal, you are already there-nothing will stand in your way once you try.

Communication: Through communication, you will learn the art of overcoming frustration. But how do you achieve it?

After a lecture to eighteen hundred successful insurance men in Boston, one fellow from Texas asked if he could drive me to the airport to catch a plane to New York.

He said, "Dr. Maltz, I'd like you to do me a favor."

I said, "What is it?"

"I have a son."

"Well, what about your son? How old is he?"

"He's seventeen."

I said, "What's your problem?"

He said, "Doc, I can't communicate with my boy."

I said, "What do you mean you can't communicate with your boy?"

"I just can't."

"Whose fault is it?"

"I don't know."

"What do you mean you don't know?' You're the father."

"Doc, I don't want to get into an argument with you. I just can't communicate with my boy, and I'd like you to help me. Can you?"

I said, "I don't know if I can; I don't think you'll listen to me. Goodbye, Phillip. I'll see you some other time."

He said, "Come on, try me out."

I said, "I'll tell you what you do. When you get home, you go over to your boy, and you say: 'Son, forgive me. It may be that I may have made a mistake about you, but isn't it possible that you could have made a mistake about me?'" I looked at him; he had turned pale.

I said, "You'll never do it. Goodbye, Phillip. I'll see you some other time."

Two months elapsed. I was in my office, busy with noontime patients, my assistants, nurses. One nurse came over to me and said: "Long-distance."

I picked up the phone.

"I did it! I did it!" I heard.

"Who is this? You did what?"

"Doctor, it works, it works!"

"What works?"

"Don't you remember me—from Texas?"

I said, "Oh! oh!—just a minute."

I went into an adjoining room where I could listen, and this is what I heard: "For two months, I couldn't get near my boy, and one day we came home from church. He went into the kitchen, chewing on a hero sandwich. I was in my bedroom, chewing on my nails. And then, suddenly, I walked into the kitchen, and I said, 'Son, forgive me. It may be that I may have made a mistake about you, but isn't it possible that you could have made a mistake about me?'"

Excitedly, he told me that the boy acted as if he was suddenly ten feet tall. He almost crushed his father as he lifted him up in the air.

They wept together and felt close, the dearest of friends.

Now, it was love that made this successful businessman communicate. Communicate! How do you communicate? Well, the first principle of communication is that you have to learn how to communicate with yourself. You've got to keep the railroad tracks within you clean and bright, unencumbered by the negative feelings of frustration, inferiority, grief, loneliness, uncertainty, resentment, emptiness. That was yesterday. The business of living, whether you are three or thirty, six or sixty, nine or ninety, is to live. First, you communicate with yourself, then with others. For you can't be a friend to others unless you are a friend to yourself, and you can't be a success with others until you are a success with yourself. You can't receive love from others unless you give love to yourself.

Don't cry in your soup because you failed in some undertaking twenty years ago. That's another lifetime!

You belong to yourself now. Forget the time when you incarcerated yourself in your own jail, in your own concentration camp, because you were unhappy over some misfortune.

The business of living, the business of being successful, the business of rising above frustration is to rise—above a heartache, a misfortune, a guilt, a negative feeling, a feeling of hatred, a feeling of bigotry.

Finally, let us study what I call The Twelve Faces of Frustration. So you can see them clearly, and win out over them. So you can make yourself an expert in the art of overcoming frustration.

## THE TWELVE FACES OF FRUSTRATION

1. *You are not true to yourself.* You fail to support yourself with true loyalty.
2. *You use your imagination destructively*—as when you have no goal. If you want to use your imagination positively, you must think of a goal, somewhere to go, a goal within your capabilities. Don't try

to be the President of the United States—he's got enough trouble. Just be yourself with your own headaches, and the beauty of these headaches is that you can rise above them to a full state of emotional health.

3. *You don't know how to relax.* Your mind seethes with complexities.

4. *Your aim is unhappiness.* Yet happiness belongs to you like your eyes, like your heart, like your pulse. Reach for it without stepping on other people's toes—without stepping on your own toes with negative feelings.

5. *Frustration is a habit.* You've hypnotized yourself into believing that you can't amount to anything . . . and . . . so you won't. You talk to a child four years of age on the phone, and if you're full of frustration, the child will feel it. Positivize your habits!

6. *You don't accept your weaknesses.* But you've got to, for you're only human, and you need a floor upon which to stand.

7. *You have no compassion.* With compassion, you are somebody; without compassion, you are nobody.

8. *You wear a mask.* You play games with yourself and with other people.

9. *You repeat your mistakes.* You've got to *grow through* your *mistakes.*

10. *You retire from life.* But no human being, when alive, has the right to do this. I cannot see how you can retire from life without doing yourself a disservice.

11. *You consider yourself a loser.* If you want to conquer frustration, learn the art of the money-player; think like a winner. If you should lose, there's always the next day. Remember that just because you're a loser once doesn't mean you're going to lose forever.

12. *You don't accept yourself for what you are.* You live in fantasy. When you come back to earth, you find it is a frustrating place.

These are The Twelve Faces of Frustration. Face up to them! Outstare them! Win out over them!

If you don't, you will not find happiness—not in this world, not in any world. Money cannot buy it for you; realistic situations of value will find you wanting; people will not give it to you. For happiness at its base is something you create from inside yourself. Happiness is something you give *yourself.*

Let this be your motto. *Pax vobiscum!* Peace be with you.

# 2

# WINGING AWAY FROM FRUSTRATION

LET US CONTINUE OUR VERY NOBLE, VERY WORTHWHILE ENTERPRISE: CONQUEST. Not conquest of foreign lands, not conquest in the name of fatherland or motherland, not conquest for gold or treasure. A noble conquest—the conquest of the frustration that eats us.

This conquest—of frustration—is not despotic. It is liberation. Our aim is to enrich our lives, to increase our worth as human beings.

I mentioned that recently I was in Salinas and San Jose, California. In each place, I spoke to about two thousand people—maybe more. I was also in San Francisco where I spoke to three thousand people. I bring this out because of a letter I received from one of the prisoners who heard me speak at Leavenworth. After reading it, I knew that this one person—this prisoner—was more important to me than the thousands I spoke to on that lecture tour.

Here is the letter:

I am a convict here at Leavenworth Prison, who has had a very pleasurable first in his life. I am presently reading *Psycho-Cybernetics*. I never had the pleasure of seeing or hearing a great author. Dr. Maltz, I think you are a great plastic surgeon, great author, great public speaker—and a very great humanitarian. Because of your visit, I have a better insight of myself than ever before. With your book Psy*cho-Cybernetics,* the rest is up to me. You have a very fine way of throwing the problem up to a man and then telling him how to solve it. Dr. Maltz, what do you think would happen if every literate person in the world could simultaneously read *Psycho-Cybernetics?* My mind cannot comprehend the total possibilities in human relations for progress. Progress needs to be worldwide now, probably more than at any other time.

I would personally like to thank you and all the people of New York and here in Kansas who are responsible for enabling you to speak to us. I am a better man for the experience, and it would help greatly to balance the ledger of bad experience in my life. The ledger, might I add, is of my own making.

May I thank you greatly and send the best wishes possible to you and all of yours for a long, happy life.

This man, to me, is tremendously significant. We have talked about people in jail and of the many factors that force people to be less than what they are; and here, in one fell swoop, you see a man who, with all the odds against him, shut away in prison, expresses his desire to make something of himself.

Are you, too, in jail? Have you thrust yourself into your own jail?

Have you announced your own jail sentence by practicing frustration? Put bars around yourself?

Pronounced your own feeling of inferiority? Have you rejected yourself? Eliminated yourself from life?

Refused to pardon your own jail sentence because you have no sense of forgiveness?

If you have put yourself in jail, you must first realize what you have done—the destruction of your self-image. Then you can embark on a campaign of rehabilitation.

Let me tell you two little stories: After a recent lecture, a young woman came up to speak to me. She was attractive, with a pretty face and a nice figure—but she was obviously burdened with frustration and negative feelings. She told me—now read this carefully—that she felt invisible. In other words, she thought so little of herself that she felt invisible. Many people feel this way, and, in a sense, she was fortunate in that she could articulate this feeling. This gave her a chance to tackle the problem head-on and try to deal with it. If you are filled with negative feelings and frustration, you do feel invisible because you think that you are nobody.

You can overcome this feeling with more positive images of yourself, when you see in your mind your past successes and see in your imagination your good moments, picturing yourself as the kind of person you admire. Use the technique of money-players in sports: they think they're out to win, and even if they lose, they start punching again in the next contest—always out to win.

Here is another anecdote. In southern France, where I vacationed not too long ago, I was sitting on the beach near the Mediterranean. Nearby, I saw two men on a stone jetty, about to go fishing. They were in their thirties and, from their conversation, I gathered that they were good friends. They both rolled up their trousers and began to fish. One fisherman got a bite quickly and smoothly reeled in his fish. And then, to my surprise, the other fellow—in anger and frustration—just quit. Furious that his friend had caught the first fish, he just quit.

Don't laugh at this story, for, in doing so, you are expressing the tragedy of this man; because laughter is a release, by which you thank God that you're not in that position. It's like your laughter when you see a person slip on a banana peel and fall. You're saying, "Thank God that I'm not in his position." So don't laugh at the tragedy of this man who quit.

You should never make success dependent on another person. It should be up to you, entirely up to you. Suppose this man had been alone; he would have been more patient. But his friend beat him to the punch, so he just gave up.

Often, people, out of hurt feelings of frustration, give up in the game of life, and they stop fishing for success because they envy other people who out-compete them. But real success is based on what you can do with your own life, without worrying about others. When you reach success, your next step must be to help others share it, so they can join in your happiness. Because happiness, in the true sense, is the only commodity in the world that multiplies by division. The more you hand out, the more you have.

There is a little island off the coast of British Columbia whose stony crags are inhabited by a certain species of bird, called a "puffin." It's a small tufted bird—a tufted puffin. The most amazing characteristic of this bird is its habit of living in that spot only. Take it away from that spot, and it perishes. It has no resistance; it cannot overcome frustration.

It just *dies* if you take it away. This tufted puffin is so fragile that it cannot endure stress.

What kind of bird are you? Are you a tufted puffin . . . with sawdust stuffin'? What kind of bird are you? A mess . . . with stress? Or are you a goal-striver, a stress-survivor? For that's what success is all about. And if you don't survive stress, you are filled with frustration. *What kind of bird are* you? You are a bird; you have wings, symbolically speaking.

There is a poem by Victor Hugo entitled Wings.

*Be like the bird that,*
*Pausing in its flight awhile*
*On boughs too light,*
*Feels them give way, Yet sings!*
*Knowing she hath wings.*

## YOUR WINGS

Do you have wings? Of course you have. Your wings are your faith and your belief in yourself. And you can *soar* to your destination if you'll only give yourself a chance. Through frustration—and despair—you clip your wings, and you cannot get off the ground; you cannot even get to first base.

What kind of bird are you? A stuffed puffin? Or can you, with wings of faith and belief, *soar* to your destination? I believe you can; you have to believe it, too.

The letter I received from prison had the prisoner's number on the back of it. It reminded me of the time, a few years after the Second World War when a woman—a middle-aged woman—came to my office. She wore a peculiar dress with long sleeves, out of fashion completely, and I could tell by the look of her that she carried some heavy burden. When she rolled up the sleeve of her dress, I saw a tattooed number on her arm.

She had been in a concentration camp. She had lost her family—her parents, her husband, her children. And many times, here in New York, she had thought of committing suicide, but something made her go on. She came to my office to have the tattooed numbers removed because she had met a man, a machinist, and she now felt she could have a new life in the northern part of the state. I operated on her; she's now happily married and has a number of children.

Have you a tattoo on your arm? Think of it. Have you? Take a look. You may say "No." But I mean your mental and spiritual arms. Have you tattooed numbers on them? Many of us have, and you, and you alone, can remove these tattooed numbers by having compassion for yourself, by believing in yourself. The man in Leavenworth, Kansas, has a number; you have a number, too; if you're filled with frustration, you must remove these numbers from the skin of your spirit—through belief in yourself, through compassion, through understanding.

When I began to practice—more than forty-five years ago—as an intern, I delivered my first baby. I was horrified when the father fainted. The child had been born with a hole in the lip, a cleft lip, and I felt it was my fault. I was overcome with remorse, and the father had fainted out of remorse, too. Subsequently, I explained to him that we could do something about it. There was a plastic reconstructive surgeon in those days who could correct the deformity. It was this experience that helped me decide to enter the field of plastic surgery.

In my practice, I have, of course, operated on cleft lips.

During and after World War II, I taught surgeons in many Latin American countries how to perform such operations on children with this disfigurement.

In one country, a boy of seventeen came to the capital from the interior. He had a cleft lip since birth, and when he was about to be put under anesthesia, he shouted: "I'm going to die! . . . I'm going to die!"

I told him that I was his friend and that he would be all right.

He tried to be calm, but I saw the terror in his eyes.

Finally, the anesthetist put him to sleep, and I repaired the hole in his lip.

Two weeks later, the final dressing was removed, and I said to him: "Take a look at yourself in the mirror."

He hesitated. I urged him. "Don't be afraid."

That minute before he slowly walked to the mirror must have been a lifetime to him. Finally, he looked—and stared at himself in disbelief. I knew what was running through his mind. He saw someone he had never seen before. He turned his head in different directions as he kept looking at his new face. Finally, he turned to me with tears of joy in his eyes and cried:

"I'm going to live! I'm going to live!"

Are you going to live? Have you an emotional disfigurement? Have you a disfigurement in your mind? In your spirit? Because of some frustration, where there is a gap between you and your integrity, where there is a hole between you and your dignity as a full-fledged human being? Many of us have. You must remove that gap. Be your own plastic surgeon, with a little belief in yourself, with a little compassion for yourself, and bridge that gap between you and your dignity with the threads of human kindness.

*Who are you?* You've got to make up your mind who you are; no one can make it up for you. Your potential rests within you, not within anyone else. *The great escape!*

The prisoner who wrote me has no intention of escaping. He has committed an antisocial offense; he knows he has to serve his time before he can leave.

But how about you? Are you going to build on your great opportunity for your escape? You're not antisocial, but those who practice frustration are anti-self. The strange thing about your escape is that, whereas the world is not anxious for a convict to escape, the world is waiting for you to escape—back to yourself. They're rooting for you because the world needs you as a full-fledged balanced human being. The world needs you in these troubled times, in your own search for peace, which you can't give others unless you feel it yourself.

One of the terrible aspects of frustration is that, because of hurt feelings, remorse, distress, loneliness, hatred, people can easily develop misunderstandings of each other.

## THE TOMORROW ILLUSION

So, in this terrible burden of negative feelings, one of the characteristics of frustration is that we like to say—since we are ashamed of our self-image—we like to say: "Well, when tomorrow comes, things will be better; perhaps I'll help myself then."

Most of us are experts at tomorrow-type thinking. We don't need any pre-schooling for that. Too many of us are born that way . . . or else acquire it very quickly. "It's too hot; I'll do it tomorrow." When we have these negative feelings of frustration, we're always pinning the blame on someone else, and we usually say, "Well, in the south, South America—it's too hot, so they're the worst offenders." But don't you believe it; one can have offenders in Scandinavia, too, let alone here.

As members of "Mañana, Inc.," we leave things till a tomorrow that is mostly an illusion. For frustration is the thief of time. You cry in your soup, lament the status quo, tell the world you have been wounded, and do nothing about it.

The business of living, the business of overcoming frustration, is to live now. Now is the time for self-fulfillment. Not tomorrow, but today.

Still, if you want to do things tomorrow, you can. Some things should be put off till tomorrow. When resentment strikes you, when hatred strikes you, when bigotry strikes you, look in the mirror and say: "Charlie, old boy; Betsy, baby; wait till tomorrow. I'll give vent to my anger, my resentment, my hatred—tomorrow." This is the only time you can be a real expert in the art of self-fulfillment, when you forget these negative feelings, these destructive forces that put a convict number on your mind—on your body that give you an emotional disfigurement.

And have a little compassion for yourself. You're only human; you're neither superior nor inferior. You came into this world to succeed, not to fail.

Any doctor who has brought a child into the world—who has spanked it and has heard the cry of life for the first time—could not ever believe that this child came into the world in sin. This child came into the world to succeed, not to fail. You, too, have a moral responsibility to succeed, not to fail. And you begin to succeed when you stop harping on your failures.

You have imagination. It's not just the gift of the poet, the philosopher, the musician, or the sculptor. Still, use your imagination as a sculptor would, chipping away the negative feelings that steer you away from the world. Chip them off your self-image, so your image can shine—an image in God's image.

A woman making dinner for her family uses her imagination creatively; she's going to make her family and friends happy. A man who visits a person in a hospital sickbed uses his imagination creatively; he wants to help someone less fortunate. And these are tremendous goals. Yet, so many people feel unworthy if they are not world-famous. They don't realize that they can be great in their own right, within their own limitations, if they use their imagination creatively, avoiding frustration and heartache. Because no one can make you feel frustrated without your consent; no one can make you feel unhappy without your consent.

On the other hand, imagination-minus is fear, frustration, no goals.

So how do you overcome frustration? You make a road map of yourself, where you're going, and what you want to do. You have a blueprint of yourself—as you look in the mirror. You must decide, on your own terms, what you want to do. Your blueprint is your opinion of yourself; if it's no good, you will fail. If you have an image within your capabilities and you sustain yourself through determination, you'll probably reach your goal.

Your image of yourself, your opinion of yourself—this, of course, is all-important. This opinion of yourself, this will make you or break you. You can't respect others unless you respect yourself. You can't admire others unless you admire yourself. You can't help others unless you help yourself.

When you have a true regard of yourself, you feel a sense of humility—with confidence. You pass on your knowledge to less fortunate people. You give your compassion to other people, your understanding to other people, your sense of direction to other people. You are on your way to worthwhile destinations.

Your self-image is the stranger within you simply because you know so little of him. Yet this stranger can be your best friend if you make it your business to get to know him better. You rule him; you can make him what you want him to be—an image of success or an image of failure.

## OTHER ASPECTS OF FRUSTRATION

Frustration means your refusal to reach self-fulfillment.

- You refuse to concentrate on a strong self-image.
- You refuse to offer it partnership in your life.
- You refuse to nourish it, thinking it is not basic to your happiness.
- You refuse to create a proper climate in which it can grow.
- You refuse to enhance the stature of your dignity as a human being.
- You refuse to enforce your sense of self.
- You refuse to develop a proper self-image every day, forgetting that only your true sense of self can make you strong.
- You refuse to realize that you came into this world to succeed—that you can improve your self-image.
- You refuse to reactivate the success instinct, the success-mechanism within you.
- You refuse to have a worthwhile goal. You refuse to understand your needs—to use the courage hidden within you—compassion for yourself.
- You refuse to play ball with your self-respect—your confidence and self-acceptance waiting to be tapped for the great adventure in self-fulfillment.

These aspects of self-denial produce the following:

**F** *Fear.* This destructive negative feeling arises when you have no goal when you are continually criticizing yourself, harping on your grievance that the world has been unkind to you. How much more creative it is to turn your back on the fears of yesterday and concentrate on a worthwhile goal today.

**A** *Aggressiveness.* Frustration produces aggressiveness of the wrong kind. You step on other people's toes to get somewhere, not realizing that in this process you get nowhere, not realizing that you are stepping on your own toes, making the road to achievement impossible. The only time you can be aggressive creatively is when you have a goal and reach for it with determination and persistence, refusing to let others steer you away from your course.

**I** *Insecurity.* Frustration produces insecurity. You feel inadequate and inferior. You forget that a mistake does not make you a failure, that no one can make you feel inferior without your consent.

**L** *Loneliness.* Frustration brings loneliness. You feel separated from others, and, far worse, you feel separated from yourself. You walk away from reality into the dark tunnel of your troubled mind—alone—without purpose. Remember that no one can make you lonely without your consent.

**U** *Uncertainty.* Frustration means uncertainty. You can make a decision to be better than what you think you are. Remember, we came into this world in uncertainty, we live in uncertainty, and we pass on in uncertainty. Remember, also, that the business of creative living—the whole principle of Psycho-Cybernetics—is to bend uncertainty to your will, fulfilling the generic innate desire of every human being to live and be happy. If you remember this goal, common to all mankind, you will fight for it and overcome your uncertainty.

**R** *Resentment.* Resentment is almost synonymous with frustration. You hate others, blame others for your inadequacy, let others run your life, complaining you never had good fortune. You forget that you, and you alone, can change your luck by turning your back on negative feelings and by recalling the confidence of past successes as you try to reach your goal in the present.

E *Emptiness*. Frustration ends in emptiness when you say to yourself that you've had it, when you give up on life, shun responsibility, give up on creative goal-striving and leave your destiny to others. Symbolically, you have packed your self-image in a valise, placed the valise in a locker at an airport, locked it—and thrown away the key.

Thus, chronic frustration produces the seven aspects of the failure-mechanism.

## OVERCOMING FRUSTRATION

Remember how destructive frustration can be. Remember that it is within your power to make a change for the better . . . to change your self-image. With a little compassion for yourself, by realizing that you are *somebody* of importance—to yourself, to your family, to your community, to your country, to the world—you can be a sculptor of your own spirit and make the diminutive image of yourself grow ten feet tall.

That's what Psycho-Cybernetics is all about. Steering your mind to productive, useful goals. Not steering your mind to unproductive, futile goals through frustration.

A few more words on fear. If you're afraid a burglar will break into your home, you pick up your telephone and call a locksmith. He'll send an expert over to put in some locks to give you protection.

But, on another level, you must not lock yourself up. You must not imprison yourself. You must free yourself to set goals and pursue them without blocking yourself with fear.

To overcome frustration, you must learn to handle your fear constructively. For, while fear can be valuable, if it's in the form of goal-oriented anxiety, unchanneled, uncontrollable fear means agitation without any purpose. It means retreat from the better side of yourself. The fearful person has succumbed to amnesia; he has lost his dignity, his identity, his potential.

To overcome frustration, you must learn to handle your resentment constructively. You must learn to channel your destructiveness into positive pursuits.

When you carry with you dreams of retaliation, TNT-type of hostility, you're carrying fifty pounds of extra mental weight on your back. Everyone has troubles, problems, complaints. You must transform your destructive goal of disbelief into a constrictive goal of belief, transformed from hostility to love. Love of self, first, before you dare offer this love to someone else. And, again, by love, I mean self-respect. When you're filled with frustration, you have acquired a certain guilt, a sense of shame. This sense of shame leads you to resentment and to all these negative feelings that steer you away from reality, from loved ones, from your goals. You must take your chances in life. If you fail, you must learn not to resent yourself.

We rise above feelings of resentment—toward self and others—by accepting ourselves for what we are; by realizing that we are capable of being better people. We must adjust to error, search for our dignity—through compassion. Compassion is a soothing balm for the world-weary. When you give yourself compassion, you give yourself a chance to improve yourself. You refuse to let your mistakes defeat you. You say to yourself, "I am only human. I still like myself."

You keep searching for the better you. You search to make money, which is fine. You search for success—but too often, we have a spurious idea of what success is. We think in terms of prestige symbols that produce resentment: Anna has a fur coat; Suzy must have one. John has a Cadillac; Bill has to have one. These prestige symbols mean nothing. You must realize that you are more than a prestige symbol, that success means more than money, that it involves a sense of direction, a quality of understanding, and a considerable degree of self-acceptance. As a success, you accept yourself for what you are; you don't try to pretend you're someone else.

Like the athlete who is a money-player, you think of the times when you were a winner, yet knowing from your mature perspective that you'll never be a champion 100 percent of the time. And you refuse to let defeat humiliate you in any way. You accept life's setbacks, realistically; you do not let them throw you.

Finally, a short assignment. See if it doesn't help you.

When you get home, even if someone is looking and thinks you're crazy, sit down with a pencil and a pad and write down something like this:

What did I forget today? Did I forget to aim at being a better person? Did I forget to conquer obsessive fears that make my life miserable? What did I forget today? Did I forget to curb my over-aggressiveness? Did I forget to fight my feelings of insecurity, of loneliness, of uncertainty? What did I forget today? Did I forget to eliminate my resentments? Did I forget my resolve that I would try to be more accepting? What did I forget today? Did I forget to be honest with myself? Did I forget to try to understand the needs of other people, as well as my own? Did I forget to strengthen my self-respect? What did I forget today?

Now, don't blame yourself if you were forgetful today. The important thing is: *did you do your best?* What did you remember to do? What goals did you achieve?

Don't expect yourself to be perfect. You do your best, and this you accept; what you forgot to do is human error. Forgive yourself your omissions.

And then, tomorrow, you will set new goals, and you will not forget so many. You will build day upon day, week upon week, improving yourself as a human being.

Until frustration is no longer a way of life.

Until you use your wings to fly with your rising spirit.

Until you use your wings to rise above your mental roadblocks.

Until you use your wings to overcome frustration as a mechanism of death.

Then you will say goodbye to The Twelve Faces of Frustration and to the other aspects of frustration that mean FAILURE.

Then you will say "hello" to life.

This could be the most important adventure of your life. The one you cannot lose. The one for the championship. The one with the high stakes. The one that determines the quality of your life that spells out your real value as a constructive human being.

# 3

## THE ROAD TO SELF-RESPECT

WE LIVE ONE LIFE, AND WE SEEK TO MAKE THE MOST OF IT.

It is an imperfect life—a series of stresses and strains—but it is the only one we have.

We must take out our compass and plot our destiny. Life's highways are many and frustrating; we seek the roads leading to self-fulfillment.

And so we re-embark on our voyage of discovery, looking for ways to stand up under stress, conquer frustration, get on the right track.

It may not be easy for everybody, but most people do have hope.

First, let me quote from another letter I received from an inmate of Leavenworth:

> Just a short note to thank you for your recent visit here with us at Leavenworth.
> It's not often that someone, especially of your stature, from the free world, comes here to let us know that, out there, there are still those willing and anxious to accept us and love us.

He goes on to write of other things. I quote this prisoner because he writes graciously and sweetly—and anyone who can do this must still have some hope.

Even though he is a prison inmate. You—outside prison walls—chances are you have hope, too.

Now, let me quote a second letter. A man wrote it, not to me, but to a restaurant in Little Rock, Arkansas, and someone there forwarded it to me:

> When I was in Little Rock the first part of this week, I noticed on two occasions, The Reader Board message at your restaurant . . . It read: "Forgive others often, yourself never!" Each time I questioned myself of the meaning—not of the first part, but the second. The message indicated that we should never forgive ourselves, and I do not agree with this. Inasmuch as our Lord Jesus Christ said that

we should forgive our fellow man of his sins toward us, as many times as seventy times seven, we are, therefore, in agreement that we should forgive others often. However, the New Testament, in Matthew 6:15, states that if you forgive others, then your Father in Heaven will forgive the wrongs you have done. Can we not forgive ourselves if our Father can? Secondly, Dr. Maxwell Maltz, in his book entitled *Psycho-Cybernetics,* states that true forgiveness comes only when we are able to see and emotionally accept that there is and was nothing for us to forgive. We should not have condemned or hated the other person in the first place. If there was no condemnation, there is no need for forgiveness. If we can truly forgive others, why is it not reasonable to say that we shouldn't condemn but forgive ourselves for our mistakes? It is fatal, psychologically, if we don't. Therefore, may I suggest a new copy for your Board: "Forgive others always—forgive yourself, as often."

It is a very interesting letter. For only through forgiveness can you turn your back on the frustrations of the past and learn to conquer frustration. The Fundamentalist concept that you are a sinner, from infancy on, long before you knew anything about Life, is not part of our thinking; this is not our belief. Psycho-Cybernetics means steering your mind to a productive, useful goal. It is when you steer your mind to unproductive, useless goals that you fill yourself with frustration.

And if you cannot forgive yourself for a blunder, a heartache, a misfortune, a hurt feeling, a resentment, then you cannot clear the railroad tracks within you so that you can communicate with yourself. And, therefore, you cannot find roads to self-fulfillment—only detours.

It is a terrifying feeling to think that, in this day and age, people feel so much bigotry. Not too long ago, we heard the drums of a parade in celebration of a great man who gave up his life for an idea of freedom. It was a terrible feeling to hear these drums, in honor of Martin Luther King, Jr. and, at the same time, to know that someone hated him enough to shoot him down. So much hatred, frustration, bigotry unrelieved, unproductive—leading to this horrible deed.

We must all overcome. We must all overcome not only personal frustrations but our cosmic and community frustrations that have made most of us less than what we think we are. We must forgive our petty mistakes, our human errors—so that we can cleanse our souls of frustration and guilt.

Recently, when I was on the West Coast, I picked up a newspaper and read about a new weapon of the United States, an anti-sub torpedo, Mark 46-0. This article stressed the deadliness of this weapon, its vast potential in bolstering the nation's defenses. This new weapon could, it was claimed, find the deepest submarine. It could, on picking up an echo, judge it had sighted an enemy sub and take action, automatically launching its attack under orders from its brain. This new weapon was equipped with a high explosive warhead, the article concluded.

This may be splendid for our Navy, for our country, for our national security. But for us—suppose we gather in a theater of our minds, use our imagination creatively and make up our own newspaper. Here's what we write:

*A lively Hunter—Man has a new anti-Frustration Torpedo*: Compassion. It is his own happiness—Mark 100. It weighs nothing; it gets its tremendous zip from understanding. Its acoustic homing system can seek out the deepest running frustration hidden within us. The brain of this Mark Happiness 100 is a simple servomechanism within us that steers our minds to useful goals. This success mechanism of confidence within us directs its torpedo to a subterranean target, deep, deep, very deep within our troubled minds. This torpedo, however, carries an extremely happy peacehead, removing our hidden emotional scars that seek to destroy us.

For us, this is more like it.

## THE NEGATIVE WARHEAD OF FRUSTRATION FEELINGS

Let me tell you a story. Sometime back, I was in Costa Rica, and there were two men, both young men in the coffee business, very successful—they were partners. One, I'll call him Mr. M., was married to a beautiful young woman, a lovely, compassionate woman who came from a family of distinction in Costa Rica. There was one trouble with him—he was suspicious, jealous. He thought his wife wasn't loyal to him, that she was carrying on an affair behind his back. And, once, when they had a charitable dance in San Jose, Costa Rica, he watched his wife waltzing with his business partner. They were smiling at each other. Suddenly, he suspected his partner was her lover.

A few evenings later, his wife wore a new print dress. She said she was going to see her mother. He wished her good luck, and she left, but he was filled with suspicion. It grew dark. He walked from his home toward a huge park in town. It was a strange type of park. It was circular, with a circular area in the center where young girls walked in one direction and a larger external circular area where the young men walked in the opposite direction. When they met each other and got to know each other, they paired off and dated.

A huge number of chairs faced this area—under huge trees; and, from the other side of the street, Mr. M. suddenly spotted his wife's print dress. She was walking with this man, and he knew, definitely, that the man was his business partner. They sat down on a bench, their backs to him. Creeping across the street toward them, he pulled out a knife and slashed the man's face—a terrible wound. The woman, shrieking, turned around—but it wasn't his wife at all. Neither was the man his partner. He was a well-known lawyer. His jealousy, his suspicion, his hatred not only affected him—it affected people he didn't even know. He suffered most of all because most of the people he knew in Costa Rica disowned him.

What am I trying to say? That these terrible negative feelings of hatred and frustration—and all that go with them—are torpedo warheads that zigzag into nothing because these types of negative emotions hurt most the one who feels them. You create your own torpedoes that take you away from your goals when you give in to negative, frustrated feelings.

Most of us are complainers. Few of us take time off to reflect on who we are, forgetting we have the great gift of being ourselves. We use a tremendous amount of energy needlessly, pursuing being less than what we really are. Negative feelings within us prevent us from reaching our daily goal of self-fulfillment, sidetracking us into a dead-end of uselessness. And the well-developed ability to complain is one of them.

Furthermore, when we complain, we usually believe it is someone else who has kept us from our goal. We all know, in our own relationships with people, those who complain. I know one, a woman who is happily married, with two married sons, grandchildren—and yet she is always complaining. She's always scratching for attention, not realizing that when you scratch for attention in complaining, it is like scratching on marble—it has no effect.

We must learn to rise to our full stature of self-respect. But when you complain, you are doing the opposite—as when you gossip. For gossip, too, is a form of self-destruction. The person you hate is not there, and yet you destroy him with your venomous comments.

It's the same thing with complaining. You're disgusted with yourself, and you destroy yourself as you complain. You must realize this. When you complain to others, you don't lose your burden at all; it is still there. Stop complaining. Start living!

Stop complaining! Tell yourself you're not a horrible person; be a friend to yourself. Then you won't have to complain.

You're complaining less, but your conscience is bothering you?

All right, let's take a look at the question of conscience.

## THE MEANING OF CONSCIENCE

Shakespeare wrote in *Hamlet*: "Conscience doth make cowards of us all." Now, what did he really mean? With all due respect to Shakespeare, surely the greatest literary genius who ever lived, I don't think he knew what he really meant. And I don't think that most of the philosophers throughout the ages knew what they clearly meant when they talked about "conscience."

Now, let's think about this for a moment: "Conscience doth make cowards of us all." Is this statement true? Oscar Wilde believed that conscience and cowardice were the same thing. But was his belief really true? Think a moment about it. Stop reading a second—and think.

What did these two literary giants really mean when they related conscience to cowardice? I don't know—but I feel strongly that they were wrong. For we make cowards of our conscience. Conscience never makes cowards of us; we make cowards of our conscience.

It's a strange thing about life. When we're happy, when we look in the mirror and say, "Charlie, old boy! This has been a great day for me"—or, "Betsy, baby, this is my day—I love you"—we forget about our conscience. We don't know it exists. But as soon as we make a blunder, as soon as we hate someone—and we're ashamed of it, as soon as we are filled with frustration, then we think of conscience. So conscience is a negative concept.

My attitude about conscience is that it's your self-image, your opinion of yourself as you look in the mirror. And if you don't like yourself, because of some error, some blunder, some hatred, some bigotry, you refuse to blame yourself; you look for some scapegoat, as Hitler did to so many unfortunate people.

Thus, the scapegoat within you is your opinion of yourself. So you blame your opinion of yourself. Your opinion of yourself is your conscience, and if you make a mistake, you refuse to blame yourself. So you tell yourself you can't live with your conscience. But what you really mean is: *You can't live with yourself.*

Remember this: When you fulfill yourself, when you win out in the battle of life, you're playing ball with your self-image, with your conscience. And remember this, too: You made the change. You. But when, overcome with negative feelings, you deny yourself self-fulfillment and don't like yourself, you think your conscience is bothering you. What you really mean is that you are annoyed with yourself, with your opinion of yourself—but you *can change it.*

You must become your own plastic surgeon and remove these scars of frustration that you bruised into yourself. Like me. Every day I operate in the hospital; I wear a cap, a gown, a mask. See me in the hospital. Here is the cap I wear. It's blue, you see, because many people think white is terrifying in an operating room. So, for the past ten or fifteen years, we've used blue, gray, or pastel shades of green. I am a plastic surgeon: I put a mask on, a gown. I put gloves on, and now I am operating to remove a scar.

And you, symbolically, join me. You, too, are doing the same thing in the room of your mind. You remove your scars, your oh! so painful emotional scars.

1. When you deal rationally with threats to yourself, you refuse to let the little pinpricks that hurt your ego cut you in two. You rise above them, removing the infection of over-sensitivity, giving yourself compassion. You cut away the scars of doubt, fear, jealousy, and suspicion.
2. You work to reconstruct a self-reliant image. You work to give to others; if you can, you will always have returns. You build your self-image not on vanity or money—but on happiness. For happiness is the only commodity in the world that multiplies by division. The more you give, the more you have. It belongs to you. Give yourself a break.
3. Play a game of tennis with your self-image, with your conscience— play ball with it. If you make a mistake, blame your self-image, if it will give you pleasure; but if your self-image is looking at you, hurt that you're not blaming yourself, blame yourself, too. And you will have a fun game that will make you laugh and help you rise to your full stature of dignity—as a person whose goal is happiness, whose goal is a healthy self-image, whose goal has value and meaning.
4. You build within you a foundation, a scaffold of relaxation for your spirit and your emotions, to cope with these emotional pinpricks.

In section 1, I mentioned the four rules for relaxation. Let me repeat them:

1. You forgive others.
2. You forgive yourself.
3. You see yourself at your best.
4. You keep up with yourself.

How do you build? Through relaxation. And through emotional flexibility. And through devotion to your most important task: the strengthening of your image of yourself.

You recall the confidence of the past, and you use that confidence in your present undertaking. You use your energy for creative rather than for destructive purposes.

You live every day to the full. Each day is a whole new lifetime that will never come back; get the most out of it.

You accept your errors, and you push to rise above them. You are on the lookout for tone—not tension.

You acquire maturity in happiness when you remember your assets: your self-acceptance and your integrity as a *person* of worth. You have maturity in your reach for happiness when you remember your assets of self-respect and confidence.

You are a person of opportunity. You can have opportunity knock on your door from now to seventeen lifetimes and never hear it. But you must listen. You are opportunity! You are opening the door to new opportunities of improving yourself—every day.

Now, let's discuss forgiveness.

## FORGIVENESS AND PEACE OF MIND

You must realize that you're not only an image-maker, but an image-breaker. You must understand that forgiveness is a spiritual weapon that will help you toward peace of mind.

*Peace of mind!* Without it, because of frustration, you are always walking back into that little jail, that little concentration camp of your own choosing—where you create your own blackout, walking into the black tunnel of your troubled mind, refusing to walk out of it into the dawn of a new day.

Forgiveness: this is your great weapon.

When you learn to operate on yourself, removing those wrinkles from the face of your mind—that age you before your time—you then become a judge without a grudge. You are no longer the offender; you have given yourself forgiveness. When you are through with the operation, you go to the mirror and notice that these "prune wrinkles" on the face of your mind are gone. You are young again!

You have found youth—in your self-image, in your opinion of yourself, in your forgiveness of your errors. If you destroy this youth with negative feelings, you are old whether you are three or one hundred and three. But if you know how to cope with frustration, you are young, whether you are three or one hundred and three. You are no longer so vulnerable to life; you are able to absorb the shocks when you take the calculated risks in living.

So now, for the first time, you realize you are not only an image-maker, but an image-breaker. You're not only a new image-maker, but an old image-breaker. You take off the mask; you stop playing games.

Most importantly, you look at a friend in your mirror: "Betsy, baby—Charlie, old boy, I refuse from this moment on to play games with you. Do you know, Charlie, old boy—do you know, Betsy, baby—there have been some rumors about your being a conscience. But what does that mean? For you're my friend. I like you." Say this as you look at yourself in your mirror.

How about trying that when you get home today? Try it when you're alone, if you wish, so none of your family will think you've gone crazy. But try it! It's a great experience to just forget your "conscience," to make friends with yourself.

You have a moral responsibility as you look in the mirror—to forgive yourself. To forgive yourself, to shed your guilt, to come alive.

You start talking to people—because you want to. You like yourself; you're not afraid of others.

You stop criticizing yourself. You practice forgiveness. You look in the mirror and say, "I'm not going to criticize you anymore. I'm wasting time; we're having a match—a tennis match. Let's play ball together." Once you stop criticizing yourself, you stop criticizing other people. You bolster your self-image, unlock your true personality.

Now, you're not ashamed to talk; you may even talk a little louder—not to shout, but to *hear* yourself talk. If you make an error, you correct it. And, most amazing, you find peace in yourself.

You let people know when you like them. This is the most rewarding thing in self-fulfillment. You've been hating everyone, fearful they're ready to knock you off. But it's just the reverse: you've been knocking yourself off.

A new sun begins to shine, through your spirit, through your eyes, when you let others know you like them. There is no shame in this; you like them, and you tell them this.

What do you lose in complimenting people—while they're alive? Why wait until they're dead and you're putting them in a hole in the ground; you look down and say, "My! What a wonderful person she was. My! What a great guy he was," at a time when they don't even bear it?

## YOUR TREASURE

I live on top of a medical building on the eighteenth floor. And many years ago, on the eighteenth floor, the people who owned the building passed away. There was a rumor many years ago that one million dollars was hidden up on the eighteenth floor. Well, the columnists wrote about it, and I decided to invite them to come have a party with me—at four o'clock in the morning—to look for the ghost who was controlling the one million dollars. Of course, no one showed up.

But, at that time of my affluence, I had a butler. He was about six feet four and had once belonged to the Hungarian Cavalry. I let him wear a splendid white coat; it made him look like a doctor. And often, during office hours, he used to stick his head way up high, as he wore this splendid white coat, and enter the room with patients—pretending he was a famous surgeon from abroad. He would then walk into another room and close the door; he would go to the mirror in a bedroom, look at himself, fix his coat to his satisfaction and march back through the waiting room—pretending he was this great surgeon.

One night—about three o'clock in the morning—I couldn't sleep, and I heard a sound on my terrace. What could it be? I wondered. It did not sound like birds; it was too loud for that. I got up to investigate. It was a moonlit night, and I could see clearly. And, lo and behold, there was my butler, in his splendid white coat—with pick and shovel, hacking away at my terrace apartment, at one of my rock gardens, hunting for the treasure.

I bawled him out—he could have killed me with one blow—but he looked at me sheepishly, nodded his head, and went to bed.

A month or so later . . . Once more, I couldn't get to sleep—it was three o'clock in the morning. So I got out of bed and tip-toed to the terrace. There was that pick and shovel. I hoisted the pick, and on impulse, I began hacking away, trying to find the treasure. And, suddenly, somehow, I knew someone was watching me. I turned around. There was my butler in his splendid white coat, watching me. I felt silly. I believe I blushed. I dropped the pick and marched back inside my apartment—chastened.

What am I trying to say? That we're all looking for treasure. That we're all hungry for treasure. That we seek it out in the most unlikely places.

But still, your greatest treasure is your dignity; your greatest treasure is your self-respect. We look at the stock market, with millions of shares traded—twelve million shares, fourteen million—up and down, up and down. But the success instincts within you, these are your blue chips; they seldom go down, they almost always go up.

Just remember that your self-acceptance, your compassion for yourself, your confidence in yourself, your respect for yourself are your blue chips. They will help you reach toward fulfillment.

How do you search for the better YOU? How do you overcome frustration?

1.  You launch a new career, set out on a new voyage of discovery. When? When you give yourself another chance; when you feel you're entitled to it. When you move toward a new self-image and learn to enrich your new self-image every day. You feed your stomach; feed your mind at the same time.

2. You realize that you must live harmoniously with your conscience, with your self-image—your best friend. Hold out your hand of friendship to it.
3. You enlist the success-mechanism within you—your confidence, your self-acceptance—to guide you to goals. You then set goals within your capabilities.
4. You visualize the better you, the realistic, better you. Don't short-change yourself. You become a better person when you look in the mirror to create a better self-image. But if you don't look, you'll never find it.
5. You make your self-image ten feet tall. Your neighbors, your friends are too busy with their own problems; they're not going to make your image ten feet tall—even with flattery. You've got to do it yourself.

## YOUR GOALS IN FOCUS

You must see your goals in focus, so you know where you're going! No day-dreams, no fantasies, no excursions to some island in the sun of yesterday, to a never-never land that never was. If you want to go to an island in the sun, go off-season for eighty-five dollars. *Your goals are real.*

You must see your creative goals in focus; you must see them clearly. Even if you fail, you are a goal-striver. When you finish one goal, you start over again for another goal. If you lose, it's not fatal; you start toward another goal. You remember that even our great money-players in sports are not champions 100 percent of the time. They don't cry in their soup when they lose; the next day, they're out to win. It will help you to be a champion . . . in the art of living every day . . . if you remember, you'll never be a champion 100 percent of the time.

Leave your regrets of yesterday behind you. Forget yesterday. Live today; set your goals for today.

You must involve yourself with new goals—even if you've failed in previous undertakings. And, even if you have succeeded, don't kiss yourself narcissisti-cally in the mirror. Get up the next morning and start looking for another goal.

Exercise the servomechanism within you to lead you toward success. We all have within us such a mechanism to steer us toward our goals—if we let it operate. Our servomechanism is impartial; it will steer you to failure or to success, depending on what you feed it. If you have a goal in mind and want to reach out toward it, call upon your past successes, let them glow in your imagination, and chances are that you will be successful. But, if you have no goal in mind and are instead filled with anxiety, sure that you'll fail, chances are that you will fail.

Use your servomechanism properly. Think of your successes, not of your failures.

Nourish your assets. They are real. I don't care who you are, you have assets. Don't be ashamed of them; be confident about them. This is not conceit—with conceit, you have no goal. And, like a complainer crying out for attention, a conceited person, shouting his superiority to a world that usually does not listen, is pleading for attention, too—but has nothing.

Along with confidence, you feel humility, and you give your confidence to other, less fortunate people.

Learn to nourish your assets, your confidence, your self-respect.

And, to repeat, concentrate on today. Forget yesterday! Ignore tomorrow!

Set your goals for today—useful goals that are very dear to you. Live to the full today with your goals alive in your mind. Don't try to be Shakespeare. Don't try to be Marconi. Don't try to be Edison. Don't try to be one of the greats of this world. Remember that you're great when you're yourself.

And—surprise!—suddenly, you are a great plastic surgeon; suddenly, you're operating.

On yourself.

You are evolving; you are shaping; you are adjusting yourself to reality. You are creating a self-image ten feet tall. Through confidence, you are creating a better you. And then? What happens then?

You keep your accent on improvement. You feel very deeply a sense of dedication for your goals. Bolstered by your mental picture of confidence, you become involved with others and find satisfaction with others for, although you may be an island within yourself, still you belong on the mainland with other people. You share your confidence with other people. You enjoy each day to the full, each day that God gives you to live, each day so precious to us all, each day that will never, never return.

And here you are, on a new road, a splendid new highway, the road which you have been seeking from the moment you opened your eyes and looked out at the world: the road to self-fulfillment.

Building a new life for yourself.

Frustration is yesterday; you have said goodbye to frustration in all its disguises.

Self-fulfillment is today. And tomorrow.

And all the many tomorrows.

# 4

# HAPPINESS AND UNHAPPINESS

WE HAVE DEALT AT LENGTH WITH FRUSTRATION AS A WAY OF LIFE. WE HAVE EX-
amined its many faces, planned strategies to eliminate it from our lives so that
we might proceed on the road to self-fulfillment.

In this chapter, we will examine happiness and unhappiness.

Recently, I read a newspaper story about Helen Keller, who had died at the
age of eighty-seven. She must have had scarlet fever, or some similar infectious
disease, when she was very young; and, in early childhood, she became blind
and deaf. Yet, with all her hardships, she overcame frustration, she overcame
the terrible adversities she had to rise above. She couldn't see; but, neverthe-
less, she saw. She couldn't listen; but, nevertheless, she heard. A marvelous,
remarkable woman!

Very often, we don't listen; very often, we don't hear. We can see, and we
can hear—but we cannot see or hear.

Long before Helen Keller was born, Socrates said: "Know thyself."

Long before Helen Keller was born, Marcus Aurelius said: "Be thyself."

You must learn from these oh-so-wise men. You must learn to know your-
self, be yourself—and to forgive yourself.

Try to listen; try to hear. You must use your vision, too; to see in front of you,
behind you, and within yourself, to remove the turner of doubt, the obscurity
of vision that constitute your frustration, your use of frustration as a way of life.

Listen! Listen to the heartbeat within you. Listen to the great man inside of
you, the great woman inside of you. Hear the voice that urges you on to self-
fulfillment. It is all within your grasp. Are you blind? Are you deaf? Listen!
See! Listen to the sound of happiness and the awful sound of unhappiness; we
will discuss them in this chapter.

Happiness is the quest to fulfillment; unhappiness is the quest to de-
stroy yourself. Happiness means your thoughts are pleasant most of the
time; unhappiness means your thoughts are unpleasant most of the time.

Happiness means you are a goal-striver, that you use your understanding and your courage to reach your goals. Unhappiness is the reverse. Happiness means you are true to yourself; you have self-respect and confidence. Unhappiness means the reverse. Happiness means you use your imagination creatively and live in relaxation. Unhappiness, once again, is the reverse. Happiness means you are creative; you grow through your errors. Unhappiness means the reverse. Happiness means you *never retire* from life. Unhappiness, once again, is negation; you retire in fright from any challenges, any danger, any adversity.

Happiness means you are compassionate. Unhappiness means you have lost compassion for yourself, and for others. Happiness means emotional and spiritual tone—freedom. Unhappiness means emotional and spiritual tension; you lose your freedom and impose your own jail sentence upon yourself. Happiness means you are a winner in life. Unhappiness means you are a loser.

You look in the mirror. What do you see? Happiness or unhappiness? Two worlds within you: confidence—frustration. Confidence repeated until it becomes a habit means instant confidence. Frustration repeated and repeated becomes instant frustration. As long as you think and see negatively, you will be negative. In frustration, you use your imagination destructively; in confidence, you use your imagination constructively.

When I spoke some time back in the Northwest—in Seattle—there was a little girl named Sylvia. She was six years of age. She rode on a bicycle, and she fell off the bicycle; and she was overcome with the fear that she would never be able to ride that bicycle again. For months she didn't. She couldn't. Then one day, her parents went shopping on a Saturday afternoon; and when they came back, there was Sylvia on a bike—riding the bicycle. And the father said, "How come, Sylvia, you're on the bike?" And she said, "Well, for two months, I was thinking how I could get on the bike; and, you know, I was thinking how I used to do it well. And just a little while ago, Daddy, I got on the bike—and I'm doing it well." She's six years old, and yet she turned frustration into confidence by utilizing her past experience. This is an excellent example of how a person can transform unhappiness into happiness.

As a young man, I wanted to be a plastic surgeon. It is quite a while since I was a young man. . . . if you believe in chronological age . . . anyway—and in those days, people knew nothing about the subject. So that when I told my mother, I wanted to be a plastic surgeon, she looked at me horrified.

"What kind of thing is that?" she gasped.

I said, "Well, it's a doctor who treats scars on the face as a result of accidents at home, on the highway, in industry, and children born with disfigurements."

She said, "Oh, that's a wonderful thing, Max. But tell me, how will you get your patients?"

"Mom, don't worry. I'll get my patients."

She said, "I don't know what's going to happen to this younger generation. In my time, we had much more sense than you people. What's going to become of you people? Why don't you be a little practical?"

I said, "How, Mom?"

"I tell you what you do; why don't you marry a rich girl?"

I said, "Mom, but I want to be a plastic surgeon."

She looked at me; I looked at her. She wept—I put my arms around her.

But I stuck to my guns. I became a plastic surgeon.

I used my imagination, way back when people knew little plastic surgery; there were just a handful of men practicing it in the United States. But my imagination was constructive in that I planned to help other people. And so I stuck to my guns; and this is imagination used constructively.

I am not trying to be conceited. I know very well that I have not always, do not always, use my imagination constructively. Nobody does; surely, I do not.

But I like to draw from my personal experience when I write, and on this occasion, I used my imagination in the constructive way that steers one toward happiness.

Learn from these two stories: the little girl and her bike, the young man and his profession. Learn from these stories to plan your goals and then use your imagination positively to help you toward happiness.

## THE UNHAPPINESS TRAP

You must keep fighting the negative forces that would trap you, that would drag you down into unhappiness.

1. You must stop the habit of complaint. That's a side of unhappiness. Stop complaining; see that you are better than you think you are.
2. You must stop thinking about your liabilities. You are only human; everyone has liabilities. Think of your assets: your courage, your compassion, your will to succeed.
3. You must stop distrusting yourself. If you don't believe in yourself, why should anyone else believe in you?
4. You must strip off your mask; throw away your colored glasses; don't believe make-believe. Be yourself; it's so much easier. The

energy you waste trying to be someone else and pretending is enough to push a ship from New York to Paris.

5. You must stop ridiculing your own weaknesses. You are not perfection, it is true, but who is? If you were perfect, anyway, chances are nobody would like to know you. You'd make other people feel inferior.

You must keep battling these negative forces inside you; you must keep fighting for breathing space. Don't let the forces of unhappiness trap you! You're a free man—a free woman! Don't give up your freedom!

You were once a little baby; God gave you life on this earth—not to be unhappy. Not to be unhappy!

God gave you life so you could fulfill your purpose, so that you could affirm your individuality, so that you could assert your identity.

Not so you could fall into the quicksand of unhappiness, living centuries of frustration, endless days of misery.

Here are some more features of unhappiness—so you can try to avoid them:

1. You play games with others, with yourself.
2. You are unfriendly—to others and to yourself. You are critical of others and of yourself. You expect perfection; no one can measure up. And who would want to?
3. You act as if failure is absolutely inevitable; and, if you think in these terms, your nightmare will come true. Your pessimistic thoughts dominate your life. You color your everyday actions with, "It can't be done, it can't be done," *and then, it can't be done.*
4. You frown all the time. Now, there is nothing wrong with frowning now and then when you're deeply absorbed in solving a problem. But if you do it a dozen times a day, you truly are carrying an overload of mental suffering on your all-too-human shoulders.
5. You react fretfully, fearfully, all the time: "The world is coming to an end" is your theme, when it should be, "It's just the beginning of fulfillment."
6. You live too much in the past: "Oh! If only I could go back to that wonderful island in the sun when I was a little child; catch the coconuts; swim in that warm, lovely water; bid servants hand me all the food I want." If this was your life, do you know you could get tired of that, too? Live in the present; make this present to yourself.

## MOVING TOWARD HAPPINESS

Enough unhappiness? Let's try happiness. Here are some features of happiness: court them, woo them, win them.

1. You are a person of confidence; you try to be cheerful whenever this is possible.

2. You try to be friendly toward others. You're not prepared to be hurt; when you try to be a friend to someone, and this individual doesn't respond; you realize he may be a "taker" in life, not a "giver" like you try to be. You aim to be less critical of yourself and of others. Knowing you're human, you forgive your mistakes; you look in the mirror and smile at yourself. You leave your mistakes in the past and give yourself another chance.

3. In your confidence, you act as if success is inevitable; this is the way you've got to feel. Your belief in yourself catapults you toward success; you realize what you can do realistically and without conceit.

4. You refuse, absolutely refuse, to let negative feelings dominate your actions. You slough them off; you turn your back on negative feelings; you will not play ball with them.

5. You try to smile at least three times a day. Do you? Maybe not, but you ought to try. When you get up in the morning, look at yourself with friendly eyes. Don't say to yourself, "Look at that nothing!" Do the reverse. Say, "Listen, Charlie, old boy; listen, Betsy, baby; I can smile at you." Smiling is good for you. If three times a day is too much for you or if you're having a bad day, how about once? If only to remember that tomorrow you will set a new goal.

No matter what happens, you react calmly, intelligently, as a mature person. Some days, everything will go wrong. So what? You can't be a winner all the time. You're a champion in life if you believe in yourself, and you will win out more than now and then.

Plato once said, "Nothing in the affairs of Man is worth worrying too much about." How true! But if you must worry, worry about something important. Worry about your self-image. Build your self-image.

Four hundred years ago, in Milan, Italy, there was a terrible plague, and thousands of people died from it. People didn't know the cause of all this. Naturally, they were frightened; they were terrified. Would the whole community die? They talked about it in fearful whispers; the dread of death obsessed them. And then the Minister of Health walked the streets to see if he could find out the cause of this plague. He had an old-fashioned ink well with a pen, and he wrote down what he saw; after a while, his fingers became dirty with the ink. He walked on and, as he walked toward some of the walls of the white buildings, he wiped his hands on them. And, after the sixth time, the women looking out of the windows, the men looking out of the windows, saw him do this. Then they saw the black stains on the walls, and they thought he was the one that was spreading the plague. And so they threw him into a dungeon where he was put on the rack. So tremendous was the pain that he confessed he was the cause of the plague—and they burned him at the stake. Not two thousand years ago! Only four hundred years ago!

Do you put yourself in your own dungeon with negative feelings? Do you burn the Spirit within you—at the stake—and destroy it, with hurt feelings of resentment, with tortured feelings of distress and frustration? Indeed, do you torture yourself? You die, much more quickly, when instead you should live much more thoroughly. Stop putting yourself on the rack with negative feelings, with frustrations. You put yourself in your own dungeon, so you must come out of it. Rely on the mental and spiritual resources within you. Turn to your self-image, to your good opinion of yourself.

Did you ever hear about "Typhoid Mary" who, many years ago, when we were plagued by typhoid, carried the gene of typhoid without being affected by it herself—not knowing that she served as an agent of destruction. And so the name came into being, "Typhoid Mary," standing for one who spreads a communicable disease.

Ah! but there is one great "contagion" that has great rewards, and it is a pleasure for you to spread that: and that is happiness. If you move toward happiness, if you win out in happiness, you can be the "Typhoid Marys" of happiness. You can spread it. Imagine if you could spread happiness to ten people; and then those ten people infected ten more; and it went on that way for about—well—two years. The whole world would be a better place to live in. There would be less frustration, less unhappiness, and more fulfillment. Such a simple thing! First, you must achieve happiness yourself, then you can be the "Typhoid Mary" of happiness.

I know I've written this before, but I'll write it again—and not for the last time. Happiness is the one commodity that multiplies by division. Remember that! When you spread happiness, it multiplies within you. Don't be afraid to give yourself to other people. Even if they take advantage of you, remember there are other people who won't. It's not so much a question of giving yourself another chance; it's a question of giving other people another chance. Remember that!

## THE HAPPINESS HABIT

Happiness! Oh! what a great story. It is the greatest of all stories. Surely, God intended this story for all of us.

It's easy to get the happiness habit—just as you get into the habit of brushing your teeth. It's all up to you; truly, only you can create a happy world for yourself; no one else will do it for you. Still, this is one goal worth all your energy.

External conditions may or may not bring you happiness. You may or may not be happy if Sally or Mabel or Mary dies and leaves you $30,000. You may or may not be happy if Celia or Rose or Sarah gets rid of her rheumatism. You may or may not be happy if your boy gets into medical school. There are no "ifs" to happiness. *You are happy now!* You do the best you can; you try to fulfill yourself. You don't try to help others fulfill themselves if they're not interested. Don't try to spread Psycho-Cybernetics to other people if they don't want to listen. You listen! You hear! You see! Another aspect of the happiness habit—a point to remember: you dig out your buried assets. You don't let your resources die inside of you. You have resources, all of you: compassion, resilience, laughter. Ah! You learn to laugh!

Laughter! A great emotion. A feeling, a feeling. What a little humor does!

I was addressing an audience once—not too long ago—when a woman came up to me at the beginning of the talk. She said, "You wouldn't remember me, Doctor, but I read your first book over thirty years ago. And then, I became interested in Psycho-Cybernetics, and I read your book on it. It didn't do anything for me." Now, many people have read *Psycho-Cybernetics,* and reading my book has, I know, helped many people. Still, how about this woman who said it didn't do her any good? Why didn't it? Because when she read it, she thought just reading it would do her good. She didn't realize she had to be more than a passive reader—that she had to do something about things. This is not positive thinking: it is positive doing! And that's what Psycho-Cybernetics is all about. You turn a thought into a creative opportunity. You set goals, and you go after them.

You wage an aggressive war on negative feelings. You push to strengthen your self-image. You try to see yourself as you have been—in your most productive past, in your most glorious reality, in your best moments. You've had a good moment—sometime! Think of it! Recapture it—relive it! At least try. Because when you try, you are already on your way. You have come out of yourself, out of your prison into the world.

And, for goodness' sake, seek out activities that will make you happy. Don't force an activity on yourself just to please someone else. Some sport, some hobby that you like for the eight hours each day that are all yours. Your eight hours free from the demands of work and the necessity of sleep. In eight hours, you can do so many things for yourself. You're a king, you're a queen, you're a stockholder—you own stock in yourself—in your free eight hours, and the better you use them, the more you will relax, the better you will sleep.

Another point to remember. Help others. It can be a glorious, rewarding experience. What have you got to lose? A little bit of your time? In helping others, you may help yourself. Some more points for happiness:

You've got to prepare for it. This is your first generic goal that makes you alive. You also live in a climate of happiness. Avoid negative people; avoid people who are filled with negative feelings and always tell you, "It can't be done; it can't be done!" You turn around and do it. And you do it by entertaining good thoughts about yourself and others, instead of poisoning yourself with depressed thoughts about yourself and other people. See yourself with kind eyes when you get up in the morning. Whether you scratch your back, or yawn, or bury your head in your pillow when you wake up, think of yourself with a little bit of kindness. I think you're entitled to it.

Unearth the negative feelings beneath you; be a great archeologist and dig-dig-dig: dig deep within you to uproot those evil, destructive forces of negative feelings.

Every morning when you look in the mirror, start with that little smile. Try to like yourself. Try—and resolve that you will do the best you know how—under whatever circumstances—to reach your goals today. And if you fail, you fail: there's no disgrace in it, and the next day, you try all over again. You must have a meeting with your self-image. You must realize that the image within you was born to greatness, to fulfillment, achievement, success. You must prepare to improve yourself. You must imbue yourself with courage. You must support yourself in time of stress or tension and rise above it. You must nourish yourself with the happiness mechanism. You live happily today; not tomorrow. You encourage this state of happiness. You help others, and you help yourself. When you look in the mirror, you see a better you.

And above and beyond all this, you must gear yourself to overcome the negative forces inside you, the forces that would drive you from that sunny land of happiness to that foggy, rain-drenched land of unhappiness.

How do you overcome the forces of unhappiness? Let's discuss this now.

## OVERCOMING UNHAPPINESS

First, you must realize you have an unrealistic attitude when you're unhappy. You may say, "I came from a disadvantaged background; I was born unhappy;

I never will be a success; I'm no good anyway." Nonsense! You can change from failure to success; you can change—from unhappiness to happiness. You can overcome these negative tendencies.

Whoever told you that you were born to be unhappy? No one can make you unhappy without your consent. You have the final say. Yours is the final judgment.

Remember that unhappiness means loneliness. No one can make you feel lonely—without your consent. What you have done—in building loneliness—you can overcome.

Unhappiness means loss of your true identity. And no one can make you lose your own identity without your consent. You must overcome this; you must support yourself, give yourself identity.

Unhappiness means undue limitations, separation from yourself, separation from other people. You put yourself in your own jail, in your own dungeon, in your own concentration camp. No one can put you there without your consent. You came into this world free. Why put yourself in your own dungeon of despair?

Psychologically, you must let the telephone ring. You create a tranquilizer between you and negative feelings. I am a professor of surgery in more than a dozen Latin American countries, especially in Central America . . . and it's mighty hot there. . . . from eleven a.m. to three p.m. So we used to operate at six o'clock in the morning. And, during the stupefying heat of midday, most people would walk around with umbrellas to avoid sunstroke. You, too, must put a mental umbrella between you and your negative feelings to avoid a "tension stroke."

In place of an old habit of over-responding to tension, substitute a new habit of delaying your response. Let the telephone ring in your mind; let someone pick it up, they'll give you the message later—you'll give it to yourself later. You break the electric circuit of distress for a moment, so that you do not over-respond to crises, so that you can renew your energies for the joys after the sorrows that will come tomorrow. You adapt yourself; you rise above your problems.

Keep your eye on the ball—your daily productive goal till you have reached it. How many deals in life have been destroyed during the last two minutes, the last five minutes? For years, you've planned on something; you are almost there; then, in the last few minutes, you get so tired you can't see the forest for the trees. Keep your eye on your goal all the time—till you're through with it, till you reach it.

Plan to get rid of your excess tension. Think of the geyser, Old Faithful, in your mind, in the room of your mind. In the playhouse of your mind, you see a sunny room. Through the window, you see a geyser—letting off steam. Isn't this a symbol for you—to let go of the pressures of the day? If your imagination won't work this way, go over to the faucet. Open the faucet; then think of the water coming out under pressure. You're letting go of that steam in your mind—and you turn the faucet back.

Learn how to forgive other people and make a habit of it. Forgiveness may bring you tremendous rewards.

I was in Spokane, Washington, not too long ago. Four couples were listening to me; they were trying to patch up their marriages. One woman said: "I forgive him, but I can't forget." But what kind of forgiveness is that? It's not easy to forgive others; when you do, you move toward fulfillment as a human being.

When you learn to forgive, you teach yourself to overcome unhappiness.

You are a unique human being in this world: God made you so. Just like fingerprints; they're never the same. You are never the same as anyone: even if you're an identical twin, you're *still different!*

Lincoln noted that God had made so many common people. No—the reverse— they are uncommon. No two people are the same. And it's your destiny to do the best you can. Don't imitate someone else. You mustn't do that at all. Your self-image is your emotional and spiritual thermostat. It's your thermometer. Keep it well regulated, pulsing with enthusiasm, not with despair. Let it tick with excitement, not like an old grandfather's clock in a deserted room.

You look in the mirror: "What kind of a day is it going to be, Charlie, old boy? What kind of a day is it going to be, Betsy, baby?" Are you going to smile? Or are you going to frown?

You overcome unhappiness—fighting through your negativism—when you feel you deserve to be happy, when you think enough of yourself to put a smile on your self-image because you are pleased with yourself.

It isn't always easy. I do not underestimate the extent of life's realistic problems—I have lived too many years to do that, I must admit. When you wake up in the morning to the harsh summons of your alarm clock, I realize that it may be to face up to a day of seemingly endless demands and irritations, in which nothing seems to go right, and in which all kinds of unforeseen obstacles to your goals seem to spring up from nowhere.

Under such circumstances—and certainly, such circumstances can surround you just as readily as everything going as planned—you may start off feeling a little grumpy, then begin snapping and snarling a little, and end up with a mind swarming with negative thoughts and pessimistic forebodings.

But this is the time!

Yes, this is the time when you need a friend. John?

No.

Jim?

No.

Margaret? Joe? Helen? Doris? Pete? No.

Yourself.

It is under such circumstances . . . it is under the painful, depressing conditions of adversity that you must give yourself a boost. No one else can give it to you.

Other people may try to be helpful—or maybe they won't—but only you, in the final analysis, can truly help yourself.

In a sense, such adverse conditions are a test for YOU. They test your belief in yourself. They test the right you give yourself—to enjoy life, to feel happy, to win out. They test the degree of support you are able to give yourself. They test your ability to turn crises into growth situations. They test your ability to climb out of frustration and unhappiness into the warm sunshine of the happy, who love life, imperfect as it is.

# 5

## WINNING OUT OVER CRISES

IN CONQUERING FRUSTRATION, WE MUST LEARN TO DEAL WITH CRISES THAT BE-
devil us. For much of life is crises and problems; we cannot run away from
challenge.

We must learn how to change crises into opportunities for growth. This
is quite a trick, but it can be done. And, in so doing, we conquer frustration.

We must say this: that any man's hope and self-respect are our hope and self-
respect, because we are all involved in the glorious adventure of self-fulfillment.
Any man's death diminishes me.

There was a death, by violence, of a great man: Senator Robert Kennedy.
Thousands and thousands of people stood outside St. Patrick's Cathedral in
New York City—watching thousands and thousands of people enter the church
to pay their respects to Robert Kennedy. And thousands upon thousands, prob-
ably over a million, all the way from nowhere to nowhere; from New York to
Washington; from nowhere to somewhere, untold thousands of people watched
a train bring his body to its last resting place.

I wondered as I watched the people going into the church, wondered if they
really understood—wondered if they really went to pay their respects to a free,
great individual who had died in violence; or whether they were paying homage
to the rebirth of their own sense of self-respect, their own sense of dignity. I be-
lieve they paid respect. The millions of people, as they waved at the train, were
not saying goodbye to a man who had passed away in violence; they were saying
hello to a man's dignity that will remain alive forever.

More than that, they were saying hello—to their own dignity. It was through
the violence and death of one man that they suddenly realized that they, too,
had greatness within them. For there is greatness within every one of us. We
must resolve to see this.

Too often, we resort to violence on ourselves—to violence on our own
dignity, because of frustration, which brings with it resentment and hatred,

brings with it the fact that we are traitors to ourselves. And, symbolically, we put a knife in ourselves, committing violence upon ourselves because of some error, some blunder, some heartache. This is the beginning of the discord—the riot within—and, to repeat what I wrote earlier, no amount of policing of the world can ever bring peace in this world unless we learn to police ourselves; unless we learn to quell the riot, the hatred, the resentment within our own hearts.

We must know that we can never be friends to other people—regardless of race, color, or creed . . . unless, whoever we are, we have two things in common: dignity and self-respect. And I like to feel that Senator Kennedy lived to show us that.

We learn to fulfill ourselves, to bring that peace of mind that we are all searching for, by learning the terrible violence we spend upon ourselves—even though passively through this terrible burden of frustrations. Now, we all have frustrations, of course—frustrations of every day—but I'm not writing about that. I refer to the chronic frustrations with which we obsess ourselves day in and day out, reliving past misfortunes, errors, old hurt feelings—not realizing they no longer live, for they are the past.

Now how do we overcome these chronic frustrations? How do we survive crises and leapfrog forward in spite of them, turning them into opportunities for growth?

Well, we must repeat: The example of Senator Kennedy should be a reminder for all of us that, through compassion and self-respect, *we* can learn to overcome frustration; through compassion and self-respect, *we* can learn to move through crisis to new life.

Your enemy within you is the conscience, the image of years which causes you to shrink to the size of a microbe. You overcome this enemy by encouraging the operation of your success-mechanism. We will discuss this in our final chapter.

But it is you who turn external chaos into constructive living. It is you who make a crisis a dynamic opportunity for growth.


## YOUR "WONDERFUL COMPUTER"

Not too long ago, I read a newspaper story about a computer that could diagnose illnesses. Information on the principal diseases and their symptoms is stored in a memory device. The physician feeds a patient's symptoms into the computer, which tries to match them with those of a particular malady.

The system uses a photographic master film as the memory device. The symptoms of each disease are recorded in transparent lines varying according to the significance of each symptom for that illness.

Fascinating, indeed; but now let me tell you of a far greater electric computer within you. Within all of us, hidden right in the mid-brain, an electronic computer—no larger than the size of a small hazel nut—something that no scientist, or all the scientists of the world put together, could ever develop. A computer that you, alone, and no one else, uses to diagnose—not your disease, but your health. Because Psycho-Cybernetics is mental health. Psycho-Cybernetics teaches you to fulfill yourself, to rise above crises, and to find in them opportunities for self-realization.

This is your "wonderful computer."

Now, if you can reactivate the success-mechanism within you, the success instincts within you, you will be able to overcome frustration. To repeat, here are the seven key characteristics of frustration:

1. *Fear.* With a goal in mind, you can change fear into an opportunity for growth.
2. *Aggressiveness.* You step on other people's toes to gain what you think is fulfillment, but it produces emptiness, for whenever you hurt someone else, you hurt yourself twice as much.
3. *Insecurity.* No one can make you insecure without your consent.
4. *Loneliness.* No one can make you lonely without your consent.
5. *Uncertainty.* When you reach for a goal, you bend uncertainty to your will.
6. *Resentment.* The twitch of the tensions, the gout of the mind, the daily cancer within us that robs us of our sense of fulfillment, bringing termites to live within us, boring holes in our mind and our spirit, leaving us empty as human beings.
7. *Emptiness.* Symbolically, we take our integrity, our self-respect, our self-image, and we put them in a valise; we then go to an airport, put the valise in a locker; we lock the locker—and throw away the key.

Turn your back on these qualities you may find in yourself. Purge your system of their poison.

God gave you more than this—much more. He brought you into the world with a purpose.

You are born to seek and achieve fulfillment; and you cannot and dare not stand in the way of that fulfillment, even though you are sidetracked by some negative feeling, derailed by a mistake, crippled by a heartache or guilt, or some other corrosion of your spirit.

You must remember that, in the room of your mind, you should set up a decompression chamber where, when you are overcome with frustration, you can get back to yourself, reassert your identity, regroup your positive instincts, giving yourself that other chance that every human being is entitled to.

At a lecture, some time ago, I spoke on the mental and spiritual potential of man. It was on a Sunday afternoon: there were a number of people on the dais—psychiatrists, a rabbi, a minister, a priest. And there was some secretary who was continually answering the telephone that kept ringing. It annoyed me and, when I got up to speak, and the phone rang, I took the receiver off the hook; there was no more ringing.

That should be a symbol to you: under pressure, let the telephone ring; don't make a mountain out of a molehill. You become self-reliant, overcoming this little problem, surmounting this small aggravation which, if you wanted, could become a major aggravation.

Learn to relax so that you can solve problems, dissolve crises. So simple, yet so difficult to achieve. Relaxation, denied sometimes even to millionaires and kings—you cannot buy it.

## THE SEARCH FOR PEACE

The world is longing for peace—peace of mind. It longs for an end to violence, to sudden death, to the explosiveness of frustrated people. It longs for people who can stand up to stress calmly and with self-respect—and then alienated, violent people destroy them. So many unnecessary deaths!

We must seek peace from within, seek it with all our hearts.

We must find peace—inner peace—even in crises. Even in times of trouble.

Marcus Aurelius said:

"Be like the promontory, against which the waves break, but it stands firm, and tames the fury of the water around it."

This is what we all must be in times of stress.

In Genesis, there is a phrase (13:8): "Let there be no strife, I pray thee, between me and thee . . . for we be brethren."

Let's change this: "Let there be no strife between you and your self-image—that great, great person within you; because you are one, an image, in God's Image."

You must learn to overcome your fears, to live with them—in crisis and in calm. Anxiety, to repeat, is a form of fear and may be useful and creative—if your imagination is creative, and if you have a goal in view. Perhaps you are fearful of not achieving your goal. But, if you have a goal, you must try; you must get your feet wet before you can swim. If there are a dozen different ways to reach that goal, you must choose one way to achieve it—you can't reach it the dozen ways at once. If you fail, you start again; and your failure does not stop you, for there are many other goals in life for you. All of us are goal-strivers; if we fail in one goal, we try again the next day for another. We don't give up.

Back to fear. I took off a little to the side of my subject here, so let me make my point about fear.

To illustrate, let me tell you a story:

Many years ago, I went to Santo Domingo. The dictator Trujillo was alive. I went there to operate on the daughter of a general who had been in an auto accident. Her face was disfigured.

The First Lady of the land knew I was to operate on this child; she insisted on watching the operation.

I thought it would be too difficult for her to watch, and I went to see El jefe (the Chief) at the Palace.

I said: "The First Lady wants to watch the operation."

He said: "Let her! If she wants to watch the operation—if she faints—that's her hard luck."

Well—I had an American passport; I was nineteen hundred miles away from New York—I wouldn't think of arguing with the dictator: I wanted to go back to New York. So I did not argue with him. I knew the First Lady would insist on witnessing this operation. I selected my operating staff. I chose two tall doctors as my associates and spoke to them in Spanish, and I said: "You two will stand on either side of the First Lady and, if she turns pale and seems about to faint, I'll nod my head and you whisk her right into an adjoining room."

They were alarmed at this—they didn't want to touch the First Lady—but I said, "Don't worry, I got the O.K. from El jefe."

I operated. They stood in caps and gowns and masks, in the operating room, alongside the First Lady—who was attired the same way. The general of the army, the father of the patient, was also attired in operating room cap, gown, and mask. This covered his military uniform; I knew he had a gun in his hip pocket.

Nevertheless, I operated—then, suddenly, I heard a "plop!"

I turned around, expecting to see the First Lady, but it was one of the surgeons who had fainted. The First Lady helped to pick him up and get him into an adjoining room; then, she returned to witness the rest of the operation.

Funny—yes; but sad. Every comedy has tragedy in it. Every laugh has a tear to it. He was a man whom I had trained for many years. He was a great surgeon—yet look what fear did to him. He fainted—out of fear. How terrifying it is to lose all your dignity—because of fear.

My point about fear is this—and I believe my story illustrates it: To have peace of mind, you must conquer fear, and fear breeds in your imagination. It will, anyway, if you let it. The most terrifying misfortunes, which you think you cannot endure, will probably never even happen. This surgeon—who fainted—was aware of the realities of the operation; he did not fear them. Some unrealistic fear took root in his imagination, and he could not conquer this fear.

You conquer fear through a process of inner strengthening. You conquer fear through building your self-image, through accepting your fears, through acknowledging your frailties, through believing in yourself no matter what happens.

When you reduce your fear, automatically, you increase your peace of mind.

Avoid aggressiveness of the wrong kind. And avoid aggressors of the wrong kind . . . the takers in life, the revengers in life, life's violent people, the people who grab and complain and take—never, never, never in a million years being able to achieve fulfillment as human beings. For they are the real robbers of the world. What? They don't rob from you? But they rob themselves—of their own integrity as human beings.

Aggressiveness has validity—if you have goals. Aggressiveness can go with a confident belief in yourself. But aggressiveness doesn't mean stepping on people, throwing your weight around indiscriminately.

The creatively aggressive person does not hurt others; he improves himself—even if he fails—because he'll give himself another chance.

When you learn to properly channel your aggressiveness, you move out toward erasing your frustrations, feeling inner peace.

You realize that you are not inferior. In the satisfaction you feel from healthy aggression, you feel better about yourself. You are a child of God, capable of blundering but capable of rising above it. And, in your dynamics, in your freed, healthy, social aggression, you move toward goals and feel successful. You feel more self-respect, you eliminate hate. You do not hate yourself; you do not hate others.

You feel at peace with yourself. In spite of uncertainty.

In spite of failure.

Your life will always be uncertainty; it will always have some failures. No matter who you are. This is unavoidable—it is an element of the human condition.

At the turn of the century, there was a man Ehrlich, a great Viennese scientist. In Vienna, people died from the terrible scourge of syphilis, that greatly feared social disease of those days. But they knew of no kind of miracle drug, like Penicillin, to cure this dread social disease. And so it was Paul Ehrlich's job to discover a medicine to cure this terrible illness.

Day in and day out, he worked on it, year in and year out. And, finally, he discovered the cause—and the cure. He called the cure "606"-because he *failed* 605 times in eleven years! Read this last sentence again; let it sink in. Now, don't you keep complaining that life has been unkind to you because you failed to reach some little goal once or twice.

I don't ask you to be a Marconi. I don't ask you to be an Edison. I don't ask you to be a Paul Ehrlich. I ask you to be something greater than that. I ask you to be—yourself. Who is the greatest human being in the twentieth century? *You* are—to yourself. You must feel this way about yourself. Not egotistically. Not narcissistically. But with an appreciation of your need for self-interest, with an appreciation (your need to give to yourself, with an appreciation that you are trying to make yourself a bigger person), and no one can do better than that.

And remember this: If you have inner peace, that little contribution you make—of peace of mind, of making yourself respected, of dignity—makes you ten feet tall. It is a community affair; it's communicable. You can spread your health. If you spread that health of self-respect to ten people, and they spread it to ten others—you are the greatest person of the twentieth century.

Because, in your own little way, you will stop the violence that caused the death of Senator Kennedy that caused the burial at night, in the darkness, of a great man. But—his self-respect is there. I can hear him talk to all of us: Live in it; grow in it; expand in it. This is far greater than all the politics, than all the wars, than all the riots. The millions of people, simple—not rich or poor—people who make up this universe, were watching, saying farewell to a man, yet saying hello to their dignity.

We must all try to stop the flow of resentment that robs us of our emotional and spiritual security. Resentment: the twitch of tension, the gout of the mind, the cancer within us that robs us of our self-respect.

One more story. About a man who worked in an insurance company, who hated his boss who didn't give him a raise in pay. He was filled with hatred: he'd get to his office five minutes to nine o'clock, and you'd think he came early to be a world-beater that day. But, on the job, he sat and hated, hated his boss for not giving him his raise. Five minutes to five, time to go home. He arrived home, still overcome with his resentment. At the dinner table, his little girl of seven spilled her milk on the table. Without thinking, he slapped her.

Then—he felt horrified. He loved his little girl. He couldn't sleep that night; he ran out of the house to go to work. Five minutes to nine, he sat down, looked at his watch. He began to hate his boss.

"What am I doing to myself?" he wondered en route home. "I'm ashamed to go home." He couldn't face his little girl; he had slapped her. But he had to go home. He got off the bus. And, suddenly, out of the doorway, his little girl came running to him; he lifted her up, she kissed him, he kissed her. Then he brought her back to the ground. He cried.

He said: "But I slapped you last night."

She said: "Oh! Daddy! That was a million years ago."

Remember this story. For, if a child can overcome resentment, can overcome the result of these small violences that destroy people, you can learn from this child. Through forgiveness, she forgot her hurt, buried it in the past.

Your hurt feelings, your failures are of another world—they are a million years ago. Your resentment—which will hurt you more than anyone else—the chances are that you are feeling this resentment against someone who doesn't even know you're alive.

Bury your resentment; find goals, and live. Stop being a zombie. Stop walking around like a somnambulist—a dream walker—in a world of reality, unable to adjust to it. You are a sleepwalker; you've hypnotized yourself with negative feelings. Wake up to a new life!

In this chapter, we have discussed violence and the healthy way to use aggression, and avenues leading to inner peace. We've discussed crisis situations—for we must learn to rise above crises, to grow through crises.

Now I'd like to give you a first aid kit. A first aid kit to turn a crisis into a golden, enriching opportunity:

1. *You let the telephone in your mind ring.* Make believe you're so loaded with money that you can have five people pick up the phone for you. You're letting the telephone ring: you're not picking it up. This gives you a tranquilizer—a buffer—between you and your negative feelings. You insist on your relaxation; you protect yourself from negative feelings. *You stop over-responding to crises.* You substitute a new habit of delaying your response for an old habit of over-responding. If you don't feel emotionally rich, all you have to do is take the receiver off the hook.

2. *You deal with crises with reason, not with worry.* Relax. Relaxation is Nature's greatest tranquilizer. See yourself at your best in crises. Keep up with yourself in crises. But stop worrying; worry will only hurt you.

3. *You make relaxation a habit.* You work to make relaxation a habit and a goal in itself, repeated and repeated, like the habit of brushing your teeth, until it becomes second nature. Eventually, you have instant relaxation. When you need it, in times of stress, you

have it. You can call upon it whenever you want to; you can train
yourself to it.

4. *You keep your eye on the ball.* By this, I mean you keep your eye
   on your daily goals. Keep your eye on the ball; never lose sight of
   your goals. Don't let crises turn you from them.
5. *You keep your self-image well-oiled.* You keep it well-regulated.
   You work on ways to strengthen it. Most people spend a lot
   of money and effort on their cars, and then they have to keep
   changing them. You invest your resources in your self-image.
   You're smarter. You keep your self-image well-oiled—with a
   little bit of compassion. This costs you nothing. You are richer
   for it. You increase your investment in yourself—and you will
   never trade yourself in.

How do you turn an aggravating crisis into a golden opportunity? How do
you survive stress? You have your first aid kit. Here's some more to help you.

1. *You practice without pressure.* You prepare for crises in your mind—
   when you're alone—you think about how to act.
2. *You react aggressively and creatively to a crisis by recalling the con-
   fidence of your past successes.*
       "But I never had any success in my life. What are you talking
   to me about—recalling my past successes?"
       But we have all had successes. No matter how many failures. If
   you hear a record that's old, and you repeat and repeat it, what do
   you do for inner peace? If you can stand the gaff . . . the noise . . . you
   change the record. Yes, you can change your own record. If you have
   within your mind the repetition of frustration, and the record begins
   to pall on you, you put another record on in its place. You substitute
   a record of happiness and of confidence. You recall the days of your
   childhood, the moments of pleasure: in the sun, a flowing brook, the
   chirping birds. Or, if you lived in the north, skiing down the slopes.
   You did something right sometime. You were happy once in a while,
   anyway. Remember these pleasant moments; make a new record of
   them. That is the beginning of a goal for now.
3. *You stop making mountains out of molehills.* We all have trou-
   bles and problems all the time. Don't make them any worse than
   they are.
4. *You keep your goals in mind at all times.* Don't let stress block
   your view. You have goals in view, and you know you'll get there,

no matter what it takes. You've got to fight for your rights, for your human dignity—to reach it and realize yourself.

5. *You take your chances in life.* You may make mistakes—even in crises. You are a mistake-maker, but you are also a mistake-breaker—and you tell yourself you will survive.

6. *You shadowbox for stability like the great prize fighters of the past.* Jim Corbett, who won the championship over John L. Sullivan, once said that, long before the contest, he practiced shadowboxing before the mirror—ten thousand times before the bout. You don't have to practice ten thousand times, but now and then, it will help you. When you get up in the morning, you go over to the mirror, and you shadowbox. Ab-ha! You gave frustration a knockout blow. Well, it sounds ridiculous; so you laugh. But even this little exercise is good for you. It's good to be able to laugh at yourself. If you learn to laugh at yourself, you can laugh at your frustration, too. Don't take your frustration too seriously; don't take crises too seriously.

7. *You refuse to fear crises.* You stop telling yourself you're unfortunate. Every crisis should be an opportunity. It's a signal for you. Make it work for you, instead of against you.

When Babe Ruth struck out, reporters would ask him what he thought about when striking out.

And Babe Ruth said that he thought about hitting home runs.

Remember this. You don't remember the times—the thousands of times—that you struck out. You remember your home runs. You see them soaring 450 feet into space. You are a winner. You are—in some way—a Babe Ruth. In some way, you're a champion.

Let me tell you another story. In San Diego, there was a minister's son—I was speaking at a church there.

He said to me, "I have been trying to play the guitar, and sing, and I get all mixed up, and it doesn't work together."

I said to him: "Well, isn't there some record of someone you like, who can play and sing the song together?"

"Yes, I'm trying to be like him."

"Well, this is the error you're making. Listen to him play and sing at the same time; but don't try to be him—try to be yourself. Learn his technique—how he does it—and substitute yourself on your own record."

A month later, I came back, and he had learned, by the technique, how to sing and play at the same time. And he did it very well. He had a goal of himself in view—not someone else to imitate.

Another story. When I was in Texas, there was a woman who honored me greatly by throwing bouquets at me about Psycho-Cybernetics—how much it had meant to her. I thanked her.

She said: "I used it on my son. He is a high school student, and he's trying to be a discus thrower; and he was terrible. He was unhappy that he couldn't be better. I gave him the book to read, and he was only seventeen. A month later, he did it so well; and then, finally, they had the contests of all the Texas high school kids, and he came out first."

He learned to relax. He learned to see his goal—how to throw the discus—and, in a few months' time, he became a champion.

Why throw a discus? You might hurt somebody. Instead of discus, instead of running, why not take your self-respect? Make a project of it. Make it a beacon. Make it the shining light of what you can be. Not just any time. In crises, too.

## OVERCOMING CRISES

The main theme of this chapter is how to surmount the many crises in your life and go on to rich, rewarding experiences.

This is easier said than done.

Still, if you apply yourself properly, chances are you can do it.

We have, in the course of dealing with this subject, dwelt upon inner dignity and senseless violence, upon the overcoming of frustration, upon peace of mind and the winning out over fear, as well as upon the proper channeling of aggression. All are relevant to the manner in which we deal with crises, and to whether we survive crises and go on to growth experiences or whether we let the crisis conditions overwhelm us and plunge us into a failure cycle that might become a rigid, tortured life pattern.

During the time I was writing the material for this chapter, a great man, Senator Robert Kennedy, was killed in an act of senseless, destructive violence. This shocked us all. Coming as it did on the heels of the equally tragic slaying of the great civil rights leader, Dr. Martin Luther King, Jr., the shock was overwhelming. Both men were sincerely constructive in the ways they lived. They died at heartbreakingly young ages; yet, while they lived, they lived richly.

They left messages for us who survived them: that we human beings must live and strive to fulfill ourselves. That we must meet crises head-on, refusing to buckle under to the forces of crisis, but overcoming crisis with the power of our determination, the sincerity of our intentions, and our reliance on an inner dignity and self-respect that will not fade away with the changing winds.

You cannot avoid crisis—except by hiding under your bed all your life and refusing to come out and meet the world. And this is no answer. Therefore, you must resolve to win out over the many, inevitable crises in your life. I hope that my suggestions in this chapter will help you. I believe they will.

And your winning out over crises is a major step in your major battle—the confrontation and final victory over the forces of frustration.

# 6

## ON TO SUCCESS!

IN ATTACKING OUR GOAL, THE CONQUEST OF FRUSTRATION, WE HAVE, OF COURSE, studied the question of frustration and illustrated the nature of frustration so we might better know our enemy.

But we have done more than this. We have also studied the importance of goal-setting. We have thought about the importance of your self-image. We have gone into mistake-making and mistake-breaking, into the acceptance of error in ourselves, into the tyranny of conscience and the hearing ability of compassion. We have discussed the constructive and destructive outlets of aggression. We have analyzed happiness and unhappiness. We have made a number of pertinent observations about the human condition.

In short, we have tried to point the way to the good life—to the overcoming of frustration and failure.

Now, suppose that we take that final giant step—and discuss the whole concept of success as a way of life.

In a sense, this is automatic. When you conquer frustration, what can you have then? Success! Right? It is so obvious.

And yet, is it? Are you ready for success? Do you easily think in terms of success? Can you handle success? What threatens you more: success or failure?

This is truly a cloudy, complicated question. For the truth is that many, many people are not emotionally equipped to handle success.

Let me tell you a story a friend told me, for illustrative purposes.

It seems that, during World War II, he was an infantryman in Europe, a rifleman in a front-line American division fighting Nazi Germany's troops. It was late November, 1944, and in Alsace-Lorraine, around the French-German border, the Americans launched a big offensive. The fighting was fierce; the Germans retreated, but my friend's company, advancing, took heavy casualties—something in the neighborhood of 50 percent in the first few hours of the attack. They seized a key ridge and withstood artillery barrages. Soon, the ridge was secured, and they could rest.

But a few days later, they moved through the countryside to a small village—their target. They attacked it frontally and ran for cover as dozens of machine guns and rifles opened up on them.

Once again, on foot, after a short wait, they attacked. Jumping to their feet, they charged forward. Again, the German machine guns and rifles barked out; back they went, behind a slope which gave them protection.

Aidmen took the wounded back; the survivors, behind their slope, looked at each other, worried. What could they do? Attacking the village from their position was very difficult. Either they had to go up a steep slope, good targets for German sharpshooters, or try to pour through a narrow tunnel—even worse. And the enemy was most certainly ready for them.

Failure confronted them, certain failure. Even if they did capture this little village—which apparently consisted of one long street lined with houses—they would face destruction in the process. Few would live to tell the story of this one.

Perhaps a bazooka could knock out the nearest houses. The bazooka-man got to his feet to take aim, then leaped back. He was most fortunate; he was untouched—but there was a bullet hole in his helmet.

And so these American infantrymen looked at failure. They sent word back to headquarters. Then they waited.

Headquarters responded shortly. New orders. A new approach. And failure turned toward success. Destruction was avoided—with a new outlook.

A new approach. The infantrymen retreated back toward their own lines, then circled around toward the other end of the village. Here, they moved in on the village from level terrain—the terrain was no longer such a handicap. The enemy did not expect them to come from this direction; they were not ready. And a tank called up from reserve completed the transformed picture. In a matter of minutes, with this new approach, they captured the village, and the surviving defenders were prisoners of war. Just like that.

One approach, failure. Another approach, success.

Now, I don't tell this story to glorify war, certainly. I don't have to tell you that I loathe violence in all its forms.

But this story illustrates very effectively one of my key points—that your approach is of fundamental importance. Just as these American soldiers had to decide on a success-type approach over a failure-type approach, so do you. So do you!

Not on the battleground that was Alsace-Lorraine, on the French-German border, but in the battleground of your mind.

For your mind is a battleground in which you win or lose; it is a battleground in which you decide on the nature of your approach to life; it is a battleground in which you lose the war against negative feelings or in which you win this essential battle and go on to face life with success-type approaches.

In each of our lives, we have to surmount unfavorable terrain every day—the problems and troubles and crises which are basic constituents of life. Sometimes we can meet them head-on; sometimes, we must bypass them, reformulate our goals and move in from another direction. But we must gear ourselves to win with success-type approaches.

Now, let us analyze some of the obstacles which we set up to keep us from success.

The world is against you?

Well, sometimes it may seem to be, but chances are you will do all right with the world if you can first do all right with yourself.

You never get a break?

Again, some days you might not, but how about the others? In the final analysis, you make your breaks—and the best break you can give yourself is to think realistically about how you can overcome the forces of frustration once and for all, as you take dead aim on success-type thinking.

You don't deserve success?

Now, this is more like it—this is the type of thinking which bars the door of success to so many people—this is what we must discuss.

## THE PERSON WHO HAS NO RIGHTS

Are you a person who gives himself no rights? No rights in terms of success, fun, inner contentment? No rights in terms of anything?

There is such a person, you know. A person who feels such strong inferiority, such overwhelming guilt, such self-hatred, that he feels he has no rights, that he deserves no rights, that he didn't deserve to be born, and certainly that he doesn't deserve to live.

And, in truth, not just one such person—many people. Many, many people who feel they have no basic human rights. So many suffering people who will not let themselves enjoy the only life they'll ever have. Perhaps they give themselves the right to own a car or a house or some other valuable material, tangible possessions, but they do not give themselves the right to feel successful, the right to feel worthwhile, the right to feel they are somebody.

Now let us suppose that you feel this way. You are always frustrated, and this feeling follows like the night the day, for you always frustrate yourself. You worry about everything (worry will kill success feelings as quickly as insect killer will kill insects). If you make a lot of money, you begin worrying about income taxes. If you're feeling healthy, you begin worrying about some disease a friend told you about. If you are humming and whistling as you pick up your morning newspaper, your face is creased with anxiety when you put it down.

Let us suppose you feel this way. You read about celebrities as if they were people from another planet. They're not, you know; they're people just like you and me. You find other people to admire and, in the process, you degrade yourself in any comparison. You find fault with your feelings; you find fault with your actions. You must be perfect; you must not make mistakes. You have no rights at all—YOU will not even allow yourself to be a human being.

What do you do about it?

You cannot allow yourself to continue to see yourself in such negative ways; if you do, you will always find yourself frustrated. You will make sure you fail—and you must see this—*you will make sure you fail because you are more comfortable with failure than you are with success.*

How do you change? How do you change from a failure-type approach to a success-type approach, as the infantrymen did?

I will now give you some suggestions to help you, but first, you must realize the extent to which you refuse to give yourself rights, the extent to which you deny yourself rights that you would give most other people, the extent to which you are an enemy to yourself. Because unless you do this, and see that you are giving yourself a hard time, you will not want to change your approaches and attitudes. Why should you if you can't see that they are not working out for your welfare?

This may help:

Go back and re-read, in Chapter 1, The Twelve Faces of Frustration.

Go over them carefully. Are they you? Be honest with yourself. Are they?

If they are, chances are that you do not give yourself many rights.

If they are, chances are that you give yourself a pretty hard time.

Now let's see what we can do to help you do right by yourself, rights-wise.

## A NEW SUCCESS APPROACH

Let's see if we can't find a new approach to your thinking about yourself—a new approach to move you toward success.

The components of this new approach are not new. We have discussed some of them, anyway. Still, this is a new approach for you, if it is not yet *yours*.

Make it yours, this old-new approach. Move to conquer frustration; move to approach success.

Our thinking is enlightened, and this is important. Bertrand Russell writes about how people in the Middle Ages, terrified during plague epidemics, clustered together in churches to pray to God, feeling that God, sensing their religiousness, would pity their plight and grant them relief from this dread disease. But their thinking was unenlightened. Objectively, they were harming themselves, for by crowding into the churches, at close quarters with poor ventilation, all they managed to do was to spread the epidemic and bring on still more suffering.

But our thinking is enlightened, and we aim to rise above the epidemic of frustration on to a new success approach.

We talk the same language now, and it is a language aimed at moving us toward better living.

And here, in our language, are a few final thoughts so that you can cement the success approach we have paved for five chapters, so that you can rise above failure to success.

1. *Appreciate your individuality.* Too many people these days do not. Sometimes I must feel a little cynical about modern "progress." *Max,* I say to myself, *when you were a kid, weren't people more themselves?* For, as a boy on the East Side of New York City, I knew a lot of "characters." And sometimes "characters" are just people who are not afraid to be themselves. They—the "characters" I knew when I was growing up—didn't have to take opinion polls before they felt or thought or did something. They didn't care if everyone loved them—they were what they were.

Today, too many people try to be someone else. To be successful, they feel they should look and act like some famous politician or movie star or entertainment personality. Then, they think, they will be successful. But this won't work. You cannot feel successful this way. The person who does this is a mass product, not a success. He is an assembly-line product, not a success.

You must learn to be yourself. You must learn to appreciate your own individuality. Don't sell yourself short! So what if you're not perfect? If you were absolutely perfect, no one could stand you. Other people would flee from you as if you carried a contagious disease. If you were perfection, you would make them feel inferior; you would remind them of their own fallibility.

God created you as an individual, not a robot. There is no one just like you—no matter what your faults or your assets, your wealth or your poverty, your opinions or your actions.

While you live, live—as an individual who appreciates himself as he is. You are genuine, the real thing—you are not an imitation. Appreciate your individuality! Accept your faults and your mistakes; emphasize your talents and your successes.

2. *Set goals every day.* It is the person who finds no purpose, no meaning in life who feels failure so intensely. You must make your own purpose . . . you must make your own meaning. No one else can do this for you. Set goals every day. Every day.

So you know where you're going. Because you have to take your day and move it somewhere; you have to make your day live. Again, no one else will do this for you.

In goal-setting, the big mistake so many people make is to underestimate the importance of their goals.

"What can I do today?" a family man may say. "Make a little money, then come home and help the wife with the kids? What sort of goals are these?" Excellent goals. Why underestimate them? So you're not a millionaire, so you won't be on television, so you won't save the universe single-handed, and you're not Superman or Batman, and you will not climb Mount Everest today. You're not a great hero—but you can be a good man, as a husband, as a father—plenty of worthwhile goals here.

"What can I do today?" a housewife may say. "I'll make breakfast, get the kids off to school, clean the house, make supper. Are these worthwhile goals?"

If they mean something to you, they are worthwhile. If they mean something to you, you are a queen in your castle; you are a success beyond success.

Set your goals. Set them every day. Stop criticizing them because yours are not a millionaire's goals; think of the taxes he pays. Stop criticizing your goals because your life is not high adventure. An insurance company will issue a policy on your life, perhaps, but not to the high adventurer. We must learn to live in reality, not fantasy. We must keep in touch with who we really are, not with the might-have-been.

3. *Keep after your goals.* In a sense, setting your goals is not enough. You have to keep after them. You must develop a persistence in realizing your goals—otherwise, they lack meaning.

If you set a goal and fail one day, this is no failure at all. Life is not perfect for anyone; no one wakes up in the morning to a day in which every road leads straight to the realization of his goals. Life involves frustration, but it also involves the overcoming of frustration. Don't criticize yourself relentlessly if you set a goal one day and cannot follow through to see its actualization. Keep after it. Set your goal for the following day, and the following day, and the day after that, until you have realized your goal.

You must not expect things to come to you. To achieve success, you must recognize that you must follow through. You must develop qualities such as patience, resourcefulness, and ingenuity, and keep your aggression efficiently channeled toward your goals. As in the story I told you, you may have to change tactics. The successful person, however, does not give up easily.

4. *Build your self-image.* And, finally, we come back to this. Because you cannot be a success unless you are a success to yourself. If you own your own house, you try to keep it in good shape. You mow the lawn, have the house painted, trim the shrubbery. You keep your driveway clear and do everything you can to enhance the value of your property.

Well and good. Enjoy your house, enjoy your car, enjoy all your material possessions.

But, above all, enjoy yourself—as you become a success to yourself. You can do this only as you build and build your good opinion of yourself, as you learn to see yourself at your best, as you see again and again your happy moments of the past, and work to make yourself the kind of person you always wanted to be.

You will not be a success if you mow your grass and trim your shrubbery, but neglect the building of your self-image, allowing weeds to grow. You will not be a success if you make a million dollars but leave your self-image impoverished.

You will not be a success if you nourish and support a dozen children but leave your self-image starved.

In the final analysis, success is a growing self-image. More on this, now.

## HOW TO BUILD A BETTER SELF-IMAGE

S *Sense of direction.* If you have a goal, then you are going somewhere. This is the beginning of your great adventure in creative living. You try to improve your self-image, you take calculated risks to be better than what you think you are, you use frustration as a stimulus to rise above a problem, a mistake, a blunder, a heartache. Remember that negative feelings have value—to stir you on to overcome them . . . to reach goals within your capabilities, within your training. In other words, your goals must be realistic and within your limitations. And, when you have a sense of direction within your limitations, your opportunities for fulfillment become limitless.

U *Understanding*. To improve your self-image, you must understand that a mistake doesn't make you a failure. It is there to stir you on to rise above it. You must understand that you cannot communicate with others until you learn to communicate with yourself. And then you have the responsibility to communicate with others, making every effort to understand them. This is the beginning of friendship—the growth of your self-image.

C *Courage*. You must have courage to take your chances in life. You must have the courage to start for another goal should you fail in one undertaking, remembering that success doesn't mean just being successful. More often, it means the capacity to rise above a blunder. You must have the courage to think creatively, then act creatively, refusing to be overcome by frustration because of momentary barriers or handicaps. You must have courage to jump the hurdle. And your courage reaches its greatest potential when you share it with someone less fortunate. Then your image is ten feet tall.

C *Compassion*. With compassion, you're somebody; without it, you are a failure. First, you must have compassion for yourself, for you are only human. And, equally important, you must have compassion for others, for it indicates your capacity to forgive. This means humility. This means maturity. This means a growing and glowing self-image.

E *Esteem*. You must appreciate your own worth as a human being. If you don't have self-respect, no one will give it to you. You can call a child on the telephone a thousand miles away, and if he hears a whining voice, a voice of frustration, a voice without esteem, chances are that he will hang up on you. Unless you feel there is good in you, others won't find it. You must see yourself as a person whose destiny is to be happy. And when you fulfill yourself as a person with esteem—when you fulfill yourself with compassion for yourself and for others—you express the God-like quality within you.

Your image is then in God's Image.

S *Self-acceptance*. Your image grows in stature when you accept yourself for what you are. Don't try to be someone else. If you try to imitate someone else, you are playing second fiddle to someone else's image. You are then behind the eight ball, a zombie living someone else's image, making your image shrink to the size of a microbe. Win, lose, or draw, you must be yourself at all times. You are neither superior nor inferior. You are you, a child of God, destined to overcome frustration only when you learn to improve yourself, improve your image, not someone else's.

S *Self-confidence.* Self-confidence comes from taking the calculated risks in living. You use the success instincts within you, you remember past successes, you use the confidence of past success in your present undertaking, refusing to let the negative feelings of yesterday sidetrack you from your goals. Confidence builds confidence. Confidence can become a habit—like brushing your teeth. You can tap confidence then whenever you need to—distant confidence. You should be proud of your confidence; it is not conceit. The conceited person only pretends he is superior; he hides his feelings of inferiority. Confidence means humility, too—and compassion.

These seven ingredients spell SUCCESS.

## THE TWELVE FACES OF SUCCESS

Now let us look at The Twelve Faces of Success. Compare them with The Twelve Faces of Frustration in Chapter 1.

1. *Truth.* Albert Camus, the famous French writer, said, "greatness consists in trying to be great." In the same way, happiness consists in trying to be happy, and success consists in trying to be successful.
   Socrates said, "Know thyself." Aurelius said, "Be thyself."
   We say, "forgive yourself." Try again. See the truth about yourself. It's not a bad truth. See your past successes; this, truthfully, is part of you.
2. *Imagination.* Imagination-plus means you have a goal within your capabilities, and you use your mind to help you strive to reach this goal with constructive aggressiveness. All of us have imagination that we can make a habit of cultivating. Your imagination is destructive not constructive when you have no goals but move in circles, in merry-go-rounds of frustration.

3. *Relaxation.* You relax when you practice and live the four princi-
ples of relaxation:
   a. Forgive others.
   b. Forgive yourself.
   c. See yourself at your best.
   d. Keep up with yourself.
      Relaxation implies that you set goals for your fulfillment. Re-
laxation means that you let your servomechanism, your success-
mechanism, work for you under ideal conditions when you learn:
   a. to do one thing at a time, with one thought at a time, one goal
   at a time.
   b. to live in the present, not in the past.
   c. to use your anxiety creatively to reach your goal.
   d. if a situation defies solution, to sleep on it, not *with* it.
4. *The Aim of Happiness.* Happiness belongs to you, like your eyes,
like your heart. See it refusing to let the tumor of doubt obstruct
your vision. Feel the throb of your self-image, anxious to win in
life. Don't let it tick like a grandfather's clock in an empty room.
Life is full of problems, but it's also full of excitement and joy. Reach
for happiness without pushing people aside, and when you achieve
happiness, you have a moral responsibility to share it with others.
And remember, your first step toward happiness starts with a goal.
5. *Good Habits.* You deliberately discard the bad habit of frustra-
tion for the good habit of confidence. All habits are forms of
self-hypnosis—like brushing your teeth, eating your breakfast, or
slipping into your shoes before you go out into the world. It is just
as easy to have the good habit of compassion as the destructive
habit of frustration. You make the decision; the responsibility is
yours, no one else's. Stop seeking excuses for your errors. When
you seek excuses, you avoid the achievement of goals, you side-
track yourself from reality and creative living. A good habit here
is to admit your errors and rise above them.
6. *Accept Your Weaknesses.* In this way, you have a floor under you
when you come face to face with a problem, a crisis. You turn a
crisis into an opportunity, not an opportunity into a crisis, when
you accept your human frailty. Every day, you are born again.
Every day is a day of creative living. You dare not resign from life
because you blunder. Don't give up the ship! You are a modern
Columbus conquering the rough seas of frustration, accepting
your limitations.

7. *Compassion.* Compassion is the basis of successful creative living. You cannot have a worthwhile goal without it. If you have it, through it, the other aspects of the success mechanism will work for you. Through compassion, you learn to overcome unproductive agitation, born of resentment—agitation that leads to elimination, where you walk away from life and turn your back on your own identity, moving nowhere into the dark tunnel of your troubled mind. Remember the blackout in New York several years ago? Thirty million people were involved in a blackout beyond their control. But what about the many more millions of people the world over who create their own blackout through frustration, walking into the dark corridors of their own concentration camps that they build for themselves. Too often, we see the dark world within our minds through a mistake. Ah, but through a little bit of compassion, a little bit of kindness for yourself, you give yourself another chance in life . . . and we all deserve another chance, another chance to walk back again into the dawn of a new creative day.

8. *Unmasking.* You stop wearing masks; you stop playing games with yourself and with others. How much energy is lost in this destructive process, a process of eating into yourself until there remains nothing of the great You that you can be. When you pretend you are someone else, you withdraw from life, removing the vital fluids of your mind and spirit, leaving you empty as a human being.

   You may wear sunglasses to protect your eyes from the sun. But how many of us wear sunglasses when we hit the pillow—I mean emotional sunglasses, to hide us from ourselves and from others while we try desperately to fall asleep. When you stop playing games with yourself and with others, you begin to play ball with your self-image. You stop hibernating, and you live creatively, communicating with yourself and with the world—where you belong.

9. *Live Through Your Mistakes.* You cannot be a champion every day of your life. Like any athlete in sports who knows he can't win all the time, you must realize that you will not reach all your goals, and that if you reach most of them, you have become a champion in the art of living. You are not perfect, and a mistake should not make you feel that you are inadequate; it should not fill you with frustration that forces you to retreat from life. Never tell yourself you are unlucky because you have failed in one undertaking, that people are inconsiderate and cruel. You are only cruel to yourself then. A blunder should stimulate you to rise above it rather than

to evade people; evade your commitment to be a full human being, and you find yourself in a pit of despair and hatred.

10. *Never Retire.* You can never retire from life—whether you are three or thirty, six or sixty, nine or ninety. Every day you must live to the full, even if you are sixty-five and have to retire from your job. Those middle eight-hour periods before you go to bed—they are the precious hours of fulfillment, when you develop pursuits and hobbies that will make your senior years productive. You cannot go into an artificial state of hibernation. It will only lead to despair. Have a goal every day, no matter how small.

   I gave a seminar, a workshop in Psycho-Cybernetics in Monterey, California, and when it was over, one man came up to thank me for teaching the course. He said: "Dr. Maltz, do you know why I took the course?" "Why?" I asked. And he answered: "I'm eighty-two, and I'm practicing to be ninety."

11. *Consider Yourself a Winner.* Call upon your confidence of past successes; use this confidence. If you consider yourself a loser, you will be fearful and without enthusiasm. You will feel oppressed as if the air from your lungs had suddenly disappeared. This feeling of oppression prevents you from reaching your goals, blocking positive feelings and positive performance, leading to weariness, ennui, boredom. Do not let your strength flow out of you. Do not let your self-image shrink. Consider yourself a winner. Strengthen your self-image.

12. *Accept Yourself for What You Are.* You are neither superior nor inferior. You are a child of God, capable of blunder, capable of rising above it. Keep up with yourself, not with someone else. Nourish your self-image, not someone else's. When you look in the mirror, see the two sides of you—the person of frustration and the person of confidence. You can't stay on the fence of indecision. You must make up your mind who you want to be. Choose confidence. Reject frustration.

## THE SUCCESS CYCLE

If you follow faithfully the suggestions given you in this chapter and in the other pages I've written, chances are you will sharply increase your ability to feel that you're a success.

Success usually leads to success—and on to more success. So that here you have another cycle. Not the destructive, heartbreaking cycle of failure, but a happy series of successes, a reactivation of your success-mechanism. What a cycle for you! Truly a life cycle! Build it. Nurture it.

And more power to you! All your life.

## THE FINAL CONQUEST OF FRUSTRATION

So where have we gone on our little voyage of discovery? To Europe?

No.

To the Caribbean? No.

We have traveled to none of the portions of the globe; you will not find our destination on any map or atlas. No ships, no planes, no rolling seas, no cloud-filled skies!

We have looked inside ourselves to see if we couldn't find potent weapons for our conquest of frustration. For our final conquest of frustration.

And I certainly hope that many of you good people, reading and re-reading my anecdotes and my advice, will find in these pages a refreshing tonic that will help you to rise above both the endlessly repeated cares of your everyday lives and above frustration itself as a way of wasting the life force that is so precious.

You, reading these pages—there are so many of you, and of course, you are all different in your ways. Your problems vary, your heartaches vary, your satisfactions vary, your lifestyles vary. For you are individuals, and, though you are the same, you are different.

Many of you, however, are similar, in that you have succumbed to a frustration that is perhaps a characteristic of our troubled times.

If my ideas will help you to rise above frustration—to happiness and success—then I will feel richly rewarded in my labors.

Then our voyage of discovery shall indeed have been fruitful. The final conquest of frustration.

# CONQUERING FRUSTRATIONS

*Commentary by Raymond Charles Barker*

MAXWELL MALTZ AND I HAVE BEEN FRIENDS FOR A GOOD MANY YEARS, AND I'VE learned from experience to respect his sense of humor as well as his integrity. But I did a double-take when he dropped into my office one day and announced: "Raymond, I'm going to jail on Friday."

He was referring, of course, to his visit to the federal penitentiary at Leavenworth, Kansas—a trip he has already told you about. He filled me in on the details by telling how his ideas on goal-striving and self-fulfillment have reached and helped thousands of men behind bars. How the principles of Psycho-Cybernetics have given them hope for the now and hope for the future when they are able, once more, to take their places in society.

Frustrations naturally beset men and women who have lost their freedom and spend most of their time locked in prison cells or prison yards.

In many cases, I've no doubt, overwhelming frustrations led to their crimes.

But you and I are *physically* free. Nevertheless, we sometimes find ourselves unable to reach a goal we have set our sights on because we are mentally locked up, locked in a prison of our own making. A prison built, bar by bar, by frustrations that we haven't conquered.

I am sure this problem goes way back to primitive man. He struggled to learn the art of speech. He struggled to learn the art of love, moving love out of the category of just a basic sex function into an enduring means of communication. I am sure he struggled with that. There were problems with food, shelter, and safety—and many other things. But step by step, primitive man conquered his basic frustrations.

And now, modern man—who has also conquered many frustrations—lives in a world of great advancement. A world where positive thoughts and feelings have moved him ahead but where negative thoughts and feelings have held him back.

The process of evolution has been, I believe, a gradual unlocking of many of the doors built up by frustrations, doors that have threatened, but failed, to keep mankind from a measure of self-fulfillment. And as a result, century after century and generation after generation, we, as a people, have become more creative, more self-expressive. We had to do this in order to get where we wanted to go.

That is a race picture, a picture of civilization in general. But what about you and me as individuals? Do you have some goal you haven't reached because you can't stay on the track because you are fearful, lack self-confidence, or feel inferior?

Well, I have a confession to make.

I consider myself a healthy extrovert, and I am unfrustrated in most things. I certainly am unfrustrated in the pulpit. But I'll tell you about a secret frustration of mine.

Some years ago, a talent promoter came to see me and said: "Barker, you are so good at speech-making that you ought to be out cashing in big money on the lecture circuit." I replied, "Of course, I know I'm good, but what does one do? How do I go about it?"

"Don't worry. I'll start you on Rotary Clubs," he told me. He did. He started me on Rotary Clubs. And what did I do?

I fell flat as could be. I managed to talk the necessary length of time, but I was not animated. I was dull. This amazed me because I like the Rotarians, a fine organization. I later went before the Elks Club and fell flat there, too.

I am totally free of frustration in the pulpit, but put me in front of a sales convention, and I am a flop. Put me in any Church of Religious Science, any metaphysical church in the world, and my message pours forth. But put me in front of a Women's Garden Club or any group of people not closely related to the New Thought movement or metaphysical beliefs, and I'm far from a success.

This is an area I should conquer. I should get over this frustration of not being able to speak effectively to non-related groups of people. I should quit making excuses that unless the members of the audience have some background knowledge of Religious Science instruction, they have nothing within them that will respond to me.

Your own area of frustration may be far different from mine. You may need money for an education or to meet a financial obligation, and you may not know how to go about getting the necessary funds. You may hate your boss but want to continue in your job. You may have a responsibility for some relative that keeps you tied down in a small town when you really want to live and work in a big city.

These are run-of-the-mill frustrations. Many people have them. Basically, they are God-given urges to get out of a rut, to move on, to progress. I believe that these frustrations are caused by the universal urge toward evolution that exists in each one of us, the urge to aim ever higher and higher in our achievements. We must remember that you and I are not finished people; we are evolving people.

We live in a world of evolving people, and we still have a long way to go. If you don't think so, read the daily papers. We, collectively, are the unfinished business of life—still evolving. Individually, we also are unfinished business.

Dr. Maltz has set a scene for us in which you look in the mirror for a few minutes after you awaken each morning. "Which face do you see?" he asks. Which face? Do you see the one that represents frustration, a down-at-the-mouth person who thinks the world is against him and knows that nothing is going to go right that day? Or do you see the face that represents confidence? The face that shines with anticipation of worlds to conquer? Small personal worlds, of course, but worlds of great significance to you, the individual.

Now, I am going to interpret those two faces in the mirror a bit differently. When I look into the mirror, I see what my conscious mind and my subconscious mind have done with me and *for* me. The two faces in my mirror represent my conscious and my subconscious mind.

I see the conscious-mind picture of myself as the Raymond Charles Barker whom I see every day. I'm familiar with that face. But the other face, which represents a deep subconscious pattern of myself, may be quite unlike my conscious-mind face; and it is not so readily seen. There may be quite a contrast between the conscious-mind picture and the subconscious-mind picture. It may be as great as the contrast between *confidence and frustration*. This all depends on what my self-image is like—or, if you are looking in the mirror, what your self-image is like.

When we refer to self-images, we move right back to the Psycho-Cybernetics field. Remember: You are steering your mind to a productive goal; or, if you are overcome with frustration, you are steering your mind toward an unproductive, useless, or destructive goal.

The self-image—the way you really appear to yourself in your own thinking—governs what happens in your life. The pattern of your self-image is firmly fixed in your subconscious mind.

One of the most important things we have learned from Freudian psychology is that, in any conflict between the conscious and subconscious mind, the subconscious will always win. What you believe yourself to be at the subconscious level is what you really are. The conscious mind has, as one of its many facets, the capacity to create delusion. So I can look into the mirror and delude myself, temporarily make myself believe that I am a better or a greater person than I am—or perhaps a worse person. I can put on a mask, and, for a few minutes, I can fool myself. But I'm not fooling my subconscious mind.

The subconscious mind is a storehouse of all your beliefs—or my beliefs. Do you like yourself or don't you? The answer to that question is firmly implanted in your subconscious mind. And you had better like yourself, or you'll never be successful in the practice of Psycho-Cybernetics—the conquest of frustration.

I frequently have someone say to me, in a counseling session, "Dr. Barker, how do I go about liking myself when I'm such a failure? When I have no friends?"

After suggesting to this person that he certainly should be able to find some points in his character worth admiring, I advise him simply to say, "I like myself." Say it over and over again—day after day—when no one is around. This is an important first step toward building the image of yourself that you want. When you say, "I like myself," you are planting a seed in your subconscious mind. If you say it enough times, your subconscious will accept it as the truth.

But too few people do that. I'm astounded at the number of men and women with whom I talk who do not like themselves. Maybe they think that's their secret, but they give themselves away by continually running themselves down. It is fine to recognize your weaknesses and correct them, or, if you can't do that, to accept them. But merely to complain about them gets you nowhere and indicates that you have a self-image that is steering you toward unhappiness and failure. Perhaps you didn't even build this self-image. You may have taken one that someone else gave you.

I frequently ask such a downbeat person: "When you were a child, which parent wanted you to fail? Which parent told you that you would never amount to anything when you grew up?"

There is a moment of embarrassment, and sometimes I see a look bordering on terror on the person's face. *Must I tell **him**?* that look seems to say. Of course, I never force the issue, but I usually get the answer.

In one case, it may be a domineering father who has called his slightly built son a runt or a weakling and declared that he would never be able to handle a he-man's job. In another, we may find a society-minded mother who has constantly bemoaned the fact that her little girl isn't pretty, that she is going to have a hard time finding a husband when she grows up.

Many sons and daughters have accepted a parent's judgment as their own and built their self-images around it. I say to the son or the daughter, now grown to adulthood: "All right. If you have let this influence your attitude toward life, then your subconscious mind is being run by an idea someone else put into it. Let's get that idea out and put your own image of yourself in its place."

I find that this complete acceptance of someone else's opinion often occurs in a marriage relationship. A husband or a wife, usually in sarcasm, makes unkind or derogatory remarks that are projected into the other person's mind as a self-image, a very wrong self-image, but one that may be hard to uproot. A sister or a brother may cause you to have a false image of your real self if you listen to the judgments that are made and accept the verdict.

There is a great tendency to go back to the little boy or the little girl you once were, to go back to those early years when other people's images of you were put into your mind and, because of their impact, these images stayed there. You see yourself as others saw you. You do not see yourself as the real you that you are.

This is dangerous. It can rob you of your happiness and peace of mind. Say to yourself:

*This image is* not *my image. I don't like it. I have let this image be* in me, *and I have let it operate me. And it is going to stop.*

Old-timers at the First Church of Religious Science in New York City know that I quite often say: "I am not George Barker's little boy anymore, and I am not Harriette Barker's boy anymore. I now am Raymond Charles Barker, an adult. Both of my parents are on their own pathway. I am an adult—I am myself."

So I talk to myself, as you will learn to do, and I say: "Wrong self-image in my subconscious, you stop! You are neutralized by my right thinking. You come to mind no more. I now declare that in my subconscious mind, there is a perfect individual known as Raymond Charles Barker. There is a man—made in the image and likeness of God. There is a creative person. I am valuable to life and valuable to myself."

I do this perhaps once every three or four days; I do this because I want my mind, not someone else's mind, to run me. Therefore, I have to put into my subconscious mind my self-image.

I look in the mirror, and I see two faces: my conscious-mind face and my subconscious-mind face. I am looking at what I am, and I am looking at that which has caused me to be what I am and that which will cause me to be whatever I may be in the future. I know that my subconscious mind is always in action producing the me that I have accepted for myself. So, if I don't like that me, I have to go about the business of changing it.

You can do the same.

Taking a look at the five roadblocks that Dr. Maltz discussed will serve as a starter. However, I am going to work them out from a positive viewpoint.

The first one, you will remember, is indecision. Start thinking of yourself as a decision-making person because you are. One of the strongest arguments I make in my recently published book, *The Power of Decision,* is that indecision is a decision to fail. Indecision is actually that: *It is a decision to fail.*

Check over your life. By this, I mean check over your present livingness. You may find that you are very decisive in certain areas and indecisive in others. Forget those where you are decisive because you are in control there. You made up your mind to do something, and you did it. Now check the areas where you are indecisive, where you are afraid to say yes or no—I will or I won't. These are the areas where you will need to work to improve.

Let's take an example.

One of the most annoying things that can happen to a host who takes three people to a restaurant is to have to watch those three people with their indecisiveness. It happens to me often. We arrive at the restaurant. I look at a menu and decide what I want to eat. That's one area of consciousness where I have no indecision. But I've wasted a lot of valuable time with people who don't know whether they should have this or have that. "What are you going to have, Dr. Barker?" they ask. It's the inevitable question. When I tell them, all three of them say, "Well, I'll have the same thing."

I've used this common-variety situation to illustrate a human characteristic that may cause real havoc in the life of a person whose indecisiveness controls most of his behavior. Remember: Indecision is a roadblock that makes you take a detour on the way to happiness and success.

Watch out. If you are indecisive in one area of your life, you probably are indecisive in many others.

I have one friend with whom I refuse to go shopping. Suppose he is only buying a tie. He asks the opinion of whoever is with him. "Do you like this tie?" If the answer is yes, he buys the tie. He takes it home, and then, ten chances to one, he returns it to the store the next day. I decided long ago to let this friend do his indecision work on his own time—not on mine.

Your indecisions may be largely concerned with small matters such as I have outlined; or, they may have to do with far more important things, such as changing a job, moving into a new house, or even deciding whom you will marry. Watch out for your areas of indecision and *do something* about them. You were born with a mind and a set of emotions. They are your vital equipment; your body is entirely secondary. Use this mind and set of emotions when you make your decisions. You are going to be making them from now on throughout eternity, and you might just as well get started now.

Indecision makes you unattractive to other people. You may lose many friends by your shilly-shallying ways. At least you'll make them impatient and hesitant to seek your company.

I'm sure you know someone like Mary, who, when she's invited to go to the movies, never knows which picture she wants to see. "It doesn't matter," she will say. "Let's go where you want to go." Trying to be helpful, her escort asks, "Well, do you like a musical? Or would you rather see a comedy? Maybe an adventure?" Her answer is, "Oh, I don't really know. I guess one picture is as good as another. You pick the show, and I'm sure I'll enjoy it."

The problem is not that Mary doesn't know what she likes. She is just in the habit of indecision, and for the rest of her life, she probably will avoid making choices. She will never announce to her friends where she wants to go and what she wants to do. But that's not my way of doing it. I announce. Yes, I announce.

So, for all the Marys and all the Johns who have read this far and resolved to remove the first roadblock in the conquest of frustration, here is a positive statement I would like you to make:

*I am a decision-making individual; I am a decision-maker.*
*Once I have made a decision, I proceed toward my goal.*

Repeat that statement often, especially when you find yourself reluctant to make up your mind.

And be sure that you don't worry about wrong decisions. You have made many of them, and you will make many more. They haven't wrecked you, and you have learned valuable lessons from them.

As a matter of fact, worry is the next roadblock we are going to consider here. It is second on Dr. Maltz's list. Worry is the greatest waste of mental and emotional energy that has ever overtaken the human race on its upward path. And I suspect we have been worrying ever since we first began to know ourselves—that first flash of self-consciousness back there somewhere along the evolutionary path.

I believe one of the reasons why religion always has been important to man is that it has given him a faith symbol—no matter what kind of religion it was. It has helped lessen his worry load. That is why different religions have helped different people. Each has *lessened the worry load.*

Here we are, well past the middle of the twentieth century, and you would think that with everything we have today, we would be worrying less. I wonder if we aren't worrying more. I wonder if our accumulation of more possessions and our ability to do more things and to go more places has not increased the worry load rather than decreased it.

What can we do about this tendency to worry about many things? Here is my suggestion to you.

Think of the place, a physical location, where you do most of your worrying. Is it a certain chair in the living room? Is it a chair at your desk? Is it in bed, after you have retired for the night? Figure out your key worry spot. If you drive a car a great deal, maybe the driver's seat is what we might call your anxiety seat.

When you have found your chief worry spot, make a decision that there is to be no more worry there. If you feel that you must worry, go to a different chair. Call it your "faith chair" or "faith spot" if it isn't a chair. After a while, you will probably feel so ridiculous that you may start laughing instead of negating.

A good laugh will often remove your tension and put you in a better problem-solving frame of mind. Remember that you are in possession of a great creative instrument—your mind. None of us truly appreciates the intricacy of this mind and the emotions that back it up. We fail to recognize its brilliance. So instead of letting it lead us to our goal, we sometimes take all of this mental and emotional energy and—whammy!—we turn it in a negative direction and get negative results.

That's not the way to progress along the pathway of life. In order to be happy and successful, you accept only the good and the positive. When you run into people who say they can't help worrying, remember that this is nonsense. Anyone can stop worrying unless he or she is a complete neurotic. It takes a bit of doing, of course. It takes finding something you are actively interested in, something that awakens your enthusiasm. When you have challenging goals to achieve, the time you allot to worrying is minimized.

That's great; worry never solves anything. It is just a roadblock.

Tell your subconscious mind, the Doer within you, that it is to stop bothering you. Here is a positive statement for you to make:

I am *not a worry person.* I am *a right-thinking, creative individual, valuable to life.*

*Failure to do what needs to be done* is our third roadblock. Dr. Maltz speaks of the importance of doing one thing at a time, not trying to do too many things at once. Naturally, if you are going to do one thing at a time, you will do the most important thing first. And if you sit around and put off doing anything, you place yourself in the class of the eternal procrastinators. Procrastination is a habit—that's all it is. It happens to be a very wrong habit. It is a habit you do not have to change unless you want to. But if you will look at the records of men and women who have won success in some field of endeavor, you will discover that none of them procrastinated in his or her chosen work. Some of these successful individuals may have been procrastinators about taking out the laundry or such trivia, but in their chosen arena of success, there was no procrastination. Whatever *needs* to be done is done by the successful person.

In our former church building, when we were without adequate help, I would do the vacuuming. It didn't bother me to mop a floor. I wouldn't do it in my own apartment. But I would do it for the church because the church was my success idea. When you have true motivation for success, you will not procrastinate in that area. If you are a procrastinator, do something about it.

The cosmic order—of which you are a valuable part—is always on time. It gets done what needs to be done at the instant it needs to do it. You can consult a meteorologist at the United States Government Weather Bureau, and he can tell you the exact time the tides will come in tomorrow or on a certain day next week or next month. Those tides, operating on exact schedule today, undoubtedly will be operating on an exact schedule a million years from now. The meteorologist can predict exactly what time the sun will rise each morning and set each evening during the present year, and the sun is expected to be on time for all the years to come.

The cosmic process is always on time. You are a part of this process. You are a cosmic process individualized as you, and you can be on time. Start saying:

*I am an on-time individual, and I do what needs to be done in order to be a success.*

If you really are a success person, you will know what an important key point our next roadblock is—*insoluble problems*. You probably have friends and neighbors who insist that their problems are too grave or too complicated to be solved. They go around announcing this, discussing the problem in question ad infinitum. But that's as far as they go.

There is not a problem in the universe that cannot be solved. The insoluble problems of a hundred years ago have, for the most part, been solved. Those of a hundred years from now will be solved in their own time.

So who are you and I to sit back and say that our problems can't be solved?

Every problem is the result of an idea, and every solution is the result of another idea. All ideas come to us from one source—the Infinite Creative Mind. If you believe that source and trust that source, you will be guided to the right answer no matter how serious your situation may seem. But when you take a negative attitude and say something cannot be done, you are planting in your subconscious mind a belief in failure. You are blocking the channels that let inspired thinking come through.

Start saying to yourself:

*Every problem I have in my world today can be solved because my mind is intelligent. I have the intelligence of the Infinite Mind within me and, when I expect this intelligence to act and give me right ideas, it does. But as long as I sit around declaring that I have a problem that can't be solved, I am* really *saying that I do not have enough intelligence to find a solution.*

*Every problem in my world today can be solved.*

You magnify and give power to problems when you dwell on them. The first thing you learn in this teaching is: Diminish the power of any negative; cut the power down. You cut the power down by giving the problem less attention, less importance, and by saying:

*I can beat this. I can beat it. There is an answer. The answer is in my mind right now, and it reveals itself in my mind right now. There are no insoluble problems.*

The fifth and last of Dr. Maltz's roadblocks is: *We refuse to relax.* He has given you some specific instructions on how to relax. But I believe all of us must first get over the idea that it is necessary to hurry and scurry through life. It is fashionable these days to be too busy; it is fashionable to always be tired; it is fashionable to feel that you are overworked; it is fashionable to feel that life today is complicated.

I wish you could move back in time and follow a typical grandmother, perhaps of your grandmother's generation, when she lived on a farm in Iowa. The water was outside the house—not inside. She pumped it from a cistern or well and carried it in a bucket into the kitchen. She often milked the cows and fed the pigs; she also tended the garden. On her hands and knees, she scrubbed the floors until they were spotless, and she baked the most wonderful bread.

There were no soap-filled scouring pads, no detergents. She often made her own soap from her special recipe. Lighting, usually by means of a kerosene lamp, was inadequate, and Grandma had no electrical equipment. If you were to follow her around for one day, you would drop from exhaustion.

So when you think that life today is too complicated, remember Grandmother.

Life today may be *just as* complicated for all of us as it was in the so-called "good old days," but it is no more complicated. Now, if you are concentrating on your own life and saying that it is too complicated, what are you doing to simplify it?

Are you wasting time with people who add nothing to your livingness? "Friends" who are just hangers-on? Who contribute nothing to your happiness? Then get rid of them and cultivate a close relationship only with the people who bring meaning and pleasure into your day-to-day living.

I know that I have precious little time to waste on stupid people, men and women whom I do not enjoy. You will never hear me say, "I am going to take so-and-so to the theater because I ought to." Either I like the person, or I don't go. I have also ended my duty trips to relatives and *old friends of Mother's.* They are forever coming to New York, and you don't know how busy I can be when I get the name over the telephone. All tied up! Sorry. I would rather read a good book than waste time on uninteresting people.

However, it may not be the other fellow who makes it impossible for you to relax. Maybe it is you yourself. Many people are afraid of a brief period of silence—of aloneness—because they don't want to face up to what they may find out if they commune with themselves. By staying overwrought, busy, hectic, they don't have to contemplate the inner workings of their minds. They put the blame for their frustrations on the office, on the home, on the pressure of social events, or maybe on the nasty weather.

You and I need to face ourselves. Do you know why? You'll find that if you look within yourself, you are really quite a nice person. You do not have to dodge the truth about yourself. Every mistake you have made is one that I have made in a different way. Your next-door neighbor has made it, and probably several people down the street, whom you don't even know, have made it. So don't let the fear of getting to know your real self keep you from relaxing.

Try five minutes without the radio, without television, without a magazine, without a book—and sit in a comfortable chair. Say to yourself: "I'm going to do nothing for five minutes." Of course, your mind will think of twenty things that you ought to be doing. I learned to do this recently.

Two or three times a week, I sit down, away from a desk and in a chair, I don't usually sit in. I sit down and say, "I'm going to do nothing for five minutes."

My mind starts to burry and bustle. What will happen if the phone rings?

If it rings, it rings; I won't answer it. What will happen if the doorbell rings? It will ring; I won't answer it. Well, maybe they are delivering something important. They can deliver it later. I argue with myself, but I do nothing for five minutes and, eventually, I feel relaxed.

Take a chair and call it your "do-nothing chair." Sit down in it and let your mind wander. You can't stop thinking, of course, so this is a good time to do some *creative* thinking.

What is creative thinking?

To those who are familiar with metaphysical teachings, or the teachings of Religious Science, the term needs no explanation. But for some readers who are bound to ask that question, here is a simple explanation.

We are not merely referring to the artist, the writer, or the inventor who thinks creatively and creates. We are referring to you, to anyone who sets a goal and strives to reach it. Visualize that goal as you relax. Picture it in your own mind and see how you will look when you have achieved it, where you will be and what you will be doing. Imagine that you have already reached that goal and feel the exultant emotions; experience the joy that goes with obtaining something that is your heart's desire.

When you create this picture, you are actually planting a seed—an idea—in the subconscious mind, and if you believe that the subconscious mind can carry out your desire once you have made it known, you have started on your way to self-fulfillment. Visualizing your goal for five relaxing minutes each day is a powerful way to attain it.

Dr. Maltz has pointed out that an important factor in the art of relaxing is *forgiveness*. This includes forgiving others and forgiving yourself. How do you do it? Just by saying, "I forgive."

I do this when I am alone. I say: "I forgive every person in my life from the day I was born to the present. I forgive everyone who has hurt me down through the years. I forgive; I bless you. You have cluttered up my mind much too much. You have caused me to waste my mental and emotional energy thinking about the hurts. I've got too much to do to carry you around any longer. I'm a busy man. I have a goal, and I am going to get there, and I cannot get there if I am worried about some dreadful thing someone said to me five years ago." Then I add: "Subconscious mind, you do the rest of the work." And it does.

Then there is the point of forgiving yourself. You and I carry a pretty heavy guilt load, you know, concerning things we didn't do and things we did do. Every time we can lessen that load, we are on the road to what we want.

So I say: "All right, Barker, you now forgive Barker for all the stupidities, minor and major, that your subconscious mind can remember you've ever committed. You now forgive yourself. You can't carry that old load around either."

When you have forgiven others and forgiven yourself, you might ask yourself this question: "Am I able to give myself away?"

The key word here is communication. Can you communicate well with other people? You see, communication is the ability to give yourself away. People who are non-communicative are afraid to do this. There is a fear of discovery, of the lack of communication, a fear that the person with whom you communicate will find out something about you that you don't want him to know—maybe something that is not very nice. You think that if you are non-communicative, no one will find out your secret.

When you give yourself away—give of yourself to others—you will probably discover that your close friends and your loved ones know far more about you than you think. I don't believe that a man who has a smart wife can keep any great secrets from her. And I doubt if a woman who has a smart husband can keep very many secrets from him, either.

Now, how do we give ourselves away through communication? When I'm talking with you, I am giving of myself to you, whether it be in a public place or whether it be shaking hands and saying "Good morning" to you in the lobby of the church. Communication is a subconscious freedom to give of yourself to others. You may have it in certain areas but not in others.

Make notes of the areas where you do have communication—such as with loved ones, with close friends, but not with strangers. Or you may have total communication in the office but not in your social life. Find the areas where you don't have communication and try to figure out what is the secret in those areas that you don't want anyone to discover. What is it that you don't want that particular group to know about you? When you have discovered that secret, sit back and say, "What difference would it make?"

Communication over a broad field, with many people, is an important factor in your happiness and your success. It is a part of the conquest of your frustrations—a vital function in your life.

## DO NOT PUT YOURSELF IN A MENTAL PRISON

You and I are mental people, and, at one time or another, we have all had the experience of putting ourselves into mental prisons such as Dr. Maltz has described. Yes, in spite of the fact that I am a clergyman, I occasionally do incarcerate myself by allowing hurts, anxieties, or resentments to invade my thinking. Only I can do this to myself; no one else can do it to me. When I become frustrated over some situation, be it large or small, it is because I allow myself to build up negative attitudes about that situation. I am sure that I do this without intent, certainly without deliberateness. It is an unconscious welling up in my mind of potentially destructive ideas that I don't bother to check when they should be checked and eliminated.

At such times, I let my fears or my worries linger too long in my subconscious. I give them a chance to take root and grow. You should never let disturbing thoughts or emotions last more than two or three hours. Just as a seed planted in fertile soil reproduces its own kind, negative thoughts, if allowed to remain in the subconscious, will eventually create negative or unhappy experiences.

If you have repeatedly, over a period of years, allowed attitudes of distrust, envy, hate, or self-doubt to control your thinking, you are indeed imprisoned in a jail of the mind. Your vision has become blurred and distorted; you cannot see clearly while looking out through prison bars. You cannot see yourself, your friends, or your loved ones in the proper light.

You are certainly getting a false picture of your own experiences.

A deeply frustrated person, looking at the world with a warped mind, sees a world of torment, a vast field of unhappiness. This must be changed! Such a person needs to find the means of letting down the bars and unlocking the prison doors. He or she needs to find the key to freedom and a new kind of livingness. That key is positive, creative thinking that helps the dynamic self-image emerge.

You can use your conscious and deliberate thought to plant right ideas in your subconscious. Then you will begin to experience the livingness that is *self-fulfillment*. I call it the sense of making one's own experience rich in living by means of one's own mind. Attaining this mind control is a one-man job. I can't achieve it for you, and you can't achieve it for me. Furthermore, neither of us can do it unless we know in quiet confidence that we can. When we know and have faith, the subconscious mind goes to work on the positive ideas we have planted there.

In my book, *Treat Yourself to Life,* which explains how to use scientific prayer called spiritual treatment in Religious Science, I say: "The basis of scientific treatment is that your subconscious mind is a part of the mind of God. Your subconscious mind is your best friend, your creator, your ally. It will go to work for you at this instant to produce all the joy, all the love, all the peace in your world that you can possibly want. Being a part of the infinite mind, it plays the leading role in the creative process. It is the part of the universal mind which is a law as unchanging and unrelenting as the law of gravity."

This is absolutely true. The trouble is that the average frustrated person has lost the ability to believe that he can become anything better than he is. He doesn't let his subconscious work for him on the positive side; by his negative thinking, he forces it to work on the negative side. His self-image is one of self-doubt and low self-esteem. He has firmly implanted in his mind the "poor me" or the "no-one-understands-me" concept. He is busy finding excuses and constructing alibis for his failures. He has no time to envision successes. In fact, he has lost sight of the thing that he really is.

And what is he? What are each and every one of us? We are *potential*. We have within us the possibility and the capability of becoming anything we want to be, if only we believe in the power of our minds and that of the Infinite Mind working and expressing through us. Once we have achieved our goal—become the person we want to be—we have achieved self-fulfillment. We are successful in some special area, and we are proud of our success. Of course, life is a process of *being* and becoming; there is no final achievement, and there will always be new goals to attain.

You have probably read some of Dr. Maltz's books and some of mine. All of these contain the necessary ideas, techniques, and suggestions for a full life. We are re-emphasizing some of these ideas here. However, after you have read this book and some of the earlier ones, you will still have to proceed on your own to do something about the ideas embodied in the books. You are the only one who can do the job, but as you reap the rewards, you will find that you are helping others as well as yourself. I often think that if each person who ever read one of Dr. Maltz's books or one of mine, had followed through with only one self-healing, the world would be a far happier and healthier place in which to live.

But books alone cannot guarantee self-fulfillment. If they could guarantee this, the Bible would have changed the whole world. But it hasn't. The Sermon on the Mount would have changed the history of the planet. But it hasn't. Historians have never attempted to record the number of sermons, based on the Sermon on the Mount, that have been preached; or the number of times this portion of the Bible has been read by millions of people. Yet, reading or hearing about this great message of Jesus has not changed the world because its teachings have stayed at the idea level; they have not moved to the practice level. In order to have self-fulfillment, you have to practice every day. At this point, I can almost hear the voices of many readers clamoring: "But I don't know how to go about it. What must I do?"

The first step is to set your goal and to believe in it. Believe, without hesitation, that you are going to reach it. What your goal is will be determined by what you want to do, who you want to be. It may be a long-range goal that you will have to travel far to reach. As you move toward it, you may be reminded of an ancient proverb that says, in essence: A thousand-mile walk starts with a single step. There may be many steps, many minor goals, on the road to your major goal. Set your sights confidently on your large objective, and then start with one of the minor goals. The pathway to self-fulfillment is made easier and brighter by each attainment of a minor goal.

Suppose your major goal is happiness. You say, "I want to be happy, but I am not." Why aren't you? What steps can you take to make yourself happier? What minor goals can you reach? Let's assume that one will be the simple matter of changing your conversation. Is what you say interesting to anyone besides yourself? Decide that the next time you see Sally or Joe, you will not re-hash things you've said many times before. If your problem is that you feel you haven't anything to say, read a book and talk about that. Read some interesting magazine articles and introduce what you've learned into the conversation. Have an exciting experience and share it with others.

At any rate, stop rationalizing your failures with trumped-up excuses, and start taking steps toward your goal, whatever it may be. That's the only way you can achieve self-fulfillment. And you'll be elated when you do achieve it. Self-fulfillment is the awareness of yourself as a satisfactory individual. That awareness gives you a wonderful feeling.

When you are lonely, miserable, and frustrated, you are not a satisfactory individual. You think of your lack of friends and pity yourself instead of doing something constructive about making friends. You let your thoughts linger on slights and snubs instead of asking yourself if perhaps you aren't to blame. Your entire attention is focused on what is wrong in your situation. Try turning it instead on something that is right or on something that you can make right.

Self-fulfillment is the feeling of self-satisfaction. There is nothing wrong with that. I believe that every person who has ever accomplished anything great has had a tremendous inner sense of self-satisfaction. It is the glorious feeling of having done something well, something worthwhile.

Perhaps you are about to say, "But I haven't ever done anything that was worthwhile." Don't say it. Start thinking instead. Use the power of your mind. Go and sit in a garden; go and sit in the park. If the weather isn't good, go and sit somewhere other than the place where you live.

Be stimulated by a new environment, and you may come up with some valuable new ideas.

The tendency of the frustrated person is always to retreat, to crawl into a shell. That shell is usually his home. There he looks at the same four walls, the same furniture, the same refrigerator, and the same set of dishes. Such a person is desperately in need of a change, if only for ten minutes. He needs to see something new, something challenging, something that will bring to life the once-bright self-image that he has successfully buried beneath his chronic negativism. He needs to find some interest that will make him hunger and thirst after a creative way of life.

We are admonished in the Bible to "hunger and thirst after righteousness," and I'm sure this means to hunger and thirst after a creative way of life. Most spiritually alert people do have that hunger and thirst because they haven't quenched it too often with hurts, loneliness, and their own misunderstanding of themselves.

It is important to realize that every time you describe yourself or your situation in negatives, you are adding to your own self-misunderstanding, which is the exact opposite of self-fulfillment. There is no quicker way to develop self-misunderstanding than to belittle yourself, to run yourself down. We all have a tendency to do that when we are feeling depressed. You can master that tendency if you remember that *self-depreciation is destructive* and that you will never find self-fulfillment through creating self-destructive images. You are never really as bad as your frustrated mind pictures you to be.

Try to see yourself as a perfect being. It isn't difficult. Shut your eyes and think of yourself as being the way you want to be. If you are one of the unfortunates who is bound to say, "I don't know what I want to be," I'm tempted to tell you to stay as you are. But try again. What would you be like if you were perfectly happy? Shut your eyes and try to figure that one out. Would you look as you do now? Would you dress as you are now dressed? Would you talk as you do in the usual conversation of the day? No. Probably not.

Right here, I am offering you some suggestions for minor goals on your road to happiness. If you want to be self-fulfilled, how would you dress if you were self-fulfilled? Then dress that way. How would you groom yourself, wear your hair, and so on if you were happy and self-fulfilled? Change your appearance to meet your ideal. How would you talk if you were self-fulfilled? Then change your conversation to that of the new image.

When you do this, the bars of your mental prison will start to shake; they will spread apart so you can begin to see your life as it really is. No creative power ever condemned you to frustration. No God, by whatever name, planned for you to be miserable. If you are miserable, you are suffering from self-created misery; and I'm willing to state that most of it is unconsciously self-created misery. No one decides to be miserable.

When you've worked with these simple suggestions long enough to see some improvement in your regard for yourself, start watching your negatives and don't allow the seed of any unwanted or unworthy idea to be implanted in the ground of your subconscious. Turn your negatives off by thinking their opposites. Learn to accept situations as they are without letting them bother you. Learn to say, "What difference does it make?"

Suppose you were fired from your job five years ago. So what! Probably the employer knew what he was doing, even though you say that you were one of the best employees the man ever had. Maybe that's just your alibi, your excuse.

Forgive yourself and your former employer for this old hurt, and forget it.

Perhaps you were ill for a long time three years ago, and you are still mentally reliving and rebuilding that illness. If so, your negative thinking will probably cause you to be ill again.

The Bible says: "For by thy words thou shalt be justified, and by thy words, thou shalt be condemned" (Matthew 12:37). Watch your words. Keep your conversation positive. You do not find self-fulfillment through self-depreciation, and you do not find it through listening to or discussing the negative thoughts and feelings of others. Nor do you end it by sitting at home and worrying. These tactics never have worked, and they never will.

As we move along in this business of looking at ourselves squarely and discovering our strengths and our weaknesses, we come to the point where we must ask, "Do I accept myself as I am, or do I reject myself?"

If you accept yourself as you are, you probably rank among the minority—the fortunate, well-balanced minority. Rejection of self is a rather common human reaction, though it varies greatly in degree of severity. This rejection stems from the fact that no one is perfect, and many people who crave perfection can't face up to their own imperfections. They continually blame themselves for every mistake they make or ever have made. Perhaps I, too, reject myself occasionally on a minor scale. But, generally speaking, I have come to terms with myself on that point. I came to terms when I reached the understanding that no mistake I ever have made is of real importance. As Dr. Maltz says, "We are all mistake-makers, but we also are mistake-breakers." When we take the importance out of our mistakes, they become dwarfs instead of giants.

If you find that you are a self-rejector, try saying to yourself:

I accept myself today, right now, as I am. Yesterday is past. Ten years ago doesn't count. I am a human being today with a creative mind, and I want to use it creatively. I have great emotions, which I can use constructively. I am a today person in a today world, and I am going to use my mind and my emotions as I should use them today. I do not reject myself. I am a rather nice human being. God created me, and if I am good enough for God, I'd better be good enough for myself. I accept myself as a valuable creative individual—individualizing life.

Add to that statement these words:

*I walk this day as a dignified, creative individual.*

What does that mean? It means that your posture matches your state of mind. If you walk in dignity, you feel important. Try it and see. Even the most casual observer can judge your personality and your outlook on life by watching the way you sit, the way you stand, and the way you walk. The person who stands erect, walks with his shoulders back and his head held high, indicates that he is unafraid; he has no fear of the future. He is a success-prone person. In contrast, the person who walks in a stooped manner, always looking down and perhaps shuffling his feet a bit, is a person who doesn't want to see the future. He has no plans for success; he actually expects to fail, and he isn't surprised when he does.

I've frequently had an individual say to me, "Dr. Barker, I was finally released from my job, but I knew it was coming." That person's mind had been preoccupied with failure for years, and there was nothing for him to do but fail. Of course, such an individual will always say afterward.

"Well, it wasn't my fault."

I'm sorry! I disagree. My mind is the center of my experience. I cannot have an experience that my mind has not caused to happen. If I were fired tomorrow from my job as minister of the First Church of Religious Science in New York City, it would be my own fault. I'd probably tell everyone that the Board of Trustees was to blame. But I wouldn't fool myself. It would be my own fault. My mind is what I am, and my experience is the result of my use of my mind. This is not only expressed in my mind/body relationship. It is expressed in every relationship I have, whether it be with people, in business, or in my home.

When I go out on any occasion, the only thing I can take is my mind. The body follows along; the body is automatic. I walk into every situation with my mind, and my mind will determine what I give to that situation and what I receive from that situation.

Let's turn our thinking now to the baby Dr. Maltz mentioned—the baby coming out of the mother's womb; its first slap and first cry. That baby arrives in this world fully equipped to be a success. It arrives with the capability of *thought* and *feeling*. Then, after the necessary months, the child will add *speech*. Here he has his three great tools for living: thought, feeling, and speech. What happens during all the rest of his life will be the result of what he is doing, or has done, with his thought, feeling, and speech.

If you want to start now using those tools in a constructive way, you may find that you are experiencing the second birth that is mentioned in the Good Book. You can change your life in any way you wish if you handle and control your thought, feeling, and speech. These three tools with which you were born are the tools, the equipment, that will take you the rest of the way.

This is a challenge. If you accept it, you can become any kind of person you want to be; the person you are five years from now will be a living example of what you did with your birthright, your total significant equipment. The individual who considers himself a miserable failure can reverse himself and become a magnificent success if he learns how to master his thought, feeling, and speech.

To repeat what I have said earlier in this chapter, it isn't easy. The frustrated person is a worrier, and he has to stop worrying. He can't stop worrying until he has a real reason for doing so. That reason is a goal. Suppose I've worried for years about my health, then I suddenly decide to make real health my goal. I start to eat sensibly, to sleep a reasonable number of hours. I take long walks, and perhaps I find suitable forms of exercise. I may add other health-promoting regimes. That's fine. But unless I think health while I walk, eat, sleep, and work, I won't reach my goal.

If health is your goal, learn to say: *"I am health."* Do this even when you are not feeling very well. Just say it. You can even spiritualize it and say: *"God is my health."* But you still have to think it, feel it, talk it, and find routines that produce it.

You can translate this into any other area of your life.

Your goal may involve a career, a happy marriage, a new home, or just a sizable bank account. Whatever it is, remember you must use thought, feeling, and speech to attain it.

I have counseled many people on the problems that come from the lack and limitation of money. While the answer to their problems is not money but rather the awakening of the creative power within them, I start counseling them on minor goals. "Put one dollar in the savings bank today," I sometimes say. The answer usually is, "Oh, they won't open a bank account with only one dollar." I reply, "Then save a dollar a week for ten weeks and walk in and plunk it down."

This doesn't usually seem to be a satisfactory answer from the standpoint of the person with a financial problem, but from my standpoint, it is a *start* on an intelligent, constructive program. When I explain that it is a most comfortable feeling to have money in the bank, beyond current bills, the person I am counseling often looks at me and says, "I need every dollar I've got." The person who says that wants to stay in his poverty. Of course, the dollar a week in the bank is nothing but a symbol; it is a valuable symbol to the mind. I have often said to someone in a financial-limitation problem: "Add a dollar a week to the payment of one bill, and gradually whittle it down." I say this because when your mind becomes really interested in paying bills, rather than in owing bills, you will find a way to get yourself out of debt. But when your entire focus is on what you owe to this store or that concern, your attention is on owing, not paying. As long as your attention is on owing, the subconscious mind will arrange more ways for you to owe. When your attention is on paying, the subconscious mind will then begin to create means for paying.

It won't be because of manna from heaven! It will be because your mind finally is organized on a success program in the particular field of finance. Self-fulfillment will come when, step by step, you have reached the point where you owe no man.

When you have cleared one department of your life, when you have completed one of your areas of self-fulfillment, you will probably want to start on another. Always remember, whatever your direction may be, you should start with your minor goals and keep on going until you have arrived at the place where you want to go. All of this starts, of course, with the concept that you are valuable to life. A frustrated person doesn't have this concept. It is essential to realize that you would not have been born if there weren't some reason for your birth and your life. You are not a biological mistake. The universe has too much order and plan to include mistakes. You were born to be a creative, valuable person. I believe that not a single person is born into this world who is not needed by the world. I believe that you and I are needed.

If you are a member of my congregation, you may say, "Yes! You! Look at the job you are doing. Everyone needs you!" I wish it were true because Madison Square Garden is still available for Sunday morning rental.

You can point to a Dr. Maltz; you can point to a person like myself; you can point to a noted criminal lawyer; you can point to all these people and say, "Look at them!" But that has nothing to do with it. You are necessary to the coordinated life on this planet, or you wouldn't be here. I don't believe the Infinite Intelligence ever makes a mistake. And I do believe that you were born at the right time, in the right place, of the right parents, to do your right work.

Start thinking this way, instead of saying, "Well, I don't know. I wish I were ten years younger; I wish I'd had different parents." You didn't. Fortunately, most of us like our parents, but if you don't, start believing and saying:

I was born at the right time, through the right family, and in the right location to do my right work.

This is self-acceptance; this is the acceptance of a new self-image, of a cause for being. Every living soul *needs a cause* for being.

Every living soul needs the sense of being needed, and if you have no one on earth who needs you, find somebody. I know it isn't easy. You have built up all your bars; you have put yourself into your own mental jail; you have been the judge, and you sat there and condemned yourself. Now change the condemnation. Let the judge in your mind say:

I now set you free to be a creative person. You are valuable to God and to man.

Even if you don't believe it, say it anyway. And if you say it often enough and long enough, it will begin to register. You will find a situation in which you are of value. You will begin to draw people to you who will find value in you. This is because you are now thinking, feeling, and talking in a way that makes people want to respond.

Each one of you has someone in your life who always says the same thing. When you pick up the telephone to answer and hear that voice, you know exactly what you are going to have to listen to. Why? Because that's what this person has been saying year after year. The locale changes slightly; the particular smaller events change, but the overall picture will be exactly what you heard last Tuesday when the same individual called.

Perhaps you should ask yourself, "Is that what I say over the telephone all the time? When I call someone, have I anything to say that I haven't said before?" People get tired of hearing the same thing. They know you are tired; they know you've had a hard week; they know that the work at the office has been extra heavy this season of the year, which is *all four seasons.* They know that the buses are crowded; they know that you don't like to go out at night anymore. This they know. This they are aware of.

Before you make a telephone call to a friend or a loved one, think of what you are going to say. Judge whether it is creative or valuable to either one of you. Perhaps you won't say it. Or, if you are seriously trying to change your image, you will, with deliberate intent, say something different.

Your thinking, feeling, and speaking make up the trinity of the creative process. With them, when they are directed correctly, you find a reason for being. Then you can literally say, "The world does need me. I am of some value to my fellow man." Then find ways of truly being of value.

Here is the situation as it commonly is found: the child is born to success; the adult grumbles, alibis, and complains that he or she is not a success. But this need not be true in your case. Change the way you handle the trinity of the creative process. This doesn't require one more degree in education; it doesn't require moving across the country to another city. It merely requires the direction of your mind, and you can direct your mind. If you say you can't, I am going to say you can. I have seen too many people do it to have any doubt. I have done it myself. I agree that it is not easy.

Dr. Maltz referred to "the stranger that is within you." To me, a clergyman, this means your spiritual self:

Many people today have dodged any search for their spiritual selves because past theological beliefs have been restrictive. People who claimed to be spiritual were not usually people whom others wanted to follow or to imitate. The older theology demanded self-denial instead of encouraging self-development.

The spirit within you is not a field of repression. It is a field of expression. I am going to emphasize that: the spirit within you is not an arena of repression; it is an arena of creative expression, an expression that will produce self-satisfying benefits for you. This stranger within you loses its strangeness as you think of yourself in spiritual terms. If the word *spiritual* is a block to you, think of yourself in creative terms. Think of yourself as possibility, potential, as being a valuable human being—then the stranger loses its strangeness and becomes your habitual, normal self.

You become a creative, outgoing, healthy, happy, prosperous individual who relates to others with ease of communication when you know this self that you are. Remember that you live in an arena of expression, not of repression. It isn't what you give up that is important. It is what you do with what you have that counts.

Perhaps you will feel impelled to confess that you have some bad habits and ask if you shouldn't give them up. My answer will invariably be: "Not unless they really hurt you in some way."

I recall a person who came to me a few years ago and said that he was on the spiritual pathway. I said, "Oh, good." He said he had given up cigarette smoking. Then he had given up any use of alcoholic beverages. Then he had become a vegetarian.

I expressed my belief that this was fine for him if he felt such self-denial were necessary. Then he continued: "But I'm uneasy. I don't feel as though I am spiritual, and these things should have done it."

My reply was, "That's not the way to do it at all. However, I have one more suggestion. Why don't you enter a monastery?" He did not take kindly to that idea.

Of course, I have no objection to monasteries. I was merely trying to point out that he was using age-old techniques that have done more to create frustration than to conquer it. They require that you give up and go without. They declare that the Lord likes those who refrain from doing things. I was about to say that these old tenets held that the Lord likes those who are frustrated. There is not a word of truth in any such rules.

The whole spirit of God within you is seeking expression through you, and there is to be no repression. You are living in a world in which the spirit within you is saying: *Be! Become! Become! Become!*

## YOUR CONSCIENCE IS YOUR SELF-IMAGE

During much of your life, you probably have considered your conscience an accuser. Many people still believe that it is a faculty of the mind devised for the sole purpose of keeping them in line, telling them that they *should do* this and they *should not do* that. Dr. Maltz has likened your conscience to your self-image, your opinion of yourself. According to his concept, when your conscience bothers you, it is because you are not making progress toward your goal, or because you do not hold yourself in high esteem.

Conscience, as I see it, is much more than a prompter telling you the difference between right and wrong, warning that you should not bridge moral gaps or cheat your fellow man. I believe that *conscience is spiritual inspiration.*

It is the still, small voice that—even in the face of profound discouragement—says: "Do it. Be it. Become it."

I believe that conscience is an inner urge to get going and to keep going, not a brake that one applies in order to stop doing something, be it good or bad. Conscience speaks to each and every one of us, but some do not listen. Some fail to hear that fervent counselor within which says to the individual in doubt: "You can be. You ought to be. Why don't you be it?" To the individual who listens, the conscience becomes an invaluable guide. You cannot live in peace with yourself until you are at least making the effort *to be what you want to be*.

Conscience may only nudge you into saying: "All right. I'll try." Those words are a good sign. They are a beginner's step in your conquest of frustration. They are the signal that you are ready to break up old patterns of failure and unhappiness which you have allowed to form in your mind.

Every frustration is a conscious or an unconscious pattern of self-limitation, a pattern that tells you that you *can't* instead of that you can. That pattern has become firmly embedded in your subconscious and will remain there, trying to keep you from being what you can be, unless you take deliberate steps to change it. These negative patterns, habits that are hard to break, are among the roadblocks we have already discussed. They are always on the inside of you, never on the outside.

That statement may seem absurd to the person who says: "I'm frustrated in my job." Or to the one who declares: "I'm frustrated in my marriage." These are life situations. They may seem to be external, to involve only persons, places, or things in the environment. Nevertheless, these troublesome situations are actually the result of unhealthy thinking on the part of the frustrated individual.

If that person has a conscience that merely tells him right from wrong, he will probably feel guilty for a certain amount of misunderstanding and resentment on his part, but he will also be ready to heap loads of guilt on everyone else remotely connected with his frustration. Let us suppose, however, that he has the kind of conscience I have called spiritual inspiration. If he starts listening to the counselor within, the Divine Spirit, he will think as follows: "You can be a valuable employee. You can learn to understand your employer and to earn his respect. You can overlook the qualities you see in him which you dislike. Perhaps you are not always so likable yourself."

Be assured. That inner counselor is there. Be still, listen, and be patient. If you are not accustomed to awaiting this inner guidance, you may have to be patient a while before you sense it. But when you do, its encouraging admonitions can be applied to any problem that troubles you.

The thoughts and emotions that are entertained in your mind are the things you need to face and understand. You must meet and solve every problem within yourself. There is no scapegoat. In the problem-solving process, you may have to change your views of yourself and your attitudes toward others. Quite often, you have to change your opinion of yourself, to revise your self-image. That is not always an easy thing to do.

Dr. Maltz has designated some of the people with whom he has to deal as "complainers." In my role as a professional counselor, I come into contact with such individuals, too. People rarely make appointments with me to tell me nice things. They come in with their lists of what is wrong with their friends, their relatives, their neighborhood, and the world. Occasionally, they admit that there is something wrong with themselves—but not often.

In my counseling work, I do exactly what Dr. Maltz has suggested in *Psycho-Cybernetics*. I have been doing this in my own way for thirty years. I help the individual to look at himself and understand himself. I start making him realize that if he is frustrated, he needs to search for the cause of his frustration within himself. The cause of frustration is never in one's job; it is not in one's marriage; nor is it in the location where a person lives.

Frustration is a mental *condition;* it is not a situation. It is a function of consciousness and consciousness alone. Therefore, the only way to cure it is to do the work in the mind that needs to be done in order to be rid of the mental block that is making you uncomfortable or driving you to desperation.

How do you do this work in the mind that needs to be done? You go right back to what we have been saying. Picture yourself as you would like to be. Count up your assets. There is not a person reading this book who hasn't some good record behind him, who does not have some commendable accomplishment. Take a moment to review your earlier years. Recall that you have done some good, some great, and some wonderful things in your life. You have been a real success in some area of your experience.

Your good, and great, and wonderful accomplishments will not be the same as mine or those of anyone else you know. You are a unique individual. Therefore, the good that you have achieved is not to be compared with the achievement of anyone else.

The good that you have done is your standard to follow. If you were once a creative person, you are still a creative person. If you were a success in one situation, you can be a success in any situation, provided you will put the same talents to work. These talents are *desire, goal,* and *enthusiasm*, an unbeatable combination.

Many persons have a lukewarm desire and a vague goal accompanied by little or no enthusiasm for doing anything about moving ahead. They have grown accustomed to the frustration of failure. They have learned to live with it. Learning to live with a frustration is psychologically dangerous. A frustration is a symptom; it is a warning that a destructive habit pattern in the subconscious needs to be replaced by a constructive one.

How does one effect such a replacement? I suggest that you pay attention to your intuition, which gives you the new idea: "You can do it; you can do it, because you have done it, before." Then look back at your former success or successes. Picture what they were and how you felt when you were a success. Relive this experience in your imagination. Then find the courage to succeed again, instead of giving way to a feeling of futility and the conviction that you are doomed to failure.

When you have the picture of your former success clearly in mind, take a look at your new self-image; see yourself as having completely broken the old frustration. This is important. You must see it as *having been done,* just as your mother saw a pie complete in her mind before she went into the kitchen to create it. She saw the finished creation, and then created it. Let us assume that your frustration has to do with your job. Ask yourself these questions:

How would I be if I did not have this frustration? What would I be like? How would it be if suddenly things changed? If I were given an opportunity to be an alert, creative, valuable part of the corporation? How would I think? How would I feel? How would I react? What would I do with my flow of conversation which now is destructive? It is destructive of the company, destructive of my employer, and it is also destructive of me. What would I talk about if this frustration were not in existence?

The gist of our everyday conversation always gives us away. It shows what is behind the facade. It divulges our secrets. When you say, "I met so-and-so on the street and had a delightful conversation," you are, in essence, saying that the person you met was not frustrated in the area you discussed. Had the person been frustrated in that area, the conversation would have been neither interesting nor vital. It probably would have been condemnatory, and your remark would have been, "I met this person on the street and couldn't get away fast enough."

Your conversation discloses your self-image, your opinion of yourself. Is that opinion as high as it should be? Does it show that you are experiencing all the health, wealth, and happiness that is your birthright? I believe in a Creative Power that the world calls God. I also believe in a creative me and a creative you. I believe that all of us are vital, dynamic producers in life. We have the equipment; we have mind and emotions. This equipment is further aided by education and experience. But, in order to get where we want to go, we have to see ourselves *as being great.* We have to come to terms with ourselves on the side of greatness.

As I have stated in my book, *The Science of Successful Living,* "Jesus could have remained a carpenter in a small village in Galilee and lived in moderate comfort all his life. Moses could have been a quiet shepherd on the plains of

Media and never worried about the Hebrew slaves in Egypt. Every great man or woman on the face of the globe who has ever moved forward in the evolution of his own soul has done so because he wanted to do so, plus devising a plan for doing it. Greatness is not inherited. It is fashioned out of the thought and feeling of the individual."

It would be easy for any one of us to make a list of what is wrong with life. But the important thing is to make a list of what is right. I often do it. You can do it, too. Make the list, then look at it and say: *I am a valuable part of life; I am contributing to humanity.*

When your attention is on the asset-man or asset-woman that you are, on the person who has accomplished and can accomplish again, your attention is diverted from your frustrations. It is diverted from your errors of omission or commission, and you are capable of self-forgiveness for any mistakes you may have made. When your full mental and emotional energy is focused on being what you want to be, on your goal, you are not guilty of self-depreciation, which, you will recall, is self-destructive. Your mental and emotional attention has to be on the side of greatness if you are to proceed into a larger arena of experience.

Imagine what would happen on Sunday morning if I were to review some of my poor lectures just before going out on the stage of Town Hall in New York. Not all of my lectures are good; some are always better than others. What would my opinion of myself be if I did such a thing? Naturally, I don't do this at all. I often, quite calmly and deliberately, stand off-stage and say: "Barker, you have done it before, and you have done it well; and you are going to do it well again." Then I walk out and deliver. I must have my mind focused in the success direction if I am going to be a success person.

This is true of me, and it is also true of you. In the important arena of your life, you need to review quite often the asset-person that you are. This gives you motivation. It gives you a disciplined thought-and-emotion consciousness. When you know what your assets are, and accept them as being yours, you are ready to proceed toward your goal with the self-assurance that you will reach it.

You actually have been on your way toward a goal ever since you were born, at which time your mother probably thought you were the greatest thing ever. Can't you imagine her saying: "My son—my daughter—is going to have a long, happy, prosperous, and successful life." She predicted everything good for you. I believe that, without knowing it, she was voicing the opinion of the universe. She was saying what the Infinite was saying about you: "Here is a destined individual."

We all forget, by the time we are thirty, that we are destined to our own personal greatness. We continue to forget it in later years. A little trick of mine is occasionally to walk up to a person and say, "You are wonderful." The reactions

I get are amazing. Always, there is bewilderment. Always, there is that sense of "What do you mean?" "It can't be so." I say it *can be so.* Somewhere, between the time of your birth and the present day, you have been wonderful. Inside you, there is that which is wonderful. When I jolt you, or someone else jolts you, you are encouraged to be wonderful. It doesn't take much intelligence to be nasty. It takes a great deal of intelligence to live with *wisdom, balance,* and *harmony*; with cordial relationships with people and a success drive fulfilled. That takes intelligence.

"But, Dr. Barker," you may say, "I'm neurotic." That doesn't explain anything. That merely means that you have accepted a frustration as a permanent thing. If you are neurotic, take steps not to be neurotic. If books such as the ones we write help you, that's great. We will never know how many people have had neuroses knocked out of them by Dr. Maltz or Dr. Barker in the last twenty years.

Both he and I lay the facts on the line. We always say to any person in any form of counseling: "You can do it." When an individual comes back and says, "I can't," we encourage that person in other ways. We point out how to do it. Conquering a neurosis is getting rid of a self-accepted frustration that you have decided to live with in order to explain your inadequacy in meeting life.

Psychologists, and specialists in the field of psychotherapy, have ways of helping the neurotic *to adjust.* We are not helping the neurotic to adjust. We are saying to the neurotic: "You do not need to be neurotic if you will take the necessary steps not to be neurotic."

I frequently say to these self-declared neurotics, "*Do something different.* I don't care what it is, but don't go on existing in the same old mold. Change your basic patterns in some way." If I get a real complainer, I may say: "What is your favorite department store? Don't go in there for a few months. Go to another store until you have improved your thinking and moved out of your frustrating rut." Of course, this is a simple illustration of how one can change basic patterns.

I have discovered that I have to keep breaking old, set patterns all of the time. If those patterns involve past mistakes, I forgive myself for them. I don't want to be reminded of them. When memory of past mistakes does come up occasionally, I simply say: "Get out of my mind. You are an impediment to what I am doing, and I don't want you in my mind." The memories I don't want will subside, particularly if I gear my thinking to their opposites.

I have done some good and great things in my life. I say this without egotism. Rather, I have self-compassion because I know that not everything I do will be good and great. I am human, just as you are. We have compassion for the sick; we have compassion for the dying; we have compassion for the poor; and we had better have it for ourselves. We had better rejoice that we can have self-compassion and self-forgiveness. This means that we see ourselves as we really are, right now, not as we may have been in the past. The only part of the past that I wish to recall is that of my moments of triumph. These moments serve as examples of what I can do; they serve as spiritual inspiration for setting and achieving new goals. It does me no good whatsoever to review past mistakes. Let memories of them be banished from my subconscious mind forever.

At this point, I would like to recommend a book called *Reality Therapy* by Dr. William Glasser, a psychiatrist who offers a new approach to psychotherapy. He believes that there are two basic psychological needs common to all of us. These are the need to love and be loved, and the need to feel that we are worthwhile to ourselves and to others.

In his efforts to help emotionally disturbed people fulfill these needs, he considers only the patient's present life. He states that he disregards the past, no matter how rejected or miserable the person may have felt. This is contrary to most psychiatric practice.

In essence, Dr. Glasser suggests that emotional confusion is not directly connected with the past, and there is no use reviewing what happened during childhood or the growing-up period. The goal he strives to help patients achieve is the ability to face the reality of their present situations and to learn to accept personal responsibility for their own experiences.

This viewpoint is, I believe, a great step forward in the psychiatric approach. For a great many years, the individual's past has been analyzed and blamed for his current problems and disturbed behavior. As a result, the past we have lived through has become our crutch; it has become our explanation of unhappiness and failure. We have relied on information about what happened in the past to furnish insight into every present problem and to aid us in finding a solution.

Let's get this straight. Your past does not necessarily condition your present. Your present is largely dependent upon what you are doing in your mind/emotion area right now. It is possible, of course, for you to point to the past and say: "I have this particular trait because of . . ." Stop a moment and think about that trait. Do you want to keep it? If you do, fine. If you do not want to keep it, it is time for you to go to work on getting rid of it.

Do you recall Napoleon's great strategy in fighting wars? It was a strategy that enabled him to make his rapid conquest of Europe. This strategy had never been used before. Its success resulted from the fact that Napoleon never hit the center of the foe's lines. He always attacked the flank. While this was a new tactic in warfare at the time, it has been used successfully ever since. We always learn from someone else's successes.

THE CONQUEST OF FRUSTRATION

I bring this up because a person with a number of frustrations to conquer often will say, "It's too much for me." My answer to that is take one problem at a time. Hit just one. Don't try to change everything in your life overnight, but do all that you can to overcome one negative.

This sounds relatively easy, but actually, it is hard work. Don't attack the whole problem at once; don't expect to be happy, healthy, and successful all at once. Take one thing at a time and, like Napoleon, hit it on the flank.

If, through reading this book, you overcome one frustration, you will have profited greatly. Even though the frustration you conquer is only minor, it will be a step forward. Your progress toward your goal is built on eliminating, one after another, the important negative patterns that are keeping you from being the person you want to be.

Your successful conquest of each frustration will require self-honesty. It will require self-examination and decision-making. It will require new goals based on new desires, and every decision will need to be backed up by sincere effort and hard work.

There are people, of course, who are so frustrated that they have lost all desire to be other than frustrated. They have built their walls; they have accepted the fact that life has passed them by. They are in a mental prison cell, seemingly without hope of ever regaining their freedom. Such persons probably wouldn't read a book like this. If they did, they would say, "It won't work." But I say, "It does work."

Once again, here is the way you wage your warfare against every frustration you have. Attack one; get rid of it. Attack another; get rid of that. You may have to keep doing this sort of thing as long as you are on this plane of life. So what! You are freeing yourself from a mental prison of your own making. You are taking down one bar at a time. Eventually, all of these bars do come down, and, eventually, you are free.

There is no virtue in unhappiness. There is no virtue in illness. There is no virtue in complaining, and there is no virtue in alibis. However, there is virtue in using time-tested methods for evoking happiness, for demonstrating health, and for reaching all the worthwhile goals in your life.

It is important to remember, as you move on toward successive goals, that there are no actual finalities in life. When you issue an encyclical to yourself, a vow in which you say, "I'll never do this again," all you are pronouncing is a finality that is unrealistic. You are setting up a self-made law which you may have to face and negate someday.

In this connection, I am reminded that, as a clergyman, one of my tasks is to conduct funeral services, and I have often heard a weeping spouse say that he or she will never marry again. I listen and say nothing, but I am not surprised when a large percent of these mourners return in a reasonable length of time and ask me to perform their next wedding service. Deep down underneath, the desire for happiness in the companionship of marriage was greater than the prison bars that were put up at a time of great emotion. Again I say, there are no such things as finalities. Mind does not work that way. Mind has no fixed positions. Its operation is one of continued progress and, in the normal individual, that progress continues forever. Mind is creative, and it cannot stop creating.

There are persons who will say, "I have found a new lease on life." They didn't find it; they created it. Everything in your experience is self-created. There is no creator in your experience other than you. Everything that happens in your life is the result of your use of mind and emotion. I know that as an absolute fact in my own life. Even when I don't like what I see regarding myself, I go to the mirror and say, "But you did it, Barker."

When I don't like what I see or experience, I know that I must refrain from complaining. Dr. Maltz has called complaining "self-gossip." I think that is a very apt term and one everyone should remember. Self-gossip is a negative discussion you carry on with yourself. You do it because you are trying to alibi yourself out of some situation. Instead of getting yourself out of something, you are getting yourself into something. You are increasing the negative mental load that you are carrying, and it is this negative mental load that impedes your progress toward your goal—nothing else. Complaints expand and make more powerful your mental *impediment load.*

Sometime, when you have the courage, sit down quietly and say:

*What is my mental impediment load? What is it composed of? What, in me, is keeping me from being the individual I know I can be?*

This is a form of mental and spiritual housecleaning.

Your mental impediment load probably is something that no one else is aware of. It is made up of the concepts that you have consciously or unconsciously accepted in a negative way; you have applied them strictly to yourself. As you explore and try to identify them, you will need to remember the importance of self-honesty.

Your inner wisdom is so much greater than you think it is. Your insight is far greater than you believe it to be. God equipped you with some very great equipment; it is there within you, and it will work for you when you give it a chance. If you say to yourself: "Mind within me, reveal what I need to know about my mental impediment," and then do some quiet, contemplative thinking, you will get your answer.

Don't give importance to the impediment that is revealed to you. Get rid of it. You do this by saying:

I now declare that the impediment in my mind has no reality, no existence, no continuity. It can never slow me down again. I now decree that it is obsolete; it has no authority. It is robbed of all emotion, and therefore, it has no existence.

You will feel a weight fall from your shoulders. You will find yourself walking taller. You will do this because you have reduced to nothing a negative, something that you had accepted as normal far too long.

This act of ridding yourself of a mental impediment necessitates self-honesty, self-exploration, and self-forgiveness. You begin to have less interest in what is wrong with you and more interest in what is right with you. You begin to have greater control of your experiences, the things that you manifest in your own life. This is making your outside or visible self take on the *look* of your true inside, invisible self.

We all are magnificent people when we behave ourselves, when we are creative and when we love other people. However, we don't live at the peak of our productivity and creativity as often as we should. Whether anyone can live there all of the time or not is a question that cannot be answered. But we ought to come up to the peak more often. We ought to sense the wonder of our very being.

The Bible says that we are "fearfully and wonderfully made." I'll take away the word fearfully. I am sure the writer of the Biblical reference was speaking of the physical body, but that isn't what I am talking about at all. I am referring to your mind and emotions—your subconscious mind. Here is the most fascinating mechanism on the face of the globe. It is a mechanism that doesn't know how to say no when you are saying *yes*. It is never selective.

You can pour into this subconscious mechanism anything you wish; it has no power to say no. Of course, you can say no to yourself, and that is what many of us have been doing from time to time. We've been saying no, and *I can't,* thereby causing our frustrations.

When you want to cure your frustration, you start saying *yes* to yourself. You affirm your own creativity. You start to self-search constructively, not destructively. You lessen your *limitation load,* and you walk free.

## HAPPINESS NEVER HAPPENS BY CHANCE.

As you take the steps toward conquering your frustrations and reaching your goals that Dr. Maltz and I have recommended, these are important points to remember:

*You are mind in action.* Every experience you have is the result of the use of your mind. As mind, you are the director of your life, the ruler of your personal world. You build your own self-image and make your own decisions. You authorize your every experience by your thoughts and your emotions. Your conscious mind is the thinker; your subconscious mind is the doer. You have the power to choose, consciously or unconsciously, to be a success or a failure. It is also within your mental province to decide, consciously or unconsciously, to be happy or unhappy.

Don't be overwhelmed by these statements. I've made them before, and I will make them again. They serve the purpose of making you aware of your potential, your responsibility to life. Everyone is born with a greatness-potential, but few of us achieve instant greatness. We need to learn the self-discipline that leads to right choices; to learn the process whereby we reach self-fulfillment. If this were not so, it seems obvious that everyone would immediately choose to be happy and successful and, therefore, everyone would immediately be happy and successful.

This is far from the way most individual lives unfold, and, as Dr. Maltz has emphatically stated, many people are actually on a *quest* for unhappiness rather than happiness. He likens this to a quest for self-destruction.

It is true that some people are subconsciously bent on destroying themselves, and if they continue their negative search, they will succeed in self-destruction. In my years of counseling, I have come into contact with many unhappy people. Happy people rarely seek professional advice. Most of the chronically unhappy individuals who have sought my help have actually been on a search for ways to remain unhappy. They subconsciously found satisfaction in being unhappy and wanted to continue to be unhappy.

You will notice that I am referring to chronically unhappy people. A person who is experiencing only a temporary unhappiness wants to overcome it, and he usually does in a reasonably short time.

Perpetual unhappiness is a result of neurosis. Persons suffering from it have seriously disturbed emotions. They do not see themselves as they are, as the cause of their own unhappiness. They blame their chronic mental state on other people, on situations that have occurred and continue to occur in their lives, on what they consider unfavorable conditions and distressing events. These are the things that the unhappy ones want changed. When it is suggested that what they need is a change in their own thinking, their own consciousness, they are incensed. They fail to see any need for such action.

These people are so geared to their unhappiness that it actually gives them pleasure. They love to talk about the "evils" that have befallen them. They will tell anyone who is willing to listen how mistreated they are; how unlucky, how misunderstood, and how maligned they have been all of their lives.

These self-pitying individuals don't know it, but their whole basic motivation is toward failure. They are heading straight for failure via the unhappiness route. If you tell them this, they will not accept your judgment. The usual response goes something like this: "If you were in my place, you'd be unhappy, too." Thank goodness I'm not in their place, nor do I ever intend to be! I am in a position where I have to be reasonably happy, because, in my profession, I have to give happiness to others. It is simple logic that you cannot give away something you do not have.

Dr. Maltz, in his work, and I in mine—undoubtedly many of you in your work—are accomplishing a great good, because we are able to give happiness. We can do this only because we have happiness in our own lives. Yet we must accept the fact that we can't give happiness to people who are not receptive, people who do not want to have happiness for themselves.

If you know an unhappy person who isn't interested in changing his thinking and developing new, creative ideas, let him dwell in his gloom and depression. Let him wallow in his "slough of despond." Remember, that is what he wants. He subconsciously desires to be unhappy. As his circle of friends grows smaller and smaller, he subconsciously experiences a perverse satisfaction because he is subconsciously attaining his negative goals of loneliness, unhappiness, and failure.

Countless unhappy people, however, do want to be helped. When one of them manifests some spark of creative interest, it indicates that he is ready to move from unhappiness to happiness.

Men and women who have spiritual understanding know that no one is hopeless, that the Spirit of God is in every human being. Those who lack such understanding will often express doubt or indicate that they are not at all interested. Most of the people with whom you have business dealings, most of the people who live near you, and perhaps most of your acquaintances are not the least bit interested in a spiritual factor in life. Most of them do not even bother to pay lip service to religious ideas anymore.

This is made obvious by the fact that if all of the churches in New York City were filled to capacity at any one time, they could only accommodate 10 percent of the city's population. We have no way of reckoning, but perhaps far less than 10 percent of the population of New York City is happy.

The person who wishes to move from unhappiness to happiness must have an interest in the *spirit* of living. There has to be a spiritual basis for continued happiness. Perhaps you know someone who is a very happy person, yet you call him irreligious because he never goes to church. I'm not talking about going to church. You don't have to go to church to have a spiritual premise for living.

A happy person is dealing with a spiritual something, whether he thinks of it in those terms or not. He is drawing upon some inner resource that is beyond his intellect. He is drawing on an inner success attitude. Without knowing it, he is using the science of Psycho-Cybernetics and the Science of Mind correctly. I repeat that there is a spiritual something welling up within the person who is happy most of the time. No one is happy all the time.

Here is an important area where mind action needs to function. Your consciousness, and the decisions you make in your consciousness, can stimulate the spirit within you, provided you recognize and acknowledge its presence. Say to yourself occasionally, "The spirit within me is a sound basis for happiness." This has nothing to do with theology. The words can be said by the Catholic, the Protestant, the Jew, or the Muslim. They can be said by the agnostic. Anyone can say, "There is something in me that is greater than I am, and that something wants me to be happy."

When you express yourself in this way and recognize the truth of what you are saying, you are already on your quest for happiness. You are seeking, and what you seek, you will find, because it has always been available to you. Everything necessary for an individual's happiness is available. The materials needed are already within his own mind.

Things do not make people happy. We live in a world of fantastic inventions. Manufacturers are offering everything one's heart could desire at prices that even those in the lower income brackets can afford. Yet unhappiness continues, and it continues among people at all income levels. Unhappy people are just as numerous in one arena of life as in another. If you are unhappy in New York, or in Denver, or San Francisco, you will be just as unhappy luxuriating in the finest hotel in Miami Beach, or basking in the sun in San Juan, Puerto Rico.

Within you, the ingredients for happiness are waiting to be discovered. This requires mental conditioning that must take place before the externals that we associate with happiness appear. When you have established your inner happiness, your spiritual feelings of satisfaction, and well-being, you will begin to experience warm friendships and make the social contacts you desire. You will love and be loved. You will know yourself as a worthwhile person. You will glory in your creativeness, and you will prosper. The manifestations that result from happiness are automatic. They happen to a person when he is inwardly ready for them to happen.

The individual who reaches out for happiness, yet holds back because of doubt or fear, needs to take a step that I often recommend. I say to such a person, "Declare that you are happy now, even though you are not sure that you are." At such times, I am often faced with a look of consternation and the reproachful statement: "That would be telling a lie." I continue by suggesting, "Well, then, tell the lie. I don't care what you call it so long as you do it." The next response usually is, "But then I wouldn't be true to myself."

Anyone who declares, "I am happy," is being true to his *real self.* The Infinite never created a single soul to be unhappy. The Divine conception of man does not include unhappiness. Unhappiness is a mental state that can be explained psychologically. For some people, it may be tied in with an unfortunate situation in early years, to parents who lacked understanding or did not give love, to an unwholesome environment, and so on. But these are explanations. They do not offer solutions.

In contrast, there are many individuals who were born in poverty and who had parents who didn't understand them, yet they are happy people. Why? They are happy because of attitudes they have built up in their own minds. They are happy because of what they have accomplished within *themselves* and what they have done to correctly condition themselves.

Happiness never happens by chance. Happiness is a result of sincere effort and, sometimes, achieving it involves hard work. In other instances, the happy person may have acquired happiness quite unconsciously. Such a person, undergoing any kind of psychotherapy, would show healthy basic attitudes. Fortunately, however, happy people do not need to go to psychiatrists.

Happiness is a phase of the mind that has received far too little attention. I am looking forward to the day when some well-known authority in the field of psychiatry will write a book about the happy mind or the psychology of the normal mind. Therein lies a great area for research. We who are working in the metaphysical field know that we are correct in saying that the ingredients for happiness are within. We know that happiness is stimulated by creativity and that both happiness and creativity are necessary in the life of anyone whose major goal is success. I amplify this in my recent book, *The Power of Decision,* by saying:

"Creative thinking gives a zest to living, and you are a creative thinker when you decide to be one. The feeling that it is great to be alive is a spiritual necessity. It lessens the strains and tensions of routine functioning. It quickens new ideas in consciousness, and alerts the mind to the fascinations that are available to us. It allows no morbidity, no boredom, and no lazy thinking. It prevents us from drifting in the past. It causes us to be *today* people expecting great things in our tomorrow."

The next time you are unhappy, say: "What's the value of this? What's the benefit? What do I get out of this, except misery?" I learned many years ago that there are certain things I can do without. By that, I mean the negative attitudes of others and the negative attitudes in my own mind. I cannot afford to have these negatives appear in my own mind. I cannot afford to have these negatives appear in my experience, and they certainly will if I entertain them in my subconscious for long. The price is too dear for anyone who is interested in mental coin as well as in a material bank account.

It is far more important for me to watch where my mind goes than to be concerned about how I spend my money. My mental bank account is entirely dependent upon the thoughts and attitudes I deposit in it. Accepting my own wrong attitudes and the wrong attitudes of persons with whom I associate is as dangerous as depositing worthless checks. Should I be foolish enough to deal in such bogus coin, my mental bank account soon would be depleted, and my happiness would be at stake.

A wealth of right attitudes is a basic requirement for the person who is seeking to be fulfilled—seeking through self-expression to reap desired results. Place respect for your accomplishments high on the list of right attitudes.

I have great respect for my personal accomplishments in life. I believe Dr. Maltz has great respect for what he has done in his career. Both of us are fulfilled individuals. This is not because we have been lucky; it has nothing to do with our horoscopes; it is not based on our parents; and it isn't because God loves us. Everything that we have done, we have done because we wanted to do it, and we have worked hard to cause our desires to materialize. We have worked hard in mind, forever guarding our thoughts and emotions, deciding where to direct our attention, seeking new ideas, and pursuing new goals. We will continue, as long as we are on this plane of life, to do just that.

Look back in your own life and recall the many times when you have been fulfilled, when you have reached a desired goal and been able to say to yourself, "Well done." Count these personal blessings and rejoice in them. Then ask yourself, "What is my next goal? Where do I go from here?" Remember, you are a today person who also is expecting great things in the future. There never is a time to stop, or to say, "It is finished." Even the most discouraged person will react to an impetus that urges him on to try once more. I think Dr. Maltz gave us that impetus in his words, "Failure is never inevitable." Psychologists frequently refer to failure-prone people. We prefer to devote our attention to success-prone people.

The Infinite did not create you to fail. The motivation of the Infinite Mind that created cosmic order, that engineered the evolution of man, was not failure. Its motivation was self-expression. This is the motivation that is passed on to you and me. The great core of your needs and of my needs is self-expression. I believe that you and I were born with an automatic success pattern. It is within us. Those of us who have tapped it, explored it, and brought its ideas to the surface have experienced our measures of success.

Initially, you are a success person, not because you want to be, but because you are. When you discover that you want to be a success person, the doors to the treasure house of ideas that are within you will open. Try it and see. Everyone wants to be a success. This is intuitive.

Many failure-prone people have changed to success-prone people. You can do it, too, if your present pattern is one of failure. Realize that you were born to succeed. I know that whatever caused me to be born, created me to succeed, equipped me to succeed, and expects me to succeed. Therefore, I had better succeed.

The way to start succeeding is to declare that you are successful. At this point, we are faced, once again, with those certain someones who will say, "But I am not successful." Perhaps you are not successfull career-wise. You may, however, be a success at boiling water, or a success at cooking a hamburger. It is important to note your areas of success. Everyone has them. Even the most defeated soul can probably fry two eggs.

Success motivation is a spiritual motivation. It, like everything else, has a creative cause and responds when recognized—just as you and I do.

You walk down the street and hear someone call, "Hey! Wait a minute, Al, I want to see you." You turn around, see an old friend, and are pleased that he recognized you. Something of this sort happened to me not long ago. I was shopping in one of our large department stores when someone called my name. As I looked up, there, standing only a few feet away, was a man I hadn't seen for several years. We had a pleasant chat, and I was pleased to be recognized by the friend who had called my name. But had he not called, I would have never known he was there. I would have had no one to respond to.

Similarly, your success motivation has no one to respond to unless you recognize that it is there in your mind and ready to be called into action. You are the one who must do the calling, just as it was necessary for my unseen friend to call me.

By the way, I told him that he looked wonderful and he was pleased. Actually, he didn't look wonderful. He shouldn't have been wearing such sloppy clothes, and this brings up a matter of considerable importance. When people look at you, what do they see? Do they see a happy person? Do they see a person in quest of happiness? Do they see a success-prone person? Study the people around you when you ride on a bus, walk through the park or drop into the corner drugstore for a soda. See if you can pick out the ones who might as well be wearing a label marked success.

Now look at yourself. Do you look like a success person? Does the word happiness shine out in your personal appearance? If it doesn't, you had better start changing. In our wonderful modern age, this is quite simple, and it isn't even very expensive. You can always change the outside of you because it is only a facade, but I am advising you to change the outside to match the inside of you, provided the inside is vibrant with the spirit of living. Look like a success person. The cost will never be too great, and changing your appearance need not necessarily be tied in with modern styles.

Wonderful Queen Mary of England, during the last twenty years of her life, wore the most outdated clothes anyone could have worn. But she looked like a success person. You knew exactly who she was, and you knew that she was born to her station. She wore skirts down to the ankles; she wore those interesting hats, and she always carried an umbrella, even on the brightest days. She was out of fashion, and it didn't bother her a bit. She had been Queen of England, and in her mind she still was, even though she had witnessed the reign of two of her sons and, later, her granddaughter. You looked at her with her erect carriage, her definite walk, and you knew you were looking at a success person.

You will find that dressing the part makes it easier to play your success role. Start tomorrow morning. You are no longer living in an era where you keep good clothes for Sunday. You need to look as much like a success at ten o'clock on Monday morning as you do at eleven on Sunday.

I am not sure what people see when they look at me. I am a person who is in the public eye almost all of the time. Some of my public may not like what they see. They may even chide me for being overweight. According to the science of Psycho-Cybernetics, I should put a pattern into my subconscious mind that would go something like this: "I am very tall, very thin, and very handsome." If I made this my constant affirmation, my subconscious mind should become convinced and get busy on the job of making me very tall, very thin, and very handsome.

The question is, would this make me any happier, and if it did, what effect would that have on my friends? Are your friends and your loved ones better people because you have lived among them? Or, when you look in the mirror, do you say, "I think I'm quite a nuisance to everyone." Do some thinking on that. Are people better because they know you? I'm not talking about finances. I'm not talking about your Christmas-gift list. I am talking about *that which you are,* and that which you radiate.

When you have answered that question to your satisfaction, here is another check you might make. Is your social life as active today as it was ten years ago? If it isn't, don't kid yourself. Something is wrong with you. Don't offer the excuse that everyone you know has left town. Think of all the people who have moved in since these friends went away. Don't use the alibi that your husband has died and no one wants single widows at a "couples" party. This may be true, but find some other widows and have a grand old time. The excuses for loneliness that I listen to are so numerous that, if laid end to end, they would reach from here to Chicago.

Unhappiness and loneliness are curable. If you are not invited out as much as you were ten years ago, get going. Do something about it. On occasion, I have asked some unhappy individual, "Do you know three people whom you could call and invite to lunch? Not all at once, perhaps just one at a time?" I've been shocked and distressed when the answer has been "No." That is serious business. It means that something needs to be done.

I know of one person in particular who has made a complete about-face. She has stepped out of her loneliness and become a moving, social person. She is sought after because people *feel better* after associating with her. What did she do? She worked in her own mind to change her attitudes. She started to devote her attention to happiness and direct it away from feeling sorry for herself. She began to take a creative interest in herself and in others. She isn't a "preacher" type—far from it—but today, the biggest compliment paid her by those who know her is, "She inspires."

In order to be a success, you have to talk and act as if you were. One of the axioms of my own teaching is: "Act as though it were so, and it will become so."

Be positive in what you say, but don't be ridiculous. I make that statement because I am reminded of one of my instructors when I attended school in a distant town. He met me at the train one day. To my greeting of "How are you?" he gave this instant reply: "I never felt better, and I never had more. But I expect to feel still better, and to have still more. I am spiritually perfect, morally okay, mentally alert, and financially improving." The man was an unmitigated bore, as you can well realize, and he always gave this stock reply whenever anyone inquired after his well-being.

I am certainly not asking you to follow my instructor's example. Just put a feeling of happiness, a feeling of success, into whatever you say. And for goodness' sake, vary the format.

Back in the days when I was a youngster, we used to have a family reunion once a year. One of our distant cousins had a son who, some folks said, "wasn't too bright;" I suppose the modern word would be neurodiverse. When I was fourteen, this distant relative must have been twenty-five, but his intellect hadn't developed along with his chronological age. Each year, he would come to my father, who was a middle-income man, and say, "Hey, Cousin George, how are you doing? How much money do you make?" My father, looking very serious, would reply, "There are a few days when I don't make $1,000." The young man would blink in astonishment and then go around telling all of the other relatives, "You know, George is rich. There's a few days he doesn't make $1,000." Luckily all of the older members of the group knew our circumstances. We had a very comfortable, middle-class home.

I am sure my father projected his own degree of prosperity, success, and happiness, just as I am advising you to do. He had what Dr. Maltz has described as human dignity.

Dignity is a quality of utmost importance to each of us. Don't mistake it for the act of behaving politely. Politeness has nothing to do with it. I'm not speaking of a dignity that has a stiff-necked, overly pompous quality; a false dignity that might be used in an effort to impress someone. I don't want to impress others. I only want to impress myself with my own integrity and my own worth. I am the only person I will have to live with, I believe, throughout millions of years.

Each individual lives unto himself alone. This is true whether a person is married or not married. It is true whether you have loved ones or do not have loved ones. It is true whether you do or do not have friends. In the last analysis, each one of us lives life alone. Because this is true, I want my dignity for myself alone.

The human dignity that Dr. Maltz and I speak of is a matter of self-acceptance. For me, it is a matter of knowing who and what I am. We are back to that question, the importance of which I so often stress: "Do I like myself?" When I ask that question, I always reply: "Yes, I like myself." This is not a matter of human ego, though I have that, too. Every successful person must have it. Never decry your human ego. Use it!

When someone tells you that successful people usually are apologetic about their success, don't you believe it. Similarly, when you are told to be "as meek as Moses," go back and read the story again. See if you can find one instance in the life of Moses when he was meek. When you are told, "YOU ought to be like Jesus," think of the man. There was nothing meek about Jesus. A man who can say, "I am the Light of the World," isn't apologizing for life. Here was a man who had accepted himself. He was a man who knew who and what he was. The who, in our cases today, is what we have made of ourselves. The what is the original self with which each of us started.

Suppose you want human dignity, but believe that you haven't made of yourself what you want to be. It's not too late. It's never too late. Start now to make yourself loved, to make yourself worthwhile. Making this effort, and building up a satisfactory self-image, are responsibilities you cannot dodge and still be successful and happy.

Dr. Maltz and I have arrived at an overall self-acceptance, I believe. Yet we make our mistakes now and then. But we don't wallow in them. We know where we are going, and we know that we must be on our way. There is no time to look back at the past and regret anything that has happened. We are today people, looking forward to tomorrow. We are both in professions that we wanted to be in.

If you are in a profession or a job you don't want to be in, get out. Quit. Then get into something you do like. You will have to take the same steps we have taken. We have worked on inner attitudes. We have worked on some of our fears. We have worked to overcome anger when we have been incensed with some people. And don't think we haven't been actually livid now and then.

The point I want to make is that everyone needs to aim for the human dignity that is one of man's most prized possessions. If you don't have it, you can go after it. It is not beyond your reach.

The thing to remember is you *can do it*. Also, if you don't have the urge, the desire within you, you cannot do it. It is up to you, and it is up to me, to be and become what we want to be.

## BEING A SELF-FULFILLED PERSON

Dr. Maltz and I have placed great emphasis on self-respect, self-confidence, self-control, and the need for being a self-fulfilled success person. We have stressed the importance of your self-image—what you see when you look in the mirror. Notice how the word self appears in each of these attributes. That is because *your self* is the only significant entity in your world.

We have also been compassionate, we hope, as we have tried to explain that perfection—or even near perfection—is something that few of us attain, and we certainly don't do it overnight. You will always be an evolving, unfolding individual because that's what you were created to be, and each time you aim for a new goal, you will run into new obstacles. You will continue to be a mistake-maker and a mistake-breaker. As you move forward, remember that your self-expression is the self-expression of the Intelligence that created you. You need the challenge and the excitement of constant change in order to function as Divine Mind intended that you should.

While you have been reading this book, you have been learning to accept yourself for what you are, an intelligent being with various weaknesses and strengths, who is living in a today world and who is capable of setting sights on a creative tomorrow. You also have been developing a mental *balance* that is your birthright. But since you are a self-willed person, you may have sacrificed some of that balance along the pathways of experience and growth. You have learned that by controlling your thoughts and feelings in a way that enables you to reach both minor and major goals, you can establish your own measure of mental health.

Mental health is the most priceless commodity that you can possess. You were born to have it because you were created to be a center of intelligence in the one Creative Mind. You also were born with free will, and therefore, your life has developed according to your own patterns of thinking and feeling. Your degree of mental health right now determines the ease with which you are able to face and solve problems.

Dr. Maltz has made it clear that the aim of the science of Psycho-Cybernetics is to help people attain mental health as they conquer their frustrations. Our teaching of the Science of Mind achieves the same thing: to help those interested in this science to recognize themselves as mind in *control of every situation*. This means having faith in oneself as a spiritual being who is an individualization of the one Infinite Mind.

Largely without any spiritual connotation, the importance of mind and its functions is being recognized in many fields of research today. You and I are fortunate to live at a time when much thought is being given to the operations of the mind and emotions and their influence on our bodies—on our failures, and on our successes. The broad subject of mental health is now one of national interest and concern. Psychologists, psychiatrists, and other specialists in the field are pressing forward in many areas of research and clinical investigation. They are gaining new understanding of the various phases of human behavior as they relate to the workings of the mind.

These are some of the down-to-earth questions being asked: Why do mentally disturbed people do what they do? Why do they say they feel as if they are "falling apart," or "going to pieces," or "losing their balance?" Why does mental illness affect people at all economic levels? Why do many patients whose minds aren't functioning properly recover in a short time, while others need prolonged understanding and care? Trained psychotherapists are asking what more we can do to help these disturbed people.

Early in this century, a person who had a serious "mental breakdown" was usually considered insane and put away in an asylum. His case was considered hopeless, and with this grim prognosis, he was left to deteriorate and, eventually, to die. In contrast, many of today's psychiatrists suggest that relatively few cases of mental illness, or mental dysfunction, should be labeled incurable. Today's goals include learning how to prevent as well as how to cure varying degrees of mental disturbance.

In the field of medicine, too, we find an ever-increasing awareness of the mind's influence on the body. The terms *psychosomatic illness* and *psychosomatic medicine* are well known to most intelligent laymen. It is fairly common knowledge that disturbance of the mind and emotions can cause peptic ulcer, high blood pressure, migraine headaches, arthritis, trouble with eyesight and hearing, and all sorts of other disagreeable ailments. But any idea that the subconscious mind, acting in a destructive way, could cause such a universal ailment as the common cold would have been considered revolutionary—practically unbelievable—less than a century ago.

I read some shocking statistics about the common cold some years back. Let me quote them to you.

"Americans will spend three hundred and fifty million dollars ($350,000,000) on the prevention and cure of the common cold during the year 1963." This statement, from market research authorities, was published in *Forbes Magazine*, March 1, 1963.

At about the same time, another research report showed that 22,800,000 Americans went to medical doctors in a single year to be treated for the common cold—22 percent of these sufferers made at least a second visit to the doctor. These figures startled me. I did some thinking about the number of days men and women lose from work annually because of the common cold, the financial losses to corporations for these lost man-hours, and the cost to insurance companies for temporary hospitalization.

All of this, to my mind, is a needless waste of time, energy, and money. I am well aware, after thirty years' experience in the field of spiritual mind healing, that the common cold and its fellow complaints—virus infection, sinus troubles, postnasal drip, and similar ailments—will yield to spiritual-mental treatment.

As a result of my thinking on this subject, I have published a booklet entitled *The Cause and Cure of the Common Cold*. In it, I explain that colds do not come from material or external causes. The weather does not cause colds. Overwork and fatigue do not cause them. Exposure to others with colds does not cause them.

There is only one cause of the common cold. It originates in the mental-emotional constitution of the individual. It is an outer expression of an inner hurt. When you know this and are able to admit to yourself that your mind and emotions alone have caused the cold, you can be cured by the spiritual ideas and spiritual treatments we have been discussing here.

If your mind and emotions make your body sick, you may be sure that the self-destructive forces in your subconscious, which both Dr. Maltz and I have already discussed to some extent, are at work. These forces seem to be present to a greater or lesser extent in each of us, but the destructive urge is rarely aimed at total destruction. An obvious exception, of course, is the person who commits suicide. Less obvious is the self-destructive subconscious aim of an individual who "worries himself to death," or the one who claims that he is "killing himself with overwork," or the person who allows himself to "pine away from loneliness." We have many common expressions of that sort that have a deeper significance than the one that is generally accepted on the surface.

Anyone who indulges in fears without trying to erase them from the subconscious is being self-destructive. Anyone who repeats a problem over and over again without trying to find a solution is being self-destructive. Anyone who nurses a grudge or allows himself to feel resentful is being self-destructive. He is not hurting the person he resents. He is harming himself.

Persons who have set their sights on the failure side of life are likely to experience the emotions I've just mentioned. They need to do something immediately to get over onto the success side. They can't do it through long worry sessions or by falling into states of deep depression. If you want to keep your mental health, stay on the optimistic side of life. This doesn't mean that you should adopt a "happy-go-lucky" attitude. It means that happiness and success come to you when you *know and believe* that they are yours, because you have made a decision to have them.

I have frequently had someone say to me: "I think I must have been born a pessimist." That's not true. Neither you nor anyone else is born a pessimist. The chronic condition may arise when you, as a child, are consistently discouraged by one or both of your parents; by other children; by your teachers; or by gloomy people with whom you come in contact. Their unhappy outlook is assimilated by your immature mind. From childhood on, after you've been under this negative influence, you never expect anything to turn out right. Since there is a universal and immutable law that operates to provide us with what we expect to get, nothing does turn out right for you.

As a responsible adult who wants to live a full and joyful life, you need to do something to correct your pessimistic attitude. Change your expectations. Expect what you want, not what you are afraid will happen. You can't change quickly from pessimism to optimism, but you *can do it*. Try being optimistic on just one subject at a time; make it one subject a day; one subject a week; or, if it is necessary to take more time, be optimistic in one situation once a month. Develop the habit of optimism.

Pessimism and depression are symptoms of an underlying subconscious danger. They indicate that something is wrong with your mental health. If you continue in these negative emotional states, you are automatically indulging in an act of self-destruction. Now is the time to catch yourself and control your thoughts and feelings. It is a time for decision. You cannot conquer any negatives until you decide to do so.

Decision opens the door to new ideas. But the door doesn't open to the pessimist or the depressed person until he makes up his mind to have no more self-destructive nonsense in his life. This is because within you, there is an Infinite Knower who can only know when your mind is operating affirmatively. Great ideas do not come to pessimists.

You may say: "Well, I knew a man who was an inventor, and he was a pessimist, but he got ideas all the time." This may be true. He got ideas in the area about which he was enthusiastic. This was at the point of his invention. He was affirmative in the area of his inventions, therefore he got ideas that helped him carry them out. He did not get creative ideas in any other area. When he wasn't inventing, he was a pessimist, declaring that the world was "going to pot."

I often have people try to tell me how terrible it is to live in New York City these days. I say to them: "Why don't you move? Try Albany, Schenectady, or Hartford, Connecticut." But they don't want to move. They're just complainers who want to harp about something that's wrong. I say to them: "Sit down and make a list of six things that are right with New York."

This provides an affirmative mental action which invites new ideas. The self-destructive instinct tends to remain inoperative and ineffective when you are in a good mental health state. It begins its action only when you move to the negative side of mind. We move to the negative side too often, because we haven't yet trained our minds sufficiently to catch our errors in thinking and make the necessary corrections in order to keep ourselves beamed toward our positive goals.

You are the only person who runs your mind, and your mind runs your life. Therefore, you are the only person who runs your life. You may declare that that isn't true. You may claim that a family situation runs your life, or a job situation does it, or a personal relationship does it. This may seem to be the case, but it is you, your mind, that is allowing a situation or a condition to control your reactions. You are granting permission to the situation or the condition so that it seems to run your life. If you don't take control, your entire existence will be run by the basic patterns already in your subconscious mind. These, at best, will probably be average or mediocre, and your life will be average and unfruitful. You will experience frustration and failure.

I have had people say to me, "Dr. Barker, I live just for my work." That's not mental health. I've heard mothers say, "I live just for my family." There is no need to do that. You have to be you. This doesn't mean that you won't do your work if you are a worker; it doesn't mean that you won't look after your family if you are a mother. It means that you are an individual. You are not to be absorbed into a situation. You are always to be the director of a situation. This means self-responsibility. You have to take complete responsibility for yourself in order to be what Divine Intelligence expects you to be.

Dr. Maltz has used the expression: "Police yourself." You do this not by watching your actions. You do it by watching your mind and keeping your thoughts on your destination. The purpose of a police force in any city is to maintain order. That is its primary function. Its secondary functions are the seeking and finding of people who break the laws of order. But the original concept of a police force is that of a body of individuals whose purpose is to keep order.

You "police" yourself when you keep your mind in order. Mental order is mental health. We have an old-fashioned expression that says, "Cleanliness is next to Godliness." But order is the first law of the universe. Behind every successful individual, there is order. Behind every creative mind, there is order. I do not believe that anyone can have a sense of well-being in life without order. That's what I call policing myself. I see to it that my mind is in order; that my *affairs* are in order; that my home and my *office* are in order; and that *life itself* is in order for me.

Some years ago, I knew a noted clergyman who, once or twice a year, would tell his congregation that everyone should have a will—a last will and testament. It is interesting to note that when he died, he didn't have one; so, obviously, he didn't practice what he preached.

Failure to have a proper will indicates that the person who fails to do this dislikes his relatives. He wants deliberately to leave a mess for other people to clean up. Remember that, and "get thee to the lawyer on time." Don't worry about getting to the church on time, as the familiar song admonishes—just get to the lawyer on time.

My seeming digression here isn't really a digression at all. Making out a will is only one of the many steps in the entire process of setting your mind and your affairs in order. Keeping your home or apartment clean and uncluttered is a matter of personal orderliness. Keeping your clothes clean and pressed and your shoes shined is another, and so is keeping your bank account straight. Developing a habit of personal orderliness in every area of your life is vital to your success.

Keeping an orderly mind is even more important, although I consider that orderly living and an orderly mind are just two sides of one coin. As you set your mind in order, you may have to get rid of a lot of mental rubbish. Get rid of petty feelings of dislike; of condemnation; of being upset by trivialities; of being confused in your thinking; and of being unable to reach decisions. Learn to take a stand on what you believe, or do not believe, and follow through on what you decide.

A successful man does not worry in the field in which he is a success. He may worry about his wife's illness, or his son's failure to get through college, but he has self-confidence when it comes to matters related to his own career. He knows that the problems there arise to be solved, not to be contemplated. That is an important statement for everyone to remember. *The problem appears in order to be solved.* It does not appear to be lingered over, to be mulled over, or to be assimilated. It appears in order that a solution can be called out of the mind of the individual experiencing the problem.

Solutions are not plucked out of thin air. They do not come from your next-door neighbor or from the policeman on the beat. They come from the Infinite Knower within you. I do not believe that a problem ever arises in the life of any individual without the answer being available before the problem arises. We often speak of the law of supply and demand. Problem-solving involves this law, and please note that the word supply precedes the word demand. I believe that the answer to any problem in my life is in my mind, as the problem appears, waiting for me to call upon it; to use it and thereby solve the problem.

I believe that the individual mind individualizes the Divine Intelligence. Therefore, I believe that the Knower in you knows what you need to know at the instant in time that you need to know it. By policing your mind, you solve problems that otherwise would bring various forms of frustration into your life. Frustration keeps the mind cluttered and disorganized and prevents the Knower in you from being able to reveal what you need to know. In other words, you can't reach a constructive conclusion about anything if your mind is completely occupied by useless and destructive thoughts.

Dr. Maltz stressed the necessity of what he called the *dignity of self-belief,* the dignity of having accepted yourself as a creative individual.

Once again, some person will say: "But I haven't done anything creative in my life. How can I accept myself as a creative person?" First of all, it is impossible to have lived to the age of twenty-one and not have done something creative. But we won't dwell on that. As counselors, we help the person who consults us to get started on something creative in his life—something simple. Here, we go back to the importance of seeking a goal. Let the person select what he wants to be or wants to do; then help him, through the use of spiritual knowing and positive thinking, to move ahead.

It is vital for everyone to accept himself as a creative person, valuable to himself and to the world.

The pessimist, of course, will say, "The world would never miss me." In his present state, that's quite true. He wouldn't be missed unless folks started noticing how much happier they felt when he wasn't around. In a short time, he probably would be forgotten.

But that isn't the point I want to make. You need this world as long as you are in it. You need to function effectively in this world as long as you are in it. You cannot function effectively without self-belief, and it must be self-belief of the right kind. The most negative person alive has self-belief, but it's on the wrong side of the track. He unconsciously has accepted himself as being no good.

This is self-belief that must be uprooted and replaced by a conscious belief in your creative value in your present world. You run your world. I run my world. I am the only thinker in my mind. I am the only person who can discipline my emotions. I am the only person who can channel my emotions into success patterns. Others can advise me. But I have to do the work myself.

This pattern of creative self-belief is the Dignity of Being. I am putting a capital "D" on Dignity and a capital "B" on Being—the Dignity of Being in existence at this time. You and I were born to live this year fully, and all of the years to come. We were born to live them, not in part but in full. This means creativity in every level of your experience.

Many people are creative at work but noncreative at home. Many people are creative in the arts and noncreative in their personal relationships. When you have achieved creativeness in every area of your present-day life, you have made the conquest of boredom.

I am always astounded at the people who exist, in the midst of life today, who are bored—because we are living in exciting, interesting, changing, and provocative times.

I am glad I wasn't around for the Revolutionary War. I am glad that I am right here, right now. I am going to be in this world, and since I am going to be in it, I am going to police my thinking so that I will have a mental health that will enable me to enjoy living. I do not intend to sit around in my present world, remembering past experiences and becoming frustrated. I am going to be spirit in action every waking moment of my life. The world was not created for people who want to remain in a rut, even if it is a comfortable and profitable rut. Dr. Maltz could have remained an excellent, very reputable, world-renowned plastic surgeon and nothing more. If he had followed that pattern, I suspect that the last years of his life would have been filled with boredom. But he didn't remain so. An *idea* bit him. He went to work on it, and he worked intelligently. Today, he is far from being bored. He lectures everywhere, goes everywhere, does everything, and rejoices in everything. I use him as an example merely because you have been reading what he has to say.

He has mentioned uncertainty, though not in the way I am going to discuss it. The law of life always has been and always will be uncertainty. There are no finalities; there never have been, and there never will be. Everything is uncertain—that's why everything is interesting.

The saddest people in the world are those who have made certain every area of their lives. They live by routine, they think by routine, and eventually, they probably will die in a routine way. These people believe in the walls they have built around themselves; they feel safe because they believe these walls protect them from uncertainty. Of course, all they have done is to put themselves into their own mental jail. They have refused to face up to the fact that everything is uncertain; everything is flexible; and everything is changing.

I can live in uncertainty. I can live with it. I can rejoice in it, because I know that uncertainty means there is always going to be a fresh experience for me.

The uncertainty of a world situation doesn't frighten me. This is because every problem that appears reveals its own answer. The negative reveals its own affirmative, according to the law of opposites. Where there is black, there is white; where there is short, there is tall; where there is thin, there is fat; and so on. And when things seem static, there is bound to be change.

It is absolutely normal to be uncertain. But you don't flounder in uncertainty; you direct it. You view uncertainty without fear. Everything in my life will be uncertain and changing for the rest of my days, and I intend to direct my uncertainties all of the way.

I do not want the boredom of certainty. I want the excitement of uncertainty. I want all the discoveries that go with uncertainty. This is because I do have the dignity of self-belief, the creative, constructive aggression that Dr. Maltz has talked about. Aggression used rightly puts us farther along on the road to success; used incorrectly, it gets us into all kinds of trouble. My aggressiveness is born of self-belief.

That which I am, I express fully.

I impose nothing on other people and, if you have true mental health, you impose nothing on other people. If you run your own life, you have ceased to have any desire to run other people's lives. I, personally, have granted a declaration of independence to every loved one, friend, and neighbor. They are free. If I don't like what they are doing, I say nothing; because they are free to do it. But I also am free to do what I want to do, as long as it does not interfere with the health of another soul.

Too often, however, we sit back and say, "Well, I don't want to hurt anyone." We continue to put up with nonsense. There is nothing in the *law of man* or the *law of the spirit* that demands that anyone should put up with nonsense from other people. Jesus certainly did not do it. He told off the Pharisees every time he got a chance. He let them know exactly where he stood, and they knew where he stood. They knew that here was one man they could not control. The reason they couldn't control him was that he was in control of himself. When you are in control of yourself, other people can't control you.

Here is a factor of great importance to you in your use of self-control. Reduce your pressures. Check to see how many false responsibilities you are carrying around. It is human ego to believe that the whole world depends upon you. If you find yourself saying, "I have so many responsibilities," reduce them. Pressures beyond a certain point will wreck your mental health.

When I ask some "overburdened" person why he feels overburdened, he frequently says, "I take on everybody's problems." My answer is, "I don't—I don't." I am sympathetic, in the right sense of that word. I have compassion. But I can't take on anyone else's problems. I know of no one but myself whom I have ever worried about all night.

A critic will say, "That is selfishness." It is not. Every once in a while, I look over my load of pressures and say, "Which one of these can I reduce to nothing?" You and I do so many things we really don't need to do. We do them because the world expects us to. Often, I make a checklist. I ask myself:

"Why am I doing this? Because I really want to?" Fine. "Because the world thinks I should?" No.

When you are enthusiastic about doing something, no pressure is involved. Any action of yours may become a pressure only when it comes under the heading of duty—one of the most unpleasant words in the English language! When a person says, "I've got to do my duty," I always know that he is going to do something be doesn't want to do. He is going to do it in a negative mental attitude. The act of duty won't help the receiver, and it will only turn the giver into a minor martyr.

One of the most insidious attitudes that can be inculcated in the human mind is that of *martyrdom*.

Looking back at the woman who said to me, "I've given my life for my family." I repeat my reply with stronger emphasis. I said to her, "You shouldn't have. You should have kept your individuality. You should have carried out your own private plans and raised the family at the same time." This is what any creative mother does. She does not submerge herself in her family. She runs the family, but she retains her own fields of interest and keeps them alive. She doesn't desert the family; she handles the family and keeps her own creative interests alive.

Your situation is much the same. Your duty is only to your own mental health. Your duty is only to yourself—to be yourself, to love yourself, and to express yourself. Don't worry—when you are able to do this, you will make a contribution to the world. You will make a far greater one than you can make if you are in a morbid, negative state. You will make a valuable contribution to your loved ones, your friends, and your business associates. All of these people, basically, want you to be happy. The only way you can be happy is by accepting your right self-image. Love yourself and continue to be yourself. Then you can create.

The genius of Jesus was that he had accepted and announced his own self-image. There is no word anywhere in the Gospels that indicates that he, at any time, disliked himself. He knew who he was, accepted who he was, and projected who he was. I believe we can say that he was a successful man. When you do the same thing—and you have probably done it already—you are wonderful. You are wonderful not because of human ego. You are wonderful because that's the way life made you.

## FACING YOUR FEARS

You and I are goal-seekers, reaching our major goals through the step-by-step achievement of minor goals. We have set forth, in previous chapters of this book, the way in which we strive and attain our goals. You have already acquired an awareness of the need for self-examination, self-honesty, and self-acceptance. Now let's concentrate on one more need, another step we must take in order to maintain the mental and emotional balance that is our necessary equipment as we move forward toward personal success and personal happiness. This all-important step is presented here in the form of a question that requires your honest answer.

*Have you the inner ability to face your fears?*

We all have fears, you know. They may be little fears or big fears. Since we are, for the most part, subjective or subconscious beings, we may have fears that we don't even know about. Subconsciously, we tend to cover up and refuse to look at some of them, just as we often try to hide our mistakes instead of facing them and forgiving ourselves for them.

Many fears are unintelligent reactions. They are emotions out of control, operating without conscious reason. When we examine them more closely, however, we discover that some fears are two-sided. They are destructive if allowed to run rampant, but when properly directed, they can often be used in a constructive way. We will go into this matter more deeply in a moment, but first, let's consider a statement that Ernest Holmes, founder of Religious Science, made on the subject of fear:

> Someone has said that the entire world is suffering from one big fear . . . the fear that God will not answer our prayers. Let us analyze the fears which possess us and see if this is true. The fear of lack is nothing more than the belief that God does not, and will not, supply us with whatever we need. The fear of death is the belief that the promises of eternal life may not be true. The fear of loss of health, loss of friends, loss of property—all arise from the belief that God is not all that we claim: Omniscience, Omnipotence, and Omnipresence.
>
> But what is fear? *Nothing more nor less than the negative use of faith . . .*

Dr. Holmes, in the words just quoted, speaks of faith in God, the Infinite Mind; but in all of his teachings, he also recognizes and proclaims the importance of faith in one's inner self. That is largely what I want to emphasize now.

If we have positive faith in ourselves, and in the Knower and Doer within, we can eventually harness most of our fears. If we place our faith in evil instead of good, however, we may remain fear-ridden all of our lives.

So let us ask ourselves in all sincerity: "Have I the ability to examine my emotions and recognize my fears for what they are? Am I willing to admit, without embarrassment or shame, that I have them and that I mean to do something about controlling or getting rid of them?"

Mentally and emotionally disturbed people who seek guidance from a professional psychologist or a psychiatrist are encouraged to uncover their fears and phobias and to learn how to cope with them. This, I believe, is one of the major accomplishments of the entire field of psychotherapy, the fact that the therapist's aim is to help the individual to know himself and to face himself.

It often takes time and patience to learn to know and understand why we are afraid in one area of consciousness and completely undaunted in another. It frequently takes concentrated effort to remove *the mask* that Dr. Maltz refers to. Most of us try—at least now and then—to dodge the necessity of taking a square look at ourselves. That is not an intelligent way to run one's affairs.

I have known people who managed, however, to go right through life into their eighties and nineties without facing themselves. Some of them died with their masks on, so to speak. In so doing, they failed to fulfill the purpose for which they were created, and they missed the excitement of great and wonderful experiences.

The point I want to make is this: You live so much more comfortably with yourself when you know yourself, and you are able to live more creatively. You lessen your frustrations when you see what you are afraid of and try to do something about it. I repeat: Everyone is afraid of something now and then. Occasionally I find a person who says, "I'm not afraid of anything. I have no fears." That person either is a great liar or be needs to shake hands with himself and say, "How do you do! Let's really get acquainted."

You may believe that you know yourself thoroughly, but the process of getting acquainted applies to you, too. I believe you will find it extremely helpful if, within the next twenty-four hours, you will sit down and make a list of your fears, as you know them. It may not be a very long list, but I imagine it will contain some significant and some petty fears.

Most people have a fear about money, not having enough to live on. Fear of illness is not uncommon or unnatural. Some individuals are constantly afraid that there won't be enough time to get things done. Others dread nightfall because they are afraid they won't sleep, afraid they'll wake up in the middle of the night and lie awake for hours. Have you ever been afraid that you wouldn't live up to the expectations of someone you love or respect? Have you been afraid people would laugh at you? That they would snub you? Are you constantly afraid that an accident will happen to you or your loved ones? Are you afraid that you may be fired from your job? Do you spend needless hours *fearing the worst* about most of your life situations?

Be honest. None of these suggested fears may apply to you. If they don't, you will probably have some nerve-wracking substitutes.

As you look at your list, here is something to bear in mind, something I mentioned in an earlier paragraph. Not all fears are destructive. Some of them are constructive. They serve as goads to keep us going, to help us attain our goals. These constructive fears are actually basic drives that are necessary to the process of our development.

Let's take, for instance, the fact that many people save money simply because they are afraid they won't have it. The fear of not having enough money to live on is in itself a destructive fear. If you keep that fear uppermost in your mind all the time, you are setting up patterns of limitation in your subconscious, and the result is that you will not have enough money. You are setting up a poverty pattern in your life through constant worry about lack. However, when you turn your fear of lack into a systematic program of saving, you are turning your destructive fear into a constructive fear. You are responding to a sound basic drive instead of cowering in perpetual dread of a bleak tomorrow in which you expect to be very poor and very unhappy.

We mentioned the fear of illness. This may be an unreasoning fear. Aunt Julia may have developed crippling arthritis in her late forties; a friend or relative may have suffered a heart attack or died of a so-called incurable disease. If, after exposure to one of these experiences or something similar, you find yourself panicking at the slightest twinge of pain, and imagining that you are about to become disabled or die, you are giving way to a destructive fear. There probably is nothing wrong with you. Go to a doctor and have a checkup; find out.

When you know that you are essentially well, you can use your fear of illness in a constructive way. Instead of reacting to it with unreasonable emotion, let it help you develop some sensible habits. Let it be a drive that starts you sleeping the right number of hours, eating the right kind of food, and exercising as much as you should. It is possible that a person who is seriously frustrated in some other areas will stay well because he has been goaded into health by his fear of being sick.

The individual who is constantly under pressure for fear that he won't get some job done on time undoubtedly is a poor planner, or he plans to do too much in a limited time. Instead of being afraid that he won't be able to meet a deadline, he should let his fear point the way to better use of his time. Chances are that while he is trying to get one job done, he is also worrying about the bills he hasn't paid, the promises he hasn't kept, and the things he believes he'll never be able to handle on schedule tomorrow and the next day. Remember, we operate in a universe of law and order.

Fear of sleeplessness bothers a lot of people. Some try to handle their insomnia with sleeping pills. Others get up the moment they are wakeful and raid the refrigerator, perform some household task, or read a book. There probably are as many "remedies" for sleeplessness as there are sleepless people. Some of these remedies work; some don't. Did you ever stop to think that when you are awakened in the middle of the night it may be for a creative purpose? Perhaps there is a Divine urge within you that is presenting you with a great idea. Think about that a bit. Wonderful and inspirational ideas have come to alert minds in the middle of the night.

Those fears that stem from someone else's opinion of you, or reaction to you, are useless fears that should be replaced by self-acceptance and self-belief. I frequently offer this reminder: You are the only thinker in your world. You also are the only person who is living your life, and you are the only person who must be satisfied with what you think, what you feel, and what you experience. If you have a fear of accidents, you can turn it into a habit of reasonable caution. Fear of losing a job can be translated into an attitude of greater personal responsibility and dependability.

I feel reasonably certain that when you look at your fears, when you make your list and give it careful consideration, you will find at least some items that will offer you a basis for correcting your thoughts and feelings. After you have made this self-examination, you will at least know where you are.

Compare this vital process of finding out where you are in your own livingness to the experience of finding your way on an unfamiliar road. You are lost. You look at the road map. You study it carefully and note the names of some towns, or the location of a river, pond, or bridge. You drive along watching for some sign that you have seen on the map. Suddenly, you come across such a sign, and you know where you are. You are no longer lost, but you still must follow the road carefully in order to reach your destination.

On my way toward my goals, I examine the negatives in my consciousness. Then I take the necessary steps to change the negatives to positives. I look at every situation that seems to be negative, in order to see what I can do about it. I'm not concerned with what the nation can do; what the government can do; or what the city or state can do. I'm only concerned with what I can do. Once I see clearly what is wrong, I usually can see what I can do to make it right. If I refuse to see what is wrong, however, I can't do a thing to correct the troublesome situation or solve the problem.

We take the steps that lead to self-awareness in order to correct our aim and to set ourselves back on the right track when we seem to be missing the mark. We are fortunate in realizing that we can do this. People didn't always understand themselves so well.

As you no doubt are aware, most people are completely self-interested. They follow the trends and new discoveries in medicine. This gives them a knowledge of their physical selves. Tremendous strides in this field have been made since 1900. Tremendous strides also have been made in man's understanding of the mind and the emotions. It has even become fashionable for the layman to diagnose himself, using such clichés as the *inferiority complex, the anxiety neurosis, the split personality,* and all the rest. His diagnosis is likely to be incorrect, but it indicates his interest in the subject of *himself.*

It is true that we know more about the physical body today than we have ever known in the history of life. We know more about how the mind and emotions work than we have ever known in the history of life. There also is something else of utmost importance that some of us know, but that not all people recognize.

This factor is the *spiritual side of life.* Dr. Maltz recognizes it; I recognize it; and many of you readers recognize it. We are the people who know, beyond any doubt, that there is a spiritual side to the mind and the emotions. There is a spiritual side to the physical body. We see a design; we see a plan. We see a something in us that will never lose hope. We see a something that will always spur us on and will always give us the "hunch," the idea. That something will always quietly say after any accomplishment: "Well done." *That is the way of the spirit in man.*

The spirit in man is that which makes you aware of evil in order to create good. it is that which stimulates you and says, "Keep on trying!" It is that which animates you as life. It is that which animates your consciousness as ideas, and that which animates your imagination so that you are always imaging yourself correctly.

The other day, without realizing what I was doing I found myself worrying about an acquaintance of mine. Suddenly I stopped and said: "Wait a minute. I'm being unfair to that person." My worry wouldn't affect him, of course. But I was building the wrong image of that individual in my mind. Realizing this, I said to myself: "Let's get this straight. This man is competent; he has lived long enough to know what to do, and he will do it. Anyway, it's none of my business."

Here was an instance where my vivid imagination was going in the wrong direction. We must not let such things happen. We need our imaginations, but we need them to further our own progress, not to fix wrong images of other people in our subconscious minds.

If you read the story of Joseph, son of Jacob in the Old Testament, you will find that Joseph's father gave him a *coat of many colors.* This coat was a symbol of the imagination, and imagination gives color to life. You are given the gift of imagination. One of its purposes is to help you envision yourself as you want to be. This is correct self-imaging. When you have seen yourself as you want to be, the next step is seeing yourself as already being that thing.

There is an ancient saying: "The ought to be is." In accordance with this statement, you first image yourself as you *ought to be.* Then you image your-self as *being.*

This is a success formula. I know of no books in the so-called self-help field, other than Dr. Maltz's and mine, which stress the importance of imagination as much as we do. I have proved the truth of "The ought to be is" many times in my own experience.

When we started plans for our new church building, which we now occupy with pride, we were faced with every possible difficulty. Difficulties with regard to finances and difficulties in connection with construction work. I refused to be daunted. Each day, I saw myself standing in the pulpit in the auditorium. This was in spite of the fact that at that time there was no floor. There was no ceiling. The designers had given me a picture of what the auditorium and pulpit would look like. They had shown me how the walls would look. They had shown me a sample of the rug, and I knew that the chairs were being re-upholstered in the same color.

With these guidelines, I was able to stand before that pulpit—in my imagination—for about one minute a day. During that minute, I visualized the complete picture as it is today. As soon as I had started this practice, which I should have started the moment we had the plans for the church, operations for its completion began to speed up.

I didn't find myself running around blaming labor for a strike dealing with delivery of steel. I did not accept as a problem the fact that certain beams couldn't be delivered. I just said: "Wait a minute. Practice what you preach, Barker." Then I would image myself in the pulpit and looking at the walls. I saw myself admiring the red carpet and looking at the seats upholstered to match. I saw the seats filled with people and imagined myself talking to them.

When I had practiced this imaging for a while, everything began to fall into line. When they told us we wouldn't be in the church by the first of March, I imaged some more. The contractors began moving the date back, and back and back. We moved into the church, which was fully equipped, on January first, not March first.

The situation I have just described illustrates the correct use of the mind. It takes courage to start such a procedure and to stick with it. But remember, any-one can wear the coat of many colors, his imagination. That is a part of man's natural heritage. I used my imagination to image the church that I wanted for myself and others. Then, using the maxim, "The ought to be is," I imaged the completed form, with myself and my audience in it.

This is an illustration of the unconscious success motivation. The church building was my success idea. We have success-motivation equipment, and it responds when we have a goal and use the correct imagination. The mechanism moves into automatic action and creates out of our consciousness whatever we have taken as a goal. This is the mechanism which Dr. Maltz stresses in his book *Psycho-Cybernetics*. He explains that it can be used as a success-mechanism or as a failure-mechanism.

Again we see the similarity between some of the principles of Psycho-Cybernetics and those of the Science of Mind. There is one law of action, but we can use it in two ways. Similarly, you can use your fears in two ways. When you clarify them and discover that most of them really are creative, you are ready to do your correct imaging.

At this point, I am back to an old theme of mine, but I want to reemphasize it. It is this: Investigate your potentials. You are greater than you think you are. You are far more intelligent than you think you are. You are far more handsome, if you are a man, than you think you are. You are far more beautiful, if you are a woman, than you think you are.

Your potentialities, regardless of your age, remain always the same. We are incomplete people seeking to complete ourselves. We are unfinished business, and we always will be. We can't ever be finished because evolution won't let us be. Call it evolution, call it God, call it what you will—it won't let us.

Your potentialities are unique to you; mine are unique to me. But they are there, and we should take a look at them quite often. Investigate the potentiality in you that will make you happy. I believe that everyone should be healthy, and happy, and prosperous. There is no virtue in illness and no virtue in sorrow or unhappiness. There is no virtue in lack. You were not created to bear a burden or to bear a cross. You were created to solve problems. Period. You were created to be happy in doing the problem-solving job.

Every problem you have actually is a blessing. It stimulates you to do new thinking, to investigate yourself a little more. Resolve that from here on, when a problem comes along, you are going to turn to the power within you and allow it to reveal the solution. It will do this through ideas. Your problem will be on its way to a solution as soon as you receive a new idea. Keep the channels of your mind open. As long as you are on the merry-go-round of worry and concern, repeatedly asking yourself why, why, why, nothing inspirational can get through. Ideas and solutions must have an open pathway into your consciousness.

Remember the importance of relaxation. When I'm looking for a new idea, I sit very still. I relax and say: "Come on, mind, I need a new idea. You deliver it to me."

This probably is what the traditional church would call prayer, just a few words spoken with sincerity and in complete faith. The Infinite is not impressed by long-winded petitions. Most clergymen pray too long. I do it quickly. I take only two minutes. I sit down, relax, and say: "Mind in me, you know what I need to know. Now give me my next idea so I can handle this problem." When I have finished that statement, I get up and go back to whatever I was doing. Soon, the idea is revealed to me.

All of us have some unpleasant experiences that come into our lives. They often involve irksome problems. They signal a time for action, action of a particular kind. Here is where we sit down and relax. Here is where we say: "Wait a minute. Life has never brought me a problem that I couldn't handle. It is not bringing me one now." That's what I call *faith*. I know that I can solve every problem because a spiritual idea is always revealed to me at the right time.

What do we mean by a *spiritual idea?* I have defined *spiritual* as intelligence in action. As I use the term, it has nothing to do with piety. The universe is a spiritual system because it is intelligence in action. You are a spiritual being because you are intelligence in action.

Getting up in the morning and washing your body is just as spiritual as saying a prayer in a cathedral. It is intelligence in action. You have received this intelligence as a free gift from life. This intelligence is a universal intelligence, individualized in you, as you. Therefore, it has the right idea to solve your problem, to cure your frustrations, and to ensure your mental and emotional balance as you move toward creative goals. Your intelligence sparks your imagination.

You are well equipped, so use your equipment. People say to me, "Well, I have the wealth and the wisdom of past experience." I know that this is true, but it is not enough. You need the wealth of hope of the future. Anyone can relive past experience, but not everyone can create intelligent future experience. That is what you are going to do from now on.

If your future is dull, it is not Dr. Maltz's fault or mine. It is because you are too lazy to use the processes we teach. Remember, the solution to each of your problems is already in your mind, as potential. You don't find the solution by studying the problem. You find it by relaxing for a minute and letting the creative side of your mind go to work. When you *review* a problem, you are using your creative process in a destructive way. But when you begin to think of the solution as being already in your mind, you move out of despair into hope. You cannot live without hope.

To me, hope is a creative expectation of a pleasant future. That is what all of us need. Do all of us have it? Watch your friends. Watch their thinking; observe their manner of speaking. You will find that many of them do not have any real hope for the future.

Anyone can be a prophet of doom today. Anyone can look at world affairs, and the affairs of this nation, and say that civilization is headed for ruin. But I don't accept that verdict. I have creative anticipation. I believe that people in high places will take the constructive actions that are necessary to make this nation greater than it has ever been before.

Anyone can join the Mourners' Union. What we need is people who refuse to join. We need people with hope; people who know that there must be change, change that has its roots in you and in me. Most of the people who want the nation to change don't want to change themselves. They go on saying, "I'm all right." That's not true. No one is *all right*. We are partially right. We may be more right than wrong. But all of us constantly need some change. Otherwise, we would be static people in a static world.

Investigate your potential for solving your problems, your potential for handling the everyday needs of living, your needs for happiness. God can do a lot more through a happy person than through a miserable one. Even if your life right now seems to be going along smoothly, remember your right to happiness. Expand your happiness. Be happier than you are. It's possible, you know.

There is another right I would like you to remember as well. That is your right to the correct kind of selfishness. I said the *correct* kind of selfishness. I recall the case of a man who came to my office one day. He wanted me to give him a spiritual treatment for one million dollars. I asked him: "What will you do with a million dollars if you get it?" He replied: "I want to give it to my three children."

I suggested that instead of praying for one million dollars for this man, we might pray for $350,000 for each of his children. He didn't go for that at all. His human ego would not have been inflated if we had succeeded in getting the lesser amounts for each of his children. He wanted that million dollars so he could buy his offspring later on. He wanted to be able to say, "Look what I gave YOU."

Gifts often carry *purchase power*. This man wanted purchase power. He wanted the million dollars only to exert power. This was selfishness used in a destructive way. I never saw that man again because he found out that I had no patience with this kind of nonsense.

There is another kind of selfishness that I recommend to you. It is a selfishness that you need if you want to maintain your own identity and to be the person you want to be. It requires that you adopt certain rules of self-preservation. *Don't let everyone walk all over you.* Have a certain point of self-privacy that cannot be invaded. You don't have to be an amateur do-gooder. There are enough professionals.

Don't let people rob you of your time. Time is a very precious element. In that connection, I am reminded of an eight-page letter I received in the office. It was handwritten, and I must say that the penmanship was very bad. I sent the letter back with a note informing the writer that if he would condense it to a single typewritten page, I would read it and give him an answer. I am too busy to waste time on inconsiderate people, and so are you.

Here is a thought worth bearing in mind as you go through your day-by-day living. Whenever you can simplify your problem and state it clearly in one sentence, it is already half solved.

I started this chapter by saying that we are goal-seekers. Now I hope I have also made it clear that we are problem-solvers. We are problem-solvers when we let go; when we stop harrying the situation that bothers us and allow the Infinite Wisdom within us to come up with the right answer.

Here I would like to quote a pertinent paragraph from my book, *The Power Of Decision.*

"Your subconscious mind is a divine instrument. Its dexterity and precision will never be fully known. It is the greatest gift that you have. It is beyond price. It is what you are as a creative individual. It accepts the impress of your thought and acts upon it. It knows neither good nor evil, yet its processes can create both. Wise men have said that all creation is the result of the Law and the Word. The subconscious is the Law. What you place in it is the Word. This is the play of life upon itself."

Learn to *know* the precious equipment for living with which you are endowed. Learn to *recognize* the potency of your thoughts and feelings. Learn to *welcome* new ideas and have the courage to follow through with them. This is living. This is life. This the purpose for which you were created.

You were created to *be and become great.*

*Dr. Raymond Charles Barker was a significant author and spiritual leader in the New Thought spiritual movement and Religious Science.*

# BOOK TWO

# THE SEARCH FOR SELF-RESPECT

# CONTENTS

# SUMMARY

Not just a book that talks about self-improvement but one that gives you an actual step-by-step action program for setting and achieving goals.

Have you ever been depressed?

Have you ever felt unloved, frightened, alone?

All of us have suffered such feelings at times. But we all have the power to change our lives by changing our attitudes. The techniques for self-discovery and self-affirmation that you find in these pages will help you every day of your life. You will discover how to free yourself from the great cripplers: guilt, remorse, and resentment. You will learn how to be tranquil in these anxious times. You will learn how to set goals for yourself and accomplish them. You will find your best qualities and use your talents to become a winner.

# 1

## YOUR GREAT NEED

### SELF-RESPECT

WHEN YOU WAKE UP IN THE MORNING, THROWING OFF YOUR BLANKETS AND blinking the sleep from your eyes, you prepare to meet a curious world.

It is a world of extravagant technological achievement. Skyscrapers thrust themselves heavenward, products of man's ingenuity, up toward the jets that whiz through our skies at speeds no one would have believed thirty years ago. Down below, on our well-built highways, unending processions of gleaming automobiles move forward. All these are products of man's inventive capacities, all reflections of a technological level of accomplishment unknown to the pages of written history before us. Computers aid us in our calculations while the telephone—once a miracle!—pulls us into close communication. Our world is full of elevators and can openers—diesel engines and lawnmowers.

What a world for people today! What a world of overwhelming achievement! There are comforts beyond compare for all the people who wake up in the morning and plunge out of the world of sleep into the world of activity.

And yet it is a world full of people reeling in confusion trying to find themselves, seeking life's answers, and, in short, searching oh-so-ardently for that inner feeling, that so elusive self-respect.

For how do you measure the value of a man's life? How do you measure the value of a woman's life? There are so many people in this huge world of yours and mine—how do you measure the value of their lives?

In dollars and cents? In totaling up their bank accounts, their stocks, and bonds, their real-estate holdings, their total net worth? In tangible property? Do you take an inventory and assess the accumulations? Automobiles, houses, fur coats, diamond rings, television sets, household appliances?

Is this how you take a human being, a creature of God born without his will into this large world of ours, and assess the value of his life? Is this how you place a value on his personal qualities, his skills, his years of experience in living?

Certainly not. Some people might use such yardsticks; I feel they are misguided.

For if there is anything that I have learned in my sixty-five-plus years in this world, if there is anything that has survived the ups and downs of my life, it is this knowledge: *That there is no more accurate measure of an individual's value than his own degree of self-respect.*

And that is why I am writing this book.

More and more, I have come to appreciate the great importance of self-respect. As the years have passed following the publication of *Psycho-Cybernetics* (and then *The Magic Power of Self-Image Psychology* and *Creative Living for Today),* I have realized more and more how the nucleus of ideas on Psycho-Cybernetics, expressed in these three books, has been the concept of self-respect as a guiding force.

And as I have traveled throughout most of the states of our great country, lecturing to people and talking to them on a one-to-one basis, this realization has become conviction. For on meeting people—young people, senior citizens, church people, irreligious people, rich and poor—I have felt that, regardless of their diverse backgrounds and the uniquely individual character of their experiences, this is what they seek for themselves: self-respect.

People reach out today—in a complicated, changing, and uncertain world—for a sense of their own individual identity. But they don't want just any kind of identity; what they seek is an identity they can be proud of. They want to know who they are, *and* they want to feel a sense of respect for who they are.

We live in a world in which respect for the dollar is considerable, and in which respect for the materialistic products a dollar can buy is also considerable.

Well and good—I like my comforts, too. But how about a more basic emphasis—on respect for one's self? Why is this more basic? Because with self-respect, you reach out toward your full potential as a human being. Because without self-respect, you are a criminal in hiding, living in a prison you have built around yourself, and even if the prison is comfortable and luxurious, it is still a prison.

So, this is why I write this book on self-respect. I make no claims that readers of my other books will find it startlingly new in concept because I carry into it ideas I have spent a lifetime developing, some of which are expressed in one form or another elsewhere. I will, of course, draw freely from my many years of experience as a plastic surgeon, and, needless to say, I will apply my concepts of Psycho-Cybernetics to this crucial area of self-respect.

Nevertheless, I do believe that readers old and new will find in these pages both fresh and arresting material to spur and challenge them, and positive, helpful, useful suggestions to aid them in moving toward a good feeling about themselves and their position of dignity and status in the world.

## REACHING OUT TOWARD THE BEST IN YOURSELF

And so, let us begin this great search of ours, this search for self-respect.

How do we begin this great process of reaching out toward the best in ourselves? How do we begin this great treasure hunt? First and foremost, by cementing our determination, by feeling strongly about our search.

To reach out only tentatively, timidly, toward the best in yourself is not enough.

To say in yourself, "I have nothing good in me, I know that, but I'll give it a try anyway"—this is not enough.

And to tell yourself, "This is an impossible world; to feel self-respect these days is hopeless, but I'll try to keep an open mind"—this also is not enough.

This is not an easy world to live in. Many people live incomplete lives, bedeviled by the swift pace of change, and frustrated by the endless chain of complications, and therefore, the search for self-respect is a difficult one. Confusion, pain, despair, dissociation: millions of people live with these feelings in today's world. Self-respect, success, dignity: these sweeter feelings are harder to come by. To reach them, therefore, you must *will* to reach them. You must feel determined to reach them. You must feel enthusiasm for your goals.

All of us experience, now and then, feelings of boredom, of inertia, of *what's the difference*. At such times, nothing looks good: steak looks like dogmeat, and when you eat it, it tastes even worse. You look at yourself in the mirror and say to yourself, *"Why does that have to be me?"*

Alright, we all get into moods like this. Laugh at them; they're just human. But the important point is this: your next move is forward, out of this inertia into determination and enthusiasm. For something. For some goal. For some *worthwhile goal.*

My goal in writing this book, your goal in reading this book, must be a determination to find—in you, in me—the self-respect we must feel to lead lives of fulfillment and happiness.

A determination. Not a halfhearted gesture, but a real determinate one. Nothing else will do.

Let me tell you about the kind of determination I mean. I found it recently when I was lecturing in Detroit.

I was about to address my audience when I noticed a woman helping a man (her husband) walk into the auditorium. He limped along, supported by the woman and by a cane; his leg was in a cast. This startled me somewhat, but I was truly amazed when I saw his clothes; under his overcoat, he wore his pajamas. Outside, there was snow on the ground, and here he came, walking slowly, in his pajamas.

I talked to him, got to know him a little, even had him up on the lecture platform with me. He was, I would estimate, in his late fifties or early sixties. He was interested in my ideas and wanted to hear me speak—and I learned that he had traveled twenty-five miles through the snow to hear me lecture. He had been very eager to come on time—thus the pajamas.

There he stood, leg in cast, pajamas—we were photographed together—and surely this man, though smiling cordially, was the very image of determination. I learned that he was living with half a kidney; that didn't stop him, either. Men with two good legs could not move; he, leg in cast, insisted on moving. In terms of determination, he was Babe Ruth out to hit another home run, Joe Louis out after another knockout. What did he want? Self-respect.

During the last couple of years, I have done a great deal of lecturing, and I have talked personally to thousands of people.

One, a young man also in the Detroit area, had studied in Psycho-Cybernetics workshops and was later a teacher for the workshops. What is so unusual about this? The fact that he is blind, that he cannot see—and yet, emotionally, he sees better than many people who have vision.

Another young man in his twenties decided to teach the inmates of a state penitentiary some of my ideas on more worthwhile living. I was impressed that a man so young, at an age where so many are often limited in their sense of responsibility, could feel so strongly for others that he could reach out even to anti-social people with a real desire to help them.

These young men, too, possess the determination that I refer to—determination to feel respect for themselves and for others.

This is the way you must feel as you start off with me on this journey. You must want to make the most of your life. You must have strong feelings about this conviction and not be ashamed of it—and why should you be? This is your life that is at stake! You should be willing, like that man in Detroit, to travel twenty-five miles through the snow, your leg in a cast, your arm in a cast, your head swathed in bandages, if it will help you just a little bit toward more self-respect.

Not to hear me speak—that is irrelevant—but to reach out toward anything that will help you to feel a greater sense of personal worth.

## THE NATURE OF SELF-RESPECT

I have already implied that there is no necessary connection between financial and materialistic success and self-respect. If I have not made my views absolutely clear, let me do so now.

I believe in positive thinking, and beyond that, to positive imagining, and then carrying the entire process forward into successful, goal-directed action. I believe in getting out into the world and achieving success in this world— which, with all its imperfections, is the only world we've got.

As a plastic surgeon, I have operated on many famous people, people whose names you would recognize immediately, people who make enormous sums of money through their talents and their positions, people whom the world labeled successes—and yet who regarded themselves as failures. Because they lacked self-respect. Thus, there is no necessary correlation between success as the world sees it and self-respect.

Today, after years of writing and lecturing and meeting people and talking to them, this is more clear to me than ever. Worthwhile goals and worthwhile achievements are very important to anyone. Successes are important, too, as is setting goals. Still, the basic feeling of self-respect is something that, initially, you manufacture inside yourself. You have the choice between self-rejection and self-respect; and in the pages of this book, we will analyze the very nature of *your feeling* of self-respect from the foundation on up.

As an illustration of what I have been saying, let me tell you about a man I met while on a lecture tour. Although, by all conventional criteria, he was a success, he lacked self-respect, and therefore, did not enjoy his success.

He was a computer salesman—a top-notch computer salesman. He had been married for a number of years. He had children. He supported his family more than adequately. He had earned the respect of his family and of people in his community. But he hadn't earned his own self-respect. With all his achievements, he could not give himself this feeling.

When he was growing up, his parents had been divorced. The product of a broken home, he had not ever been able to put himself together again to his complete satisfaction.

I talked to this man—he was very likeable, I thought—and gave him some advice that I sincerely hope helped him to feel better about himself, for he deserves his self-esteem.

Our aim in this book is to achieve a kind of self-respect that is real and dependable, that does not hinge on either your financial condition or the state of world affairs, that can weather the disapproval of your neighbors or the anger of your boss at work. This is Self-respect with a capital S, and this, in the final analysis, is the only factor that can make the world inside you go round so that you feel truly secure, regardless of all the external forces which you cannot possibly control.

This is SELF-RESPECT!

## USING YOUR MIND

Self-respect, then, is basically something that you manufacture for yourself in your mind. You must, therefore, learn to use this mind of yours. You know how to use your automobile. You know how to use your television set. Now—and so much more essential to your self-respect as a human being—you must learn how to use your mind.

Let me digress for a moment or two at this point and tell you about my father. Preparing to write this book, I spent an afternoon once just thinking and smoking my cigars, thinking about starting to write a book about self-respect—and I began to think about my father, who had, while he lived, taught me so much about other people and about how to live, and who, in so many ways, as most fathers do, helped me to shape my destiny.

My father came to this country from Austria. He was a great designer of clothes, and he set up a business in this country as a clothes designer. He was wonderful at using his hands, and, in retrospect, I realize how I gravitated toward the field of plastic surgery, which, of course, also requires deft, skillful hands.

My father was a very religious man, and he always tried to apply his ethical principles to people in a practical way. In our community on New York's Lower East Side, where I grew up, more than once I saw him arbitrate a dispute among neighbors, or perhaps break up a brewing fistfight between two of the hotter young bloods out to prove their manhood.

He believed strongly in giving people a square deal, and he never failed to return a favor or to give people the benefit of their good intentions—even if these intentions were not obvious on the surface. And he prided himself on his sense of self-respect. He nurtured it as one would a flower by placing it in the sun to flourish. He lived for his sense of self-respect—the feeling that he was a worthwhile, positive person, and he worked to develop it.

I remember once—I was very young, not yet even a teenager—and I went to his place of business, where people were working with the cloth that was an essential in his life. It was early in the afternoon, and the workers had just returned from lunch. One man handled the cloth with greasy fingers; my father saw him do this and became enraged. Grease on his cloth! On his cloth! He felt his artistry being sullied, his goodness being dirtied. Dad had a violent temper, and he started toward the irresponsible laborer, hand raised, ready to strike him in his sudden wrath.

It hurt him that his rage would overcome him like this, and he started away from the man, mortified, his sense of self-respect endangered, and walked into his own private office to sit there quietly until he could control his anger. Then, restored, he returned to tell the man calmly and quietly not to soil the cloth.

I have always remembered this—how upset he had been, and how.he had retreated in order to advance toward his sense of self-respect.

At home, too, my father, usually friendly and agreeable, would sometimes find himself threatened by his temper. One of my brothers or sisters would do something to outrage him, and, in a flash, his hand would be raised to spank the offender. He didn't like this in himself; he would draw back his hand and re-treat to a little room where he could be by himself—his bedroom or the kitchen, perhaps. When he came back, his sense of self-respect would be restored; he would have kind words for the children and a friendly smile for everybody.

There were, as you can see, two sides to my father, and he battled mightily to win this fight with himself—self-respect would win.

Many years later—after my father died in a tragic, sudden accident—I re-membered my father's habit and incorporated it into my theories of Psycho-Cybernetics. You can do yourself a good turn and give yourself relaxation from your tensions if, instead of plunging headlong and heedless into a difficult and frustrating situation, you go to rest for a while—in a quiet room in your mind where you can be alone. Think, refresh yourself, and prepare once more to go out and meet life's battles head-on with your self-respect restored.

But, to return to my point, you must learn to use your mind to develop your sense of self-respect, and in the pages of this book, we will examine ways in which you can do this. For as it was in his mind that my father was able to quiet his surging emotions and restore to himself his dignity, so must you—in your way, with your special problems, with your unique assets and liabilities—give yourself your self-respect.

In your mind.

Where good things start.

## FINDING THE SELF YOU LIKE

We hear a great deal about identity problems these days. We hear about mil-lions of people caught in an over-mechanized and impersonal society, losing themselves in the midst of the vastness and the impersonality. And, truth to tell, we live in a world that is growing and growing. One billion people in 1830, two billion in 1930, three billion in 1960; experts predict a world population of seven-and-one-half-billion by the year 2000, and a population of three hundred million in the United States before 2000.

How do you keep a firm hold on your identity in such a huge world? How do you feel the importance of *yourself* as a human being?

Studies have shown that teenagers growing up into adulthood in this world underrate themselves. Adults, according to this study, consider teenagers more worthy than the teenagers consider themselves.

As for adults, their dissatisfaction with themselves is reflected in the rising incidence of alcoholism, of divorce, and an increasing cynicism about whether or not there is meaning in life.

Some people seek identity in the way they clothe their selves, and old-fashioned people, used to conventional manners of dress, easily are startled when they go out into the streets and see identity-seeking people parading around in down-to-the-ground overcoats, up-to-the-thigh skirts, peekaboo dresses, and plunging necklines—and that's not all, with outlandish hair, makeup, and so on.

Many people seek to find themselves through promiscuous sex, but does it work? I doubt it. Studies have shown that promiscuous men and women gain little sexual satisfaction from their adventures and have difficulty relating to other people. It is also interesting to note that research has shown that sex workers—glamour figures of today to some people—lack the capacity to establish wholesome, worthwhile interpersonal relationships.

And so, people—struggling people, seeking to do something with their lives, earnestly reach out for identity for themselves. In conventional ways. In unconventional ways. But the question is, or should be, *What kind of identity?* For you can come to grips with what you are, you can *identify* yourself, but still not like what you are.

So you have to do more than find an identity for yourself. You have to build a sense of self that you like. To live the good life, you have to learn how to give yourself something of priceless value—self-respect.

That is what we will think about in this book—how you can build inside yourself a sense of self-respect, of dignity as a human being, that you can feel secure with.

These are not hollow words. Self-respect is our great need today. Obviously, we live with materialistic plenty and super-plenty. All you have to do is go shopping in a department store or supermarket, and you can see this. Or, if you read the financial section of your daily newspaper, chances are you know the indexes are going up.

Prosperity is not around the corner, but here and now.

Still, what good is this prosperity if you don't *feel* prosperous? Affluence. A chicken in every pot is depression talk; today, the talk is about two cars in every garage. Still, you are as affluent as you feel you are. There is a character in a short story who feels affluent when she has potatoes, beef, and onions, even though penniless. On the other hand, if you don't feel the inner assurance of your respect for yourself, you can earn an income in seven figures and still feel impoverished.

What is the great, crying need of people today? Prosperity is not enough; affluence is not enough. A sense of full, dependable self-reliance is needed—the supporting feeling that they respect themselves.

We will do more than treat self-respect as an intellectual concept or a vague verbal formulation. In accordance with my theories of Psycho-Cybernetics, we will set practical goals that we can accomplish.

I hope that you will not be lazy in reading this book, but that you will try to turn ideas into practice, so that you can truly reactivate the functioning of your success mechanism.

Learn to use your imagination constructively, and help yourself in an active, responsible way toward respectfulness toward yourself—as you are—as an individual and as you function in your world.

"Nothing is good, I see, without respect." William Shakespeare wrote this hundreds of years ago, and, as so many of his lines, this one lives in the present as well as in the past and in the future. For our purposes, let's amend *respect* to *self-respect,* and then let us start our search for self-respect.

# 2

# UNDERSTANDING

## THE KEY TO HUMAN DIGNITY

AND SO, WE ARE OFF ON OUR MISSION. WE SEEK THE KEYS TO UNLOCK THE TREA-sure chest of our sense of self-respect. We seek to find, to recapture, to reinvigorate our human dignity.

Our weapons are invisible but potent. Understanding is one of our key weapons. For to live fruitfully in a subtle, civilized society in which complexities are not always spelled out for us, in which we must often seek beneath superficial appearances to discover truth and to differentiate reality from fantasy, we must be understanding people. We must understand ourselves—complex people that we are—and we must understand other people, even while they may hide the essence of their personalities behind various affectations and poses.

And, in truth, we must accomplish not one, but two tasks. We must become more understanding, and, at the same time, we must become less misunderstanding. Anatole France was a writer who believed there was great misunderstanding in the world. He thought that the development of just a little understanding was a far greater achievement than building one's life on the quicksand of many and monumental misunderstandings.

We read volumes and volumes on the nature of racial and religious prejudice these days—and yet is not prejudice, in essence, misunderstanding?

A recent study of Catholic schools showed that 53 percent of the students had unfavorable opinions of Jews and 33 percent thought ill of people of color. But what caliber of understanding was behind these opinions? What experience of people of color or Jews are they based on—if any?

A poll on anti-Semitism in France indicated that half the population was opposed to the idea of a Jewish president; one-third was against Jewish representatives in government; and one-fifth would not consult a Jewish doctor (they feared poisoning, mostly). Misunderstanding running wild.

What is even more shocking, perhaps, is that in a study, out of 505 American country clubs, 498 indicated that they were opposed to accepting Jewish members.

These studies, these polls, were made quite recently. Hear often—and with good reason—these days of injustice; abuses inflicted on Black people because of irrational prejudice and misunderstanding, so much that this needs no documenting; but the misunderstanding rampant in the world spreads out in many directions, and the ignorance behind these misunderstandings is truly staggering. It is especially interesting to note that, as regards the poll on anti-Semitism in France, researchers found the strongest prejudice in communities with no Jews.

I don't bring these studies up to write about the problems of these two minority groups; although, it is interesting that the Catholics, who are prejudiced against others today, have been the object of prejudice themselves—that none had been elected president of the United States until just a few years ago. My main purpose in mentioning all this, nevertheless, is to write about the enormous human problem of misunderstanding, a global problem of almost unbelievable dimensions. We must become more understanding, less *mis*understanding of individuals if we would aspire to make the world—and our internal world—a better place to live in.

And thus, we reach out, attempting to reach full awareness, toward our full self-respect as human beings, judging ourselves charitably, coming to grips with our true personalities, appreciating ourselves with friendship, and then reaching out toward others, not with animosity or prejudice, but with the same helping hand of friendship and of constructive intentions.

This is no easy thing to do. We are more likely to misunderstand than to understand ourselves and other people. In truth, this may be a protective phenomenon in which we defend ourselves against possible enemies; thus, we may come to use misunderstanding as protective armor, but it leads to more misunderstanding, and the setting up of a vicious cycle in which you just can't win.

## MISUNDERSTANDING AS A WAY OF LIFE

More on misunderstanding. Why? Because it is so prevalent over the world, over our great nation, among all age groups, among all income groups, among children, and among senior citizens. Before we can erect our great structure of self-respect, we must select the site and clear the foundation of debris— and the debris obstructing the building of *understanding* is *misunderstanding*.

When I was a young "tough guy," everybody misunderstood everybody. We had lots of gang fights on New York's Lower East Side. We had them every day sometimes; teenaged terrors clustered in gangs and warred on each other. We armed ourselves with sticks (from stickball), broken bottles, and bricks. For protective shields to ward of blows of the bloodthirsty foe, we took the tops of old-fashioned wash-kettles that the women used to wash clothes in those days.

Thus, the young bloods of one block would come to us, and it was not exactly love thy neighbor. The two would clash, *boom!*

How did the fights start? It was pride that did it; stubborn pride. A member of one gang would seem to affront a member of the other gang, the little misunderstanding would become a grudge, the grudge would become a mortal injury and . . . You know the rest—bricks, bats, sticks, stones, wash-kettle tops. The adults would rush into stores and buildings to take shelter, and we kids would smash each other around until the police came rushing to the rescue.

It was Armageddon; D-day; Custer's Last Stand! From cement roofs, the neighborhood snipers crouched with BB guns, and the marksmanship was superb. When, finally, the fighting was over, usually no one even remembered how it started! Yet someone was usually hurt, and occasionally, wagons came to cart away the most seriously injured to the hospital.

It is true that it could have been worse—I understand in more recent times, teenage "rumbles" with switchblades have resulted in deaths, whereas our gang fights never, to my knowledge, ended in anything so tragic and final.

Still, ours were bad enough. To a degree, of course, they stemmed from overflowing teenage energy and from aggression seeking an outlet. But they also stemmed from an appalling lack of communication between people— then as today.

For today, we still find ourselves in a chaotic world where adults, not teen-agers, cannot seem to communicate with and understand each other. Witness: suspicion among the Great Powers; race riots in American cities; rising crime rate; rising divorce rate; and alcoholism as a way of life. These are among the leading symptoms of twentieth-century life, and they spell out an inability of people to accommodate themselves to each other.

In 1968, I was lecturing in Washington to about eight hundred executives of insurance companies. At that time, Washington was aflame with violence, riots, and looting—products of centuries of misunderstanding. A fundamental human right had been abridged: that one person is as good as another, and that we are all children of God, born with rights to happiness and to the feeling that we are human beings of dignity.

The police rushed out in force to cope with the situation, and eventually, they restored order to our nation's capital.

Still, police are no answer to the worldwide problem of misunderstanding. We do not have enough police to stop all the inner and outer riots in all the streets and highways and byways of the world. We do not have enough police to stop all the violence and resentful fury of the world's teeming population. There are never enough police, and there never can be enough police.

The victory of understanding over misunderstanding starts when you police yourself first. It starts when you take charge of the riot inside you, and when you police the potential fires of violence before they erupt. It starts when you come to terms with your anti-social impulses and police properly, channeling them into healthy, aggressive, directed outlets.

By "policing yourself," I do not mean that you put yourself in jail. Nor do I mean that you emotionally imprison yourself. My concept of understanding is this:

1. You seek to identify your needs, and to work to their realization.
2. You try to find out who you are in relation to people.
3. You understand that there is greatness in yourself, there is greatness in other people, that there is indeed greatness in all people.

You don't have to be a hero to be great. Your name doesn't have to be Franklin D. Roosevelt or John F. Kennedy or Dwight Eisenhower; it doesn't have to be a name any one side your family recognizes at all. Your greatness comes from your recognition of the best in yourself, from the humanity that you give yourself, from the sense of self-respect—it's your present to yourself from yourself every day of the year—not just on Christmas.

This is how you police yourself in a kindly spirit, so lead yourself away from misunderstanding and redirect yourself towards real self-commitment. When you do this, you are free, and you are on the road to respect.

## THE POWER OF UNDERSTANDING

When you understand yourself, when you understand others, you are a powerhouse. Because you are honest with yourself, no one can stump you.

Still, to misunderstand is easy. To understand is more difficult.

Our news media headline the "generation gap," but what is this but a much-publicized series of misunderstandings between young people today and their elders? I can't help but wonder why there should be such a "gap." I'm over sixty-five years old, and I think I get along pretty well with teenagers, and, at the same time, I understand the different perspectives with which older people look out at the world. Why can't everybody bridge this "gap" between the generations and accept the fact that people differ, and times change, and values do not remain static?

I know a middle-aged woman who is very unhappy because her daughter—married and with a young baby—will not tolerate her in her home. The older woman is attractive and lives in one of the wealthier communities in Connecticut on a thirty-acre estate with tennis courts, swimming pool, bridle path—the American Dream.

Yet she cries to herself because her daughter has so completely rejected her. Sometimes, she telephones and knows the daughter is home, but the daughter does not answer the ringing if she thinks it is her mother. When the mother offers to come over to help with the grandchild or to babysit, the daughter always turns her down flat.

Now life is often like tennis—it goes two ways, back and forth—and there is a reason for the daughter's total rejection.

I know about it. The mother was too domineering when the daughter was young; she was so bossy then that the daughter still defends herself by keeping her away. This gap is even wider than the generation that stands between the two. Oceans separate mother and daughter. Misunderstanding keeps them gulfs apart, stranger than strangers to each other. The mother keeps trying to bridge the gap; the daughter keeps rejecting—rigidly cold, chillingly polite.

The mother has erred; but does not the daughter err still more, in refusing to make the smallest concession, in refusing to take the tiniest step toward even a token reconciliation in the name of forgiveness, of human error and attempted understanding?

Anybody can misunderstand; anybody can turn grievances into lifetime grudges. The person who concentrates on building his own sense of human dignity, who also insists on human dignity and sincerity and understanding for other people, is the exceptional person.

The daughter in this case lacked understanding—both of herself and of her mother. She did not realize that she was no longer a little girl, that her mother could no longer dominate her. She did not grasp the reality that she had nothing to fear, that she need not flinch from the forceful nature of the mother's personality. Moreover, she did not see her mother—then or now—with sensitive understanding, empathizing with the difficulties she had lived through in her lifetime, feeling for her conflicts and her problems, her ups and her downs, the human imperfections of a woman, not a goddess.

The daughter—it is not easy for her to understand; deep scars are painful—but I feel that she must if she is to make peace with herself. She must have compassion for herself and for her mother as well. Perhaps she will never feel close to her mother, but she must try to understand.

Now let me tell you about two other people—more fortunate people in that they are closer to their need to understand themselves and other people.

One is in a most unglamorous occupation—she is an elevator operator in the building where I live and work when I am in New York. Every day—with amazing evenness—she is friendly and smiling, glowing with good nature as she takes me up or down on the elevator.

This is a monotonous job—up and down, up and down, up and down—and I confess that if I were an elevator operator, I believe I would be very evil-tempered and spend half the time scheming to change occupations.

But this woman—a pleasant, middle-aged woman—glows with inner self-understanding and projects this to the many people who ride in her elevator. Perhaps she doesn't have much money, but she shares her wealth with others and turns the monotonous up-and-down into an adventure in pleasantness.

The second person is a young fellow whom I don't really know. Someone sent me a clipping from a Toronto, Canada, newspaper with this story about him.

His name is Jim Dillard. He is a football powerhouse in Canada—he was, anyway, until he went into a slump. He just could not get going. He was out of touch with himself; he could not mobilize his feeling about himself as he had been.

Then he read my book, *Psycho-Cybernetics*. I understand that members of the champion Green Bay Packers claimed my book helped them, and so did Dillard.

He understood himself once more. He understood that he had to forget the times he'd blundered, and concentrate on his past successes. He understood that he had to carry confidence of what he had done into the present, in the most of his ability, leaving worry and negative feeling behind.

Jim Dillard regained his old feeling. Once again, he is running and blocking crisply, a potent force for his team. His understanding of himself as a success was back—and so was his sense of self-respect.

## UNDERSTANDING YOURSELF

There is one common denominator in these three different stories: That understanding must start with yourself. You live in a complicated, mobile world. The twentieth century has brought with it new freedoms: of children, adolescents from parents, of women from men, and minority groups from the Establishment. Our morals are changeable, our values may fluctuate.

One thing you must keep constant: you understand yourself.

This is basic.

According to one research project, the difference between "normal" people and mental patients centered around the degree in which they found—or did not find—meaning in their lives. The critical factor, in other words, was they either understood how to give themselves this meaning or they did not.

Studies of high school dropouts indicated that 8 to 10 percent had IQs of 110 or over. They dropped out not due to lack of intelligence, but through lack of self-understanding and through an inability to realize and cope with themselves. Other surveys of scholastic underachievers emphasized that they are negative in self-evaluation, and, at the same time, resentful in evaluating others. Again, we find the emotional component: the lack of human dignity.

"I work so hard," you may say, "and I'm always in debt. When I get hold of some money, I'll take time off from my job and then I'll find my self-respect."

Well, maybe you will. I hope so.

Still, leisure time is certainly not the answer for many people. Maybe they start out with great expectations, but studies have pointed to an increase in depression and in suicides on vacations and holidays. Other surveys have shown a correlation between leisure time and juvenile delinquency.

Cicero claimed that, "Leisure with dignity is the supremely desirable object of all sane and good men." Although he gave this measured opinion many centuries ago, it still stands up today—with one qualification: *if you understand yourself and your needs,* and if your understanding is friendly and supporting.

If not, you will be better off busy, hustling, bustling, but moving toward understanding yourself in a positive way. Busy as you are, you can always find a little time every day to be alone with yourself and to be quiet, to think peacefully, retreating temporarily into a room in your mind to reinvigorate yourself for life's struggles. One thing I understand about myself in my own busy life is that I need a break like this every day. Perhaps you do, too.

But more on this later. For now, let us now discuss principles of understanding that will lead you to a greater sense of human dignity.

## NEW DIGNITY FOR YOU

I believe that if you apply my ideas faithfully, you will be in a strong position with yourself and with your world, and that you will find a new sense of human dignity in you.

1. *Understand that you are as good as the next.* This is extremely important because envy is such a common feeling—perhaps among

people of all time, certainly among people today. The other pasture's always greener; the other fellow has always got it better. You feel you are always getting a raw deal. Too many feel that they are inferior. They feel that the others feel more worthy—or less guilty—than they are. They feel, he is more mature or more of a man, or that he has more money and that this makes him better. (Or that she is more feminine, giving, or intelligent, and that these make her better.)

You must understand that you are as good as the next fellow. More than this, you must evaluate yourself by your standards and stop thinking about the next fellow in repetitive terms. Do you feel you have to "keep up with the Joneses"? Well, stop it. Let the "Joneses" keep up with you. If you have to compete with somebody, compete with yourself. Every day when you wake up, resolve to make this day a day in which you feel even more strongly the pull of your human dignity. This is a constructive form of competition.

*You* must determine how good you are. *You* must umpire. Forget the next fellow. He's probably moping about what he thinks is *his* inferiority. So help him out. Tell him he's as good as you.

2. *Understand the individual nature of your needs.* For you *are* an individual; no one else is quite like you. Your needs are individual. You must learn to identify them out of your insight, channel your energies toward goals to realize them.

Once again, stop thinking in terms of the needs of other people. Stop bowing to conformist pressures. The needs of this friend or that acquaintance should be irrelevant; you identify and seek to satisfy *your* needs.

People differ. Some people need to work with their hands; others thrive on mental work. Some come alive when they go to the country or the seashore; others prefer the hustle and bustle of the city. Some people fear and run away from heated arguments; others thrive on them and couldn't live without them.

You must not only *understand* the very individual nature of your needs, you must also *accept* them without self-recrimination if you feel others would feel they make you an inferior sort of person. Remember, you must play the game according to your own rules. Just so long as you don't hurt others in the process, you have a perfect right to call the shots for yourself. Indeed, it is your responsibility to yourself.

As a creature of God, living in His universe, you are an individual, and you owe it to yourself to develop in yourself the qualities that arise from your unique needs and to develop to the fullest extent your creative capacities.

*Understand that you have a right to a life of contentment.* This should be self-evident, but it isn't.

So many people feel so negatively about themselves. So many people accuse themselves unceasingly of so many crimes, so many guilts. So many people do not feel they deserve to feel content. They feel guilty about too many things in the past. They keep remembering their past mistakes, their past failures, and when they look at themselves in the mirror, they may even hate the sight of themselves.

I know people who always seem to feel guilty. I know people so afraid to express their positive feelings like joy and exultation they seem to be soldiers on parade, drilling themselves with self-denial, anything not to reach a state of peace as if that would threaten them.

During approximately forty years of practice as a surgeon, I have given "new," improved faces to more people than I can remember. It is a thrilling experience for me; it is an electrifying experience for the patient who can accept the happiness of it all.

Feel it with me. The operation is over. I have removed the wrinkles or strengthened the chin or the disfiguring scar. The tissues have been healed. Now it is time to remove the bandages from the patient's face. I feel humble in my expectation, and I remove the bandages; I hand the patient a mirror and await the reaction.

Often this reaction is pure joy. Exultation, excitement, marvel. A "new" face, a new world, a new life. Fantasy may temporarily outdistance reality at this point, granted, but this is legitimately a time of excitement for the individual. Often, however, the patient is still dissatisfied. The operation has been successful, but he cannot accept his good fortune. He feels he has no right to be happy. His guilt smolders within him. He does not understand that it is his to feel contentment.

You must understand that you were born into this imperfect world to be happy—imperfectly happy, perhaps, but happy. It is your right to achieve this feeling; you must not take it away from yourself. You don't give up your money to anybody who asks for it, do you? Well, then, don't give up your right to contentment.

It doesn't matter if at times you have sinned, erred, blundered; it doesn't matter if you've been inept, weak, stupid; it doesn't matter if you've been clumsy, insensitive, arrogant. All of us at times succumb to our weaknesses; you have, and you will again. The important thing is not to let your guilt and the whole impact of crushing negative feelings take away your knowledge that you have the right to a life of contentment and human dignity.

## UNDERSTANDING OTHER PEOPLE

So far in this chapter, we have analyzed how to apply understanding to give you a greater sense of human dignity. As we have seen, this understanding must start with an understanding of yourself and of your basic needs and rights. It is an understanding you must give yourself. You owe it to yourself. Convicted criminals in our penitentiaries are trying to help themselves through applying my theories of Psycho-Cybernetics; they have committed anti-social acts, and yet they feel they deserve another chance. So why can't you shed your guilt and give yourself a chance to achieve self-respect through understanding?

But once you give yourself this great gift, do not keep it and hoard it narcissistically. This would be a waste. Exercise your understanding; bring it out into the world of people and share your understanding with others.

Refuse to let narrow-minded hates and prejudices eat into you. Try instead to understand other people—as individuals, not as stereotypes. Other people are unique individuals, too, and you should apply your emotional capacities to relating to them with as much sensitivity and integrity as you have inside you. Once you no longer feel inferior to them, don't turn around and develop another irrational feeling—one of superiority. This, too, would be self-defeating.

Misunderstanding. There is so much misunderstanding in our struggling, fighting world of people; and understanding among people is so rare by comparison.

Still, if you can give yourself understanding, then you can take one more step and give your understanding to others. As you do, you give yourself the key to your sense of dignity because the person who can understand and accept both himself and others cannot help but feel his power as a human being with dignity.

You should understand that the other fellow is as good as you—that other people have needs, some quite different from yours. That other people have the right to happiness. Reach out a helping hand to other people, and think twice before passing judgment on them. You should attune yourself to their aspirations. Nourish yourself as you help them and accept nourishment in return.

As you make a habit of building attitudes of understanding and helpfulness, your respect for yourself grows.

# 3

# THE ACTIVE POWER OF SINCERITY

WE ARE IN THE PROCESS OF ASSEMBLING YOUR POWER TOOLS FOR THE BUILD-ing of your self-respect: The bulldozers and drills with which you—a construction worker, self-employed—are making yourself a bigger person.

Did you ever watch a building going up, growing day by day through the sweat of many good working men? It is no overnight project. Just laying the foundation takes many weeks. If you observe closely, you may see minute progress daily; weekly or monthly observation may show you more surprising developments.

And so, it must be with your sense of self-respect. You must work on it, patiently, with dedication, persevering in stormy weather, surviving the winds of bad fortune, refusing to let the inevitable onslaughts of negative feelings pull you under. Sometimes your progress may seem invisible to you—because you are often unobjective and, of course, see yourself every day—but someone who hasn't seen you for months or years may see a striking change.

In building self-respect, we must acquire the ability to develop sound habits that will help us function in a directed, constructive, and humane manner. Such a habit is a wholesome orientation toward life, an orientation of sincerity.

This is not as easy as it seems. Our world is complicated; our mores are changing; our values are confused. In such a climate, millions of people feel cynical. Double hypocrisy may seem the only sane way to play the game. Sincerity as a way of life may seem to you foolhardy.

Still, we must more resolutely define our term *sincerity* as an active force, and this concept may be new to you. Indeed, in this book, I will recommend concepts which most people think of as passive—the idea of forgiveness, for example—in an active and dynamic sense.

Sincerity is an active power, if you harness the realistic best in yourself, and project it out into the world where you belong. Sincerity is a dynamic approach to living if you express your God-given individuality aggressively but constructively.

To know that you do your best to be ethical and honest in your relations with others—in terms of your own willingness to choose this way of conducting yourself—can only improve your feeling of respect for yourself.

What do I mean by sincerity as an active power? I will spell this out for you in this chapter.

First, let me say what I *do not* mean. We will not discuss sincerity as a passive concept, in which you exercise naiveté in your dealings with others and turn your other innocence to people who might wish to exploit and humiliate you. I see no special virtue in a childish form of sincerity in which you assume that all people are honest and therefore you might stand helplessly around, a perfect potential victim for any trickster or slickster who might come along scenting an easy mark.

Sincerity, in my meaning—and it is rather a new shade of meaning for me, too—involves an active exercise of constructive power as well as a highly developed sense of sophistication, and it involves also a strong ethical motivation which I feel is at the heart of any individual's genuine self-respect.

## THE DESIRE TO DO GOOD

In order to discuss sincerity as an active concept, let us now discuss the ingredients of sincerity.

First, there is the desire to do good. One must feel the desire to make the most of oneself. One must strongly feel the need to be honest with oneself. As an extension of this, one must yearn to give the best of himself to others. When you keep your goodness inside, it stays inside, and it does not warm others. It remains a secret to others; and, sooner or later, it may become a secret to yourself, too. Then it is lost, perhaps forever.

Let me read you a letter I received recently. It is a beautiful example of the desire to do good.

> Yesterday, the world was ugly and reeked of deception.
>
> At least that is the way it appeared to someone I used to know. A person who had incurred an emotional scar of such proportion that it sank him to the bottommost rung of a ladder suspended in space. All he would have had to do would have been to let go of that last rung and fall to remain forever suspended in the eons of time and fantasy.
>
> But from that pitch blackness of despair came a meager shaft of light in the form of your superb and startling book titled "Psycho-Cybernetics." Word by word, sentence by sentence, and page by page, the intensity of the light grew, and one by one, the rungs of the ladder were ascended. At times, most painfully. With

each rung, the next became easier to reach until firm ground was sighted, and the world surrounded and bathed him in the warmth of its brilliant glow of sunshine.

He told me of being reborn in the image upright, firm in stature, positive in thought and deed, and of being ALIVE! Reincarnation in the truest sense of the word. As if by the stroke of a pen, the word "impossible" was stricken from his language.

The person I used to know is dead. He is alive. He is I. Today the world is beautiful.

It was concluded with "I thank you—Your friend for life." Now I do not write about this letter because my book helped this man—although, of course, this pleased me more than I can express in mere words—but as an example of what I mean. For this man wanted to do good. Though he had known terrible despair and frustration, his desire to be a sincere, positive person with self-respect remained alive, ready to be ignited—and luckily, my book ignited this desire.

In the heat of our competition to outdo each other and to win all our tempting forms of material splendor, we may lose track of this crucial desire to do good and surrender this essential component of sincerity, which in turn is one of the key building blocks of self-respect.

We must win the battle in our minds—our great battle—our battle with negative feelings. The man who wrote this beautiful letter, expressing his gratitude, would light up my day for me; he won this battle. It was obviously no easy one for him; he had to pick himself off the floor after he almost went down for the count. Once he regained contact with the positive side of himself, he was not content with this. He wanted me to feel good, too. This is what really impressed me about this letter: his desire to do good.

The great Albert Schweitzer, who wrote about reverence for the life force and about oneness with the many forms of life in the universe, made his words reality with his many acts of of kindness to others. In an active sense, as a healer in a primitive land, he made obvious his desire to do good toward others and, in the process, lived a life of sincerity and enormous dignity.

This, too, is what I write about.

## KEYS TO SINCERITY

You will note, already, that the people I use as examples of sincerity exercise this quality in an active sense.

The man who was helped by my book could have sat in his chair, said "Thank you, very sincerely," and let it go, and it would be a passive expression of sincerity, but what would it do for him? It was far more freeing for *his self* to come out of his shell and project his good feeling out into the world in an active and potent way, to enrich another human being.

Albert Schweitzer was one of the great geniuses of our time. Schweitzer was a living embodiment of sincerity in action. His desire to do good was no secret. He healed people with his hands, with his books, with his music. He spanned the continents with his active and commandingly potent energy for constructive effort.

Now suppose that we search further for the other keys to an active sincerity that will leave us not passive children to be whipped into submission by the world's bullies, but active builders, potent in the sense of our constructive intentions.

1. *Focus on the truth about yourself.* It is clear that you cannot be sincere with others until you can focus on the truth about yourself. While this is fundamental, it is doubtlessly the most difficult thing for you to do. You may choose to think charitably about someone else, but you probably expect perfection of yourself. And if you expect yourself to be perfect, you might begin next to hide your faults from yourself, so you can find life tolerable.

The trouble is that this sets up a vicious cycle that never ends; insincerity becomes a way of life for you, and you forfeit your feeling of self-acceptance.

You must learn to focus on the total truth about yourself—your assets and your liabilities. You must develop the courage to do this. Especially, you must inventory your past successes and your capacity for future successes. The truth need not be negative; truth can be most bolstering.

Focus on the truth about yourself—past, present, and future. Bring back the past now and then to see yourself in proper perspective but recognize that you cannot live in the past. Look into the future again to see things from a balanced point of view, but understand that you cannot live in the future, either. Then see yourself as you are in the present and see what you can do to keep focused on this truthful sense of yourself as you are now.

Once again, your chief obstacle to this strengthening, honest type of thinking is your own perfectionism. It is one of the greatest tragedies of our times that so many people expect such impossible things of themselves and cannot allow themselves to see truth because they fear the truth.

The truth about yourself should not disturb you; it should not cause you sleeplessness and self-loathing. You must understand that you have the right to make mistakes sometimes! Everyone does. You have the right to wallow in negation sometimes. Everyone does. And sometimes, you have the right to be thoughtless, inconsiderate, fearful, hostile, indecisive, rude, timid. I do not believe that there is an individual in this world who now and then is not a difficult, even impossible person. People are human—not made of marble. Stop feeling you're a criminal when you see yourself in focus. Stop making yourself feel guilty. When you do this, you are a vindictive judge, a vicious jury—you are not giving yourself a *fair* trial.

In my lectures around the country in recent years, I have stopped off to talk to inmates of more than one penitentiary, including Leavenworth. I have found many of these men convicted of anti-social offenses eager for self-improvement, anxious to find the road back to constructive living, quick to ask me questions about my theories of Psycho-Cybernetics, honest about the negation in much of their lives, searching to remedy it. I was gratified by the response of many prisoners to my lectures, and more than one wrote me following my visit.

My point is this: If these men, who have committed crimes against our very social structure, can forgive themselves, why can't you? What monstrous crime have you committed that you will not allow yourself to take an objective look at yourself without hating yourself?

Focus on the truth about yourself; and then, with full knowledge—the fullest you can give yourself, anyway—accept yourself.

2. *Develop an inquiring mind.* For proper perspective, you are curious to know the truth about others, too. In a healthy way, you exercise your curiosity. You are interested in them; you try to know them as they are and to appreciate their individuality. You try to learn from their achievements at the same time; you try to profit from their errors. Through others, you strive to improve yourself; if they need you and seek your help, try to help them too. Thus, your attempt to know the truth about yourself is an active process, is attentive and mobile; you adjust yourself to the realities as they appear.

In doing so, you extend your curiosity toward the world you live in—people and all—projecting yourself out toward the world enthusiastically when you wish, or with reserve when you think this approach proper. Your desire for expanding knowledge is alive and active. Your approach is as direct as is practicable. You want to know about life—about yourself, about other people, about your world.

This is not easy. Appearances are often deceiving, and you cannot always be sure your judgment is accurate.

Let me tell you a story; I mentioned it in my book *New Faces: New Futures,* which I wrote over thirty years ago.

Three men who were convinced that they could estimate character on the basis of facial appearance were in my office—a playwright, a lawyer, and a doctor. They studied masks of patients made before surgery.

"This person is a weakling," said the playwright, "this one with the receding chin."

"No," I said. "He is a direct man of business, a stockbroker."

"This fellow with the gash on his cheek," said the lawyer, "he must be a gangster."

"Wrong," I said. "He is a self-effacing businessman who was involved in an auto accident."

It was the doctor's turn. He carefully studied a cast with a broken nose and then gave his opinion: "This man seems to have taken part in a number of fights. He is either a fighter or a racketeer."

"Wrong again," I said. "He fell on his nose when he was a little fellow. He's a schoolteacher."

At this point, I showed them the casts made of these patients after surgery, and they expressed their amazement. They found it almost unbelievable that these normal faces had at one time been so disfigured.

Too many of us, however, still hold to the belief that the face is an infallible guide to character and that we—in our great wisdom—can study someone else's face and read his character.

As a plastic surgeon of long experience, I know better, and you should, too. Your quest for knowledge about others and about your world, your development of an inquiring mind, is no overnight matter. You learn actively, interestedly, with a constructive, charged curiosity—but slowly, day by day.

Reject snap judgments. Is a person stupid because he has big ears? Of course not. Is a person swinish because he has a nose with a thick bulbous end? Though even Aristotle believed this was true, it is not so.

Just as you continue to focus on the truth in regard to yourself, you continue to focus on the truth as it applies to others and to the world you live in.

3. *Build your confidence.* You cannot reach out to sincerity without confidence. Unless you feel confident, an attitude of sincerity will be merely threatening to not supporting at all.

"I do not feel confident," you say?

Well, then, you must build up your confidence.

How?

By reminding yourself of your past successes, by reliving in your mind your past successes, and by daily keeping your eye on the ball.

I close my eyes, and in the room of my mind—in my imagination where I see myself—I am playing golf. I take the proper stance, legs apart, handgrip on the club. Now I prepare to stride into the ball and club it. As I do this, I keep my eye focused on the ball. Wham! I follow through. Most important, I follow through.

This is, of course, a symbolic exercise, but it is most meaningful. Success will give you confidence.

And what will give you a good chance to nail down successes? Keeping your eye on the ball—your goals and then following through until you wallop it far and high down the fairway to achieving those goals.

You must remember that life is split-second timing, and you must face the reality of this. We live in a fiercely competitive world; inches may mean the difference between winning and losing, between success and failure. Contrary to popular belief, there may be just a hairline separating the well-paid, confident executive from the lower echelon clerk. Similarly, you may find it hard to discern between the .300 major-league hitter and the fellow who has trouble hitting 230 in the minor leagues.

You build confidence—and, therefore, a springboard toward an attitude of sincerity—when you keep your eye on the ball and continue to follow through even during days of discouragement. This will win you the successes you need day after day.

4. *See reality.* See it as fully as you can, focusing on the truth about yourself, projecting your inquiring mind toward others, building confidence with your active mental approach. Then make your thinking as realistic as you can, refusing to float away into fantasies and refusing to indulge yourself with daydreaming, which may momentarily be pleasant, but which will give you no lasting benefits.

One thing should be clear to you: Sincerity will fill you with strength; insincerity will exhaust you. When you deceive yourself and deceive everybody else, you do little or nothing for yourself or others, and keeping up the pretense may so tire you out that you have no energy left for real productive activity.

The more sharply you see reality, the less involved you are in fantasy, the more sincere you are capable of being—this is obvious.

What may not be obvious, and perhaps I repeat myself but this is such an important point—is that seeing reality is no simple process. Reality is not always beautiful—sometimes it is very painful—and you may find it more pleasant temporarily to live in a fool's paradise than in the sometimes-bleak world of what is.

Far back in history, men believed in fire and wind gods, and in spirits of the mountains and of the waters. These were aids to them in thinking about the precariousness of their actual existence.

Today, among still-primitive peoples, medicine men still hold sway, reassuring their fellows with their "magic" and sacrificing animals to "appease the gods"—anything to feel a sense of power in coping with the many uncertainties of a dangerous existence.

Well, we may thank our lucky stars that we live a less treacherous existence than this; uncertain as our reality may be, we can usually feel safe in the assurance that the all-powerful natural elements will not bring immediate destruction upon us and that, therefore, we can face life without the protection of "magic" and "magical thinking."

Even then, facing our realities head-on is not easy. But you must do this to reach your full stature as a human being of dignity.

## A CHANGING YOU

These are changing times—oh, are they changing times! The world seems to change a little almost every day; we try to keep pace with the changes.

But the most important changes are usually internal; and a positive change for you is one in which you adjust your attitudes—toward yourself, toward others—in the direction of greater sincerity.

If insincerity and pretense, and endless affectation have been your habitual pattern, you may not find change effortless. Adjusting to newness is rarely effortless. Children have been shown to be disturbed by listening to altered rhymes. Dogs have barked and whined at the unfamiliar sight of their masters walking on their hands. Any newness—any change in habitual pattern—may cause anyone emotional upset. The adult who overeats or smokes or drinks too much may find the adjustment to moderation positively unsettling.

Still, our objective is a changing you. To move toward your full self-respect as a human being, you must move toward the greatest degree of sincerity that you can attain, however difficult that may be at first.

To review my main points, this is an active form of sincerity, in which you go beyond lip service, helplessness or wishful resignation—to a kinetic, functional, and dedicated participation in your own improvement as a person who lives in a particular local community which is part of a larger community which is part of a world community.

The passively sincere person may be in favor of improved education for disadvantaged children and let it go at that. Time for a nap.

The actively sincere person will—if he possibly can—do something about it. If he is a school administrator or teacher, he will practice what he preaches. If he is not, he may make an active attempt to implement his ideas as a PTA member or community helper, or perhaps as a donor of money, or he might help to campaign for political office-seekers who agree with his ideas.

The passively sincere person may believe in more ethical business dealings—in principle.

The actively sincere person will put it on the line. In his business dealings, he will be as ethical and honest as he can possibly be without jeopardizing his position vis-a-vis his competitors. True, he will not always be able to reach his ideals in actual conduct; sometimes, this would amount to cutting his own throat—which he would not do, and I certainly would never suggest that he should.

As I mentioned earlier, I am not suggesting that you turn the other cheek and let people without ethical scruples push you around. I am also not suggesting that you assume that just because you are moving toward sincere attitudes and sincere actions, others will reciprocate. I am also not trying to make you believe that this is a world of inexhaustible goodness, a world in which you can blindly put your faith in others who have not proved that they merit your faith.

My concept of sincerity—and you may find it a rather new concept—is one in which you try to be honest with yourself and with others and to play a worthwhile constructive role in your world *when this is possible.*

It goes without saying that sincerity is not always possible, that it would be foolish to try to be sincere with some people. Adolf Hitler, for example, was such a man. Perhaps Neville Chamberlain thought his best path was to be candid with Hitler. I don't know what he was thinking, of course—but, if so, he was unwise. Hitler is the perfect prototype of the person you should not try to be sincere with.

Still, with yourself, and with many people, you may work toward sincerity—as an active power giving meaning to your life and substance to your budding skyscraper of self-respect. There are doctors who, above and beyond financial reward, want to help people feel healthier. There are lawyers who, of course, want to get their fees paid, but also want to help their client. We have entertainers who want to give enjoyment and judges who want to render just decisions, waiters who want to make your meal pleasant, and typists who try to make letters look attractive. These people are living examples of my conception of sincerity as an active dynamic life force.

Carlyle believed that society was based on hero worship. I think he was right—and I think it is too bad he was right, because you must be your own hero.

What good does it do you to look at someone else—a "hero"—and tell yourself that he is wonderful? You must tell yourself that *you* are wonderful. You must give yourself credit for what you are as a human being. You must build in yourself a sense of self-respect that can make you feel wealthier than any millionaire. Start by building with understanding; then move the emphasis to sincerity. Start today, start now.

I have a friend who has a little girl who resists going to sleep. When bedtime comes, she seems to sense it and is ready to fight. She will go to bed on time, she says, "Monday, Tuesday, Wednesday." Her parents are indulgent, and therefore the result is predictable: She never goes to bed on time.

Don't you put off your building of self-respect until "Monday, Tuesday, Wednesday." That really means "Mañana," "mañana" means "tomorrow," and chances are that "tomorrow" means "never." So, start today.

Are you building your bank account? Fine. Are you building your professional status? Wonderful. Are you building a family? More power to you. Whatever you are building for yourself and for others in your world is fundamental to your *life*.

As you build, as you set your goals and move toward them, make self-respect the cement that binds them and that gives them meaning. Give your activities meaning and power as you intermesh them with understanding and sincerity.

# 4

## WINNING OUT OVER UNCERTAINTY

OUR APPROACH TO SELF-RESPECT WILL BE ACTIVE AND FUNCTIONAL. WE AIM AT a sense of human dignity that is real; we descend from our ivory towers and plant our feet in the solid soil of our common humanity. What we want is more than an abstract concept, more than a fleeting thought—useful as these may be to us. We will transcend passivity and, hopefully, go on to the implementation, not only of ideas and images that will help us respect ourselves, but goals that will improve our station in life and bring us inner satisfaction as well.

First, in other words, we build our good feeling about ourselves. Second, we do something about this good feeling. We use it. We extend it out into the world of people and feel the power of exercising it constructively.

In this book, we will do more than verbalize abstraction. Later on, we will get very practical and tackle some exercises together, exercises for the stimulation of your emotional muscles. Goal-builders, I will call them. We will see what goal-building we can do together in furthering our common search for a self-respect that has its roots both in inner acceptance and in an adaptation to reality.

We will focus on the positive. We will be Walt Whitman's all, as we "sing" of the positive and try to channel our energies into our drive for the positive.

But we are forgetting something—my long experience tells me this. You were not born yesterday? Shake hands on that, friend; neither was I. What about our negative feelings? What about our fears of disaster? What about our impossible mornings? What about those days when even a quick glance in the mirror is traumatic?

I strongly feel that to build the positive and ignore the negative is building on quicksand. Although we must continue our positive approach, of course, we must also prepare ourselves to deal with the negative feelings that threaten to destroy us.

And first of all, we must learn to cope with uncertainty. We must not let life's uncertainties frighten us into a retreat from life. We must refuse to let them make us immobile and dissociated, to play everything safe, and to take no chances, straddling the fence at all times.

We must win out over uncertainty; we must lose our fear of uncertainty; and we must live with uncertainty.

We must look upon life's many uncertainties with adult eyes. They will not vanish if we wave our "magic wand" and say "go away"—that is, if you will permit me a very small joke, no self-respecting uncertainties will do this.

Uncertainty has always been with us. When the world was born, uncertainty was born. Birth and death—we have always known these uncertainties. Weather—we have always lived with the sudden onslaughts of lightning and blinding rains from the skies, of violent typhoons sweeping over our seas, and of ferocious hurricanes swirling over our land, destroying with a frightening and impersonal fury.

Down through history, people have felt an insecurity about each other, and this almost inevitable insecurity has led to the possibly endless series of wars which have spread-eagled the pages of our history books. In a sense, one could characterize the story of civilization as a story of wars—national wars, religious wars, civil wars—and in recent years, as transportation's and communication's progress makes the world grow smaller, we have world wars. Human civilization has not been able to escape from wars and the scars that come from wars, these destructive manifestations of uncertainty.

Today uncertainty is still with us—in all these ways and more. We are uncertain of our civilized rules, which are changing constantly. We are uncertain about our objectives; we do not seem to know where we are going. Further, we are uncertain of our status; we live in a highly mobile and competitive world, and in our struggles to keep up with others, we lose touch with ourselves.

So, in summary, to build self-respect, we must learn to live with the potential negation of uncertainty; and that's what we will discuss in the pages of this chapter.

## LIVING HOPEFULLY WITH ANXIETY

And so, how do you win out over uncertainty?

First, I feel strongly that you must learn to live with the fear that uncertainty brings, on positive and hopeful terms. If you can handle this fear, this anxiety, if you do not allow it to dominate you, then you are on the right track.

This is not always easy to do; it goes without saying. In my travels around the country, hundreds—no, thousands of people have talked to me about how their uncertainties have obsessed them, making their lives little but painful question marks: Will the boss fire them? Will their spouse leave them? Will the dreaded nuclear holocaust come to reality?

Will they lose their money? Will a loved one in the hospital die?

What can I tell them? How can I help them? With no miracles, surely. Just with common sense and with insight. I tell them that their problems are not theirs alone—they are universal. Everywhere we find problems and uncertainties. The person with self-respect wrestles with them; the person who lacks self-respect drowns.

Let me tell you about a tragedy from my own life; it might help you with the tragedies in your life, so that you can adjust to them.

A birthday party for my mother was in progress. I gave it for her, and many, many people came to my apartment on top of a medical building in central Manhattan. Actors, doctors, lawyers, businessmen, wives, career women filled the apartment and overflowed onto the terrace. Music, dancing, drinking, eating, laughter, spirited conversation. An orchestra serenaded us. Life seemed joyful. It was a happy occasion for me—at first.

My mother's old friends were there, too, her old friends from many years gone by; one was singing her old favorite songs.

I had a splendid evening. I talked to my friends, I reminisced with my mother's old friends, I enjoyed what I thought was my mother's pleasure in the occasion. In a way, I felt detached; I mostly savored the feeling that something made my mother happy. Too many of my mother's birthdays had come and gone unnoticed; not this one.

But at three in the morning, when the guests were gone, my mother and I stood alone on the terrace. She told me then that she had cancer of the breast. My satisfaction vanished, and in a second, I felt only fear and despair and sorrow. Her death, about a year later, was one of the big tragedies of my life.

It was not easy for me to recover. For a while, I sat around and moped; I could not accept such a terrible thing happening. I cried for my mother—and for my loss. But what could I do? I could not forever bemoan life's sorrows, life's dangers, life's uncertainties.

One day I remembered an old Irish proverb one of my mother's friends had told me many years before, when I was a small boy: "If God shuts one door, He opens another."

I couldn't complain to God, I realized. I must fight my way back to my feet and feel again the way I had when I was planning my mother's birthday party. Even though it was in a sad way, *I had* given her pleasure with her birthday party—her huge birthday party—before she died. I realized that I had to place my hand, once again, on the knob of the door, ready to open it and walk into the opportunities of today and tomorrow, leaving the disappointments of the past behind me and not fearing the uncertainties ahead.

That's what I did, and that is also what you must do. You must learn to live with the anxieties and the depression that life's uncertainties bring—and you must live hopefully, too.

You, too, know your disappointments, your tragedies, your heartaches, and your frustrations—and you must learn to rise above negation to surmount them and live as best as you can, with your sense of self-respect still alive in the midst of imperfection.

Many social critics have called this an "age of anxiety." Maybe so. But it can also be an age in which, despite your anxieties, you live most productively.

Close your eyes now and, in your imagination, see this picture: A doctor is checking a patient's blood pressure. He finds that a condition of high blood pressure exists. As tactfully as he can, but honestly too, he tells the patient this, and he advises him on relaxing and getting adequate rest, and perhaps he prescribes some medication, too.

Now, if you have high-blood-pressure-type reactions to the anxieties that uncertainty brings, you must "prescribe" for yourself.

For one thing, you must understand that your frequent frustrations and small crises are not unique. Life is no bed of roses for anyone, and people who think it is must adjust such unrealistic preconceptions. Anticipate the uneven flow of life so that the shocks do not unseat you.

In his book, *Don Budge: A Tennis Memoir* (Viking Press, 1969), the tennis great tells a classic story of successful adaptation to an anxious, uncertain situation.

It was 1936, and Budge was locked up with Fred Perry in a tense semi-final match at Wimbledon as 18,000 people watched from the stands. They had split the first two sets, and every point was crucial. Then, during a volley, a little piece of newspaper drifted down from the stands—and Perry, about to make an easy shot, paused, neglected to hit the ball, and instead watched the paper as it sailed to the ground.

An outstanding tennis player, Fred Perry also had great presence on the court. While 18,000 watched, stunned, he calmly walked over, picked the paper off the ground, and began to read it. Then he started to laugh. He laughed and laughed. He laughed so hard he had to hold his stomach.

His laughter was infectious. Soon the crowd, bewildered as they were, joined him in his laughter.

At the other side of the court, Budge waited, his curiosity growing. Finally, Perry beckoned him, and he ran to the net to see what was so funny.

It was nothing at all. Something very mundane—maybe a weather report—

was on the piece of newspaper, but out of the side of his mouth, Perry told Budge to laugh.

And laugh Budge did. He laughed, Perry laughed, and everybody who had come to see the semifinal match at Wimbledon laughed and laughed.

Suddenly Perry decided it had served its purpose. He stuck the paper in his pocket and went back to play tennis once more. Things quieted down again, the sedate atmosphere returned, and Perry and Budge slashed at the ball once more—with the same old efficient fury. But, doubtless, they were more relaxed and more competent than before, if that was possible.

A semifinal match at historic Wimbledon. What a creative, masterly, daring way to eat into the pressure! What a superb reaction to anxiety and uncertainty! What a lesson for living in our "age of anxiety"!

Of course, there are some things you can't laugh at. There is nothing funny about poverty, disease, war, death, deprivation.

But for the ordinary uncertain, anxiety-producing crisis situation, tennis player Perry's tactics are superb. While you're here, while you have the great gift of life, laugh whenever you can; and, extracting the real meaning from this story, those times can be frequent if we aim at creating the laughter.

## DON'T TAKE UNCERTAINTIES PERSONALLY

I have, especially in the last three or four years, talked to many people around the country and am coming to realize that many people who feel most hopeless about their anxieties and their uncertainties seem to believe that their problems are unique.

This, of course, is not so. Everyone is at sea these days, and everyone feels at times that he is drowning. So don't take your uncertainties so personally, and then maybe you will be able to navigate your fragile craft through the stormy waves to the safety of the shore.

Everyone must cope with problems and uncertainties, and anxieties; everyone makes mistakes, even dangerous mistakes. Everyone in living exposes himself to the dangers others may bring him and exposes others to the dangers he may bring them.

One evening I wanted to get to a hospital quickly. But it was six o clock, and New York's streets were jammed with traffic, as usual. I jumped into a taxi at Fifty-seventh Street, asking the driver to enter Central Park at Sixth Avenue and go through to the West 106th Street exit. I thought that this route would help us bypass the heavy traffic.

The cab driver didn't listen too well. He drove to Seventy-second Street, swerved left, and headed westward. Near the West Seventy-second Street exit, I reminded him that I had asked him to take a different route.

"Oh," he said, "I forgot." I could see he was not acting; he was truly annoyed with himself.

"Anyone can make a mistake," I said. "Forget it."

"I hate to make mistakes like that," he said. "I don't know what's the matter with me." He cursed himself out with a few unprintable remarks.

"It can happen," I said. "We'll get there just about as fast anyway. Don't worry about it!"

"Yeah, but I don't like myself when I make mistakes like that." He continued to berate himself while we waited at the Seventy-second Street exit for the traffic light to change.

"It's all right," I said.

"I shouldn't do that," he said.

Finally, he got me where I wanted to go, but he was still angry with himself. On the way, we witnessed a near-disaster. A car made a left turn as a pedestrian crossed. The pedestrian, who had the right of way, kept walking, raising his hand imperiously toward the superior strength of the vehicle, which kept moving. It was a close call. Two more mistakes: A careless driver and a stubborn, in-the-right pedestrian.

On this one short cab ride to a hospital, there were three mistakes in all—and the two-sided mistake was almost a disaster. This is the human condition, so face it resolutely. Of the three persons who made mistakes, my driver's mistake was by far the most harmless. All he did was delay me a few minutes. Yet he was doing such damage to himself! He lashed into himself as critically as if his small mistake was tragic and unique.

But we must realize that mistakes are part of us—mistakes and problems and uncertainties and anxieties and frustrations—like bacteria in the throat or tension in our urban, fast-moving environment. We need all these imperfections, in a sense, so that we can master them and develop in ourselves a tough and resilient strength in order to live imprecisely yet resourcefully in our scrambling world.

Remember this:

If your boss fires you, you are not the only one who ever lost a job. Stop hating him or blaming yourself. Be practical about it; rest up and when you're ready, go look for another spot.

A friend may reject you—a good friend, an old friend; shocking as this may be, you are not the only one to whom this has happened. Hating him will do you no good—it will harm you. You can do without such a friend. Your best friend is yourself, anyway; and you can make another friend later on when you meet someone you like.

If you get sick—you are not the only one.

You lose your money—you are not the only one.

With very few exceptions, no matter what happens to you, you are not the only one.

It is important for you to remember this, so that you don't take uncertainties, heartaches, and problems too personally. Then you can concentrate on the main point—accepting yourself and respecting yourself as you wrestle with your crises and seeking practical answers that will help you to improve your status in the world and give richer meaning to your existence.

## A WINNING APPROACH TO UNCERTAINTY

And so, we all live in uncertainty. We must build self-respect despite uncertainty.

We are not omnipotent, and we must admit this to ourselves. Hard as we may try to exercise a constructive control over our destinies, we can never be successful all the time. I have my tragedies and my defeats and my depressions to endure; you have yours.

The question is: How do you rise above uncertainty? How do you develop a winning approach to uncertainty?

1. *Renounce passivity as a way of life.* You refuse to give in to helplessness. You don't just sit back and let things happen. You do not see yourself as a victim of life's vicissitudes—even when things go wrong. You do not retreat in a panic during stormy weather.

2. *Renounce neutrality as a way of life.* Perhaps neutrality works all right for nations (Switzerland survived two world wars thus), but the neutral person does not live fully. When life's uncertainties and insecurities frighten you into repeated assumptions of neutral attitudes, you give up part of yourself in the process. There may be times, of course, when it would be prudent to straddle the fence, to remain silent, or to express no opinion. To ensure your survival, sometimes your best approach may be one of absolute neutrality; I would never recommend that you ever expose yourself or loved ones to any danger through reckless or needless actions or statements.

Nevertheless, though you may at times find it expedient or wise to assume neutral attitudes, you must still renounce neutrality as a way of life. Whenever you can, get off the fence. Whenever you can, shrug off life's insecurities and take a stand. Whenever you can, you take pride in the expression of your individuality. Whenever you can, you come out of hiding—knowing that you are a person of genuine worth.

3. *Choose an active approach to life.* Instead of letting life's insecurities floor you, hang in there and counterpunch like a courageous boxer. Stop thinking about what life can do to you and start thinking about what you can do for yourself.

In this book, I stress an active approach because I am coming to understand more and more that ideas and images though crucially fundamental in importance—are not in themselves always enough. Thus, I have written of sincerity as an active concept, and in a later chapter, I will discuss my conception of active forgiveness.

It is the passive person who is always obsessed with what the world will do to him; the active person may be too busy *doing* to worry.

Though Babe Ruth may have struck out many times, I doubt if he worried about it much when he stood at home plate, bat in hand; he was too busy thinking about hitting a home run.

Similarly, every time Joe Louis stepped into a ring, he could have mulled over the possibility that he'd get hurt; he probably didn't, however—he was too busy planning a quick knockout of the other man.

The active approach is the approach with which one has a fighting chance to win out over life's multiple dangers.

4. *Set goals.* Every day set goals, then move out to achieve them. The nature of the goal is not important; what is important is what you feel for it. If you feel real enthusiasm for your goals, you will keep thinking about the steps you will take to reach them; you will not waste your time worrying about every adverse possibility.

In my theory of Psycho-Cybernetics, I stress the basic importance of goals for the individual who wants to get the most out of his life. Later we will consider goals in greater detail in terms of your achieving maximum human dignity.

5. *Allow yourself mistakes.* Allow them just because you aim to be reasonable with yourself, and it is reasonable that you will make plenty of mistakes during your lifetime. It is obvious to anyone who thinks

objectively about it that the only person who can avoid making mistakes is the person who never tries to do anything.

This is a key idea—life is uncertain enough, and if you compound its uncertainties by criticizing yourself for your mistakes, you are likely to remain passive through fear and buckle under to life's forces.

Here's a thought that may help you: You win out over life's uncertainties, as a rule, only when you are able to accept your own uncertainties.

## THE SECURE PERSON IN AN ANXIOUS AGE

I think it is possible for a mature, thinking, productive person to feel secure—even in an anxious age such as ours.

Anyway, is this such an anxious age? Is this century more difficult than past centuries? Today, it is true; we live knowing that devastating weapons exist which could blow up the world. It is also true that this century has witnessed the most horrifying tragedy in human history—the massacre of six million Jewish people in Hitler's Nazi Germany.

Basic personality change through "brainwashing" is, on a lesser scale, another frightening development in our hectic times.

But other ages have known other inhumanities and other terrors.

In the eleventh, twelfth, and thirteenth centuries, the Crusades to the Holy Land brought brutal savagery and destruction to people in the name of religion.

From Genghis Khan to Napoleon, power-mad despots have over and over again bloodied the face of the world.

Human history has endured many barbarous customs: Legal authorities, many centuries ago, had the power to remove a man's tongue if he was an alleged blasphemer; insane people many decades ago were kept in chains; witches—in reality just simple women—were burned to death. Kings held absurd and total power over people, and the insidious practice of slavery cheated millions of their right to freedom.

All this is very morbid—I write of it only because I hear, in my travels, so much about how impossible it is to live sensibly these days, whereas to the best of my knowledge, insecurity and injustice have always been part of the human condition.

I am merely trying to indicate the insecure nature of our world and the necessity of your overcoming these negative abilities to move toward your attainment of our common goal—self-respect.

Once again, I reaffirm my belief that it is possible for a mature and sensibly directed person to feel both security and self-respect in this age of anxiety, as it has been possible in all the ages of anxiety throughout history.

In sum, to do this, you must: Learn to live with anxiety; understand the universal, not personal, nature of uncertainty and of ill-fortune; and adopt a dynamic approach to life so that you can outlast bad times and go on to good times.

In the process, you must accept yourself when external events let you down or when you let yourself down. You must not be like the cab driver I wrote about who was so intolerant of his minor mistake.

There have been recently quite a few carefully designed programs to help children with learning differences achieve reading skills. One of the fundamental aims was to change the emotional orientation of these children, averting them from the stumbling block of their anxiety and sense of inadequacy and motivating them toward goal attainment.

Most of you have no trouble reading, but you may have plenty of trouble dealing with life's uncertainties. I hope that this chapter helps you to free yourself from anxiety and, as in the case of these children with learning differences, moves you toward a sense of goal attainment.

If you are a housewife, keeping a home that is safe, clean, and attractive is commendable, and your family will appreciate it. Something is wrong, however, if you spend all your spare time worrying about it.

If you are a salesman, it is reassuring that you have just made some strong sales. There is something off-center if you find yourself tortured about your next sale.

If you are a college student, it is promising that you have earned good grades in all your courses. Why then are you fretting about your senior year?

If you are a business executive, your raise in pay is good news—your wife will be happy. Why do you keep getting upset every time you speak to your boss for more than five minutes?

If you are a single person and finding a mate is a satisfying goal, why worry about it? Let it happen.

Uncertainties here? Yes, legitimate uncertainties. The question is: Can you win out over your many uncertainties—or do they win out over you?

When your uncertainties are winning out over you, re-reading this chapter should help you to turn the tables.

This is very important for you. If you can win out over your uncertainties and over your other negative feelings, you are well on the way to consolidating your feeling of inner strength and of respect for yourself.

# 5

## YOUR STRUGGLE TO OVERCOME RESENTMENT

WHEN I WRITE, I DO MORE THAN POUND A TYPEWRITER OR FILL UP PAGES OF PA-per. I try to visualize the people who will read the book. Who are they? What are they like? What do they want from me? How can I help? I ask myself these questions.

In a very real sense, I have a head start here because, lecturing in almost every state of the nation during the last ten years, I have seen your faces, and I have talked to you, and I know more than a little about your problems and responsibilities and worries.

I have seen in my audiences businessmen, absorbed in the competitive money-fight, scrambling to make enough money to rear their children, involved in tensions at work and at home—in many cases.

I have seen housewives, wrestling with their own special pressures, unsung heroines of the home, trying to adapt their thinking to changing ways, trying to figure out sound ways to bring up their children.

I have seen youth—high school and college—earnestly seeking to formulate values, looking for the road to good living, trying to get off on the right foot.

And I have seen senior citizens—often (too often) retired from life's battles, sometimes still in it—seeking answers for their own special problems.

I have lectured to many, many thousands of people—so different, and yet so similar—about making something of their lives, about finding themselves, about achieving for themselves a sense of their unique human dignity.

Self-respect; that's what it's all about.

But, as I've said, in seeking self-respect, you must do more than sharpen your positive forces; you must also develop the capacity to overcome your negative, destructive tendencies.

Such as uncertainty, which we discussed at some length in the last chapter; and such as resentment, which we will now consider.

Resentment is a fundamental component of the failure mechanism, which I have written about often in detailing my theory of Psycho-Cybernetics. It is a dread enemy, because at one time or another, everybody feels it. It is a universal phenomenon, unfortunately.

I close my eyes and see again in my imagination the tens of thousands of people who have come to my lectures—many different types of people, but all sometimes must wrestle with their resentment.

I close my eyes and imagine you, the many people who will read this book—so many different types of people, but you, too, will all at times find you must try to smother the fires of your resentment.

And I, too—again and again—must marshal my constructive forces and put to rout my own resentment. The terrible thing about resentment is that it may become a marathon—unending, chronic, spreading.

Indeed, resentment spreads like an infectious disease. When we feel strong resentment, we spread it to others because others react to our resentment with more resentment. Moreover, feeling annoyed with us for initiating the feeling and irritated with themselves for latching on, they may then drench themselves in resentment and unleash it on others who, by bad fortune, find themselves in their path. This is the negative contribution that a resentful person has to make to other people.

Suppose that you are eating foods which are causing you to become overweight. You become sluggish, and you find that you are beginning to worry about your health. What do you do? Well, if you are making a genuine effort to be constructive, perhaps you change your diet.

Now resentment is one of the foods in our emotional diet. It is an unpalatable goulash of negativism and unrelieved frustration. It is an unappetizing stew seasoned with bad temper, envy, and revenge—a horrible concoction worthy of the witches from *Macbeth,* but not worthy of you.

The result? Emotional indigestion, a mental ulcer moving toward becoming a very real physical ulcer.

What to do? Again, change your diet. You need more nutrition, with less waste and over-sharp seasoning.

You must eliminate the resentment from your emotional diet. It won't be easy; the feeling of resentment warms like fire and has the fascination of fire. You must struggle to overcome this negative and destructive inner fire; you must struggle to pour water on its crackling flames. You are your own fireman; you brave flames and smoke and heights to win over fire and save a life—your life.

Yes, it is your life you save when you extinguish the spreading flames of resentment. For, with resentment, you may or may not hurt others, but there is one person you are certain to destroy—yourself.

In fighting resentment, we fight to save our most human and most precious feeling—our feeling of self-respect.

## THE RESENTMENT COMPLEX

We all know about the inferiority complex. We have read about it so much that we may cringe at the impact of the mere phrasing.

But what about the Resentment Complex—that ghastly marathon, that dance around destruction, that cycle of endless negation?

Here are its components, briefly spelled out for you to escape, not to emulate. In dodging them and embracing positive qualities, you enrich yourself. Afterward, I will spell it out in greater detail.

1. Revenge
2. Envy
3. Sulkiness
4. Elimination from life
5. Narrow-mindedness
6. Temper
7. Mistake-mindedness
8. Enmity
9. Negligence
10. Tension as a habit

1. *Revenge.* You feel you have been wronged. You are a victim of injustice, you tell yourself. So, you plan your revenge—not just for a few minutes, or a few hours, but every day, as a way of life.

   Maybe you have been wronged. But why dwell on it for a lifetime? Whom do you destroy with your fantasies of revenge? The person you hate? No, you destroy yourself. The fires of revenge consume you. You do not sleep well. You do not work well. You do not eat well. Your obsession with revenge spins you round and round, trapped in your Resentment Complex.

2. *Envy.* Another feeling you can do without. When you envy someone else, you depreciate yourself, and you resent the other person. Again, you trap yourself in an endless cycle of negation.

   Stop envying! Instead, work to build your self-image. If you feel good about yourself, you will not waste your time feeling envy.

3. *Sulkiness.* The honeymoon is over, and you find yourself in an unglamorous world, living your usual unglamorous life making compromises and moving from problem to problem.

Your bright moment—whatever it was—is over, temporarily at least. Your reality is not constantly exhilarating. How do you react to this? With sulkiness? Pouting, sluggish sulkiness? If so, you head straight for negation; for a cycle of negation I call your Resentment Complex.

The alternative? Set new goals for your imperfect self in our imperfect world and move toward creative living.

4. *Elimination from life.* You fear competition. "Suppose I lose," you tell yourself. And so, taking no chances, you eliminate yourself from life.

But, when you do this, you also eliminate yourself from joy and usefulness, and eventually, you become useless to yourself as well. Frustrated in your web of fear and withdrawal, you quickly fall prey to resentment—and living with a Resentment Complex is no joyride.

5. *Narrow-mindedness.* You restrict your outlook. You tighten your feelings. You put tight shoes on your feet, handcuffs on your wrists, and pull up on your necktie until you fear you won't be able to breathe.

Then what?

Resentment comes. It flows through you like spreading fire, in reaction to imprisonment. Your narrow-mindedness plunges you into resentment, and until you learn to look at life with a gentle perspective and kind eyes, you will live in the dark world of resentment.

6. *Temper.* Temper is the explosive end product of the Resentment Complex. Envy, disappointment, and frustration build up in our lives, until smoldering resentment finally bursts into the flames of temper.

7. *Mistake-mindedness.* When you live with resentment, you live with mistaken-mindedness. We are all mistake-prone, but there are questions of degree. We will make mistakes as long as we live, but the mistake of resentment is especially regrettable because it is self-destructive and leads us into pockets of tension from which we find it very hard to escape.

8. *Enmity.* The sharpest and deadliest claw of resentment. It can be even more destructive than revenge because your revenge obsession may

focus on one or two people, while your feeling of enmity is a disease which you wish to unleash upon all people.

Enmity as a way of life is cancerous. You must destroy it, or it will destroy you.

9. *Negligence.* When you wake up in the morning, do you scramble out of bed and, without hesitation, rush out your front door and head for your place of employment?

Of course not. If you did, you would be guilty of negligence toward yourself since other people at your office or factory would see you, disheveled and in your nightclothes and well, let's not carry this fantasy any further, because I can't bear to describe your boss's reaction.

Thus, on arising mornings, you dress, brush your teeth, and so on. You do not neglect your appearance.

This is one form of negligence; another is emotional negligence.

The emotionally negligent person wallows in resentment. Instead of steering himself toward constructive goals, he lives aimlessly, drifting in frustration, developing a Resentment Complex.

10. *Tension.* When resentment becomes a habit, so does tension. For resentment and tension are twins—not identical, but twins nonetheless. Everyplace one goes, you will find the other. They are not pleasant either: you would be better off not knowing them.

The Resentment Complex is a composite of negative forces; of revenge and envy, negligence, and narrow-mindedness—the culmination of which is tension.

This negative, destructive buildup of poisonous, unreleasable feeling leads inevitably to resentment and tension.

Resentment Complex: DANGEROUS, KEEP AWAY.

How do you avoid this complex? In a way, that is the subject of this book. For resentment and self-respect do not mix well. And, in the process of building your sense of self-respect, and reaching out with it to other people, chances are that you will deliver a knockout blow to your resentment.

## THE DESTRUCTIVENESS OF MISGUIDED RESENTMENT

Earlier, I described the wild gang fights of my boyhood. Bricks, bats, sticks, stones, kettles, and shields—two gangs of boys unleashing resentment upon each other.

These were warm-weather battles, most of the time. As in today's riots, warm weather seemed a fact in firing up physical outbursts of violence. But we smoldered in winter, too. It would snow, and we would build huge mounds of snow on street corners and the violence would take on a different—and generally milder—pattern. Throwing snowballs at each other was harmless fun, but ice balls were products of nastiness.

I remember one fight vividly: This kid stood on top of the pile of snow, crowing that he was the leader, when another kid came up and at short range hurled an ice ball at his head, knocking him down. Slumped in the snow, unconscious for a while, the leader did not move, and everyone was scared: blood trickled from a horrible gash on his forehead, blood flowing over his right eye, then onto the snow, dyeing it red-brown. Luckily, he recovered consciousness in the hospital and was stitched up—one victim of resentment who recovered.

"Well," you can say, "boys will be boys."

But if you say this, you don't get the distinction. Growing boys need outlets for their aggression—this goes without saying—and such outlets as competitive athletics (or snowball fights) are helpful in this sense.

But ice balls are not snowballs, and the kid who threw the ice ball aimed at the leader's head was expressing destructive resentment. He was, incidentally, from the leader's own gang and perhaps was trying to hurt him out of envy of his status.

Surprisingly, the victim, once recovered, gloried in his wound, feeling that the scar on his forehead was some kind of medal for bravery. In summertime, when we swam in the East River, he would repeatedly call attention to the scar on his forehead.

What a mistaken concept of bravery! How much braver the policeman who, that same winter, saw a kid struggling in the ice-cold waters of the East River and who, with his overcoat on, plunged into the waters to save him!

## THE TORTURE OF RESENTMENT IN FANTASY

Now these gang fights of ours, resentment exploding into action, were externally destructive.

Resentment does not always take this path. Sometimes it stays inside, and smolders, and the poor, suffering, resentful person must endure the torture of his unhappy fantasies and obsessions, poisoning himself with his thoughts, destroying his self-respect, reducing his positive instincts to ashes with the fire that burns inside him.

Recently, two unhappy men came to see me to talk over their problems and to see if they could help themselves in the process. Both struggled under the burden of their resentment. Both buried their creative, positive energies under the fury of their hate. Both could not find the sense of human dignity to which they were entitled.

Coincidentally, both tortured themselves with repeated, intense fears that followed an identical yet opposite pattern. They both feared choking to death—one, that he would choke somebody; the other, that someone would choke him. Resentment smoldering within—a terrible force.

In telling you their stories, I will, of course, not reveal names or identify them in any way. I tell you their stories—in this anonymous way—so that you, reading my book, can benefit from their experience without injuring them in any way.

One man was a middle-aged salesman. He was living in the past. He had grown up with a sense of inferiority, and he projected this feeling toward me.

His mother, he told me, talking to me in my living room, was an old woman now. But still, he hated and feared her.

He feared being close to her. He feared that if he were close to her, living with her, visiting her, she would choke him. He feared that she would kill him.

Obviously, this was extremely unrealistic. To find out how he came to think this way, I asked him about his background.

It was an unfortunate one—he had come from a broken home. He was only a few years old when his father deserted his mother. He had been an only child, and his mother gave up her life to tend to him. She left a good job to take a less lucrative one so that she could take better care of him. She gave him all her attention, fussed over him, centered her life around him.

This, of course, was terrible. A boy needs to get out into the world, to explore it, and to feel confidence as he experiences a growing ability to deal with that very real world. He was deprived of all this. His mother, deserted, needed him—or, at least, she felt she did. So she smothered him. Deep into his adolescent years, they spent much time together. In fact, they were inseparable. He needed to feel separate and on his own, with an identity that was his.

This was the unfortunate background of this middle-aged salesman who came to see me in his unhappiness, struggling to find fulfillment in an uncertain and competitive world, struggling to overcome the burden of a past which had been none of his doing.

His life was not all negative. He was a fairly adequate salesman; he had some satisfactions now and then. But, still, he drifted from job to job, was frightened by a self-destructive urge in himself and, unmarried, he had few good friends. He drank too much, felt guilty, and was worried by the perverse pleasure he felt in doing the wrong thing. Sometimes, he told me, he seemed—against his conscious will—to be trying to lose his job.

Most pronounced, though, was his strong feeling of resentment toward his mother. He hadn't lived in the same home with her for many years, in a physical sense, but his mind was full of her, of his hate for her, of his endless resentment of her.

He was free of her, but he was not free of her—the resentment burned on, an endless marathon dancing around in his imagination day and night.

Another man came to see me recently—a good-looking man, married, with one child, who told me how one night he woke up and, horrified, found that he was beginning to choke his wife.

Another story of a burning, long-smoldering resentment—not really toward his wife. It was toward his father that he felt this.

Still, his wife became the unwitting object of his almost-acted-out resentment. She considered it a bad dream the first time it happened, but it happened again. Several other times, it did not reach such an extreme state, but nevertheless, he felt the urge to choke her.

Anxious and horrified with himself, this man sat across from me and told me of all this. He loathed himself for this because, you see, he loved his wife, too.

I asked him more about his earlier life. He told me of his father, a successful businessman, who preferred his brother to him. He told me how his father had no use for him, how he had ridiculed him all his life, how his father had downgraded his ability and belittled everything he tried to do.

Resentful, he had left his father's place of business, where he had been employed, and got a job as a salesman. He made out fairly well as a salesman, well enough to support his wife and child, anyway. But he continued to seethe with resentment at his rejecting father; he could not get his father out of his mind for long. He, too, could not rise above the hatefulness of his past.

Still, he lived a fairly decent life—holding his own as a salesman, husband, and father. Until, in his sleep, semi-conscious, he found himself trying to choke his wife—and tortured himself with the knowledge of what he had almost done. In this tortured state, fantasying further attempts at unleashing his resentment so destructively, he came to see me.

Two men, so alike and yet so different. Self-torturing, denying themselves self-respect, the fires of resentment destroying them from within.

"But why not?" you may say. "Look at their backgrounds. They were hurt. Why shouldn't they feel resentment?

True, why shouldn't they? They were hurt; no one can deny this. The man with the smothering mother was badly hurt; so was the man with the rejecting father.

But if you stop here, you are missing my point, which is this: How do we help them? By encouraging them in nursing their feeling of deprivation and thereby helping them stoke the furnace of resentment?

I think not. But, before I tell what I said to them and how I feel about their potential adjustment to life, let me tell you about a formerly obese taxi driver who won out over his resentment.

## ONE VICTORY OVER RESENTMENT

I boarded a taxi at Kennedy Airport. I was tired and closed my eyes, but the cabbie was talkative and told me a story of one victory over resentment.

"Where you coming from?" he asked.

"Los Angeles."

"It must be hot out there."

"So-so."

"It's been cold here. What's your business?"

"I'm a doctor."

"A doctor! Boy, do I need a doctor!

"You do?"

"Yeah, didn't you notice how overweight I am? You know how much I weigh? Two hundred fifty-five pounds."

"Why don't you try to reduce?"

He held up a paper bag. "See this. Half a chicken and some pot cheese. That's my diet."

"Does it help?"

"It did. I lost thirty pounds, but then I get depressed and angry, and I start eating a lot again."

"What's the matter?"

"Well, I get mad."

"What about?"

"Would you be interested?"

"Yes."

"Oh, you would not, buddy. I'm a hopeless case, I guess."

"Are you married?"

"I was. I got married when I was very young. I have two kids, both boys, sixteen and seventeen."

"Were you so overweight then?"

"Yeah, but she loved me anyway. At least she seemed to at first."

"So?"

"She began talking about how she was ashamed of me because I was so obese. I figured she was right, so I went on a diet. I ate pot cheese and chicken all the time. I lost over thirty pounds."

"Good."

"No, it was no good. I thought that when I looked thinner, my wife would be happier with me, but it didn't work out that way. Something was wrong. You know, you can tell when a woman likes you; she doesn't have to say anything, just the way she looks at you. Well, I'd look at her and see something was wrong. She had this faraway look."

"What then?"

"I went to see my best friend. I've known him for many years. He said he would straighten things out; he told me not to worry."

"Did he?"

"Oh, sure. You've heard the story before—nothing new—I found them together in bed one day. I don't know what stopped me from killing him. I could have choked her too. I felt like it. Instead, I ran out of the house, and drove. And drove. And drove. I drove for two days, till I hit Florida. I felt so mad, that was all I could think to do."

"I'm sorry," I said, "about what happened. Guess you're divorced now?"

"Yeah, sure. She married him. I felt sorry for her."

"And for yourself? Don't you feel sorry for yourself?"

"Sure. Look at me, driving around with a paper bag full of chicken and pot cheese. Why am I trying to get thin? For whom?"

"You're doing it for yourself."

"I hate myself," he said. "I hate them. Maybe I hate almost everybody."

"Be responsible to yourself," I said. "Lose weight so you'll feel better about yourself. That's the main thing."

"I don't know."

"I know it's not easy, but you've got to get over your resentment and regain your self-respect. Lose weight. Stop feeling sorry for yourself. Look, here's my card. I dare you to come see me when you are thin."

It was about a year later, and there he was in my office. I had trouble recognizing him. He looked like a different person. All the fat was gone; he couldn't have weighed much more than 160 or 170 pounds. And, biggest change of all, there was a broad smile on his face.

"I did it," he said.

"I'm happy for you," I said. "You look fine."

"I feel fine."

"You look like you won out over your anger."

"I won," he said.

"Will you ever get married again?"

"I did," he said. "I did that, too. She's my soulmate. I'm crazy about her. Here's a picture of her."

One victory over resentment. From fat to thin, change one. The biggest change: from resentment to happiness.

## A POSITIVE APPROACH TO RESENTMENT

So, now, let us put our heads together and plan a positive approach toward resentment. To find self-respect, you must find in yourself the weapons to use against the negation of resentment—and, to define my terms more precisely, what I mean is "chronic resentment."

First, you must disabuse yourself of any idea that you are alone when you feel resentment. Everyone feels resentful sometimes because everyone, at one time or another, experiences frustration, grief, disappointment, and despair. The distinction is this: The person who lacks self-respect stays resentful, fails to get over it, inflicts his hostility on others; the person with self-respect climbs out of the pit, gets over it, goes on to a constructive life of which he can be proud.

Now, what do you do?

Well, first, let's go back to the two men I wrote about. They were so resentful that (in different ways) each kept fantasizing about choking or being choked—to death.

What did I say to them?

Well, the first man had, I felt, been especially unfortunate in being so smothered by his mother, and of course, I understood his resentment and his fear. His mother, perhaps fearing another desertion, kept him by her side and thus blocked his growth as a person. Indeed, you might say that she used him as a substitute for the husband who had deserted her.

So, in his early formative years, this man had been deserted by his father and imprisoned by his mother. Good God, why shouldn't he feel resentment? I thoughts, but I didn't say this.

Because resentment was no solution for his problems. Feeling resentment as he moved out into the world, he would get resentment back from others and would spend his life in a never-ending cycle of negation, a death-in-life cycle of misery. Obviously, his early experiences would limit what he could do with his life; still, this did not mean that he could not, within limits, lead a good life.

"I cannot blame you," I said, "for feeling resentment toward both your parents. Don't feel guilty if you feel this way. But, at the same time, recognize that it won't do you any good and that you must change your ways of thinking."

"How?" he said.

"You have had some good moments in your life, too," I said. "You just told me about some of them. Think about them, not about your mother; bring them into the present. Feel these successes now. Live now. Set your goals today. Set them every day."

"I'm not sure I have any goals," he said. "And if *I* did, they wouldn't be important anyway."

"They would be important," I said. "If you set a goal, say, of approaching a customer in a positive way or stopping your critical thoughts about yourself, I would call either an important goal. A very important goal."

"But what about my mother?" he said.

"If all you can feel is resentment when you think of your mother, live in the present and don't think about her too much. Concentrate on defeating your resentment and accepting yourself, and going toward goals that will make you feel good about yourself. Someday maybe you'll forgive your mother—when you feel better about yourself, maybe you will feel compassion for her failings. When you are able to think this way about her, without resentment, then think more about her. I hope that someday you will forgive yourself and forgive your mother, too."

What about the second man?

"As far as I can see," I said, "you are so full of resentment toward your father that you transfer this feeling—almost unconsciously, perhaps—to your wife and, though you do love her, in your ambivalence, you fantasized choking her and found yourself almost doing that very thing.

"You must understand this: You cannot be responsible for your father's belittling attitude toward you. You don't have to see him all the time if you don't want to. You don't work for him anymore. So why the continual resentment?"

"I can't help it," he said. "Look what he did to me."

"You have a good job, a wife, a child," I said. "You have problems, I can see, but you have good solid qualities too. Maybe your father was far from perfect, but he did not destroy you. Build a new life for yourself.

"Forget your father; forgive your father. Live for today, without resentment destroying your day. You are more than your father thinks you are. You are what you think you are. Forgive yourself for what you almost did; accept yourself, get over your resentment, set new goals. You have finer goals to set, a rich life to lead, a good marriage to build—if you will forgive yourself and your father and get over the resentment that burns inside you like a cancer."

Postscript: Months later, the man phoned to tell me of the improvements in his life. There were no more choking fantasies or near-attempts. He was earning more money and enjoying his work. He and his wife were feeling closer and re-experiencing their natural affection for each other. His child was thriving. He saw his father seldom, but no longer felt submerged in his resentment toward him.

The first man I have not heard from. He has much to overcome. I hope he succeeds.

I have indicated my idea of a positive approach to resentment in my advice to these men. But let me summarize this advice:

1. *Rise above the deprivations of your past.* This is not easy, but neither is bathing yourself in self-pity and hate.
2. *Set goals every day.* You are worth it. Your goals are important if they are important to you. Stop turning your resentment in on yourself. Move toward your goals instead.
3. *Forgive others.* Anyway, try. Have other people let you down? Try to forgive them anyway. They are not perfect; you are not perfect. Forgiveness is the soothing balm that takes away resentment.
4. *Forgive yourself.* Forgive yourself every day. When you let others down, when you let yourself down, forgive yourself. I have made my mistakes, and you have made your mistakes. Forgive!

And overcome the fallacious concept you may have—many people do—about the heroism and "guts" of expressing resentment in a belligerent way. There is nothing heroic about lashing out at other people with destruction, and there are no "guts" in using as a model some renowned tough guy criminal who ended up in jail or incorrigibly alienated from society. It amazes me sometimes that so many people admire these anti-social types in their hard-bitten and negative resentment.

The person with real "guts" is a big enough person to rise above his resentment, to adopt a constructive way of life, to contribute all he can to other people, to reach out—in his imperfection, in his all-too-human imperfection—toward life with the best he has in him.

This kind of person has felt resentment and has even been submerged in resentment, but he has won the battle to overcome it. He has won this great battle. He does not have to show off and prove that he has "guts." Deep down inside, he knows that he does.

He feels self-respect. He bestows this great gift on himself. When he looks in the mirror, he may chuckle a little—but he does not cry, and he does not flinch, and he is not in pain.

This is the gift you must give yourself: self-respect.

# 6

## YOUR THIRD ENEMY

### EMPTINESS

YOU ARE ON THE ROAD TO SELF-RESPECT. YOUR CAR IS SLEEK, THE GAS TANK IS full, the highway is firm. There are no detours; your direction is forward.

You harness the supercharged powers in your understanding and in your feeling of active sincerity. These are awesome powers; do not doubt this. They are subtle and positive powers that will lead you toward a good feeling about yourself and others—fundamental components of any self-respectful orientation in this our complicated twentieth-century world.

Thus, when we win out over the negative and self-destructive forces in ourselves—the uncertainty and the resentment—we then call on our positive capacities to build our sense of human dignity, to move us toward our goals, to make the most of our lives.

Before we go on to a consideration of more positive aspects leading to your sense of self-respect, let us learn about your third enemy: emptiness.

Like resentment and uncertainty, this is a dread enemy.

Perhaps it is man's greatest enemy these days. Because of my extensive travels and lectures, I talk to a pretty fair cross-section of people. Not everyone can articulate what is bothering him, but a common thread runs through what I hear. Many people today suffer from a constant sense of incompleteness, of non-being—of what I would call emptiness.

This may seem strange to you: That in a land of material plenty, in an era which economic indexes herald as a time of unparalleled prosperity, so many people should feel so empty. That living as we do, well-fed, well clothed, whisking around in cars and jets, so many people should feel an internal lack. That in an era of rising personal incomes, rising savings, and rising participation in ownership of such tangibles as shares of stock, so many people should wonder who they are and spend their days in a fruitless and often bizarre identity.

And yet it is so. Too many people have passively withdrawn from life and from themselves, cut themselves off from the glow of their creative powers, and turned their eyes toward externals in an effort to fill the void of their emptiness. They seek to erase this inner lack by turning to alcohol or drugs, indulging in excesses of food or entertainment, or trying to identify with the lives of celebrities.

But this is not the way to take away emptiness. In the final analysis, you must give yourself substance, and you must overcome your sense of emptiness yourself. This is your responsibility to yourself, your joy in doing, your sense of accomplishment when you succeed.

If a sense of emptiness haunts you, you must win out over this third enemy. First is uncertainty; then, resentment, and finally, emptiness. These are the principal negative forces that stand between you and the full sense of self-respect that you deserve to feel.

When I was a boy, we used to hear other kids (usually a year or two older, and braggarts all) talk about the horrifying "haunted house" in the neighborhood. Remember? Most neighborhoods had one.

Sometimes we would walk past this "haunted house" and look at it with a peculiar mixture of curiosity and fear—keeping a respectful distance, of course, and crossing our fingers or some such nonsense.

Finally, prodded on by curiosity and an effort to show how brave we were, we gathered up our courage, launched ourselves piously into prayer, and crossed the threshold.

To discover . . . what?

To discover that the house was just an ordinary house—no ghosts at all— just empty.

My point is that we must learn to do away with our childlike haunted-house-type illusions—they are empty. We must be strong enough to live in and to face the solid world of a reality.

Further, we must rebuild ourselves from the ground up, so that our foundations are strong. Insight is our window; inner peace, our furniture; and the excitement of our goals, the fuel for heating. Thus, we build ourselves, become strong persons, and overcome the despair of emptiness.

## EMPTINESS AND FULFILLMENT

Before I give you my ideas on dealing with emptiness more concretely, I will tell you three short stories about people I know. These people are of my world, and of your world, too—for their problems may be your problems, and their anguish may be your anguish.

The first is about a man who came up to speak to me after a lecture in Florida. He was a big, heavy-set man, and he talked to me about his feeling of emptiness and his lack of trust in people—including his wife and three children.

"This emptiness, this lack of trust—maybe it came from the war," he said.

He had been in the infantry in Europe in World War II, and more than once, he had killed other men. "Maybe that's why I feel so bad," he said.

"I doubt it," I said. "You were fighting for your country, and you were forced to either kill or be killed yourself." Then he told me about his childhood. How he was the least favored of his family. His parents thought him worthless, and he grew up with a poor feeling about himself.

"There's where your problem comes from, probably," I said, "from the poor opinion of yourself that has stayed with you from your childhood. You still believe what your parents thought of you. This empty feeling, this bad feeling, you cannot win over it until you learn to live today, in the present, to forgive yourself for what is not your fault—to set goals for today."

Here is another story. It is about a couple who married and divorced. About emptiness, several years of emptiness.

They came to see me after one of my lectures, about themselves. They had remarried. Both had read my book *Psycho-Cybernetics*—separately—and had learned to stop hating each other and start forgiving. Their sense of emptiness, mixed up in this resentment, grew less and less. Finally, they decided to forgive each other for all their grudges in marriage, and they began to think of the good times they had shared.

They thanked me for writing my book.

How did I feel when they told me this? How would you feel if someone walked up to you on the street and handed you a million dollars?

Another story came singing to me over the phone, three years ago, spanning the thousands of miles between New York and Texas.

"I did it."

"What?" I said.

"I did it."

I looked at the telephone. What a funny instrument it was, I thought.

"It worked," said the voice booming over the telephone. "It worked."

I was in my office. I had just finished operating. My mind and body were both just a little tired. "Who is this?" I managed to ask.

"Don't you remember me?" The voice roared out of the telephone at me. "I drove you to the airport, and I told you about me and my son."

"Oh," I said.

"I'm the salesman from Texas. The guy who made a lot of money talking to other people, who couldn't talk to his son."

"How are you?" I said. "I'm glad to hear from you."

"It worked," he said.

"Oh," I said.

"I did it," he said.

"Congratulations," I said.

"It worked," he said.

"Great. But I'm kind of tired, please forgive me—what worked? What did you do?"

He reminded me of what he'd talked to me about—the great emptiness in his life, his inability to communicate with his son.

The emptiness of it! He was making a good living; he had a fine teenage son—but he couldn't reach him.

He was driving me to the airport; I had to catch a plane and didn't have much time. "Talk to him," I had said. "Even if it's difficult—and painful. If you've failed him in any ways, ask his forgiveness. Tell him something like this: 'Son, forgive me. I may have made a mistake about you, but isn't it possible that you've also made a mistake about me?'"

Behind the steering wheel, his face was full of despair. He had nodded his head, but he seemed empty to me.

I had advised him some more—on forgiveness of himself, and of his son, and on making a fresh start—and then we had shaken hands goodbye.

Now here he was, materialized from out of this little miracle gadget we take for granted. "It worked," he said.

"What happened?" I said.

"I stopped being so proud," he said. "I humbled myself. I forgave myself; I forgave him—and I couldn't believe the way he reacted. We embraced. We cried. He became the son I used to be close to. My son and I are close again."

"I'm happy for you."

It was three years ago when this man had phoned me to tell me of his victory over emptiness and to thank me. I had talked about him to people, here and there, and written about him a little, too.

Then just the other day, as I was writing this book, I picked up the telephone, and there he was again.

"I want you to know, Max," he said, "that as I travel around the country, I keep hearing the story of me and my son."

"My lectures," I said. "I like to talk about you."

"I'm glad you're telling my story," he said. "I hope it helps other people. My son and I are closer today than ever. We have been the best of friends since I talked to him in a humble way—finally."

"You did it," I said.

"What?"

"It worked," I said.

"What?"

"You did it," I said.

"You're kidding," he said.

"I am. But I'm laughing with you, that you let down your pride and found your human dignity, that you won out over your emptiness. This is something to laugh about. It is something to feel happy about. People don't laugh enough these days; they have to learn how to laugh."

"Thanks," he said.

"I talk too much," I said. "But call me again."

Three stories about people who I have helped feel less empty. And they have helped me feel more fulfilled. Indeed, I do not tell of them to show how they are in my debt; for, most assuredly, *I am in their debt.* I tell these stories of people grappling with emptiness because emptiness is one of the prime obstacles to the attainment of our sense of self-respect.

## TWENTIETH-CENTURY EMPTINESS

Do you suffer from a feeling of emptiness?

If you do, take heart; you are not alone. You are one of many people wrestling with one of the dread diseases of the twentieth century. To reach up to your full feeling of dignity, you must overcome this emptiness.

Too many people wake up to feelings of aimlessness, substancelessness, and go to face days which lack meaning and a sense of direction.

Too many people today suffer from a kind of twentieth-century emptiness—with excuses for their voids, endless complaints for anyone who will listen, and a mañana philosophy underlying and poisoning their lives.

Some people think they feel empty because they are not married; but this need not be so. Some people think they feel empty because they have no children; but this need not be so. Others believe their emptiness stems from the fact that they are not overwhelming successes in their work, but this need not be so.

*You* create your own feeling of emptiness to a great degree, and *you* must accept responsibility for overcoming it.

In reality—not fantasy.

Too many people wish they were somebody else.

When you wake up in the morning, do you say to yourself, "If I only had a million dollars"?

I hope not. Because if you do, you are licked before you start. You are rejecting yourself as you are, leaving yourself empty and unfulfilled.

Or perhaps you say to yourself, "If only I were a beautiful Hollywood actress."

Again, I hope not. I might add, I have known beautiful Hollywood actresses who wished that they were somebody else too.

Or maybe you think, "If only I was twenty years younger."

You were twenty years younger once. What did you do with your youth when you had it?

Stop wishing you were somebody else; start enjoying the unique privilege of being yourself. Wishing is an evasion—and it leads you only to despair.

I used to know a man many people would consider fortunate—because he was extremely wealthy. He and his brother owned a number of business enterprises years ago; they had amassed a considered sum of money—or, so I was led to believe.

Still, he was always bored. He found little to interest himself. He suffered from an enormous sense of indifference.

There were hordes of nice girls in New York, but he went to the south of France to meet a countess whom he would marry. With him, he took a sense of emptiness and illusion, and he fell into the hands of some people who played games with him and tricked him. A fake baron introduced him to a fake countess and her daughter, both of whom fawned on him—and he was blissfully unaware of the manipulations going on around him.

To the best of my knowledge, he emerged from all this unscathed. I hope so, anyway. He was really a decent fellow. But he suffered from a terrible sense of emptiness that drove him into such illusion and made him a target for such confidence people.

Do you think you wouldn't feel empty and bored if you had a lot of money? Here was someone who had a lot of money—and he still felt an appalling emptiness.

Now, what do we do about this? How do we fill ourselves so that we no longer feel empty? How do we discard all our elaborate excuses and get down to brass tacks?

## FIVE WAYS TO VANQUISH EMPTINESS

Here are some suggestions I have to give you. I think they may help you.

1. *Stop sleepwalking.* Approximately eight hours a day, you should sleep and sleep soundly—you need sleep to renew your energy and bring you back to yourself.

When you are awake, stay awake. Concentrate on what you are doing; stop doing things halfheartedly. If some project is important enough for you to undertake it, throw yourself into it with concentration and enthusiasm and with your full life force.

Will all this exhaust you?

Not at all. Concentration is a fine art; in sharpening your focus on the things that interest you, you become more fully alive, and this is exhilarating. Instead of sleepwalking, you will live more while you are awake, and chances are you will then also sleep more soundly and wake up, not exhausted, but refreshed.

The sleepwalker feels empty because he just wanders around in a daze and does nothing. Stop sleepwalking, make your activities purposeful, fill your days with vitality.

2. *Resign from Mañana Incorporated.* I have written about this bankrupt corporation in some of my other books, but just a few more words about it in connection with emptiness.

Members of Mañana Incorporated—addicted to the tomorrow-type thinking—put off everything until mañana (tomorrow). Thus, they never realize their goals because they always delay going after them until a "mañana" that no one I know has ever even experienced.

Members of Mañana Incorporated never get any dividends. They are in the business of rationalizing why they cannot do something today, but must put it off until "tomorrow." They live fiercely in the future, disdaining to dirty their hands with the sordidness of the present.

The result of all this?

Emptiness, of course.

Because they never do anything.

So, you millions of members of Mañana Incorporated, do yourselves a favor and resign.

3. *Renew your sense of direction.* Because you cannot go around in endless circles. If you do this, obviously, you get a listless, aimless, indifferent kind of feeling about your life.

Yet many people do just this—and see nothing wrong with their lifeless, empty orientation.

Suppose you boarded an airplane which left New York, whisked over Philadelphia, circled back to New York, changed direction and jet-propelled itself to Chicago, then moved toward Canada, only to circle back to Chicago and then back to New York, where it did not land but continued to circle for hours, until it moved again toward Philadelphia.

"Ridiculous!" you say. "What kind of an airplane is this? An airplane that goes nowhere. Absurd!"

Truly, an airplane with no sense of direction is a horrifying thing to contemplate. But what about a person who has no sense of direction? Is this not also a terrible waste?

Of course, just as boarding an airplane which does nothing but go around in circles is an experience in emptiness, so an individual who spends his precious time going around in circles lives with emptiness.

You must renew your sense of direction to break through the feeling of emptiness and give valid meaning to your life. Every day set your goals. Don't downgrade them; give them your full enthusiasm. You deserve to feel that the goals that are important to you are worthwhile. So, you won't make a million dollars. So, your name won't be in the headlines. It doesn't matter. What does matter is that your goals mean something to you. What does matter is that your zest for them helps you lift yourself up out of your feeling of empty nothingness into a feeling of doing something and being somebody. No one else has to sanction that you are somebody either; this is something that you give yourself.

4. *Enrich your self-image.* When you have a good opinion of yourself, when you use your imagination productively you enrich your self-image, and you dissolve the empty, negative feeling you have about yourself.

You have already seen too much of your failures; seeing your failures again and again in your mind has produced only negation and has engendered in you a sense that you are empty and inferior—lacking in worth as a human being.

See your successes instead! Your imagination has enormous power and can help you picture your successes and bring enrichment to your self-image.

I have said this before, in other books, but I cannot possibly repeat it too

much—it is too fundamental: When you see your successes in your imagi-
nation instead of your failures, you precondition yourself for more and more
success, for a reactivation of your success mechanism. In the process, you en-
rich self-image and move out into the world with a confidence that is reality,
not overcompensation or fantasy.

As you enrich your self-image, it goes almost without saying, you dissolve
your feeling of emptiness.

> 5. *Reach out to other people.* This, too, is fundamental, and just as, in
>    a sense, you dissolve emptiness as you enrich your self-image, so
>    you also dissolve emptiness as you reach out—in a constructive
>    way—toward other people.

And this is the common denominator I had in mind when telling the sto-
ries of five people fighting to win out over their feelings of emptiness. Their
feelings of emptiness or of fulfillment had much to do with their lack of ability
to reach out and communicate successfully with other people.

One man feared closeness with his family—he did not trust them—but he
was probably well off the mark when he blamed this on his killing enemy sol-
diers during the war.

The couple, who felt able to forgive and forget, were able to overcome their
sense of emptiness and reach out toward each other once more.

The father and son, too, were able to bury their past grievances, were able
to feel a warm bond again, and, as they did, fulfillment replaced emptiness.

In short, to win out over emptiness, material achievements are not enough. You
must value more than the material; you must reach out with friendship to people.

People values: sharing with people; living on friendly terms with them; and
loving. These are the values that will bring you fulfillment instead of emptiness.

## OUR FINAL GOAL: SELF-RESPECT

Our final goal is self-respect and, moving toward this goal, we have examined a
trio of deadly enemies that might block our path toward our goals. These enemies
are negative feelings: uncertainty, resentment, emptiness. They are invisible but
are dread enemies, nevertheless.

We have devoted a chapter to each of these possible pitfalls because stressing
positive concepts is not enough if we do not have an awareness of the negative
forces inside us.

A friend of mine who was a soldier in World War II told a story which is

illustrative. He was an infantryman, a squad leader, and his outfit was fight-
ing the Germans door-to-door in a town near the German border.

One night, after midnight, his platoon went on patrol behind the German lines.
They crawled through the snow to a house at the end of a block and my friend
was to lead the charge. He did, rushing across a barbed wire-strewn minefield,
to the house across the street. A German sentry guarding the entrance fled, and,
after hurling grenades in the house, the GIs rushed in. Four Germans waited in
the cellar, surrendering hands overhead while they were searched.

But the soldiers were not completely vigilant—or they were too excited or
frightened—and the fourth German was not searched (or handcuffed or tied).
To my friend's horror, this German soldier reached over to hand him two gre-
nades with which he could have wreaked fearful destruction. He handed him
the grenades; he could as easily have hurled them in his face.

The patrol was a success. The platoon returned with the four prisoners, who
faced interrogation at headquarters.

But what might have been! Because the American soldiers had not coped
properly with the enemy, their mission might have been a disastrous failure.

Our mission is self-respect and, before moving full force on it, we too must
search search our negative for the destructive grenades before they can explode
and ruin our mission.

We cannot keep moving forward toward self-respect while we are arming
our negative forces of uncertainty, resentment, and emptiness.

We cannot build and face destruction at the same time.

But now we know a good deal about the negative forces inside us, and we
will resume our positive emphases.

We know our rights; we will not short-change ourselves; we will seize our
opportunities to build for solid human dignity.

# 7

## DEVELOPING THE STRENGTH TO SEIZE OPPORTUNITIES

WHAT IS OPPORTUNITY, AND WHEN DOES IT KNOCK? IT NEVER KNOCKS. YOU CAN wait a whole lifetime, listening, hoping, and you will hear no knocking. None at all.

*You* are opportunity, and you must knock on the door leading to your destiny. You prepare yourself to recognize opportunity, to pursue and seize opportunity as you develop the strength of your personality and build a self-image with which you are able to live—with your self-respect alive and growing.

Opportunity covers a wide area: some people may constrict the totality of its meaning and apply it only to work or financial success, but your opportunities in living are really much wider than this. Opportunity may also mean warding off negative feelings. It may also mean functioning under pressure. It may also mean rising above vanity, bigotry, and deceit as you strive to live with dignity. It is your opportunity to be an archaeologist digging under the debris of tension and conflict to uncover for yourself a sense of self-acceptance that will give you inner peace and comfort in our swiftly paced, always troubled world.

Accessible to you may be the exciting opportunity of steering yourself to a productive goal through your growing awareness of who you are and where you can channel your assets in practical terms toward achieving your ends. Developing your strength as you build your self-respect, you mobilize yourself for action and place yourself—practically, in an external sense, and emotionally, in an internal sense—in a position to seize opportunities at the proper times. You build the caliber of your thinking, propelling your thoughts into and through your imagination. Then with internal strength, you move toward your goals of fulfillment and happiness.

*You* create opportunity. You develop the capacities for moving toward opportunity. You turn crises into creative opportunities and defeats into successes and frustration into fulfillment.

With what? With your great invisible weapons: your good feelings about yourself, your determination to live the best life you can, and your feeling—that only you can give yourself—that you are a worthwhile, deserving person.

You must fight for your right to fulfill the opportunity that God gave you to use your life well. You do this when, in your mind, you support yourself instead of undermining yourself. You do this when, in your mind, you develop your creative and imaginative powers instead of worrying about what other people think or foreseeing endless disasters.

What are explorers? Men alive to opportunity and adventure. Men not afraid to challenge uncertainty and seek new horizons. Men alive to possibilities of expansion and innovation.

Suppose, in 1492, Columbus had said to himself, "But trip weather may be stormy" or "I'd better not go. I might get scurvy."

What are inventors? Men who see opportunity in things where others see none. Men whose senses are alive to creative possibilities. Where would the world be today if Thomas Edison had been unable to see opportunity where others saw nothing—and then to seize it?

You must stop complaining about your unfortunate past or your bad luck and open your eyes to the opportunities that exist for you. You have limitations, sure, and no matter who you are, you will sometimes meet frustrations—but you have opportunities too, and you must search for your creative goals so that you can move toward them. In a sense, you become Columbus, you become Edison; you explore and invent and originate and adapt.

Who gives you this right? You give it to yourself because you respect yourself.

## OPPORTUNITY IS NOT JUST FOR THE OTHER GUY

From New York to California, I have gone back and forth lecturing for quite a few years now, and I have talked to thousands of people about things that worry them—so let me anticipate a few thoughts of many people reading this:

"The other guy gets opportunities. I know that. But I'm just unlucky."

Or "I have this handicap, so you can see that I'm licked before I start."

Or "I have no right to try something like that. Who am I, just a nobody."

This is self-defeating; you must fight to overcome this type of negative thinking, or you block yourself off from opportunity as an eclipse blocks off the sun.

You must understand that opportunity is not just for "the other guy," opportunity is a possibility for you, too—if you can accept it and make it welcome. A plant may wither and die if you don't water it and give it enough sunshine. So will opportunity.

Don't let opportunity die for you! Don't kill it with negative feelings!

There is much concern in education today about "disadvantaged" children in our schools and in many communities university teams are helping public school teachers to improve communication between school, students, and parents and thereby to get the "disadvantaged" children more of a chance to climb up the educational and vocational ladder.

Well, as adults, we all have disadvantages and limitations. If we get help—as these children are getting today—wonderful. If we don't, we must nevertheless move toward whatever opportunities are realistic for us anyway

Many people sit around moping, envying others, complaining, resentful. If they hear about people like Helen Keller, who overcame drastic handicaps to seize her opportunities for achievement, they say that this is an isolated case.

Indeed, in the case of Helen Keller, her handicaps were so severe that perhaps she is an isolated case.

Still, in general, many people who have pursued and seized their opportunities and risen to prominent positions in our world have had no easy road.

A study was made of four hundred eminent men and women of this century, and the researchers concluded that three-fourths of these celebrated people had been handicapped in their youth by tragedies, disabilities, or great frustrations and had overcome these problems to achieve their position of renown and make their contributions to others. Three-fourths of these four hundred people fought through their handicaps: an important statistic. Thomas Edison and Eleanor Roosevelt were included among those who had risen above handicaps to achievement and opportunity.

Opportunity is not just for others. But you must make opportunity for you.

## DON'T CLOSE THE DOOR ON OPPORTUNITY!

Opportunity won't knock on your door; nevertheless, you must not close the door on opportunity.

Apply creative Psycho-Cybernetics, and rise to meet opportunity, forgiving yourself for your failures and continually moving toward new goals.

To close the door on opportunity is, unfortunately, common. You must guard against this type of tendency in yourself. Let me tell you an illustrative story:

It's about a doctor who shut the door on an opportunity to advance himself.

He was already a doctor, and he wanted to become a plastic surgeon.

"Can I watch you operate?" he asked me.

"Tomorrow," I said. "Eight a.m., okay?"

I wasn't sure the "eight a.m." pleased him, but I figured I was probably imagining this. He nodded his head. "I'll be there," he said. "Eight a.m."

He was as good as his word. He was there at eight a.m., and he watched me operate. He said he was fascinated. Could he be my pupil? I agreed that I would teach him.

The doctor came a few times, expressing fascination with plastic surgery and for the opportunity for fulfillment that this work could be for him.

I was delighted with his enthusiasm.

But one morning, he was not there.

The morning after that, he was also absent.

Finally, a few days later, I walked into my office, and there he was. "Where have you been?" I said.

"I overslept a few times," he answered, rather sheepishly. "When I woke up, I looked at the time, and it was too late to come."

"You won't learn this way," I said mildly.

"I know. Tell me, do you operate in the afternoon? I like to sleep, and it would be easier for me."

"Sorry. I always operate in the morning. The patient has just awakened, and I feel it is best for the patient psychologically."

"Oh," he said.

And, fascinated as he was with plastic surgery (it represented a creative opportunity for him, and I do not believe he faked his interest), he didn't follow up. He couldn't get up early in the morning. He shut the door on his own opportunity. He was qualified to succeed, but he denied himself success on his own terms.

Learn from this story. Are you, without knowing it, blocking yourself from opportunity? You have this great gift of life, and you must make the most of it. When you fail—and sometimes you will—let it be after you have done your best, not as a result of your own inertia.

Now let me tell you a story about a scrubwoman who found opportunity.

## A SONG OF HAPPINESS

I met her, this scrubwoman, in the elevator one evening. I had enjoyed my dinner in a nearby restaurant, returned home about eight o'clock, and stepped into the elevator to go up to the eighteenth floor, where I live. She was armed with a mop and pail. A small woman, in her late forties, she had worked about ten years in the building, but we didn't know each other any better than to nod our heads and say hello. That's what we did this night: we nodded our heads and murmured "hello."

She came up with me to my place, with mop and pail, ready to empty the wastepaper basket and mop the floors. While she started on a front room, I walked to the living room.

I made myself comfortable. I was smoking my pipe, my feet were up, I was reading a play. I had forgotten about the scrubwoman's presence. She might have been on another planet.

Then I heard singing from another room—no, humming. Someone was humming a lullaby. It was soft and sweet and happy-sounding, a song of happiness.

I got out of my chair. In another room, the woman was mopping the floor, humming her lullaby. She looked up as I entered the room, and we exchanged greetings again.

"Did you have a busy day?" she asked me.

"Yes. And you?"

"About the same as usual."

"But today is different, isn't it?"

"How?"

"You're smiling, and you're humming a song."

"I often do. It makes my work more pleasant. I'm cleaning up, and I'm singing while I work, so I'm happy."

"I never heard you before," I said.

"Perhaps not."

"And," I said, "we never talked before."

"That's true."

I asked her about herself. Her life had been enough to crush many an individual who could not endure grief and rise above it to regain herself. Her husband, a truck driver for the government, had been killed in a car accident twelve years earlier. She had one child—a daughter—nine at the time of the accident—now twenty-one, unmarried, a college girl. She and her daughter were in the car with her husband when it crashed, and he died; by some miracle, the woman and her daughter had survived.

Grief-stricken at her husband's sudden and horrible death, consoling her daughter, who at such a young age had seen such a frightening tragedy and suffered such a catastrophic loss, she had nevertheless found in herself the courage to go on. She had for many years supported herself and her daughter, who was soon to graduate from college in Wisconsin.

"What will she do then?" I asked her.

"She majored in psychology. She'll go for her master's degree, and then she's going to get a job teaching underprivileged children."

"May I congratulate you?"

"Do you want to?"

"I do. I think you deserve it. I think you should be very proud of yourself."

"I am proud."

"You should be."

"And I'm happy."

"Good."

"About my daughter."

"That's fine," I said. "But I feel also that you should be proud of your great achievement—of the way you came through for your daughter when she was a little girl, and you didn't let her down."

"Thanks, doctor."

"You know, we've never talked before—all these years, but I've seen you now and then, and you look different somehow. What is it?"

"My wig?"

"Oh." I looked at her hair. "Oh. That's it. Yes."

"Do you like it?" She was suddenly shy, almost a little sensitive; in a flash, she seemed to wait, depending on my opinion, hoping for my approval.

"I like it."

"Does it make me look like a lady?"

"You always were." I hate to flatter people, but I felt an honest respect for her that made me enjoy complimenting her.

She stood there with mop and pail, her eyes gleaming with pleasure. No princess or countess on the French Riviera ever gleamed with more inner pride. "I wanted to look better for my daughter. I'm so proud of what she's learning and what she's planning to do with her life. She wants to contribute to the children of the world—she is sincere in this—and then she wants to have children of her own and teach them to lead useful lives and to assume responsibility as human beings."

I went back into the other room to continue my reading; strange, all these years, coming and going, nodding hello as people whose lives meet on no level at all—and suddenly, I knew so much about the woman who scrubbed my floors and cleaned up. Some people might look down on her because they thought her work demeaning: I could only respect her for her courage in rising above misfortune and maintaining her self-respect in the face of a tragedy that would have crushed many people.

Humming again, soft, and sweet. Happy. A song of happiness from a scrub-woman. She wore a wig to cover her hair, but she needed no artificial aid to cover her sense of purpose. It was there.

Husband alive, husband dead—just like that—but she had overcome her grief and terror to find opportunity once more. Still, she had reached out to find opportunity in helping her daughter toward a life hopefully easier than her own had been.

Even while working—tiring, painstaking, ill-rewarded work—she found opportunity to sing a song of happiness.

## HOW TO MOVE TOWARD OPPORTUNITY

This world is far from perfect—you don't have to be brilliant to perceive that—but it nevertheless contains many opportunities for fulfillment and achievement.

Some people spend all their time criticizing the American culture and, while some of their criticism may be quite valid, still we must be pragmatists. We must ask: "Where have men grouped together in civilizations and behaved like angels, with absolute justice and absolute constructive effort and absolute brotherhood and peace of mind?"

Even ancient Athens, home of so many great philosophers whose thoughts have lived through the ages, even ancient Athens had serious defects as a culture. The worst of which was its lack of an adequate sanitary system. The lack of a sanitary system helped spread a terrible plague which was largely instrumental in destroying ancient Athens.

All right, we live in an imperfect world, in an imperfect culture, and as you settle in your easy chair after a hard day's work to read your newspaper, all the frightening headlines upset you further, and finally, thoroughly irritated, you throw the newspaper at your cat. But the cat slinks away. Even the cat doesn't want to read about all the world's troubles.

Yet ours is a world of opportunity, too. The frontiers are not all closed, and the doors are not all shut. We can still look forward and move forward—toward exciting new opportunities.

How?

1. *Keep an eye on the red light.* I mean the red light on your mental dashboard, with which you stop yourself from moving toward your opportunities. Red lights on our streets are necessary for

safety, of course. But when you stop yourself, you must ask your-
self this: Am I stopping myself for realistic reasons, because I
am moving into a danger area, or am I just stopping myself be-
cause my opinion of myself is too low, and I do not believe I de-
serve success?

Stop wasting fuel worrying about yesterday. Just as you would take care of
your car, change the oil, and check it out—take care of your emotional car, so
that it moves you toward your objectives.

Stop when the red light on your mental dashboard signals a necessary
slowdown—but change it to green when, for no real reason except negative
feelings, you would keep yourself from moving forward down the main high-
way toward opportunity.

Stop, and start—this is the way to move toward your goals.

As you formulate them and move toward them, remember your past suc-
cesses and, even more important, see them in your mind as if they were hap-
pening *now*. Thus, your success lives again, in your imagination, so that you live
and breathe the success of the past and project it into the present, thus pouring
psycho-cybernetic oil into the creative engine of your mind.

Stop, but then start again.

2. *Live in the present.* The past is gone; the future is unknown—but
   the present is real, and your opportunities are now. You must see
   these opportunities; they must be real for you.

The catch is that they can't seem real if you're tied in past failures, if you
keep reliving old mistakes, old guilts, old tragedies.

Creative Psycho-Cybernetics means that you focus on goals today and
use the past only to sharpen your success feelings as you move toward your
goals. You forgive yourself for your mistakes and your failures, and you take
a friendly look at yourself and understand that you must stop torturing your-
self and start living.

Fight your way above the many inevitable traumatizations of your ego,
escape damnation by the past, and look to the opportunities of the present.
I don't mean some vague moment in the present—next week or next month,
perhaps. I mean today, this minute.

The past may not be your only obstacle; tomorrow-type thinking can also
block you from your goals. Yearning for a new tomorrow may often be unre-
alistic and negative—especially if you foresee some angel coming to your res-

cue and pressing a magic button for you. There is no magic button—as you formulate your goals and move toward them, remember your past successes and, even more important, see them in your mind as if they were happening *now*. Thus, your success lives again, in your imagination, so that you live and breathe the success of the past and project it into the present, thus pouring psycho-cybernetic oil into the creative engine of your mind.

Stop, but then start again.

3. *Stop belittling yourself.* Too many people do this. Maybe you're not a celebrity or a millionaire or a football hero or an astronaut hero. You can be great if you're a salesclerk or a housewife, or a car washer or a dishwasher, or a garbage collector or a bill collector. Learn from my story about the scrubwoman with pride and courage. A scrubwoman can be a great human being.

Stop belittling yourself. If we were all movie stars, there would be no food on our tables, no production in our factories—and maybe no one to watch movies.

Accept yourself as you are. Otherwise, you will never see opportunity. You will not feel free to move toward it; you will feel you are not deserving.

4. *Try to set constructive goals.* We have enough negativism these days, enough violence, enough cynicism.

Experiments in Australia have indicated that kangaroos do not like loud noises. Well, I'm with the kangaroos. I'm in favor of quiet, purposeful, constructive people who move toward their goals without unnecessarily loud fanfare.

I know of some people who have adopted a child; the youngster's parents died, and he was needy. He needed affection; he needed a home. This couple wanted to help him, and so they adopted him. But they did it quietly. They did not boast loudly about how great they were. They just did it. I admire them as much for the way they handled themselves as I do for what they did.

I feel proud of my nephew Joe also; his goals are quietly, modestly constructive. He seeks opportunity—the opportunity to help other people lead longer, more secure lives.

I went with my wife, Anne, to Cambridge, Massachusetts, to see the Commencement Exercises. Our nephew was graduating from Harvard. Thousands of people had come to attend. We sat with Joe's parents in the rear, under a tree near a dirt roadway. The sun was shining, and it was hot; waiting for the formal exercises to begin, I thought about my talk with my nephew the night before.

He had told me about his plans. He had been on scholarship at Harvard, in organic chemistry; now, he was about to go on to his master's in biological chemistry. He told me that some research on wound healing that I published many years ago had excited him very deeply and had influenced his thinking to the point that he was determined to pursue research in chemistry, on the life of the cell. He told me of his determination to do research, to find a clue to the cure for cancer, to make a serum that would prevent it.

This was no wild-eyed boasting, no loud conceit. We discussed some technical points; we exchanged opinions. His feet were on the ground; his goal was straight ahead.

I was most pleased with his quiet purposefulness. That night I couldn't sleep. I was excited by his determination, by the wonder of his youthful belief in himself, by the thrill of the commencement exercises the next day.

The commencement exercises were stormy. A student was allowed to criticize the learning process in a ten-minute lecture to the audience, and following his talk, one hundred students—boys and girls—walked out.

Still, the commencement exercises proceeded, and our nephew Joe, along with many others, received his degree. An important step toward the implementation of his constructive goals.

A move toward opportunity.

5. *Stand up to crises.* Don't let them throw you! Fight to stay calm. As I've written in other books, even surmount the crisis completely and turn a crisis into a creative opportunity.

Refuse to renounce your self-image. No matter what happens, you must keep your good opinion of yourself. No matter what happens, you must hold your past successes in your imagination, ready for showing in the motion picture screen of your mind. No matter what happens, no matter what you lose, no matter what failures you must endure, you must keep faith in yourself. Then you can stand up to crises, with calm and courage, refusing to buckle; then, you will not fall through the floor. You will be able to support yourself.

Look in the mirror. That's you. You must like yourself; you must accept yourself; you must be your own friend. In crises, especially, you must give yourself support. That is you in the mirror. Don't look at yourself narcissistically, telling yourself you're the most perfect, wonderful, godlike individual on earth, but give yourself appreciation. Remember other crises you've lived through.

See in your mind the ones you handled successfully, the ones you turned into opportunities for growth. Don't let yourself down!

## OPPORTUNITY AND SELF-RESPECT

Five suggestions for moving toward exciting new opportunities. I hope they help you. I think they will.

I feel that this is a key chapter in this book on self-respect because few of us are spoon-fed everything we want and need in life, and we must learn to take advantage of our constructive opportunities if we are to build good lives for ourselves—the kinds of lives that encourage us to feel a strongly embedded sense of self-respect.

In a physical sense, the American frontier and many other frontiers throughout the world are closed—but opportunities remain very much alive. And not just in Outer Space. Some of the greatest opportunities gain momentum in the Inner Space of our minds before they are ready to be propelled out into action.

In the field of education, we find people using "talking typewriters" to help children learn skills such as reading. One group of children, helped by the Typewriter procedure, at the end of the first grade read at the sixth-grade level—according to a prominent test.

New opportunity for children.

And adults? Plenty of opportunity for adults who go at it intelligently, rejecting the passive approach of waiting for opportunity to knock, and instead of building the inner strength they need to open their eyes to opportunity, to move toward opportunity, to seize opportunity.

I mean constructive opportunity, of course, not the kind of opportunism which would enrich you while you trample all other people en route. This kind of anti-social and inconsiderate aggression could not bolster your sense of self-respect.

Indeed, one of the greatest opportunities in your lifetime must be a direct attempt to build your respectful attitude toward yourself. To respect our cultural celebrities and leaders, and institutions is not enough. To live well, you must respect yourself.

Living in this huge world—so heavily overpopulated that some eminent people fear the possibility of a drastic shortage of food at some future time—we are not omnipotent and must sometimes compromise or surrender.

By surrendering, we must win.

You surrender to compassion, however, not to resentment.

To courage, not to cowardice.

To your assets, not to your liabilities.

And you surrender to the opportunity within you that you create for yourself—an opportunity that will lead you to richer living and greater self-respect.

Complicated person that you are, frustrated and yet confident, negative, and yet positive, failure-oriented and yet success-oriented, you count down in the Inner Space of your mind, strengthen yourself, and then launch yourself toward today's opportunities in your world.

# 8

# REAL FORGIVENESS

## ACTIVE FORGIVENESS

AS A TAILOR GIVING HIS FULL ATTENTION AND SKILL TO THE DESIGNING OF A handsome custom-made suit, we build the full and rich power of our sense of self-respect. Each day this is our major objective; each day is D-day, and we sail forth heavily armed with weapons of peace to make new conquests—inner conquests—overcoming the shoreline-to-shoreline resistance of our internal negative feelings and removing from our path the mines that would detonate and destroy us. Forward we march, earning the money that gives us the realistic tools to live, and then using this precious life in a constructive way.

Ours is a very special D-day. As with the D-day of World War II in which General Eisenhower gathered together the full forces under his command and, mustering his courage and intelligence and troops, unleashed his complete concentrated drive on the enemy, we too must concentrate, and focus to move out. But our enemy is invisible, negative feelings; and our goal is invisible: self-respect; and our weapons are invisible (and peaceful), our ideas and feelings and images.

For us, each day is D-day, and we brave the stormy seas in our fragile craft, rising above the fears of our aloneness and our mortality, rushing out of our landing craft, wave upon wave of purposeful determination, hurling ourselves upon our day's goals and grimly bayoneting the self-depreciation that would keep us from our goals.

To repeat, ours is a very special D-day. Our war is not only an invisible one; it is also a humane war, bloodless, constructive, and without casualties. On our D-days—on all our D-days—we seek only our self-respect, only our status as rich human beings.

Even more, we strive to join others—of all nations and races and colors—in this battle for self-respect. On this D-day we wish self-respect for all humanity.

Furthermore, we forgive: We forgive others for their faults. We forgive others for their imperfections. We forgive others for the wrongs they have done us—and we forgive others for the wrongs which we imagine they have done us.

On this D-day—in which we cherish self-respect, and forgiveness—we condemn all war. We condemn war against others, as well as war against ourselves.

For we forgive ourselves, too. We forgive ourselves for all the mistakes of our lifetimes. These are many, but we forgive ourselves for them. We forgive ourselves for all our human flaws—and they are many. As Jesus Christ did, we do—we bring with us into our life forgiveness.

This is a formidable task, this nurturing of forgiveness, one of the key ingredients of self-respect—thus, when we undertake to forgive every day, each day is a D-day. No half effort, no tentative stumble—a real thrust, all-out, D-day.

Let us face it, the history of humanity has been a history of grudge-holding and hatred. From all the religious wars through the revolutionary wars and through our bloody twentieth-century wars, the world—as Alsace-Lorraine and Vietnam—has been a battleground in which Suspicion and Resentment and Greed have joined forces to throw and pin Forgiveness to the mat.

So, on our D-day, we must marshal the forces of our maturity and seasoning, to launch ourselves upon a momentous day of self-respect through forgiveness. No headlines in the newspapers, but we move forward.

What is forgiveness?

I ask this question because what we must seek is a form of forgiveness that is real.

Is forgiveness just a word? Someone wrongs you, you mumble to yourself, "I forgive him," and that's that. Is this forgiveness? Is forgiveness a magical word that you no sooner mouth than—abracadabra—you have wiped the slate clean?

Unfortunately, I do not think that forgiveness comes that easily. It seems to me that forgiveness is much more than lip service. In this sense, noting this objection, I will outline my ideas on forgiveness—which may well be different from the concept of forgiveness on which you have been reared.

To many people, forgiveness is a rather passive concept. You forgive yourself or someone else, lie down to take a catnap, and that's that. You return to the passive void and go back to half-living.

I know a very responsible middle-aged man, who is only half-alive. I meet him in the street now and then and ask, "How are you doing?"

He shrugs his shoulders, bored, and says, "I'm still alive; I get by."

Six months later, I met him and said, "How do you feel?"

He shrugs his shoulders, bored, and says, "I'm still alive; I get by."

A very intelligent man, decent instincts, a good worker, a responsible family man—still, life to him is only a matter of, "I get by."

His boredom, I always feel, arises from an essentially passive way of look-ing at things.

To be passive is, all too often, to be half-alive.

So, with forgiveness.

Passive forgiveness is not good enough. Traditional lip service forgive-ness is not good enough. For full living, we need a more active concept of forgiveness.

Real forgiveness, that which gives you a full sense of living and self-respect, is active forgiveness.

I feel that two stories—one of passive and one of active forgiveness—will clarify my point.

First, let me tell you about a husband and wife, a "forgiving" married couple.

They came to see me. They felt troubled, guilty, and confused. Her mother had given them money to use to buy a house, and somehow, they had lost the money. This was typical of them; I could see quickly. They lacked a sense of direction and moved toward frustration. The woman was obviously too ag-gressive; the man was obviously too passive.

The man had been overseas in the service. While he was away, I learned, she had been unfaithful.

Still, she apologized for what she had done, and he said, "I forgive you." Surely there was hope.

Their personalities seemed to clash constantly. He worked in the chemi-cal industry. She was pushing him, "Why don't you ask your boss for a raise?" He was timid, and so her aggressiveness threatened him; he evaded trying to improve himself vocationally and, in an attempt to escape her domination, warned that he was intending to start flirtations with other women.

Thus, she was unsure of him, but "I would forgive him if he did," she said. "I would forgive him."

All this forgiveness, all this mouthing of the words, but what did it come to? He forgave her; she forgave him. They were still frustrated with each other in all kinds of ways, and, despite the words they used, they seemed bent on destroying each other's self-respect.

My feeling was that they had to learn to forgive in a real and active sense—first themselves, then each other—helping each other to fulfill themselves. She, for example, needed to curb her aggressive dominating ways and to help him to assert himself more forcefully in his work, while he needed to help her as-sume a more balanced role by rising to his responsibilities with more assurance.

This was what they needed: real, active, functional forgiveness going be-yond words to the world of goals and of meaningful activity.

Were they able to do this? I don't know. Time will tell; I am hopeful.

Now, a forgiveness success story—from a failure, an outcast, an inmate of a federal prison.

What this man had done, the nature of his crime—or crimes—I do not know, but he had been a prisoner at Leavenworth before going to the Texarkana institution in the federal prison system.

So, he had much for which to forgive himself; and he did.

In an active way. He did more than mutter to himself as he moped around his chores, "I forgive myself."

At Leavenworth, struggling mightily to do something to help himself, he enrolled in a Psycho-Cybernetics course. Feeling himself on the road to rehabilitation, he transferred to Texarkana and got a Psycho-Cybernetics course started, working to rehabilitate not only himself but other inmates as well.

This is active forgiveness. He forgave himself and others. He did something about it by building his self-image, working to rechannel his life focus, accepting responsibility for himself and his actions, and by trying to help others in addition.

Quite a success story. Here was a "failure" who gave himself forgiveness, did something about it actively, started a twelve-week course to help others forgive themselves too.

This is active forgiveness.

## ACTIVE FORGIVENESS IN ACTION

How do you forgive so that, in doing so, you improve yourself as a human being and increase your sense of self-respect?

1. *Use foresight.* You must build your vision of a good day; this means you exercise clear thinking.

The first principle of clear thinking is to realize you are living in the present where forgiveness does not apply—for forgiveness arises out of yesterday's problems. To start forgiving, you think in terms of the here and now. Renouncing grudges, you plan your present goals, rising above the regrets of yesterday and looking forward to what the new day can bring you if you plan actively for it.

Stop looking backward to misery and mistakes; look forward to new goals and new excitement.

2. *Seize opportunity.* We talked about this already, and therefore I need not remind you that in seizing opportunity you do not trample on

other people's toes or infringe on their rights. Opportunity-building is constructive.

When you look for opportunities and move toward opportunities, you tear yourself away from the hurts of the past. Even if these hurts remain with you somewhat, you neutralize their effect as you build your enthusiasm for new adventures. Thus, you feed your soul and, satiated, you feel no need to keep piling the fires of resentment which come, to a considerable degree, from hunger and frustration.

When you reactivate your success mechanism by reaching out toward new opportunities, you drown out your frustrations with the flood of your fulfillments, and with this active approach, you forgive yourself and others in your generous feeling for your new living.

3. *Develop your insight.* Into what? Into yourself. Into other people— Into the life process itself.

As you develop insight, increasing the scope of your awareness, you build your capacity for forgiveness. Because you move out of a narrow channel of self-centeredness into a wide swath of thinking.

Understanding the imperfections of life, the imperfections of people, the limitations of circumstances, the unhappy reality of death and danger, you stop expecting perfection of yourself and of others. Thus, when you make a mistake, you can feel compassion for yourself, refusing to condemn yourself and to reduce your self-image to the size of a microbe. You can accept yourself, with insight and with the humility that insight can bring, and you can accept others too.

In developing insight, recognize the importance of your thinking and your imaging. Your sense of dignity is a full-time job, a lifetime accomplishment. Your capacity for forgiveness is a marvelous yardstick to measure your value as a human being. No matter what your age, you aim at daily growth and at productive involvement in your world, and at assuming responsibility for yourself and for other people.

4. *Concentrate on compassion.* To feel compassion—for yourself or for someone else—is a wonderful feeling. The compassionate person identifies with the problems of other people and, indeed, feels empathy for others in their troubles. He feels for himself, too— one individual in a vast universe fighting for his place in the sun.

This is not self-pity, which is a negative attitude. It is a positive reaching out with brotherliness.

When you feel compassion, forgiveness comes easy because you understand the frailty of the human situation and the inevitability of mistakes and frustrations.

It is all right to work on your concrete goals—job, money, investments, or whatever. But break free from your more materialistic goals from time to time and concentrate on concession, which leads to forgiveness.

5. *Forget yesterday.* Not completely, of course, but forget the negative quicksand in which you submerge yourself; in a spasm of agony, you go to your doom.

Not that your yesterdays don't have a certain importance, but still, today is your realistic time for living—not yesterday. Too many people yearn for yesterday in a self-pitying way, yearning perhaps for days that were not nearly as wonderful as they think they were. Or they obsess themselves with the mistakes of yesterday, and the grievances of yesterday, refusing to forget them.

Forget and forgive. Or perhaps the more proper order should be forgive and then forget.

Then take an active approach to living and move forward to today's exciting goals.

6. *Try to relax.* Make this a daily goal. Because when you relax, you automatically forgive—yourself and others. You cannot relax while you're holding a grudge; when you hold a grudge, the resentment burns inside you and keeps you from relaxing.

You relax when you rise above resentment with forgiveness to pleasant thoughts and images and feel good about yourself, other people, the world you live in.

Forgiveness to relaxation to pleasure to self-respect is a fine success cycle.

## FORGIVENESS A LA CARTE

This is a rather silly label for this next story, I must admit. Still, the story did feed me—and I hope it will also nourish you.

One day I was in Philadelphia, I climbed into a cab, and the cab driver started talking. I was trying to think about a lecture I was to make to a group of one hundred executives on the art of communication, but the cabbie was very talkative.

"You know," he started in, "the funniest thing happened to me. My wife phoned me at three o'clock in the morning."

"Does she stay out that late often?" I asked.

"Well, actually, she's not my wife anymore. I should have said, 'my ex-wife.'"

"When were you divorced?"

"Twenty years ago. And this is the first time she's called me since then."

"The first time in twenty years?"

"The first time in twenty years—when we got divorced. She woke me from a deep sleep. At first, I thought maybe I was dreaming. But it was her."

"You recognized her voice?"

"Yes—after a minute."

"Why did she call you after all these years?"

"She just wanted to say hello."

"At three o'clock in the morning?"

"Right."

Hello at three o'clock in the morning after twenty years of divorce. Hello, indeed! I shoved my lecture notes back in my jacket pocket; I would talk off the cuff. Hello at three o'clock in the morning after twenty years!

"What did you say to her?"

"I said hello."

An obliging Philadelphia cab driver—why not hello? I leaned forward in my seat. "You mean you never got in touch with her for twenty years?"

"That's right."

"What went wrong with your marriage?"

"I don't know. She was all right, I guess, but she kept telling me what to do and what not to do and what was right and what was wrong and—I tell you, she almost drove me crazy. She wanted to have her way all the time—in everything."

"And you couldn't take it?"

"That's it."

"So, she got sore and left you?"

"No, buddy, I left. I left her. I was up to my ears with all her opinions. One day I couldn't stand it anymore, so I bawled the hell out of her. So, she says, 'If you don't like it, why don't you leave?' I didn't say a word. Why should I? She always got her way no matter what I said. I ate my dinner that night—a good meal, I remember it, she's a great cook—and I went to bed. I had a good sleep. I got up very early. She was snoring. I took a hot tub and brushed my teeth. Then I had some cereal—and left."

"Just like that?"

"Just like that."

"No words, no fight . . . ?"

". . . . No, I had some cereal and left."

"That was twenty years ago?"

"Right."

"And you haven't seen or talked to her since?"

"Yup. Wow, wait till I tell my mother she phoned me at three in the morning!

"For three months. Then I disappeared. I went around the world on a boat—as a deckhand. She had the police after me, but they couldn't catch up with me."

"Where is she now?"

"Down south. She said she has a beauty parlor there."

"Did she tell you why she called?"

"She just wanted to say hello."

"Was she mad at you?"

"Nah."

"Were you mad at her?"

"Nah."

"Was she drunk?"

"She doesn't drink."

"Did she get married again?"

"Fifteen years ago, she said."

"Is she still married?"

"I don't think she is."

"Did you have any children together?"

"A boy. He was four when I left. He's twenty-four now."

"You haven't seen him since? You must miss him."

"Sure, I do. But not her."

"Did she tell you what he's doing?"

"Oh, he's in the army—for good. She said he's six feet two and weighs two hundred thirty pounds." He laughed. "Can you imagine what he'd do to me if he ever got his hands on me?"

We rolled along through the streets of Philadelphia as he laughed and laughed. We passed dozens of grim, worried-looking people as we rode through the streets. The cab driver laughed and laughed as he thought of the son he hadn't seen in twenty years.

"How old are you?" I asked him.

"Forty-seven." He was still laughing.

"Did you remarry?"

"No."

"Do you intend to marry again?"

"Not me, brother. Once is enough."

"How did you feel talking to your ex-wife?"

"It was a nice feeling. We talked about old times, and we had a lot of laughs."

"No hard feelings?"

"What for?"

"No old grudges?"

"Nah."

"Maybe she missed you."

"Maybe."

"Maybe she's sorry—"

"Maybe."

"Maybe she'd like you back."

"She asked if I'd like to come down there and visit her."

"Will you?"

"No, sir."

"Why not?"

"Well, it's like this." He braked the cab and came to a stop in front of my destination. "I may not have much dough—I'm just a taxi driver—but I have one thing nobody can take away from me. And I mean nobody. That's my self-respect. She could never take that away from me. Maybe that's the only thing I do have, but do you know something, I sleep fine at night."

I got out and handed him a bill. "I've sure been talking," he said. "What about you? Are you married?"

"Yes," I said.

Then he gave me my change. "How does your wife like Philadelphia?"

"She's in New York." I tipped him.

"Oh," he said. "You left your wife, too."

"For the day only," I said. "I'm lecturing here."

"Good luck in your marriage," he said. "As for me, I'll be fine just so long as my son doesn't catch up with me." He laughed, waved, and off he went.

Forgiveness a la carte. That's what I like to call this story.

I tell you this story because it has a certain offbeat charm, for one thing, but also because it is good medicine, I feel, for those of us who keep blaming ourselves and other people and who find it so difficult to forgive. A marriage broken so abruptly, yet both principals gave forgiveness to the other—in a real sense, not mouthing the words at all, but refusing to hold grudges, and going about the day-by-day job of living. Such fantastic drama—twenty years between scenes—and yet they could forgive each other without words and say hello at three in the morning.

Now, although I rather liked the cab driver, I am definitely not holding up his actions in any positive light—for one thing, his apparent irresponsibility to his son is far from commendable. The same goes for his apparent irresponsibility toward his wife, too. Still, from all appearances, he forgave himself, his ex-wife forgave herself, each forgave the other; and, in light of their forgiveness under such drastic circumstances and the independent kind of self-respect that both people seemed to seek for themselves, perhaps the little boy had a pretty fair childhood too. I don't know, but perhaps.

I do not tell this story to praise (or to condemn) the character of either husband and wife, but primarily as a helpful aid for those who find it so hard to forgive minor mistakes. In other words, if this cab driver could forgive himself even for these actions, why can't you forgive yourself for your small blunders?

## FORGIVENESS AND SELF-RESPECT

Admittedly, forgiveness is no easy matter. We live in a difficult and uncertain world, and, to the best of my knowledge, the world has always been difficult and uncertain.

Perhaps we can see an individual's problem in forgiving other people if we enlarge the scope of our inquiry and project it onto an international scale.

Here we see the nations of the East seething for decades in resentment at western invasions and at their repeated subjugations. We see little forgiveness or understanding on either side.

Or the people of color murdered and enslaved many decades ago, brought from Africa and debased. Little forgiveness or understanding to this day—on either side.

Or the Irish, impoverished by Great Britain, humiliated, and enraged, cornered in their arid potato farms, hungry. Decades of little forgiveness or understanding on either side.

Or Germany, never forgetting her defeat in World War I, never forgiving—until Hitler came and drove her to her doom in a spasm of maniacal resentment.

Yes, the world has seen great trouble and injustice, little understanding, and formidable violence. And very little forgiveness.

Now, a person who is hounded and deprived and victimized has, in my opinion, every right to insist on fair treatment and to fight for his rights. To discriminate against anyone because of race or color or nationality, for example, is obviously an abomination—but that is not my point. My point is that nations have practiced little forgiveness through the centuries, and great bodies of people have persecuted minority groups most cruelly. Seeing this unforgiveness demonstrated on a world-size scale, we can appreciate how hard it is for individual human beings, fragile human beings, to forgive each other.

When someone hurts you, do not turn the other cheek. I do not advocate turning the other cheek at all. In this and in other regards, my concept of forgiveness is active—not at all passive.

But—and here is my point—after you have actively done what you can to protect your rights and move toward your goals, at this point, you would do well to see what has happened from the other fellow's point of view and try to forgive him for being human.

Maybe he didn't realize he was injuring you. Maybe he was blindly pushing forward on his goals and did not even see you in the way. Maybe he was brutal at the time but regretted this afterward. Forgive him.

Forgiveness for other people is a great achievement, the achievement of a lifetime. You rise above resentment to your real worth as a human being.

Forgive others if you can—but, more importantly, forgive yourself.

For this is the great forgiveness: self-forgiveness. Forgive yourself, and you soar to your greatest dignity as a human being. Like Neil Armstrong, you walk on the moon. Forgive yourself, and, like Galileo or Newton, you explore new areas—in yourself—areas free of guilt and taint, inner areas in which you can build yourself, a giant among men.

You can be a giant among men, because you forgive yourself; an ethical, religious man, because you absolve yourself; a philosopher, because you think of your virtues; a plastic surgeon, because you remove your emotional scars; and a human being, because you thrill to the feel of life without guilt.

If you have erred, forgive yourself—not just with empty words, but actively. This is real forgiveness. Actively forgive yourself, and with your forgiveness, give yourself the inner strength to move out toward your goals. Climb Mount Everest as you ask your boss for a raise you have long deserved. Fight your way through the rough waters of the English Channel as you live through a failure and, forgiving yourself, calmly eat your food and go to sleep. Hack your way through tropical jungles as you communicate sincerely and honestly with a fellow human being.

Real forgiveness. Active forgiveness. More than words. Forgiveness in living.

Thus, each day is D-day for you, a peaceful D-day in which you plot your goals and move on them, actively forgiving yourself and others and winning your great battle for self-respect.

# 9

## THE DYNAMIC POTENTIAL
## OF MIRROR WATCHERS

THIS IS AN AGE OF JETS AND COMPUTERS, AN AGE IN WHICH MAN, EXPLORING Outer Space, has even landed and walked on the Moon. Still, we have with us in our households some of the old, familiar objects.

Like mirrors.

And we can use mirrors usefully and creatively, as a dynamic potential for our emotional growth.

Many people have said that this is an age infected with too much spectatoritis— too much watching. People render themselves too passive to life. Instead of going outside and swatting a tennis ball or belting a golf ball or swimming a few quick laps, they tend to station themselves in front of their television sets and watch someone else performing, armchair participants.

Watching. Not "doing." Just watching.

I am focusing on athletics here to illustrate my point, but I feel that we can apply this concept of too much spectator-like passivity to many areas of modern life. Too many people try, without success, to make watching a substitute for doing.

You can do it.

Because your mission in life is greater than this. You were not born into this huge, sprawling, amorphous world to passively surrender your unique God-given nature to become a depersonalized absorber of impressions, an automaton.

Try mirror watching instead.

Mirror watching can be—if exercised with an honest, creative approach—a most rewarding, enriching pursuit, in which you can combat the depersonalizing forces in our modern world and assert your individuality in a constructive sense.

The creative mirror watcher has a goal in mind; and that goal is not vanity, not narcissism, but focusing on the image within. He builds onto his self-image so that he can use this day, and the next, to move toward a more strongly entrenched feeling of self-respect.

We all know the story of Narcissus, the handsome youth who, seeing his image reflected in a pool of water, fell in love with it. According to the centuries-old legend, he was then transformed into the flower bearing his name.

We know about narcissism—or self-love—in which an individual may fixate his admiration on himself.

The creative mirror watcher, however, is not engaging in narcissism. He is not looking at himself in order to idolize his face. What he seeks is a clarification of who he is, in an emotional sense, and a sharper refocusing on the person he can become.

The man who is a creative mirror watcher, straining to make his day an exciting one, does not aim at admiring the color of his eyes or at worrying about his receding hairline; and the woman is not out to congratulate herself on her latest permanent or to criticize hastily applied powder on her cheek.

Interested in his growth as a person, the creative mirror watcher looks penetratingly for the negation of frustration or for the inner smile of confidence.

Looking at himself with kind eyes, he seeks to find in the image behind his face his sense of identity, his potential for emotional development, his capacity for self-fulfillment, his readiness to forgive himself and others and, blending all these subtle ingredients; he seeks to cook up a nourishing feeling of self-respect.

In the final analysis, this mirror watching is an exercise in orientation. What is it you see as you look at your face in the mirror? Is it not success or failure?

I have, of course, treated the success and failure mechanisms at great length in my book *Psycho-Cybernetics*, outlining the components of these mechanisms in detail, so I will not do that here—though I will in this chapter emphasize several.

My main point is this: As you look in the mirror, searching, on one day or another, for the negative or positive forces behind your outward features, you are then placing yourself in a position to reinforce your success orientation and to fight to overcome your failure orientation.

You may make use of all your faculties and your capacity for adaptation to your environment, or you may not. The following story illustrates how important your orientation is.

## THE MALADJUSTED PIGEON

Circling my apartment in New York City is a terrace with rock gardens, trees, and boxes of growing green shrubbery. Between these boxes of shrubbery are massive stone pillars, two feet square, topped by four heads of sheep; the pillars are solid stone, built in an old-fashioned way—Gothic style, perhaps—and connecting the sheep heads are U-shaped slabs of stone. These U-shaped ornaments—almost V-shaped, because the bottoms come to such sharp points—are a foot high and four inches wide. At the base are crevices slanting downward about three inches deep.

Many pigeons live on my terrace. Now and then, on a summer's day, while I relax on my terrace, drinking a glass or two of beer, I feed the pigeons breadcrumbs.

One day a young pigeon hopped off the head of a stone sheep, where it had been perching, and wobbled toward me. It was a strange gray-white pigeon whose beak was distorted, twisted severely to the side. I threw some breadcrumbs, but the only way this pigeon could pick up the food was to twist its head to the side.

It was a warm summer day—late in the afternoon—and having finished an especially hard day's work, I decided to reward myself with *two* glasses of beer. Which accounts, I guess, for the following conversation—which I relate with, of course, some artistic license:

"You see, doctor, it isn't easy for me to eat."

I nodded my head, appraising its twisted beak. "I know."

"Last time I flew down here, I wanted to ask you—you're a plastic surgeon—can't you fix my beak?"

"It's not easy," I said.

"I see. You don't want to do it because I haven't any money."

"No, that's not it."

"Then why don't you give me a break?"

It was a lazy, hazy summer afternoon. Below, people were surging from the skyscraper office buildings, milling underground in the hot subways, homeward bound. Above were sunshine, sky, and clouds—yellow, blue, and white—with little birds and huge jets whirling through the skies. Reality and unreality, meeting and separating.

"Okay," I said. The pigeon seemed a nice little fellow. "We'll admit you to the hospital later. We'll give you a checkup, and if your blood pressure is normal, we'll go ahead and operate."

"Thanks, doc. You don't know what it will mean to me eating like every normal pigeon."

Then this small, twisted pigeon—"The Runt"—flew off, fluttering its wings to say goodbye, then soaring higher and higher and gone.

I noticed Brownie then—a pigeon I had nicknamed Brownie—this pigeon had visited me dozens of times.

Brownie, with a swishing of wings, whirled from atop a box of shrubbery to take up position on a U-shaped crevice between the heads of two stone sheep. It was only four inches wide.

How could she balance herself in such a narrow crevice? I did not know how, but she did it.

Facing south, she balanced herself on her left clawed foot, hiding the other in her feathers. Aside from moving her wings now and then to keep her balance, she remained immobile in this absurd position for close to an hour.

I was fascinated by the awkwardness of her posture, and by the stubbornness with which she maintained it. I glanced at my watch—time for dinner soon— but still, Brownie continued to face south, balanced in her narrow U-shaped crevice on her left foot, the other foot concealed beneath her feathers.

Then, by some miracle, she managed to turn around in her constricted resting place. Now she was facing north, balanced on her right foot. Five minutes passed, but she stayed in her new, equally uncomfortable position, seeming to remain unruffled in spite of making the worst of all possible adjustments to the possibilities in her pigeon world.

I had to talk to her about this—again, exercising my imagination just a little:

"Hello, Brownie," I said.

"Hello."

"What are you doing there?"

"I live here."

"You mean you sleep here?"

"Of course. Where have you been?"

"All the time?"

"Sure. For months."

"But you must be uncomfortable. You must feel cramped. You are off balance."

"It is my home."

"But there are so many nicer places on my terrace."

"I'm used to this place."

"Brownie, now let's be reasonable." I leaned forward in my chair. "Why stand on one foot facing the wrong direction when you can stand, comfortably, on one of my shrubbery boxes on both feet, facing the right direction?"

"But I'm used to this."

I must make a confession: occasionally, I lose my temper, and I lost it now. What triggered it was the sight of this pigeon—still awkwardly balanced on one foot, twisted to face the wrong direction in terms of the configuration of its body, unmoving. "Look," I shouted. "I just want to help you. You can't feel happy in such an uncomfortable position. It's impossible."

"But I'm used to it." Pointing her nose upward, pigeon style, she indicated her annoyance with my attempts to make her change.

My conversations with pigeons were over for the day. It was almost seven o'clock. New York's office buildings were now strangely deserted, but people, in lesser numbers, walked the streets below. Above, the sun was cooling and, on my rock-gardened terrace, with the massive stone pillars, one small pigeon, body twisted, clung stubbornly to her adopted home.

I went in to dinner.

## WHICH WAY ARE YOU FACING?

Look in the mirror to focus more clearly on your orientation. Which way are you facing? Are you headed toward success, or toward failure?

Too many people live one-dimensional lives, tragically clinging. With pigeon-minded persistence, they refuse to change even when they can improve the quality of their living through doing so.

Too many people—like Brownie the pigeon—use only one leg when they have two legs, in the sense that, fearfully, they lead over-limited lives, refusing, because of their sense of inferiority, to step out strongly into the world on two firm legs that give them genuine movement and mobility.

Too many people—like Brownie the pigeon—fail to see possibilities for improvement and, emotionally distorted, lack perspective.

To repeat. Which way are you facing? Ask yourself this, mirror watchers, as you look for the image behind your physical image—your self-image.

Do you insist on holding fast to a dull non-living existence because of past guilts, mistakes, or fears?

Mixed deep in a sense of your inadequacy, do you move about on one leg instead of two, unable to capitalize on your resources?

Do you, clinging to false beliefs about yourself, encase yourself in a tiny niche, limping through life with complaints and worries, telling yourself that's all you can make out of life?

Do you paralyze your sense of adventure with stand-pat clichés, adapting yourself listlessly to small-mindedness and a merry-go-round without music that goes around in circles of inertia?

Pigeon-headed, like Brownie, do you tell yourself that life is boring and that there is no better outlook for you and that you're "used to" things as they are?

Standing at the poolside, looking down into the glistening blue waters, cool and refreshing, do you refuse to take the plunge? In short, mirror watchers, do you orient yourself toward failure as a way of life, "pigeonholing" all your worthwhile goals until mañana?

If so, communicate this to yourself as you look at yourself in the mirror—your mirror for finding truth. Communicate this to yourself and set about changing your orientation.

Stop facing toward failure!

Resolve to change direction and face toward success!

It may not be easy, but this must be your goal: to use both legs, both arms, all your resources—emotional and physical—to drive you toward success, on all cylinders.

Move toward success, in many-faceted terms. Look, not just for financial success, but for success as a human being who can give to other people, as a human being who can be a brother, as a human being who feels respect for what he is or for what he can become.

Are you willing to make the effort to find the uniqueness within you, the potency, the self-respect?

Or are you willing to settle for a life of dullness and changelessness, living in a narrow space, on one leg, constricted, your potential crushed?

The other pigeon in my little story, who I called "The Runt," tried (with a little imaginative help) to improve herself, tried to get help to overcome her handicap.

You must do this constantly: Work to overcome your handicaps, whatever they may be.

This is real movement toward self-respect.

## STOP COOKING UP FAILURE!

In *Macbeth,* surely a masterpiece of mood, Shakespeare uses the three witches to build a feeling. They circle malevolently, cooking up a premonition of evil fully as noxious as the nauseating ingredients which they put in the pot. You sit in the audience watching the witches, and—even if you never saw *Macbeth* before or read it—you cannot escape the sense of evil that they convey.

This is one of the basic functions of mirror watching: To intercept not evil, but failure. To catch impending signs of failure before they develop. To see failure in the making, head it off, and reorient yourself toward success.

Let me tell you another story:

A man came to see me. He had read *Psycho-Cybernetics.* He was forty years old and very unhappy. He had been an only child in a troubled family. Other professional help had failed to change him.

"I lost my job," he said, "two months ago. I was selling insurance, but I wasn't selling enough. I really prefer the investment business, anyway. I was glad to get rid of this job."

"How do you feel about your chances now?" I asked.

"Now? "

"Yes, now."

"Well," he said, "you write about having a goal, a worthwhile goal that is right for you. I think of good ideas, and I want to follow through, but then the same thing always happens. Always."

"What?"

"I can't control the negative thoughts that hit me—I feel that I'm no good, that I'm a failure, that I'll lose. These negative thoughts—I don't know what's the matter with me. I end up getting drunk, and I get fat from overeating."

I could see he was overweight, though not drastically so. But drastically, he was overloaded with depression and failure, and self-defeating drives. Here he was truly overweight.

"The other day," he said, "I was driving in Boston. I was thinking what a failure I am. I tried to resolve to diet and think thin. But then I started thinking of this pizza place in the suburbs. I tried to shake this thought, I was trying to lose weight—but I couldn't shake it. Well, you know—pizza, beer. Some diet."

His background had been troubled, and he described it despairingly: masochistic mother, alcoholic father, alcoholic uncle, alcoholic grandmother and grandfather.

"I never felt loved," he said. "I'd like to love somebody.

Maybe I don't know what I feel—anyway, I get drunk maybe three times a week."

"Your mother didn't drink?"

"No, she never drank. She had a sense of shame and guilt for the whole family. She hated herself, and hated that I had to grow up with all the drinking going on."

"She wanted you to grow up with self-respect?"

"I guess."

"But you haven't?"

"No. I try, but I fail at everything."

"Did you ever have a good girlfriend?"

"Who would want me?"

"Girls could like you."

"Oh, come on."

". . . if you liked yourself."

"I try."

"How?"

"I do what you say. I try to relax—I close my eyes—and I try to picture my-self happy."

"And then?"

"Nothing happens," he said. "But nothing. All I get is lots of thoughts about what a failure I am. And let's be frank about it—I'm not much good."

"Is there anything you want to accomplish?"

"Sure."

"What's that?"

He leaned forward. "I want to feel good," he snapped.

"And what else?"

A spark in his eyes; for the first time, I saw determination. "I want to have good thoughts. I want to make money. I want a good emotional life."

"Anything else?"

Lightning sizzling from the heavens, the words bolted from him. "I don't want to be poor anymore. I've been poor since I was a kid. I don't want to be alone. I want friends. I want leisure. I want a good life."

Ah, I thought, here, in this passion for life, here was the hope for him. Aloud, I said, "You must feel better about yourself."

His shoulders slumped, and he fell back, dejected once more, into his chair. "That's not easy."

"That's true," I said. "It's not easy. It's not easy at all. You've had some rough experiences. Rising above them is not easy. But what you have to feel is this: It is possible.

"Every day, you must work to improve your opinion of yourself. You must forgive yourself for your failures and forget them; you must forgive your mother, too. You are not responsible for your family problems; you did not create them. You must have compassion for yourself, for your own troubles and problems—but you must not drown in them. You are more than troubles and problems and failures. You are a human being—you fight, you try, just now, I saw you fight-ing; in your eyes, I saw you fighting for your right to lead a good life, and I heard you, too. You have a right to feel happy and successful—if you work for it. You have a right to block off negative feelings and give yourself peace of mind. Do you want to exercise these rights?"

He nodded his head.

"Every day, make it a goal to try to feel better about yourself. Forget the past. Concentrate on the present. Live today.

"Every day, look at yourself in a mirror: You have two images you can see—the unloved, deprived, frustrated person from an alcoholic home or the confident, successful person you can be."

"I have no successes to see."

"Yes, you have. They may be few—but you have successes—and if you can regain your successful feeling, your successful image of yourself, if you can bring it full-strength into your imagination, if you can keep this good feeling about yourself alive in your imagination, then when you look in the mirror you will see there possibilities for moving toward success."

He shook his head. "I can't remember any successes. I get drunk, and I eat too much. I'm overweight. I can't hold a job. I haven't even got a girl.

"Why, I . . ."

"All right," I said. "You've had more than your share of failures. But you have had that success feeling. Maybe not often—but a few times, anyway, and that's all you need. I know you've had it. I saw it just a few minutes ago. Your eyes flashed with determination—I saw you—and you talked like a man who had a goal, many goals, that he believed in. You talked passionately about them, without guilt or fear for a few seconds—and that was a success."

"It was?" he said.

"Yes," I said, "that was one of your moments of success. Forget your failures; remember that moment."

He soon left, but came to see me four months later. He was still depressed. He was trying hard, but he could not feel good about himself. I told him to keep trying.

A year later, he came to see me. He had lost twenty pounds and was in the investment business. He felt better about himself at times, though at other times, he still hated and despised himself. He was trying hard to live in the present; time would tell whether or not he would make it. We shook hands, and I told him to keep trying.

## MIRROR WATCHING AND YOUR POTENTIAL

We live in a world of positives and negatives—and we ourselves, citizens of this world, are composites of positives and negatives.

Injustice in this world? Yes. I never bury my head in the sand to deny it.

Humanity, by and large, has historically lived through centuries of enslavement. Until the Industrial Revolution, the common man labored from dawn till dusk. Until the Reformation, the common man had no freedom to think about religion.

In India, grave injustices have for centuries been inflicted upon groups of people called "untouchables." These poor people have for centuries been chained to an inferior status because of some supposed wrong committed in a previous life. Brutally unjust—yet reality for many, many years.

In our nation today, we have great privilege—but injustice, too.

Still, the greatest injustices today, by and large, are the injustices you inflict on yourself:

When you consign yourself to failure.

When you refuse to forgive yourself for past mistakes.

When you deny yourself the right to happiness.

There is a scientific experiment that was performed on frogs. Live frogs were placed into tubs of water, and slowly, ever so slowly, the water was heated. The question was this: When would the frogs, feeling the danger of ever-mounting heat, become alarmed and leap out of the tub to save their lives? Slowly, more heat. Slowly. Ever so slowly. More heat. Still more heat. But applied so slowly, so imperceptibly, the frogs did not notice it. Without even attempting to escape, the frogs boiled to death.

Which brings me back to Brownie the pigeon, who had grown accustomed to her uncomfortable perch on my terrace. These frogs were "used to" what seemed to them the same temperature of water, so slowly was the heat applied.

In accepting uncritically what they were used to, the pigeon endured endless discomfort, and the frogs met their horrible fate.

And my point is this: You must not accept a life in which—because you are habituated to it or because you are afraid of change—you bore yourself to death.

You must not short-change yourself, denying yourself the right to live fully, insensitive to the possibilities of more successful adaptations to a world in which you must create your own justice for yourself.

Every day, be a creative mirror watcher, looking for success, not failure, out to find your dynamic potential—even if you are over sixty-five, like me. At least, I think I am over sixty-five—I don't really waste my time counting, I just love to use my time living.

Look in the mirror for the image behind your physical image.

Don't be afraid! That face won't bite you. It's you—and you must give yourself justice. You must be your best friend.

You've seen that face before? You're tired of looking at the same nose, the same eyes?

Oh, but you're not looking at nose or eyes. You're looking behind them into your self-image.

A creative mirror watcher, you look through failure to success. You look through obstacles to goals. You look through mistakes to accomplishments. You look through a sense of inferiority to a sense of self.

A creative mirror watcher, you seek to unearth your full potential as a human being.

Doing the best job with yourself that you possibly can, congratulating yourself for your determination to better yourself, you move toward a feeling of self-respect that gives sunshine to your days.

# 10

## TEAR DOWN THOSE PRISON WALLS!

ON WE GO IN OUR GREAT TREASURE HUNT, SEARCHING FOR OUR SELF-RESPECT. Ours is a hunt which requires effort, application, and determination—not a children's game, in which we scamper around digging up objects superficially hidden here and there.

To locate our treasure—our self-respect—we must gather all the energies we possess so that we can overcome the defeatism of negative feelings, preoccupation with meaningless superficialities, and our empty, non-living tendencies.

How do we do this?

Explaining this, plotting the route, is the purpose of this book. Summarizing our progress to this point, we place stress on developing our understanding of ourselves and of others—and on building an attitude of sincerity, carried forward into the world. We, in addition, stand guard vigilantly, sentries always alert, protecting ourselves against the internal undermining triumvirate of deadly enemies: uncertainty, resentment, and emptiness. We will refuse to compromise with this trio—we will not let them take hold of us.

What then?

We look for opportunity. We do not wait for it to knock; no, we actively seek it. We will look for opportunity on worthwhile routes toward objectives which will enrich us, aiming to build our success feeling without hurting or trampling on our fellow brothers and sisters of the human race.

We forgive ourselves and others—actively, not passively. We rise above lip service, to ideals of forgiveness that float meaninglessly heavenward, to a sense of forgiveness that is active, concrete, visible, and human.

Our tools are thoughts and images, success—feelings and goals—they are very powerful tools. We can use them in many creative and individual ways—as in mirror watching, when we look in the mirror to discover or rediscover the good in ourselves, the success in ourselves, the meaning for our lives.

Now, let us tear down those prison walls!

Prison walls?

Yes, now let us tear down the prison walls that you have built around yourself, walls inside which you serve your life sentence, stone which blocks your emotional movement, confines you rigidly so that you live your days passive and bored, and isolates you from other people until, in solitary confinement, your soul dies while your body lives on.

A drastic statement?

Maybe so, but I do not doubt that millions and millions spend their lives, eating themselves up with guilt and shame, punishing themselves for their past mistakes or even their very human feelings, submerging themselves in a beehive imprisonment in which they sting and sting themselves as a way of life. They have political freedom, but they are not free; they have life and breath but are not really alive; and they have mobility but are emotionally immobilized.

Our convict population consists of human beings waiting inside prison walls, dreaming of freedom.

Millions of other people—who are free to walk the streets, the parks, and the beaches, free to work in offices, factories, and on farms—build walls around themselves. They sabotage their own positively channeled aggression, and, in deformed and excessive conformity, they crush their best human feelings. Even worse, they are "stool pigeons who inform on themselves; they accuse themselves of crimes; and they condemn themselves to their bleak internal prisons.

The aim of this chapter is liberation from self-imposed imprisonment.


## HANDLING TRAGEDY AND DISILLUSIONMENT

First, why do people build walls around themselves? Why do they restrict and confine themselves—unnecessarily straitjacketing their emotions and handcuffing their natural aggressiveness?

There are, of course, many reasons; complexity is, unfortunately, often the rule in life. But I think it is likely that many people imprison themselves in shocked reaction to terrible tragedy or disillusionment.

Someone beloved has died or suffered a grievous misfortune, or some close friend or member of the family has given them (or so they think) an unforgivable blow, depriving, deserting, rejecting. Worse still, many people feel responsible for a catastrophe that happened to someone else.

Recoiling in horror from life's uncertainties and dangers, fleeing from difficult reality, they then may build prison walls around themselves in frightened defensiveness, resigned to spending their lives imprisoned, bored, not really living *but safe*.

Now we must face this: Our lives are not Cinderella stories—there is no magic coach with horses and no one waving a wand over our destinies. Most of us will have to cope with tragedy and disillusionment at least a few times in our lives; so, we'd better learn to deal with it.

A loved one may die—that is reality. We may suffer the loss of job, or money, or status, or our business may collapse. That is reality. We may be rejected: by a friend, a sweetheart, our wife or husband, our mother or our father—that, too, is reality.

How do we deal with tragedy and disillusionment? How do we handle despair and grief? How do we live with the disappointed awareness that sometimes we are powerless to control crucial forces in our lives?

We feel sorrow—we are human beings, and it is as simple as that. We feel sorrow, we feel deprivation, we feel resentment. We are not made of stone, so we react. Unashamedly, we may feel depressed; without guilt, we may feel discouraged. It may take us time to rally our fighting spirit and get back to ourselves, but we will.

We must get back to ourselves—this is the key to handling crushing tragedy or disillusionment. We must fight our way through our depression, our sadness, and our rage and get back to our successful way of seeing life, and of seeing ourselves. It may take time, but we must rally our feelings of enthusiasm and adventure and begin living fully again.

The alternative is building stout defenses to protect us—prison walls.

It may be that you have imprisoned yourself emotionally without experiencing the trauma of tragedy or disillusionment. In any case, my basic point is this: If you have built prison walls around yourself, you are only half alive. You owe yourself more than that. You must tear them down if you want to live fully. There is no other way. Money cannot do it for you, and neither can property or material goods or travel or anything else.

Only you can do it.

Prisoner, tear down those prison walls!

## THE BUS DRIVER AND THE SALESMAN

Let me tell you two more stories—one about a bus driver and one about a salesman.

The bus driver was in his early thirties. He was a slim, good-looking, young fellow, but I noted a listless and unhappy look in his eyes. He came to see me, and we had a long talk.

"You have to help me," he said. "I feel rejected. Maybe I'm not much; I don't know. I feel filled with rejection. Every time I meet a girl, she rejects me. They all do."

We saw things through different eyes, he and I. I saw a slim, clean-cut, good-looking young fellow—he saw only "rejection." I asked him about himself.

"Girls turn me down," he said. "All the time. They don't like me."

"You're a good-looking guy," I said.

"They reject me. Well, not completely. Twice I almost got married, but they were pushing me so hard for marriage that I rejected them."

"You rejected them?"

"Yeah, come to think of it, I did."

"Tell me about yourself. About your family."

"My father's dead; he died when I was twelve. He was a good father, I guess, but he smacked me around, I really didn't like him much. I liked my mother better—she was kind of bossy, though. Anyway, sometimes I used to wish my father was dead. When he died, I think I felt responsible."

"What did he die of?"

"He had a heart attack."

"And why did you feel you were responsible?"

"Well, I remember I wished he was dead. More than once, I wished that. Then he died."

"Did you kill him, or did he have a heart attack?"

"He had a heart attack—of course."

"Then it's ridiculous to think you were responsible for his death. Don't you realize that?"

"Yes, but. . . ."

"You must stop blaming yourself for your thoughts. He used to hit you, and sometimes you hated him—but you are not responsible for his death. He had a heart attack."

We talked about his current life. He was a bus driver, lived with his mother, and rejected himself constantly. As he talked, I could see the walls of inhibition and of limitation he had built around himself—perhaps in reaction to his father's sudden death when he was twelve. (I couldn't really be sure of this.) He thought of himself as a prisoner; he had even built his own prison.

"As far as I can tell," I said, "you are living in the past. You keep rejecting yourself—maybe it's because you still blame yourself for your father's death. But remember this: You are thirty-one now, not twelve. Your father has been dead nineteen years. You must stop blaming yourself for whatever happened in the past, especially since you didn't even do anything. It was a tragedy for you that your father died when you were twelve, but you've got to stop hating yourself and live in the present. Today. Accept yourself. Look at yourself kindly. Forget the girls who have rejected you. Forget the girls who you have rejected. Live today."

Now the salesman.

I met him in Memphis, Tennessee, where I was speaking to a thousand or so salesmen on the art of communicating to other people through your own self-respect.

I was on the speaking platform early and watched the people crowding into the auditorium. It was hot. People came in, took their seats, then removed their suit jackets.

A man in a light summer suit walked down the aisle, he was gray-haired, slim, in his fifties. He caught my attention as he moved halfway down the aisle—because I could not see his hands.

I watched him as he worked his way past other people and took a seat at the side. Laboriously, he removed his suit coat. In his shirtsleeves now, he sat down again.

Now it was clear; he had no hands.

It didn't seem to bother him at all. Two other men came over to join him, and they chatted companionably until I began my lecture.

He listened attentively as I talked. I was fascinated by him because he seemed so contented despite his handicap, and I found myself frequently facing in his direction.

Later, I talked to him. He told me about himself, and I felt extremely moved. About eleven or twelve years before, he had been crippled in a railroad accident.

Before the accident, he was physically sound. Afterwards, he had no hands. For a while, he thought of suicide. Finally, he rejected this idea, but what next for him?

A few years passed, and then he read my book *Psycho-Cybernetics*, which, he told me, gave him new hope.

He had a goal in mind—selling machinery parts for a local concern. He moved relentlessly toward his goal. He began thinking once again in terms of success; he began setting in motion his old success images. He was selling; he was selling well. Now—with no hands—he was a top-flight salesman.

He talked with me a while, then turned to greet someone else he knew. A friend of his came over to talk to me about him. "He's not this way all the time," he said. "He has artificial hands. Why he even drives his own car."

The "handicapped" man turned around, a smile on his face.

"Too damned hot," he said. "I didn't feel like wearing them."

Without a trace of embarrassment, he laughed. His friends laughed, too—without self-consciousness. No need for self-consciousness, or pity, or tact.

This handicapped man had no handicaps. For a few years after the accident, he had lived in his own prison, yes. But now, the walls were gone. He had no hands, but he could laugh—and he was free.

He had brightened my day for me.

## UNLOCKING YOUR TRUE PERSONALITY

Now, how about brightening your own day?

How?—by tearing down those prison walls and unlocking your true personality.

Here is the crux of the problem. If, in fear, you have built prison walls around yourself, defending yourself against your feelings and against your basic humanity, you are only half alive. Your true personality is imprisoned—you might not even be aware it exists. Don't you want to get in touch with yourself as you really are, hiding behind those stout walls?

Here are my ideas on how you readjust yourself if you wish to try to liberate yourself from your self-imposed jail:

1. *Get in contact with your aggressiveness.* Understand that you have the right to be aggressive if you don't use aggressiveness to hurt and destroy other people.

Misdirected aggressiveness is oriented toward failure, but constructive aggressiveness is essential if you are to express yourself fully, build your sense of self, and move toward your goals. If you have denied yourself the right to exercise constructive aggressiveness, you must unchain yourself from this prohibition.

2. *Focus on your goals.* You are ready to do this when you have given yourself the right to aggressiveness. Indeed, aggressiveness needs goals just as goals need aggressiveness.

Each day, have a goal, or goals. Ask yourself where you're going and what you want to accomplish. Don't accept inertia and aimlessness. It's great to be alive; it really is. You can move in all kinds of exciting directions—life is full of rich possibilities.

Sometimes you'll be frustrated, sure. Sometimes you will defeat yourself, or others will, or external forces beyond your control will defeat you.

But then, there's always another day—and new goals. Goals that mean something to you. Not to others, to you.

Set your goals. Then feel that aggressive spirit and channel it so that you move toward the realization of your goals. Toward success. Out of prison and moving forward. Concretizing the fresh feel of your real personality, free to seek constructive self-expression.

3. *Accept your individuality.* Understand that you don't have to be just like everyone else; you have a right to differ from other people.

In *The Magic Power of Self-Image Psychology*, I wrote at length about the problems of conformity in our increasingly mechanized and standardized civilization. This is still a difficult problem for many people, who may inhibit themselves drastically and needlessly, imprisoning their true personalities, so they can act the way they think other people expect them to act.

Now, civilized men pay a price for the safeguards and the rewards of civilization; they must follow a number of rules for the good of all. When you're driving a car, for example, you stop when the light turns red. This is a rule—and there are others—to which you must conform.

But you have a right also to preserve the uniqueness of your personality; you have a right also to insist on your individuality. When you place yourself emotionally behind prison walls, locked up behind bars, you overconform. In an emotional sense, you wear the same uniform as everyone else and live cooped up in a tiny cell; you cannot let yourself expand when the opportunity arises.

It is basic to my theory of Psycho-Cybernetics that you live in your own image—not as someone else would like to see you. This is liberating; you create and build.

If you have locked up your real personality, hiding it from a world you fear, fight for the courage to unlock it—to give it freer and more constructive expression. Then build on your new, success-oriented, goal-bound, self-created personality and feel the self-respect grow.

## THE WOMAN WHO COULDN'T TALK

"Okay," you may think, "I'm more inhibited than I need to be. I never assert my opinion—not even with friends. But these prison walls you write about, I just can't tear them down."

Why not?

"Because I'm used to them, I guess."

Lo and behold! We are back in the last chapter with our stubbornly misoriented pigeon-facing in the wrong direction, awkward, but unable to change. This is the power of habit, the tyrannical power of habit.

Change is no easy process. Our habits help us to function without thinking; changing basic habits may be painful.

Even with young children, who must change their habit patterns in order to grow up, we see the slowness of change often. A very young child may throw a ball and forget it. It may take many, many months before he thinks to observe the trajectory of the ball in the air.

With adults, habits are deeply embedded. Change can be most difficult.

But impossible?

Not at all.

Let me tell you, for example, about the woman who couldn't talk.

There was no organic problem. She *could* talk, but she didn't because she was terribly shy and dreaded talking to people.

I met her after a lecture I delivered. She came up to me and started telling me about herself: How shy she had been! How, although a woman, she almost felt like standing up when other people came into a room where she was sitting!

How lonesome she felt! She was married, had two children—but she often wondered why her husband had married her. At many social occasions, she couldn't talk to anyone, so great was her feeling of inferiority.

Most gratifyingly, she told me that she had begun to change, to talk, to break out of her unreasonable prison walls two years before after reading my book *Psycho-Cybernetics*.

She set a goal for herself: a job in real estate, selling houses. This goal fired her with enthusiasm. She got her job, and she worked at it. She began to find her proper image and to lose her shyness. To sell, she had to talk, and she did talk. She talked enough to sell homes to people, and more people. She talked with enough enthusiasm to become one of the top real-estate salespeople in the area.

Talkative, friendly, she told me of how once she just couldn't get herself to talk.

In two years, she had changed. She had broken through her self-imposed imprisonment to real achievement and self-respect. This woman forgot her awkwardness and self-consciousness while involved in the dynamic process of doing. Out in the world, doing, concentrating on her goals, feeling her love for life, she used a practical activity as a fulcrum through which she climbed to a new sense of confidence.

This points to one of the key concepts of Psycho-Cybernetics: that you use your imagination to build your success feelings and formulate goals, and then take action in constructive ways.

You all have interests—and they may lead you, too, along the road to creativity and productive self-realization.

When you express yourself through them—positively, purposefully, assertively, and bubbling with life—you are tearing down those prison walls.

## THANKSGIVING EVERY DAY

Do you remember, when you were a youngster, reading about the first Thanksgiving?

Our ancestors in New England decided to set a date for giving thanks for the year's harvest. It was a rather disappointing harvest that year—1621—but they were grateful for it. Feeling a spirit of generosity, they also sent an invitation to the nearby Native Americans; Chief Massasoit and his followers accepted and dispatched their contribution to the feast: five robust deer. The joyous feeling of reaching out in friendship was contagious; the Plymouth Colony sent out a hunting party to shoot wild turkey and other game, and they returned from the wilds with game aplenty. At home, the women were busy making cornbread and preparing cranberries. At our first Thanksgiving, the tables were piled high.

Huge fires blazed outdoors; turkey, deer, and other delicious meat sizzled as the New Englanders and the Native Americans, in friendship, enjoyed the first Thanksgiving feast in our national history.

It lasted three days. There was feasting, singing, and dancing and wrestling and running races and even a cannon salute. Everybody gave thanks—for the food, the warm fires, and the joy of being alive in an era when people lived short lives and had to take full advantage of their opportunities for celebration. You, too, give thanks that you are alive. Make the most of every day.

We are, I fear, living in an age of pessimism. Too often, we overlook our blessings and obsess ourselves with our anxieties. Unlock your real, basic personality. Seek your real wealth—your creative self-expression, your freedom to accept yourself as a dynamic and unique individual, and your ability to see yourself as a person of importance who has the right to happiness.

To stop the flow of your happiness is easy. You can always find a newspaper headline to frighten you or a negative thinking acquaintance to depress you. You can always find a disease to worry about—or economic pressures, or taxes, or other images of some vague impending catastrophe. You can always feel rejected when others frown instead of smiling at you.

But you are the provider of your happiness. You are the host at your feast of Thanksgiving. You are the one who must stoke high your blazing fires of contentment.

You, with your good opinion of yourself, through the good graces of your self-image, can pile your tables high with the emotional food that can sustain you through good days and bad—until you reach out to the Thanksgiving feast that is success.

Even when your harvest is disappointing—when your income falls, or your marriage is at low tide, or you have a fight with your boss, or your car needs overhauling and you don't have the money—if, in your imagination, you feast on vibrant images of your past successes, you can heal your wounds, feel the strength of your resources and give thanks.

You can even, exulting in your resurgent strength, extend the hand of generosity to other people, giving them your spirit of Thanksgiving and of self-accepting plenty.

Thanksgiving can come every day in which, unafraid of the unknown terrors of inner space, you tear down those prison walls that block your constructive, goal-directed aggressiveness and keep your self-image weak.

Thanksgiving can come every day in which, freeing yourself from unrealistically constricting inhibitions, you live for that day (for your new creative day), feasting on the joys of what the new day will bring you.

Thanksgiving can come every day in which, rising above your past failures and forgiving yourself for all your mistakes and human imperfections, you choose to warm yourself with images of success and feast anew on what you can make of the new day.

And, most important, Thanksgiving can be celebrated even on a bad day, a wretched day, a day in which everything goes wrong, a day in which you move from mistake to mistake. Even on such days, you can still accept yourself, still you support yourself, still you feed yourself.

But, first, you must tear down those prison walls and, unchaining your inner resources, find yourself and develop yourself as the kind of person you want to be.

This is no easy task. It takes hard work, and it takes patience and determination.

Moreover, the freedom you seek is a responsible form of freedom. In terms of your actions, you must, of course, follow some rules and obey our laws. I advocate freeing your personality of unreasonable limitations, not irresponsibility. When you escape from your emotional imprisonment, you don't go around stepping on other people's toes; you use your new, hard-won freedom constructively.

And then?

Self-respect.

You must respect yourself because you are trying, oh so earnestly, to find yourself as a free person.

You must respect yourself because your aims are constructive, and you seek to give—to yourself and to other people.

You must respect yourself because your goal is so worthwhile, and because it is necessary to achieve your greatest possible fulfillment as a human being.

# 11

## TRANQUILITY AND SELF-RESPECT

Into the second half of the twentieth century we go, where the great masses of struggling humanity search—for food to eat, clothes to wear, and money to give them security. Rising above these basic considerations, they search for their identity as creative, well-motivated, integrated people—no easy task in an overpopulated, changing world in which an individual may feel like a meaningless speck in an endless universe.

This search for the best that is in us is our search for self-respect—with tranquility.

When you go to buy a suit, you try it on first to see if it fits. The shoulders, the waist, the back of the suit jacket, do they fit? The trousers? How about the waist and the length? Do they fit? No matter how exquisite the suit, it will not look good on you if it doesn't fit.

The same principle applies to self-respect; a turbulent, volatile self-respect will not wear well. It will not give you satisfaction. The suit of self-respect you wear each day must come from stronger material; look for 100 percent tranquility on the label.

Tranquility is next in our voyage in search of self-respect. We must not bypass this stop; for if we do, we may destroy the meaning of the whole voyage.

Recently we were, via television, witnesses to one of the great exploratory voyages in the history of the human race: landing a man on the moon. Who would have believed it? When I was a kid, we talked about moon travel as something silly and impossible—like Santa Claus or "haunted houses." Who would have believed it: a man on the moon?

Yet, there they were, our three astronauts, on their way to the moon. With our own eyes, we saw them reach the moon. We saw it on television; when I was a kid, we didn't even have television.

There was Neil Armstrong, the first human being to set foot on the moon in the history of the world. Deftly, they avoided a crater, and there they were on the surface of the moon in their lunar module. Armstrong walked on the moon. Then Buzz Aldrin walked on the moon. The two men walked on a Sea of Tranquility; they walked on the solid surface, weighing only one-sixth of their weight on earth, and their small footprints carved out a "giant leap" for the entire human race.

What did they find? Superficially, they found rocks, dust, craters, a barren wasteland with no sign of life. Further findings? Time will tell.

Thousands and thousands of people, and thousands more, were involved in this great adventure of mankind—and billions and billions of dollars financed it. Man on the moon. What a magnificent adventure; what can approach it in excitement?

There is just one personal adventure for which you do not need billions of dollars or the teamwork of thousands upon thousands of helpers. This great voyage is particularly remarkable in that transportation is free.

Your destination? The land of tranquility.

Others have made it before you—but it is a crucial voyage for you to take in your determined search for self-respect. You may not make headlines with your spectacular technical virtuosity. Your tools are not even visible. But *you* will understand the importance of your accomplishment.

A momentous success in Outer Space, wonderful! A soul-building exercise in Inner Space, more power to you!

There are millions of anguished, suffering people in our world, forever running, jumping hurdles, vaulting over obstacles, tripping themselves up, tying themselves in knots, and rushing—forever rushing.

Your destination is more promising. The land of tranquility has no rocks or craters and no dusty, barren wasteland without life. You will find greenery all around you, refreshing and stimulating; gorgeous flowers of all colors scent the air lovely with their perfume; luscious fruits grow on strong trees; and nourishing vegetables can be found in abundance. Is this what the land of tranquility looks like? Or is this fantasy?

You tell me because you create this land. As the director of your destiny, as the governor of your personality, as the commander of your forces, you create this land of tranquility inside yourself.

How?

That is what we will consider in this chapter—the creation of tranquility leading to self-respect. The heart of your search for the good life.

A voyage of exploration, in the most genuine sense. Don't wait for tomorrow; start today.

## YOUR DAILY DOZEN FOR TRANQUILITY

Now, in reverse, I will briefly spell out your daily dozen for tranquility: twelve negative forces that you must combat if you are to succeed in reaching the land of tranquility. Afterward, I will spell it out in greater detail.

Every day, in your mind, while you are taking a walk or quietly sitting in a chair, when you have time, focus on these twelve negative forces and wage war on them—so that you can have peace.

Tranquility, how to lose it:

1. Tension.
2. Resistance.
3. Arrogant aggressiveness.
4. Negation as a way of life.
5. Quandary.
6. Unbelief.
7. Inferiority.
8. Life of loneliness.
9. Laissez-faire.
10. Irritation.
11. Trepidation.
12. Yesterday Incorporated.

Succumb to these negative forces, and you will never know what tranquility is. Combat these forces, overcome these destructive forces, and then your voyage will be underway: toward the land of tranquility.

1. *Tension*. Tranquility and tension are opposites; they cannot co-exist. Life brings with it problems and tensions, but stresses and strains are there for you to overcome, not to retain as a way of life. You can look at tensions as stimuli giving you creative opportunities to prove yourself and find renewed respect for yourself. With an active approach to living, you move through life's tensions to your goals; then, with tension shrugged aside, you can relax.

Change creates tension because people must readjust to newness, and this is always difficult. Change is so rapid in our swift-moving world, vibrating to the constant dynamism of our complex technology and its multifaceted products, that many people give in to the tension habit.

Above and beyond the load of tensions that we cannot avoid, we burden ourselves with unnecessary tension; we worry about things that never happen and bury ourselves in obsessive anxieties. We take a passive view of life's uncertainties. This passivity renders us helpless to forces we cannot cope with; so that we can only tie ourselves up with tension in our helplessness.

To overcome tension, you must take a more active approach to living. Wake up in the morning and think of something constructive to brighten your day. Then get off your back and, fighting off your worries and your doubts, get out into the world and live the best way you can. After a good go at your goals, you are ready for your trip to the good land—tranquility.

> 2. *Resistance.* Resistance can be positive. Take, for example, the "resistance movements" that were organized in France and other European countries during World War II to oppose the Nazi tyranny by slowing down troop movements, blowing up bridges and railroad tracks, and hiding and protecting people the Nazis wanted to kill.

When your resistance consists of negation of your successful goal-directedness, you produce only frustration and destroy not your enemy, but your emotional friend—tranquility. When the French Resistance in the early 1940s dynamited a train full of Nazi war munitions bound for the front, saving the lives of American doughboys, that was a good thing; when you sabotage your worthwhile daily goals, placing roadblocks all around you in resistance of your legitimate satisfactions, that is not so good.

For your peace of mind, you must fight off your own self-defeating resistance to your worthwhile plans. You must appreciate that you have rights, that you are deserving, and that you are a decent human being with an overpowering need for happiness. You are not inferior and unworthy. You must not stop yourself in your tracks with the crippling negation of your inner resistance to your growth.

When you overcome your resistance, cast off your chains, and reject your prison, you can travel to the golden land of tranquility.

> 3. *Arrogant aggressiveness.* We all need aggressiveness to move toward our goals. When you move toward goals which are within your training and your other capacities and which are socially constructive, your aggressiveness in pursuing these goals serves you well. Indeed, this constructive type of aggressiveness spurs you on to achievements.

But arrogant aggressiveness is a different kettle of fish. It is asking for trouble—and trouble is what you'll get.

The arrogantly aggressive individual is ruthless and inconsiderate. He will tolerate no interference with his goals; he cares nothing for other people's feelings and will step on their toes or crush their egos with his dominating personality to reach his goals. In his arrogance, he recognizes no limitations; in a sense, he's a baby reaching for his bottle; he wants that bottle and will raise an earth-shaking commotion if he does not get it and now.

This arrogant type of aggressiveness naturally disturbs the equilibrium of other people; it then rebounds from others back to the initiator of all the trouble. Thus, arrogant aggressiveness leads to all-around chaos.

Thus tranquility begins when you learn the difference between taking from life and giving to life. When you learn to give to life, you will be able to take happiness from life, because happiness belongs to you. You will also give consideration to other people, because happiness belongs to them too. Your aggression will be goal-directed and constructively channeled—not an exercise in ruthlessness or unbounded egotism.

4. *Negation as a way of life.* Will this lead to tranquility? Of course not. Anyone can see that. But is your vision clear—or is it blurred?

I met a man who had "blurred vision."

His wife phoned me recently. She said, "I'd like to see you with my husband. He has blurred vision."

"Well, that's not my . . ."

"He was just examined by specialists," she went on. "They found nothing wrong with his eyes."

"Oh?"

The words poured out, overflowing. "We love each other. I read your book *Psycho-Cybernetics.* We have our children. The last one was a Caesarean. I studied for the opera."

"All right," I said. "You're going too fast for me. Why don't you and your husband come to see me?"

And there they were, opposite me. He was slim, in his early forties; she was shorter and stockier. They talked about themselves. He was an engineer. He said he liked his job, but he kept insisting he could get more pay if he switched. She had studied singing for many years. She had always loved to sing but had made no professional appearances.

"How long have you had blurred vision?" I asked.

"Two years."

"Tell me about yourself. About your background."

She answered for him. "His mother died when she gave birth to him, and his father died when he was two. His grandma took care of him. He told me when he did something wrong, his grandma would not hit him; instead, she hit her own head against the wall."

"And you? What about your singing?"

He answered for her. "It's my fault."

"Why? "

"We met in Germany years ago. We were married. One child came, then another."

"The last one was a Caesarean," she said.

"I love my wife," he said, "and my children. But I'm not happy."

"He doesn't feel he deserves to be happy," she claimed.

"I see trouble ahead of us," he said. "I always worry about what will happen. I keep worrying about everything. I don't relax very much. Maybe we'll go back to Germany. I can get a job in West Berlin for five thousand dollars a year—maybe I'll take it. But I don't know. Maybe I shouldn't."

I handed him a book. "Can you read this page to me?"

"It's blurred," he said.

"But the eye doctor said there was nothing wrong with your eyes?"

"He found nothing wrong."

"I find something wrong," I said.

"You do?"

"But not with your eyes—"

"What, then?"

"Your image of yourself is blurred—you do not see yourself clearly. You use negation as a way of life. Apparently, your eyes are fine—the specialists told you that—but you are still living in the past, blaming yourself for all your painful yesterdays. You probably blame yourself for your mother's death and your father's death, and you keep feeling guilty. And do you blame yourself for your grandmother's hitting her head against the wall?"

He said nothing; he just sighed.

"You keep rejecting happiness and choosing negation," I said, "you blame yourself because your wife had children instead of a singing career. You love your wife and children, and yet you bury yourself in yesterday's pains. Then you start dreaming of tomorrow—you'll change jobs, you'll go back to Germany, you'll do this or that—but that ends up in negativism too. You have a yesterday-tomorrow complex and it's all negative. You see images of yesterday and tomorrow—and they lead you only to negation. Your image today is blurred; that is what is blurred."

"What should I do?"

"See today," I said, "and live for today. To focus your vision, look for a happy today. Forget the painful images of your past and your fantasy images of your tomorrow; concentrate on today, every day, and do your best every day to defeat your negative feelings and create happy days for yourself and your family *now*."

He nodded.

"Now. Today. Those are your keywords. Not yesterday. Not tomorrow. Now."

Incidentally, I heard from this man about a year later. His vision was no longer blurred.

Back to you, reading this book: How is your vision? Do you seek tranquility, or is your vision blurred?

5. *Quandary,* you may spend your life in a constant quandary; many people do. Your days are unfinished symphonies of indecision. You stop and start; you turn around. Who is that worried-looking fellow staring at you? Oh, it's you. You saw yourself in the mirror.

The hard-to-face reality is that many of your decisions will be extremely difficult. You will suffer through the twin tensions of conflict and uncertainty; indecisive, you may find yourself in a continual quandary, wandering around in circles, searching for your sense of direction.

The Louisiana Purchase—now that was a bargain! For $15 million, the United States bought from France an enormous mass of land—room for fourteen new states. Overnight, with this fantastic purchase, the United States was almost doubled in size, extended through the Mississippi Valley and west to the Rocky Mountains. It was perhaps the greatest real estate bargain in history; our nation bought all this land at a price of about two cents an acre. Napoleon felt he had to sell cheap. His troops had been disastrously defeated in Haiti, and, giving up his dreams of empire in the Americas, he sold us the Louisiana territories at bargain-basement prices. The decision was then in the hands of the United States government: We bought the territories from France in April 1803. A good decision. But an easy one—and this is my point. A very easy decision. A fantastic bargain. A rare, almost once-in-a-lifetime opportunity.

Just as the United States, as a nation, must ordinarily make decisions of much greater complexity, drawing hairline conclusions and weighing all sides with great care, so must we, as individuals, make many difficult decisions every year, every month, perhaps every day.

Do we then spend our time in a quandary? Are we never to know what it is like to feel peace of mind?

No, we achieve tranquility by transforming a destructive quandary into a constructive certainty. We do this by accepting ourselves when we make poor decisions as well as when we make wise decisions. We do this by looking at our failures through kind eyes and by consigning them to the past where they belong. We do this by building an image of ourselves that will stand up under trying conditions. We do this by seeing our full potential as human beings.

6. *Unbelief.* Another non-component of tranquility is unbelief. When you do not believe in yourself, you waste great amounts of precious time trying to imitate others. This is a great destroyer of inner tranquility: carrying someone else's image in your imagination; giving someone else this power in your mind when this power rightfully belongs to you.

Unbelief is a passive attitude stemming from self-doubt and leading to defeat and despair. Doubt comes from error, and when you decide to forgive yourself and forget yesterday's errors, focusing instead on the confidence of your past successes, you take a giant step toward destroying unbelief and laying the foundations for peace of mind.

7. *Inferiority.* When you walk around day in day out, feeling a sense of inferiority eating away inside you, obviously you cannot know what it feels like to attain tranquility.

So, you must out-wrestle this self-dooming sense of inferiority; you must throw off this blanket of gloom that keeps you passive to a world in which you make other people superior to you.

Are others as superior as you think they are? No, they are just people—people with problems and anxieties and eccentricities, some of which they try to hide from you, so you won't think they are inferior.

Why do you see them as superior? Because you make mountains of your mistakes. Because you cannot forgive yourself for your human imperfections. Because your enormous and surely unreasonable guilt chokes off your creative self-expression, and you punish yourself constantly for your mountainous mistakes. You feel, then, if you do this, that since you are so worthless, other people, by comparison, are superior to you.

Furthermore, since you feel you are so inferior, you may carry this inner destructiveness out into inadequate performance in the world. Thus, you may reinforce your inferiority complex, as you prove the inferiority of your image in life.

To alleviate this self-destructiveness and move toward the land of tranquility, you must forgive yourself for your mistakes—past, present, and future. You must develop more human attitudes toward yourself. Tell yourself you deserve another chance. Wouldn't you say that to a friend?

8. *Life of loneliness.* You feel lonely sometimes when you are in a crowd of people, just as you can feel a substantial feeling of brotherly warmth when you are alone. Thus, loneliness is a feeling, not a physical state.

Loneliness is also a feeling of dread—you are separate, you are cut off, you must cope with the pain of your sense of isolation.

But, as the late Wendell Willkie insisted, we are One World. Even before our modern jets and spaceships, we were, in a sense, one world. European culture through the centuries is a prime example of how cultures influence each other. Europeans learned much of Greek science from the Arabians. The mariner's compass came from China. Other inventions that helped revolutionize European culture were the spinning wheel from India, and the hot-air turbine from Tibet.

Just as European culture was no isolated phenomenon, you too are no island. You are more than an individual—you are also a member of human society. At times you may separate yourself, to feel your unique selfhood more fully, but for peace of mind, you must also feel a sense of brotherhood—and perhaps of identification—with other people.

9. *Laissez-faire.* I do not mean the economic philosophy urging a governmental policy of non-interference, but rather your attitude of accepting things as they are with an overly passive attitude. You don't even try to change things.

You may think that such a non-interfering and "laissez-faire" attitude toward life brings tranquility, but it does not. It brings passiveness, apathy, and inertia—not the same thing as tranquility at all.

Contrary to what many people think, you must adopt an active approach toward tranquility. You must work for it.

You must fight for it. You must want it very much. You must move toward your goals; you must keep fighting for them; you do not give up easily. You feel your energy bubbling in you as you move. Then, when you stop driving and relax, you are truly tranquil.

10. *Irritation.* A disease of the age? A symptom of our "age of anxiety"? Maybe so—but maybe irritation has always been a precondition to living.

Either way, my point is this: We must consider how to handle our irritation.

We cannot run and hide. You will always meet people who will irritate you. You will always face situations which will irritate you.

What do you do?

You utilize the healing power of forgiveness. After you have tried your hardest to make the best of your irritation, and your continuing irritation is only a form of self-destruction, you forgive. You forgive others, and you forgive yourself. There may have been considerable provocation, but you forgive and forget.

As you do, you move toward the cool green pastures of tranquility.

11. *Trepidation.* In the chronic sense, trepidation means anxiety as a way of life: Tranquility-minus—as in the case of a young woman who came to my office not too long ago.

She was a beautiful woman, married, in her early twenties. Before she married, she had been the beauty queen of her country, Santo Domingo. Life had been good to her.

Then, suddenly, it happened. While riding in a car that her husband, a financier, was driving, there was a terrible collision. The husband and six-year-old daughter escaped injury. But the wife suffered a terrible deep wound of her cheek running into the angle of her mouth, and the skin over the left nostril was torn from her face.

She burst into tears as she told me her story. She had lived in despair since then. Many times, she had thought of suicide. She forgot how to laugh. How could she regain the inner peace she had once known?

In the operating room, she was placed under general anesthesia, and I began to repair the damage. I removed the scar tissue of the cheek, undermined the opposing edges of the wound, and approximated the skin edges with interrupted sutures of fine silk. The angle of the mouth was now normal—so was the tissue of the cheek. Except for the stitches, both cheeks were once again symmetrical. A circular piece of skin about the size of a nickel was removed from behind her left ear and grafted into place over the nostril defect; it was kept in place with interrupted sutures of silk.

Ten days later came the big day; time to remove the final dressings; time for the fearful confrontation.

She was the picture of dread. She insisted that she would not look in the mirror. I coaxed her. Finally, she looked apprehensively. Then, joy swept over her, and she wept.

"I thought I'd never be myself again," she cried.

"But you are," I said.

She kissed her husband. She kissed her daughter. She even kissed me. We all laughed. The cloud of trepidation was gone.

I do not really tell this dramatic story for illustrative purposes. I tell it for comparison, to help you who must overcome the emotional scars—not the physical ones—that cause so much anxiety in people. You must be your own emotional plastic surgeon. With compassion for yourself, you must forgive. Your emotional scars are invisible—not as in the dramatic case of the beauty queen—but they may cause you chronic consternation. You remove them when you forgive yourself for your past thoughts, for your past actions, and for all the mistakes of yesterday. When you have successfully removed your emotional scars, you will begin to live in the present—with tranquility.

12. *Yesterday Incorporated.* I have written, in *Creative Living for Today,* about mañana-type thinking. The members of Mañana Incorporated have dedicated themselves to delaying almost everything until tomorrow. Their belief in "tomorrow" is so fervent that they never do anything today.

The members of Yesterday Incorporated also do nothing, or very little, today. They live in the past, not the future—but the result is the same: very little creative living today.

Recently a lovely woman, married and in her early thirties, came to my office. She was beautiful, but her eyes mirrored a deep sadness.

She told me about her father, and how she had loved him. He had died four months before, and she grieved for his passing. She insisted, again and again, that she could not get over her father's death.

"He was a poet, a philosopher, a great man of the Bible," she sobbed. "He was such a fine liberal man—so compassionate. I loved him so much."

She told me about her husband, a high school teacher of French, and her two children, a boy, and a girl. But inevitably, she returned to her father. "I married out of my faith, but my father understood."

"Is your mother alive?"

"She lives in Jerusalem."

"Permanently?"

"I hope so."

"What do you mean by that?"

"I can't get along with her. She was against my marriage. She complains all the time. She always complains about her health, but there is nothing physically wrong with her. I think she plans to come back to New York, but I don't know how to get along with her. I miss my father."

"You want my advice?"

"Yes. I've read your philosophy; it is simple, easy to understand, compassionate—it is as if you were writing about my father."

"That's fine," I said. "But you must understand that you can't live in yesterday. To have peace of mind, you must live today. It's wonderful that you loved your father, but you can't keep living in the yesterday when he was alive, protecting you, inspiring you. You can't hide behind your father of yesterday away from your mother of yesterday. Respect the memory of your father—but live your own life today. He would have wanted you to. That is the way to reward him—and yourself. Live today."

You, too—if you are a member—resign from Yesterday Incorporated. This corporation has no earnings, declares no dividends, and is headed for bankruptcy; so, resign. You will find the land of tranquility only when you live for today.

## TRANQUILITY: AN ACTIVE CONCEPT

I have spelled out the roadblocks that keep you from tranquility. You must defeat these negative forces in order to make your voyage to the land of tranquility.

You will notice that—as with sincerity and forgiveness—you should look upon tranquility as an active concept. Many people connect tranquility with lying passively in a hammock, rocking gently, stirring yourself only to brush a fly from your nose or to answer the call for dinner.

I do not agree with this. I see the passive person as one who, in his inertia, makes himself helpless to cope with life's dynamisms and therefore lives with fear and uncertainty, not tranquility. I don't really refer to the occasional hammock user who enjoys resting there now and then.

The person who moves toward tranquility is the constructively aggressive, goal-oriented individual—brotherly in a doing sense—because he gives himself the weapons with which he can master his destiny.

Change does not unsettle him because, reacting to life with an active philosophy, he moves out to deal with change and to adjust to it in a successful way. Thus, he is able to live with tranquility even in an era of rapid change—even in our swiftly moving twentieth century.

Serene, quietly confident, he moves to cement the positive orientation of his life. Calmly, he builds his house brick by brick—and no fleeting wind can knock it down.

Actively, with faith in his powers to create and to make decisions; in his reality and in his mind, he manufactures for himself that greatest of nonmaterial products: tranquility. As a by-product, proud of himself and of his creation, he also creates self-respect.

Tranquility—and self-respect.

# 12

## THE ACTIVE LIFE

### NO RETIREMENT CLOCK

WHEN YOU SEARCH FOR YOUR SELF-RESPECT, ONE THING YOU CANNOT DO IS RE-tire from life. This is inconsistent with self-respect. When you throw in the sponge, you throw away your dignity. Retreating from life's battlefields, resigning your commission in the great human army, you are then a traitor to yourself and render yourself vulnerable to attack and defeat by onrushing hordes of negative feelings.

In the last chapter, I wrote about a man with "blurred vision," who needed to refocus his emotional forces. Well, people who retire from life also suffer from "blurred vision." People with foresight stand up to life's problems and, though they may seek physical or emotional solitude now and then, they rally their inner strength and return to a sense of full participation. Like General Douglas MacArthur, they come back to win.

Or at least they try.

No retirement clock for them—they prefer self-respect.

What is a retirement clock? Is it the clock that chimes out the age of sixty-five, ushering you into a land of rocking chairs and soft cushions?

No. I have written enough about the perils of age sixty-five. I have written many pages about the quicksand philosophy with which too many people doom themselves at sixty-five, dragging themselves down to an inner death as they tell themselves that they are too "old" to do anything or have any fun.

No, this retirement clock is a mechanism that knows no distinctions of age. For people may withdraw from life at five or fifteen as well as at sixty-five.

There is a retirement clock in all of us. It ticks away useless seconds, useless minutes, useless hours. It ticks away in people of all ages when, submerging themselves in negative feelings, they waste their precious time in worry, frustration, and retirement—from life and from their sense of aliveness.

Our world is fast-moving, and time is a key element in our lives. How could it work without clocks—in airport terminals, railroad stations, savings banks, telegraph offices, mass production factories, and department stores?

In the home, too. What kind of clock do you have in your home? Is it electric, or do you have to wind it up? Is it an alarm clock? A grandfather's clock, ticking away? Or do you have a wristwatch? Is that the "clock" in your home?

It really doesn't matter—just so it tells the time, just so it keeps you in tune with the world.

The worst clock in the world is your retirement clock. A stopwatch doesn't really stop you. You may use it to temporarily "freeze" time and show how fast your friend can run. Your retirement clock, however, can stop you. If the ticking of your retirement clock hypnotizes you, pulls you away from your belief in yourself and in the world of people, and draws you away into a desert where nothing grows, you must cast off its influence and escape from the monotony of its beat. You need an alarm clock to ring out harshly, awakening you from your stupor, shrieking out against your inertia, warning you that you must wake up to the meaning of life—which is living.

You need an alarm clock to summon you from a life of sleepwalking to a life of constructive doing, to bring you back to a concentration on your goals, to shock you into movement toward life, and to jet-propel you from vague dreams to stark reality.

I have long felt that most people do not really understand the meaning of self-respect.

Self-respect does not mean perfection. It does not mean complete realization of all your dreams. It does not mean that you are better than everybody else. It does not mean anything ideal, absolute, or all-powerful.

Self-respect means this: You seek, and you search. You do your best. You are sincere in your desire to make yourself the best kind of person you can. You accept yourself as you are, with all your limitations, and accept other people too, with compassion and brotherliness. You forgive others, and yourself, in an active sense, making your forgiveness real—in action as well as in thought.

When you exercise your resources, day after day, week after week, developing yourself as a human being, reaching out to other people in friendliness, moving toward constructive goals in your world, overcoming your negative feelings to feel more life, refusing to let external defeats and your own mistakes stop you, relishing life's daily challenges, then you feel self-respect.

Then no retirement clock inside you ticks away minutes of withdrawal from life.

Then you fight off the guilts of yesterday, and the fantasies of tomorrow.

You must stop accusing yourself of past crimes; you must refuse to let past mistakes force you into self-hate and panicky withdrawal from life.

And tomorrow?

Stop fantasizing about tomorrow also; live today.

Live in your precious hours and minutes and seconds. Now is the time for living. There must be no retirement clock.

## RETIREMENT OR LIVING: YOUR CHOICE

You have a choice: retirement from life or full living. This is your problem; this is your choice. You are on the fence—which way will you jump?

The retirement mechanism—or clock—ticks away emptiness. We will now examine and spell out its components along with their opposites, giving you both sides of the coin in one toss.

| | | |
|---|---|---|
| 1. | Retreat | RETURN |
| 2. | Eviction | CONVICTION |
| 3. | Tendency to withdraw | COURAGE TO ACT |
| 4. | Impotence | IMAGINATIVE POWER |
| 5. | Resignation | REAFFIRMATION |
| 6. | Evasion | RESPONSIBILITY |
| 7. | Mañana | TODAY |
| 8. | Ennui | EMANCIPATION |
| 9. | No direction | GOAL ORIENTATION |
| 10. | Traitor | FRIEND |

Retirement: an enemy to avoid. These are the components of the retirement mechanism, of the retirement clock, which ticks away emptiness and despair. Alongside them, you also find your alternatives, the components of a rich life, components that bring you closer to your feelings of success

Now let us first examine the dangers you must skirt, one by one. Then let us examine your alternatives, which direct you toward fuller living and self-respect.

1. *Retreat. (The alternative is: Return.)* This is the fundamental concept of retirement. You presuppose a dangerous, threatening world; as soon as you can, you retreat from it. You walk away from its problems and its responsibilities; if you are truly frightened, you run away.

You find much evidence to support your stand. The world is difficult; it changes too fast; people are always fighting with each other, you can't win.

And so, you retreat. You move away from people. You keep to yourself. You go into hiding.

Now I cannot deny that critics of our world score with some of their attacks. Certainly, the world is difficult, anyway. But you can win.

I say to you: Retreat if you must—but then return.

Life is never a series of smoothly flowing victories. Everyone knows defeat and despair. But the fighters, the battlers struggling to fulfill their potentials, return.

As did Richard Nixon, who survived crushing political setbacks and returned—to become President of the United States.

As did the late Franklin Delano Roosevelt, who survived physical misfortune and returned—to lead our nation out of economic depression.

As did the ballplayers on the New York Mets, for years characterized as one of the most inept teams in baseball history, who returned in 1969 to play each game one at a time, living for the day, until they had amazingly climbed the ladder to the top.

Life may seem tough to you, problems endless, obstacles insurmountable. You feel tired and defeated. But keep going, and, following the example of the 1969 New York Mets, underrated and chronic losers, return—to win.

2. *Eviction. (The alternative is—Conviction.)* Are you a victim of eviction? That is, have you instituted eviction proceedings against yourself from the world? From life? From the world of people?

Have you so completely evicted yourself from yourself, having no faith in your own powers, that you flee from a world in which everyone seems so superior to you because you feel so inferior?

Many people do evict themselves, saying they cannot help it, they have had bad breaks, no one ever befriended them, they are inferior.

Maybe they have had bad breaks.

Recently I read about a study of an orphanage in Teheran. Whereas most children sit up alone at about ten months, 60 percent of these orphaned children could not sit up alone at the age of two years. While most children learn to walk alone at about fourteen or fifteen months, 85 percent of these orphans could not walk alone at the advanced age of four years.

Now obviously, many of these children were severely handicapped at the beginning of their lives, slow starters. Here is real misfortune.

But what would you say to them, victims of really bad breaks: Give up? You can't win? Don't even try? It's not worth it?

No, sir. This is eviction, and it is destructive. Deprived children may have to face the reality of their limitations, but must they be forced to face a life without hope?

Conviction is the answer. Belief in oneself. These orphaned children or you—maybe you can't do everything, and maybe you're not perfect, and maybe some people can outcompete you in some areas, and maybe you're not even a little omnipotent. Still, you feel inside yourself a conviction.

You know as a certainty that you do your best and, beyond any shadow of a doubt, you know that you don't give up easily.

Further, it is your strong conviction that your goals are worthwhile.

And you move toward life with conviction; no eviction for you.

3. *Tendency to withdraw. (The alternative is: Courage to act.)* Once again, another "moving-away" symptom—a failure-oriented tendency. This is a reaction to a feeling that life is too tough; it represents helplessness and panic as a way of life.

You must overcome this tendency, if you have it, with all your determination. You must develop the courage to act, even in very trying circumstances, even when you're frightened, even when you make mistakes, and feel foolish or alarmed.

I have my disagreements with some of the existentialist philosophers, but I must agree with their emphasis on a person's facing life, exercising responsibility, making choices.

In my own theory of Psycho-Cybernetics, I stress the concept that, as valuable as positive thinking is, and it is extremely valuable, you must go beyond positive thinking and develop the courage to act—with constructive goals in mind.

In creative Psycho-Cybernetics, you combat your fearful tendencies by refocusing on your past successes, making your happy moments live again in your imagination, over and over, fortifying your sense of self-esteem, so that you can reverse your orientation toward failure and build in yourself the courage to act constructively.

4. *Impotence. (The alternative is: Imaginative power.)* Lack of power, lack of drive. Everyone feels impotent sometimes; that's nothing. But when you feel impotent day after day, week after week, that's something else.

Nobody can exercise a steady control on all areas of his life all the time. This does not indicate impotence, but lack of omnipotence. We should recognize this and understand that when things go wrong for a while, we should not withdraw from the world and from ourselves. We should stay in the world, with its winds and its rain and its lightning and thunder—until we weather the storm.

A short story about a good friend of mine: She came to New York from a small town. Her family was large—many brothers and sisters—and the church played a big role in the life of the community.

She got a good job. She built a fine life for herself in the big city.

Then, one afternoon, she thought of the small town in which she had grown up and of the church. She wanted to do good. She would send the church a check for fifty dollars.

She did. A check was sent from a big-town girl to a hometown priest.

Fifty dollars.

Five thousand pennies from heaven.

And it bounced.

She told me about it, embarrassed. She had only wanted to do good. But she had forgotten to add up her checking balance. Temporarily, she felt powerless. She deposited more money in her account and sent the check out again, but for a few days, she felt she could do nothing good until the church received her new check. Until then, she felt a spiritual impotence—as if nothing could go right with the world.

What do you do when you feel this way? Friend, stay with it! Use your imagination to help you out. Let your imaginative power pull you to your feet—with images of your past successes to help tide you through your period of emotional impotence.

5. *Resignation. (The alternative is: Reaffirmation.)* Your life is bleak. Your wife screamed at you as you left for work, your boss screamed

at you at the office, the traffic cop screamed at you as you drove home (and gave you a ticket). You are batting 100 percent—all wrong.

What do you do? Resign from your job? Divorce your wife? Do you tear up your driver's license? Renounce your citizenship? Resign from the human race?

No, you reaffirm. You reaffirm your belief in yourself (no matter what others think). You reaffirm your rights—to happiness, to pleasure, to self-respect. You reaffirm.

In ancient Rome, toasts were a common formality. The people customarily pledged the health of their friends as they drank their wine. Then the Roman Senate decreed that diners toast the health of Augustus at all gatherings.

Surely there was much pledging of good health in those times.

Reaffirmation? Of a sort, I guess, but not quite what I had in mind for you. When you feel low, when you feel depressed, when you feel like resigning from life, bestow on yourself a liquorless toast. Pledge yourself richness in living, reaffirm your faith in yourself, get back in the ring, and start punching.

6. *Evasion. (The alternative is: Responsibility.)* You can spend your lifetime being evasive, but where will it get you? You can hide, and you can run away; but where?

There is no absolute justice in life. So, how do you react to life's inequities?

I jotted down some statistics on the education of women. One 1966 study showed that women's presence in our labor force was related to their education; that the more educated woman was more likely in the labor force. According to this study, only 45 percent of women who had graduated from high school were in the labor force or looking, compared to 53 percent with four years of college, and 72 percent with five or more years of higher education.

Another study, of gifted college students, indicated that about 50 percent more gifted women than men dropped out of college.

Both studies indicate inequities, though along different lines. I will not analyze them. That is not my concern here.

My point is this: Assuming that these statistics apply to you, or identifying with them in some fashion, with yours the sub-par status, how do you react?

With the feeling that life is not worthwhile, so why not run away and hide?

Or with the determination that, come what may, you will hang in there, take your punches, and continue to accept your responsibilities in our imperfect world?

The choice is yours, but accepting reality and responsibility leads you away from the destructive retirement mechanism to self-respect.

>   7. *Mañana. (The alternative is: Today.)* When you keep putting things off for mañana (tomorrow), you never do them; in your nondoing, you retire from the realities of life.

Today. That's the word for real living. Today.

Recently I delivered some lectures in Miami Beach. At one, I spoke to six hundred women, and before my lecture, they had a raffle. Some women won perfume, a hairdo set, a radio, and some won fine silverware. Others, of course, won nothing.

You take a chance when you bet on a raffle. When you live in the present, you also take a chance. But the rewards are great—when you participate, when you are involved, when you are a doer.

Still, that's the road to self-respect. Living for today. Not for mañana.

>   8. *Ennui. (The alternative is: Emancipation.) Ennui* means boredom, and boredom means you're only half alive. You're not collecting Social Security or any form of pension, and maybe you're still in your teens or twenties, but you are retired.

The powerful boa constrictor eats, sleeps, and keeps right on sleeping until once again hungry.

Not much of a life. If you'll permit me a small joke, not much pressure.

To rise above ennui, you must feel a sense of emancipation. Emancipation—the freedom to feel confidence in yourself and live without unreasonable and constricting guilt crushing your spirit, a boa constrictor crushing your bones.

Free yourself from the past, from the guilts that torture you and the mistakes that haunt you. You deserve to live, a free human being, today.

>   9. *No direction. (The alternative is: Goal orientation.)* If you have no direction, you feel empty. Each day is a dilemma because you are aimless: there is no goal, no movement, no sense of achievement. Soon you do nothing at all. You end up retiring from life.

With goal orientation, your sense of being alive bubbles. You are no longer asleep; you wake up to the opportunities around you. Your sleepwalking is in the past; today is what is important. Your goals bring you out of your daily retirement into a life of meaning.

As I write this, the great cellist Pablo Casals, although over ninety years old, is still a young man. Because he lives for the day. In a recent interview, Casals told a reporter how each day he is born again to live a new lifetime. Casals has lived more than ninety years of goals and excitement. This is real living.

10. *Traitor. (The alternative is: Friend.)* Concluding this discussion of the negation of retirement from life, I suggest that you ask yourself this: Are you a "traitor" or "friend" to yourself?

When you retire from life—and from your image of yourself—you are truly a "traitor" to yourself.

You need all the friends you can get, as the saying goes, and there is realistically one friend you must have—yourself. Befriend yourself, and never retire.

## THE GENERATION GAP

Now let me tell you a story. We have spelled out the destructive retirement-mechanism—the retirement clock and the life forces with which you can oppose it, in young and old. This story, too, is about young and old; it is about what I might call a "generationless gap."

A quiet, friendly, gray-haired man in his sixties came to see me. He was an engineer of Swedish extraction. He came from New Jersey to talk about his problem with his son, twenty-three years old, unmarried, and who lived with him.

He had two other sons; they were married. He was worried only about his youngest son. They never talked to each other after "hello" and "goodbye." What should he do about it?

It was a strange meeting, in that I repeatedly found myself forming interpretations which were then suddenly shattered.

The first came quickly—"generation gap," I thought but later I thought of this as a "generationless gap."

Shortly, I asked him about his wife, and he told me a most unusual story.

Years before, he said, his wife had said to him, "I'm going back to Sweden," packed her valise, and left.

Eight or nine months later, she was back—for two months, then back to Sweden.

It turned out that she had left for Sweden because an elderly man, of eighty, had invited her to live with him in Sweden. She had met this man in New York.

A pattern set in: Each year, she went to Sweden for most of the year, and then she came back to her family for two months or so.

"What a terrible problem this man has," I thought to myself.

Of course, it was, but, to my surprise, the man's problem did not seem to be with himself at all. He evidenced little sense of being rejected. He accepted the situation, unconventional as it was, and did not want a divorce.

"Would you take her back for good?" I asked.

"Would I, yes! The trouble is with the boys."

"What do you mean?"

"This man is eighty," he said. "If he died, I would take her back. I would feel sorry for her."

I marveled at his compassion for a woman who had basically left him. "What's that about the boys?" I said.

"They think we're both doing what's best for us. They accept the way things are."

Another preconception destroyed. I had pictured the boys seriously disturbed by their broken home. "But you indicated the trouble was with the boys?"

"The youngest boy."

"What is the problem?"

"Oh, I don't know. He doesn't talk to me."

"Why not?"

"Oh, I don't know."

"You have no idea?"

"Nope."

"Do you think it has something to do with your wife leaving you to go to Sweden?"

"Maybe."

"Your youngest son is twenty-three, you told me. What kind of work does he do?"

"He has no job."

"He's unemployed?"

"Yes."

"Does this bother you?"

"Now and then."

The man was friendly, but not very talkative. Words just didn't come easily for him. I would see his son, I thought.

The boy was another surprise. The father had made him sound lazy; instead, he was an alert, good-looking six-footer. He wanted to get a job in the banking business; he had confidence he would get what he wanted.

"Why don't you talk to your father?" I asked.

"Oh, I just don't."

"Is it because you don't respect him? Because of what your mother did? "

"Oh, no. I respect Dad."

"Does he keep telling you what to do? Does he pester you because you don't have a job?"

"I want a job."

"Does he blame you because your brothers are married and you're still living with him?"

"Nope."

"Do you have a girlfriend?"

"Yes. For three months."

"Do you want to get married?"

"Yes."

"And you don't hate your father because he's dominating you?"

"Nope."

"Or because he's weak, because your mother left, and he just takes her back?"

"Nope."

"And he doesn't try to force you anyway?"

"Nope. Dad's a great guy."

And, looking into the boy's friendly eyes, remembering the father's friendly eyes, with mounting surprise, I realized that once again, my preconception was false. This was no "generation gap" brought about by the hatred between generations. This was a "generationless gap."

Its cause: like father, like son. The father didn't talk much, and the son didn't talk much. They didn't hate each other; the father was perhaps a little worried about his son, but there was little if any hate. The son really liked the father. Their trouble was that they did not know how to communicate, that their shyness and clipped speech operated as destructive barriers which separated them from each other, bringing about an enforced retirement.

No hatred operated here, but a retirement clock which ticked away in both men: Minutes and hours were wasted. Through mutual ignorance, so common in so many families, they sat silent, withdrawing from each other though they wanted to be close.

I talked to the son about the importance of opening up lines of communication with his father. I told him it was his responsibility—he was younger. I stressed that he had to gather up the courage to do this; that this was a goal of major importance in his life.

I felt that father and son had learned from me—I hope they learned as much from me as I learned from them.

## THE ACTIVE LIFE AND SELF-RESPECT

Which brings me back to an earlier point: The retirement clock is the worst clock in the world. It ticks away wasted time, and it respects no generations. It ticks away in young and old alike.

In this chapter, we have spelled out the destructive components of the retirement mechanism, and we have stressed the positive forces which you can harness to overcome the negatives which would pull you away from fully living.

My theory of creative Psycho-Cybernetics involves an active approach. I believe in an active life, with goals, and with enthusiasms. I believe in constructive thinking and imaging and doing. I believe in full living each day, even though this may mean that, since you are less protected than if you remained passive, you may make mistakes every day.

With an active approach, moving toward living and doing rather than away from it, I feel that you reach out toward your most complete sense of self-respect.

One of your great comforts is that you accept your mistakes; you live amiably with them; you refuse to expect perfection of yourself.

This comforting cushion enables you to come out of your shell, secure in the knowledge that you will give yourself compassion and understanding when you need it. Then you no longer need to listen to the ticking of the retirement clock; because inhibiting fear and crippling self-reproach are muted, you do not waste time worrying obsessively about your actions in the world.

You exercise sensible caution, when necessary, but you refuse to coddle yourself. You refuse also to retire from life's problems, and life's anxieties, and life's uncertainties.

In an active sense, you do your best to make yourself the best human being you can be. What a superb goal! It follows naturally that your sense of self-respect will grow.

# 13

## INTEGRITY AS A WAY OF LIFE

MANY OF US, SUCCUMBING TO THE PRESSURES OF OUR MODERN TECHNOLOGICAL civilization, live fragmented lives. We rush around in all directions, cornered, and misdirected in our confusion, unnerved in our rush to scoop up what we think is good in life, and assuming appropriate facades for self-protection, as we seek to master the many complicated situations we encounter

Too many people lose track of themselves. They probably know where their automobile is because they have just driven it into the garage. They feel secure about the location of their bankbook, they have a special place for it; jingling the keys is reassuring, the key to the house or apartment is right there. The key to the mailbox, to the automobile, to the safe deposit box, are all present and accounted for. It gives people a good feeling to know that everything is in order. But have they kept in touch with themselves?

In most cases, unfortunately, the answer is no. For many people today are not close to themselves.

A couple of years ago, the title of one of my lectures was "The Whole Man: Let's Keep Him Whole." But, come to think of it, I might have rephrased my lecture title and made it "How to Become a Whole Man." Because, though our gross national product statistics are huge and impressive and we are a wealthy nation of hard-working and energetic people, not too many of us are complete people.

But we want to be complete people, and that is our blazing hope. We want to be people of integrity, and that is our saving grace. We seek integrity as a way of life, and this ardent seeking makes us great.

Integrity means wholeness, and a man or woman cannot be whole if he or she is internally divided, at war with himself, with herself. The battleground is not only in Vietnam and the Middle East; it is in the heart of every individual who seethes with negative feelings and who builds a thick wall of resentment inside himself, separating himself from himself and from other people. A man can be financially wealthy but if he slashes at himself with negative feelings, he is emotionally poverty-stricken. He must negotiate with himself; he must declare a cease-fire; he must move toward integrity as a way of life.

You must keep track of many things to survive. The wife must remember to turn off the oven, to lock the door when she leaves to go. The breadwinner must remember to pay his taxes, to meet his insurance deadlines, to get to work on time. Functional essentials. You want to survive—so you remember.

But you want to survive as a whole person. You want your integrity; you want your image of yourself to be a support, not a handicap; and you want your self-image to be hearty and expansive, not shrunk to the size of a microbe.

It is self-respect that we seek and a sense of wholeness or integrity.

Let us keep track of more than our survival functions. We want more out of life than physical survival to an old age. We want to survive whole, and with self-respect. We want to do more than total up years; we want to total years of integrity.

We want to spell out for ourselves a master plan leading to integrity. And that's what we will do now.

## THE "GRIT" IN INTEGRITY

This is no easy task. We must all cope with many pressures and conflicting demands. Survival itself may be difficult. Survival with integrity may be an enormous challenge.

Still, if you spell it out, you will find "grit" in "integrity" and this "grit" you must also find in yourself to make yourself whole.

The components of integrity? Let's spell them out now.

1. Inquiring mind.
2. Natural good tone.
3. Thoughtful focusing.
4. Encountering the you in you.
5. Goal of confidence.
6. Reaching for reality.
7. Industrious involvement.
8. Tenacity in thinking.
9. Yearning for emotional nourishment.

When you go into a restaurant, sit down at a table, and place your order, you hopefully await the return of your waiter with strengthening food. Here, too, we move toward feeding: a basic and strengthening feeding of your capacities for development. Self-service style, though. For you must do more than read; you must want to help yourself.

1. *Inquiring mind.* What is the great gift that distinguishes you from animals? Your mind. It is a great gift if you use it. But the question remains: Do you use it? Do you use it to make yourself a whole, growing, responsible being? Or do you let it stagnate?

You cannot touch your mind as you can your skin, but it is there to use. You respond continually to the needs of your skin—in hot weather and cold, in rain, and in snow. You bathe and don clothing. You use soap and apply lotions. You never are passive about your skin; you react to any threat and move quickly to protect your skin, which covers your vital organs. What about your mind? Do you use it? Creatively? Inquiringly? Remember this: If you do not use your mind, your mind is useless to you.

Looking in the mirror, you see your face. But now, go beyond that; use your imagination to see the face of your mind behind your eyes. Ask yourself: What can my mind do? What is its potential? Am I holding it back from operating—with timidity, or fear of making mistakes? How can I exercise my mind so that it will work for me instead of against me? How can I use my mind so that I feel more complete as an individual? Ask yourself these questions.

You can, of course, survive by playing second fiddle all your life, but why not gather up your courage and lead the orchestra? That orchestra plays beautiful music when you use your mind to see your successes instead of your failures.

With an inquiring mind, you see yourself in perspective. You see your past in focus, but you also see your current and future possibilities. Realistically you see yourself as you are and what you can become. You feel complete as you see the whole picture.

You see other people too. You watch them walking on the sidewalk, talking at restaurant tables, relaxing on planes and trains and buses, browsing in department stores. When you are personally involved with other people, you may not be objective, but when, as a stranger, you observe them, you can assess their virtues and their shortcomings. You can learn from their pluses and profit by avoiding their minuses. As human beings, we share many common tendencies. The person with an inquiring mind can give his energies to the rewarding pursuit of self-improvement—every day, in many ways, and all his life.

2. *Natural good tone.* Just as the natural good tone in the muscles of your body may lead to good health, so may the natural good tone

in the "muscles" of your mind. How do you achieve this? You do so, once again, by exercise.

People will move heaven and earth to get physical exercise—and with good reason, for it's good for them. They will go through agony for physical exercise. During the summer months, people will get in their cars and head for beaches or lakes, crawling bumper-to-bumper, and inch-by-inch for miles until they can break through the city traffic blockages that seem inevitable. Even in the winter, weekend trains are jammed—with skiers and ice skaters. There is also the army of walkers who reject modern technological progress in favor of stretching their legs.

Of course, in getting physical exercise, there is a right way and a wrong way. As a very young man, shortly after World War I, I learned to bicycle in Amsterdam, Holland. I bicycled everywhere. I even used to follow my professor over narrow lanes and bridges, pedaling to the clinics and to the university. Fine exercise, the right way. But later, on vacation in Bermuda, I tried it the wrong way. Showing off for friends, I took off on my bike down a very, very steep hill, full speed ahead. When I picked myself up off the ground, I found I was fortunate—no broken bones.

Physical exercise gives you good natural tone. In stimulating the healthy functioning of your body, you also beef up your feelings of emotional well-being.

Many people swear by setting up exercises to get their day off to a good start. Breathe in deeply, then breathe out. Exercise mornings for good physical tone.

Natural good tone is also essential for you on an emotional level. When you wake up in the morning, walk over to a mirror and look at yourself. You've seen that face before—and you'll see it again and again, hopefully—but what you're looking for is a feeling that you're glad you're you and you're glad that you're alive. Over and over as the days pass, aim at giving yourself this good emotional tone each morning, seeing all sides of your personality, striving for self-acceptance, and wholeness. Reread Chapter 9 on mirror watching for more detailed ideas on this.

3. *Thoughtful focusing.* To achieve integrity as a way of life, you must learn to focus with thoughtfulness and concentration on the complexity of your life—your past, present, and future; your limitations and your possibilities—and weave all the strands together into a coherent pattern. Thoughtful focusing means razor-sharp observation in three dimensions: within you, behind you, and before you.

Before we go into this, however, suppose we all try a little experiment. Seat yourself in a large-sized room and try to focus on all the objects in this room. Spend a few minutes concentrating; your goal is to remember every object in

the room. Now walk out of the room and write down every object you can re-
member. Then re-enter the room and note the objects that slipped your mind.
Chances are that you did forget a number of items, for sharp focusing is no
easy task. I have tried this exercise on some people, using my living room as
the experimental area, and most people overlooked many things.

Why? Because sharp, thoughtful focusing is an art that you develop with prac-
tice. Most people appraise superficially and incompletely. So do not expect your
three-dimensional appraisal to achieve lightning-quick results for you. Focus
thoughtfully but give yourself time. Develop your perceptiveness with practice.

Each day, remember to:

*Focus within yourself,* taking stock of your assets as well as your liabilities,
making an in-depth inventory of yourself, cutting the red tape and the fat, em-
phasizing your past successes and your positive qualities.

*Focus behind yourself,* seeing the past to give you perspective on today—not
to brood over past mistakes and failures—reminding yourself of past blunders
only so that you can avoid repeating them.

*Focus before yourself,* looking to the great day that lies ahead of you, clear-
ing away the smog and fog with your creative enthusiasm.

4. *Encountering the you in you.* Integrity means not only wholeness;
   it also means impeccable honesty. The person with integrity is
   trustworthy; he pays his debts and honors his promises; and his
   word is good.

We are, beyond question, extremely complicated human beings. We are
composites of positive and negative feelings and images. We rise above our
failures only with great effort to our full stature as human beings.

This is how you encounter the you within yourself—the you that you like,
the you whose integrity is unquestioned, the you whom you respect. It takes
great effort and a positively oriented selectivity.

The power of selectivity operates in all of us. The playwright uses his good
material and discards the irrelevant as he weaves his plot and moves to the cli-
max of his story. So do you. You are a playwright too, and your drama is the story
of your life. The big question is: Do you select the you in you? The you that you
like? The you that is sincere, determined, successful? The you with integrity?

In weaving your plot, discard your negative feelings and choose your assets.
Build your play around your success feelings. Your stage props are confidence,
forgiveness, courage. Your lighting is bright; you have nothing to hide. When
the curtain rises and the audience encounters you, you will find that you are
well-received.

5. *Goal of confidence.* Confidence generally leads to a sense of com-
   pleteness and to honest and equitable relations with other people;
   so, we must list it now, in our analysis of integrity, as a worthy goal.

You develop confidence when you keep your eye on the ball.

When you play golf, you keep your eye on the golf ball, then you belt it.

If you don't like the idea of driving for an hour through traffic to the golf
course, then try my version of indoor golf in your living room.

Your wife is glaring at you? She is lifting her most expensive vase above her
head? She is about to throw it at you?

Reassure your wife: her furniture is safe. You will play symbolic golf only.

No golf clubs: you will assume the correct golfing stance, keep your eye on
the imaginary ball, then follow through.

Silly?

Not at all. This exercise is a basic and worthwhile reminder that to reach
your goals you must keep going—all the way to your goal. This is the road to
confidence.

Almost everybody has experienced many near-misses: a big business deal
that fell through at the last minute, a promotion that almost happened, a nearly
successful interview. People with confidence know that they must follow through,
keeping their eyes on the ball even though they are tired, until the signature is
on the dotted line. This symbolic golf exercise can remind you that you must
keep your eye on the ball all the way and follow through completely, or you
will hit the ball glancingly off to the side and into the trees.

Persistence is the basic answer. How did I become a plastic surgeon? By be-
ing persistent and by keeping my eye on the ball, I succeeded.

I grew up on the lower East Side in New York, as I've written, and I survived
the numerous perils of a youth living in a rough neighborhood—enjoyed some
of them, too. I proceeded with my education and finally decided I wanted to
become a doctor.

But it was not until I was about to graduate from medical school that I
decided to become a plastic surgeon. I delivered my first child, and it came
into the world with a cleft lip (a hole in the lip). It seemed insufferably cruel
for a baby to come into the world disfigured, and I made my decision: I would
be a plastic surgeon. I would train myself to help human beings born with
disfigurements, and those victimized later on, from accidents at home, on
the highways, or in industry.

I got little encouragement. My mother, anxious to protect me, afraid I would
not make a good living in what was then a little-known specialty, urged me
to forget my wild dreams, and become a general practitioner. I asked my pro-

fessor for advice; he too discouraged me. When I talked to my friends about plastic surgery, I received blank looks as my answer.

But I continued to keep my eye on the ball and follow through. Because I knew what I wanted. I overcame a great many obstacles, traveled to Europe to study, and finally returned home to practice plastic surgery.

My situation was still difficult. Many people were critical of what they called beauty surgery. They didn't agree that it was the natural right of every human being to have normal features. Furthermore, they didn't understand that behind the physical disfigurements were serious, inner, emotional scars. I opened my office, but my first patient was a long time coming.

Nevertheless, I kept my eye on the ball and followed through; and whatever successes I have enjoyed through the years, and whatever confidence I feel, I attribute to this. Today, more than forty years later, people recognize the value of plastic surgery, and almost any good hospital anywhere keeps a capable plastic surgeon on its staff.

Success in our undertakings, and the confidence that follows, is your goal as well as mine.

How do you achieve this?

Through keeping your eye on the ball and following through.

Through your daily game of symbolic golf in your living room.

6. *Reaching for reality.* Certainly, there are vast surpluses of fantasy in people these days—our mass media sees to that. But, to face reality, that is to face yourself with honesty and with a multi-faceted, complex approach—with integrity, in short.

When you reach out for reality, you may experience pain and depression to some extent, but you nevertheless strengthen yourself. The greatest of the ancient philosophers—Socrates, Marcus Aurelius, many others—believed in a realistic approach to self.

There is one hurdle you must jump, however, before you can accept reality. You must learn one great art: the art of forgiveness.

This is not the first time I have mentioned forgiveness in this book, but if you can't forgive yourself for your mistakes, how can you see yourself other than arrogantly—as a person who never makes mistakes?

Of course, you must learn to forgive others too, but first, you must learn to forgive yourself.

Then you can develop the capacity for sincerity. But remember this: sincerity is strengthening, whereas insincerity produces exhaustion.

We go through life taxing our physical equipment to its limits. We run here and there; we never seem to have enough time. We even bolt our food on the run, producing indigestion and other gastric complaints so characteristic of our age.

But equally exhausting is insincerity. Indeed, insincerity is the mother of exhaustion. People who spend their lives putting on airs, blowing up the balloons of their egos, live in constant danger. Someone may take a pin and, as with a balloon, poof! There go their egos. People who spend their lives fencing, shadowboxing, waging cold war after cold war—what is left to them but to crawl back home exhausted from their arduous life of dodging reality.

The wholesome way to life is reaching out to reality. You do not exhaust yourself; you fortify your energy when you face up to the facts, even when they are unpleasant.

Of course, you can go to the other extreme too. Instead of dodging reality, crawling into a womb of fantasy, you can confront yourself with all the most morbid facts all the time, destroying your peace of mind.

A lovely girl came to see me a year or two ago. She was young and beautiful, and she held the hand of her little girl. But her face was tense with horror. "Doctor, I'll do away with myself." She tried to talk calmly, but it all came out almost in a scream.

"What is the trouble?"

"It's all my fault." She clutched the little girl's hand like a drowning woman grabbing a life preserver.

"What?"

"I'll never forgive myself."

"For what? Tell me what happened."

"She's so active," she wept. "Always running around the apartment. I could never control her. She tripped, and her face struck the glass table." Tears were streaming down her cheeks.

"Let me examine your little girl's face."

"I've ruined her life. She will never forgive me."

The little girl's face was bandaged. She was four years old and frightened by her mother's crying. I removed the bandage. She had a deep, jagged wound on her right cheek near and below her lower lip, A beautiful child, with one cheek severely deformed. The wound was bleeding; I stopped the oozing and rebandaged the cheek.

"My little girl will always hate me. I should have done something to protect her."

"What?"

"I don't know, but it's my fault."

"Why? You didn't do it."

"But—will she be all right?"

"We will have to operate on her immediately."

"She'll be disfigured all her life. I'll run away. I will run away somewhere where nobody knows me. I'll . . ."

"Stop blaming yourself," I said. "Try to calm yourself."

"They'll all hate me."

"Who? "

"My husband's parents. They never liked me anyway. They'll blame me."

I tried to soothe her, but my words had no effect. She was imprisoned in a dreadful reality, a reality-beyond-reality, in which she ended up assuming a totally unrealistic burden of guilt. The torrent of self-blame in her kept overflowing; she could not stop accusing herself.

"And my husband," she cried. "How can he ever forgive me? I have betrayed his trust."

"It was not your fault."

"It was. I'll never be able to face them. My husband will never forgive me. And neither will his parents. My darling little girl, I should have been quick enough to catch her before she struck her cheek against the glass table. Why wasn't I watching her more closely? Why wasn't I able to catch her when she tripped? I can see it all in my mind clearly; how could I be so careless as to let it happen."

My efforts to comfort the mother were useless. The picture of the accident was clearly framed in her mind; nothing could pry loose the horror, or the self-reproach.

I operated on the little girl. Then the days passed. I changed the dressing on the child's face, and I tried to comfort the mother, but she clung stubbornly to visions of the accident and of her guilt.

The little girl and I would play. We didn't talk much, but we played. I would ask her her age. She would shake her head—she wouldn't tell me—I had to guess. I held up the five fingers of my right hand. She said nothing. I showed her ten fingers. She shook her head. Six fingers. No. Three fingers. No. Finally, I held up four fingers, and she smiled and nodded her head. We were friends.

Finally, I removed the stitches. The little girl was calm enough. The mother was tense. One by one I removed the stitches. Finished.

I turned around to see an incredibly sudden transformation. Not that it surprised me; I had seen it before. The young mother's face was a study in mobility—a jet airplane whisking through blankets of fog into blinding sunshine. Her eyes sparkled for the first time in days, and big happy tears poured from them.

"You're still crying," I said.

"Oh." She sat down to wipe her eyes. "Oh."

"Is that all you can say?"

She nodded her head, and I thought to myself: tears for tragedy, tears for happiness. The same, but what a difference!

I have two reasons for telling this story:

First, I want to warn you how you can face up to reality in an obsessive, destructive way.

Second, I want to *show* you how, in facing up to reality, by not minimizing the situation and by coming quickly to see me to try to remedy the damage, this woman had initiated positive action to bring about a happy ending.

Reach out to reality in a healthy way; this is the way to reach out to integrity.

7. *Industrious involvement.* Involvement in what? In making yourself the best human being that you can be. For this is worth industry, and it is also worth involvement.

The world's population continues to grow. I read, somewhere, that experts anticipate an approximate 2 percent increase in the world population each year. This deepens the already-severe problems involved in supplying adequate food for the entire population of the world. At the same time, it makes the successful application of scientific, agricultural techniques for increasing food production even more urgent than it is already. A person with integrity hates to see anyone go hungry and accepts his new role as a world citizen, trying to identify with the needs of all people in our vast world.

Still, his fundamental responsibility is to himself. His industrious involvement centers on himself. His goals: completeness, maturity, creative adjustment to life.

8. *Tenacity in thinking.* Creative thinking, that is.

As a full, complete person, you insist on your right to think for yourself. Many people let others think for them. As you move toward integrity, you refuse to allow this. This is not being arrogant; you are merely asserting your right to individuality.

Integrity, as we have said, implies wholeness, and the well-integrated person sees the world from a balanced perspective. He sees that God has created millions and millions and millions of human beings, all unique individuals, each owing it to himself to nurture the roots of his uniqueness. In an age of conformity, he insists on his right to think for himself.

9. *Yearning for emotional nourishment.* Finally, in spelling out the components of integrity, we come to "yearning for emotional nour-

ishment." While you may aspire to be honest, principled, and complete, you need a feeling that you can reach out to feed yourself, in abundance, to feel the full satisfaction of well-balanced integrity.

There is an old Saxon toast. The devoted lover, letting the sharp edge of his poniard lightly cut his forehead, dribbled his blood into his wine cup, and then drank the mixture in honor of his beloved. Physical nourishment? Emotional nourishment? I know it's too strong for my tastes.

But this custom, centuries old, and now a barbarous anachronism, seems to me symbolic of the human yearning for an overpowering nourishment process which seems basically of an emotional nature.

If you don't eat, you don't live, but in our technological age, eating is an emotional process. To be a full person, you need "food" for thought, "substance" in your relationships, a "wholesome" motivation.

## INTEGRITY AND SELF-RESPECT

Reread this spelling-out exercise whenever you have some spare time.

Integrity is a key component of self-respect; because the individual with integrity is balanced, thoughtful, and responsible. He gives other people a sense of security; surely, he must give himself as much.

"Integrity," you may say. "Who has time for it?"

You.

"Me? I'm so busy most of the time I could hardly tell you my name."

But you have to find time to develop integrity. Just as you must find time to build in yourself such fine qualities as sincerity, understanding, the capacity for active forgiveness, and creative mirror-watching. What are you without integrity? A hunted animal? A clock watcher? A robot?

"Words," you may say. "More words. They don't mean anything. Integrity. One more word."

You think so? Then you are wrong. In my theory of creative Psycho-Cybernetics, we move from words, to images, to action. To see how, turn to Chapter 15, "Goal-Builders," in which we will work on practical exercises for self-respect.

But for now, take time to develop your capacity for integrity. Do you have time to cook supper? Or wash your car? Or go to the salon? Or the barbershop? Do you have time to pay your income tax? Or make a bank deposit? Or to open your mail and read it? Then you can find time to work with yourself on your most important emotional level, building a sense of wholeness, of rational perspective, of sincere trustworthiness.

Integrity. If you have it, how can you not respect yourself?

In a dinner, dessert and coffee follow the main course. In your emotional life, self-respect follows integrity.

Our search for self-respect is no wild, far-out scramble. We build qualities and capacities; we focus on positive concepts and images. We go from integrity to self-respect.

# 14

## SURVIVAL WITH SELF-RESPECT

SURVIVAL IS, OF NECESSITY, A BASIC HUMAN GOAL. IT IS A TIMELESS GOAL. DOWN through the centuries—from the flowering of Greek culture to the savagery of the Crusades in the Middle Ages to today's dynamic, ever-changing world, everyone has struggled for survival.

Life, a precious gift. We fight to preserve it. We fight with all our resources.

Still, we seek more than mere physical surgery in the theme of this book and, indeed, of cybernetics. We seek a constructive form; seek a survival that is meaningful and honorable. We seek a live, give-and-take form of survival.

Physical survival is in itself a fine, instinctive aim. That many people are successful in living to an advanced age is obvious; social security statistics will illustrate this, I am sure.

But we seek more than this: We seek a qualitative survival. A survival with self-respect.

This is no small accomplishment; you cannot reach it overnight or by pushing a button or mouthing a few magic words. It takes hard work and purposeful thinking—imaging which surfaces into positive action.

Where do you start?

By understanding, to begin with, that survival with self-respect is a human possibility. That you can make it a lifetime goal and still cling to sanity. That you can make it a lifetime goal and rise above sanity to full living.

This is an age of confusion and cynicism, and millions upon millions of people have come to doubt themselves. It is one of our greatest tragedies that so many people today feel disillusionment, not hope; humiliation, not pride in self; debasement, not self-respect.

When you set a goal, you must believe in that goal. Therefore, if survival with self-respect is your goal, you must believe you can achieve it. When you have your goal in focus, only then can you move toward it effectively.

In the early 1900s, man was still struggling to fly; and it was a struggle.

Many were skeptics and felt that man would never fly. Samuel Langley was one of the world's most eminent scientists. The newspapers gave enormous publicity to his flying machine. When it failed, skepticism about man's possibility of flying rose to a new high. This lent still greater stature to the achievement of the Wright brothers. Where others doubted, they believed; and they backed their belief with intensity. In their experiments—both near home and at Kitty Hawk, North Carolina—the Wright brothers backed belief with a creative, realistic approach. When they failed, they analyzed the reasons for their failures. As no one before them, they applied themselves with a keen, excited concentration to each problem. They solved the problem of flight control, and, early in the twentieth century, they made the skeptics blink their eyes and reassemble their thoughts.

What about you? You, too, can fly. Don't let the skeptics tell you it's impossible.

You fly when you set survival with self-respect as your goal, and you move toward it.

You fly when you believe in such a meaningful goal and believe you deserve such an attainment.

You fly when you resolve to rise above your failures, your dissociations, and your disappointments to reclaim the better side of yourself, to stake a claim in that better side—courageous in your powers.

Here is my main point: You have this better side. No matter who you are, no matter how difficult your life, no matter how many your frustrations and your failures, you have this better side.

Reclaim this better side. I congratulate you on your physical survival but take one giant step farther and work toward a survival with self-respect.

The pace of the world moves forward. Yesterday, the Wright brothers pioneered flight. Today, the astronauts pioneer the moon.

Not too long ago, astronauts Armstrong and Aldrin descended onto the moon—on the right side of the moon—and Neil Armstrong stepped out of his landing craft to make history.

Then it was the turn of astronauts Conrad and Bean. Another fantastic technological achievement. There they were, Conrad and Bean, landing near a crater on the Ocean of Storms—also on the right side of the moon.

Once, people had said it could never be done. But, backed by billions of dollars and hundreds of thousands of people, they did it.

What an achievement!

From science fiction to reality: Men on the moon—on the right side of the moon.

But let us hypothesize. Let us assume a miscalculation, a failure in communication, a misdirection. Our astronauts, through error, might have landed on the dark side of the moon, there to be lost forever on that bleak and barren landscape—on the wrong side of the moon.

But how does this apply to you?

You, too, have two sides: a side that leads you to failure and frustration, and a side that leads you to success and confidence. Every day, through torturing themselves over their errors, their guilts, their misfortunes, millions of people step out into the world on the wrong side of themselves, the one that leads to failure: the wrong side. You may survive the misery, in the physical sense, but where is your self-respect?

Whizzing around the earth at unbelievable speeds, our astronauts see an earth which is half the time in shadow, half the time in sunlight.

And you? You must become a psycho-cybernaut, steering through your mind toward inspiring goals, weaving through your negative feelings toward the person you want to be, jet-propelling yourself through shadow into sunlight. Your instrument panel is not complicated, and you do not have to be a trained technician. All you need is to win that crucial battle in your mind, between your negative and positive forces, reactivating your success mechanism, not your failure mechanism, fighting through to your better side, then carrying your emotional triumph out into the world of action.

Psycho-cybernauts, too, are creative and courageous adventurers. They venture into a land that many people fear, the land of inner space. They seek control over this area in themselves, positive and constructive control of an area which many people mark as "off-limits."

Psycho-cybernauts, brave and hardy, seek the raw materials in themselves with which to manufacture that champagne of the emotional life—self-respect.

They steer themselves toward the best kind of life—survival with self-respect.

## NO SURVIVAL (WITHOUT SELF-RESPECT)

Now let us examine the components of No Survival, by spelling them out:

1. Negative feelings.
2. Oppression.
3. Separation.
4. Unacceptableness.
5. Resistance to living
6. Vacillation.

7. Indifference.
8. Vulnerability.
9. Absenteeism.
10. Lamenting yesterday.

The airplane that buckles before it gets off the ground. The flight to the wrong side of the moon. The earth in shadow. NO SURVIVAL.

1. *Negative feelings.* You can't get off the ground. Your negative feel-ings are weighing you down. You can't forget your past mistakes. You can't forgive yourself. You move forward with turtle speed. You go on living, but your days are agonizing.

2. *Oppression.* You are a living embodiment of the failure mechanism. Your life is a morass of failure. Fearfully you walk around, lonely, and uncertain, choking with resentment, empty and despairing. You go through the motions of living while under the cloud of a sense of inferiority, reacting to your chronic frustrations with mis-channeled aggressiveness, antagonizing others, and humiliating yourself.

   You go on living? Fine. But what is the caliber of your survival? Do you survive, with self-respect? No, you oppress yourself with failure.

3. *Separation.* You separate yourself from more than the mainstream of people. You estrange yourself from yourself. You deny the worth of your self-image.

   You separate yourself from an appreciation of your assets, of your capacities, of your possibilities.

   You separate yourself from your feelings of success and from your smile of confidence.

   Yielding to futility, you drift into nothingness as a status quo.

   You discontinue your dialogue for your emotional improve-ment, and the resulting monologue signifies that you are growing older, not wiser.

4. *Unacceptableness.* Who is unacceptable? You are. In whose opinion? In your own.

   This is an intolerable state. You blow the whistle on your self-esteem. You call yourself out on strikes. You mark the papers and grade yourself "F." You sentence yourself to life imprisonment.

   You are referee, umpire, teacher, judge. You will not give your-self the same justice you give others. You refuse to accept yourself and, without your acceptance, you will not give yourself a chance to give your life meaning.

5. *Resistance to living.* Too many of us chip away segments of our self-respect every day because we resist living in the present and bury our creativity in the quicksand of the past. But coddling our regrets leads us into cycles of defeat, and therefore such resistance to living in the present leads us into a life of boredom and, blinding ourselves to possibility, into crosscurrents of cynicism.

6. *Vacillation.* When you vacillate, again and again, you deny yourself the world of action.

If, through vacillation, you block off your goals, inhibiting yourself from action, you will find yourself slowly drowning. In a way, it is a safe form of drowning since your body survives.

But, by playing it so safe that you continually vacillate, by never taking a chance, you drown emotionally. You go under. You refuse to surface for action. You deny yourself artificial respiration. Your body lives on, but your emotional self is drowning, and you do not hear your own cry for help.

7. *Indifference.* This is, beyond doubt, one of the most horrifying words in the English language. To feel indifference when one breathes life—what an inhuman fate! To feel indifference when one enjoys God's great gift of life, this is most pitiful. To survive the years, to win out in the great battle for time, what a feast for the human being! To squander this time, feeling indifference and emptiness, what waste! It is dying to spend a life in the shadows when there is sunshine. Real living, with real self-respect, involves human feeling—not indifference.

8. *Vulnerability.* Vulnerability is an integral component of nonsurvival. You leave yourself vulnerable to defeat when you fail to support yourself emotionally. In defeat, you vanish from yourself, and from your world. You become one of those invisible people of modern times, one of the millions of visible/invisible people who survive without a sense of real participation.

Feeling vulnerable, you succumb to dizziness when you try to move toward your goals. This is emotional dizziness. You are seasick, carsick, plane sick—without ever going out to meet the world.

9. *Absenteeism.* A great problem in industry is absenteeism. Millions and millions of dollars lost. Production schedules disrupted. Corporations hold meetings to deal with the problem.

But we refer here to your greatest industry—YOU—and your problem with your own absenteeism. When you are not on the job, helping yourself, strengthening your self-image you lessen your productivity and find yourself wallowing in a form of survival that lacks any real meaning.

10. *Lamenting yesterday*. This is a sad song. Don't sing it again, Sam—or Mabel—or Harry—or Joan. Don't sing it again, this lament of yesteryear. It is not harmonious. The melody is discordant. Further, it is inappropriate to the occasion. Pull out another sheet of music. That's it! Sing a song of today!

## THE TALL LITTLE PERSON AND THE "LITTLE SELF"

Living with or without self-respect, that is the question. We have spelled out NO SURVIVAL. Now SURVIVAL.

But first, two stories: One, about a Little Person who lived with a full sense of self-respect. The other, about a normal-sized woman who felt chronically humiliated and who thought of herself as a "little self."

I met the "Little Person," in Toronto, Canada. It was a few weeks before Christmas, and I sat in the lobby of a Toronto hotel. It was a huge lobby, and some people were putting up a Christmas tree. I was waiting to lunch with a friend and had nothing to do, so I watched them setting up the Christmas tree—a huge tree, twenty-six feet high, someone said—installing lights and decorations. I watched the Christmas tree glitter awhile, and then my attention strayed to a tiny bellhop whose job it was to call out people's names into a microphone, or loudspeaker system, or whatever. His appearance was striking. Apparently in his forties, he seemed little more than three feet tall. He was engaged in his work, paging people, then smiling and joking with co-workers in a most amiable way. I could not take my eyes off him for, tiny as he was, he breathed forth a feeling of confidence and good nature.

He left his post for a minute and walked over to look at the tree. There he stood, under the tree, looking almost like a happy little doll, a present to go with the tree, talking to the men putting it up, laughing with them, a talking, laughing doll.

Then back to his post, calling out people's names in clear, friendly tones, functioning smoothly in his job—calm, mature, full of self-assurance. Maybe he was physically a "Little Person," I told myself, but his self-image is as tall as that twenty-six-foot Christmas tree. Growing up deformed, he had outgrown his physical defects and reached the full stature of his self-respect.

When I returned home to New York City, a girl in her twenties came to see me—a normal-sized girl, pretty too, and I found myself thinking of the emotionally tall "Little Person," and contrasting him to this attractive, physically normal girl with a tiny self-image.

"My 'little self' is killing me," she said.

"What?"

"My 'little self.' It's killing me."

"I hadn't noticed," I remarked.

"Noticed what?"

"Your 'little self.' What about your 'big self'?"

"I don't have a 'big self.' I'm not much. I don't kid myself. My 'little self,' it's killing me."

She came from out of town, she told me, her father and mother were always bickering. One argument after another, that was her home life. She thought of herself as a "little self."

She wanted to be an actress, but found she was blocking herself from her goal with constant feelings of inferiority. Her mother had also wanted to be an actress when she was younger but had failed. Resenting the child, her mother had ridiculed her for her ambition: How could the daughter make a success as an actress when she, her mother, had failed! What was the daughter, anyway? Only a "little self."

She sat across from me, this attractive, intelligent girl in her twenties. "How can I become an actress? My 'little self' is killing me."

"You have a 'big self,'" I told her. "And maybe you can make a go of an acting career. Let me tell you a story. There was this fine teacher of drama, and she had this young girl pupil, a marvelous actress, who pitched into every new role with such vigor that she was successful in all of them."

"I wish I was half as good."

"She hated herself so much in real life that she loved to pretend she was someone else, and she played fictitious roles with great zest. The teacher then asked her to enact the role of her better self in real life. She did and became a better human being as well as a fine actress. You'll try this, won't you? Develop your skills as an actress, escaping from yourself to become someone else; then, in real life, work at playing the role of the better you. Maybe you'll be a better actress and a better human being, maybe you'll find you're your 'big self,' and maybe you'll forget about your 'little self' and start living."

Eight months later, she came to see me. She was radiant. She had finally found her better self—her "big self," and she had landed a job in the cast of an off-Broadway musical.

We have spelled out NO SURVIVAL; now, let us spell out SURVIVAL.

## SURVIVAL

First, our list:

1. Sense of forward movement.
2. Upgrading.
3. Relaxed attitude.
4. Vitality.
5. Imaginative power.
6. Values.
7. Aspiration for happiness.
8. Living now.

That's our chart for survival with self-respect. Now let us work on it.

1. *Sense of forward movement.* You move forward toward your goals. You will not find meaning in your life through adding up your birthdays or sitting around worrying about the world's dangers. Set your goals; then move out toward them. This is your first step toward a form of survival with real meaning.
2. *Upgrading.* Many people spend their lives downgrading themselves, heaping contempt upon themselves, then accepting or resenting the humiliations that other people push upon them.

   Stop downgrading yourself and making excuses for yourself. Upgrade yourself. See your past successes and feel them. Give yourself credit for your accomplishments. Stand up to pressure and to fear. Re-evaluate your self-image, and reevaluate with kind eyes, befriending yourself and giving yourself the benefit of the doubt.
3. *Relaxed attitude.* Forgive—yourself, first of all, then others too. By doing this, you can build a relaxed attitude that will help you survive with a good feeling about yourself.

   Forgive completely—not on the installment plan. A little here, a little there is not good enough.

   Pick up your eraser and wipe the chalk off the blackboard, all the chalk. Leave a clean slate with no grudges, no lifelong condemnations, and no obsession with past grievances. Wipe the slate absolutely clean.

   Then approach yourself and your world with a relaxed attitude, which will smooth your path to living with self-respect.

4. *Vitality.* Concentrate on what you're doing. Act with intensity. When you have formulated a goal, release your full vitality in your attempt to achieve that goal. Halfhearted actions seldom succeed. Put your full energy into cementing your goals.

   Remember this: A near-success is a failure. You must follow through to your goals with all the vitality that is in you.

5. *Imaginative power.* Used creatively, this means survival with dignity.

   You use this enormous power creatively when you use your imagination for building a positive image of yourself, for seeing, again and again, your past successes, for envisioning goals that inspire you, and foreseeing tactics to move you toward your goals.

   Stop using your imagination for storing the memory of all your past mistakes and miseries. Use it to build, not destroy, yourself.

6. *Values.* What is there in life you need, and what is excess baggage? What is valuable, and what is irrelevant? You must adjust your values sensibly so you can stress helpful focuses in your search for dignified living.

   You must learn to value solid human values: constructive motivation, compassion, forgiveness, and self-fulfillment, a strong self-image, and a feeling that you are a winner as one of life's money players.

   You build survival for self-respect on the bedrock of strong values.

7. *Aspiration for happiness.* Your aspiration is universal. You aspire to help yourself to happiness, and you aspire to help others too. You fight to bolster your courage in withstanding life's pressures; you try to give your courage to others.

   Don't replay that old record of frustration. It is a long-playing record; sometimes, it never stops. Play a new record: of aspiration for happiness as a fundamental goal. Place it on the turntable now.

   This is a rough, competitive world, and you cannot always live up to your ideals; but try—at least, try—to act in a brotherly way toward other people whenever this is practical. Some will reciprocate, and your aspirations for happiness will reap rich harvests.

8. *Living now.* Now that you have my ideas for survival with self-respect, I must ask you when you will go to work on them. Did I hear you say "Tomorrow"?

   *Please.* I can't stand that word. I've heard it for over sixty-five years now, and I can't stand it, because I know it really means never.

   Live now. Today. You survive with respect when you live today and forget the fantasy of "tomorrow."

Live today. Reactivating your success mechanism, channel your sense of direction toward positive and attainable goals, accept yourself for what you are, and work on creative attitudes toward yourself and other people. Survival with self-respect means *SUCCESS*, and success begins today.

## THE ANATOMY OF SELF-RESPECT

In these first fourteen chapters, we have dissected the anatomy of self-respect.

We have discussed the nature and importance of self-respect. We have analyzed the role of understanding and of active sincerity, in the attainment of human dignity. After treating, at length, some of the roadblocks to self-respect, we have analyzed the proper application of active forgiveness and the constructive use of mirror watching, among other factors, in the anatomy of self-respect.

We have stressed the active approach—thoughtful imaging which leads to constructive action. This active approach is basic to my theory of creative Psycho-Cybernetics.

To illustrate my point, I have told a series of stories about myself, my friends, and people who have come to talk to me, while preserving the anonymity of people where there is confidential material.

Now, we will sing about survival with self-respect. Why "sing"? Well, isn't this something to "sing" about? To many people, life is arithmetical. You live to the age of fifty or sixty or sixty-five or—but let's stop here. Because at sixty-five, most people believe in survival—period. Most people abandon all creative living and, with it, a good measure of self-respect as they retreat into an absurd state known as retirement.

Survival with self-respect. How that reminds me again of the great cellist Pablo Casals! This wonderful man seems to get younger all the time. Last I heard, he was ninety-two and still going strong.

Casals, exiled from his native Spain for almost half his life, is a man of courage and moral principle, a brave fighter for just causes. He spent years fighting to bring good music at reasonable prices to the common people of Spain. Having recovered from a heart attack, he went right on working, participating in his music festivals, and embarking on a peace crusade.

Casals is a young man in his nineties, surviving the many years with an enormous amount of self-respect: Truly, he is an inspiration to all of us.

Casals has always been too in love with life to worry himself about arithmetic, too enthused about his great lifelong goal of giving to people through music, to let chronological numbers eat into his sense of constructive participation in the world. When this book comes out, will he still be alive? No matter, he will long be an inspiration.

Survival with self-respect. This finishes our analysis of the anatomy of self-respect, except for a short physical examination.

When you go to see a doctor, he examines you. Perhaps your heart, lungs, and blood pressure are normal, but then he puts you under a special kind of microscope. A worried look on his face now. "Your self-respect," he tells you. "It has vanished. Physically you're okay, but emotionally—I'm sorry to tell you this—you are invisible."

You leap to your feet. "What's the prognosis, doctor?"

*"No survival."*

"What can you do for me, doctor?"

"The point is, what can you do for yourself?"

"I don't understand."

"You have lost faith in yourself. Your blood pressure is fine, and all the tests check out fine, but emotionally you are invisible. You have lost self-respect. But I can't help you regain it. You have to do this for yourself."

A horrifying fantasy? True.

But my point is this: You must assume responsibility in this great search for your self-respect.

Ask yourself this: Would you fail this examination? Would your self-respect be invisible?

If so, your search is not over.

Go on to the final chapter, "Goal Builders," in which we will work to turn theory into reality, with a series of exercises I've designed to help you find your full self-respect as a human being.

# 15

## GOAL BUILDERS

NOW WE HAVE REACHED THE END OF OUR VOYAGE OF DISCOVERY. WE HAVE COM-pleted our search; now we have found our self-respect.

Or have we?

We have launched a major drive toward self-respect. We have analyzed its components; we have focused on its importance; we have shuffled our values and rearranged our priorities, but what about self-respect? We have concentrated our energies to seek out a direction of thinking that will bring us self-respect, a utilization of our imagination that will bring us self-respect, a constructive orientation toward the world, and our human brothers and sisters that will bring us self-respect.

Still, we have not concluded our search. And perhaps we never will. For the search for self-respect is a lifetime job. When you feel self-respect, you still seek more, and when you find more, you keep your momentum alive and give your self-respect to others. You share. You give. This is the creative spirit that enriches you as you devote yourself to enriching others.

In this final chapter, we end our voyage, but for a while only. For, just as we like to save our money week after week and month after month and year after year, we must also attune ourselves to the importance of continually building our sense of self-respect. Self-respect is even more basic than money. If you are frugal, you can survive with "just a little money" and live a good life—but life without self-respect is a wasteland.

I call this concluding chapter "Goal Builders" because we will now focus, one by one, on the goals we have outlined in the previous chapters of this book. For each chapter, I have devised an exercise to help you take firm hold of the goal that is stressed. I feel that this is the key to this book. Because my words will not help you enough if they remain passively on the paper; you can make them come alive if you use them to strengthen your emotional muscles by working on these exercises. This is my concept of creative Psycho-Cybernetics.

You move from constructive thinking to constructive imaging, and on to constructive action—goal builders for self-respect.

This is a fourteen-week building-up process. Here is how you go about it. Give each goal builder one full week: work on it for six days, then take a day off. You are a creative mirror watcher for self-respect. Six days a week—for fourteen weeks—you build. Fourteen chapters, fourteen goal builders. Your first goal builder is self-respect itself. Your other goal builders are the components of self-respect. In Chapter 9, I stress the enormous impact of creative mirror watching. Use it as you work on these exercises, moving from goal builder to goal builder. One full week on each: six days of application, then one day of rest. They add up to what we're starting with—self-respect.

## GOAL BUILDER 1. *SELF-RESPECT*

Do you feel guilty and keep blaming yourself for all your past mistakes, downgrading yourself as a human being? Help yourself; try this.

Close your eyes; sit down in a quiet place; imagine that you are a convicted criminal living behind bars. You've seen your share of prison movies. See them again in your mind, but you're one of the actors. You're playing one of the heavies; you are ruthless, embittered, totally antisocial. You are unmanageable. You shake the bars of your prison cell, screaming curses at the guards. Eating with the other prisoners, you beat your plate with your fork, trying to stir up an inmate riot. You never talk; you only snarl. You are so mean you make James Cagney's old gangster roles seem angelic. The warden, a kindly man, comes to see if he can reform you; you try to attack him, and the guards wrestle you to the ground howling threats of revenge.

Now, back to reality. Are you really such a terrible fellow that you should deny yourself self-respect, feeling guilty about everything? Why?

This criminal you imagined you were, he was guilty of all kinds of irresponsible, antisocial behavior. But you? You were just imagining you were like this. Are you like this—in reality? Of course not.

Then why do you keep treating yourself as if you were loathsome, distorted, guilty? You do your best; you try to be a constructive human being. Give yourself credit for this. Stop convicting yourself of crimes. Stop putting yourself behind bars. Feed yourself self-respect. Remind yourself of your virtues once in a while.

But go beyond this. Walk over to a mirror in your home and look at yourself. Ask yourself: "Do I see a distorted version of myself? Do I fail to see my value? Do I shortchange myself and deprive myself of self-respect?"

Take out a lipstick or an erasable pencil and in large capital letters—don't
be afraid—write on the mirror SELF-RESPECT. You can erase it later. Mean-
while, leave the word on the mirror, look at it, and at yourself.

Say to your image in the mirror: "Today, I will try to respect myself. I de-
serve to respect myself."

Back to my prison movie, let me, in fairness, add a footnote because in
lecturing around the country, I have talked to many convicted criminals, in-
mates of our penitentiaries: I suggest this Hollywood-type criminal image to
help you feel how ludicrous it is to obsess yourself with guilt and deny your-
self self-respect, but this image is largely a distortion. I have talked to men in
prison who had fine, constructive attitudes. Some criminals have paid for their
offenses and want another chance to build wholesome lives; they deserve our
compassion. Self-respect is their right too.

## GOAL BUILDER 2. *UNDERSTANDING*

Walking down the street, you look at all the people. You have walked down
this street before—in New York or St. Louis or wherever—but this time, you
get more than physical exercise. You get mental exercise too. For you are try-
ing to focus on an understanding that has often eluded you: the understanding
that you have the right to live happily, pleasurably, and with self-respect. This
is a basic understanding.

You glance at the people you pass on the sidewalk. They are so alike—yet so
different. You are concentrating on observing one thing that differentiates them:
their feeling that they have rights or their conviction that they have no rights.

With this in mind, you study the people you meet. You look at this person
or that person, and you ask yourself, "Does he (or she) believe he has the right
to be happy?"

In many cases, on such superficial consideration, you can come to no sure
conclusion. Some people may be in "up" moods while others are in "down"
moods. Many successfully hide their feelings. Others register neutral or mixed
impressions on the most careful observer.

But some people, you will see, slouch and stumble as they walk, avert their
eyes in an excess of timidity, seem empty of any feeling but fear. A percentage
of these people may be only temporarily down, but it is a fair assumption that
many habitually short-change themselves, refusing to understand that they are
as good as other people and have the right to a life of happiness and self-respect.

You see other people who, without swaggering or stepping on other peo-
ple's toes or overcompensating, walk proud and erect, looking others in the

eye with friendliness and a smile of confidence. Again, you cannot be sure, but it is a fair bet that many of these people give themselves rights and feel they are deserving.

You have finished your walk; you walk back home. Now I'll use this mirror again and again. Go to your mirror; you win. Once again, take out an erasable pencil or lipstick and write on the mirror—in capital letters, bold and clear, UNDERSTANDING.

Say to yourself, looking at yourself in the mirror, "I have seen people who feel they have rights and other people who feel they have no rights (and also, of course, people with mixed feelings). But how about me? Do I have rights? Yes.

"Yes, I do."

Erase the word UNDERSTANDING from your mirror but keep alive in you the feeling that you do have rights. Subject to the restrictions of our civilized laws, you have the right to enjoy life and to respect yourself, and to make each day a good day.

## GOAL BUILDER 3. *SINCERITY*

People disagree on many issues, but most people would agree to this statement: Sincerity is not a quality many human beings possess these days.

This is tragic.

Sincerity is a fine trait. The sincere person gives substance to human relations. He enriches himself, and he also enriches others.

But sincerity requires confidence; it requires enough belief in yourself so that you can face up to reality without evasion.

So, the question is: How do you build confidence in yourself?

This is no overnight proposition, but I think this exercise will help:

Once again, seat yourself in a quiet room and close your eyes and let your imagination go to work for you. This time you will visit an amusement park in your mind. See it—the merry-go-round, the barkers, the roller coaster, and all the other thrill rides. You walk by a crowd of giggling girls and then a young couple, arm in arm, and a man in work clothes munching a hot dog.

Your destination? The "fun" mirrors.

Remember them? The mirrors that distort your form so ludicrously that you stare at yourself in amazement? Short? Tall? Thin as a pencil? Bulging with fat? People come to laugh and laugh as they see themselves in the "fun" mirrors; their reflections are too ridiculous to threaten them.

In your mind, now, you see yourself in one of these distorting mirrors. How ridiculous you look! How can anyone take you seriously?

Back to reality now; open your eyes. Walk over to your mirror; write the word SINCERITY on it.

The grotesque physical distortions of the "fun" mirror did not disturb you. But how about your real image?

Look at yourself in the mirror, and ask yourself this: "Do I emotionally distort myself, taking away my confidence and my capacity for sincerity? Do I see myself as a distorted person when other people disapprove of me? Do I feel I am ridiculous when I make a minor mistake?"

If you do, remember the distortions of the "fun" mirrors.

"They are ridiculous," you say?

True—but when you distort yourself emotionally, taking away your feeling of confidence and your capacity for sincerity, is this not equally ridiculous?

I feel strongly that this amusement park "fun" mirror exercise can help many people. If you can see that when you torture yourself for your imperfections, you are distorting your self-image "fun-mirror" style, and if you can use this comparison visually to laugh at yourself as you would do at an amusement park, then perhaps you can begin to stop yourself. With practice, you will be able to do this with more and more ease until you can finally see yourself with a smile of confidence. Then you will be able to practice sincerity in your relations with other people.

## GOAL BUILDER 4. *DEFEATING UNCERTAINTY*

Once again, the only tools you need are a place to seat yourself, some quiet, and your imagination.

You close your eyes and see a motion picture.

It is World War II. You are a Marine in the Pacific. You have landed with your buddies on a heavily fortified island. The first wave of attackers was wiped out by the enemy soldiers defending the island. You are fortunate; you were in the second wave, and you survived. You and your fellows advanced into the jungle— perhaps half a mile. Now, you are in darkness. Suddenly you realize you haven't seen one of your buddies in fifteen minutes. You can't see anyone. You can't shout; the enemy might be behind the next tree. You are cut off—perhaps for the whole night. Will you still be alive the next morning?

Scared? Sure you are; I am, too.

My point?

That your life, no matter how filled with uncertainties, could be worse. The nightmare you just lived through in your mind, suppose this was your reality?

If you find this revisualization of World War II in the Pacific too unsettling to bear, see any other terrifying experience in your mind—another war, an automobile accident, your house on fire. My point is that you must learn to deal with life's uncertainties in order to feel a real sense of self-respect; seeing such a terrifying "motion picture" may (assuming your reality is not so monstrous) help you to return with relief to your own life situation.

It may make your problems seem smaller by comparison and therefore more manageable. Thus, it may help you to stand firm and cope with them instead of running away from life into fantasy.

Go back to your mirror once more. Walk over and with erasable pencil or lipstick write DEFEAT UNCERTAINTY.

That is your goal.

Look in the mirror and say to yourself, "I know that life is uncertain, but I will try to face my problems and troubles as best as I can and not run to hide at the first sign of danger. When situations test my patience and courage, I will try to stand up to them."

It is basic to my theory of creative Psycho-Cybernetics that you do more than theorize about handling uncertainty. When it is practicable, translate theory into action, moving toward your objective with wisdom and determination—in spite of uncertainties.

Difficult? Yes. But you will respect yourself for your courage, and this is most rewarding.

## GOAL BUILDER 5. *OVERCOMING RESENTMENT*

Resentment is a way of life with too many people. How do you overcome it?

One helpful technique is to work at handling your anxieties more rationally, because anxieties lead to resentment.

Today you are worried about this or that. How do you manage your fears?

Think back to last week. What were your anxieties then?

Write them down.

Think back to last month. What were your anxieties then?

Write them down.

Can you remember what you were worried about a year ago? If you can, write these fears down.

Now take your list and study it. Check out your anxieties. Was this one realistic? Did it make any sense? Or that one?

Many people worry about things that never happen, and there is a splendid chance that, as you check out your list of anxieties, you will find that many—perhaps most—of your worries were unrealistic.

If you discover this, hopefully this insight into your overreactions will help you deal more realistically with your present fears and thus reduce your resentment. And, with less resentment, you move toward richer living and heightened self-respect.

Now, to the mirror, and write: OVERCOME RESENTMENT.

Tell yourself that you will overcome your resentment. Say to yourself, "I will try to overcome my resentment every way I can. I will try to reduce my anxieties. I will set constructive goals. I want self-respect."

## GOAL BUILDER 6. *GETTING RID OF EMPTINESS*

The empty person lacks goals. His emptiness is linked with his indifference about the events of his day.

If you feel this apathy, rise above it. To the mirror and write NO EMPTI-NESS. Then work to make these words meaningful.

Look at yourself in the mirror and tell yourself, "I will make my life mean something. Time is my treasure, and I will not waste it. I will set goals to give meaning to my precious days."

Then take a pad and pencil. Think of a goal and write it down. Weigh it. Is it your goal? Does it mean something to you? Can you achieve this goal? Do you have a fighting chance, at least? Keep writing and thinking until you have found goals to give purpose to your life.

Or perhaps you may prefer putting away pad and pencil in a drawer, seating yourself comfortably, closing your eyes, and once more using your imagination, searching your mind for meaningful goals, inventorying your past experiences, and visualizing current possibilities.

These are two techniques for formulating goals; perhaps you can devise a technique that works better for you than these would. The main point is that you must orient yourself toward goals and self-respect and full living and away from an inner sense of emptiness that is a repudiation of your life force.

## GOAL BUILDER 7. *OPPORTUNITY*

Recently, a friend of mine with small children showed me a wonderful children's book by Dr. Seuss called *Green Eggs and Ham*. It is a most comic book. There is a small, nondescript, mischievous-looking animal trying to induce a larger, more grouchy, equally nondescript animal to eat green eggs and ham on a platter. This small animal—Sam-I-am—keeps prodding the big grouch to try the green eggs and ham. He is a high-pressure salesman without peer. He follows the other animal over hill and dale, cross-country, and finally underwater in his single-minded determination to get him to eat the green eggs and ham. The big animal keeps refusing to try the dish, insisting he does not like it, thwarting Sam-I-am in a Keystone-Cops-type chase; under no circumstances, he insists, will he eat green eggs and ham.

But finally, he gives in; and, to his surprise, he finds that he likes green eggs and ham. He likes them very much.

Why do I tell this story?

Certainly not to commend to you green eggs and ham. To tell you the truth, even the words make me feel mildly nauseated.

For me, this story has an allegorical meaning. It suggests that people shy away from new experiences, run away from experimentation, fail to explore life's many opportunities for satisfaction. Many people will explore new avenues of opportunity only under compulsion.

Do you welcome constructive opportunities, or is your fear stronger than your sense of creative adventure?

When you wake up in the morning, walk over to your mirror and write: OPPORTUNITY.

Then ask yourself, "What opportunities await me today? How can I make today a good day?"

Close your eyes; see them in your mind. Take out paper and pencil and write them down. Then plot your course of action.

Back to Goal Builder 2, *Understanding,* remember that you have the right to move toward opportunity—without trampling on others' rights—and to feel happy.

## GOAL BUILDER 8. *FORGIVENESS*

On the mirror, draw an arrow and say: "From forgiveness to self-respect." For this relationship is fundamental. If you do not forgive yourself for your limitations and your failures, you cannot give yourself the wonderful gift of self-respect.

Do you find that you cannot stop blaming yourself? You cannot stop the flow of self-condemnation? Your self-critical thoughts overwhelm you?

Try another movie in your imagination. This time picture a "torture scene"—a gruesome, horrifying scene of physical torture. The "enemy" holds you prisoner and tries to force secrets from you. "So, you won't talk, eh? We'll see about that."

Is this too horrifying? I agree. Do you want me to stop? Then I will.

But what about your own cruel self-torture? Is this not equally horrifying?

Equally inhuman? Can any "enemy" with whatever ruthless refinements of physical torture inflict more damage on you than you can inflict on yourself with your ceaseless critical self-mutilation?

On your mirror, erase the arrow and write FORGIVENESS. Say, "I will try to forgive myself. I will try to forgive others. We are all human and imperfect."

The next step is self-respect.

## GOAL BUILDER 9. *CREATIVE MIRROR WATCHING*

I decided to insert the word "creative" because if you misapply mirror watching, you can make it an exercise in narcissism, superficial apathy, or critical self-destruction. Your aim is seeing behind your face to the mature, dynamic, and compassionate person you want to become.

Step to the mirror. Don't panic; it's only you.

Look at yourself this time in absolute honesty, evaluating yourself. No, don't run away. The mirror won't break; don't let it break you.

About face! You weren't in the army? All right, then, just turn around. And walk away.

Now think. The sight of your face, did it evoke a torrent of critical thoughts? If it did, ask yourself this: Do you feel this hostile when you see the face of a friend when he comes into your home or when you enter his home?

Back to the mirror.

But this time, look at yourself as you would look at a friend. Close your eyes for a moment and see the face of this good friend; select a specific friend and see his or her face. You feel a positive feeling at the recollection? Alright; now, open your eyes. That's you in the mirror. Write FRIEND on the mirror; that's you.

Say to yourself, "I will be a friend to myself. I will look at myself with kind eyes. With compassion for my imperfections. With appreciation of my capacities."

Tackling Goal Builder 3, *Sincerity,* we emphasized the physical distortion of amusement park "funhouse" mirrors and compared the harmless and amusing effect of these images to the crippling impact of emotional distortion. Be creative: Stop distorting your self-image and take a giant stride toward self-respect.

## GOAL BUILDER 10. *TEARING DOWN PRISON WALLS*

You feel imprisoned in your own home or at a party? Even walking down the street, swinging freely, you feel unreasonably trapped? Civilization imposes limits on what people can do, but perhaps you over-inhibit yourself beyond these limits. Tear down those prison walls!

I think this exercise will help you because over-inhibition usually stems from lack of confidence, which comes from chronic failure.

Once again, seat yourself comfortably, quietly, and close your eyes. Imagine you are playing baseball. It is your turn at bat. You swing a few bats, to warm up, hand one to the bat boy, and stride to home plate. You assume your stance, crouching slightly and facing the pitcher. You want to get a hit.

But you know from past experience that this is a tough pitcher. His fastball is overpowering; his curve is sharp; his change of pace throws you off balance. His control is his strongest asset; he keeps the ball away from you and nicks the corner of the plate. In the past, he has struck you out repeatedly. You feel defeated the moment you look at him. What can you do?

Ah, you remember something. In the past, you came to the plate determined to hit home runs. But this pitcher is too tough for you to hit for home runs. Trying to belt home runs and striking out, again and again, you tie yourself up in knots of frustration. Your goal is unrealistic.

You can and must realign your goal. You can stop trying for the skyrocketing home run blast and aim at meeting the ball squarely. A line drive between the infielders is good for a solid single, and that will do fine.

So, you shorten up your grip on the bat, eliminate the unrealistic fantasy that you are Babe Ruth, and aim at punching out a single. This pitcher may still get you out—he is tough—but you will get your share of hits now that your goal is realistic.

Along with your share of hits, you will gain confidence.

With confidence, you need no longer imprison yourself so cruelly.

On your mirror write: PRISON. Tell yourself, "I do not deserve to imprison myself. I committed no crimes against society. Instead, I will accept myself."

## GOAL BUILDER 11. *TRANQUILITY*

Close your eyes, but this time make use of another vital organ, your ears.

Listen, and hear sounds that will bring you a sense of tranquility. This is individual; we all have our unique tastes. Use your imagination and listen.

Some people love to hear the sound of rain falling on city streets.

Others like to hear the roar of the ocean pounding on the shore.

Many people respond to beautiful music. For this, of course, you do not need your imagination; you can play your favorite phonograph records or listen to the radio.

Soothe yourself with the sounds you love to hear. You owe yourself this relief from life's struggles, so often full of discordant noises.

Now open your eyes and walk to the mirror. On it write: TRANQUILITY. Tell yourself, "I will be tranquil today. No matter how discordant the world and its problems, I will give myself tranquility."

## GOAL BUILDER 12. *NO RETIREMENT CLOCK*

Once again, you listen. To the ticking of a clock. If you have a clock that ticks, use it. If not, imagine the ticking.

Time is ticking away, and time is precious. Time is ticking away, time that comprises your life, and this is your great gift.

Walk to the mirror now and write: CLOCK. Tell yourself: "I must not use this valuable time to retire from life. I must not resort to 'killing' time. My life is for translating constructive thinking and constructive imaging into constructive action."

This is what creative Psycho-Cybernetics means.

## GOAL BUILDER 13. *INTEGRITY*

The person with integrity is whole, honest, honorable. He feels self-respect.

Do you feel that you cannot qualify?

Your life is a potpourri of failures?

You are unreliable?

You have lived uselessly, disconnectedly, irresponsibly?

Are you sure?

Take out paper and pencil. Close your eyes and roam through your life, connecting it up. Think of your proud moments, see them in your mind. Then write them down on paper. Draw up a list of your moments of integrity. Forgive and forget your mistakes and your irresponsibilities. Bring back your shining experiences, then list them.

And your qualities of integrity, list them too. Perhaps they are not absolute, but just because you were irresponsible in a minor way three or four times in your life, does this make you an irresponsible person or a responsible person? A responsible person, I would say, and a person with integrity. List this quality: RESPONSIBILITY. Draw up a list that gives you a fair shake.

Then read your lists and reread them later. If you are a person of reasonable integrity, see yourself this way; don't let your perfectionism take away your right to see yourself as a person of integrity so that you frustrate your need to respect yourself.

Then walk to the mirror and write: INTEGRITY.

And say to yourself: "First, I shall look at myself with kind eyes. Second, I shall see myself at my best, as a person of confidence, rather than at my worst, as a person of frustration. Third, I forgive myself for the mistakes of yesterday. Fourth, I forgive others. Only then will integrity be a living thing for me. Only then will self-respect be a living thing for me."

## GOAL BUILDER 14. *SURVIVAL*

Survival with self-respect. In a world of uncertainty this is quite a chore!

Another movie—in your mind. You are scheduled to deliver a speech to a huge crowd of people. Workmen have been enlarging the stadium in which you are to speak so that 125,000 people will come to hear you if it doesn't rain. You can't imagine looking at such a crowd of people? I can't either. You are so nervous that when you look at yourself in the mirror, you can't recognize yourself. You even forget your name. How will you survive with self-respect? You pray for rain, but the weather is ideal. Who is that stranger telling you it's time to get dressed so you can take a cab to the stadium? Oh, it's your wife (or husband)! Hurriedly, you brush your teeth with soap and wash your face with toothpaste.

You check yourself. Thank God, you have a shoe on each foot, and you're wearing clothes. But your hysteria mounts to super terror when you think of 250,000 eyes watching you as you speak. How will you survive with self-respect?

Okay, you've got the picture. Obviously, it's a caricature.

I am a veteran lecturer, and this picture scares me, too. The question remains: How to survive?

Go to the mirror and write: SURVIVAL. Look at yourself and tell yourself this: "I will accept my fear. And my nervousness. And my panic. My key to survival with self-respect is this: I will accept myself no matter what all these people think of me. I will stop expecting myself to fail no matter how imperfect I am. No matter how imperfect I am, I will accept myself."

How else can a person deal with such an imagined crisis? Bring images of your past successes into your mind. This will serve a dual purpose: it will encourage your success feelings to surface and replace your nervousness; second, if you make a terrible speech, these past successes will make acceptance of this failure easier for you.

Then do your best, knowing this will help you to survive such a crisis experience with self-respect. Do your best in reality, too.

## YOUR LIFELONG GOAL

I hope that these exercises help you move toward self-respect. Many of them—such as the last one which involves such a dramatic situation—are purposely exaggerated and unreal so that when you come back to earth, you can cope with your more common problems still more effectively.

Our tools are invisible, but extremely potent: understanding, forgiveness, success imaging, confidence building, goal orientation, and emotional readiness for constructive action.

In this chapter, as in this book, we have applied creative Psycho-Cybernetics to forward our search for self-respect.

Temporarily, our search is over.

But self-respect is a lifelong goal. It is one of our basic human values. If you own a plant and love it, you keep watering it as long as it lives.

Walk over to your mirror now and say this: "As long as I live, I will strive to make myself a complete person, in my own image, with a sense of mature responsibility, rising above my human limitations to realize in good faith and with constructive intentions toward other people my full potential for self-respect."

# BOOK THREE

# LIVE AND BE FREE THRU PSYCHO-CYBERNETICS

# CONTENTS

# CONTENTS

# SUMMARY

Dr. Maxwell Maltz wrote the book *Live and Be Free Thru Psycho-Cybernetics* to help you bring the wisdom of this groundbreaking discovery into your daily lives. Most personal development and motivational teachers of today can trace their roots to Dr. Maltz and these techniques.

*Live and Be Free Thru Psycho-Cybernetics* "will deepen your knowledge and show you how to be 'goal-directed.' You will live a more successful, happy life because you will have learned how to live and feel free now!" Maxwell Maltz, M.D.

From the original:

Now! You can teach yourself how to use Psycho-Cybernetics in 21 days!

Why do people who seem to have everything needed for success fail to succeed? Why do others without such natural advantages achieve outstanding success in business, family, and life? The people who get to the top know what they really want and go after it.

This book will show you how to learn more, do more, be more—

We promise you that if you use the simple ideas and formulas in this book, the results will be tangible, they will be measurable, and they will be soon.

In just 21 days . . .

You can start a new life—a life in which you will achieve your goals for happiness and success.

There are no hidden secrets or mysterious truths; the reasons for a person's happiness and successes are plain and simple.

*You Can Learn Them*
*You Can Master Them*

Dr. Maxwell Maltz, who discovered the "Self Image," one of the most important psychological insights of this century, has reached literally millions of readers with his book *Psycho-Cybernetics*.

LIVE AND BE FREE THRU PSYCHO-CYBERNETICS is the first practical "do-it-yourself" handbook of Psycho-Cybernetics. Here are step-by-step instructions that you can use now to bring the power of Self Image thinking into your own life.

You can start the 21-Day Course in Living Free *right now.*

# PREFACE

I have written more than eight books on Psycho-Cybernetics, which have been read by tens of millions of persons throughout the world.

What you are about to read is the first "Self Study" program on Psycho-Cybernetics. It offers you practical tools; new,easy-to-grasp techniques for achieving greater personal growth. You will learn to form the habit of thinking positively, and it will reflect itself in your daily life. Now, through this book, you will have a program to follow to learn how to improve your life in the privacy of your home or business.

I predict the start of a new life for you—living free—in just twenty-one days. I know this book will deepen your knowledge and show you how to be "goal-directed." You will live a more successful, happy life because you will have learned to LIVE and FEEL FREE!

Maxwell Maltz, M.D., F.I.C.S.

# 1

## THE CHIEF PURPOSE OF THIS BOOK

THIS BOOK INTENDS TO ASSIST YOU IN BECOMING A TREMENDOUSLY MORE *effective* person, not just in one area but in every phase of your life. The knowledge gained from this book will help expand your thinking to understand yourself. It differs from many books of this nature in that it deals with an emphasis on practical, usable tools.

You will find that all these techniques work if you will let them.

As you progress from step to step in your understanding of the principles involved, undoubtedly, you will *accept them in one of two fundamental ways*:

You may regard them as an interesting mental exercise whereby you may gain knowledge of practical psychology worthy of careful evaluation. If this is your attitude, you will achieve a greater understanding of how and why people act and react as they do and will vaguely sense that if you *wanted* to do something about becoming a more effective person, you *could* do so.

This attitude is a passive approach. You may even try some of the techniques and think about them, but that is where it will end.

On the other hand, you may test the tools and ideas given and find it is not necessary to *believe*—the mere knowledge that you *tried* them, and they did work is enough for you to continue the journey. You will find that all these techniques work if you will let them. If you acquire this state of mind, you will surely be entering one of the most exciting periods of your life, and the learning and growing process started will extend far beyond the reading of this book and will change the rest of your life.

### CONFIRMED BY OUR OWN EXPERIENCE

Perhaps the best introduction to the philosophy I wish to advocate would be to tell you that I believe a person is not born happy—he *learns* to be happy.

I make only one claim for the formulas and ideas offered; I have confirmed them by my observation and experience, and they have increased my happiness and peace of mind whenever I have acted in accord with them.

Many of the ideas and techniques I will review are as old as recorded history—thoroughly tested and proven. Some will be familiar to you; some even may seem over-simplified.

## CONTENTS SHOW YOU HOW

We are all attempting to get more living out of life, make more of ourselves, *learn* more, *do* more, *be* more than we are.

This book will show you how to:

Reach more of your goals

Use more of your potential

Develop attitudes that will get you what you want

Become a more successful person

## YOU CAN ONLY PROVE THIS BY DOING

The only way to demonstrate the ideas presented in this book is to translate them into action; put them to the test, and then decide how effective they are. No amount of debate or discussion can give you proof that these theories work. Still, if you follow them for twenty-one days, you will be able to judge the outcome for yourself. (For a person to experience a noticeable change in a mental picture, a minimum of twenty-one consecutive days must elapse.)

## PROMISE

I promise you if you make use of the simple ideas and formulas contained in this book, the results will be tangible, they will be measurable, and they will be soon. The time investment you make in the program is not just an investment in a success program; it is an investment in your future, your dreams, and your happiness. Only you know how you measure success. This realization is something else you will discover. Once you see your goal clearly, you will be able to achieve it. That is the promise.

## BASIC FACTORS FOR SUCCESS

There are many books written about the secrets of success, as though there are dark, mysterious truths that lie in the back of it. There are no hidden secrets or mysterious truths; the reasons for success are plain and simple—you can learn and can master them.

## WHY PEOPLE DON'T SUCCEED

Countless individuals seem to have all the needed requirements for success, yet they do not succeed. They have natural ability, education, attractive personalities, outstanding talents, yet they fail to make good.

Why?

On the other hand, some individuals lack all these advantages. Yet they make outstanding successes in business and their family and social life.

People, with rare exceptions, do not fail because they lack knowledge, education, or talents. They fail chiefly because of what they do not do.

One of the big reasons that most people go through life getting so little out of it is that *they do not really know what they want.* Things happen to them more by chance than by choice.

When a person stops seeking idle pleasure and begins *truly seeking success and happiness,* that is the *turning point* in his life. There is such a turning point in the life of every successful person. Therefore, the first step toward your success is for you to cause this turning point. *You and you alone can do it.*

Suppose this turning point has already come with you, and you are moving toward greater success and happiness. In that case, this will strengthen your determination and show you how to mobilize your ambitions and skills for a rich and happy life of accomplishment and fulfillment.

## DETERMINING FACTORS FOR SUCCESS

Do you know in what way the mind and a parachute are alike? They both must be open to function properly.

Psychologists have determined that only 15 percent of our knowledge is in technical training, and the balance of 85 percent is represented in *personal qualities*, such as the following:

Goal Orientation

Memory (recall)

Creativity

Calm Reaction

Enthusiasm

Diplomacy

Relaxation

Personal Confidence

Friendliness

Decisiveness

Aggressiveness

The Ability to Get Along with Others

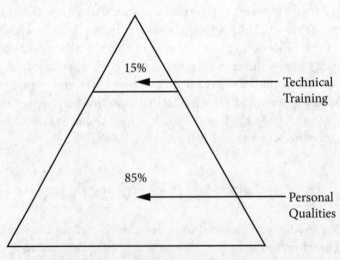

**DETERMINING FACTORS FOR SUCCESS**

## THE CONQUEST OF INNER SPACE

Why can we move at such breathtaking speed to conquer the vast wonders of outer space yet make virtually no progress at lighting up dark inner recesses of the human mind?

The giant rocket that carries our astronauts on their magical journey to the moon and the tiny cameras that let us more or less journey with them—these are testaments to man's rationality, and mastery of logic. But the stories told by the crewmen of the U.S.S. *Pueblo,* (the navy vessel captured by the North Koreans on its maiden mission as a spy ship for Naval Intelligence and the National Security Agency in January 1968) that speak of the hatred and uncontrolled emotions that go back to Cain and Abel, have dogged mankind down through the course of human history.

Of course, a reporter need not speculate on Vietnam or North Korea [or all wars since] to see this darker side of man's nature. 1968, the year of *Apollo 8,* was also the year of the murders of Senator Robert Kennedy and Dr. Martin Luther King and many other violent indications that man is not nearly so smart as his technology would suggest. [Apollo 8 was the first crewed spacecraft to leave low earth orbit and the first to reach the moon, orbit it, and return.]

Enjoyment of the magnificent technological feats involved in space travel is diminished by the certain knowledge that probably more people are at work trying to figure our military applications than are busy trying to determine in what ways these achievements can be turned into the uplift of the whole human family.

We marvel at the ease with which man unlocked the secrets of the universe. *Why cannot they also uncover some of the dark mysteries within themselves?—* The internal mysteries are the things that make us the frail and destructive creatures that we are.

We may go down in history as the age that got a man on the moon before we had figured out a way to get the pigeons off the statues.

## AVOID DEBATING

The ideas discussed are as old as recorded history and confirmed by all those who have tried them. The most unimportant thing in studying the information in the book, right from the start, is to avoid debating about who is right and who is not.

A debate always follows discussions where one person deals in generalities and the other counters with specifics—the use of false analogies and syllogisms fuels the fire.

Why is it that another person sees things we do not see, or he fails to see things we see? Seeing things as they are is not as simple as it is always supposed. The ability to deceive ourselves is boundless. We build our illusions of reality.

What you see (in your imagination) is what you get

What you think (about) is what you get.

You receive the net results of what you think (about.)

It is silly to think that those who make no effort and are undisciplined could possibly know what these things are and, presuming that, the other person knows it is absurd to enter into a debate with this false assumption as a premise.

Another false assumption that infiltrates through debate is that the other person can suddenly change his fundamental values. This is not true, and the reason it is not true is that at any given moment, we have become who we are because of our past (conditioning). We remain as we are or change due to more or other conditioning. To suppose that something so laboriously built up can be altered suddenly by rational (intellectual) argument is remote.

Changing people's values and understanding occurs only when the change or idea was in the works for some time before it surfaced publicly. It is ridiculous to assume you can produce changes in people suddenly and only by means of argumentation. To change someone's mind is the result, not the cause, of changing him, since argumentation occurs from the kind of person he is already, not the other way around. Since arguments result from the sort of person one already is, it is easy to see why it is wrong to think you can argue someone into being another way.

To benefit from this book, if an idea or technique does not agree with your present thinking, you will not attempt to debate it but learn its validity by trying it in your life. It is an unassailable fact that all of us possess infinitely more talent than we use. Therefore, it is logical to conclude that the measure of success we achieve depends not on how much we possess, but on *how much we utilize.*

## WE CAN ALWAYS BE BETTER

An individual can't communicate to others all the knowledge of his real self. No one can ever exercise the full potential effectiveness of his authentic self. Every one of us has much room for improvement. Our real self is continuously moving toward but never reaching its ultimate goal. The real self is not passive but is forever in motion; it is never really perfected and is perpetually in a developmental state.

Consequently, no one should merely aim to be a success but should strive to be successful.

## DISCOVERY FOR SUCCESS

We will draw a triangle representing one person's potential and a second triangle representing another person's potential. The first person has a great amount of natural ability, outstanding talents, broad education, and an attractive personality. The second person does not have all of these advantages and has a much smaller potential. Which of these two persons would we say would be more successful?

We would likely all agree that it would be number one. But when this doesn't happen, how is it explained? The number two person far exceeds the number one in the degree of tangible success accomplishments. Most people are at a loss to explain this. What happened to number two to allow him to do this? The explanation is simple. He simply *used* a lot more of what he had and thereby

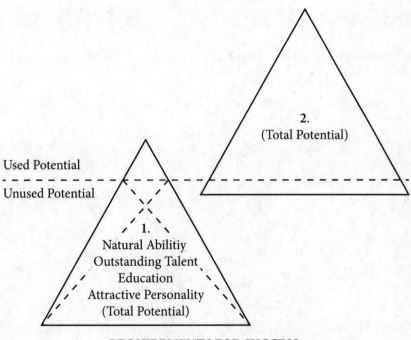

REQUIREMENTS FOR SUCCESS

attained a greater degree of success. To reiterate, if we draw a line across the drawing of triangles in the lower part of triangle two and extend it into triangle one, we see the amount of potential used. It then becomes apparent why person number two will become more successful than number one.

The training, exercises, and techniques you will use will enable you to bring out your unused potential, so you can be eminently more successful than you ever dreamed you could.

# 2

## TWO IMAGES

YOU HAVE WITHIN YOU A DEEP DESIRE TO PERFORM SOMETHING OR TO BE SOME-
one who will bring real happiness, satisfaction, and peace of mind into your
life. While you usually consider this desire to be no more than wishful think-
ing, being impossible to attain, you never forget it.

The fact that you have this desire is evidence that it is attainable. You hold
two pictures of yourself in your mind. The first is a picture of the person you
know yourself to be—a person with whom, in many ways, you are dissatisfied.
The second is a picture of the person you'd like to be—a relaxed, enthusiastic,
confident, decisive person ready to meet any situation and master it, respected
by all those who know you.

The contrast between the person you are and this inner vision of what you
might be is the *Divine Discontent* in you; it accounts for all your growth and
progress. It is not a device by which nature tantalizes you. It is not contained
within you as a seed of frustration and unhappiness.

It is the creative urge within you that builds the desire to grow. Nature has
equated this urge within you with a piece of built-in equipment that enables you
to grow and to continue growing mentally and spiritually as long as you live.

You want to feel secure, to be loved, to be important, appreciated, needed,
and to be respected. You are not unique in these feelings. All human beings
have them.

In this book, I will outline a program for you and show you how to put this
built-in equipment to work, and how to handle it in such a way that you may
become the person tomorrow that you envision today.

# 3

## ACQUIRING KNOWLEDGE

### ACQUIRING KNOWLEDGE IS PASSIVE, EXPERIENCE IS ACTIVE

People gain knowledge through the reading of books, pedagogically, but to *experience,* one must react psychologically and imaginatively to that knowledge.

### EXPERIENCE IS NECESSARY

If you follow the ideas set forth here, you will be forced to *experience.* Merely talking about the ideas will not verify their worth in your life. The only way you can prove they are valid is to try them out and then decide for yourself what effect they have upon you as an individual. Put them into action, and reserve your judgment until you have allowed them to work for you.

What is the magic of carrying out these rules, regulations, and suggestions? Just this—a deep driving desire to learn and a vigorous determination to start today and never stop. The only way we can develop such an urge is to continually remind ourselves of how important these principles are to us.

### THERE IS NO OTHER WAY

Say to yourself over and over and over:

*My peace of mind, my happiness, my health, and even my income will, in the long run, depend primarily on applying the old, obvious, and eternal truths that have been described in this book.* Write this material down. Keep this knowledge near you. Glance at it often.

Remember that the use of these principles can be made habitual and unconscious only by a *constant and vigorous* campaign of review and application. *There is no other way.*

When you acquire knowledge only intellectually, you will never *learn*. You can *learn* only by doing. If you want to master these principles, study them thoroughly. Then do something about them in *applying* them at every opportunity. If you don't, you will forget.

Until knowledge is activated into a useful advantage, it is worthless.

Only knowledge that is used flows to the conscious mind. You will probably find it difficult to apply this all the time. You are not merely trying to acquire information; you are attempting to *form a new habit pattern*. This change will require time, persistence, and daily application. Use these principles, and they will achieve magic for you.

## KNOW THYSELF

From Socrates, the first great teacher of success, down to the present day, wise men have said, "Know thyself." This statement is essential for you. You are unique. There is not now, nor will there ever be, another human being exactly like you. However, you indeed have the same basic desires that every other human being has. What makes the difference is the degree of intensity of these desires. This intensity defines what is important to you, and what you think is important determines what you do.

## BASIC DESIRES

Human beings are all moved by four basic desires; they are, at the same time, man's four basic goals:

Security (physical-emotional-financial)

Love

Ego Satisfaction

Bodily Comforts and Possessions

The difference in the level of these four desires is what distinguishes one person from another. What makes you an individual is the strength and degree of your desire to meet these basic goals.

## OBJECTIVES

We define objectives as duties and responsibilities. They set the pattern of your behavior. You cause a "turning point" in your life when you recognize your duties and responsibilities to *yourself, your loved ones,* and to the *company, career, or business* which provides your livelihood and then accept these duties and responsibilities and proceed to carry them out to the full extent of your ability.

I repeat for emphasis: The "turning point" in your life will come when you recognize your duties and responsibilities to yourself, your loved ones, and your company, career, or business; when you accept these duties and responsibilities and proceed to carry them out to the full extent of your ability.

You will carry out your duties and responsibilities when you define your goals, lay out a plan for reaching them, establish controls, and generate within yourself the power of self-motivation.

## VALUE OF SETTING GOALS

The value to you in setting definite objectives or goals is that you link your thinking to a purpose. You no longer daydream. You know where you are going, and you concentrate your thoughts and actions on getting you there. Your personal improvement is the most significant consideration in your life—Yes, without question or a doubt, your personal development is the essential thing in your life.

## CHANGE IS NECESSARY

As you follow these suggestions, you will begin to improve immediately. You will note a decided change in your thinking, in your power of understanding, in your ability to solve your problems, and to express your thoughts forcefully, fluently, and convincingly.

Does this sound as though you are being offered the world in a neat package? You are. It is not a wild promise, and it will surely be fulfilled. There have been remarkable changes in the lives of men and women who have made the sincere effort and followed these simple procedures.

## A GREAT DISCOVERY

But first, each one of them changed their attitudes of mind. In the year 1900, William James, professor at Harvard, Medical Doctor, Psychiatrist, Philosopher, and one of the foremost thinkers this nation ever produced, made a profound statement.

Nineteen hundred—this was the year when the electric light and the automobile came into being. William James did not mention them. "The greatest discovery of my generation," he said, "is that human beings may alter their lives by altering their attitudes of mind."

Everything in your life depends on your mental attitude, and the important thing to remember is that *you control* your mental attitude. In fact, it is the one thing in your life that you can *absolutely control.*

## DESIRE TO SUCCEED

When you decide that you are going to make your hopes and dreams realities, turn wishes into facts and desires into solid achievements, you are taking the first step on the path to success. You have generated within yourself the desire to succeed. Daily, as you work with this program, your confidence will grow and hasten your progress toward your goal. Your mental attitude will undergo great change. You will believe you can. And when you believe you can—YOU *CAN.*

Nature has given every human being at birth a built-in automatic success mechanism. Human beings are gifted with creative imagination and can formulate their own goals. We must do this for our peace of mind and happiness, or the internal desire to use our potential will nag at us as an unfulfilled desire. The ideas in this book are designed specifically to help you achieve the goals that you set for yourself. It deals exclusively with the one most important factor to *you—your own personal goals.*

## YOU MUST DO IT

You must realize that you are the only one who can make the program effective. This program will tell you *what* to do and *how* to do it. But *you must do it,* consciously following the directions on how to get to where you want to go.

## BECOME EMOTIONALLY INVOLVED

Reading this book will not make you a success. You must become emotionally involved and tailor the principles enumerated to fill the needs and requirements for your own progress. Therefore, do not rush through this book. Take as much time as needed and work out the pattern for your success with careful thought. The more sound thinking you do at this time about your future progress, the better will be your plan and the greater your success.

## GENERATE ENTHUSIASM

Many books and talks by the thousands tell you that you must be self-motivated, that you must be enthusiastic; that enthusiasm overcomes all obstacles; that nothing great is possible without enthusiasm; that the enthusiastic individual, while often dissatisfied, is never discouraged or negative. This is all true, but these books and talks do not tell in plain, understandable language *how you can generate this enthusiasm* and become self-motivated.

Yet, the way is simple. You must be motivated toward something. You must be enthused about something. That is why you must *set a goal* for yourself— one that you can reach. Then you must use the most powerful force in all of the history of humanity's achievement, IMAGINATION.

# 4

# THE STRANGEST SECRET

EVEN THOUGH THIS KNOWLEDGE, AS WE HAVE SAID, IS AS OLD AS RECORDED history—the the early wise men and women discovered it, and it appears again and again throughout the Bible—it remains a secret. This is strange, because most people who know about it do not understand it. Therefore, it remains the strangest secret. But you can dare to be different. Then you will be different from the millions of unhappy people in this world. *You will know the truth that will set you free.*

## SECRET OF SUCCESS

If you were able to stop people on the street and ask them, "What is the secret of success?" maybe one out of fifty could tell you. Of all people, 95 percent are actually searching for the right to fail.

Suppose I were to tell a person that there is a mansion ready and waiting for his or her occupancy just over the hill. This person wants to believe me, but he or she is unable to. This person has been fooled too many times by too many people and is not willing to risk being hurt again.

But the mansion exists whether this person moves toward it or not. Whether he or she claims it or not, it is always there ready for him or her. This is the problem: the man or woman will not walk toward the mansion until he or she sees it, and he or she cannot see it until he or she walks toward it.

This seems to be the dilemma we are all undertaking, and it is our job through this program to get you to move forward far enough to catch your first glimpse of the mansion. Maybe you'll see only a small portion of it, but that is enough. You will have seen something that will make you curious, excited, and eager.

The real secret is *goals;* people succeed with them and fail without them.

## SOMETHING TO THINK ABOUT

*Grant me the serenity to accept the things I cannot change, the courage to change the things I can, and the wisdom to know the difference.*

What has now been called the Serenity Prayer and used in 12-step groups applies to everyone. We all must discern the things we can or cannot change, so we put our energy into the things that will help us succeed rather than wasting our time in futility.

# 5

## EXPECTATION OF CHANGE

### HOW SOON CAN YOU EXPECT CHANGE?

How long will it be before you can use or experience these principles and notice a change?

Changes take place immediately, the very moment you read or learn in any way some fundamental principle for a more superior life. You will then experience some reaction. This reaction may be somewhat clouded, but if you are persistent, a more distinct understanding will emerge. A typical response is, "I'm not sure what is happening, but something different is occurring."

The constructive, positive changes you make inside you will have a beneficial effect on your personality and all your activities.

### CONFUSION IS HELPFUL

As you think about what you are reading, do not be concerned about being confused. *Confusion is a genuine emotion.* A man has begun to understand himself when he can say, "I don't know," without being afraid. To realize you don't know is the beginning of knowing.

If an idea seems to be outside your comprehension, do not disregard it. No idea or principle is incomprehensible to man. No matter how obscure, it exists in every human being.

As you progress toward change, a strange thing happens. Your confusion will grow just before you realize the truth for the first time (darkness before the dawn). A simple explanation is that you have become more aware of your confusion. You've brought it up to the conscious level, and you now discover that you didn't comprehend as much as you thought; this gives you a genuine understanding. The reason you fail to be happy and to attain personal freedom is that you are unaware that such a state is attainable.

## NEED TO BE AWARE OF ITS EXISTENCE

For us to be motivated toward something, we must at least have a suspicion of its existence. We are not discussing anything far-out or of no practical value. I am offering you a far better way to live that you can benefit from today. Finding it is only possible through an awareness that it does exist. What is strange—we already know, but we are not aware that we know. You don't need to understand the basic mechanical principles of an automobile to drive it or ride in it. Therefore, you do not need totally to grasp the numerous changes that will take place within you. Let them happen. Relax with your studies of Psycho-Cybernetics. Read with a sense of exploration, seeing everything as good news, and enjoy the adventure.

# 6

## AS A MAN THINKS

### AS A MAN THINKS, SO HE IS

As a man thinks, so he is; and as he continues to think, so he shall remain. This thought not only embraces man's being, but is so comprehensive as to reach out to all circumstances of his life. A man is what he thinks. His complete character is the sum of his thoughts, and as long as he maintains those thoughts, he remains the same.

> *SOME MAY REACH FOR THE STARS,*
> *OTHERS WILL END BEHIND BARS,*
> *YET, WE WOULD ALL LIKE THE RIGHT,*
> *TO FIND THE KEY TO SUCCESS,*
> *THAT ELUSIVE RAY OF LIGHT,*
> *THAT WILL LEAD TO HAPPINESS.*

*What do you think is holding this man behind bars?*
There are many ways he can get out. All of us are sometimes captured by some idea or situation and put ourselves behind bars. We feel locked in. What could he possibly be saying to himself that is holding him there?

He could be saying:
"I don't want to get out."
"I don't see a way out," or simply, "I can't get out."
If he thinks and believes he can't get out—he can't.
As a man thinks, he is.

## PSYCHO-CYBERNETICS DEFINED

We define Psycho-Cybernetics as a method of steering yourself.

Where do you want to steer yourself? If you don't know, you're in trouble. You are somewhat like the man who stands at the airline ticket counter and when asked, "Where do you want to go?" replies, "I don't know," or says, "Give me a ticket to anywhere you choose." Does it make sense not to know, or to let somebody else choose your goal for you?

*Psycho-Cybernetics is positive doing.*

It is a guide, a gateway to creative living. It is a way of life. *Psycho* means mind, and *Cybernetics* is taken from a Greek word meaning "helmsman," a man who steers a ship to port. The term, Psycho-Cybernetics has been coined to mean "steering your mind to a productive, useful, worthwhile, predetermined goal" so that you can reach the greatest port in the world, *peace of mind*.

From the beginning of recorded time, man has held, in one form or another, the concept that something is guiding him, a guiding force outside himself. This belief has taken thousands of forms but has persisted from primitive superstitions to the philosophy of our modern cultured societies.

## ESSENCE OF PSYCHO-CYBERNETICS

The essence of Psycho-Cybernetics is that *our basic ultimate goals have already been predetermined.*

Man is teleological. He is motivated toward some ultimate goal having an ultimate meaning. Man, in his existence on this earth, does not know what this ultimate meaning is. But when he is not moving in this direction, he gets negative feedback (Divine Discontent). We all came from someplace, and we're going someplace. The architect of the universe did not build a stairway going nowhere. By his very nature, man is acting freely and normally when he is pursuing a precise objective and is working actively toward it. The feeling of contentment is a by-product of his goal because when a person is working toward a definite goal, he is usually happy, no matter what his situation may be.

Only when man moves for accomplishment does he begin to fulfill the purpose inherent in the existence of life. Life calls for activity, and for man, this activity needs to be purposeful to bring the realization that it is meaningful.

Man's big goal is toward creative accomplishment

*Man is Similar to a Machine*
*You are guided by your mind.*

Have you ever seen a tractor, a giant earth-moving machine—a tremendous, incredible machine, with a man sitting way up on top with a wheel in his hand guiding it? It occurred to me that there was a similarity between the human mind and this machine. Suppose you are at the controls of such a vast source of energy. Will you settle back and fold your arms and allow it to run itself into a ditch, or are you going to hold both hands on the wheel and control and direct the power to a specific, worthwhile goal? It's up to you.

Let's say we had two ocean liners—again, enormous machines. One, we staff with a full crew and give it a goal. It surely will get where it starts out to go 9,999 out of 10,000 times. The other, we provide no crew and no goal. We start the engines and let it go. It will surely run itself up on the beach before it can get out of the harbor.

Our mind is standard equipment. Did you ever think that because your mind came to you free, you place little importance on it? Yet, the opposite is true. Your mind is of the utmost importance.

## SOME THINGS TO THINK ABOUT

*"Whatever the mind of man can conceive and believe, it can achieve."* Napoleon Hill

What a man can imagine or conceive in his mind he can accomplish. *"Impossibles are as impossible as thinking makes them so."* Henry J. Kiser. (The father of modern shipbuilding)

*I am limited only by the thoughts I choose to encourage.*
*I have the power to select and control my thoughts.*
*I have nothing to deal with but my thoughts.*
*Present thoughts determine my future.*
*Thought is action, in rehearsal.*

IF

*If you think you are beaten, you are.*
*If you think you dare not, you don't.*
*If you like to win, but you think you can't, It is almost certain you won't.*

*If you think you'll lose, you're lost,*
*For out of the world we find,*

*Success begins with a fellow's will.*
   *It's all in the state of mind.*

*If you think you are outclassed, you are.*
   *You've got to think high to rise.*
   *You've got to be sure of yourself before you can ever win a prize.*

*Life's battles don't always go to the stronger or faster man.*
   *But sooner or later the man who wins*
   *Is the man who Thinks He CAN!"*

# 7

## SELF-IMAGE

### THE SELF-IMAGE

What is this self-image, and why is it so important? Without question, the essential key to human personality and behavior is the self-image. Even our achievements are limited by how we view ourselves. If we alter our self-image, our behavior and personality are affected by the change.

Self-image is the overall average of the various attitudes we hold towards our capabilities in a multitude of areas. It is the "picture we have of ourselves." Our self-image, therefore, is of utmost importance because we cannot be any more effective, more successful, better coordinated, more creative, or more anything other than what our self-image says we are. It is the *ceiling* on the *effectiveness* with which we can use our *true potential*.

The data in the subconscious mind governs the self-image and, the self-image controls our effectiveness. It then becomes evident that if we want to change our actions or attitudes and thus change our behavior, we must add information to the subconscious that will reflect itself in our behavior.

Human beings are always changing and growing. They have an insatiable, never-ending need to better themselves. Around the self-image is built everything they do. It is the core of their being.

### BEHAVIOR DEPENDENT ON SELF-IMAGE

Suppose we have a vertical line and calibrate it to represent bits of knowledge (the brain contains about three trillion information facts by age thirty). We place an arrow at the top representing ever-increasing knowledge. Next, we select a self-image in a certain area. This self-image is surrounded by an effectiveness range. Our performance is effective only within this range. This picture given to us by our subconscious tells us to a very fine degree just how we will perform. We can only act according to this picture. It is our comfort zone. Any performance outside this zone will produce tension.

The only way we can change our performance is first to change the self-image. It raises the ceiling on our effectiveness and allows us greater use of our potential.

## BETTER SELF-IMAGES RELEASES ABILITY

To change your self-image, it is not necessary actually to improve yourself. It can be revised merely by repainting the *mind-picture* of yourself you carry in your imagination—your own private opinion and concept of that self. The change that comes from the development of a new self-image can produce rather fantastic results.

A person is usually more superior than he thinks he is. When he changes his self-image, he doesn't necessarily improve his skills and gifts. He only puts to use the talents he already possesses.

## WHEN POSITIVE THINKING WILL NOT WORK

The realization that you lack learning and wisdom is the initial step toward acquiring them. Beginning to be a more proficient person starts when you first realize you are incompetent.

We have discovered a fresh viewpoint about the *power of positive thinking*, which seems to answer why some people use it with success and yet others find it useless. When it is compatible with a person's self-image, *positive thinking* does undoubtedly function, but when it is incompatible with the self-image, it absolutely will not work.

As long as you hold any negative view of yourself, you will find it out of the question to think in positive terms.

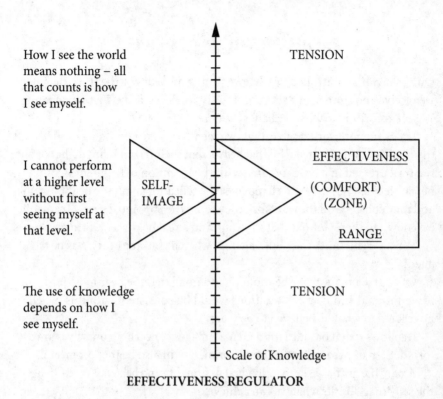

How I see the world means nothing – all that counts is how I see myself.

TENSION

I cannot perform at a higher level without first seeing myself at that level.

SELF-IMAGE

EFFECTIVENESS

(COMFORT) (ZONE)

RANGE

The use of knowledge depends on how I see myself.

TENSION

Scale of Knowledge

**EFFECTIVENESS REGULATOR**

## HOW YOU VIEW YOURSELF IS ALL-IMPORTANT

How you look at the world means nothing. All that counts is how you look at yourself. Because how you look at yourself determines how you look at the world!

Everyone has the power to grow and to change.

## WHAT MAKES YOU GOOD

Do you know what the largest room in the world is? It is the room for improvement.

Dizzy Dean was one of the greatest big-league baseball pitchers. When asked why he practiced so much when he already was the leading pitcher in the world, he replied, *"When you stop getting better, you stop being good."* This sums up the need for continued learning. The thing that makes you *good* is attempting to be *better*.

## WHAT WE THINK—IS TRUE

Our behavior is controlled by what we think and believe to be true. The image we receive and store in our subconscious is not necessarily what is happening. We act according to what we believe is true.

Let us suppose, for example, that two men are walking on the trail—let's call them Bill and Jim. Jim tells Bill that he has sent their friend John further out on the trail dressed in a bear costume with the intention of frightening Bill. But he has decided not to let this happen, so he tells him about the bear costume, and they continue on the trail until they reach the appointed spot. Meanwhile, unknown to them, John didn't show up, and a real bear was waiting!

What do you think were Bill's feelings when he saw the bear? Was he frightened?

Of course not, because he thought and imagined the bear to be John, and his emotional and nervous reactions would be consistent with this belief, so he reacted to what he believed to be true.

It follows that if our ideas and mental images concerning ourselves are distorted, then our reaction to our environment will also be inappropriate.

Again, the primary key to individual personality and behavior is self-image—the self-image limits what we can achieve.

## SOURCE OF IDEAS IS UNIMPORTANT

You must remember that it makes no difference how or by whom you have been programed with the various ideas you now have. No matter if they have been received from relatives, schooling, your friends—even from yourself, you are presently behaving in a manner based upon the belief that these ideas are true.

You have the ability, knowledge, and potential capacity to perform whatever is necessary to attain a happy life of accomplishment and fulfillment. This capacity will be used by you as soon as you alter the beliefs that are inhibiting to you right now.

## INFERIORITY

Feelings of inferiority are experienced to some degree by almost 95 percent of the world's population. To a major portion of these people, these feelings are a severe disadvantage in attaining fulfillment and satisfaction in life.

Inferiority feelings do not usually arise from actual experience, but from our own judgments and interpretations of events and experiences.

Inferiority complexes, which can intrude upon our lives, are developed from the feelings of inferiority that originate because we judge our performance and measure our abilities against someone else's and not against our own. When this happens, we will always be only a runner-up. When we evaluate our achievements by these criteria, we feel second-rate and unhappy. Consequently, we arrive at the erroneous assumption that we don't measure up.

Feelings of inferiority and superiority are conflicting feelings.

*The plain reality is:*

You are not *superior* to another person

You are not *inferior* to another person

You are merely *you*. Period.

A continuing feeling of inferiority soon deteriorates into an inferiority complex which causes a decline in a person's performance. It is interesting to realize how this situation can be artificially created in a psychological test. Some kind of mean level of performance is set up, and then the test subjects are persuaded that they are below this average.

To illustrate this theory, a professor passed out a written test to his class, telling them that the normal time of completion was fifteen minutes. In reality, the test required about an hour to finish. After fifteen minutes, even the most brilliant students became upset, believing they were inadequate or mentally deficient.

*Keep up with yourself. You are not in competition with anyone in this world.*

Don't compare yourself and your performance with another person's accomplishments. You can never possibly attain their standards, nor can they achieve yours. When you can unquestionably accept this truth as a fact and apply it in your daily life, your feelings of inferiority will evaporate.

## SOMETHING TO THINK ABOUT

*I'm not selfish. I'm simply deeply committed to me.*

# 8

## DEFINITIONS

IT IS NECESSARY THAT WE DEFINE CERTAIN WORDS. WHEN UNDERSTOOD IN THE terms given, these words will aid you in a better understanding of the subject.

PSYCHO-CYBERNETICS: "Self-steering" Helmsman or Steersman [from Greek] Method of steering, guiding, or directing yourself toward a useful, productive, worthwhile, predetermined goal. (Positive Doing)

POTENTIAL: "Total knowledge." (innate plus experienced)

EFFECTIVENESS: Degree of use of potential.

SUBCONSCIOUS: "Storehouse of Knowledge." (innate plus experienced) Vast unbelievable capacity to store knowledge. Controls all automatic body functions. Stores as memory all perceptions of the five senses.

SELF-IMAGE: "The picture we have of ourselves." Sets the boundaries of human accomplishments—the key to human personality and behavior. How *I look at the world means nothing. All that counts is how I look* at *myself.*

HABIT PATTERNS: "Automatic Response." (conditioned, without thinking)

1. Constructive (helps you reach your goals)
2. Restrictive (stops you from reaching your goals)
3. Compulsive (have to)
4. Inhibitive (can't)

PERSONALITY: "Outer expression of inner attitude or self-images." Something that attracts and is obscure and inexplicable. Something that is freed from inside a person—easily sensed, but hard to explain.

DATA REVISION: "A direct and controlled method of changing the self-image." Method of programming experience, training response to high performance. A method to control input to control output. (G. I. G. O. Garbage In-Garbage Out) Action in rehearsal.

ATTITUDE: "Habit of thought." Basic attitudes are formed up to seven years of age (formative years). Our success or failure is dependent upon these attitudes, yet we had no choice in their formation. The child starts with an open mind, and that is the last time he ever has one. He either becomes a bank president or a bank robber, or a diplomat who argues the question of the day, or a pool shark who argues whose shot is next. In other words, he is either the victim or the beneficiary of these attitudes. Our firm belief is that a person does not have to go through his entire lifetime a victim of attitudes formed when he was a child—he can create attitudes that will get him the things he wants and help him reach the goals he sets for himself.

MOTIVATION—"The quality of human emotion that produces the drive that moves you to *action*" (puts action in the doing).

Let's think of how people are motivated.

There is *incentive motivation* based on *reward* and *fear motivation* based on *punishment*.

An example of *incentive motivation* is the story of the donkey being led by a small boy riding on a wooden cart down an unpaved country road. In his hand is a long pole with a rope tied on the end of it. A carrot dangles from the rope in front of the donkey's nose. The donkey then moves toward the carrot and pulls the cart—if he is hungry. This type of motivation eventually wears itself out, based on the need being satisfied.

An example of *fear motivation*—assume in the above story that the boy stops the cart at the side of the road and the donkey munches on some dry grass until his appetite is satisfied. What happens when he holds the carrot in front of the donkey? When the donkey doesn't move, the boy removes the carrot from the pole and commences to beat the donkey with the pole. If the donkey is afraid, he will move, but at some point, he will become immune. *While incentive motivation and fear motivation* both do work, there comes a time eventually when they do not produce the desired results.

What percentage of people in business today do you think are using either incentive or fear motivation, or both? My premise is that an individual does not have to be lured with a prize or driven with a whip in order to accomplish anything. I believe a person can be moved by his own attitudes, which are lasting. This is called *attitude motivation* based on *change*.

The world is not short of people *who know how,* but it is in desperate need of people *who will do it.* They must, of necessity, put *action* into the *doing* rather than the *knowing.* People properly motivated will *go;* they *will move and do things.* It is the action idea of motivation that brings results.

*No one gets far without motivation. Motivation is the number one need in achievement.*

Since all action is based on *emotion* despite logic and reason, the action itself springs from *feelings and emotions,* not from reason. Until the emotions are aroused there is no action.

The answer to becoming motivated and enthusiastic is simple—you must first be motivated toward something—and be enthusiastic about something.

*A person who has a goal and a plan to achieve it then develops the emotion needed.*

Goal

Plan

Desire (increased desire for the goal)

Confidence (develops the confidence he can reach the goal)

Determination (finally he develops the determination that says, "I don't care what anybody says, thinks or does, I will reach my goal.")

SUCCESS—"Success is the progressive realization towards a productive, useful, worthwhile, predetermined goal."

It is necessary that you understand what success is. The dictionary defines success as "The accomplishment of a goal sought, a favorable outcome of something attempted, the attainment of wealth, fame, etc." indicating that success is in the obtaining of something. In other words, this implies that when you do accomplish your goal, you are a success, and therefore you are not a success until you do. However, defining success in these terms would mean that your success was only momentary.

Think of success as a *journey,* not a destination. When you are not actively progressing toward a goal, you are not successful. No matter how you measure success, no matter how much you attain of what you think you want, you will never arrive at a point called success. When you get where you think success is, you'll still find the road stretching invitingly ahead.

*Success is related to potential.*

*Success is dependent on our effectiveness.*

Simply stated: Success is the result of attitude and habit.

This places the attainment of success within the reach of everyone, because success attitudes can be developed, and success habits can be formed.

Financial success is a rate of exchange of effectiveness. In business, people earn money by providing products or services which are needed and useful.

Financial success is not the result of earning money—earning money is the result of financial success.

HAPPINESS: "A state of mind when your thoughts are pleasant most of the time" (happiness and success are synonymous). Happiness is a by-product of actively seeking a goal.

# 9

## DO WE SEE WHAT'S REALLY THERE?

A VERY WELL-KNOWN QUOTE FROM THE BIBLE IS, "KNOW THE TRUTH, AND THE truth will set you free." This could mean that the truth that sets you free is the truth about *yourself*. Most of us underestimate ourselves and overestimate the problem. Now, what will this truth set you free of? It will set you free from fear. Inhibition is always based on fear. Therefore, the only real freedom is being *free from fear*.

### EXAMPLES

Many of the ideas and techniques we will review are as old as recorded history, thoroughly tested, and proven. Some will be familiar, some may seem oversimplified, and some may seem obvious.

Take your wristwatch and place it upside down next to you. Now write a description of the face of the watch. What kind of numerals does it have, color, second hand, dials, make, and any other details you can think of? Statisticians tell us the average person looks at his watch (Editor's addition: or cellphone) 5,000 times in one year. Multiply 5,000 by the number of years you've had the watch. Wouldn't you say that anyone who has looked at something that many times should know what it looks like? Let's see if you have described your watch. How many things did you leave out or get wrong? The reason is that you only look at your watch to observe the time. This makes the point—how many things do we look at and not really see?

Now try this. What does it say?

PARIS IN THE
THE SPRING

It does not say Paris in the Spring. Read it again. If you
read it correctly, it will say "Paris in the the Spring." The
third word "the" is repeated. Why didn't you see it? Be-
cause you have been conditioned not to see it.

TEST YOUR AWARENESS
First, read the sentence enclosed in the box below.

> FINISHED FLIES ARE THE RESULT OF YEARS OF SCIENTIFIC
> STUDY COMBINED WITH THE EXPERIENCE OF MANY YEARS.

Now count the Fs in the sentence. Count them only once and do not go
back and count them again

How many did you get? Did you get three? That's normal. The correct an-
swer is six. That's how many there are. Why did you miss them? Conditioning?

The sound of the "F" in "scientific" is different from the sound of the "F" in
"of." One is an "F" sound, and the other is a "V" sound. The result is that you
block it out, and you neglect to read it.

Read the following word:

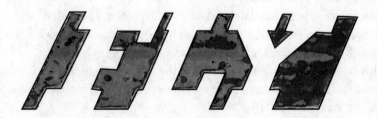

What is it? Now concentrate on the white spaces instead of the black. it's "FLY"
of course. Do we see what's really there? No, we can only see what we have been
conditioned to see. We read black on white, not white on black. The thing that
determines what we see is the assumption we have made when we look.

With the aid of the exercises in this book, you will become aware. You will then be able to see much more of what is really there. It will open up a whole new world for you, and life will become more interesting and exciting.

Let's try another one.

What do you see in this picture?

Do you see a young woman in a three-quarter view to the left? Or are you the one in five who immediately sees the old hag facing to the left?

In either case, you probably will find it very difficult to "turn off" the picture you first saw and reorganize its elements into the other figure.

This is a simple demonstration of how the mind tends to "lock on" to apparently satisfactory solutions to problems, blocking out alternatives and sharply curtailing creativity *and effectiveness*.

*What does all this show us?*

It shows that there is much more to our "image of reality." It shows that it is incomplete, inaccurate, and there is *always more*. By being able to see and interpret more you increase your awareness and, consequently, your creativity. The more we see of what is really there, the more accurate is our view of reality.

*"It isn't that you're stupid—it's that you understand so many things that just aren't so."*

*"It's not what you don't know that harms you, it's what you know for darn sure that isn't so."*

*"People don't think; they just think they think.*

What are they doing? They're reacting to what they think and believe to be true, they are reacting to past conditioning.

## VICTIMS OR BENEFICIARIES

We are all bombarded constantly, from the day we are born we're bombarded with limiting suggestions. You, at present, are either the victim or the beneficiary of ideas you were exposed to as a child.

Following are some examples of the victim of erroneous ideas:

Opportunity knocks only once

Born loser

Not artistic (can't draw)

Never could do anything right

Children are seen, not heard

Can't teach an old dog new tricks

Clumsy kid (all thumbs)

I'm not a businessman (got a "D" in geometry)

The following paragraphs are *examples of conditioning.*

## CIRCUS ELEPHANTS AND LIMITATIONS

An elephant can easily pick up a one-ton load with his trunk. Have you visited a circus and watched these huge creatures standing quietly tied with a light rope around one leg, which, in turn, was tied to a small wooden stake driven several inches into the ground?

*How was this accomplished?* By cruel but effective conditioning.

While still young, and weak, the elephant is tied with a heavy chain to an immovable iron stake embedded in several feet of concrete; no matter how hard he tries (and he does try) he cannot break the chain or move the stake. Then, no matter how large and strong the elephant becomes, he continues to believe that he cannot move as long as he sees his leg tied to the stake in the ground beside him.

## THE PIKE AND THE MINNOW

Picture a four-foot glass cube filled with water and a little minnow swimming around inside. The cube is divided in the middle with a glass partition. A pike is dropped in the water on the opposite side of the minnow. He makes an immediate dash for the minnow, and, of course, he collides with the glass partition. After repeating this maneuver many times, the glass is removed, and he never again will try to attack the minnow.

These two stories will help illustrate the tremendous effect of conditioning by the process of repetition. When we are conditioned to believe something that isn't true, our behavior becomes consistent with our belief.

There was a *Peanuts* cartoon by Charles Schultz in which one of the characters was spouting off about Charlie Brown and his lack of understanding of life and girls and even baseball.

She arrived at his house saying, "He plays a lot of baseball, but I doubt if he even understands baseball." With that, she knocked on the door, and Charlie Brown put his head out. She said, "I don't think you understand *anything*, Chuck," turned around and walked away, leaving him standing with a blank expression on his face saying, "I don't even understand what it is I don't understand."

This is sort of an example of your dilemma. But you're *going* to understand what it is you don't understand!

# 10

## THE PROCESS OF THINKING

### HYPOTHETICAL ANALYSIS OF THE "THINKING PROCESS"

The following is a hypothetical analysis of the "thinking" process. Science is rapidly coming to regard the "mind" and the "body" as separately acting entities. Actually they are one complex interacting whole. Yet it is more convenient to separate them and look at each area of activity. It is necessary to carry this a step further and look at three different parts of the mind in terms of the functions they perform for us. This is not the actual way they are divided, but it is how our "thinking process" is. It is a hypothetical process and seems to explain the functioning of these entities.

We will divide this process into three functions, the *conscious, the subconscious,* and the *creative center.*

### CONSCIOUS MIND

The part of the mind with which we are most familiar and, of course, of which we are most aware, is the conscious mind.

The chief functions of the conscious mind are:

1. The *perception* of incoming information from the environment and from inside the person.
2. The *association* of current information about the environment and the functions of the body with partial information or data which is in the memory files of the subconscious mind. (If the perception is of something not previously contained in the subconscious, the only function is to store this information.)

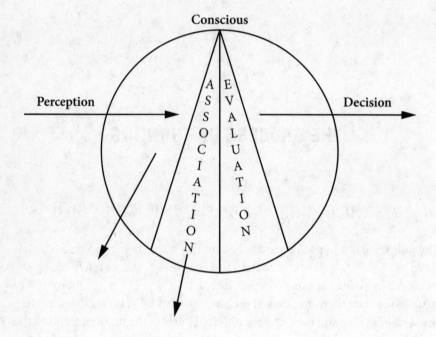

3. The *evaluation* of this association with respect to the best inter-
est of the individual.
4. *Decision* and direction of action (or inaction).

As you can see, each of us spends all of our waking hours running through these four steps: *Perception, Association, Evaluation,* and *Decision.* The process is exceedingly rapid and perfectly accurate, based on the information. Only two things can lead to a decision, or action, which is not in the best interest of the person.

One is the failure to perceive something. This might happen because of failing eyesight or hearing, etc. The other possible reason for error would be inaccurate information or data, either from an external source or from the memory files in the subconscious. The accuracy of the conscious mind, as with any good computer, is no better than the data available to us (G.I.G.O.- Garbage In-Garbage Out.)

If the airline information clerk tells you on the phone that Flight 703 is sched-uled to leave at 8:15 p.m., and you arrive at the airport at 7:45 p.m. only to find that the plane left at 7:15, then your directed action was wrong only because the data available was false. Many similar errors happen to us every day because of false data or the interpretation of this data in the remarkable memory storage files in the subconscious.

## SUBCONSCIOUS

The Subconscious Mind has two primary functions:

1. It controls all the *automatic* functions of the body, such things as the beating of your heart, breathing, glandular secretions, etc. Even when the conscious mind is disconnected, whether through sleep, hypnosis or a concussion, the subconscious continues to operate automatically the various functions of the body.

2. It stores as *memory* everything that happens to the individual. And, as part of this memory storage capability, it is able to develop automatic or preprogrammed courses of action to thoughts which are called Habit Patterns. An important aspect of the subconscious mind is its inability to discriminate. It accepts input just as transmitted to it by the conscious mind. If the conscious view is distorted, then the recorded data will be distorted. Here is something that is a great description:

*I am very accommodating*
*I ask no questions.*
*I accept whatever you give me.*
*I do whatever I am told to do.*
*I do not presume to change anything you think, say, or do; I file it all away in perfect order, quickly and efficiently, and then I return it to you exactly as you gave it to me.*
*Sometimes you call me your memory.*
*I am the reservoir into which you toss anything your heart or mind chooses to deposit there.*
*I work night and day; I never rest, and nothing can impede my activity.*
*The thoughts you send to me are categorized and filed, and my filing system never fails.*
*I am truly your servant who does your bidding without hesitation or criticism.*

*I cooperate when you tell me that you are "this" or "that," and I play it*
     *back as you give it. I am most agreeable.*
*Since I do not think, argue, judge, analyze, question, or make decisions,*
     *I accept impressions easily.*
*I am going to ask you to sort out what you send me, however, my files*
     *are getting a little cluttered and confused. I mean, please discard*
     *those things that you do not want returning to you.*
*What is my name? Oh, I thought you knew!*
*I am your subconscious.*

                                                    *By Margaret E. White*

There is two-way communication between the conscious and the sub-
conscious minds. Of course, the conscious is able to *transmit* information
to the subconscious at will, whereas some of the bits of information in the
subconscious are more readily available to conscious recall than others.
Many of the memories which we have there are right on the surface, bits
of information which we use all the time. We have an almost unbelievable
scanning mechanism capable of looking over all of the available informa-
tion instantly. Plus, we can tell immediately what a particular moving ob-
ject is. For example, a new Chevrolet convertible has two doors, is blue, has
disc wheels and whitewall tires, etc. If we had to go through each individual
bit of logic and piece each bit of related information together consciously,
it would take two to three weeks to come to the same identification. There
are approximately ten billion memory cells in the human brain, each capa-
ble of storing 100,000 different bits of information. Every single thing that
has ever happened to you is recorded there, every sight, every smell, every
sound, and every feeling that you have ever had since you were born, and
maybe a little before that. At age thirty, the average person has accumulated
about three trillion memories. (Of course, some of these memories have
been repressed—blocked off from conscious recall).

## THE CREATIVE CENTER

There is the third mind—the Creative Center.
     The function of the third, and in many ways the most important, part of
the mind is:

1. To maintain sanity.
2. To find creative solutions to problems.

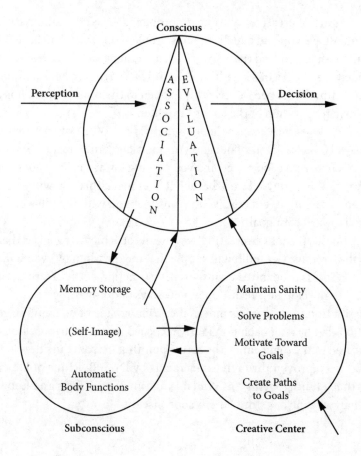

3. To motivate the individual in the direction of his goals.
4. To develop new, creative means of achieving goals.

The Creative Center has only recently been recognized and researched. It has always functioned. Yet, specific methods by which the tremendous power of this section of the mind might be purposefully used have been developed only in the last twenty years.

When it is not used in a directive manner, the Creative Center functions automatically. It performs all four of the above operations whether or not you are aware of its existence, whether or not you direct it to do so. The maintenance of sanity is accomplished largely through dream therapy. The Creative Center is completely aware of all the pressures, tensions, and emotional conflicts that are disturbing you. It is capable of reducing the effect of these reactions on your mental health by giving you a dream which is symbolic.

The finding of creative solutions to problems is equally automatic. How many times have you had a really serious problem on which you have worked for hours without finding the answer? Then, perhaps, you have laid the problem aside to take care of something else, only to have a perfect solution pop into your mind. Most people have this happen to them quite often. It is a perfectly normal operation of the Creative Center.

The third job of the Creative Center is motivation. When you have a properly defined goal (and I will talk about goals in detail later), the Creative Center does an extremely effective job of keeping you moving toward it. This does not necessarily mean that you will work harder. It does mean that you will work more intelligently and more effectively. It means that you will like the work which takes you toward your goal.

And, finally, the task of creating new means of achieving goals is the function of the Creative Center. It will supply the "means whereby" you will reach your goal. This is probably the most exciting function of the creative center— its ability to develop new techniques, new ways of doing things.

The solution to your goals may come from outside of you, giving you information that has not been previously recorded in your subconscious mind, as indicated in the diagram by the arrow pointing in from outside.

It has been proven through experiments by Dr. J. B. Rhine of Duke University that a human being has available to him certain facts and knowledge other than what he has stored in his subconscious.

# 11

## THE SECRET OF CREATIVE THINKING

ORIGINAL THOUGHTS AND IDEAS ARE NOT CONCEIVED AT THE CONSCIOUS LEVEL but come out of the subconscious, seemingly "out of nowhere." When the conscious mind has freed itself from the question and is actively thinking about something else, creative ideas emerge. However, they do not materialize without first giving some conscious thought to the problem.

First, a person must be concerned with seeking a solution in order to activate an "inspiration." One should consciously gather all the facts of the situation and weigh the possible alternatives. Then, after analyzing the problem and mentally picturing the most satisfactory outcome, it is necessary to relax and allow one's subconscious imagination to go to work.

*Conscious effort is the greatest impediment to effective creativity.* When you use conscious effort, you restrain and prohibit your automatic success mechanism from working.

It has been shown that when you try to use willpower or effort of any kind to change your beliefs or to correct bad habits, there is a negative rather than a positive result. Deliberate effort is one of the major factors in a person's falling short of his goal.

In his "law of reversed effort," Emile Coue said, "When the will and the imagination are in conflict, the imagination invariably wins."

Other scientific discoveries showed that effort is one of the main forces prohibiting a person from discontinuing a bad habit or acquiring a new one. It has been found that a habit is, in reality, strengthened when a person makes an effort to curb it.

Physical relaxation, when practiced daily, brings about an accompanying mental relaxation and a "relaxed attitude," which aids us to consciously control better our automatic mechanism.

## THE HUMAN MIND'S POTENTIAL FOR CREATIVE IDEAS

The potential of the human mind for creating new ideas is unlimited. Everyone's subconscious mind is a *storehouse* of thousands and thousands of *stored facts*—and these facts can be combined in an endless variety of combinations to create endless numbers of ideas.

When the mind comes up with a *creative idea*, it has selected two or more separate facts that were unconnected and flashed their relationship to the conscious level.

When you need an original answer to a specific problem, no matter in what area of endeavor—whether in business or the arts—you must have a desired end result in your mind. Even if this result is obscure and indefinite, you will recognize it when you come upon it.

The main consideration is to apply yourself as diligently as possible, feeding into your subconscious all available information on the subject. Then, if you allow your creative success mechanism to go to work, it will automatically sift through the data available and will come up with a solution to your problem. Sometimes, when you least expect it or when you are thinking of an entirely unrelated subject, your conscious mind will take over, and you suddenly realize you have the answer.

*EXAMPLE:* The following four facts were existing separately and unconnected in a person's mind:

1. Six months ago, he saw an obscure news item in the local paper stating that the county was going to surface the roads in the area bounded by Black Canyon Road, Glendale Road, Bell Road, Carefree Road.
2. A week ago, he learned that the 100-acre Butler Farm was for sale. (The farm is within the area mentioned above.)
3. He is aware that ABC Corporation is planning a new plant in town and will hire 3,000 new employees.
4. He recently went house-hunting with his son (for his son and his family). He found there was an acute housing shortage.

It is easy enough to see the relationship of the above four facts now that they are put together. Now they suggest a money-making real estate opportunity, such as:

Buy Butler Farm—now easily accessible over improved roads—and sell it as a real estate development to house the new employees of the ABC Corporation plant.

The mind, in order to develop this relationship and produce the *idea* had to choose these four facts from among thousands. All of us need some kind of discipline that will start the unconscious mind into its creative process (servo-mechanism). An essential part of creativity is *not being able to fail*.

Nothing is new, and everything is new. It's a matter of *exposure and absorption*. It is what your mind does with what funnels through your five senses.

In your search for originality and creativity, remember, it requires no special genius—what you need is:

OBSERVATION RETENTION SELECTION.

Age has little to do with it—ideas come from "young minds." It's not how *old* you are but how *bold* you are.

---

*ACCUMULATION Stock up on facts* (collect-amass-increase)

*CEREBRATION Ponder on it*—let the function of the cerebrum taste it (act of thinking) and toss it around "upstairs."

*GESTATION Let it work and wait* (mental development of idea). The subconscious plan in the mind takes over and stews over it. (You stop thinking.)

*ELATION You've got it—you've* (feeling of success) *struck oil!* The idea starts gushing.

---

## SUCCESS MECHANISM

You have within you a mechanism that will locate a goal automatically when you have previously set this goal. To illustrate this goal-seeking mechanism, sit at a table blindfolded and have someone set a small object within your reach. First, your job will be to locate this object. You will do so by a trial-and-error method until you finally locate it. Then, after picking it up, replace it exactly where it was originally placed, leaving the blindfold over your eyes. Now sit back in your seat, reach out and pick it up.

Let's review what happened here. When we set out to locate the object, we made a number of errors, each time possibly saying to ourselves, "No, it isn't there," until we finally located it. We did not relate the errors or mistakes as failures. In the second attempt, you undoubtedly reached out and touched it on the first try; you forgot the errors and recorded the success by creating a picture of it. This picture led you to your target.

## SOMETHING TO THINK ABOUT

*When the will and the imagination are in conflict, the imagination always wins. The greatest hindrance to effectiveness is conscious effort.*

# 12

## THE QUIET PLACE

MARCUS AURELIUS SAID: "MEN SEEK RETREATS FOR THEMSELVES; HOUSES IN the country, seashore and mountains; and you, too, are wont to desire such things very much, but this is altogether a mark of the most *common* sort of man. For it is in your power, whenever you shall choose to retire into yourself. Constantly then, give to yourself this retreat, and renew yourself."

### NEED FOR FINDING A PEACEFUL RETREAT

It is necessary for every person to have a peaceful place within himself to which he can retreat for self-renewal. This place should be completely isolated from the outside world. Everyday stress and tension can cause frayed nerves and can cause him to be upset. A quiet place should be available to him to restore his serenity. He needs to go to it at least once a day, in order to calm himself and to revitalize his inner strength.

### CONSTRUCT IN YOUR IMAGINATION

Teaching oneself the art of seeking out the quiet center is one of the most well-received ideas ever suggested to my students. The easiest way to retreat into this quiet center is to mentally construct it in your imagination; to plan, build, paint and decorate it according to your own taste and preference so that it will be comfortable and attractive, to you. You must truly feel "at home."

When you create a place where you can be alone with yourself, you are escaping from reality. It's necessary for you to shield yourself and be free from the daily attack of outside distractions. Everyone needs an occasional vacation, a change of scene to get out of a rut and away from daily obligations.

When you retreat into your *quiet place,* your nervous system gets a rest every day. As you mentally do this, a feeling of freedom takes over and calmness and peace will come over you. This tranquility will undoubtedly carry over into any actions that follow. The quiet time will literally clear out the cobwebs and free you for new and challenging activities.

It is not outside events that are your key to being agitated or calm, but your own response to the things that happen around you.

## HARRY TRUMAN'S QUIET PLACE

It is important that we have a place in our minds where we can relax. Harry Truman claims to have had such a place. He referred to it as "a foxhole in my mind where I allow nothing to bother me." He would retreat into this foxhole in his imagination when anything bothered him.

## WHAT IS IT?

It can be a sort of a retreat strictly of your own making, a secret place somewhere where you will be perfectly safe, all alone—a room with mystical, if not magical qualities. It can be furnished simply or luxuriously—soft chairs, special pictures on the walls. A hi-fi stereo with a complete collection of the world's music, and even a very sophisticated computer that can solve any problem. It can be a small house on a quiet beach on an uncharted island in the Pacific dotted with palm trees and a light breeze blowing the waves ashore. The house may have a picture window taking in this whole view, or it can just be on a cloud, or deep in the earth or on a distant planet millions of light-years away. Don't tell anybody where your quiet room is. You are the only one that knows. Nobody can go there but you. This is the atmosphere where you are anything you care to be.

## HOW LONG TO ARRIVE

Just close your eyes and recall the last time you were in San Francisco, New York, Chicago or out in a park. Did you get a picture of the Golden Gate Bridge, Fifth Avenue, Michigan Boulevard or the trees and greenery in the park? It takes just an instant to get to any of those places in your imagination. That's how long it will take you to get to your secret place. It's that simple.

## PRACTICE EXERCISE

Go to your quiet place at least once a day for relaxation and renewed energy.

# 13

## RELAXATION

"STRESS" DOES NOT HAVE TO BE AN ACCEPTED PART OF THE WORLD WE LIVE IN.
Our lives could be much more serene and carefree if we would only recognize that God has given each one of us a built-in success mechanism which allows us to live as successful individuals. We create and compound our own problems when we force ourselves to employ conscious thought in finding the solution to complications which intrude on our lives.

As mentioned previously, you could compare your creative success mechanism with an electronic brain or high-powered computer. Your forebrain is the operator feeding data and problems into the computer which, in turn, is unable to *create* anything. Its job is to recognize the problems, sort out the data and relate to them. It was never designed to solve problems. Therefore you must not try to solve them with conscious effort.

## THE ART OF RELAXATION

If you happen to be traveling through a good, smooth period of living, then allow yourself to *feel* happy. Go the limit to sense the cheerfulness and pleasantness of the present moment.

John A. Schindler, M.D., has said, "Good emotions are the best medicine and the greatest power for good health. The physiological effects of good emotions are just as great in the right direction as the effects of bad emotions are in the wrong direction. Healthful living is more a matter of having the right kind of emotions than anything else. It is then apparent that the most important aspect of living consists in training and handling our emotions."

He has given us a few simple rules that will help us make our lives richer.
*Keep life simple.* Be responsive to the simple things near at hand—get your

pleasures from the world that lies immediately before your five senses. Then life becomes a tremendously interesting adventure.

*Avoid listening for the knock in your motor.*

*Learn to like your work.*

*Have a good hobby.*

*Like people.*

*Make a habit of saying the cheerful, pleasant thing.*

*Meet your problems with decision.*

## BE CONSCIOUSLY AWARE OF YOUR ENVIRONMENT

You should attempt to develop a more conscious awareness of your surroundings; to what you are presently responding and reacting in relation to your five senses.

A highly-developed awareness and understanding of what is going on *right now* will actually help you to reduce tension. When you find yourself tightening up, ask yourself this question:

"What is there in my present environment right now that I am able to react to in a positive way?"

The function of your creative servomechanism is to develop the appropriate response *right now* to your immediate environment. If you are not aware of your reactions you will continue to react by habit to some other event out of your past. If you react in this manner, you are not responding to what is going on now, but to that past event.

Actually you are reacting to a possibility, not to a reality. When you have understanding of the situation this knowledge can often effect an overwhelmingly instantaneous remedy.

## RELAXATION IS LEARNED

Relaxation is an acquired talent—like driving a car, sewing, hitting a baseball, cooking and selling. It is necessary that you relax in order to allow the automatic success mechanism to work. Relaxation tends to cut off the conscious mind and to accelerate the subconscious mind.

Relaxation is a way of immunizing yourself against external disturbances by refusing to respond to them.

## PSYCHOLOGICAL RELAXATION

Let us review four vital aspects of psychological relaxation:

1. Forgive yourself
2. Forgive others
3. Keep up with yourself (not others)
4. See yourself at your best

If you find yourself tensing up, check on the four vital rules and see if you are not breaking one or more of them!

## PRACTICE EXERCISE

Begin each day in a new and better way by reciting the following:

This is the beginning of a new day.

I have been given this day to use as I will. What I do today is important, because I'm exchanging a new day of my life for it. When tomorrow comes this day will be gone forever, leaving in its place whatever I have traded for. I will pledge to myself that it shall be for gain, good, and success, in order that I shall not regret the price I paid for this day.

My thinking and my attitudes are calm and cheerful.

I act and feel friendly toward other people.

I am tolerant of other people, their shortcomings and mistakes, and I view their actions with the most favorable understanding possible.

I act as though attainment of my goals is sure to happen. I am the kind of individual I aspire to be, and everything I do and the way I feel expresses this individuality.

I will not allow my judgment or attitude to be affected by negativism or pessimism.

I try to smile as often as possible; at least several times a day.

I respond in a calm and intelligent manner without alarm, no matter what the situation.

If I cannot control a situation, I try always to react in a positive manner, even to negative facts.

I know that if I apply myself to forming habits to enable me to act in the above manner, it will have a positive influence on my self-image in a most constructive way. By making these actions a part of my life, I will notice a definite growth in my self-confidence.

READ THE ABOVE EVERY DAY FOR TWENTY-ONE DAYS

# 14

## THE PSYCHOLOGY OF GOALS

THERE IS NO REAL HAPPINESS, NO SENSE OF ACHIEVEMENT, OR CONTENTMENT in life if a person has no goals to accomplish.

### MOVE FORWARD

When you are moving forward, you are able to correct your course as you go. Your automatic guidance system cannot guide you if you are standing still.

You have a real sense of direction when you are able to concentrate on your goals. When you have this sense of direction, when you're looking toward something, you maintain your balance. When you have no personal goals which mean something, you may go around in circles, and feel lost and purposeless.

### ENERGY TO REACH GOALS

First, in order to cause our goal-seeking mechanism to operate, the goal must be within the scope of the self-image. Second, the greater the desire for the goal, the more smoothly and energetically the machine will function. The creative center will be stimulated to provide the necessary "means whereby" for reaching the goal and to supply whatever energy is needed. The person who drags out of bed in the morning and limps through the day has goals way below his potential. His creative center is barely working. Even though the energy is there, the goals are so low that very little energy is needed.

The man who always seems to have an unlimited supply of creative energy has learned to set goals at a higher limit of his potential. The higher the goal, the higher is the self-image expressing itself. Aim high, rather than low, and you will become energetic and creative.

## GOALS SHOULD BE CONSISTENT, COMPATIBLE, AND CONSTRUCTIVE

Each goal should be *consistent and compatible* with others, in other words, you don't set a goal of a $250,000 home while earning $10,000 a year. Make it a harmonious picture and blend them together to form the complete picture.

Your goal should also be *constructive,* a goal which is high enough to stimulate the creative center. Set goals at the outer edge of your self-image. For example, a man driving a 1967 Ford does not set a goal for a 1968 Chevrolet. On the other hand, he doesn't decide on a chauffeur-driven Rolls-Royce, either.

It is just as wrong to set a goal so low that you can reach out and have it without any effort at all as to set one so far beyond your present self-image. In either case it would have no stimulating effect whatsoever. If you can almost believe it possible, but not quite, then it is high enough. Sometimes people fall into the trap of setting a goal so inconceivably high that they don't bother reaching it.

"Goals by the yard are hard—Goals by the inch a cinch."

Set intermediate or short range goals to reach long range goals. Short range goals are more believable, while long range goals are more meaningful, but you must, in both cases, *clearly see the end result.*

## THE ANT AND THE STRAW

A story that illustrates all this work we are about to do is comparable to the story of an ant and a piece of straw.

A biologist tells how he watched an ant carrying a piece of straw which seemed a big burden for it. The ant came to a crack in the earth which was too wide to cross. it stood for a time, as though pondering the situation, then put the straw across the crack and walked over upon it.

What a lesson for us! The burden becomes the bridge that will aid you in reaching any goal.

*Why do men with goals succeed and those without fail? Involvement in goal-setting* is the *Secret of Success.* The key to success and failure is, "We become what we think about," or, "As a man thinks, he is." When a person is thinking of a productive, useful, worthwhile, predetermined goal, he absolutely succeeds. The things that are important to you that you really want should fill your thoughts.

"Imagination is more powerful than knowledge." Get an image in your mind of where you want to go and keep it there. Think of where you want to go, not where you don't want to go.

## HOW DO YOU DO THIS?

First you must select your goals. As already mentioned, your basic goals have already been determined. There are *no others*—they are all categorized under these four headings:

Security (Physical Emotional Financial)

Love

Ego Satisfaction

Bodily Comforts and Possessions

It is the degree of these desires that makes people unique.

*Security*—the assurance that we are guarded against the hazards and dangers of life. This implies the protection of self and the desire for safety, health, food, clothing, shelter and preservation of a long life.

*Love*—the assurance that we are loved and we can safeguard our loved ones. This implies protection of loved ones and includes sex, romance, marriage, parenthood and family.

*Ego Satisfaction*—the inner assurance that, as individuals, we are to be admired and are capable of winning admiration. This implies protection of one's feelings and includes respect, approval, importance, appreciation, pride, prestige, recognition, status and personal satisfaction.

*Bodily Comforts and Possessions*—the provision of a life standard that will assure physical satisfaction. This means the acquiring of material things that can be bought with money; such things as conveniences, luxuries, a home, a car and physical surroundings of ease and beauty.

They determine what is important to you and what you think is important determines your actions.

## TWO-REASONS WHY PEOPLE DO ANYTHING

There are only two reasons why an individual does anything. They are:

1. to gain a benefit (something he does not have).
2. to avoid a loss (something he now has).

If it would be possible for you to consult all the sociologists and anthropologists who study people in groups, all the psychologists and psychiatrists who study individuals, or any other human behavioral scientists, you would find that they cannot come up with one single, additional reason why an individual does anything.

The process of living becomes very simple when you understand that man has only these four basic goals and only two reasons why he does anything.

A human being always acts, feels and performs in accord with what he imagines to be true about himself and his environment. This is a basic fundamental law of mind. Your selection will determine how you wish to satisfy these goals.

*For example:* No one needs a $10,000 car, when a $2,000 car will get him where he wants to go. The $10,000 car satisfies a need other than transportation.

*For example:* If you have a home that performs the basic need of security, then you have satisfied this need. However, wanting another home that is larger and more elaborate, surrounded by things of ease and beauty, you are satisfying a need for respect, approval, importance, recognition and prestige, or *ego satisfaction*.

Set up your present goals under these four headings. Remember—the degree of the intensity that you desire these things defines what is important to you.

## HOW CAN YOU APPRAISE YOUR CHANCES FOR SUCCESS?

What can you do to improve your chances and exploit your opportunities? What you do tells a lot, but why you do it tells even more. What you want out of life is significant, but how hard you work to get what you want is even more significant.

Look for signs of "motivation" in your ambitions, attitudes and the way you feel about yourself, your job and everything you have done or plan to do. "Good motivation" is probably your most important quality and the lack of it is a most serious drawback.

Have you been enthusiastic in attacking opportunities in the past? What do you get excited about and why? Do you get a real kick out of doing things well? Do you take advantage of time off? What have you done to broaden yourself, to think more and to be more useful? What do you get out of your learning experiences? What have you made out of your opportunities? Are you goal-oriented? Do you make plans? How specific? Do you have the ability to communicate? Can you put your thoughts across in writing or in words? Do you have leadership ability?

The only real gauge you have to judge motivation is *what has moved you in the past and what you have your eye on for the future.*

*Get yourself a goal* or a series of goals. Get yourself a project. Determine what you want out of life. Never stop looking ahead toward something that will bring you satisfaction and happiness. You will find when you're not looking forward, not actually striving toward a goal, you're only existing, and not really *living.*

Again, no one can feel really happy or content if he tries to exist without goals to accomplish.

I'M SATISFIED
WITH MYSELF,
BUT THE FEELING
ISN'T MUTUAL.
I'D TRY TO
KNOW MYSELF BETTER,
BUT I DON'T WANT
TO GET INVOLVED.

## SOMETHING TO THINK ABOUT

*Goals need desire.*

*Goals provide motivation and enthusiasm.*

*Goals create awareness of opportunities.*

*Specifics give direction.*

*Men of accomplishment seldom reach their goals, their goals keep moving ahead of them.*

# 15

## GOALS

THE PURPOSE OF THE FOLLOWING EIGHT STEPS IS TO HELP YOU ANALYZE YOUR-self and help you determine your goals. When you have completed these, you will have a good idea of what your goals are today.

1.  Following is a list of ten areas in which you will rate yourself. The degree of the liabilities shown in this exercise determines the need for a goal.

| Assets / Liabilities | (degree of use) | (degree not used) |
| --- | --- | --- |
| a. Ability to earn money | % | % |
| b. Leadership ability | % | % |
| c. Work ability | % | % |
| d. Getting along with others | % | % |
| e. Sports and hobbies | % | % |
| f. Family relationships | % | % |
| g. Persuasion ability | % | % |
| h. Memory (ability to recall) | % | % |

| i. Awareness of potential | % | % |
| --- | --- | --- |
| j. Confidence | % | % |

For the above exercise fill in the Asset column from 0 to 100, then subtract this figure from 100 to get the Liability. (Don't spend much time thinking about this. Your subconscious will provide the answer.)

2. After this exercise is completed you will develop a *composite self-image* rating by totaling your ten asset scores and dividing by ten.

a. %
b. %
c. %
d. %
e. %
f. %
g. %
h. %
i. %
j. %
Total %÷10= %
This is my composite Self-Image rating.

3. Next you will arrive at the things you need right now. If I offered to give you anything you wanted, what would you choose?

Suggestions: new furniture; car repair; new clothes; dental work; medical insurance; new refrigerator, etc.

I need the following:

_____

_____

_____

_____

_____

The above items you would list if I offered to write a check for anything you have listed. Don't be hesitant to write everything that comes to your mind.

4. This will help you arrive at the personality qualities you need in relation to the goals you have set.

*Suggestions:* ability to concentrate; real personal confidence; to be more aggressive; to finish what I start; more original creativity; to be friendlier to others; to be a leader; to be in good health; to be enthusiastic; to react calmly; to organize my time; to have a good memory; to be more diplomatic; to be goal-oriented.

I need and want the following:

_____

_____

_____

_____

_____

_____

5a. Personal Characteristics To Be Acquired

*Greater use of potential (knowledge)*

*Understand myself better*

*Understand other person better*

*More alert (to opportunity and new ideas)*

*More tactful and diplomatic*

*Get along with others better (handle people skillfully)*

*Better health (maintain good emotions)*

*Think clearly and accurately*

*Communicate more effectively*

*More aware*

*Friendlier person*

*Better memory (recall)*

*More tolerant*

*More aggressive*

*More relaxed*

*More goal-oriented*

*Enjoy my work*

*Be a happier person*

5b. Now analyze some of your personal characteristics that help you arrive at your goals.

| | |
|---|---|
| Concentration | Speech |
| Imagination | Reading |
| Efficiency | Emotions |
| Courage | Relaxation |
| Self-confidence | Decisiveness |
| Self-respect | Maturity |
| Self-organization | Composure |
| Self-liking | Interest in People |
| Self-starter | Planning |
| Self-education | Accomplishment |
| Self-discipline | High Quality in Work |
| Time-organization | Motivation of Others |
| Perseverance | Calmness |
| Creativity | Cheerfulness |
| Energy | Enthusiasm |
| Memory (recall) | Communication |

6. Analyze the feeling of "I Can't."

a. Is there some job or some particular duty you would like to perform, but feel that you can't?

b.  Ask yourself why you can't.
c.  Do you base your inability to perform on real truth, or just on what you assume to be true?
d.  Do you have a real reason for believing this to be the truth?
e.  Could you possibly be mistaken in your belief?
f.  Would you hold the same belief if the situation applied to someone else?
g.  If what you believe is not the truth, why do you continue to act in this manner?

Because we have so many memories of past failures and unpleasant experiences in our subconscious does not mean they have to be "dug out," exposed, or examined to effect a personality change.

If you are constantly reminded of your former blunders, you will likely find it difficult to change your behavior pattern. Remembering these past mistakes tends to have a detrimental effect on your actions. When you continually remind yourself of them, you are not using your power of reason.

It is certainly not logical to conclude that because you may have failed once you are doomed to failure again.

To say to yourself, "I can't" before even trying and in the absence of evidence is certainly not rational. Your answer should be like the man who, when asked if he could play the piano, replied, "I don't know, I have never tried."

These past failure experiences do not harm you as long as your conscious thought is centered on what you do want, not on what you don't want.

7.  Fill out your personal balance sheet.


PERSONAL BALANCE SHEET OF:

---

KNOW-HOW
    Assets, liabilities
    Total experience, knowledge (degree of formal education), training, (of use not used) developed talents

ENERGY
    Ability to perform
    Physical drive (physical health)
    Ability to work at top efficiency

TIME
    How to organize it, make it work for you, ability to properly use it
    How efficiently you use it

IMAGINATION
    Creative spark
    Ability to foresee and solve problems (picturing power of the mind)

PEOPLE
    Family, friends, business associates (how they help you)
    Knowledge of human relations, behavior

RESEARCH AND DEVELOPMENT
    Investments of time and/or money in improving performance in all areas
of living

8.   ANALYSIS TO BE USED IN THE SELECTION OF GOALS

Answer the following questions YES or NO.

LEADERSHIP
    1. Should people have to pay school taxes if they do not have children?
    2. I try to see what others think before I take a stand.
    3. I would rather have people dislike me than look down on me.
    4. I must admit I am a pretty fair talker.

INTELLECTUAL EFFICIENCY
    1. Do I read at least ten books a year?
    2. When faced with a problem, do I find I act on impulse to solve it?
    3. Do I like science?
    4. Do I feel teachers often expect too much from their students?

AMBITION
    1. Do I always try to do a little better than what is expected of me?
    2. Did I like it very much when one of my papers was read to the
       class in school?

3. Do I believe that in many ways, the poor man is better off than the rich man?
4. Do I believe that planning my activities in advance is likely to take the most fun out of them?

## RESPONSIBILITY

1. Do I feel that when prices are high, I can't blame someone for getting all he can while the getting is good?
2. Do I feel every family owes it to the city to keep its sidewalks cleared of snow in the winter and its lawn mowed in the summer?
3. Do I feel we ought to take care of ourselves and let everybody take care of themselves?
4. Do I feel any guilt or shame if I fail to vote in the elections?

## CONVICTION OF SUCCESS

1. Do I think there are as many opportunities for an ambitious person as there ever were?
2. Do I often have doubts as to what action will win approval for me in my work?
3. Do I doubt that I will ever be an important person? . . . that I will make a real contribution to the world?
4. Do I get nervous and upset when I feel I have been placed in competition with another?

The answers to these questions are at the end of this chapter.

## SELF-ANALYSIS QUESTIONS

The self-analysis questions on the pages that follow will serve as a guide and a stimulus in arriving at your goals in each of the six most important areas of your life.

| | | |
|---|---|---|
| SOCIAL | MENTAL | FAMILY LIFE |
| SPIRITUAL | PHYSICAL | FINANCIAL |

These self-analysis questions are merely stimulative.

They are by no means the only questions you are to ask yourself, but they are designed to start you thinking in the right direction. You will then see an amazing thing happen. These questions will quickly suggest other thoughts, ideas and other questions in each area of your life that will give you the correct goal to pursue.

If you are too close to achieving your objectives, you need to set higher goals. If the attainment is too far away, you need to set up intermediate steps. Remember, "Success by the yard is hard, but by the inch is a cinch."

These questions will aid you in setting more "challenging" goals.

## SOCIAL DEVELOPMENT

1. Do you consider yourself very sociable? Moderately sociable? Antisocial?
2. Do you get along with your children?
3. Do you genuinely like people?
4. How many people have you invited into your home in the last three months?
5. Into how many homes have you been invited in the last three months?
6. How many times have you gone out with friends in the last three months? At who's invitation—yours or theirs?
7. Do you look forward to parties and social affairs? Are you more anxious to have guests in or to be invited out?
8. Do children make friends with you quickly? Slowly? Or not at all?
9. What is your general attitude toward "society?" Are you objective? Optimistic? Pessimistic? Indifferent? Resigned? Completely unaware?
10. Do people seem to like you? What can you do to make them like you more?
11. In social affairs, do you consider yourself a leader? A follower? An average participant? Which would you like to be?

## SPIRITUAL DEVELOPMENT

1. Do you consider yourself a religious person?
2. Do you adhere rigidly to your moral or ethical standards?
3. Do you modify your beliefs to allow free expression?
4. Do you practice flexibility by deciding right or wrong on the merits of each situation?

5. Do you ever make decisions based on axioms, proverbs, or "wise sayings" you learned during your childhood?
6. Do you count among your close friends any people you consider to be spiritually sound?
7. Do others come to you for counsel or advice? How many in one year? Are you able to help them?

## MENTAL DEVELOPMENT

1. How do you consider your intelligence level? Above average? Average? Below average?
2. Do you consider your learning rate to be fast? Average? Slow?
3. What was the extent of your formal education?
4. If you could turn the pages of time back, would you extend your education to a higher level?
5. What supplemental training have you had in your present field?
6. What training or refresher courses have you taken in the last five years?
7. What steps have you taken to complete your mental development?
8. Do you consider your education and training to be well-rounded?
9. To what magazines do you subscribe? Where do you get your information?
10. What types of articles interest you the most?
11. Have you a strong desire to know more?
12. Are you embarrassed because you know so little?

## PHYSICAL DEVELOPMENT

1. Do you consider your state of health excellent? Good? Fair? Poor?
2. Are you the outdoor type?
3. How many days have you lost from work in the last five years due to health? What was the length of each absence? Cause of illness?
4. When did you have your last physical check-up?
5. Do you have a regular program of seeing your doctor, dentist, and optometrist?
6. Are you a weight-watcher? What foods do you enjoy? Dislike?

## FAMILY LIFE DEVELOPMENT

1. Was your childhood home a close family unit? Did you do things as a family? Did you enjoy them?
2. How does your present family life compare or contrast with what you experienced as a child?
3. Do you reserve time for your children?
4. Do they ask your opinion about personal problems or decisions?
5. Who makes decisions in your family—husband or wife? Or both?
6. Who decides where the family will go on vacation?
7. Do your children invite their friends to your home?
8. Do you have specific "home rules" of conduct that are clearly established to recognize the rights of the individual?

## FINANCIAL DEVELOPMENT

1. Do you consider your income to be average? Above average? Below average?
2. Is your spending compatible with your earnings?
3. Has your income increased yearly?
4. Do you have a regular savings program?
5. Do you regularly make up a personal financial statement?
6. Do you have an operating budget?
7. Have you ever dreamed of inheriting a large sum of money? Was it specific? What was it? What would you do if you received this amount?
8. Do you have an insurance program?
9. How do you evaluate your present worth to your current job? Are you paid what you deserve? More? Less?
10. What can you do to increase your worth?

## SOMETHING TO THINK ABOUT

*Goals need desire.*

*Goals provide motivation and enthusiasm.*

*Goals produce awareness of opportunities*

*We move toward that which we dwell upon.*

ANSWERS:

## LEADERSHIP

1. Yes
2. No
3. Yes
4. Yes

## INTELLECTUAL EFFICIENCY

1. Yes
2. No
3. Yes
4. No

## AMBITION

1. Yes
2. No
3. No
4. No

## RESPONSIBILITY

1. No
2. Yes
3. No
4. Yes

## CONVICTION OF SUCCESS

1. Yes
2. No

3. No
4. No

Each correct answer is 25 points—grade yourself.

# 16

## SYNTHETIC EXPERIENCE

### REVISING DATA IN THE SUBCONSCIOUS MIND

The principle of affirmation (a statement of belief) has been known and used for as far back as recorded history. It has been used by schools of religion and philosophy. Only recently have we had a functional understanding of why the repeating of an affirmation has had such a dramatic effect on a person's behavior.

### NOTHING SUCCEEDS LIKE SUCCESS

*It is a direct and controlled method of changing the self-image;* we learn to function successfully by experiencing success (nothing succeeds like success). Our memories of past successsses are our stored information which give us the self-confidence for our present position. But how does a person draw on memories of past successful experiences when either he has had no experience or he has experienced only failure? His dilemma is comparable to the man who cannot secure a job because he has had no experience and cannot get the experience because he can't get a job.

### HUMAN NERVOUS SYSTEM CANNOT TELL THE DIFFERENCE

Clinical psychologists have proven experimentally that it is impossible for the human nervous system to distinguish between a real experience and one created in the imagination. (The brain waves of the real event are the same as the imagined.) This provides us with a very potent and effective tool.

Successful affirming requires three things:

Desire          Information          Repetition

## THE TIME TO RECONDITION THE SUBCONSCIOUS

There are many times during the day when revising the data in the subconscious is effective. Basically, they are any time when you can be thoroughly and completely relaxed and *be aware of only your thoughts.* These are the times when the communication channel with the subconscious flows most freely: immediately upon awakening in the morning (when you are still in an unaware state, unmindful of anything except your thoughts); just before you fall asleep at night; immediately after returning from lunch or at any other time you are alone and can relax.

The first step in making an *affirmation* is to take the goals analyzed from the previous eight steps and then make a written explanation (for yourself) of why you want to acquire a particular goal or personality trait. In other words, describe it to yourself in as much detail as you can (Descriptive Statement). Then prepare a simple *Statement of Affirmation,* the purpose being to help you create clear mental pictures.

When you are in a relaxed state (physically and mentally) repeat this statement in your imagination and form a mental picture of yourself *performing* appropriately.

Then sense the emotional feelings that are a result of having performed accordingly.

Begin by knowing you have arrived.

Words          Pictures          Feelings

If you are wondering whether you go through all three phases each time you are attempting to revise the data in your subconscious mind, the answer is an unqualified YES.

In using this technique, it is important that you stand aside and let it work. Revising the data by using this technique brings results. *Let it work. Don't try hard to change. Don't continually check your progress.*

Just let it happen, especially don't talk about it with other people. Do not predict the things that are going to happen to you. Just quietly use this technique, and you will feel the changes soon enough, or possibly your friends will begin to notice the change. That will be time enough for discussion.

## DETERMINING WORDS FOR AFFIRMATION

The following are rules and suggestions for choosing the words used in an affirmation:

1. Be strictly personal. Use I, me, *or* my.
2. Be absolutely positive—move *toward* what you want; avoid the words *not* or *don't.*
3. Use the present tense.
4. Do not be progressive. Avoid *I am going to.*
5. Do not be comparative. Never compare with the *past* or *others;* do not use *more than* or *better than.*
6. Avoid the words *able to* or *can.*
7. Affirmation should be balanced. *Do not use opposites or extremes.*
8. Be realistic. *Do not use absolutes or perfection.* Always write for yourself, *not for others.*
9. Do not set time limits. *Time limits are deadly; they create tension.*
10. *You Supply The Goal.*

Your automatic creative mechanism functions according to the goal you set. Once you give it a definite objective to achieve, you can depend upon its automatic guidance system to take you to that objective much better than you ever could by conscious thought. Your automatic mechanism will supply you with *how* you will reach your goal.

IF YOU DESIRE TO IMPROVE YOURSELF, REMEMBER THIS FACT. ACT THE WAY YOU WANT TO BE (IN YOUR IMAGINATION) AND YOU'LL BE THE WAY YOU ACT.

### CHECKLIST TO BE USED IN THE WRITING OF A DESCRIPTIVE STATEMENT

1. Do I "really" want this? (This must be something I "really" want, not something that will "sound" good if someone else reads it.)
2. Is the goal compatible with my other goals?
3. Is it positive? (State what I want, not what I want to get rid of.)
4. Is it expressed in "total" detail?

5. Is it realistic? (Is it possible for some human being to achieve it? Not just, "Is it realistic for me today?")
6. Is my goal high enough? Reach out! Set the goal limit high. Nothing should enter my mind at this point as to how I will achieve these goals.
7. Am I including personality factors necessary to achieve my goals?

*An example of a Descriptive Statement:*

I want to be able to speak in front of a group of people, but I seem to lack confidence that I can do this. I am always nervous and fearful that I will make a mistake or forget something. I know if I can build confidence to do this, it will rub off in other areas, especially in my job.

I can see myself giving a talk on creative thinking in front of about 200 people. I'm an expert on the subject, because I know more than anyone present. I'm standing on the rostrum, and as I give my talk, the audience responds with applause and appreciative laughter. At the conclusion, as I leave the speakers' platform, several key people offer me congratulations, giving me a feeling of importance and self-esteem:

*Affirmation:* I AM A CONFIDENT SPEAKER.

## SOMETHING TO THINK ABOUT

*Whatever you vividly imagine, ardently desire, sincerely believe, and enthusiastically act upon, will inevitably happen.*

## CREATIVE WORDING AND THE SUBCONSCIOUS

We are going to consider only words, written and spoken, and their effect on you. Your subconscious responds to your words, especially when they are repeated over and over again. It takes your words literally—it cannot reason like your conscious mind.

### CASE HISTORY

The following case history demonstrates the use of creative wording showing a bad or negative result.

A person was going to a doctor for headaches. The doctor had prescribed many drugs for the relief of pain, but as time went on the person did not react to the drugs and consequently did not get rid of the pain. We had a conversation that uncovered the cause of his headaches.

During the first half-hour of discussion, it was particularly noted that he frequently used the phrases, "that gave me a headache" and "he gave me a headache." He was using creative wording to give him a headache, and it created a real one for him. His headaches were caused *only* by his repeated statements that these things or people gave him a headache.

This man was using his subconscious to work against him. He soon realized that the repetition of such statements actually did create the end results. He now knew he could get help from the subconscious to do anything he wanted to do. He only had to use words that would give him the end result he wanted. Your mind is so powerful; it will give you exactly what you want once you understand the method of getting it.

## ACTUAL PHYSICAL MANIFESTATION

Here are some examples that are often used and are converted into actual physical manifestations.

I get tired of

I can't see

. . . gives me a pain

I can't stomach that

I can't swallow that

I'll be damned

. . . drives me crazy

. . . makes me sick

. . . gives me a headache

I can't stand . . .

. . . gives me a pain in the neck

. . . gets under my skin

## BECOME AWARE OF WORDS

When you say things like these, your subconscious is being conditioned to what you say. *Beginning right now, become aware of the words you use.*

Examine what you say and think and all that is said to you. Remove these words or phrases from your vocabulary and become aware when they are said to you. Replace them with something that will bring good results.

## CASE HISTORY

One day a young man came to me with a desire to be in one of our Psycho-Cybernetics Workshops. He explained his predicament. He had no money, and he was hopelessly in debt (he thought) and deeply depressed. He was unmarried, and his mother lived with him. He owned an art shop in Scottsdale, Arizona, in which he featured his own work as well as the works of other artists. He was a very talented sculptor with a very bad "self-image." We agreed to have him attend the Workshop Sessions after having him make two promises: first, that he would attend all the Workshop Sessions and do all the techniques and exercises prescribed; secondly, that he would pay us when he was able.

When we were working on Data Revision, he made six affirmations:

1. The art shop would be sold at a figure sufficient to pay all of his debts.
2. He would be released from his house.
3. He would have a place for his mother to live.
4. He would have $10,000.00 in the bank.
5. He would have freedom from financial worries and time to sculpt.
6. He would fulfill a desire to travel.

When he had completed several weeks assuming in his imagination that these things had already taken place, he came to me one evening and said, "I must be going crazy because I'm experiencing happy feelings and my situation has not changed one bit." I told him what he was experiencing was change, and when this change had taken place inside he then would experience what he had been affirming.

This is exactly what took place. All six of his affirmations became a reality within six months.

This case is not as unusual as it seems. He owes this success to his discipline in following the techniques and exercises prescribed in this book.

## CASE HISTORY

One day a furniture designer described her difficulties in working with a prominent manufacturer. She was convinced that he unjustly criticized and rejected her best work and that often he was deliberately rude and unfair to her.

Hearing her story, it was explained that if she found the other person rude and unfair, it was a sure sign that she, not the manufacturer, was in need of a new attitude. She had learned *that the power of this law of assumption or data revision and its practical application could be discovered only through experience;* that only by assuming that the situation was what she wanted it to be could she bring about the changed desires. Her employer was merely bearing witness, telling her by his behavior what her concept of him was. It was suggested that it was quite probable that she was carrying on mental conversations with him in her mind, which were filled with criticism and recrimination. There was no doubt that she was mentally arguing with the producer for *"others only echo that which we whisper to them in silence."*

She confessed that every morning on her way to work, she told him just what she thought of him in a way she would never have dared address him in person. The intensity and force of her mental arguments with him *automatically established his behavior toward her.* She began to realize that all of us carry on mental conversations. Unfortunately, on most occasions, these conversations are argumentative; that so many people are mentally engrossed in conversations, and few appear to be happy about them. The very intensity of their feelings must lead them to the unpleasant incidents that they themselves have mentally created and therefore must now encounter.

When she realized what she had been doing, she agreed to change her attitude and to live this law of assumption faithfully by assuming that her job was highly satisfactory and her relationship with the manufacturer was a very happy one. She would follow the method prescribed and *imagine* that he had congratulated her on her fine designs and that she, in turn, had thanked him for his praise and kindness. To her great delight, she soon discovered for herself that *her own attitude* was the cause.

The behavior of her employer miraculously reversed itself. His attitude, echoing, as it had always done, that which she had assumed, now reflected her changed concept of him.

What she did by the power of her imagination, her persistent assumption, influenced his behavior and determined his attitude toward her. This is one way we can see it is not facts but our *imagination* by which we create and shape our lives.

# 17

## MENTAL PICTURING

ALL THROUGH THE AGES, PHILOSOPHERS, SCIENTISTS, AND VARIOUS TEACHERS
of religious principles have been constantly confronted with a major question:
*How can we reach the human mind with a major truth that will set it free?*

When they had achieved the answer to this question, it seemed that all they
would have to do would be to tell people about the new life that was open to
them, and everyone would be naturally anxious to try it. But experience indi-
cated and proved the contrary. The mind of man has always opposed change
with a strong intensity; it does not welcome progress. When the human mind
has been provided with the actual power that could set it free, it has used vari-
ous evasions, rationalizations, and oppositions, which have prevented it from
accepting the truth.

Teachers of the truth did come upon a method, and it worked. It enabled
people to take charge of their own lives. They received great inner strength. They
solved their daily problems, and physical difficulties became a thing of the past.
As each new day appeared, it became fresh and meaningful to them. They be-
came calm, and a whole new self-image developed. *What was this method? The
method was the mental picture.*

## ADVANTAGES OF MENTAL PICTURES

1. Everyone understands a mental picture.
2. Everyone has the ability to form mental pictures and to draw mean-
   ing from them.
3. A mental picture is a scene played upon the "screen of the mind."
   Its value is extensive. The thinking process itself is largely a pro-
   jection of mental scenes.

4. The mental picture gives the mind a positive course of action to follow.
5. It provides a powerful and accurate guidance system.
6. It guides the individual into doing what is necessary to reach a goal.
7. It creates the mind as to a positive course of action to follow.
8. We can all understand a mental picture that illustrates an idea.
9. The picture becomes the bridge that helps us reach the unknown.
10. It connects one level of understanding to a higher level of understanding.
11. We move up from a literal understanding to a psychological understanding.
12. A mental picture, once implanted, works ceaselessly and effortlessly.
13. When a mental picture is absorbed, it begins working immediately.
14. It transforms our thinking and supplies energy and wisdom even when we are not consciously aware of it, working quietly, giving us whatever we need to reach our goal.

This wonderful "secret" was known and practiced by all the great teachers of the *truth*.

## RESULT OF MENTAL PICTURING

We have come to a greater understanding, through the science of cybernetics, of the reason mental imagery yields such astounding results. They are not produced by the supernatural or trickery, but are effected by the spontaneous and instinctive workings of our brains and intellects.

The brain and nervous system, together, are regarded as a cybernetic device or a complicated *servomechanism*. It is an involuntary machine that *directs* itself toward its goal target by using negative feedback based upon stored data, shifting its course when necessary.

An example is a self-guided missile with a predetermined target. When it is traveling on a correct course (positive feedback), it actually needs or gets no direction; it continues on its way and does not react to positive feedback. When it gets off its course (negative feedback) it does respond to the information that reaches its mechanism, telling it, for example, that it is off its path too far to the left. The corrective device automatically causes the steering mechanism to veer back to the right. When doing this, if it *overcorrects*, it will then steer back to the left. The missile reaches its goal by moving forward, making mistakes, and constantly correcting them. It makes a series of zigzags, finally arriving at its target.

The important thing for us to note is that when it was on a failure course, it did not consider this a *failure;* it kept moving forward and correcting its course.

The straight line is the shortest distance between the release of the torpedo and its goal. The zigzag is the path the torpedo actually follows, always moving towards its goal.

The reason mental pictures are so significant is that fully 83 percent of what we perceive is through the sense of sight.

## CREATE A MENTAL PICTURE

This letter describes a rather complicated accident that supposedly occurred to a bricklayer in the British West Indies. Follow along and create the mental pictures:

> *Dear sir:*
>
> *When I reached the construction site, I found that the hurricane had knocked some bricks off the floor of the main building.*
>
> *So I rigged up a beam with a pulley at the top of the building and hoisted up a couple of barrels full of bricks. When I had repaired the building, there were some bricks left over.*
>
> *I hoisted the barrel back up again and secured the line at the bottom, and then went up and filled the barrel with extra bricks. Then I went to the bottom and cast off the line.*
>
> *Unfortunately, the barrel of bricks was heavier than I was and, before I knew what was happening, the barrel started down, jerking me off the ground. I decided to hang on, and halfway up, I met the barrel coming down and received a severe blow on the shoulder.*
>
> *I then continued to the top, banging my head against the beam, getting my fingers jammed in the pulley. When the barrel hit the ground it, burst out the bottom, causing all the bricks to spill out.*
>
> *I was now heavier than the barrel and so started down again at high speed. Halfway down, I met the barrel coming up and received severe injuries to my shins. When I hit the ground, I landed on the bricks and received several painful cuts from the sharp edges. At this point, I must have lost my presence of mind because I let go of the line, and the barrel came down, giving me another blow on the head and putting me in the hospital.*
>
> *I respectfully request sick leave.*
>
> *Your servant,*<br>*Ricardo*

## SOMETHING TO THINK ABOUT

*Your mental picture of yourself is the strongest force within you.*

   *Hold a picture of yourself long and continuous in your imagination, and you will be drawn toward it.*

   *Picture what you want—not what you don't want.*

# 18

## THINK SHEETS

THIS BOOK HAS BEEN DESIGNED TO INCREASE YOUR ABILITIES IN MANY AREAS of human endeavor. Perhaps one of the most important areas of improvement will be a tremendous increase in your ability to visualize your goals in preparation for their accomplishment.

All of the puzzles that will be given to you are of a purely logical nature as distinguished from riddles. They will contain no plays on words, no deliberate deceptive statements, and no guessing. In short, no "catches" of any kind.

The puzzles are of a completely non-mathematical nature, requiring thought and mental imagery. That is, they will use native mental ingenuity, which utilizes the store of acquired information you already possess.

It is interesting to observe that solving puzzles of the purely logical type epitomizes the scientific process of reaching your goals, as stated in *Psycho-Cybernetics*. At the onset, one is confronted with a mass of more or less unrelated data. From these facts, a few positive inferences can be drawn immediately, but it is usually necessary to set up a clear picture in your mind of just what your goal is. For in reaching your goals, as in solving these puzzles, a knowledge of the feeling of victory will be your greatest asset.

As you solve these puzzles, you will find that you are calling upon many of the mechanisms you use in reaching your goals. In both cases, inconsistencies will appear. Your success mechanism will be called upon to reject negative assumptions and substitute positive affirmations until a consistent set of conclusions—a clearly defined goal—emerges.

We reflect on the fundamental processes of rejecting negative influences and reinforcing positive affirmations, drawing conclusions from them, and examining their consistency (within the framework of the problem at hand). Thus, the solution of the problem, as it is with the achievement of our goals, is ultimately brought about from the mass of seemingly unrelated information initially provided. So it is in science, too. A great mind once said, "When learning ceases to be fun, it ceases to be learning." To this end, the following THINK SHEETS are presented.*

It is inherent in the nature of logical puzzles, as in the achievement of our goals that the solution cannot be reduced to one fixed pattern for all.

## THINK SHEET NO. I

CONSIDER THE FOLLOWING:

1. Having to catch a 6:00 a.m. flight, I woke up while it was still dark. Not wanting to wake my wife, I went to the closet to get a pair of shoes and socks without putting the light on. I found my shoes and socks, but I must confess they were in no kind of order—just a jumbled pile of six shoes of three brands and a heap of 24 socks, black and brown. How many shoes and socks did I have to take with me into the bathroom to be sure I had a pair of matching shoes and a pair of matching socks?

2. We are watching the midnight news on Channel 4, and the weatherman says, "It is raining now, but we can expect the storm to pass in 72 hours, at which time it will be a bright, sunny day." What is wrong here?

3. A contest was held with three contestants, one of whom was a graduate of the Psycho-Cybernetics Seminar and Workshop. The moderator made this statement to all three contestants:

"Every pain has been taken to make this a perfectly fair contest, as all three of you will be given exactly the same information at every point of the contest."

At this point, the three competitors were blindfolded. A white piece of paper was taped to each one's forehead, and they were told that not all of the pieces of paper were black. The blindfolds were removed, and the prize was to go to the first man to correctly deduce whether the paper on his forehead was white or black and write his answer on a sheet of paper out of the view of the other two contestants.

My Psycho-Cybernetics graduate wrote his answer immediately, while the other two contestants took two minutes to solve the problem. All three wrote "white." How did our Psycho-Cybernetics graduate come to his conclusion so quickly?

4. At the local bank, the positions of cashier, manager, and teller are held by Brown, Jones, and Smith, though not recessarily respectively.

    1. The teller, who was an only child, earns the least.

    2. Smith, who married Brown's sister, earns more than the manager.

What position does each man fill?

(*Reprinted, with permission, from the book "HOW TO RAISE YOUR I.Q." by Sheldon Howard.)

## THINK SHEET NO. 2

1. When was the most recent year that reads the same upside down?
2. A tramp makes cigarettes from the butts he picks up on the street. He finds that four butts make one new cigarette. How many cigarettes can he smoke from a haul of sixteen cigarette butts?
3. I always sit in the same pew at church; the third from the front and the seventh from the back, on the right-hand side. Each pew seats five persons on each side of the center aisle. What is the total capacity of the church?
4. A lady bought a hat with a floral decoration for $10. If the hat costs $9 more than the decoration, how much did the decoration cost?
5. A non-stop train leaves Los Angeles for San Francisco at 6:00 p.m., traveling at a constant speed of sixty miles per hour. At 7:00 p.m. the same day, a freight train leaves San Francisco for Los Angeles at a constant speed of forty miles per hour. Los Angeles is 400 miles from San Francisco. How far apart are the trains one hour before they pass each other?
6. A boy has as many sisters as brothers, but each sister has only half as many sisters as brothers. How many boys and girls are in the family?
7. Bob, Paul, Richard, and Sam are four talented, creative artists; one a dancer, one a painter, one a singer, and one a writer (though not necessarily in that order).
    1. Bob and Richard were in the audience the night the singer made his debut on the concert stage.
    2. Both Paul and the writer have posed for portraits by the painter.
    3. The writer, whose biography of Sam was a bestseller, is planning to write a biography of Bob.
    4. Bob has never heard of Richard.

What is each man's artistic field?

## THINK SHEET NO. 3

1. I asked my math teacher to sell me a copy of his new book. He said he would for this amount:

"Put two silver dollars in front of a silver dollar and two silver dollars behind a silver dollar with one silver dollar in the middle.

What is the least I would have to pay?

2. If a salesman and a half can sell an order and a half in a day and a half, how many doctors will six salesmen sell in seven days?

3. Three women each have two daughters, and they all get on the bus to go shopping. There are only seven empty seats on the bus, but each has a seat to herself. How did they manage it?

4. A doctor in Los Angeles had a brother in San Diego who was a lawyer, but the lawyer in San Diego did not have a brother in Los Angeles who was a doctor? WHY?

5. My daughter put a dime in an empty wine bottle, then replaced the cork and challenged me to remove the dime without breaking the bottle or taking out the cork. How can this be done?

6. I happen to notice at exactly the moment of low tide a boat tied to a buoy at the local marina. A rope ladder was hanging over the side with ten rungs a foot apart. The bottom rung was just visible above the surface of the water. The water will rise eight feet at high tide. How many rungs of the ladder will be visible at high tide?

7. Two lawyers were both defending a young man in a civil action regarding a contract for the purchase of a used car. One of the lawyers was father to the son of the other lawyer. How could this be true?

8. If I drive at an average speed of thirty miles per hour from my house to the Railroad Station, I just catch the train. On a particular morning, there was a lot of traffic, and at the exact halfway point, I found that I had only averaged fifteen miles per hour. How fast must I drive for the rest of the way to catch the train?

## THINK SHEET NO. 4

1. A twelve-inch phonograph record is recorded from the outer edge to two inches from the exact center while a seven-inch phonograph record is recorded from the outer edge to one inch from the exact center. (Each record is recorded on one side only). The twelve-inch record revolves at thirty-three revolutions per minute and plays for fifteen minutes, while the seven-inch record revolves at forty-five revolutions per minute and plays for three minutes. How many more grooves on the twelve-inch than the seven-inch record?

2. The math teacher said to the student, "I have looked over the twenty-five test papers you have turned in this year, and I can't make up my mind whether to give you an "A" or "B." You are right on the borderline. However, I will give you the "A" if you can solve this problem: I'm giving you back all of your test papers

and six paper clips. Fasten an odd number of papers with each paper clip, with no papers or paper clips left over." The student got his "A." How did he do it?

3. I weigh ninety pounds plus half my weight. How much do I weigh?

4. If I can build a square wall around a one-acre lot with 12 truckloads of bricks, how big a square lot can I enclose with a similar wall containing twenty-four truckloads of bricks?

5. Mr. White, Mr. Black, and Mr. Green were having lunch together. One was wearing a white tie, one a black tie and one a green tie. The man wearing the white tie noticed that each was wearing a tie matching the names of the three men. Mr. Green agreed and also noticed that none of them was wearing a tie that matched his own name. What color tie was each man wearing? Is there enough information given to solve this problem?

6. Bob, John, Harry and Chuck all work for Apex Inc. as clerk, foreman, supervisor and manager. All are paid in whole numbers of dollars. The manager earns twice as much as the supervisor. The supervisor earns twice as much as the foreman. The foreman earns twice as much as the clerk. Bob does not earn more money than Harry, and Harry does not earn twice as much as Bob, yet Bob earns $10,753 per year more than John. What position does each hold?

7. Two trains are thirty miles apart. They start toward each other at fifteen miles per hour and as they start, a fly takes off from one train toward the other at forty miles per hour. As soon as the fly reached the other train, he reversed his direction and headed toward the first train. He repeated the process of flying back and forth at a constant rate of speed until the trains met. How far did the fly fly?

## ANSWERS

### THINK SHEET NO. 1

1. Three socks, four shoes.
2. It will be midnight again.
3. Every pain—etc.
4. Brown is the manager, Jones is the teller, Smith is the cashier.

### THINK SHEET NO. 2

1. 1961.
2. Five.
3. Ninety.

4. Fifty cents.

5. One hundred miles.

6. Four boys and three girls.

7. Richard is the writer; Bob the dancer; Paul the singer and Sam the painter.

## THINK SHEET NO. 3

1. Three silver dollars . . . $3.00

2. Total of twenty-eight orders.

3. One is a woman who has two daughters, each of whom has two daughters.

4. The doctor in Los Angeles was his sister.

5. Instead of taking the cork out, just push it into the bottle.

6. Ten rungs.

7. The other lawyer was his mother.

8. It was too late; I had already missed the train.

## THINK SHEET NO. 4

1. No more grooves in the twelve-inch than the seven-inch. They both have one groove.

2. Use one clip on each group of five sheets. Then clip the total together with the sixth clip.

3. I weigh 180 pounds.

4. Four acres.

5. Mr. White was wearing a green tie. Mr. Black was wearing a white tie. Mr. Green was wearing a black tie.

6. John is the clerk. Bob is the foreman. Chuck is supervisor. Harry is the manager.

7. Forty miles.

# 19

## IMAGINATION

*Imagination is more important than knowledge.*
*—Albert Einstein*

CERTAIN WORDS HAVE TAKEN ON SO MANY STRANGE MEANINGS AND CONNOTA-
tions in the course of time that they almost cease to have any meaning whatsoever.
One such word is "imagination." This word seems to serve many ideas—some
of which are even directly opposed to another. The word imagination has such a
wide variety of uses and so many diverse meanings; it has no fixed significance.

For example, when we say to a man, "Use your imagination," we mean his
present outlook is much too restricted. Next, we suggest to him that his ideas
are "pure imagination," implying his ideas are unsound. When we refer to a
jealous or suspicious person we say, "He is a victim of his imagination," mean-
ing his thoughts are untrue. Therefore, the word imagination seems to have
no definite meaning.

The dictionary defines imagination as, "The picturing power or act of the
mind; the process of forming mental images of the objects of perception or
thought in the absence of concrete external stimuli; the mental ability to re-
produce the images of memory; the reproductive faculty of the mind."

Imagination is said to be "the gateway to reality." By our imagination, we
have the power to do or be anything we desire. If we realize this, we then real-
ize that only as we live by imagination are we "truly living" at all. *It is the inner
world of continuous imagination that is the force that will make it happen in the
outer world.* It enlarges the vision, stretches the mind, and challenges the im-
possible. It projects your thoughts in search of creative achievement. You must
firmly implant in your mind a picture of the person you want to become with all
of the benefits and advantages this stature will bring you. See yourself winning
the admiration and respect of your family, friends, and business associates.

Our success mechanism is activated by our imagination, which has given us a picture of our goal. A common misbelief is that action is taken, or we fail to act, because of willpower. The real source is our imagination. A person's behavior, actions, and feelings are based upon what he imagines to be the truth about himself and everything around him. This is an elementary and essential mental law.

It is impossible for the nervous system to distinguish between a real experience or one created in your imagination. What you *believe, think, and imagine* to be the truth will determine how your nervous system responds.

Hold this image constantly in your mind. It will transform your outlook on life. It will spur you on to further study and thought, generating within you an unquenchable enthusiasm, a zest for a fuller and richer life, and motivate you to do the things necessary to attain it.

## SOMETHING TO THINK ABOUT

*Before imagination can flow, you must let go.*

# 20

## THE METHOD

TEN MINUTES EACH DAY SHOULD BE RESERVED FOR SHEER IMAGINATION. DURING this period, you should be by yourself and without distractions. Now, with your eyes closed, start to *exercise your imagination.*

### VIVID IMAGINING

The mental pictures you create in your imagination should be as close to actual experiences as you can make them, as lifelike and as complete in every detail as possible. This can be accomplished by becoming aware of and by focusing your thoughts on all the minute particulars that you perceive with your five senses. (For all reasonable intentions, details relating to the environment are extremely vital because if the experience you create is intense enough, your nervous system will accept it, the same as a real one.)

### IMAGINE YOURSELF SUCCESSFUL

During these ten minutes that you envision and feel yourself performing in a natural way, your past actions are unimportant. It doesn't really make any difference how you behaved on another occasion. It isn't essential to be absolutely confident and behave in an entirely satisfactory manner. Your nervous system will accept the fact eventually, if you imagine yourself the way you want to be. Picture yourself already as you would like to be. How do you feel? If you have behaved in a tense and unsure manner, imagine how you would feel if you were acting in a calmer manner, more intelligently and with more assurance.

## CONCENTRATE IMAGINATION ON GOAL

Concentrate your attention upon the *feeling* that you *already are that person*. The great secret is a controlled imagination and well-sustained attention. Firmly, repeatedly focus on the goal to be accomplished. Suppose you could not afford a trip; that your financial status would not provide for this. Would imagination be sufficient to produce this goal? Suppose you are capable of acting with continuous imagination and capable of sustaining the feeling of this goal as already accomplished. Will your assumption in your imagination produce the fact? Is your imagination a power sufficient to assume the feeling of the goal already accomplished? Is it capable of producing the reality of this idea?

Experience has convinced me that an assumption (though false) if persisted in, will produce the goal; that all our reasonable plans and actions will never make up for our lack of continuous imagination.

## CONCENTRATE IMAGINATION OBJECTIVELY

*A word of caution.* We use our imagination correctly, not as an onlooker (objectively), but as a *participant* (subjectively). *We actually must be there in our imagination.* This is not mere fantasy but a truth you can prove by experience. Every goal is already there as a mere possibility as long as you *think* of it, but is *overpoweringly real* if you think from it.

Determined imagination, thinking from the end result, is the beginning of all miracles. We would like to give you belief in miracles, but a miracle is only the name given it by those who have no knowledge of the power and function of imagination.

## THE FUTURE BECOMES THE PRESENT

*The future must become the present in the imagination of the person who wisely and consciously creates the circumstance.*

We translate vision into *being* when we are thinking from instead of thinking *of*. This, reason can never do. By its very nature it is restricted to the senses, but imagination has no such limitation. Through imagination, man escapes from the limitation of the senses and the bondage of reason. There is no stopping a man who can think *from* the end result. It does not matter what he has been or what he is; all that matters is *what he wants,* because he knows by use of his continuous imagination, his assumptions will harden into reality.

This inner journey into imagination must never be without direction. Man attracts what he is. This is a firm law of the universe.

"Man attracts to himself that which he sets out from himself."

The art of living consists in sustaining the *feeling* of your goals as *already being fulfilled* and letting things come to you.

## ONLY NOW COUNTS

It is only what is done *now* that counts. The present moment does not recede into the past, as so many people commonly believe. It advances into the future to confront us.

## A GREAT TRUTH

When man discovers that his world is his own mental activity made visible, then no man can attract to himself anything other than what he has set out in his imagination.

It was a momentous day when we realized this great truth: *that everything in our world is a manifestation of the mental activity that goes on within us,* that the conditions and circumstances of our lives only reflect this.

Therefore, practice frequently *in your imagination* the feeling that your goal has already been fulfilled. This is creative magic, and in this way you become the master of your fate.

*When you understand this function of the imagination, you hold in your hand the key to the attainment of all your goals.*

The truth that sets you free is, "You can experience in your imagination what you desire to experience in reality, and by maintaining this experience in your imagination, your desired goal becomes a reality."

## INCREASE ATTENTION ON FEELING

The success of this method is to focus your attention on *feeling* that your goal has already been fulfilled, without permitting distractions. All of your progress depends on the *increase of attention.* The ideas which move you to action are those that dominate your consciousness and possess your attention.

To the unenlightened, this may seem like fantasy, yet all progress comes from those who do not accept the world as it is.

When you set out to control your attention, you then will realize how little you actually presently control your imagination and how much it is dominated by the five senses.

## GO FORWARD WITH IMAGINATION

"Man either goes forward in imagination or remains imprisoned in his senses."

## CONTROLLED ATTENTION

Your imagination is able to perform in direct proportion to the degree of your attention. Attention is attracted from outside of you when you are consciously aware of external impressions. It is directed from within *when you have chosen deliberately what you will be preoccupied with mentally.* There is a great difference of thought attention directed objectively and subjectively. This control is achieved when you concentrate on the thoughts you have deliberately predetermined. You will no longer be dominated by outside circumstances and conditions.

To help you create more control, here is a practice exercise. Just before you fall asleep at night, attempt to hold your attention on the day's activities in reverse order. Place your attention on the last thing you did—getting into bed, and then go backward in time to the first thing you did—getting out of bed. This may not be the easiest exercise, but remember, just as specific exercises help develop specific muscles, this will help you develop the muscles of your "attention." Your attention must be developed, controlled, and concentrated in order for you to effect a successful change in your self-image and your future.

## PRINCIPLE OF LEAST ACTION

You must imagine yourself experiencing your goal as already being achieved, together with the accompanying "feeling." You attain deliberate conscious control of your imagination.

"Begin by knowing you have arrived."

This method employs the principle of "least action," which governs everything in physics. Least action is the minimum of time multiplied by the minimum of energy. The *future* becomes the *present* when you imagine you are or already have what you have assumed in your imagination. You then assume the "feeling" of possession of these things.

## ACTIONS ARE AUTOMATIC

This is a method of revising data in the subconscious mind, which controls your nervous system. After you have practiced this for twenty-one days, you will find yourself behaving differently, without conscious thought or effort.

Now, you do not have to try in order to feel insufficient and inadequate because you have stored up in your subconscious mind memories created by faults, both real and imagined. These memories generate your feelings of ineffectiveness automatically for you.

These actions have come about from the negative thoughts programmed into the subconscious. Conversely, this method will work just the same on positive thoughts and thereby will create a new *self-image*.

## CONSCIOUS NOT RESPONSIBLE FOR RESULTS

A person decides upon an objective with conscious thought. Then he gathers all the data, he evaluates it, and finally reaches a decision. The final outcome of this decision is allowed to take its course.

## POINTS FOR THE SUCCESSFUL USE OF THIS METHOD

*Essential:*

1. A strong desire for whatever it is you want (goal).
2. Cultivate the physical state of immobility described. You must learn to induce this state at will. The greater energies of the mind are available only when the body is still and the door to the senses is closed.
3. Experience in your imagination the "feeling" of already having achieved your goal. Experience daily for 21 consecutive days.

## LAW WORKS IMPERSONALLY

One of the prevalent misunderstandings is that this law is workable only for those who have a devout or religious principle. This is definitely a fallacy. It works impersonally, just as the law of gravity or electricity.

## HOW TO UTILIZE THE POWER OF RATIONAL THINKING

Your automatic success mechanism is completely detached and disinterested. It performs much like a computer operating from data in the subconscious mind, creating the proper feelings to complete predetermined goals for you. It functions on data which you have programmed into your subconscious in the form of thoughts, views, convictions, evaluations, and impressions.

Our future and present are not decided by constantly turning over and reviewing the past. When a person does this, he becomes obsessed with underlying emotional problems that do not allow him to remember or regulate and direct his present thoughts.

*IN THE THEATER OF MY MIND*
*At night, upon my bed; my eyes closed tight,*
*I inward glide, collecting scattered thoughts to reap,*
*And reassemble as a script desire did write,*
*To be performed upon the imaged stage of sleep, entertaining GOALS.*
*While affirmations wing in flight*
*Thru thin, pale scenes of thought my visions keep.*
*To hear, to see, to touch, to be what ere I might,*
*Creates a play, with props from fancies formless heap.*
*And the Hero is me.*
*What fleeting, filmy feelings will my mind achieve,*
*As senses, with my dream fulfilled are sate?*
*What if this inward drama I do then believe,*
*And store within my heart, and calmly wait?*
*Then in a way, tho surely one I can't conceive,*
*One day, that dream will be my waking state.*
*And when I know a web of life that I did weave,*
*I'll also know that I control my fate.*
*My dream and I are free.*

                    *H. J. Halverson—a Psycho-Cybernetics student*

## SOMETHING TO THINK ABOUT

*Imagination is more important than knowledge.*
*Man attracts to himself that which he sets out from himself.*
*Man goes forward in imagination or remains imprisoned*
in his senses.
*Begin by knowing you have arrived.*
*Take imagination and enthusiasm and hitch the two together. Then fix your*
gaze on the farthest star and forgo about the weather.
*You can experience in your imagination what you desire to experience in*
reality, and by maintaining this experience in your imagination, your goal
becomes a reality.
*Before imagination can flow, you must let go*

Introduction to *Rod Serling's Twilight Zone:*

"There is a fifth dimension beyond that which is known to man. A dimension
as vast as space and as timeless as infinity. It is the middle ground between
light and shadow, beyond science and superstition, and it lies between the
pit of man's fears and the summit of his knowledge. This is the dimension
of imagination."

# 21

## HOW TO MAKE USE OF NEGATIVE FEEDBACK

### GLANCE AT NEGATIVES, BUT CONCENTRATE ON POSITIVES

The instrument panel of any modern feedback system contains negative indicators in the form of light panels, which become illuminated when anything goes wrong. If this happens, it does not mean that the system is defective, but merely an indication that steps should be taken to correct the problem. If the signal is disregarded, the mechanism may be damaged. When one of the panels lights up, no one becomes upset.

However, it is not necessary to give the instrument panel one's undivided attention. An occasional glance at the negative indicators is all that is required. There is no need to concentrate on them, and major attention is focused on the positive aspects of the mechanism.

### HOW TO USE NEGATIVE THINKING

We need to learn to appreciate the power of negative thinking when it is applied in a constructive manner. We only should recognize negatives in order to avoid them.

For example, a tennis player does not need to be aware consciously of the net; a golfer, of the sand traps and water hazards; a bowler, of the channels; or a high jumper or pole-vaulter, of the bar. They all concentrate on their objectives or positive goals.

When this type of negative thinking is used, it operates to our advantage, not against us. It will always help us attain our various successes.

We need to take the following steps:

1. We must be aware of the negative so that it can warn us of possible danger.
2. We should evaluate the negative as being unwanted, objectionable, unacceptable, and something that cannot result in happiness
3. We should then take whatever measures are necessary to correct the situation at once.

By employing this method and reacting in this manner, a form of *automatic reflex* is created. These correct reactions become part of our stored data. Thus we are using *negative feedback* as an automatic control that can actually guide us and help us remain clear of failure, thereby producing success.

## RECOGNITION OF NEGATIVE FEEDBACK

If we see *negative feedback* for what it is, a signal in the wrong direction, it will help to steer us toward the successful accomplishment of whatever we strive for. We need to be aware of our feelings about it but must not concentrate on it. We also need to perceive it as objectionable and something we do not want to happen. It does not aid us in any way in producing happiness or success.

The inhibited individual is frustrated in almost every area of living when he cannot, to his own satisfaction, give voice to his thoughts and be himself. This feeling of unfulfillment will very likely extend into all of his activities.

## NEGATIVE FEEDBACK

In a feedback system, a negative signal is the same as disapproval, telling you that you're going in the wrong direction. It is necessary for you to take proper action that will guide you back in the right direction. The main concern of negative feedback is to alter and adjust the direction, not to halt it. Negative feedback is never a STOP sign. Its basic objective is to correct or change its forward direction and not to stop the action in its tracks.

## INHIBITIONS CAUSED BY "WHAT OTHERS THINK"

An inhibited personality is always aware of what other people think of him to the degree that he is too self-conscious about his actions. He is always weighing everything he says and does in an effort to please other people. Then he is too easily offended, or his feelings become hurt by what someone thinks of him or by what he *thinks* they think of him. Consequently, he acquires an inhibited personality and behaves in an unsatisfactory manner, merely because of excessive negative feedback.

To be effective with other people:

1. Avoid trying too hard at the conscious level to impress them.
2. Avoid doing or saying anything for the effect you believe it will have on them.
3. Avoid thinking about what they think or feel about you.

## SOMETHING TO THINK ABOUT

*Accentuate the positive, eliminate the negative (in terms of its influence on your actions).*

# 22

## ATTITUDES CAN BE CHANGED

ATTITUDES CAN BE CHANGED. HOW DO WE DO THIS? THROUGH A PROGRAM OF repetition.

Read the following each day for seven days, and it will impress on you the value of a daily, methodical, systematic affirmation.

I am involved in a *daily, methodical, systematic* program toward the direction of my chosen goals. By daily association with my positive attitudes—contained in my program, I will *think positive thoughts* and *form the habit of thinking positively.* As this positive daily repetition builds up, it reflects itself in the difference between my *positive* and my *negative* thoughts.

Example:

(+direction of your goal)

(–away from your goal)

I will concentrate on the positive and omit the negative in terms of their influence on my actions.

I will take positive action in the direction of my goals. This will start a constant upward spiral stimulated by the very simple fact that my mind is like the film of a camera or the tape of a recorder, in that it absorbs everything it is exposed to. The net result is that, by exposure to my *daily systematic, methodical program,* I am involved in my *optimistic, goal-oriented ideas.* My mind will then *associate and form habits* that will *show and express* themselves in my ACTIONS.

# 23

## PLAN OF ACTION

THIS *PLAN OF ACTION* IS TO BE DISTINGUISHED FROM THE SYNTHETIC EXPERI-
encing method (Data-Revision) in that it is in writing and carries a deadline
for its attainment of goals. Some of the thoughts and ideas generated by the
synthetic method upon reaching the conscious level will be written down in
the *Plan of Action.* Each of these methods will work separately, but they will
work amazingly well if used together.

It is a well-organized method of goal-setting. You already know that this
is the "secret of success."

Goals are divided as follows:

*Long-range Goals* (tangible and intangible)
Must be meaningful—distant point of reference something to
aim at.

*Short-range Goals* (tangible and intangible)
There must be believable steps toward long-range goals.

*Success by the yard is hard—by the inch is a cinch.*

*Motivational*
Must be able to clearly see end results.
Must be compatible.

When goals are compatible, you have a relaxed feeling that you are doing
what you want to do every day. Your life will be what you desire to make it.

Some people have more opportunity, money, and talent, but within certain
limits. They do not have more time than anyone else. Therefore, *planning* is
critical. Can you imagine the tremendous exhilaration that comes from having
your life planned and doing what you want to do so that you don't waste time?

## "PEOPLE DON'T PLAN TO FAIL, THEY FAIL TO PLAN"

*Blueprint of finished product.*

Plan in advance what you want your life to be. Every day aim for what you are trying to accomplish. A written plan helps you visualize what it will mean to you if you continue this course. What do you do if you lose sight of the end result? The same is true in planning your life. Do you see how this would work for you? Do you see how this would make a tremendous difference in your performance?

> *"ALL MEN SEEK ONE GOAL: SUCCESS or HAPPINESS. The only way to achieve TRUE SUCCESS is to express yourself completely in SERVICE to Society. First, have a definite, clear, practical idea—A GOAL, AN OBJECTIVE. Second, seek the necessary MEANS TO ACHIEVE your ends—wisdom, money, materials and methods. THIRD, ADJUST ALL YOUR MEANS TO THAT END"*
>
> —*Aristotle*

The *plan of action* is designed to put theory into *practice,* turn knowledge into *know-how* and thought into *action.* It discourages procrastination and will move you to greater utilization of your potential.

## YOUR OWN PLAN OF ACTION

A word of caution: *Do not* under any circumstances identify the *plan of action* as anything other than *yours.* Unless you make it your own plan it will remain forever outside your grasp, and it will never make a significant change in your life. The "failure to identify" is critical. When you recognize the plan as *your plan,* you will sense the power of your own talents, abilities, and capacity *to change.* Hereafter all references to this plan must be to *my plan of action.*

## CRYSTALIZE YOUR THINKING

The first step is to crystalize your thinking. It is a well-known fact that only 5 percent of all people have definite, concrete plans for their achievement in life. Therefore it comes as no surprise that only 5 percent are highly successful.

With such clear-cut evidence of the *results* of planning, why are so many content with so little?

Two reasons stand out prominently.

1. Very few people know how to plan.
2. Even fewer know how to *turn thought into action*.

They have never really discovered the power of visualization. Thought is only the beginning of the process. Without "vivid imaging," without a crystal clear visualization of the "event" before we act, it never comes to pass. Everything we do, we must first accomplish in our "imagination."

When you speak or think in vague generalities as "someday, I'm going to have . . ." that day never comes. Before your energies can be directed toward your goal, you must *first crystalize your thinking* and say exactly what you mean and exactly what you do want.

Set your *long-range goals HIGH.*

Set your *short-range goals.* (Progressive intermediate steps that are easy to reach.)

Visualize yourself as already being there.

## DEVELOP A WRITTEN PLAN AND A DEADLINE
## FOR THIS ATTAINMENT

The second step is to have a written plan and a deadline of its attainment because *writing crystalizes thought, and crystalized thought stimulates action.*

Definite plans produce definite results, but indefinite plans produce *no results.*

Unless a plan is committed to in writing, it is seldom definite.

The written plan will give you *direction,* now you will know:

Where you are now, and where you want to go.

1. A properly conceived plan in writing helps you in *both* to see yourself in your present position clearly, exactly, and honestly—and to define your objective just as accurately.
2. Planning conserves energy. You accomplish a great deal more with half the effort because your energies are *directed toward a goal.*
3. Planning assures compatibility. By reducing your goal to a written plan, incompatible goals become more obvious.
4. Planning makes visualization habitual. The power of visualization has already been defined. No painting was ever painted that the artist could not clearly see in his imagination. Reducing a plan to writing makes visualization a habit—a habit that, once acquired, will open up a new world you never dreamed existed.

Each separate goal requires a deadline. A deadline gives a challenge to action. Without it, failure will follow because your goal will be forgotten.

But deadlines carry hidden dangers unless you make them your slaves and not your master. What if you miscalculate and do not reach your goal by the deadline? What then? This is where most people accept temporary failure as defeat. If you have set the deadline, you can change it.

The man who succeeds is the man who alters the *deadline, but not the goal*— who resets his sights in view of changing circumstances and keeps going until the goal is achieved (to be distinguished from Data-Revision in which no deadline is used.)

| Long-Range Goals | PROGRESS DATE Annual or Semiannual | Visual Aids |
|---|---|---|
| Tangible 1. 2. 3. Intangible 1. 2. 3. | | |

| Short-Range Goals | PROGRESS DATE Weekly or Monthly | Visual Aids |
|---|---|---|
| Tangible 1. 2. 3. Intangible 1. 2. 3. | | |

## DEVELOP A REAL DESIRE

The third step is to develop a real desire for the things you want from life.

Desire is based on a powerful emotion generated by crystalized thinking and vivid imagining.

Desire can be tested exactly and accurately by answering these seven questions:

1. What do I want? (Analyzed from previous procedure under goals.)
2. Where do I stand now?
3. What are the obstacles and roadblocks? (What's between me and what I want?)
4. How can I overcome these obstacles? (Plan)
5. Target dates for overcoming obstacles?
6. What are the rewards?
7. IS IT REALLY WORTH IT TO ME?

When the answers to the questions are an integral part of your plan of action, you not only test your desire, but you can develop it and use it.

## DEVELOP SELF-CONFIDENCE

The fourth step is development of confidence in yourself and your ability. Confidence is a reliance on the positive (instead of the negative). Thoughts give direction to our conscious actions. All thoughts are basically positive. Only the direction is different.

A human being is limited by his self-imposed bonds of limitations. We can never come out from underneath these bonds *unless we believe we can change*—and we can change if we *think we can!* Everything tells us we can change; history speaks of progress, and progress is *change;* biology speaks of evolution, and evolution is *change*. Yet some people stubbornly continue to believe that "others can change, but they cannot."

People resist change for many reasons. Even when they decide to change, they try to change conscious actions before they change their self-image, their attitudes, and their habits. Much of our activity is directed by the subconscious mind. Therefore any attempt to control the conscious is always ineffective.

Knowing how to change by changing our self-image, attitudes, and habits, we build self-confidence in our ability. This self-confidence then becomes a way of life affecting everything we do.

## DEVELOP DETERMINATION

The last remaining ingredient is the development of *determination* to succeed regardless of circumstances or what "other people" say, think, or do. In step three, if you have answered the question "is it worth it to me?" affirmatively and honestly, then you can find no circumstance that will allow you to sway from reaching your goal. You will develop your determination by:

1. Reviewing your written plan.
2. Concentrating on the rewards.

Your desire will stimulate an endless flow of dynamic, positive *direction* to keep you on course until your goals are reached.

Set goals and make plans for their achievement in the following areas of your life:

1. Spiritual
2. Mental
3. Physical
4. Social
5. Family Life
6. Financial

This kind of program will tell you *what to do and how to do it,* but you must do it. You link your thinking to a purpose. You know where you are going, and your thoughts and actions are then concentrated on getting you there.

# 24

## TIRED PEOPLE

### WHY ARE THERE SO MANY TIRED PEOPLE?

Let's take the familiar problem as is so often expressed by doctors and psychologists whose patients declare, "Doctor, there must be something wrong with me. I seem to have so little energy." After a full examination, the doctor reports there is nothing physically wrong. What do you suppose is the problem? Why do you think there are so many tired people? Once a person sees the tremendous amount of unnecessary and pointless burdens he is carrying around and disposes of them, he will no longer be tired. He must first become aware of these burdens. This is the problem of many, many people who are carrying around unnoticed loads of energy-robbing negative thoughts that steal their energy. No wonder they are all so tired.

Everyone has his special brand of energy-robbing burdens. The quicker we throw these away, the sooner we will feel better.

*The feeling of being free is not a matter of gaining anything. It is purely a process of ridding ourselves of something. This is one of the most surprising, most rewarding, and helpful ideas you can ever grasp.*

The simplicity of this idea escapes most of us. We are all used to thinking in terms of joining, uniting, and building, but our inner freedom lies in the opposite direction. *Happiness is a process of getting rid of these unnecessary burdens.* This is a vital truth. We must be able to clearly recognize the way to this truth doesn't lie in creating anything that does not now exist or in acquiring anything not presently available. (It is all within our potential right now.)

# 25

## HAPPINESS

### THE HABIT OF HAPPINESS

Dr. John A. Schindler (author of *How to Live 365 Days a Year*) explains happiness as, ". . . a state of mind in which our thinking is pleasant a good share of the time." This is a remarkable, deceptively simple definition. We don't think it could be stated more clearly.

### WHOLE PHYSICAL SYSTEM WORKS BETTER

When you are contented, you are usually in better health, are more efficient at your job, and enjoy it more. Your brain works with greater competency, and your memory is better when your mind is in a relaxed state. Your five senses are more acute when you think agreeable thoughts. Unhappiness and stress are causes of psychosomatic ailments.

It has been pointed out that when people in business have a bright positive outlook, they are more apt to succeed than those who are depressed.

### ARE YOU BEING MANIPULATED?

When you react automatically to outside circumstances that tell you to be angry or to get upset, you are being manipulated into behavior that you might normally wish to avoid. You are letting outer conditions dictate how you act and feel. If you learn the *habit* of happiness, you are the master instead of the slave.

## HAPPINESS IS A BY-PRODUCT OF A GOAL

As we have said before, when a person is motivated toward a worthwhile, predetermined objective, he is usually a cheerful person. When someone is happy, he will probably be successful. No one is really ever alive unless he is striving for a series of goals.

## HAPPINESS CAN BE METHODICALLY CULTIVATED

Anyone, by careful concentration, can develop the ability to keep his thoughts on a happy level a major portion of the time and methodically make cheerfulness a part of his behavior pattern.

On the surface, this may sound ridiculous and impossible. However, from our past observations, we have found that it is really unlikely anyone can make an optimistic outlook their way of life without earnest, intentional effort.

You may wait forever if you expect happiness to come to you as a matter of course or for someone to bring it to you. If you wait for your state of affairs to be perfect before you can have a pleasant frame of mind, you are destined to be gloomy, because that condition will probably never exist.

Nothing is ever all black or all white. Our lives are filled with gray days, and it is entirely our own decision as to which direction our thoughts will take. Whether or not we maintain optimistic thoughts is determined wholly by the type of thoughts we choose to keep in our minds.

## HAPPINESS

Happiness is the rarest, most prized, sought after state of man and, sadly, the least understood and most misunderstood.

We, as human beings, have a creative urge within us, which gives us a deep desire to grow, solve problems and reach our goals. Accomplishing these things is the only way we can obtain peace of mind, fulfillment, and happiness.

There can be no real happiness if the things we believe in are different from the things we do.

HAPPINESS is a by-product of a goal.

HAPPINESS is a mental attitude.

HAPPINESS is a state of mind in which our thinking is pleasant most of the time.

HAPPINESS is purely internal.

HAPPINESS is learned and is practiced only in the present or never experienced at all.

HAPPINESS is a feeling of being glad, pleased, contented, doing well, peace, freedom, responding to life, being interested in life.

HAPPINESS is a mental habit.

HAPPINESS is an "emotional feeling" of satisfaction coming from having experienced or expecting something that, in your own opinion, is good or to your liking.

HAPPINESS is in your own personal terms, by your own standards, in your own way, in your own time, by yourself, and for yourself. There is no comparative norm.

The achievement of a serene and lasting happiness is not an accident, nor is it a gift. It is something that each of us must construct for ourselves. We are not born happy. We learn to be happy.

## PERPETUAL HAPPINESS IS NONSENSE

It is pure absurdity to expect to be happy all the time. A periodic depression is normal. We all have enough common sense to know that anyone who is happy all the time may be in fact, quite mad. After all, reality sometimes warrants unhappiness, and you don't need to be apologetic or depressive about it. There's no need to feel that discontent is an occasion for immediate psychiatric suspicion. Perpetual happiness is nothing but nonsense. It is necessary to direct your attention to what is good, useful and productive and ignore all the rest.

## LIMITATIONS ON THINKING

We must literally limit the scope of our thinking. If we think of days gone by, we should create pictures in our minds of nostalgic occurrences, like happy, carefree events of our youth. When we think of the present, we must focus our minds on things that we strive to improve, our homes, our jobs, and all our aspects for success. We must intentionally disregard situations that appear to have a dead end. When we think of the future, we should take for granted that all the things we want are a definite possibility.

## OTHER CHANGES COME FROM THE INNER

The most amazing effect of limiting our thinking is the dramatic change in the outer aspects of our lives which come about as a direct result of the inner transformation.

## SELF-IMAGE CONSISTENT WITH HABITS

Your habits are spontaneously altered when you change your self-image because these two things are closely allied. The self-image is compatible with your behavior pattern. Consequently, when you intentionally bring new patterns into being, you leave behind your old ones.

## HAPPINESS DOES NOT LIE IN THE FUTURE, BUT IN THE PRESENT

One of the problems shared most frequently by unhappy people is that they allow their lives to be governed by what may happen tomorrow. They are always waiting for some incident to come about in the future to make them happy—the time they get married, when the mortgage is paid off, when the children complete their education, when they make more money, when they get a new car, complete some job or overcome a difficulty. They are continually let down and frustrated.

If the art of being happy is not experienced and related to the present time, it will not be experienced at all. You cannot base happiness on an uncertain event or possible occurrence. Another problem will always come along just as you find the answer to the previous one. Your whole life is a connecting succession of difficulties and problems—both large and small. The only time for happiness is right now.

## HAPPINESS MUST BE EXPERIENCED

Happiness means being interested in life, or responding to life, not just with one's brain, but one's whole personality, and to become truly independent. Happiness can be negated by separating intellect and emotion. It requires a combination of experiencing, through intellect and feeling. Without this combination, man is incapable of experiencing anything but thought.

Being happy can be a decision between full human development and full marketplace success. It is tied into the capacity to see, to discern fact from fiction, not to indulge or live by rationalizations and illusions which block authentic experience. Care more for happiness than success.

## THE ONLY CURE IS THE CURING OF UNHAPPINESS

A difficult person is an unhappy person. He is at war with himself and consequently is at war with the world. No happy person ever disturbed a meeting, preached a war, promoted bigotry, nagged a husband, wife, or children. No happy man ever committed a theft or murder. All crimes, hatred, all wars can be related to unhappiness. How does unhappiness arise, and how does it ruin human lives?

*Happiness is emotional tranquility. Unhappiness is emotional stress.*

## LEARNING MATURITY CONCEPT

Most people conduct their lives poorly because they have never been taught maturity. They have simply never learned to grow up mentally. Most of us continue to react to adult problems with childish reactions (conditioning). *It is by trying to meet adult problems with childish reactions that we generate emotional stress and unhappiness.* There is no place people are taught maturity. It does not come as a natural process. Maturity must be learned.

## MATURITY IS A MATTER OF ATTITUDES

Maturity is not a matter of being crammed full of technical or classical knowledge or information, nor does it consist of being able to make important judgments correctly. It is essentially a collection of attitudes—attitudes that are more effective and helpful to the individual in meeting situations than are the attitudes of a small child in the same situation.

An attitude is an established way of reacting to certain classes of experience (Habit Pattern Conditioning). The more mature a person is, the more complete the stock of effective attitudes he can bring to the variety of experiences that arise in his day-to-day living. Areas which *require* the possession of maturity are Business, Sex, Old Age.

## IS FINANCIAL SUCCESS A DETERRENT TO HAPPINESS?

We believe there is a battle that every earnest human being has to fight with himself to make his life according to his beliefs. The instinct of acquisition hurries on from gain to gain, but the moral consciousness is very conservative. It has its roots deep in the tradition of the past, and therein come each man's complications.

As soon as we get out into the world, there are only two possible courses open to us. Either we can try to make our lives conform to our beliefs, or we can modify our beliefs to fit our lives. True happiness, we know, depends on which path we take.

Many men force themselves to take the latter to achieve financial success. They lose their idealism and become "practical" and indifferent toward "moral consciousness." Their material returns are high—but so is the price they pay. The moral consciousness eventually obtains its revenge—in ulcers, high blood pressure, alcoholism, and in the kind of emotional collapse we wrongfully call "nervous breakdown."

The other task—that of shaping our lives to the pattern of our deepest beliefs is infinitely more difficult, and only a saint can perfectly succeed at all. But psychologically, *it is the effort that counts,* not the achievement. When the moral consciousness is satisfied, a man can live comfortably with himself.

The unhappy man is constantly striving for the approval of others, yet the more applause he gets, the more he requires. The happy man is concerned only with his own approval, with the knowledge that what he does is consistent with what he believes to be right.

Success is a blessing when it comes without compromising moral sense and the greatest of curses when it is at the expense of silencing the inner voice.

# 26

## HAPPINESS CONCEPT

### RECOGNIZING THE REAL SELF FROM THE FALSE SELF

Inside every human is a "real" self and a "false" self. If the "real" part of your personality becomes a powerful force, you will undoubtedly become happier and more productive in all areas of your life. But if you permit the "false" self to take over control of your thoughts and behavior, you will probably become frustrated, with a feeling of emptiness and futility in your life.

In essence, you are the "real" self—positive, without negative qualities. It is really YOU, and you have always possessed it. The "false" self is negatively oriented, and even if it temporarily controls the "real" self, the real self is always there.

What does this have to do with personal happiness?

In order to be happy, a person must not permit the false self to dominate because the false self remains miserable all the time. On the other hand, the real self, being positively oriented, is always happy.

When you are able to distinguish between your real and false selves, you will be taking a step toward your goal of inner happiness. Your real self sends messages that tell you what to do, if you will merely listen.

Occasionally you may wonder why you should even try to develop new attitudes and forget your old negative ideas. What is the value and significance of understanding yourself and continuing to strive for self-improvement?

The value is uncomplicated and clear. Perhaps this is why many people do not understand it.

VALUE involves these facts:

You want to live the way you really want to.

You want control of your life.

You want to avoid mistakes.

You want an abundance of energy.

You want to always feel youthful.

You want to feel free of pressure.

You want to know who you are.

You want to look forward to a brighter tomorrow.

You want to feel free from fear.

These facts make up the VALUE, and they are available to everyone.

If you are aware that the complete value is to get the things you truly desire out of life and keep this in your mind, you will inevitably reach your goal.

Some people would like to get out of their rut and change their entire lifestyle. However, they don't break away and live as they would like to because "they" have an artificial sense of morality.

"They" try to establish a false idea as to what your responsibilities are to them and what you owe them. The real fact is that "they" expect something from you. There is NOTHING you owe them. Remember that your primary obligation is to yourself.

Behaving in a manner that does no damage to you or to anyone else is genuine morality.

Think of your friendships and other relationships. It is a known fact that you are drawn to people who occupy the same level of consciousness that you do. When you change your self-image and thereby change your level of awareness, you will have less in common with some of your friends and associates, including your shared psychological concerns. When you find associations at your new awareness level, they will probably be more rewarding.

Feeling obligated to help others is disturbing to some people.

You must learn not to confuse yourself with any notion as to how you can be of assistance to your fellow human beings. This idea is a terrible pitfall. Your wholehearted effort should be directed toward creating a new self-image. You should make this your primary obligation, the way in which you can be of service to others in the most beneficial way.

A person instinctively knows that you have within you firmness and power if he realizes you are trying to be someone to him and not necessarily trying to do something for him. Never try to do anything for anyone if it requires conscious effort; there is no need to help someone until it is automatic and you truly want to do so. You really don't want anything from someone you care for.

The way to be of the greatest service to someone else is by first changing your own self-image and developing your own inner strength. When you have accomplished this, you will never again be troubled about helping others. Your mental state will enable you to be someone to them rather than to do something for them.

After this change has taken place and you have found your real self, you may be surprised at the extraordinary calmness and assurance you possess. Your relationships with other people will be more straightforward and open because you don't expect anything from each other. You can be close to one another and yet be independent at the same time.

Genuine kindness is what you are. It is not what you do. The greatest kindness you can ever offer anyone is the *truth*.

# 27

## EXERCISES AND TECHNIQUES

BEGIN EACH DAY A NEW AND BETTER WAY BY RECITING THE FOLLOWING AND practicing each day for 21 days:

This is the beginning of a new day.

I have been given this day to use as I will.

What I do today is important, because I'm exchanging a new day of my life for it.

When tomorrow comes, this day will be gone forever, leaving in its place whatever I have traded for it.

I pledge to myself that it shall be for gain, good, and success, in order that I shall not regret the price I paid for this day.

My thinking and my attitudes are calm and cheerful.

I act and feel friendly toward other people.

I am tolerant of other people, their shortcomings and mistakes, and I view their actions with the most favorable understanding possible.

I act as though the attainment of my goals is certain to happen. I am the kind of individual I aspire to be, and everything I do and the way I feel expresses this individuality.

I will not allow my judgment or attitude to be affected by negativism or pessimism.

I try to smile as often as possible, at least several times a day.

I respond in a calm and intelligent manner, without alarm, no matter what the situation.

If I cannot control a situation, I try always to react in a positive manner, even to negative facts.

Each of the above habitual ways of acting, feeling, and thinking does have a beneficial and constructive influence on your self-image. Experience them daily, and you will find a marked decrease in worry and sense of guilt and hostility, and an increase in self-confidence.

Mark off 21 consecutive days after reciting each day.

*IT'S DONE WITH MIRRORS*
*When you get what you want in your struggle for wealth*
*And the world makes you king for a day,*
*Just go to the mirror and look at yourself*
*And see what that man has to say.*

*For it isn't your father or mother or wife*
*Upon whose judgment you pass,*
*The fellow whose verdict counts most in your life*
*is the one staring back from the glass.*

*Some people may think you're a straight-shootin' chum*
*And call you a wonderful guy,*
*But the man in the glass says you're only a bum*
*If you can't look him straight in the eye.*

*He's the fellow to please, never mind all the rest*
*For he's with you clear to the end,*
*And you've passed your most dangerous, difficult test*
*If the man in the glass is your friend.*

*You may fool the whole world down the pathway of years*
*And get pats on the back as you pass,*
*But your final reward will be heartaches and tears*
*If you've cheated the man in the glass.*

Practice this exercise by substituting first-person pronouns (I, me, my).

## SELF-IMAGE BUILDERS

### YOUR MIRROR MAGIC PRACTICE

Every morning, when you get up, do breathing exercises for a few minutes. Tell yourself you are taking in oxygen not only to satisfy your physical lungs but the lungs for your soul. Picture yourself not only stimulating the heart muscles of your body but also the heart muscle of your mind and spirit. Tell yourself that you are making yourself strong enough to hurdle yesterday's fears and defeats to be strong for TODAY.

Go to the mirror every day for a few moments. Look at yourself. Ask yourself: "Am I a friend to myself? Remind yourself that you must be a friend to yourself before you can be a friend to others. Remind yourself again and again that you must rise above an error or a mistake of yesterday to be friendly to your self-respect as a human being TODAY. Make a habit of it.

> *"Do the thing, and you will have the power."*
> *—Emerson*

If you desire to improve yourself, remember this fact: Act the way you want to be (in your imagination), and you'll be the way you act.

## MORE SELF-IMAGE BUILDERS

### MIRROR MAGIC PRACTICE

Are you the one in charge of wastebasket-emptying and garbage disposal in your home? If not, elect to be for at least six days. Utilize this usually onerous household task in a positive way as follows: As you throw away the garbage and useless accumulation of a busy household, discard, at the same time, the emotional and mental garbage that you have allowed to accumulate in your mind. Thus, both your home and yourself can start a new day clean and free.

Every day for six days when you leave your home and close the door, see this act as a symbolic closing of the door to the past—that moment in the past when you made a mistake or failed in some undertaking, resolving that the past shall no longer intrude into your new day.

## SELF-IMAGE BUILDERS

When you are driving your car or walking in the street and come to a red traffic light every day for six days, think of the red light as an expression of your negative feelings, your fear of failure holding you back. Realize that no circumstance holds you back indefinitely. Expect the green light to go on, opening the way for you to go ahead. Then when the green light flashes on, move forward as if you are moving toward a useful goal with the confidence of past successes, guiding you—giving you that winning feeling of accomplishment.

When God shuts one door, he opens another.

## IN PURSUIT OF SUCCESS

The most useful rules are so deceptively simple as to escape recognition by most people. Heed the following very simple advice. These rules may not be easy to follow, but they are easy to understand.

1. *Do one thing at a time*

    Remember, no man can do more. Two or three things at a time are less than one thing at a time. Here mathematics stand confounded, for here always—more is less.

2. *Know the problem*

    Don't waste time trying to find answers to a problem when you don't know the problem. Be sure you have clearly stated the problem first.

3. *Learn to listen and listen to learn*

    Open your ears before you open your mouth—it may open your eyes.

4. *Learn to ask questions*

    The ability to ask questions made Socrates a wise man. Make it a point to ask questions if only to double-check your position.

5. *Distinguish sense from nonsense and be brief!*

    Be not among those who expound brilliantly on "trivial matters." Be known for your succinct clarity and not for the "gift of gab."

6. *Accept change as inevitable*

    Heraclitus said that "no man can step in the same river twice." Not only does the river change, but the man himself changes as well. Beware of the pat solution. Everything can be improved.

7. *Admit your mistakes*
   Avoid the great temptation to rationalize your mistakes. Do not be afraid of making mistakes.
8. *Be simple*
   If a child can understand, then so can an adult.
9. *Be calm*
   Sound judgment is more likely to thrive in a contemplative atmosphere than in a hurricane.
10. *Smile*
    A man with no humor can never have the warmth and personality of a great leader.


*THEY GO EVERYWHERE*
*A smile is quite a funny thing,*
*It wrinkles up your face.*
*And when it's gone you never find,*
*Its secret hiding place.*

*But far more wonderful it is,*
*To see what smiles can do.*
*He smiles at someone since you smiled,*
*And so one smile makes two.*

*He smiles at someone since you smiled,*
*And then that someone smiles back.*
*And that one smiles, until, in truth,*
*You fail in keeping track.*

*And since a smile can do great good,*
*By cheering hearts of care,*
*Let's smile and smile and not forget,*
*That smiles go everywhere !!!*

## TAKE TIME TO . . .

| | |
|---|---|
| THINK | SEE YOURSELF AT YOUR BEST |
| PLAY | COUNT BLESSINGS |
| READ | USE CREATIVE IMAGINATION |

| | |
|---|---|
| LOVE | UNDERSTAND YOURSELF & OTHERS |
| PLAN | FEEL HAPPY |
| BE FRIENDLY | BE HAPPY, (NOW) |
| LAUGH | FORGIVE YOURSELF & OTHERS |
| GIVE | BE CONSIDERATE |
| WORK | LEARN |
| RELAX | MAKE DECISIONS |
| BE HAPPY | BE CHEERFUL |
| FEEL FREE | DEVELOP HOBBIES |
| APOLOGIZE | SMILE |
| ADMIT ERROR | BE HAPPY |
| BEGIN OVER | BE RESPONSIVE (TO THE THINGS NEAR AT HAND) |
| SET GOALS | DEHYPNOTIZE FROM FALSE BELIEFS (REEVALUATE) |
| DREAM | |

MY GREATEST MISTAKE IS TO:

be afraid to make a mistake.

live in the past.

worry about tomorrow.

compare myself (with others).

doubt myself.

not have confidence.

pass a negative judgment on myself and others.

not be happy NOW (not enjoy the present moment).

not improve my self-image.

not be a friend to myself.

not set goals.

not have a PMA (positive mental attitude).

not use my creative imagination.

not like my work.

get uptight and not relax.

not keep promises to myself.

not laugh at my mistakes.

not have a good hobby.

abuse my health.

inhibit my real personality.

say, "I can't, or I have to."

think I am not important.

not try to understand the other person's point of view.

not react calmly and intelligently.

give up.

ignore negative feedback.

be too concerned about what others think.

## HOW TO MAKE DECISIONS

### DECISIONS

1. Get the facts.
2. Analyze and interpret the facts.
3. Arrive at a decision and then *act* on it.

*"You have no right to an opinion until you have examined the evidence."*
If a man will devote his time to securing the facts in an impartial, objective way, his worries will evaporate in the light of knowledge. Merely writing the facts down and clearly stating them goes a long way toward a sensible solution.
*"A problem well stated is half solved."*

1. What am I worried about?
2. What can I *do* about it?

3. *Decide* what to *do!*
4. *Start* immediately to *carry out* this decision.

Unless we do something about carrying out and actually *acting* on a decision, all our fact-finding and analyses are just whistling in the dark. Once a decision is made and acted on, dismiss all care and responsibility of its outcome. Don't reconsider, don't retrace. It's the same as a roulette player having placed his bet and worrying about the outcome while the wheel is spinning, even though he has no longer any control.

> *"If you are going to worry, don't do it*
> *If you do it—DON'T WORRY."*

## NOW NEVER WAITS!

*What happens to unused nows?*
   *They turn into unusable thens.*

*JUST FOR TODAY*
*I will live through the next twelve hours and not tackle all my life's*
   *problems at once.*

*JUST FOR TODAY*
*In one thing I know, I am equal with others—TIME. All*
   *of us draw the same salary in seconds, minutes, and hours.*

*JUST FOR TODAY*
*I refuse to spend time worrying about what might happen.*
   *It usually doesn't. I am going to spend my time making things*
   *happen.*

*JUST FOR TODAY*
*I will stop saying, "If I had time . . ." I know I never will*
   *"find time" for anything. If I want time, I must make it.*

*JUST FOR TODAY*
*I will improve my mind. I will learn something useful. I will read*
   *something that requires effort, thought, and concentration.*

*JUST FOR TODAY*
*I will be agreeable. I will look my best, speak in a well-modulated voice, and be courteous and considerate.*

*JUST FOR TODAY*
*I will not find fault with friends, relatives, or colleagues. I will not try to change or improve anyone but myself.*

*JUST FOR TODAY*
*I will have a program—I will save myself from two enemies—hurry and indecision.*

*JUST FOR TODAY*
*I will exercise my character in three ways:*
*I will do a good turn and keep it a secret. (If anyone finds out, it won't count.)*
*I will do two things I don't want to do, just for exercise.*
*I will be unafraid. Especially will I be unafraid to enjoy what is beautiful and believe that as I give to the world, the world will give to me.*

*JUST FOR TODAY*
*I will have a quiet half-hour all by myself and relax. During this half-hour, I will get a better perspective of my life.*

*JUST FOR TODAY*
*I will be happy.*

Read every day for seven days.

### What's The Problem?

Problems that complicate my life,
That interrupt my plan,
Might be no task at all to solve,
In the hands of another man.

Troubles I have, may not trouble him,
and so it's plain to see,
If that problem's not there for the other one,
The complication must be in me.

To Have A Friend

I'd like to have a friend, sincere, loyal, considerate, and kind.
Who's reliable, dependable,
with a forgiving mind.

Unselfish, understanding,
How patient he would be. It would be especially nice,
If the friend I had was me.

*H. Jay Halverson*
A Psycho-Cybernetics Student

What I *have* today is a direct result of what I *did* yesterday; what I *will have* tomorrow is a direct result of what I *do* today. For this reason, it is useless and silly for me to weep over my present situation.

Yesterday is gone, and the past cannot be changed.
If, however, I take action now, I can form the future.

Work with what I have at the moment and build upon
        it is what I must do, as it is in this way only that I may have
        what I want.

*—Ray Gilbert*
A Student of Psycho-Cybernetics

# ABOUT THE AUTHOR (FROM THE ORIGINAL BOOK)

Maxwell Maltz, M.D. has achieved a national reputation as the foremost authority on Psycho-Cybernetics.

Dr. Maltz is one of the first pioneers and fathers of plastic surgery in the United States. In New York from 1920 to early 1960, Dr. Maltz studied the changes that took place in his patients' personalities after he had corrected facial scars and disorders. Arising out of thousands and thousands of cases came his remarkable discovery of the "Self-Image," the most important psychologic discovery of this century. He is best known as the originator of the term "Psycho-Cybernetics" and is author of the bestseller of the same name. His concepts were first printed in the book *Psycho-Cybernetics* in 1960 and since that time over 15 million copies have been sold. This book is an important, valuable contribution to man's knowledge of himself and his ability to improve himself. Most of his efforts since 1960 have been devoted to writing, traveling, and lecturing worldwide on personal growth and understanding thru Psycho-Cybernetics.

# BOOK FOUR

# THE MAGIC POWER
# OF SELF-IMAGE
# PSYCHOLOGY

# CONTENTS

# SUMMARY

Here, at last, is the secret of bridging the gap between what you have now and what you desire. This book shows you what you must do to unleash the colossal forces of your mind and drive forward to greater prosperity.

This book from the Dr. Maxwell Maltz Psycho-Cybernetics Library shows you the new way to a bright, full life.

Poverty miraculously transformed into riches . . .

Loneliness into love . . . disgrace into glory . . .

Failure into success . . . all by using

The Magic Power of Self-Image Psychology.

Some examples:

The Secret Strength in Relaxation

Sex and the Self-Image

Master your habits and control your destiny

And other ways to find peace of mind in a troubled world.

*Every man who knows how to read has it in his power to magnify himself, to multiply the ways in which he exists, to make his life full, significant, and interesting.*

—*Aldous Huxley*

# 1

## YOUR SELF-IMAGE CAN GIVE YOU A STARRING ROLE ON LIFE'S STAGE

IMAGINE THAT YOU ARE SEATED IN A THEATER, LOOKING AT THE CURTAIN WHICH hides the blank screen, as you wait for the feature picture to begin. You anticipate the film, and many thoughts run through your mind.

Will the film be interesting?

What will this picture do for you?

How will it affect you?

What impact will it have on your life?

Will you feel moved—perhaps even to tears?

Will you laugh at a comedy? Or feel terrified at the crises faced by the hero or heroine?

Will you feel wonderful waves of love and compassion? Or surges of resentment?

All these feelings will pulse through you—and more. The picture is about the most fascinating person in the world—yourself.

This theater is that of the mind. It is in the heart of each of us, and although you may not realize it, you are the producer, director, writer, actor or actress, hero, or villain. You are the film technician up in the booth and the audience which reacts to this thrilling drama.

The exciting story unfolding upon this inner screen is one which you invent every second of your life—yesterday, tomorrow, but most importantly, right now.

You watch the image upon that screen, and you invent it at the same time.

Will the story have a happy ending? Is it full of happiness and success or sorrow and failure? The storyline is already there, and the discerning eye can tell how the story will go.

But one realization can comfort you. Since you are the dramatist, the director, and the actor, you can change the story as it unfolds. Now. This instant. And for your whole lifetime.

You can make this a success story. You can be the hero and conquer the villain. And you can make this a heart-warming tale that will enrich the lives of all who know you rather than something drab and mechanical, a chronicle of boredom.

It's all inside you.

You may already understand the concept of choices. Everything depends on the image you carry inside you. Your self-image is your most important tool for good or for ill.

Your story depends on you and your self-image.

## MAKING A MOTION PICTURE OF YOURSELF

What do we mean by the self-image? Is there such a thing?

We know there is a mind, even though no one has ever seen it. Beyond the physical brain filled with neurons and electrical impulses, the mind thinks, hopes, fears, grows happy, becomes sad, remembers, and envisions, invents molehills and mountains.

The mind has just as much reality as the brain—even if we can't touch, feel, or examine it under a microscope.

And the self-image has reality, even if we can't touch, feel, or see it. In the pages of this book, we will come to grips with this reality. Because success is real—and failure is real. Energy is real—and lassitude is real. You may be tired of a life which feels out of your control. But that is because you have not understood that you do not need to be a passive observer. In this book, you will see how much input you have in how your story plays out.

I will help you use your self-image to develop the picture you've always wanted to see—a picture of you surmounting difficulties and driving on to a successful, happy conclusion.

Why is self-image so important?

As I explained in my first book, *Psycho-Cybernetics,* the self-image is your conception of the sort of person you are. It is a product of past experiences, successes and failures, humiliations, triumphs, and how other people react to you, especially in early childhood. From these factors, and others we shall discuss later, you build up a picture of yourself, which you believe is true. The image may be false—and in many cases is false—but the critical fact here is that you act *just as if it were true.*

"Then," you ask, "in that case, my picture of myself as a weakling, as a victim, the person to whom everything happens is true. What comfort is that?"

There is a beautiful comfort in one fact, embodied in two little words—"as if." You see, I said you act *as if* the picture were real. But is it? Since this picture, your self-image, can change and *has* been changed in thousands of cases, there is no cause for despair. You don't have to accept it.

Understand this: You are the writer; you are the director; you are the actor starring in this picture. All you have to learn is how to change that picture by investing a little more time and energy in it, by following time-proven methods that are so easy and so close to each of us that it's no wonder we've overlooked them. It just takes a new insight.

There's a story told about the famous Russian philosopher and mystic Ouspensky. To pursue his research into the nature of consciousness, he took a drug. While under the influence of this narcotic, he suddenly realized that he had found the secret of existence, that it had come from his subconscious where it had been all his life and was there, in simple terms, released by the drug. Eagerly, he seized a pencil and wrote down the fantastic formula for success. Then he dropped off into a deep sleep.

On waking up, completely conscious now, he examined the precious piece of paper. There, scrawled in his handwriting, he saw the words: "Think . . . in new categories."

This simple realization is what I hope to help you do. Think, feel, act in new categories. Re-examine what you've taken for granted. Become dissatisfied with "proof." Broaden your beliefs. In other words, change your self-image.

We will work together to change this mental picture of yourself. We will discuss the factors that go to make up this self-image. Over and over, because concentration is necessary, we will use the powerful tool of mental picturing to redefine your concept of yourself to enhance the appreciation of the unique individual you are.

Words are not enough. In the pages of this book, you will find seven practice exercises, exercises in imagination, each of which will help you break through the barrier of your previous limitations. The power of mental picturing will help you burst through the self-imposed obstacles that are blocking your dreams.

These exercises can be the most important ones upon which you've ever worked. I planned them carefully to help you see yourself new, on the rise, going forward to realistic successes that are within your grasp.

Don't defeat yourself by feeling skeptical about these exercises! And don't do them passively. Reading about them won't help you change. Take the time to do them if you want to see results.

They are not tangible; you cannot reach out and touch the concepts in them, as you would a chair or a table. But the images you will see, the pictures of anticipation you will manufacture—these are products of rare power. This power of your mind pictures is awesome; it may be difficult for you to understand the impact of their power. Perhaps you must have *faith*. I hope you will because I can help you so much as I have helped so many others.

Aside from these exercises, I will offer you specific suggestions for living happily in this challenging age, ideas which will help you to feel more kindly about the only self you've got.

## YOUR MENTAL BLUEPRINT

Certainly, the self-image discovery is one of the most important finds of this century and perhaps the next. For, though we may not realize it, we all do carry with us this mental blueprint or picture of ourselves. We may not be conscious of it, but it exists. We believe firmly in it and do not question its validity.

Furthermore, all our actions and emotions are consistent with our self-image. You will act like the sort of person you think you are. You simply can't act otherwise, even if you exercise all your willpower. The man who thinks he is a "failure type" person will find a way to fail, no matter how hard he tries to succeed, even if a few good breaks do come his way. The person who thinks he's just "unlucky" will manage to prove that he is indeed a victim of "bad luck."

The self-image is the foundation stone of our whole personality. Because of this, our experiences seem to verify, and thereby strengthen our self-images, setting up a vicious (or pleasant) cycle. A salesperson who thinks he or she is unworthy will face a prospect with a dejected expression. He or she will almost apologize for his or her very existence, literally inviting rejection. He will shake the prospective buyer's confidence and have "proof" that his self-image is correct. She will confirm her belief she is unlovable, inferior, and a failure.

The high school girl or boy who thinks of themselves as ugly and unattractive will find a way to prove that their self-image is accurate. They may ignore compliments or awkward efforts of others to connect by focusing on all of their faults. They will assume others don't like them, perhaps even before thinking about how they feel about someone else. Teenagers are the best example of how self-image can be torturous. They will fixate on the smallest things and present themselves defensively to drive away rejection. When rejection is perceived, it confirms their self-image of being undesirable while experiencing it in their minds.

## YOU CAN CHANGE YOUR SELF-IMAGE

Because of this so-called "objective truth," people rarely realize that the trouble lies in their evaluation of themselves. If you tell the salesperson that he or she only thinks they cannot sell, they will skeptically look at you. They only know they have tried and tried, with no results. They don't see any connection to what they present to others. If you tell the teenage boys or girls that they are quite attractive, they will also try to prove you wrong. After all, they have no girlfriends or boyfriends.

Anyone can change this. I will tell you true life stories of real people:

- salespeople who have made almost miraculous changes in earning capacity; and
- defensive, almost antisocial teenagers who had adapted beautifully to the opposite sex when they understood the importance of changing their self-image.

For, this is basic; you can change your *self-image*. One is never too young or too old to change their self-image and start a new, more productive, more creative life.

I fully believe that before discovering the tools of Psycho-Cybernetics, it has been nearly impossible for people to change their basic habits because they directed their primary efforts at the circumference of the self rather than at the core. Many people have tried to use "positive thinking" to conquer some external obstacles or character defects ("I will relax more next week," "I will pass the examination"). But they had not tried to change their thinking about the self that was to do these things.

"Positive thinking" is not a bad thing. But it is not enough. Some people use it as a crutch and do not see that using it with the same negative self-image can't be effective. How can one think positively about some situation if one carries a negative opinion about his very self with him? This positive thinking without underlying change is a setup for a fundamental conflict. Many experiments have shown that once the idea of self is changed, other things consistent with this new concept may be accomplished—often without significant strain.

Prescott Lecky, a pioneer in self-image psychology, did some convincing experiments. He regarded the personality as a system of ideas, all of which must seem to be consistent with each other. Ideas inconsistent with the system are rejected, he believed, while those which seem consistent are accepted. At the center of this system of ideas is the person's "self-image," his conception of himself.

A schoolteacher, Lecky, was able to test his theory on thousands of pupils. *(Self Consistency, a Theory of Personality,* The Island Press, New York, N.Y.)

Lecky believed that if a student had difficulty learning a subject, it could be because learning it would be inconsistent for him from the student's point of view. However, he reasoned that if you change the student's self-conception underlying this attitude, he will look at the subject differently. If the student would change his self-definition, he could also change his learning ability. This theory proved to be so. He had many examples of his finding put into practice.

One student who was a poor speller and failed so many subjects that he lost credit for a year made an excellent grade the following year and became one of the school's best spellers. Another boy, who dropped from college because of poor grades, became an "A" student at one of the country's most respected universities. A girl who had failed Latin four times finished with a fine grade after receiving guidance. A boy, told by a testing bureau he had no aptitude for English, won honorable mention for a literary prize the following year.

These students were neither stupid nor lacking in basic aptitude. Suffering from inadequate self-images, they identified with their failures. When they failed a test or a subject, they classified themselves generally as "failures." Their change in self-conception merely released latent abilities.

Lecky, using the same method, cured students of nail-biting and stuttering.

My files contain equally convincing case histories:

The schoolteacher who had to drag herself out of bed to face her class each day; now, seeing herself more accurately, she enjoys relating to her pupils. The movie star whose frayed nerves were forcing her into semi-retirement; today, unafraid to expose her feelings, she faces the cameras without panic. The executive whose timidity interfered with his work responsibilities; today, he likes himself, and because of this, other people at the office find him relaxing.

These are true stories. Other people, struggling human beings like you, have changed their pictures of themselves and their lives. So can you.

## DISCOVERIES OF A PLASTIC SURGEON

At first glance, one would think there was little connection between plastic surgery and psychology. Yet, my work as a plastic surgeon made me realize the importance of self-image, raising questions that led to critical psychological conclusions.

For, upon starting the practice of plastic surgery many years ago, I was amazed by the dramatic, sudden personality changes that often took place when I corrected someone's facial defect. In many cases changing the physical image seemed to create an entirely new person. My scalpel often seemed to have magical powers, capable not only of improving the patient's appearance but of transforming his whole outlook on life. Fearful people became bold; the angry became friendly; the self-effacing were now outgoing.

A "mean," aggressive adolescent boy, who always fought with his schoolmates, won the acceptance of his peers when he dropped his defenses and just tried to be friendly.

A listless middle-aged man who was just going through the motions felt new hope rise within him; his once despairing eyes mirrored a life they had not shown in many years.

Explaining the successes was easy. For example, a girl with a cleft lip had been teased about it by her classmates and felt inferior. Her thinking was negative. She was obsessed with the thought that none of her friends had a cleft lip. That was her trouble, she thought, the cleft lip. Why shouldn't she feel afraid of attack? She stood out because of her physical defect, was a natural target for the cruel. When I corrected her cleft lip with surgery, it was natural that she would feel less defensive, more hopeful in her thinking, and her concept of self. That she improved emotionally was no surprise.

But what about the exceptions who didn't change even after I improved their physical features through surgery?

Yes, as a plastic surgeon, my "failures" really taught me the vast importance of a person's self-image. When I improved a person's physical features without an accompanying lift in his spirits, I had to ask myself what was wrong.

One day many years ago, a woman in her mid-twenties came to my offices. She had a deep indented scar on her left cheek, a constant reminder of an automobile accident she'd been in. She seemed unhappy with herself and her life. I asked myself, "Who wouldn't be in her situation?"

I thought about how, as a child looking in the mirror when she brushed her teeth or combed her hair, she saw a perfectly normal face and began to take it for granted. Now, when she looked in the mirror, she must think, "Gosh, I look awful! I used to have a normal face; now I have two entirely different cheeks." I told her that I'd remove the scar, and, after surgery, she'd look fine once again. "Don't worry," I said. "We'll take good care of you." She asked how she would look, and I reassured her and tried to soothe her fears.

Later, I operated on her. After a week, she came back. I took the bandages off and handed her a mirror. Her scarred cheek was a thing of the past. Then I waited for her reaction. Many patients are delighted when they first see their new, improved image. But her response was uncertain; she expressed no real positive emotion.

I waited a few seconds, then said, "What do you think? Do you like it?"

She responded, "I really don't see any improvement."

I was stunned. My surgery had been successful. "Would you like to see the pictures of your face before the operation?"

She looked at the "before" pictures, then surveyed her new face in the hand mirror. "It looks better," she admitted, "but I don't feel better."

Cases such as this one (and there have been many) helped me understand that not all our scars can be seen, that some are worse than physical scars, that they are deep inside us and infinitely painful.

Upon talking to this young woman, I learned more about her inner, emotional scar—about an unhappy, frustrated romance that had ended two years before, many months before the automobile accident. The grief was still with her; her self-image was poor. She was still unhappy after the removal of her physical scar, which was comparatively superficial. She still longed for her lover and felt that she could not be happy without him.

What could cure her? What could she hope for? Physically, she was young and attractive, but what could remove her despair? A changing, a strengthening of her self-image, of her feeling about herself! If she could improve her opinion about *herself,* she would feel renewed courage, go out more confidently into the world, meet another fine young man, and work toward greater fulfillment of her natural life impulses.

But would she? The sad part of this was the change for her was unlikely. I had done all I could for her physically. It caused me to ponder what would provide real and lasting change for the better. I could see her core issues as they were apparent outside, as if they were still scars on her face. But she had to see it and want to make things better. She had rejected herself and any possibilities for future happiness.

## ARE YOU TRUE TO YOURSELF?

"This above all: to thine own self be true," wrote William Shakespeare many, many years ago.

It astonished me how many people are not true to themselves. Like the girl whose case I've just told you about, they reject themselves. She was not the only patient who, after surgery, has dramatically improved their appearance, negated the change, refused to acknowledge it, insisted that they look the same as they did before the operation. Showing them "before" and "after" photographs does no good; it even arouses anger.

People's images of themselves, good, bad or neutral, depend on past successes and failures. This concept of one's worth is so important, more profound, and more meaningful than a mirror. People carry this self-image into present activities and into plans for the future too.

If a person nourishes their self-image on past successes, it will be pleasant.

But if inhibitions have blocked off the road to success, and past failures clutter up the mind, one's self-image will be low, as in this girl whose case I have described.

What do you think of yourself? I mean, what do you feel about yourself, deep down inside?

- Do you like yourself, or do you regard yourself with distrust?
- Do you expect too much of yourself, or do you sit back passively, waiting for life to come to you, for people *to do things for* you?
- Do you set reasonable goals for yourself, goals whose accomplishment will help you feel whole and alive, or do you let other people tell you what to do, what to think, and how to behave?
- Do you think you are good-looking or secretly think of your too-long nose or too-big mouth?

*What* you think is very important.

Over the years, many people have come to my office complaining of purely imaginary defects, by-products of what these people *thought of themselves.*

- Middle-aged women are convinced they look "old" even though their appearance is normal and often very attractive.
- The young girls are positive they are "ugly" just because physically they are not exact duplicates of the latest movie queen.
- There are men whose false beliefs about their physical image defeats their life goals.

These people are their own worst enemies; they think themselves into a living death.

## HOW TO LIVE JOYFULLY

How, then, does one live a happy life? How does one find joy living in this busy, complicated world of ours? What is the secret?

It is so simple. To really "live" to find life enjoyable, you must have a realistic, adequate self-image, one with which you can live. You must like and trust yourself. You must feel that you can express yourself without fear of exposure;

you must feel no need to hide your true self. You must know yourself well. Your self-image must be realistic, what you really are. You feel good when your self-image is intact and adequate. You feel full of confidence. You are ready to show the world what you are. And you are proud of it. You breathe life, give deeply to life—and take happily from it.

Think beyond the physical. When I have corrected a facial defect by plastic surgery, dramatic psychological changes occur if there is a corresponding change of the distorted self-image. Otherwise, the difference is only superficial. If you have a distorted self-image, no amount of cosmetic surgery will fix it for you.

## MAKE FRIENDS WITH YOURSELF

In the theater, you will look at yourself on stage to act out the concepts outlined in this book, take a mirror in hand and look at yourself. Look long, and look deeply, and do not be afraid of what you will see.

Do you know how to look? What to look for?

Do I hear someone say, "I'll see myself"?

Will you? You will see someone with ears, eyes, nose, legs, and arms, but are these physical features you are looking for?

Now, look behind the physical—to the inner face, emotions, beliefs—the hidden stranger within you, which you cannot see in a mirror.

This is your self-image.

If your self-image is an enemy, it uses the past failures to undermine you and make you a failure in the present.

If a friend, it draws from past successes and confidence to give you the courage to live and grow.

Make friends with yourself. Only then will you be happy and attain status as a human being!

On this stage, in the playhouse of your mind, we will act out dramas in which you will be the central character, with your self-image as a friend.

"But," you may tell me, "I have no outer scar; my face is normal. Is this book for me?"

It certainly is. Less than 1 percent of the U.S. population has facial defects requiring plastic surgery; over 99 percent have normal faces. But of this 99 percent or so, many of you have scars within—distorted self-images. *So many of us sell ourselves short!*

In this book's pages, you will find practical suggestions for improving your self-image and exercises designed to accelerate your pattern of positive change. You will set yourself the goals you long to achieve—success, happiness, friends, money, and relaxation. Whatever your dream for success, if you have reasonable goals, we will move toward them utilizing the power of mental imagery. Unlike simple positive thinking, you are not waiting for the magic to occur. You are creating magic with the power of your mind and the harnessing of your mental energies.

To improve your self-image, you must be willing to apply your mental energies in doing these vital practice exercises. If you work hard at them, you can change. More than that, the changes may seem miraculous to you and your friends. But you must work hard, stepping out on the stage of your mind to practice. The famous actor Sir Laurence Olivier's superb craftsmanship did not just happen. You will first flub your lines and miss your cues—don't worry about it, and don't blame yourself. Change takes time and effort. But if you keep at it, the production will be smooth later on.

Aldous Huxley, the great English writer, once wrote, "There's only one corner of the universe you can be certain of improving, and that's yourself."

That's just what we're going to do!

# 2

## TRUTH

### THE FIRST KEY TO YOUR PERSONALITY

YOU ARE GOING TO CHANGE YOUR SELF-IMAGE. YOU ARE TIRED OF TEARING YOUR-self down, heaping criticisms on your thoughts and actions. Perhaps you're still not convinced you're worth the trouble, but still, you're determined to see yourself with pride. You will, too, if you're willing to work. I promise you that your mental picturing can be changed—and your life with it.

First, however, we must select the equipment we will use in this overhauling of your self-imagery.

Our first tool is extremely powerful. It is simply the truth.

- "Ye shall know the truth, and the truth shall make you free"—(John viii:32)
- "Rather than love, than money, than fame, give me truth"—Henry David Thoreau
- "The man who fears no truth has nothing to fear from lies"—Thomas Jefferson

Yes, truth either sustains us or lets us down. Its importance in our lives is overwhelming.

What is the truth about yourself? Are you convinced that your image of yourself is a true one? Do you look at yourself as a fool, a buffoon? As a coward? A hero? A master of your fate—or a victim?

As you stand on the stage of life and look at yourself in the mirror, how do you judge yourself? What are your good points and your bad? Do you like yourself? Are you a friend or an enemy?

The most crucial exploration that faces humankind and you, personally today, is not exploring outer space but the exploration of inner *space*. It can change whole civilizations—and it can improve your life through the most rewarding adventure of your entire existence.

## WHAT IS THE REAL TRUTH ABOUT YOURSELF?

Perhaps you are thinking, "Of course I know the truth about myself. If I don't know myself, who does?"

Psychologists and psychiatrists have repeatedly pointed out that the most challenging person to evaluate objectively is oneself.

Indeed, if you stop to think of people you know, you'll agree with me. All of us know intelligent people who think they are stupid, good-looking people who imagine themselves ugly, and the people who downgrade themselves constantly, evaluating all successes as failures.

In my practice as a plastic surgeon, I have often met people whose self-evaluations were grossly inaccurate. One patient comes to mind, a timid teenage boy. His "truth" about himself was that he was weak, that his receding chin had doomed him to a life of misery.

When he first came to my office, he was 18, ready for college, but he didn't even want to go. He felt he was worthless. His high school record had been poor; he had listlessly dawdled his way through four boring years. He had taken part in no physical activities, had no real friends, kept to himself, and died inside. Why should college be any better?

He believed I was his last hope. Could I do anything with the chin with which Fate had saddled him? Something was wrong with his self-image, I saw quickly, for though his chin was not classically perfect, it was no different from millions of other chins. These other millions of people surely did not give such a mild imperfection even a second thought. But he was obsessed with it.

The recession in his chin was too mild to require plastic surgery, so I talked to him about it instead. I asked him when he had begun to worry about his chin and why he associated it with weakness.

After seeing him several times, I got the whole story. When he was ten, he had overheard his parents talking about him when, in reality, they thought he was asleep. "I wonder whom he takes after," his father had said. "He hasn't got the family chin, isn't that odd?"

The young boy looked at himself in the mirror the next day. He never noticed his chin before, but now it looked terrible to him. How had he overlooked the way it receded?

He went to the family album and looked at pictures of his family—uncles, grandfather, cousins. "Strong faces, especially the men," he thought. "Not one receding chin! I'm the only one!"

Unfortunately, he did not tell his parents he had overheard them, and he did not seek help for his torment. At the age of ten, considering himself an outcast, he kept the concept of his weak chin to himself as his own personal sorrow.

As he grew into adolescence, his sensitivity about his chin grew and grew. He was afraid to show his profile to people, so he would face them directly. This obsession got him into ridiculous situations in which he would constantly move about to prevent the offending profile from showing. People began to notice how nervous he was and laughed at his eccentricity. Finally, he told his parents how bitter he was about his chin, and they took him to see me.

Luckily, I was able to help him. I told him that objectively his chin was not a bad one at all, that his "truth" about himself was pure fiction. Not only that, I told him that he was no weakling, that he had to realize that he was as good as anyone else. I enlisted the help of his parents. His father had, of course, long since forgotten that he had ever made the remark—and he had made it casually and innocently at the time. They both assured him that he was a fine-looking young man and that his chin was normal while not the typical family chin.

Naturally, a concept which one has held of oneself for eight years doesn't go away in a day. But after several weeks, with his parents helping him see the real truth, he began to feel more at peace with himself.

Slowly, his truth about himself changed. He went to college, and, along with his rising self-esteem, he became an outstanding student. He majored in languages, became a successful writer, got married, had children, and today he doesn't waste his time worrying about an absurd, untruthful idea. People's actions always depend on what they think is true about themselves and their environment. This is fundamental; it is the way we are built. We act as if our concepts are valid, no matter how misguided they are. Experiments with hypnotism also illustrate this point.

Don Newcomb, nicknamed "Newk," was an American professional baseball pitcher who began in what was at the time the Negro Leagues (editors note: this was the language of the time) and then Major League Baseball. He was the first pitcher to win the Rookie of the Year, Most Valuable Player, and the Cy Young Awards. At one point in his brilliant baseball career, he was afraid to travel on planes. The big pitcher known for his size thought he knew the truth: that an airplane he boarded would crash. Newcomb went to see a hypnotist. He was told, under hypnosis, that his plane would not crash, and the practitioner bought round-trip plane tickets for himself and Newcomb to fly from New York to Detroit and back. Convinced of this new truth, Don relaxed on the plane and enjoyed the trip.

Hypnotism also helped Maury Wills, another famous Major League Baseball player who was the Los Angeles Dodger's shortstop. An electrifying base-stealer, Wills at one time began to worry about his legs. He thought that they pained him, but there was no cause for the pain.

Putting him in a trance, the hypnotist said that it would be too bad if his worry undermined his base-stealing ability. To Wills' amazement, his pain vanished. Indirectly, the hypnotist had told him the truth about his legs, and Wills had accepted it.

People under hypnosis have taken action on the most unlikely truths. Told that water is champagne, they have become intoxicated. Informed that the weather is warm, they have perspired, then told that it is cold (same situation, same temperature), they have shivered and put on additional clothing.

Told he was Frank Sinatra, a hypnotic subject reached for a nonexistent microphone and began singing until the hypnotist told him a new "truth," to which he quickly adjusted.

These people, under hypnosis, accepted new truths—some false, some true. But enough of them. How about you? What is your truth about yourself? Take the time to ask yourself the following:

- Do you undervalue yourself?
- Most people do.
- Is your truth about yourself that you're too thin or that your nose is too long or that you're stupid, or that you'll never succeed at anything, or have bad luck?

Make a list. What do you believe is true about yourself? Be truthful. Don't lie to yourself. We all want to paint a better picture of ourselves on paper. But what good will that serve you? This list is not a time for shame or self-doubt but a time for TRUTH. It is not the truth of what is. It is the truth of what you believe about yourself.

Now, look at your list. Are there negative statements about yourself? Not only are these "truths" negative, but they are also false. You must remember that God created you for a purpose: to do good on this earth for yourself and your fellow human beings. You must remember that each of you, no matter how painful your past experiences, has something unique and positive. You must understand that each of you, no matter how downtrodden, has something good to offer.

Too many of you hypnotize—and that is not too strong a word—yourself with false beliefs about yourself. You are your own worst enemy; you undermine yourself with critical "truths" that even your actual real enemy wouldn't think. You base feelings of inferiority on evidence that any fair-minded jury would reject. Your "truth" is not the truth at all; it is often just a prejudiced case directed against yourself—one more unkind than you would level against any of your acquaintances. You give yourself as much justice as would a lynch mob.

## YOU ARE UNIQUE

God did not mass-produce the human race; people do not roll off an assembly line uniformly like the latest model automobile. He made people of different shapes and sizes and different skin colors. God created people with many more subtle distinctions. He made each of us unique and individual—and He didn't set up standards to which we must conform. Believe it or not, God created each of us with the same unconditional love as another.

You are unique; this is an obvious truth. You should see this fact as a positive life force, not as a fact to substantiate a feeling that you're inferior.

Yet most people mar their lives with inferiority feelings, thus putting obstacles between them and success and happiness.

Every person on earth is in some way inferior to some other person. Indeed, I cannot hit a golf ball as far as Arnold Palmer. I cannot dance as well as Fred Astaire. For that matter, I cannot equal Muhammed Ali in either boxing or showmanship or whoever are the standouts in the future when you might be reading this book. There will always be people whose talent seems superior. That is their purpose. Acknowledging these lacks in myself does not make me feel inferior, not in the slightest. I do not compare myself to them; I accept myself just as I am. Every day I meet people—bookkeepers, salespeople, corporation presidents—who are superior to me in some areas. So what? These people cannot improve a scarred face, and there are other things I can do better than they can. And they have no cause to feel inferior to me for these reasons.

When we feel inferior, it is because we measure ourselves against somebody else and convince ourselves of the entirely ridiculous idea that we should be like "somebody else" or even "everybody else." Certainly this is a false conception, for "everybody else" is made up of individuals, no two of whom are the same.

We stack evidence against ourselves and base the evidence on false premises.

In the Ten Commandments, God said: "Thou Shalt Not Covet." One of the reasons for this is likely because we, as human beings, spend too much time in comparison. Then we covet, which is another word for yearning for something. Comparisons are dangerous. Perhaps God was warning us not to covet because our human nature is to be cruel to ourselves. If we look to others to determine our worth, we often believe we are inferior. Then to make life tolerable, people then strive to be superior. They then drive and drive themselves, making themselves thoroughly miserable in their enslavement in a web of untruth.

Inferiority and superiority are merely opposite sides of the same coin—and the cure lies in simply understanding that the coin, itself, is counterfeit.

The simple truth is that you are neither "'inferior" nor "superior" to your fellow human beings.

"You" are "You," and that's the whole story.

The truth is that, as a personality, you are not in competition with anyone else. God made you a unique individual. You will never be the same as another person, and you were never meant to be.

This statement is not something phony, something sugar-coated to make you feel better. *This is the real truth.* It is your negative "truth," which is false.

## THINKING CAN MAKE IT SO

You might be thinking, "This is all well and good. But my 'truths' about myself are negative, and they've been that way for a long time. Can I change them?"

Yes, you can.

- Think new thoughts about yourself.
- See yourself in a new light, as an individual like no one else on earth.
- Forget your past failures, bury them, and think of your successes, no matter how few.
- Remember that you have an obligation to yourself to make your life on this earth as happy as possible.

Believe in this new truth, and act on it. Resolve to be your friend, not your enemy.

I'm not telling you that it's easy to change your fundamental truths, but if you keep at it, following the suggestions I outline in this book, applying yourself to the practice exercises, I assure you that you can do it. In doing so, you change the self-image with which you rise and fall.

## PRACTICE EXERCISE: WHAT IS YOUR TRUTH?

1. Make a list of all the words you would use to describe yourself.
2. Make a list of words you think other people would use to describe you.

3. List all the words you would like to describe yourself.
4. Write a short biography of the person you would like others to see in you.
5. Write a list of all the reasons you believe this would be impossible, and the people, things, or circumstances in your life that have stood or still stand in your way.

# 3

## THE POWER OF IMAGINATION

*"There is a boundary to men's passions when they act from feelings, but none when they are under the influence of imagination."*

—Edmund Burke

### HOW TO TURN "AS IF" INTO REALITY

Your first item of equipment was figuring out what you believe to be the truth about yourself. Your second item of equipment is functional and creative and will help you develop an accurate and successful self-image. It is your imagination.

Imagination is as elusive as joy or sorrow. You can't put it in a bottle or get it out of one. It has no shape, and yet it gives you shape.

Imagination is what puts the "I" in "Image." It enters into our every act. It is imagination that gives us the goal for which we head. We act or fail to act; our actions are accelerated or frozen because of imagination.

If you use your imagination positively, you can make yourself a bigger person.

In the Stanislavski school of method acting, we find an excellent example of imagination put to use. A method actor playing a king in a Shakespearean drama tries to think *as if* he were that king. He tries to put himself entirely into this king's shoes. He stands on the stage and projects this *as if* into a living reality for the audience.

Actors, in general, can do this. One day last year, I visited an acting school and observed a director's class. I joined a group of people standing around informally, watching a scene the director had mapped out for two young people, one a well-known actress. In this play, the girl acted as a 16th or 17th-century girl who was accused of witchcraft. When she imagined she was this girl, she performed the part so well that when on trial, being accused, looking up angrily at the heavens, she seemed to be the very force of evil.

Some Golden Age Hollywood actors, using their imaginations, completely changed the images they projected from one movie to the next. Dick Powell

changed from a song-and-dance man to a tough-guy detective and was suc-
cessful as both. James Cagney has been equally convincing as "the good guy,"
the vicious killer, or an eccentric ship's captain. June Allyson played a cun-
ning manipulator and was believable after many years of being cast as a sweet,
wholesome girl.

Some actors can change their self-image with such skill that when you
see them on the screen, it is hard to even recognize their face as the same one
you've seen in other films. But the use of imagination is not limited to the ac-
tor or other creative artists.

You use it as they do—every day.

Are you worried? You are using your imagination—seeing yourself and
what can happen to you.

Worry is a state of mind before the event happens.

## DO YOU WORRY ABOUT THINGS THAT NEVER HAPPEN?

Too many of us use our imaginations negatively; we worry. Not that worry
doesn't sometimes have a positive function; it can prevent catastrophes, even
save our very lives. But many people worry destructively. They stop up their
creative energies, keep themselves from relaxing, and continually imagine
things that never happen.

There's one man I know, a businessman, whose father smoked a lot and five
years ago died of cancer of the throat. Ever since his father's death, this man has
worried about cancer. First, he stopped smoking, which was a good thing. But
this did not stop the torrent of anxiety. At the first sign of a cold or even a husky
voice, he rushed to see the doctor. He thought about cancer all the time. When he
read articles in newspapers and magazines about cancer, his worries increased,
and he read less. Eventually, his imaginings dominated his life, and, deciding
he'd had enough worry, he retired from his lifework, thinking that might help
him relax. He still worries, though, and his health is still fine.

A woman, a former patient of mine, has an imagination that tortures her
every day of her life. Instead of one worry, she has many. She fears heart at-
tacks, nuclear holocausts, stock market catastrophes, deaths of dear ones and
devotes her God-given gift of imagination to harmful ends.

Now, of course, unpleasant things do happen now and then. I don't mean
the "never" to be taken literally. But people like this who worry constantly
imagine things that, to be exact, rarely happen. And their worry is more apt
to do harm than good.

## YOU CAN GET THAT PAY RAISE FROM THE BOSS

Let's take a common situation and see how you can use your imagination positively or negatively and what the results will be in each case.

You work in an office. You've held down the same job for two years, and you want a raise in pay. You're entitled to more money, you feel, since you've done good work.

But you feel discouraged when you imagine what the Boss's reaction will be. You picture the upcoming interview in your mind. You'll knock timidly on his or her door—you always were afraid of the Boss—and enter the private office. He (or she) will be talking on the phone and signing letters simultaneously, and you'll sit down and wait for him to finish his phone call. You'll fidget in your chair and wonder if it's such a good idea to ask for a raise—you could wait another six months, couldn't you? After all, he is such a busy man (woman). You worry about what you should say first. Perhaps he'd be annoyed if you asked for a raise too directly. Maybe you should start talking about some neutral subjects like the weather.

All right, do you think you'll get the raise? It is doubtful. Your imagination has betrayed you. You see yourself as a failure or at least unworthy. And so you'll probably fail. Although your imagination is something inside, its energy is projected outside through your expressions and emotions.

Now, let's put imagination to use again, but this time on your side.

Once again, mentally picture the situation. You'll knock on the Boss's door. You won't smash it in, but you won't feel timid about it because you're asking for a raise that you know you deserve. You'll walk up to his desk, stride crisply and confidently, and sit down, waiting for him to finish his phone call. When he finishes, you'll ask him for your raise, knowing full well that you're worth every nickel for which you are asking. And you know that the Boss realizes that too. You are confident that you'll achieve what you're aiming at—your pay raise.

Do you think you'll get it now? I do because you are using your imagination to enhance your self-image. Put simply, you *are betting on yourself!*

I know people who have used their imagination to see opportunities where other people saw nothing. There's one fellow who wasn't well educated, in terms of college degrees—who 25 or 30 years ago bought some small brownstone houses in an undeveloped area about a half-mile from Central Park in New York City. He was not a wealthy man, but he saved his money and bought this property.

People laughed at him, called him an idiot. But he was the bright one, actually; he had a vision. He saw that a day was coming when this area—not too far from the huge park—had to improve. Today he is a millionaire, and people call him a genius in business. In truth, this man had confidence in his imagination.

If I am a well-known plastic surgeon today, it is because I used my imagination and set goals for myself. When I started my medical training over 30 years ago and told people I was interested in plastic surgery, they scoffed. At the time, it was a little-publicized field. "Where can you study?" they asked.

My mother wept. She wanted me to be a general practitioner, become an assistant to our family doctor, work up a safe, sure practice.

But I had this vision and imagined ways to help others as a plastic surgeon and give people new faces that would help them feel better about themselves.

I assured my mother that I knew what I was doing, and I made it my business to reach my goals.

I studied with men in Paris, Berlin, Vienna, London who had done plastic surgery during World War I. Then I came back home and opened my office. Everyone predicted failure.

But my imagination told me that people would need a good plastic surgeon, and I was right. The first month was difficult, but then my practice started growing.

## PUTTING A SMILE ON YOUR SELF-IMAGE

"How about me?" you may ask. "What can I do?"

You can do plenty. I'm going to show you how to use your imagination as your friend, to improve your self-image and give you new life. I say "new" because too many of us have given up on life; our imaginations have let us down.

Napoleon Bonaparte once wrote, "The human race is governed by its imagination."

But to many people, unfortunately, imagination is not a good government. It is a breeder of death and failure. ". . . But the Imagination is conscious of an indestructible dominion," wrote the great English poet William Wordsworth.

True, but will your imagination's dominion lead you to success or failure, happiness or misery? In these pages, you will learn to use your imagination as a tool for happiness, a healthy self-image constructor.

Our recent realization that our behavior stems from our images and beliefs gives us a new, potent weapon in changing personality. It opens up a new door leading to a good life.

You act and feel according to the image your mind holds of what things are like, which might be quite different from reality. Moreover, if our mental images are twisted, our reaction to our surroundings will be doubly unrealistic.

If we picture ourselves functioning in specific situations, it is nearly the same as the actual performance. Mental practice helps one to perform better in real life.

A psychologist, using controlled experimental conditions, found that mental practice could help people throw darts accurately. His subjects sat each day in front of the target, imagining they were throwing darts at it; it improved their aim as much as actually throwing the darts.

Golfers use this technique. When you next watch a golf tournament, note how the pro rehearses his shot and imagines what will happen before he strokes the ball.

Shadowboxing is a classic example of people using their imagination to prepare them for a prize ring's successful experience.

How can this help you? You can "shadowbox" in the areas that are meaningful to you. I gave you an example of mental picturing when I discussed getting the pay raise from the Boss. The man (or woman) who probably got the raise saw him or herself as smiling and efficient and imagined the Boss responding to the integrity of his or her self-image.

This mental picturing can work for you; you can become a more positive person. You can imagine the self you'd like to be and see yourself in new roles. You can change your personality, become more whole than you've ever been if you build a healthier self-image.

Let's get one thing straight, though. The aim of self-image psychology is not to create a fictitious self, which is omnipotent. Such an image is as untrue as the inferior image of oneself. We aim to find the best we have in us, realistically, and bring it out into the open. Why should you continue to shortchange yourself?

## YOUR SUCCESS MECHANISM

Your imagination is crucial because it can trigger your success mechanism, the great creative mechanism within you that can implement your success in life. I described this mechanism at great length in *Psycho-Cybernetics,* which you should read if you want a complete technical understanding of it.

The science of cybernetics has led us to understand that your so-called "subconscious mind" is not a "mind" but a goal-striving servomechanism consisting of the brain and nervous system that the mind directs. We do not have "two minds," but a mind or consciousness which operates an automatic, goal-oriented machine. This machine functions like an electronic servo-mechanism, but it is more wonderful than any man-made electronic brain.

This inner mechanism is impersonal. It will work automatically to achieve the goals which you set for it. Feed it "success goals," and it functions as a "success mechanism." Feed it negative aims, and it operates as a "failure mechanism."

Like any servomechanism, it must have a clearly defined objective toward which to work.

Our automatic mechanism seeks to reach objectives presented in mental pictures, which we create by using our imagination.

The main goal-image is our self-image, which defines our endeavors' limits, the areas in which we must operate.

Our creative mechanism works on the data we feed it, just like any other servomechanism. Our thoughts are funneled into it, describing the problem which it must tackle. In this sense, our beliefs and our mental pictures predetermine the final results. Suppose we provide our automatic mechanism with information about our inferiority, a reflection of a poor self-image. In that case, it will process this data, working as a "failure mechanism," translating this into an objective experience. Too many of us do this.

To accelerate your determination to get more out of life, you must learn to use your great creative mechanism as a success mechanism, not as a failure mechanism. You must develop new ways of thinking and imaging to build a strong, reality-oriented self-image, which will nourish your success mechanism, leading the way to happiness.

In the practice exercise in this chapter and in succeeding chapters, I will show you how to use your imagination to put a smile on your self-image and a spring in your stride, and a song in your soul. I will show you how to picture your past successes—not your failures—and carry this successful self-image forward into the operational success that constitutes the good life.

## PRACTICE EXERCISE NO. 1: BUILDING A NEW SELF-IMAGE

You formed your present self-image from mental pictures of yourself in the past, growing out of judgments you placed on your experiences in life. We will now work on building a healthy self-image with this same use of imagery. But first, remember this: Change will not come without effort. You must work hard to realize inspiring results. You must be willing to set aside time daily for this exercise, as well as for the other practice exercises in this book. I would suggest an hour a day. Don't make yourself a slave to this schedule but discipline yourself so that you're working on these exercises until you get the results you want nine days out of ten. If improving your self-image is important to you, and it should be—you'll find the time.

Sit down or lie down somewhere that is restful and quiet. Relax and make yourself as comfortable as you can. Then close your eyes and let your God-given imagination work for you.

In the theater of your mind, picture yourself as you truly like yourself. Imagine that you are looking at a movie screen, watching a picture of yourself. See yourself in a problem situation, as you've been in your best moments handling this situation. I can't tell you specifically what areas to focus on—this is individual. But I can give you a fictitious example, and you can take it from there.

Suppose you're a young woman, 22, single, and you've quit your job because you didn't like it. You want a job as a personal assistant, and you know you'll be good at it.

Your trouble is that job interviews make you nervous and inhibited. Every time you've ever looked for a job, your self-image has been weak.

No, that's not true. There was once a successful interview when you were 16, and you wanted a job as a swimming counselor at a girls' summer camp. You felt *good* that day. Fine! Picture that interview, *seeing, and feeling every detail* in your imagination.

You walked into the office building, high heels click-clacking in the lobby. The camp's office was on the 13th floor, and you laughed at their lack of superstition. You smiled at the elevator operator, and he said, "Good morning."

The camp's office was one small room, but you didn't feel cramped. You sat down and smoothed your dress. You were wearing your black dress with gold buttons, and your hair sparkled. You felt confident, and you weren't worried about the interview—you felt too good for that. The interviewer, sitting in a leather swivel chair, seemed friendly to you because you felt friendly.

Keep visualizing this scene in detail, feeling once again the confidence you felt during this interview. See everything in your mind—the mahogany desk, the interviewer's eyeglasses—until this past success is part of you, and you are ready to act on it, forgetting your fear of other interviews, making this new confidence part of a growing self-image.

I created this example in my imagination just to show you generally what I mean. Now apply this potent method to your realistic case. Perhaps you're a man in your sixties. You no longer work and devote much of your time to community activities. You enjoy belonging to organizations, but when there's a public discussion, you can't seem to talk as you'd like to. You crawl into a shell instead, fearful of being the center of attention. Still, there was that time ten years ago.

Perhaps you're a younger man, in your thirties, and you love to play tennis but feel self-conscious and awkward when you get out on the court. Still, how about that time you beat Frank, the only time you ever beat him?

Maybe you're a woman in your fifties. Your children have grown up and married, and when you see them, you feel like a stranger to them, unable to relate meaningfully to their world, unable to meet them halfway. Still, how about the warm, sincere talk you had six months ago with your daughter-in-law before you both put your defenses back up?

Only you know what your problem situations are; you feel them in your heart. During this practice period, focus on a basic problem situation with an important switch. *This* time *see yourself in the theater of* your mind, *handling this situation as you would like to handle it.* This time you are successful, and you bring this success back onto your inner movie screen and see it again and again. During this extremely vital practice period, see yourself over and over— acting and reacting the way you would like to in a difficult situation, activating your success mechanism. How you acted yesterday doesn't matter; how you act tomorrow doesn't matter. See yourself as a success; keep this image alive. Imagine your feelings if you were to become the kind of person you'd like to be, in terms of your real potentialities. If certain situations have frightened you, picture yourself mastering them, winning out over your inhibitions, slaying the dragon of failure.

The power of your imagination is so tremendous that it may take you weeks to realize it. You may doubt this great power for a while because it is intangible— you cannot touch it. But Jesus Christ's message was intangible; so are the beliefs of most religious and political philosophers. Faith itself is one of our greatest possessions, and it is not material.

As time goes on and you continue to use your imagination positively, funneling information into your success mechanism, you may be surprised to find that your new picture of yourself is becoming a reality. You are going out into the world with more confidence, and you are acting differently. Your image of yourself is getting stronger with each passing day.

# 4

# THE SECRET STRENGTH IN RELAXATION

"AH, WHAT IS MORE BLESSED THAN TO PUT CARE ASIDE, WHEN THE MIND LAYS down its burden and spent with distant travel, we come home again and rest on the couch we longed for?" So wrote Catullus, the great Roman poet, several thousand years ago.

But so few of us rest these days. Relaxation seems to be a lost art. Is it the hustle and bustle of modern civilization? The frenzied scientific and technological discovery pace? The expectation of achievement? Are these too much for mere human beings?

Doubtless, current conditions are not ideal but consider this: God gave each of us life to enjoy, not bury in countless anxieties. He meant us to savor His world in calmness, not to rush around it in perplexed consternation.

Many call these times "the age of anxiety." Some people even accept worry, insomnia, stomach ulcers as the price for living in today's world.

But it does not have to be like this, and in this chapter, I'll give you some ideas on how to relax and be at peace with yourself—whether you are watching a peaceful pastoral scene or working in a crowded office. At the end of this chapter, you will find a practice exercise to help you relax; I will show you how to achieve calm, no matter what your circumstances.

## EASY DOES IT!

People today try too hard, push themselves too hard. They frantically drive themselves in their struggle to make money, become beautiful, or overcome their inferiority feelings. Too often, the end does not justify the means; certainly, material wealth cannot compensate for losing one's good health. We see so many anxious, driven people every day. Others seem relaxed but are merely masters of the art of concealment. What price material success? Is it worth hypertension? Is it worth the sacrifice of one's health?

Millions of people today suffer from excess tension, a disease more common than the so-called common cold. It is a rare person who is calm. In one way or another, hypertension probably afflicts more people and is more destructive than all the diseases we lie awake worrying about, such as cancer and cardiac trouble. But just as tension can make you sick, relaxation can make you well. Medical authorities have cited relaxation as an aid to sufferers of heart trouble. They have prescribed relaxation as a relief—even a cure for people in high-pressure occupations who have heart trouble. Researchers in the field of psychosomatic medicine have documented the close connection between emotional and physical health. In writing this book, however, I am not primarily interested in physical disease. I want to show you how to be good to yourself, change your self-image, and enjoy life more. And, in this chapter, I want you to learn how to relax.

Why don't you start right now? If you're sitting in an armchair, nervously tapping your feet, a frown on your forehead, relax, settle down, stop worrying while I tell you a story about a man I've known for many years.

He's a businessman, and he's made a fortune. He's earned millions, and he's saved quite a bit too. But—and I've seen him hundreds of times—he never seems relaxed.

Relax in the playhouse of your mind and watch the scene as I unfold it for you. See it with your own eyes!

He's just come home from work, and he's just stepped into his dining room. The furniture is rich mahogany, a long table, and six chairs, but he doesn't notice it. He sits down at the table, but he's restless, so he paces around the room. He bangs the table absentmindedly and almost trips over a chair. His wife sits down; he says hello and drums the table until a private chef brings in the meal. He gobbles the food down as fast as he can, as if his hands were two shovels hurling it down a hole.

Dinner over, he gets up quickly and walks into the living room. It's a decorative room, with a long, beautiful sofa and plush, upholstered chairs, wall-to-wall carpeting, and rich paintings. He hurls himself into a chair, picking up a newspaper in almost the same motion. He ruffles a few pages, scans the headlines, throws it to the ground, picks up a cigar. He bites off the tip of the cigar, lights it, puffs twice, and puts it out in the ashtray.

He just can't find himself. But suddenly, he springs up, goes to the television, and turns it on. After some channel changes, he turns it off impatiently. He strides to the hall closet, grabs his hat and coat, and goes out for a walk. This man has done this hundreds of times. I know. I've seen him do it. With all his success, he has not learned to relax. He is a dynamo of tension, bringing home from his office the spasms of his occupation.

He has no economic problems; his home is an interior decorator's dream; he owns two cars; his domestic employees attend to his every command—but he cannot relax. Not only that, he has even forgotten who he is. In his drive toward success and prestige, he's given all his time to achieve material success, and in the process of making money, he's undone himself.

Suppose we bring him back onto the stage of your mind so that a friend can question him. This friend wants to help him to relax and become himself. The conversation goes like this:

FRIEND: Who are you?

HE: You know who I am. I'm Mr. X.

FRIEND: Is that all you are? Just a name?

HE: Are you crazy? I'm head of Y Corporation. I'm the head of the whole industry.

FRIEND: Yes, I know, but you're a failure in a much more important industry, in your industry, in the most significant industry in the world. You've forgotten who you are. You're made up of assets and liabilities.

HE: What! Don't you think I know that?

FRIEND: You don't understand. I'm talking about other liabilities—not the business. I am referring to your status as a human being. You have no dignity, no understanding, no sympathy for yourself. You've got research to improve your business product, but how about improving your product—yourself? Is money everything? Or is self-direction important too? How about some compassion for yourself, for your self-image? Give it the relaxation it needs. How about accepting yourself as you are instead of always outdoing the Joneses?

HE: I think well of myself. I—

FRIEND: No, you don't. You like yourself as a businessman, not as a person. When you're not working, you don't know what to do with yourself. Don't outdo the Joneses; just keep up with yourself. Find yourself. Then you'll be able to sit still and relax, find out who you are, work at improving yourself.

Maybe you, sitting in the playhouse of your mind, are the friend who helped this man. Perhaps this advice has inspired him, put him on the road to relaxation. You can see it for someone else, but how about helping yourself? Can you help yourself to relax?

But do I hear you say, "He has position and money, while I have none"?

This doesn't matter. You, too, can relax if you just do the best you can and then accept yourself realistically, as you are, with your limitations. Stop punishing yourself! Have compassion for yourself. See your strengths as well as your weaknesses. *See yourself as you are, a* human being *with unique, individual qualities. Relax with the image of yourself and, as you relax, others will relax with you and appreciate you more and* more.

I know this sounds simpler than it is. But you have picked up this book, so you have committed to wanting a better life. The first step is becoming conscious of where you are now. Do you have trouble sleeping? Are you worried all of the time? When good things are happening, do you wait for something terrible? Does unscheduled time make you uncomfortable?

You have real problems to solve. We all do. When you're grappling with a problem, do your very best. You may not figure it out because you don't have the answer. But if you did your best with what you have, that is all you can do. And if you achieve your goal, wonderful! If you don't, and you've already done your best, give yourself a little common-sense advice: that you can do no more. Take a walk, go to a movie, go to sleep—in short, let go, give up all conscious responsibility for the outcome.

You will be surprised how often the answer you've been struggling for will come to you out of nowhere while you're doing some menial task or thinking about something entirely different. Trying too hard, combined with worry, never achieves the answers. It blocks the natural mechanism of your problem-solving self.

Surely an intelligent person should set his goals, gather his information, arrange his materials, and work earnestly and efficiently. I'm not telling you that magic will come to your aid. But when you've reached your limit, and everything still isn't just the way you'd like it, learn to take it easy. Learn to relax and treat yourself as a human being put on this planet to enjoy life. Your imagination surely needs a rest now and then if it's to function as a friend.

## LET BYGONES BE BYGONES!

*"And their sins should be forgiven them" (Mark iv:12).*
*"Father, forgive them, for they know not what they do" (Luke xxiii:34).*

These quotes from the Bible point up the great importance of forgiveness—of yourself and others. You cannot relax and be at peace with yourself if you carry grudges around with you. If your job was to unload heavy crates of oranges from a truck and bring them into a supermarket, wouldn't you feel overburdened if you had to lift a crate on your shoulders instead and carry it around with you all day? Could you relax? Of course not. Well, you cannot relax and carry grudges around with you all day long, either. The two just don't go together.

There are many fallacies about forgiveness, and one reason that its therapeutic value has not received full recognition because real forgiveness has been so rare. We have been told that we are "good" if we forgive, but have seldom been advised that the act of forgiveness can relax us, can reduce our load of hostility.

Another idea is that forgiving places us in a strategic position as a means of winning out over our foes. This is a way of saying that forgiveness can be used as an effective weapon of revenge—and it can be. But revengeful forgiveness is not real.

Real forgiveness is not as difficult as you might think. It is much easier than holding a grudge. There is only one essential condition. You must be willing to give up your sense of condemnation; you must cancel out the debt with no mental reservations.

When we find it hard to forgive, it is because we enjoy our sense of condemnation. We get morbid satisfaction from it. As long as we can condemn another, we can feel superior.

In nursing a grudge, many people also derive a perverse sense of satisfaction in feeling sorry for themselves. When we forgive, we are not doing someone a favor or showing off our righteousness. We cancel out the debt not because we have made the other person pay long enough for the harm he has done us, but because we have come to see the debt itself is not valid. True forgiveness comes when we can see that there is and was nothing for us to forgive. We should not have condemned the other person in the first place.

Some people will hurt you and do wrong. But the main point is that if you want to relax, you must learn to bury grudges to enjoy peace of mind. You must become a forgiving person. Be a lover, not a hater. In the words of the great French writer La Rochefoucauld, "One pardons in the degree that one loves."

## THE SECRET OF LIVING WITH YOURSELF

As human beings, we all live with or near other people and learn to live in harmony with them. We must learn to compromise, give and take, shine in the spotlight, and yet surrender it gracefully.

Learning to live with people and machines, changing customs and the threat of nuclear war, or other kinds of challenges that the future may bring, is not easy. But the most important secret of all is learning to live with yourself. If you can learn to do that, you'll get along somehow—no matter what is going on around you. And you'll be able to relax.

In his essay "Self-Reliance," Ralph Waldo Emerson wrote:

"There is a time in every man's education when he arrives at the conviction that envy is ignorance, that imitation is suicide or worse as his portion; that though the wide universe is full of good, no kernel of nourishing corn can come to him but through the toil bestowed on that plot of ground which is given to him to till. The power which resides in him is new in Nature, and none but he knows what that is which he can do, nor does he know until he has tried. Trust thyself: every heart vibrates to that iron string."

We can learn much from his message today. We have made scientific discoveries in the past 20 or 30 years that stagger the imagination. Technologically, we are an amazing people. The cleverness of our minds seems to know no limits when it comes to grappling with mechanical problems. Haven't you ever marveled at our astronautical accomplishments at Cape Canaveral? I know that I am sometimes astounded at New York's skyscrapers, which I see every day. Once in a while, I wonder how they were so well made of steel and concrete, so perfectly planned.

*And yet we have not learned to live with other human beings and relax!*

Moreover, most people today cannot be alone—for even a short period—and find it tolerable.

It's no accident that a New York radio station told listeners that they'd never be alone while tuning in its programs, feeling that this would be a comforting statement to many people.

In his popular book *The Lonely Crowd* (Yale University Press, 1950), David Riesman stresses modern man's fear of being alone. ". . . What is it that drives men who have been surrounded with people and their problems on the day shift to see often the same company on the night shift. Perhaps in part, it is the terror of loneliness.

"When I asked young people in interviews how they would feel if, for some reason, the radio should be shut off, quite a few were frightened at the prospect. One veteran of the Pacific campaign, who had spent two years in Korea, said he had once been at a summer place in Wisconsin where there was no radio for two weeks. He said he couldn't stand it; nothing in the army where he had the Armed Forces Network was so bad. Without the noise of the radio, it seems, people feel as if their receptors are dead. And indeed, they have used the noise of others to deaden the noise of the self."

I've met many people to whom a day—even a few hours alone, is sheer torture. One comes to mind right away. He was a good salesman, a "jolly good fellow" type, he could sell anything to anybody, but he never sold himself on himself. His eye was always on business. When he played golf, there was no enjoyment in it; he was just after business deals with his partners. He never found release or relaxation and dreaded being alone; he would go to any lengths to avoid solitude, even if it meant buying people supper or drinks or entertaining them with an endless repertoire of anecdotes.

This poor fellow died of a heart attack in his forties, and I doubt that he ever enjoyed one good, sincere talk with himself during his lifetime.

I'm sure that many of you find it most challenging to be alone. At the first hint of peace and quiet, you panic and head urgently for the radio or television, to be soothed by the thunder of horses' hooves as the "good guys" chase the "bad guys" through western prairies that look mighty familiar by now.

This is a far cry from the days of Henry David Thoreau. In *Walden*, he wrote that ". . . I went to the woods because I wished to live deliberately, to front only the essential facts of life, and see if I could not learn what it had to teach, and not when I come to die, discover that I had not lived."

I do not advocate solitude as a way of life, but being alone is good in small doses. You can then return to the people around you, refreshed, to give them the best you've got in you. But, as a way of life, solitude is an evasion that defeats you. However, one should have the capacity to find one's own company entertaining—alone or with others. One should be able to relax—alone or with others.

The whole art of relaxation is to accept yourself, be part of your fellow human beings in give-and-take relationships, respect them as human beings with faults, and respect yourself.

In learning to live with yourself, the final key must be the health of your self-image. If you see yourself realistically, giving yourself the respect you deserve, picturing your successes and your loving feelings, keeping faith with yourself despite your faults, forgiving yourself for your mistakes, then you have found the secret of living with yourself without fear.

## HOW TO RELAX ON THE JOB

People have to make money to live; therefore, their most realistic fears often center around their jobs. Since fear and tension are twins, it's not surprising to hear people complain that they just can't relax on the job.

One confidently completed dozens of bombing missions over Germany as an Air Force pilot during World War II. He revealed to me that he feels great anxiety in his routine office job.

In *The Split-Level Trap,* by Dr. Richard E. Gordon, Katherine K. Gordon, and Max Gunther (Bernard Geis Associates, 1960–1961), there are some interesting case studies of people's emotional problems, many of which center around their vocations.

One man returned from World War II to a lucrative selling job. He moved with his wife and three children to a larger, more expensive apartment and filled it with furniture bought on credit. Shortly after, his job vanished when his company merged with another organization. He was told he could quit or take a job at lower pay in the parent company's sales office.

He took the job.

His drive to succeed was strong. With real economic pressures pushing him, he drove himself ruthlessly, paid off his debts, and became a star salesman. When a minor executive position was offered to him, he was not ready for it but felt he could not refuse.

By now, he had bought a house in the suburbs, along with a new load of furniture and appliances, and a new car. He began to assume an air of confidence to fit in with his status. His wife, striving for social acceptance in the community, gave expensive cocktail parties and joined the country club.

He could not relax. The drive to get ahead had come to dominate him, and anything that did not contribute to that goal was an irritation. A day's adventure with his son, a quiet afternoon in the shade of a tree, a good book, a symphony, these things lose their magic when the mind is too strongly preoccupied with material striving. Relaxation comes in well-practiced activities that are not associated with danger, punishment, fear, or strain. He developed an ulcer.

He began to feel pinned down to one job in one company because, realistically, all his eggs were in one basket. He knew of no other economic areas he could turn to if he failed in this job. He became tenser and tenser on the job.

Finally, he began to see how diversifying could improve his position. He began to chat with people about job possibilities in other companies. He found job areas in these companies where he might fit in. This reduced his fear of failure in his job and set off a series of dynamic improvements in his personal life and that of his family.

This study, which has profound sociological implications, offers one very practical suggestion on how to relax on the job: *diversify.* Be as independent of your boss and your company as you can, so you need to fear nothing.

This is an uncertain, changing world, and the more possible sources of income you have, the more you can objectively afford to relax. The other day I hailed a taxi and struck up a conversation with the taxi driver. He told me he'd been hacking just two months; for years, he'd owned a butcher shop with a partner in the Bronx. They had made good money for a long time, but now incoming supermarkets were taking the profit out of their formerly thriving business. He had not foreseen this happening and felt depressed for months. Finally, being a resourceful man, he turned to driving a taxi part-time and making reasonably good money. With a second source of income available, he was no longer worried about his declining butcher trade.

Try not to carry grudges on the job. Don't be resentful of the guy making more money than you do, don't hate the boss because he can give you orders.

The best way I know how to relax on the job is to do the best you can every day and allow this to give you contentment. Perhaps you can get a better job someday, but in the meanwhile, feel proud of your daily performance and see yourself as you are—someone who does his best and who has every right to relax in this knowledge.

## YOU CAN HELP OTHERS EASE THEIR TENSION

The great joy of relaxation is that it's contagious. If you are at peace with yourself, you can spread relaxation to others—and happiness too. Relaxation is the first stage of happiness.

I know an amazing man with great inner wealth. His eyes are calm and friendly, and he has a warm smile for everybody he meets. He helps others ease their tension far better than tranquilizers because he is full of peace and love.

Every week he goes to a particular hospital to visit the patients, many of whom are tense, uncertain of the future. He sits with them for 20 or 30 minutes, listens to their worries, and calms their fears. They are strangers to him, yet he goes to cheer them up.

He does not expect a reward; this is his Nature, to sit with people and chat, to be cordial and concerned.

Many times he has painted the day in bright colors for some suffering human being. How wonderful it would be if his relaxation could spread like an infectious disease, bathing the world in his kindness!

## DON'T DRIVE YOURSELF!

A few years ago, a friend said to me, "I like my work, I love my family, I've had a good life, and I can go home and relax: I think I'm a lucky man. But when I get in a car and get out on the highway and head for the city, I get tense all over, and it takes me a few hours before I can shake off this feeling."

My reaction was immediate. "Don't drive," I told him. "You don't have to.

You can take the train to work. If you're not relaxed when you drive, it's doing you harm."

He took my advice, and today his life is more restful. He hadn't equated his tension with something so simple.

I'm not concerned with driving here—it tenses up some people and relaxes others—but with the avoidance of *driving yourself.*

Too many people force themselves to do things because they feel others expect it of them. Most adults drive today, so my friend, a successful man in many ways, thought he had to drive—even though he hated it.

You cannot relax and force yourself; the two don't together. While there are some things in life that you are compelled to do, you often have a free choice that you do not exercise. As individuals, we must choose the kind of life that is good for us.

## YOU CAN ONLY DO SO MUCH

Unfortunately, we often are our worst enemies. Many people just keep driving and driving, pushing themselves harder than even a terrible boss would do. They may rationalize their on-the-go life, stating that they're trying to make money or get something out of life, but they're just destroying themselves. Often, they're also undermining what they consider their objectives to be. Moreover, they are blurring the outlines of their self-image.

To relax, you must know your limits, know when it's time to pack in the work and play a little. If your responsibilities are demanding, you must know when to seek release and how to find it.

You must understand that you are just a human being, not a whole organization or an army and that there is only so much you can do. Don't expect the impossible of yourself. Sometimes circumstances force people to perform beyond their limits, for a time anyway, making them tense and resentful. It is better to explode at times like this, to let the anger burst out into the open like water pouring out of a dam. Keeping it locked inside poisons the system, makes relaxation unattainable.

## YOU CAN'T PUSH YOURSELF INTO SLEEP

Sleep is our moment of supreme relaxation, the time when we should forget all our problems, forgive all whom we think have wronged us, accept all our limitations.

*Dream who love dreams, forget all grief;*
*Find in sleep's nothingness relief.*

—*Lionel Johnson (English Poet)*

Yes, sleep should bring us relief. It should refresh us, give us strength for the demanding day ahead of us.

But to many of us, it is something else to worry about. It is a challenge, something we must accomplish. Millions of Americans take to bed each night, grimly muttering to themselves, "Sleep! I will go to sleep!" It's like an order, and it doesn't work. These people spend their nights tossing and turning, torturing themselves with resentful thoughts.

To sleep is to relax, and then relax some more, until waves of drowsiness steal peacefully through your body and soul, engulfing you in gentleness, until you are at peace and know no more.

Modern-day insomnia points out once again the magnitude of our real problem: our inability to relax. Sleeplessness is one of the most common symptoms of emotional distress.

The easiest way to fall asleep is to stop worrying about it. Many people, fearing they will contract illness if they don't get their quota of sleep hours, stay up into the night, preventing themselves from sleeping through their fears. Yet, in lab experiments, people have stayed awake for close to 10 consecutive days without suffering permanent ill effects. Naturally, they had trouble concentrating and were short-tempered, but just 12 hours of sound sleep brought the rest-deprived man back to normal.

So our fear of not getting enough sleep is groundless. We attack the question of sleep just as we attack other areas—hustling, bustling, pushing, trying too hard.

How easy it is to sleep is emphasized by the sleeping customs of other cultures. The Maori of New Zealand, for example, sleep squatting on their heels with a mat tied around the neck to keep out the rain. The Japanese use a block of wood as a pillow. And you say you can't sleep on a nice, comfortable mattress with a soft pillow?

Live your day spiritedly, doing your best to achieve your goals and to live in harmony with your fellows, realistically accepting yourself, and you won't have to worry about sleep; it will just come.

First, do your work, which should take about eight hours. Then relax and enjoy yourself, leaving your work troubles where they belong—at the office or factory. Roughly, this should take about eight hours. Then you will be ready for sleep, and no one will have to hint that it's getting late. You'll know it. You'll be tired, in a pleasant way, and you'll just fold up on the bed, relax with your thoughts for a while and be asleep before you know it.

When you wake up in the morning, you'll feel renewed. You'll feel energetic, ready for the day that lies ahead.

## YOUR SELF-IMAGE AND RELAXATION

You must relax to be happy, and I consider this area so important that I've devoted two chapters to it. Consult Chapter 15 for some more ideas that will help you find calm.

The suggestions I've already made in this chapter can be vital to your well-being. They can not only help you to live a longer life, but they can also make your years more enjoyable.

I did not just jot them down on impulse; they are concepts I have formulated from my 60-plus years of trial-and-error. They are the fruit of a lifetime of contemplation, and in some cases, you will be able to profit from my own mistakes.

They will aid you in living more calmly, and when you're tense, I know it will help you to re-read the ideas in this chapter.

The basic idea, once again, is the health of your self-image. It cannot be otherwise because this picture you have of yourself brings you success or failure and triggers your automatic mechanism's functioning.

You will find this theme repeatedly on these pages because it is so fundamental to your happiness. I cannot write enough about it; if anything, I write with understatement because this inner quality is your one great possession in life. If you work tirelessly to change this conception of yourself, seeing yourself with ever-increasing tolerance, believing in yourself with more and more conviction, you will find the state of relaxation that you seek.

## PRACTICE EXERCISE: HINTS TO HELP YOU RELAX

As you're doing this exercise, you're once again sitting in a quiet place where you can concentrate on your thoughts, which can be amazingly useful tools.

In the last chapter, I tried to familiarize you with one of your greatest potential allies: your imagination. Once again, we will use the extraordinary power of mental picturing to help you solve your problems.

This exercise will help you when you are tense. Work on it now, but also go back to it any time your nerves are jangled, and you feel like screaming or taking your irritation out on a friend.

Simply sit in the playhouse of your mind and envision a physical landscape that is relaxing to you.

If you like to go to the beach and stand at the ocean's edge, looking out at the seemingly endless expanse of glistening water, go there in your mind. Relax in these surroundings that you love. Recapture the full beauty of the scene in every detail; feel the sun beating down on you, hear the waves breaking against the shore, smell the refreshing, salty breeze. See the clear blue of the sky above and listen to the happy laughter of children playing at the seashore. Feel your part in Nature's plan.

If such a beach scene brings you peace, picture it over and over, feeling that you're there, relaxed, worrying about nothing. Keep analyzing it until sunshine flows through you, driving the dark thoughts out. See every detail, bring a happy feeling back.

You'll be amazed at how quickly such a positive use of your imagination can help you find peace of mind.

Naturally, I'm using this beach scene as an example. You might not find a beach relaxing at all. Picture an environment that you love, which brings a feeling of contentment to you. Once you feel less tense, do some concentrated thinking on two significant roadblocks that keep you from relaxing.

1. *Accept your limitations.* Understand that you are just one person and that you can do only so much. Tell yourself that you should stop driving yourself beyond human capability, that you should slow down. If you find yourself rushing around at a frantic pace, tell yourself to stop. Ask yourself what you're accomplishing. Would you rather drive yourself into a heart attack or relax with your human limitations? Ask yourself this question over and over because it makes a lot of sense.

2. *Learn the healing power of forgiveness.* Tell yourself to stop holding grudges against others *and against yourself.* You cannot afford this burden of resentment; you cannot have peace of mind while you hate. Compassion and love are parents of relaxation. If you want an inner calm, make every effort to become more charitable and discard your grudges.

Now go back once again into your inner powerhouse, feeling more relaxed as you do. See again, on your personal movie screen, the drama we enacted early in this chapter. Picture in your mind this pressure-driven man who cannot even relax in his own home, cannot even enjoy his dinner, cannot even sit down without jumping up and pacing the floor.

It is essential that you see this man, clearly, the worried lines on his forehead, the fist-clenching of his tense hands, the stiffness of his movements. Bring him to life in your mind as you see him, based on my verbal description. Bring your mental camera in for a closeup to help yourself because you must not just think about him; you must *see* him in your mind. For once you do, you will do everything in your power to avoid being such a personal failure, as you see. This exercise is the same for women who work too hard, who try to be all things to all people.

Focus on this mental image because it is the image of unhappiness, our enemy.

Now let us bring in another picture, a visualization of what we're aiming at, a model for you in your efforts to change your self-image and improve your life.

Think of a person whom your heart tells you is happy. Bring his or her image into the theater of your mind and see him or her as clearly as you can. Once more, focus on his or her face and bring out every detail: the calm eyes, the warm smile, the relaxed facial muscles.

Mentally imagine this person carrying on activities and note the easy confidence with which you have seen him or her functioning. Feel the attitude toward problem situations and imagine the philosophy of life. Visualize relationships with other people, perhaps yourself, and note the friendliness with which this person shakes hands and listens when you talk.

See this person over and over in the theater of your mind, for this is one movie you must not miss; this is the picture of happiness. This image is the one toward which you will aim: this is the type of photo you must have stamped in your mind as you work at readjusting your picture of yourself, making yourself a relaxed, easygoing person on the road to happiness.

*This new image is the way you want to see yourself,* not just in your glass mirror but deeper, in the mirror of your mind. When you see yourself this way, you will trigger the success mechanism in yourself, and you'll be on your way.

I must make one thing clear: You can't see yourself as exactly like this happy person you want to emulate. You are different people. It is the quality of happiness, the face of joy, the identity with happiness—this is what I want you to capture.

If you keep working on these exercises, understanding more and more the extraordinary power that resides in your image and yourself, you will change your self-image. Your picture of yourself will be happier, and you will be in the process of becoming a happy person. You will be calm, knowing that you will not hurt yourself with disrespect and overwork. You will allow yourself the privilege of mastering relaxation because it is your God-given birthright.

I wish you, my readers, a great gift: the ability to relax. You can relax in this turbulent world of ours; you are a fortunate person and you are blessed. As you read this book absorbing the concepts and *practicing* them on the stage in your mind, you will find that you can attain peace of mind, which you never dreamed was possible.

# 5

## WHY NOT BE A WINNER?

STEP OUT ON THE STAGE OF LIFE AND PREPARE TO FACE THE STRUGGLE, FOR IT will be a struggle. You are one of many, and it is easy to get lost in the shuffle.

Take your mirror in your hand and apply your makeup. But, first, what is the role you will try to play? Clown or villain? Failure or success?

You say to me, "All my life, I've seen myself as a failure." That doesn't matter. You can succeed if you want to and if you're willing to work hard at it.

"But I'm no youngster," you say. "I'm not 21—or 31, either. I'm past the prime of my life. It's hard to change when you're my age."

Changing may indeed become a little more challenging if you're older, but the important thing is that you *can still change*. The road to success is rarely smooth.

It is common knowledge that the great scientist, Albert Einstein, was thought a mediocre student by some of his grade-school teachers. His name is practically interchangeable with the term genius.

The eminent French scientist, Louis Pasteur, was considered a failure for many years. Lillian Roth was a famous actress who started on Broadway at age six. Her stage parents pushed her, but she had the talent to succeed. The pressure was high, and her fiancé's death caused her to spend decades in and out of mental institutions. She waded through years of alcoholic fog to regain stardom. Thomas Edison had such a difficult time in school that his father feared he was stupid.

Recognition did not come immediately to any of these people—and it won't come immediately for you. Probably, you'll have to set more modest goals for yourself; you must be realistic. Few scientists have the stature of an Einstein; few actors have the appeal of a Gable.

Set goals that are reasonable but, at the same time, don't underrate your potential. See yourself as you've been during your best moments.

For, even if you've failed at things most of your life, you can succeed if you change your self-image.

## SEE YOURSELF AS A SUCCESS

Step out on the stage of life and look at your audience. Don't pay any attention if they jeer at you or throw tomatoes. Remember that you have a good part, the best you've had, and you will be a success!

You may be nervous in the spotlight; don't worry about it. A little nervous energy will not harm you; it will not spoil your performance if you accept it as natural and do not let it overwhelm you.

You may miss your cues at first—you probably will. Don't let it bother you. You cannot be perfect, you never will be, and if you've been used to spending your life sitting in an audience, watching others shine, you'll have to get used to your new self-image. You'll have to break it in gently.

But these are the things to remember: you *can change,* you *can succeed.* While you're sitting backstage, in the darkness, just with yourself, see yourself as the kind of person you want to be and resolve to make yourself that kind of person. Don't shoot for the moon; don't be unrealistic. If you failed high school math, you'll probably never be a physicist. Be yourself as you've been in your finest hours—no matter how fleeting—and recapture the feeling of what you can *be* and what you *can do.* You've got the raw material in you. Dig out your buried treasure, and don't be afraid to show it to yourself and the world.

## THE MEANING OF SUCCESS

Success means different things to different people. To some, success and money are the same things. To others, a good marriage and family life spell success. Some people feel successful only when engaged in the creative sense of artistic achievement.

I know one man who feels the warm glow of success when he puts through a clever business deal; it's not just the money, it's the feeling that his tactics have won out, that he's won a victory on the battlegrounds of business. He plans his deals with the imagination and careful attention to detail of a General Eisenhower planning the D-day invasion in Normandy. When his manipulations have been effective, this man feels the exhilaration, the heady wine of success.

Another acquaintance thinks of business as vulgar and greedy, a seamy side of life that one must put up with. He feels successful when he's doing something with his hands at his country home: painting the house, plastering, building a barbecue pit.

Success is an individual thing, so you must define it for yourself. Ask yourself what you want to achieve and what will make you feel alive, most joyous. Forget what others would like you to think—think for yourself. You are a unique human being, like no other on earth, and only you can know your meaning of success.

## TAKE DEAD AIM ON THE TARGET

Once you have defined success for yourself, you have taken your first stumbling, awkward baby steps. No easy road lies ahead of you; there are no traffic-light-less thruways with signs pointing out: SUCCESS, 50 MILES. You must be your own navigator, and your compass is in your mind.

But your built-in "success instinct" is on your side. Animals have these instincts, which help them to deal successfully with their environments, guaranteeing their survival. And the human success instinct is much more developed than that of animals. God blessed humans with prime equipment for the achievement of success. For animals do not choose their goals—reproduction, self-preservation, food gathering—they are all instinctive.

Humans, however, have the power of creative imagination, a power that animals do not possess. More than mere creatures, we are creators. Utilizing the imaging ability of the imagination, we can set goals. We can be masters of our ships; we can choose to go to Europe or the South Seas. We can select our targets, take dead aim on them, and direct our energies to hit the bull's-eye.

Humans can also rely on the marvelous, built-in success mechanism to take over once the stage has been set for it. We have this wonderful mechanism geared to aid us if we just whirl it into positive motion.

## HOW YOU CAN PUT A BUILT-IN MECHANISM INTO ACTION

First, choose your goals, but make sure they are your goals. Too many people kid themselves and aim at what they think other people want them to achieve. They are not the master of their ship. They are galley slaves shoveling coal into the ever-hungry furnace and, though they may shovel furiously, sweat pouring down their backs, the ship they are propelling forward is not theirs. *Even if they succeed, they will fail,* for they are slave labor.

But once you have probed into your mind and your own heart and know what you want, you are on your way to success that is genuine. You are a free person, a unique creature in the eyes of God, and when you wake in the morning, you have goals. You are on your way to a successful day!

Remember, first, select goals that are *yours*. Second, be sure that they are realistic in terms of your talents and the world you live in. Third, visualize your goals and use your creative imagination to direct you toward their realization.

## YOU HAVE AS MANY RIGHTS AS THE NEXT PERSON

On our security exchanges, traders buy and sell the stock of business corporations. When a stock is trading at $100 share, and a trader thinks it is worth $50, he may sell short. He feels the stock is overvalued; he anticipates that other people will see this too. If he sells short, he hopes to profit if the market price of the stock declines.

But too many people sell themselves short, and they do not make a profit out of it at all. Quite the contrary, they lose their shirts; they treat their aspirations with contempt, despising themselves, pouring cancer into their souls.

We come to a fundamental concept here. You, reading this chapter, have gone over it carefully so far. You've defined success for yourself; you've thought of goals you really want that are also reasonable for you; you've even figured out a few ways to go about things and pictured them in your imagination. But, *if you sell yourself short, you will fail!*

Millions of people in their hearts feel they were born to be failures. If success were handed them on a silver platter, they would find a way to fail. They do not think that they have the right to succeed; success would be criminal. In their minds are rows and rows of freshly plowed fields waiting for the harvest. But the crop is a failure.

Have you ever tried raising your own food? It's fun; lots of people get a kick out of it. But, when you plant lettuce seeds, will you get asparagus? Of course not! But, by the same token, when you plant the seeds of failure, how can you hope to harvest success?

You must replant your mind, inserting the seeds of success, seeds labeled the "will to win." You must realize that you have as many rights as the next person, no matter how successful he or she is.

People have ingenious ways of failing, methods that are hard to believe. I know one man who inherited apartment buildings worth perhaps a half-million dollars. Feeling he was unworthy, however, he neglected them, forgot to collect the rent, and, inside of a few years, threw away $70,000. Luckily, he realized his will to fail and righted himself before he destroyed all his good fortune.

A patient of mine felt comfortable as an economic failure but made the mistake of making a lot of money. Immediately he developed anxieties. He became a hypochondriac, afraid other people were out to rob him of his money. He visited doctors, took out insurance, worried all the time. He preferred failure to success.

One woman came to my office, seeking plastic surgery for her nose. There was nothing wrong with it; it would have been a crime for me to operate, and I refused to do so. She was trying to destroy herself unconsciously.

It seems to me that many people who regard success and money as the same thing are the ones who fail. This is a serious mistake; a successful person may not have a dime in the bank. Wealth is in a person's heart. It may be associated with the making of money, or it may not.

But one thing that all successful people share is a belief that they deserve to be happy, that happiness is their very birthright, that the sun rises each morning to usher in a day of successful living.

## SUCCESSFUL PEOPLE: HOW THEY DID IT!

Clark Gable was this kind of person. He was a star during the Golden Age of Hollywood and, in his films, portrayed cocky, cheerful men who enjoyed life.

Before he became well known, Clark Gable was never afraid to try new things; he enjoyed new adventures. He was a water boy in a mine and a timekeeping clerk in a steel products plant. After World War I, he worked part-time in a clothing store. When about 20, he was a garage mechanic and later worked long hours learning to be a tool dresser. He tried acting for a stock company, spending two years with a tent show at $10 a week. Later he worked as a lumberjack. These were not years of failure leading up to great triumphs, for Gable was a success even then. To him, success and living dynamically were synonymous, so Gable was successful even while economically poor.

To Harlow Curtice, former president of General Motors, success has mainly centered around the forceful drive in economic areas.

A country boy, Curtice had little more than a high school diploma when in 1914, he got a bookkeeper's job with a partly owned subsidiary of General Motors. At 35, he was president of the company. Curtice was only 40 when he was appointed general manager of General Motors' prized Buick division.

Curtice had always relished action. A dynamic executive, he pressed for daring designs on the new models, revised Buick sales channels, and traveled across the country to see Buick dealers, giving them faith in the product they were selling.

During four years in the middle of the depression, he quadrupled Buick cars' sales, installing his division as the second biggest money-maker in the General Motors setup.

Curtice's success netted him a salary of about $750,000 a year, but it was even more significant than his enormous salary at the time indicates. He enjoyed setting goals for himself and his subordinates, took delight in overcoming the obstacles that cropped up, and developed the habit of winning.

Charles Allen was a man who made it big in the world of finance. Quitting school at 15 to become a Wall Street runner, he began his own investment house at 19. Unbelievably, he made and lost close to a million dollars by the time he was 26.

Allen believed in his ability to evaluate securities; this confidence helped him invest large sums of money. Able to make vital decisions quickly, he could speak out when millions of dollars were at stake. That was the basis of his success.

Allen never let temporary failure throw him. Initially, he had neither money nor connections, and he made a fortune only to go under in the stock market crash. Some men committed suicide during those grim days, but he wasn't floored. Building up his business once again, he made his banking house wealthy and influential.

Althea Gibson, the Black tennis star, wrote a book called *I Always Wanted to Be Somebody* (Harper & Row, 1958), in which she described her concept of success: "I always wanted to be somebody. I guess that's why I kept running away from home when I was a kid, even though I took some terrible whippings for it. It's why I took to tennis right away, and I worked at it, even though I was the wildest tomboy you saw, and my strong likings were a mile away from what tennis people wanted me to do.

"I was determined that I was going to be somebody too—if it killed me."

Althea Neale Gibson was a tennis player and professional golfer who was one of the first Black athletes to cross the color line of international tennis. Althea's will to win was so strong that she became a "somebody," one of the big names in women's tennis for many years. In 1956, she became the first Black athlete to win a Grand Slam title.

Romain Gary, the great French novelist, felt that his success would repay the mother he loved; she had given him tenderness and devotion. Through his art, he felt he was giving to mother *something that he wanted to give her*.

In *Promise at Dawn* (Harper & Row, 1961), Gary wrote:

I knew that my mother's artistic ambitions had never been fulfilled and that she was dreaming for me of a career she had never known herself . . .

I was determined to do all I could to make her, by proxy, so to speak, through my achievements, a famous and acclaimed artist: it was only a matter of choosing the right field; and, having hesitated for a long time among painting, acting, singing and dancing, after many a heartbreaking failure, we were finally driven to literature, which has always been the last refuge, in this world, for those who do not know where to lay their dreaming heads.

To most people today, the name Houdini is synonymous with the word "magician" and the very act of magic. His story is enlightening because he was a self-made man who worked very hard at his craft, keeping faith in himself even amid defeats.

Houdini was comparatively unknown for many years, working in the circus, beer halls, and vaudeville. Tirelessly, he kept practicing his magical feats. His family opposed him, the world did not recognize him, but he kept going, improving his trade until he finally achieved renown as a magician.

To some men today, baseball means success, and centerfielder Jimmy Piersall was a successful ballplayer for many years.

Piersall, once a high-strung young player on the Boston Red Sox, broke down under the emotional strain. He did this while in the public eye—major league baseball players are potential headline-makers for newspapers and media—and could have quit baseball to avoid personal embarrassment. However, Jimmy was a fighter and came right back to play more than ten years in the American League, a target for those who attend baseball games to bait ballplayers, and he even hit .322 for the Cleveland Indians in 1961.

Success doesn't always come easy. Sometimes winning in life takes a lot of good, old-fashioned courage.

## BELIEVE IN YOURSELF, AND YOU'LL SUCCEED

Ralph Waldo Emerson once wrote that "Self-trust is the first secret of success," which is true. But some people connect success with "luck." The winners, they say, are those who are "lucky."

I do not believe in "luck," and I think it is a dangerous concept, for once a person believes that he is "unlucky," he is very likely to give up on life. It's true that some days seem to go better than others, things may be more to one's liking, but these factors even themselves out over the long run. Too often, the person who believes in "luck" is waiting for someone to help him out instead of having the confidence in himself to take the initiative.

I've already gone over some of the ingredients of success, but one maxim is fundamental: *Believe in yourself, and you'll succeed!*

The successful people I've written about in this chapter are so different in their concepts of success, their fields of endeavor, their strengths, and weaknesses, but they all have one thing in common: a belief in themselves. In some people, this belief was at war with failure instincts, and they had to fight to win out. But at its core, the belief in themselves was part of their personalities.

There is nothing in this world beyond your grasp, which you need to live successfully.

Edmund Burke, the great eighteenth-century Irish political philosopher, once said: "Those things which are not practical are not desirable. There is nothing in the world really beneficial that does not lie within the reach of an informed understanding and a well-directed pursuit."

Yes, but with one caveat. It is only valid if you believe in yourself and believe that you are the kind of person who deserves success and happiness.

But not many of us live up to our potential.

In an article entitled "Man's Potential and His Performance" in the *New York Times* Sunday magazine in 1957, Dr. Joseph W. Still writes:

"The charts reproduced here are based on observation of human physical and intellectual behavior made during nine years of research in gerontology, the study of aging. They indicate the potential of normal men and women as compared with their usual performance. Each contains an upper 'success' curve and a lower 'failure' curve. I believe that not more than 5% of the population follows the upper curve. The rest fail for lack of motivation and understanding of their abilities.

"First, as to the chart of physical growth. No one can doubt that the 'failure' curve represents the physical development of a great many people today. They get almost no physical exercise, and they eat, drink, and smoke too much. Their physical fitness declines rapidly after the early thirties. As for the chart of psychological growth, again we have a 'failure' curve that describes the intellectual development of far too many today. Too many people reach the peak of curiosity and intellectual growth in high school or college or early adult life and cease growing and begin to decline."

Why does this informed observer find a "failure" curve instead of a "success" curve? There is something wrong when so many people reach their intellectual peak so early. Life should be a process of continuing growth until death.

The answer is that too many of us don't believe in ourselves. We watch baseball games on television when we might be better off playing baseball. We watch soap operas on TV instead of living full lives ourselves. We have come to be "watchers" instead of "doers" and have lost faith in our creative powers. We are becoming passive people who observe life while it passes us by.

To be one of life's winners, you must recapture your belief in yourself. You must set worthwhile goals for yourself and believe in their worth—no matter how insignificant these goals might seem to someone else.

## NO ONE IS PERFECT

Remember that old proverb: *If at first, you don't succeed, try, try again.* I first heard these words when I was a little boy in public school, and I never heard truer words. We can all learn from it, too.

If you feel that you must succeed all the time, you will be a failure, for no one is perfect.

The person who feels his or her house must be perfectly clean will be miserable. Homes are not sterilized test tubes. No one can make them antiseptic.

The student who feels he must get an "A" in every subject cannot win. Life is just not perfect. Even if his mastery of every subject is commanding, he will sooner or later have a teacher who rarely gives students "A" grades.

The man who feels he should never show emotion is just building a wall around himself. He is not noble or perfect; he is imprisoning his success mechanism.

The woman who thinks all her features should be classically perfect degrades her human qualities, turning herself into a puppet.

The night watchman who berates himself every day because he isn't a doctor or wealthy business owner is a traitor to his positive qualities.

Now, let's get back to our proverb. Many people can't succeed at things because they won't even try. They are afraid of failure; they must be perfect even the first time they attempt something. If their perfectionism is extreme, they will try nothing new, for, at first, they expect they will not succeed.

Perfectionism is an enemy to success.

## TO ERR IS ONLY HUMAN

You cannot succeed at anything if you don't treat yourself as a human being. And a human being makes mistakes. To err is only human; if you were really perfect, you'd have no friends. No one could relax with you.

All babies, learning to walk, stumble, and fall. Do we call them failures? Of course not. We readily see that walking is at times difficult for them and expect them to make trial-error progress.

But suppose you have to do something equally difficult for you, at your present level of maturity. Suppose you're a housewife and your husband brings the boss home to dinner, and you've never been in this situation before. You're more nervous than usual and make a joke that just doesn't come off and, getting flustered, ask a question that is embarrassing or tactless. You've erred; are you a failure?

Of course, you're not. You're a human being who faced a trying situation and stumbled. Why shouldn't you have as much compassion for yourself as you do for a baby trying something new?

Forget your failure and try to do your best to make the remainder of the evening pleasant. The boss might even like you and your husband better because he sees you're human. You don't know what his problems are.

As the great English poet John Dryden once wrote:

*Presence of mind and courage in distress*
*Are more than armies to procure success.*

Just as a spouse wants to fulfill expectations successfully, the young married man wants to prove himself as a breadwinner. The baby is only two months old; it's their first child, and never before has he felt such a desire to support his newly enlarged family. But along with the desire goes a feeling he's not familiar with—pressure.

He's been an insurance salesman for 15 months, and he's done well for a beginner, but the pressure changes his personality a little. He's more anxious when he deals with a customer, more forcing in attitude, thinks of his own need for money rather than the customer's need for insurance. He blames himself for messing up a few sales he should have made and soon thinks of himself as a failure.

Is he? Certainly not. He's going through a period of readjustment and is temporarily disturbed. *His only real mistake is that he is not accepting his mistakes.*

Problems are a big part of life and, to live successfully, one must live with them. Pressure, mistakes, tensions, misjudgments—these are parts of life too, the lot of a human being. Sometimes all of us feel inadequate to the demands made upon us.

The Roman Publilius Syrius once wrote, "If you wish to reach the highest, begin at the lowest," which is not bad advice.

## IF YOU DON'T LIKE YOURSELF, WHO WILL?

In this chapter, I've given you a few ideas to help you make yourself a winner. If you work hard on the practice exercise following, I'm sure that you will also find this helpful.

In the long run, it is your self-image which is the determining factor. Your success or failure rides with the adequacy of your self-image. In Chapter 1, I describe the type of salesman who simply will not sell well; his self-image is too weak.

He can change, and so can you. You can change your self-image and become more successful in life if you see the truth about yourself—if you use your imagination to see yourself as you've been at your best and project yourself through imagery to play new roles within the limits of your physical and emotional capabilities. If you can relax and accept your weaknesses, if you can feel compassion for yourself as a human being alone in the universe—such a small part of the scheme of things, you can see what is good in yourself and stop torturing yourself with what is negative.

For it is this pictorial concept of oneself as a failure that makes one fail.

And it is this generous, loving, giving self-image which makes a person successful and happy.

This new self-image does not imply the idealization of oneself. We are struggling in a world full of problems, and we simply do the best we can to live each day givingly. We all have faults and try to overcome them; sometimes we can, sometimes we can't. Most of us have friends and enemies.

If anyone should be your friend, it should be you. If you don't like yourself, who will?

And, if you are your own friend, if your self-image makes sense, if you know what you want and set your sights on realistic goals, using your imagination to guide your effort, you will be a winner!

## PRACTICE EXERCISE: HOW TO ACHIEVE SUCCESS

In this exercise, I will suggest concrete ways for you to attain your life goals.

1. *Encourage your success mechanism* by discarding your negative, "failure" thoughts; instead, picture yourself as a success. Recapture, in your mind, every happy experience you can bring to consciousness. Do not indulge in vague positive thinking; picture your moments of triumph. See them in technicolor;

make them live again in your mind. Rise above images of failure; imagine, instead, how you will overcome your obstacles.

2. *Set definite, realistic goals for yourself.* After you've determined what you want, visualize the steps you must take to accomplish your objective. Don't let past failures discourage you. If your goals are within the range of your potential, they make sense. Your success mechanism needs goals to function at its maximum efficiency.

3. *Understand your rights.* Many people think along these lines: "I've had this same dull job for 12 years, but I don't deserve any better." Or "All I do in my spare time is watch TV, but I guess I just have no get-up-and-go." If you think in these channels, your trouble is that you do not have a high enough opinion of yourself; you do not feel that you have the same rights as successful people. Often the difference between success and failure is one's conviction of what one deserves. Tell yourself that you are a deserving person. Think of people you regard as successes and tell yourself that you have the same rights they have. Keep on thinking about this concept until you feel the truth, which, in different words, is part of our great American Declaration of Independence: that each of us has rights to the good things of life.

4. *Believe in yourself.* If you feel that you have too many faults and made too many mistakes in life, remember that no one is perfect. The whole business of being successful is to rise above failure. To achieve success without problems confronting you is one thing. To achieve success by overcoming failure and rising above it is a far greater victory, for, in that very act, you improve your self-image and your stature of self-respect. Tell yourself, again and again, that your failures are in the past; that, beginning right now, you will be a success.

# 6

# YOU CAN MASTER YOUR HABITS
# AND CONTROL YOUR DESTINY

THERE'S AN OLD SAYING THAT WE ARE ALL "CREATURES OF HABIT" AND I THINK this is quite true. We all tend to follow specific habit patterns in leading our lives.

Some habits are culturally determined. Almost everyone shares them in a given society. If you live in the U.S.A., for example, I can predict that one of the first things you do is brush your teeth when you wake up in the morning. Most Americans have this habit, and it's a good one. Your breath smells better, your teeth are healthier, and your mouth feels fresher. Some habits are more individual. A friend of mine, with whom I now and then debate a philosophical question, invariably gestures with his pipe when he makes a point. He has done this for as long as I can remember him.

If your habits are wholesome, you *must be* a happy person. If they are not, you should make every effort to change them so that you can live a fuller, more vibrant life.

Some people say that "you can't teach an old dog new tricks." I don't believe this at all. You can change—it's just more difficult because first, one must undo negative habit patterns that have been part of the individual for many years.

In writing this chapter, I aim to help you cement your good habits and replace your poor habits with ones that will make your life happier and more successful.

The word "habit" is a negative one for many people. In this age of materialism and loss of moral and spiritual vision, with playwrights and authors writing about heels and destructive people, with good people no longer considered interesting, we hear about the "drinking habit," "smoking habit," "drug habit."

But habits can be good, even inspiring, and the whole art of living is to overcome bad habits and rise above them to habits that make for a good life.

## THE IMPORTANCE OF HABIT

Your habits govern your life, and you need them to function in the world. To give an elementary example, upon waking up on a weekday morning, you habitually brush your teeth, wash, put on your clothes, button them, and eat some kind of breakfast. If you hadn't developed these and other socially acceptable habits, your community would not tolerate you.

Without the aid of habits, you would be slowed down to a walk in your daily activities. You would be in conflict with yourself about the simplest functions. You would need a full 24 hours to get your day's work done, and you'd have no time for sleep.

Are you a housewife? Where would you be if you forgot how to cook breakfast for your husband, make the beds, and wash the dishes?

Are you a department store salesman? Where would you be without the habits of dressing neatly, greeting your customers politely, and knowing the prices of the merchandise?

But, useful as some habits are, others may be destructive. The person who automatically smokes three packs of cigarettes every day has formed a habit that is his implacable enemy.

## HOW HABITS ARE BORN

Growing up, the child learns ways of doing things from his parents and later from his friends. Soon these actions and thinking tools become part of him; they become automatic. He repeats them again and again for months and years, perhaps for the rest of his life.

Habit patterns operate not only in an action, such as tying one's shoelaces or driving a car. Our emotional reactions and feelings also depend on habit patterns.

You can develop a good habit of thinking of yourself as a worthwhile, constructive citizen with goals for every day of your life. Or you can think of yourself as a failure, a person of no worth. This way of thinking is a habit.

In *The Road to Emotional Maturity* (Prentice-Hall, 1958), Dr. David Abrahamsen writes:

> All of our habits, in fact, express something basic in us since they reflect our unconscious feelings. This is the reason why we do not think of the way we eat, talk, or walk or the way we carry out our daily routine.

Pavlov's simple experiments with dogs were the first proof that habits were the result of pre-conditioned responses to given stimuli, and that these habits would continue even when the situation no longer remained exactly the same.

To prove this theory, he held out a piece of meat to a dog and rang a bell at the very same moment. At the sight of meat, the dog's salivary glands began to work. Each time Pavlov repeated this procedure, the dogs reacted in this same way. Eventually, no meat was offered; only the bell was rung. The dogs' glands still secreted saliva because the reactions had become automatic and spontaneous—it was unconscious. It would be a long time before anyone could dissociate this repetitive pattern of action from the original factors that related to it.

And so we see that while we accept our habits as a definite part of us which was always there when in reality they were acquired as we grew up. . . .

Just as Pavlov's dogs were conditioned, so are people. You can think of yourself as a winner or a loser; either way of thinking is a habit pattern that can jet-propel you toward life or force you to retreat into a shell.

I know of a girl with great talent as a pianist who was into the habit of thinking that she was incompetent. She told me the story of how, when younger, she used to perform brilliantly at the piano keyboard, her ability outstanding. Yet if she made one small mistake, her mother would scold her.

Today she criticizes herself for the slightest mistake, putting her extraordinary talent in a straitjacket. Her negative habit of extreme perfectionism has ruined a career that had every possible potential.

And so, in our childhood, habits are formed, and they persist for a long time. But *you can change them* and, *in this chapter, I'll show you how.*

## STOP DRINKING AND START LIVING!

Drinking is a self-destructive habit. I don't mean the custom of taking a drink or two after work to ease the pressures of the day—I see nothing wrong with drinking in moderation. I mean the habit of turning to the bottle in any crisis and swallowing drink after drink in a frantic effort to escape from life. This behavior is known as "alcoholism."

People often mistakenly think of alcoholics as happy, imagining the "happy drunk" they may have seen in a movie. In truth, when alcohol consumption is a habit that the individual can no longer fight, it is a terrible disease. The film *Days of Wine and Roses,* which shows the sufferings of an alcoholic married couple, is a classic picturing of the tragic consequences of alcoholism.

The attraction of alcohol is that, under its influence, one can escape the outer and inner world of problems into a dream world for a while. A few drinks, and you can forget all about income taxes and parking tickets and that argument with your mother-in-law. A few more drinks, and you'll even forget about how inferior you feel on the job. A few more, and if the atomic bomb went off in your face, you'd grin stupidly.

If you're troubled, however, your relief is only temporary. The next day your head will feel as if carpenters had assaulted it with hammers. Your "escape" from reality did not bring you joy. Over the long run, drinking heavily will dull your senses and ruin your physical constitution.

People who drink habitually do so to escape from more than realistic pressures; they are running away from a negative concept of themselves, a feeling of inferiority that obsesses them. The drinking habit is a pernicious one and, if you drink too much, you should see this clearly and work to change your ways. Before you can break a habit, however, you must admit that it exists.

Alcoholics Anonymous, which has helped people break the drinking habit, asks that its members begin talks to groups announcing, "I am an alcoholic." This admission is necessary, for many alcoholics insist on kidding themselves, telling themselves that they are not alcoholics but just "social drinkers."

Dr. Harry J. Johnson, in *The Life Extension Foundation Guide to Better Health* (Prentice-Hall, copyright Life Extension Foundation, 1959), writes that: "An authoritative study, which dug into the history of more than 5,000 families and covered three to five generations, once yielded the conclusion that moderate drinking did not shorten life span by a single day. Neither, however, did it increase life span. I merely want to point out these facts because there are so many fallacies in circulation regarding drinking. All existing evidence strongly endorses the potential benefit to be derived from an occasional drink."

So don't be afraid to take an occasional drink! There's a vast gulf between the bona fide social drinker and the real alcoholic. But, if drinking is a habit with you, you must resolve to break the pattern. Later on in this chapter, I will give you the tools to help you stop drinking and start living!

## THINK YOURSELF THIN!

Another typical American scourge is overeating. The twin to this habit is the condition of being overweight, which sends many people on sporadic diets from which they emerge, hungrier than ever, to knife-and-spoon their way back to their pre-diet weight.

Comedians find good material for humor in kidding people who are overweight, but it is not funny.

According to Dr. Johnson, "Long life and excess weight do not go together. Overweight is perhaps the most significant health hazard of the twentieth century. It is like a plague. There is overwhelming evidence that for each 10 percent increase in overweight, mortality increases by 20 percent.

"Overweight, as a cause of death, does not show up on mortality tables. But I believe—and so do most of my medical colleagues—that it is, directly and indirectly, responsible for more disability and illness than any single disease. Heart disease, kidney disease, strokes, and diabetes occur two and a half times as frequently among people 25 percent over normal weight than those of the same age.

"In more than nine out of ten cases, excess weight is caused by nothing more than eating too much. Only rarely is it the result of some organic disease."

This is not a pretty picture, and one might well ask, "Why do people eat too much? Why don't they know when to stop?"

The simple answer is that it has become a habit with them, which provides temporary satisfaction and which they thus hate to renounce. People whose lives are full do not overeat. They feed themselves with worthwhile goals and activities that are exciting. They *nourish* themselves with living relationships with other people and feel that each day is an adventure. They relax with themselves and sleep the sleep of happy people and need only an average amount of food to eat.

If you overeat and are overweight, your overeating habit results from an emotional grievance, conscious or buried. You overeat to make up for what you feel you are missing or have missed at some time in your life. You are trying to soothe all your frustrations with food, and it can't be done.

Keep reading, and I'll give you some hints on how to "think yourself thin."

## DON'T SMOKE TOO MUCH!

Smoking is a habit that has a hold on many people who puff away day after day on cigarettes, pipes, and cigars. Cigarette smoking is, to my knowledge, the most common, and there have been studies attempting to connect cigarette smoking with cancer, heart conditions, and other serious diseases. Amazingly these studies have not broken the national habit. I don't think they've even made a dent in it.

The American Cancer Society and the Public Health Service have both published statistics demonstrating a relationship between cigarette smoking and disease. *Reader's Digest* surveys have also suggested a link between cigar smoking and lung cancer.

An American Cancer Society study on the smoking habits of 188,000 men between the ages of 50 and 70 disclosed a frightening coronary death rate for smokers—some 70 percent higher than the rate for non-smokers.

*The Readers Digest* is a widely read magazine, with a circulation of over 23,000,000 at this writing, but its findings seem to have gone unheeded. Many people need to smoke; smoking cigarettes relieves their tensions.

Cigarette smoking, I believe, also artificially helps many people to think well of themselves. The endless repetition of TV cigarette commercials has had its desired effect: a young lady puffing daintily on a cigarette may identify herself with the smiling blonde standing by a waterfall, her hair blowing in the breeze. A young man exhaling vigorously may think himself the brother of the muscular six-footer who showed all his teeth in the 60-second break.

Aside from the danger of relying on a habit that may be injurious to your health, this is no way to strengthen your self-image because it is artificial and, in most cases, unrealistic. You must make your self-image of stone and mortar, not of smoke floating away into the air.

I do not think smoking an occasional cigarette can hurt anyone physically. Still, when it becomes a habit, and a person must run through two packs a day to exist, it can be dangerous if we believe in medical reports.

How do you stop smoking?

In *How to Stop Killing Yourself,* Dr. Peter J. Steincrobn (Wilfred Funk, revised and enlarged edition, 1962) writes: "Here is a helpful trick for the inveterate cigarette smoker. Recognize that for most of us, smoking is a reflex action. The easiest way to break a habit is to substitute another one for it. Keep pieces of hard candy on hand. Whenever you have the urge to smoke, reach for the sweet instead of the cigarette. The reaching, the unwrapping of the candy, the putting it into your mouth, the sucking on it—not to mention the slight rise of blood sugar that ensues—are a series of reflexes equivalent to reaching for the pack, removing a cigarette, lighting it, and puffing. Try it. It is a pleasant way to fool your reflexes. And it works."

## DON'T WORK YOURSELF TO DEATH!

A full person has good work habits. As a community member, one can often make his most significant contribution to others through his work. A person who doesn't work will usually feel like a parasite; he will probably think little of himself, and others will most likely confirm his opinion.

But some people habitually overwork themselves. They work long hours in their offices and, when the working day is done, they carry home briefcases filled with papers so they can continue their work at home. Work is not part of their life; *their life is work.*

Overworking is too great a burden for a mere human being. To live well, a person should work, relax, sleep. He should devote time and attention to each part of this threefold daily schedule. All work and no play does a man no good in the long run, and he may be heading for an early heart attack.

Why do people overwork? First, because they are slaves to the idea of great material success. Second, because through continual work, they can escape the problems they have with themselves and other people.

John Tebbel, in *The Magic of Balanced Living* (Harper & Row, 1956), writes:

> Running like a strong current beneath all the discussions of work and health is the 'success' fallacy that dominates American life. Most men have to contend with it, and they had better recognize the enemy as early as possible if they are not to be defeated by it.
>
> It is both a fallacy and an enemy. No one is a success who has made a great deal of money and hasn't the time or the good health to enjoy it. The record is full of 'successes' who single-mindedly pursued the goal of Success, achieved it in their late forties or early fifties, and died of a heart attack or succumbed to another disease generated by worry, anxiety, and tension. Of course, it is quite possible to be both successful and healthy, but the percentage of American men who have achieved that goal is small.

Remember this: *If Success to you means material Success and vocational attainment, more power to you! See yourself as a success and go out and achieve your goals. But to overwork and overdrive yourself, to ruin your health and exceed your limitations—this is folly!*

Some people accept themselves only when they're working. Outside of work, they are at a loss; they do not know how to relate to the world of people except through work. In over-working themselves, they satisfy a need to prove that they are worthwhile human beings. In doing so, they can ruin their health. The tragedy is that they are worthwhile, as people, and don't even know it.

If you overwork yourself, tell yourself that you live once and that there is more to life than work. Live each day as if it were your last! Resolve to face the problems that drive you away from your true self and into work. Redefine your concepts of Success, developing your full emotional qualities as well as your work abilities.

## DRESS AS IF YOU THINK YOU'RE WORTH IT

The way you dress is another of your most important habits. While clothes do not necessarily make the man, people will often judge you—sometimes unfairly—by your appearance. When you dress well, you present a positive picture of yourself to the world. Nowadays, many people pay too much attention to clothes, ignoring spiritual qualities that make us better people. Still, if you are a sloppy dresser, you have acquired a negative habit. You are putting your worst foot forward.

It does not take great effort to dress neatly and, if you are habitually slovenly, you should ask yourself why you think you are so worthless—for you must think this. When you think more of yourself, as you should, you will take the trouble to dress as if you thought you were worth it.

## YOU CAN CHANGE YOUR HABITS

Now I'm going to get down to brass tacks and tell you how you can change your bad habits. But, first, you must *believe that this is possible.*

In October 1957, *Science Digest* published an article related to an experiment in which about one-half of a group of 57 college student nailbiters cured themselves of this habit or showed marked improvement in less than a year.

The late Dr. Knight Dunlap devoted many years to studying habits and helped people stop nail-biting and thumb-sucking.

Alcoholics Anonymous has helped great numbers of suffering souls break away from a habit that ruins their lives. The U.S. Health Service at Lexington, Ky., has even helped sufferers from the dread drug addiction to regain their pride and self-control and lick the habit.

Surely each of you knows one person who has dragged himself out of a rut of negativism and developed new, successful ways of thinking.

You can change your habits. It's not as easy as rolling off a log, but you can do it. If you really want to. Your negative habits stand between you and happiness. Why go around in the same circle when it leads you nowhere? If you overeat or drink too much, or if other bad habits plague you, and you want to change them, here's what you do:

1. *Believe that you can change your habit.* Have faith in your ability to control yourself and to bring about changes in your basic makeup.

2. *Understand the physical consequences* of these habits so well that you're

willing to undergo temporary deprivation, even suffering—so great is your desire to change. Face the reality that being overweight puts a strain on your vital organs, that alcohol undermines your tissues, that overwork drives you into premature death, and so forth.

3. *Find something satisfying* which will comfort you during the temporary period of pain that you will go through while you are depriving yourself of a prop that has sustained you for a long time. A hobby such as photography or gardening or piano playing might help wean you away from, say, smoking too much.

4. *Discover the fundamental problems* that drove you to excesses. What is your frustration? Do you undervalue yourself? Why are you such an enemy to yourself?

5. *Come to grips with these problems.* Realign your thinking; accept your failures, and rediscover your triumphs.

6. *Direct yourself toward positive habit patterns* that will make your life rewarding. Set new goals for yourself. Get the feel of Success in constructive activities that will bring out your ability and your enthusiasm.

If you have faith in these concepts' potency and dedicate yourself to applying them, you can change any negative habit pattern. You can thrust aside the bottle that brings more pain than satisfaction or the extra helping of strawberry shortcake, which will never really console you for your past deprivations. Go over my suggestions once more and, when your will falters, read them again and again. They will work for you if you have faith and patience and are willing to work to achieve the results you want.

You can change your habits and lead a better life if you'll stop relying on miracles and get in the habit of realizing that you've got to work to get what you want.

## THE MOST IMPORTANT HABITS OF ALL

You can develop good habits that will improve your self-image.

A child finds that his parents brush their teeth in the morning and imitates them until it becomes second nature. He also learns to tie his shoes before going to school. He can soon perform these functions automatically, and he can think about a problem in his chemistry or physics course while brushing his teeth.

When he grows up, he can eat his breakfast, tie his shoes, and think of his job responsibilities simultaneously without straining because his habits are sound.

If these simple physical habits help a person, how much more valuable it is to develop more important ones: parents might teach a child to stop fighting with his brother or respect his sister.

In any family, the inception of good habits occurs when parents teach the child that he is not alone in life and must respect others' wishes, not only his own.

The growing child should have as his proudest possession a habitual way of thinking: feeling self-respect and dignity. Schools develop children's habits—in arithmetic, geography, English, history—and these are fine. More importantly, there should be a course at an early age, teaching them the respect of themselves and others.

They should learn positive habits of thinking: how to feel successful, how to respect other people, how to feel compassion for one's fellow men.

Boy Scouts taking older people across the street have learned outgoing, friendly habits. If their heart is in what they're doing, they are rewarded—not by money, which is not everything but with their self-respect and the fellow feeling of other people.

People are not born with courage. When one feels respect and compassion for others, he'll fight for them against injustice—and this is the basis of courage. When a white man stands up for a mistreated Black man in the South, the threat of physical violence doesn't bother him.

Compassion, charity, self-respect—when you can reach these feelings, you will like yourself.

With the habit of profiting from mistakes, getting a sense of self-direction, you're on the right track here. Driving toward your goals, moving toward them despite obstacles, is the beginning of a habit—for habit is repetition.

One of the most significant habits to develop is accepting yourself for what you are instead of pushing yourself to be what you're not, which is one of the world's worst habits today. Accepting yourself as you are gives you confidence, whereas scrambling to keep up with the neighbors produces a sense of continual tension. It is a terrible undermining habit, and it will inflict cracks in the core of your self-image.

If you understand this, you realize that worry is a bad habit, just as happiness is a good quality. Happiness is the habitual glow of excitement you feel from your positive anticipations.

Resentment is a vicious habit because it is repetitious. Anger breeds fear of retaliation, which brings on more anger and feelings of uncertainty—the vicious circle never ends. It does not pay. Resentment will hurt the person who is your victim but will inflict far greater harm on the person who hates.

If you have developed negative habits such as worrying, resenting, fearing, and dreading the future, you must see clearly how these habits corrode your self-image. When you can visualize yourself as you really are, you can change the habits that destroy your self-image's dignity.

What kind of person do you want to be? In the theater of your mind, project the witches of Macbeth, cackling as they stir the cauldron on the flames. You're the audience, so you can clearly visualize them. Do you want to have their traits of maliciousness and sly cunning? Or would you rather have the nobility of a King Arthur of the Round Table?

It's all up to you, the person you will be. You can be a witch or knight in shining armor. You can be Dr. Jekyll and Mr. Hyde, with good and evil coexisting, but you certainly would be more fortunate if you developed the kind of emotional habits that lead to happiness.

In the final analysis, habit represents the use of imagination, positive or negative. If you use your imagination as an ally, you will ensure your well-being. It is your imagination and, if you feel that you have the rights of a valuable human being, you can use it to give you the emotional patterns that will make your life a joy.

## PRACTICE EXERCISE: MAKE HABIT YOUR FRIEND

Your habits can be your friends or your enemies; they can help you or hurt you. Apply your energies to develop constructive habits, which will channel you into happy activities.

Here are three winning habits:

1. *Do the practice exercises in this book.* This activity is a wonderful habit to form. These exercises have a definite purpose: to help you think better of yourself and relax with a self-image that you like. I'm confident they will help you, but only if you get into the habit of doing them regularly—just like washing your hands or combing your hair. Understand that they are just as important; indeed, your self-image has as much meaning as your appearance and cleanliness.

2. *Understand the importance of your mind.* It is such an extraordinary force. The ideas I stress in this book—mental picturing, concepts of yourself and the world, attitudes toward success, happiness, and people—are all products of your mind. They consist of thoughts and images, vague in that you can't see them.

You might, therefore, say to yourself, "It's just an image in my mind. How important can it be? I can't touch it, and I can't see it. Maybe it really doesn't matter."

Don't fall into this trap! The pictures your mind produces are essential to your stature as a human being. The ability to produce and sustain a single mental picture can often be more significant than the attainment of monetary Success and materialistic accompaniments.

Your concepts, your mental images—more than anything, they are you. Tell yourself over and over just how important are the workings of your mind.

   3. *Realize the power of your self-image.* Your self-image is another intangible, but its power is also real. You rise or fall, succeed or fail, depending on your self-image. For your own good, don't forget this!

Get out of the habit of rationalizing away your defeat, then crawling into a shell of resentment at the world's failure to recognize you. First, you have to recognize the good in yourself.

Tell yourself repeatedly about the power of your self-image and get into the habit of working to improve your concept and image of yourself, for this is your great hidden wealth. Let's take an outstanding case, that of our late President John F. Kennedy. Politics is no one-way street, and during his career, Kennedy met challenges and refused to buckle under them. What was his great secret? The strength of his image of himself. If you ever saw President Kennedy making a speech, surely you could feel the relaxation in the man, the at-homeness even in front of TV cameras. Only a man who sees himself favorably can be so comfortable when the eyes of millions are on him, and their ears hear his every word, sometimes with the fate of the world at stake.

As further testimony to the fantastic power of the mind's imagery, consider this: Months and months after his death, as you read this book, you can picture this man in your mind. Though he is dead, you can see him still alive and vivid. In a sense, this power of your imagery keeps him alive. Thus, with newsreel tapes to refresh our memories, he will never die in the theater of our minds.

Why not apply this same power of mental picturing to your advantage? Use this overwhelming impact to see yourself in your most successful moments, upgrading instead of downgrading yourself. Do not let your successes die; keep them alive in the theater of your mind. Keep on picturing your victories in life, doggedly focusing on your success pictures until they become a part of your personality, and what *might* have been, becomes *what is.*

# 7

## SEVEN RULES FOR HAPPY LIVING

"IT IS ONE MAIN POINT OF HAPPINESS THAT HE THAT IS HAPPY DOTH KNOW AND judge himself to be so," wrote Samuel Taylor Coleridge, the great English poet.

If you're happy, you'll know it. You'll feel it in your bones; you'll find excitement where some people find boredom.

Everyone has this right: to know what it feels like to be happy. You don't need to earn this right. You were born with it. Our great Declaration of Independence affirmed this right. Written mostly by Thomas Jefferson, it asserted that "We hold these truths to be self-evident, that all men are created equal, that they are endowed by their creator with certain unalienable Rights, that among these are Life, Liberty and the pursuit of Happiness . . ."

But how many truly happy people do you know? Answer this question honestly. Use the fingers of your hands to count them; unless you know very unusual people, your ten fingers will be adequate for the task.

### YOU LIVE ONLY ONCE

Whenever I think of the many unhappy people in the world, I find it amazing. Surely God did not mean us to spend our days in misery; life is too short for that. As human beings, we are God's proudest creatures. *We should be happy.* You live only once—remember this when you're feeling blue. Make the most of your days; dedicate your energies to making yourself and others happy. Instead of sitting around moping, thinking of ways to waste time, understand the great value of time. Would you throw away money if you were in your right mind? Of course not. Then why throw away time, which is also precious?

Time is one of your most treasured gifts. Alfred Lord Tennyson once wrote:

*"Time driveth onward fast,*
*And in a little while our lips are dumb."*

These are words to the wise. Don't waste your time letting life pass you by.

## LIVE EACH DAY AS IF IT'S YOUR LAST

I know many people who live for the future. They are always saving for "a rainy day," or they are always putting their money away "so I can retire and go to Florida," or they work themselves to death, "so I'll be taken care of when I'm older."

Foresight is a fine quality; I would not dream of criticizing it. Plans are fun, and they're often wise. But—

Many of these people plan for the future *at the expense of the present.* This choice does not make sense to me. Life is uncertain, there are no guarantees, and a person who sacrifices the present for a future that might not ever come may be sacrificing his happiness.

If you can live each day richly and *still* lay the groundwork for a happy future, wonderful. But if you must surrender present joys, I say to you, "Don't do it!"

I speak from more than 60 years of experience in this world, some of it sad. And the saddest stories I know are of people who lived for "tomorrow" and died before they could ever reach it—or who saved for the "sunshine years" only to see unexpected expenses wipe out life savings—or who overworked themselves all their lives and arrived at the "golden years" with plenty of money but with their health shattered.

To live happily in the present and the future:

1. *Live each day* as fully as you can.
2. *Set goals for every day.* Don't be afraid if some people think them trivial; if they have real meaning for you, that's all that counts.
3. *Tell yourself that you have the right to be happy;* don't let people worry you with their negative thinking.
4. *Set aside several hours for relaxation every day;* do the things that give you peace of mind and release from the practical problems of living.
5. *Accept yourself as you are,* with your strengths and weakness. Don't try to be someone else!

You could also try to *live each day as if it's your last.* If you imagine this to be true, you will shed minor irritations that ordinarily plague you. You will be surprised at what a calming effect this thought can bring. You will stop worrying about the many little things that, added up, destroy happiness. For, on your last day on earth, why worry about trivia?

## HAPPINESS IS A STATE OF MIND

Money's a nice thing to have, but, in the final analysis, you can't buy happiness. You can, however, think yourself into a state of happiness.

If you feel good about yourself and think you deserve to be happy, you will resolve to create happiness wherever you go. If you want to be happy, you will find happiness all over the world. You will enjoy each bite of breakfast; your morning shower will be refreshing; you will feel content in the routine of getting dressed. When you go out into the street to go to work, you will feel happy to see your fellow human beings because they are brothers. They are not perfect—are you? and if some are unresponsive, you will understand that they may have problems that bother them. You will give them the best you can, and if there is no immediate response, you will not care. Your act of giving will make you happy. If it's raining, you will go to buy an umbrella and get enjoyment from the simple act of flicking it open and shut, appreciating its mechanical functioning with the simplicity of a child having fun with a toy.

Much is good in our imperfect world if you want to see it with eyes that seek contentment.

Did you ever read Robert Louis Stevenson's short poem, "Happy Thought"?

*The world is so full of a number of things,*
*I'm sure we should all be as happy as kings.*

You can be "as happy as kings," but you must first think yourself into it. You must get rid of the negative feelings that are enemies of contentment; fear, worry, resentment. If you are infested with these phantom diseases, you cannot feel well and cannot even know what it means to be happy.

If a horde of mosquitoes were to invade your home, would you attempt to live with them? I doubt it. More likely, you would spray them with insecticide or declare war with fly swatters. You might enlist the support of an exterminator. But negative thoughts are infinitely more dangerous. You cannot coexist with them, for they will not let you "live and let live." You must root them out and knock the props from under them; you must destroy them before they destroy you. Nazi Germany was a threat to world peace, and her defeat in World War II was essential, so it is with negative thoughts, which are annihilators of your peace of mind.

## YOU CAN BE HAPPY IF YOU REALLY WANT TO BE

It is your attitude toward yourself, which determines whether you are happy or miserable. Do you see yourself as a weakling and a failure? You will be unhappy. Do you see yourself as a nice guy? You'll do fine.

*You can be happy if this is what you want for yourself.*

A positive mental attitude reinforced by your powerful mental imagery will bring you all the Success and happiness you desire. Such a positive attitude implies a feeling of faith, an impulse toward charity, and a dose of good common sense. It is topped off by the full potency of your imaginative processes.

These qualities will lead you toward happiness, provided your self-image is healthy enough to allow you. Your concepts—about yourself and the world you live in are powerful; it is sometimes difficult to comprehend just how powerful they are.

In *The Power of Your Subconscious Mind* (Prentice-Hall, 1963), Dr. Joseph Murphy tells of a man who wanted happiness.

"A number of years ago, I stayed for about a week in a farmer's house in Connemara on the west coast of Ireland. He seemed to be always singing and whistling and was full of humor. I asked him the secret of his happiness, and his reply was: 'It is a habit of mine to be happy. Every morning when I awaken, and every night before I go to sleep, I bless my family, the crops, the cattle, and I thank God for the wonderful harvest.'"

Dr. Murphy also found that other people craved misery.

"I knew a woman in England who had rheumatism for many years. She would pat herself on the knee and say, 'My rheumatism is bad today. I cannot go out. My rheumatism keeps me miserable.'

"This dear elderly lady got a lot of attention from her son, daughter, and the neighbors. She really wanted her rheumatism. She enjoyed her 'misery' as she called it. This woman did not really want to be happy."

He points out that "There is one very important point about being happy. You must sincerely *desire* to be happy. There are people who have been depressed, dejected, and unhappy for so long that were they suddenly made happy by some wonderful good, joyous news, they would actually be like the woman who said to me, 'It is wrong to be so happy!' They have so become accustomed to the old mental patterns that they do not feel at home being happy! They long for the former, depressed, unhappy state."

## THE HABIT OF CONTENTMENT

In the last chapter, I talked to you about the importance of habit in your life. Happiness is a habit, a wonderful one. Happiness is the kind of habit that you should try to develop.

I never met the farmer Dr. Murphy writes about, but probably he's not financially wealthy—few farmers are—and he's probably had his share of heartaches. The odds are that he's not much different from most of us, but he's developed the habit of reaching out for happiness. He sings and whistles while others worry about their troubles and complain to anyone willing to listen.

We all have troubles. Problems are part of life. They are always with us, "and if it's not one thing, it's another."

But ask yourself this. When trouble comes, do you crawl into a shell of misery and resentment, or do you keep on whistling while you seek a solution? Do you mope and sit around feeling sorry for yourself, or do you think back to better moments and plan for a successful future?

Your mind is such a potent tool. Remolding your truths, harnessing your imagination, and driving yourself into Success channels, you can use your mind to make you relaxed and happy. You can make contentment the essence of your life!

## LAUGH YOUR TROUBLES AWAY!

Get into the habit of laughing; too many of us have forgotten how to laugh. As people grow older, they sometimes forget that they ever laughed. It is a part of their childhood that they can no longer remember.

Did you ever see a happy baby? He crawls on the floor, picks up a toy and sticks it in his mouth, then drops it and gurgles delightedly. When he laughs, he opens his mouth wide in an expression of sheer, uninhibited joy. There is nothing halfhearted about the baby. He looks up at Mother, and his whole face is a map of laughter. If she responds to his good nature, he lets out a howl of glee and claps his hands together, and crawls ecstatically across the floor until another joyful object strikes his eye.

As grownups, our needs are much more complicated than a baby's. When a baby needs food, the Mother comes with a bottle. When a grownup needs something, he often must be more patient until he reaches satisfaction and must accept a compromise or defeat instead of what he wanted. A grownup's life is usually demanding and, at times, frustrating.

Still, to laugh is to let joy bubble out to the world. We all feel joy sometimes, and when we do, we should use it, sharing it with other people, giving it a spirit of completeness that will make it last longer. Learn to laugh like a happy baby!

Sometimes, when you're feeling depressed over something that has defeated you, think of past Success or something funny that happened to someone else. Throw your head back—don't be afraid—and laugh, with all your heart and soul, and see if you don't feel better for it.

## ACCENTUATE YOUR ASSETS!

You can't laugh easily, however, if you dislike yourself. If you think poorly of yourself, you feel like crying, not laughing. So, first, you must build yourself up. Not artificially. That wouldn't do you any good at all. You can't kid yourself, and I am not advising you to be unrealistic. But you can build yourself up if you'll take a good, hard look at your positive qualities.

You have them. I don't care who you are; these qualities are there. They may be hidden, it is true, but you must dig them out and show them to yourself and the world so that you can feel pride in yourself and laugh once again.

I have, during my many years as a plastic surgeon and human being, met so many people who buried their finest qualities: warmhearted, human men who felt forced to wear a mask of stoicism that cut them off from the world to prove that they were masculine; women so ashamed of a mild facial deformity that they never dared to show their basic generosity; people so obsessed with vocational frustration that they downgraded all their other creative activities.

If your positive qualities are buried treasure, get out a pick and shovel and dig them out. Show them to yourself so that you can appreciate yourself, and then you'll be ready to take that treasure with you on the road to happiness.

## HELP OTHERS, AND HAPPINESS WILL BE YOURS

In *Success Through a Positive Mental Attitude* (Prentice-Hall, 1960), Napoleon Hill and W. Clement Stone write that "One of the surest ways to find happiness for yourself is to devote your energies toward making someone else happy. Happiness is an elusive, transitory thing. And if you set out to search for it, you will find it elusive. But if you try to bring happiness to someone else, then it comes to you."

This is the fundamental truth. We are brothers and sisters, but we don't realize it and withdraw from each other in our minds too often. Or we devote our energies to armed combat, in which we seek to outmaneuver each other—usually to gain material possessions which never give us the sense of joy we could experience in human kindness.

When you help others, you help yourself. You feel a sense of relatedness to others, and others are your world. You feel that you are a useful and meaningful person, a contributing member of society. In addition, if the people you help are appreciative (and most people are grateful for kindness), you feel the warmth of their reaction to you, and your social interaction can be a friendly one. You feel more comfortable in the world of people and less need to retreat into an inner shell that is a living death.

To be happy, you must learn the art of give-and-take, which is the lifeblood of civilized living. A person who is just a "taker" can never be happy. A man whose whole life is grabbing money like a shark killer or a woman who accepts others' gifts like a pampered pet—neither can be happy in this kind of role. One must know the joy of giving, the spine-tingling thrill of making somebody else happy, to know the real meaning of contentment.

## HAPPINESS IS CONTAGIOUS

I can't remember his exact words, but an older friend, when I was growing up, once told me something like this, "When you are with negative-minded people, don't let their ideas take hold of you!"

This was good advice, and I've tried to follow it. Negative thoughts are deadly; they are as contagious and as devastating as any bubonic plague that ever infested a population.

A few months ago, I was walking down the street from my office in midtown New York. A casual acquaintance stopped me with a greeting. "Hello," I said. "How are you?"

"Not so good. I was 60 last month and, you know, you get to feeling your age. You get to wondering how long you have to live."

"I feel fine," I said, "I enjoy myself, and I don't worry about that. And I'm past 60."

"Did you hear about _____?" he said. "Too bad. Cancer. He was only 54."

I expressed my regrets and asked him to convey them to the man's widow.

"Oh, well," he sighed. "The weather's so hot; it's unbearable anyway. Besides, the air's no good anymore with all these buses spewing out carbon monoxide. And, with income taxes coming up, life's too miserable to care about."

I shook hands with him, said goodbye, and went back to my office. My nurse said a patient was waiting, so I erased the negative conversation from my mind and prepared to do something useful. But, if you let such negative people's thoughts take hold of your mind, you're a goner. You will waste your God-given days on this earth in worry.

Here's the main point, though: just as misery loves company, so does happiness. When you are happy, you can spread it everywhere you go. You are a carrier of beauty and love, and you can give your gift to others.

Laughter is contagious when it's genuine. It can spread like wildfire through gloomy talk of nuclear annihilation, wiping the worry from people's minds and keeping your thoughts well lubricated, ready for positive action.

Quiet happiness is also catching. When a person quietly gives to another from his great storehouse of contentment, he makes the other person glad he's alive. His compassion turns suffering to acceptance and inhibition to the expression of feelings. He turns worry to joy and hate to love. The streets don't look dirty and paper-littered anymore; they look like efficient transportation tools in a functioning civilization. The country fields don't look lifeless; they look mellow green with the throbbing growth of grass, watered by God's great natural force: rain.

## PERFORM AN OPERATION ON YOUR THOUGHTS

When I was in my early twenties, studying to be a plastic surgeon, I learned to perform an operation that would improve a person's appearance. I learned how to handle nasal instruments, delicate tools used within the nostril in so small an area to remove a hump on a nose or straighten a crooked nose, all done within the nostril to avoid an external scar.

I learned to be completely accurate in removing a scar and bringing the edges together, with fine forceps that hold the skin edges while bringing them together with a very fine, curved needle and stitches as fine as horsehair. I learned to bring these skin edges together with complete precision to prevent future scarring.

But you, too, can perform an operation—on your thoughts. Don't laugh, because this is a tremendously important operation. The patient, you, can emotionally live or die. You need no surgical instruments, just the will to make yourself happy.

You will remove no scar tissue, just negative thoughts. You will try to cut out of your mind worry, fear, resentment and replace them with thoughts that give you pleasure.

At the end of this chapter, you will find guides for making this happiness operation a success.

## ACTIVITIES THAT BRING HAPPINESS

Your mind can function for your happiness; activities can also bring you fun.

For example, Former President Dwight Eisenhower, when under the pressure of being Chief Executive, used golf as a way to relax.

The late President John F. Kennedy, and others of this famous clan, played touch football and were strong advocates of physical fitness.

Britain's great Sir Winston Churchill has often painted natural scenes to bring him a few hours of quiet enjoyment amid days of struggle.

The famous artist Grandma Moses, who lived to be one hundred and one, took up painting as a relaxing hobby in her eighties.

Hugh Downs, the TV personality, devotes much of his spare time to work for an association to better national health.

Bob Hope found rewards in traveling around the world, entertaining our troops overseas during World War II.

Doing things will be fun for you if you select the activities you enjoy and are not doing them to win others' approval. No one can tell you what to do; you know what you enjoy.

## HOW A POLITICIAN GOT DOWN TO BRASS TACKS

A friend of mine told me this story, and I think it's an instructive one. It's about a professional politician and his rise from misery to happiness.

This man had devoted his life to politics as a paid representative of a major political party. He talked politics every day of the week, and he worked himself around the clock. He was a stranger to his wife and children; he provided for their material needs but gave them no attention. He smoked and drank too much to help his tension but was able to keep going.

One year a cycle of trouble hit him. His oldest son began running around with a rowdy destructive group of teenagers and was becoming more like them all the time. His wife had for years been gradually withdrawing from him; she insisted on their having separate bedrooms. Finally, this man, in his early fifties, had a heart attack.

He was fortunate. He recovered, and his near-death was a blessing in disguise. For the first time, he realized the meaning of the gift of life. He understood that there was more to life than overwork: that he had a family, a wife, and a body that would be good to him if he was good to it.

This hard-headed man, who had previously prided himself on how practical he was, began to reform his life. It wasn't easy because he had let things drift so far for such a long time. He began spending time with his wife and children; he gave of himself to make them happy. He worked his 35 or 40 hours a week and did his best. Then, recognizing the transitoriness of human life, he went home and relaxed. The shock of his close call propelled him into efforts to build a happy life day by day. His family, feeling his earnest desire to give, gave back to him, and, for the first time, he experienced the thrilling sparks of devoted family life.

He now had work, family, relaxation, hobbies, good sleep, freedom from tension. He and his wife grew back together, and his rebellious son received the benefit of his guidance. He was on the road to happiness.

## SEVEN RULES FOR HAPPY LIVING

You can make your life happier and richer. I'm sure these ideas can help you.

1. *Get the happiness habit.* Smile inside, and make this feeling a part of you. Create a happy world for yourself; look forward to each day. Even if some shadows blot out the sunshine, there is always something to feel good about.

2. *Declare war on negative feelings.* Don't let unrealistic worries eat away at you. When negative thoughts invade your mind, fight them. Ask yourself why you, who have every natural right to be happy, must spend your waking hours wrestling with fear, worry, and hate. Win the war against these insidious twentieth-century scourges.

3. *Strengthen your self-image.* See yourself as you've been in your best moments, and give yourself a little appreciation. Visualize your happy times and the pride you've felt in yourself. Imagine future experiences that will be joyful; give yourself credit for what you are. Stop beating your brains in!

4. *Learn how to laugh.* Adults sometimes grin or chuckle, but not many can laugh. I mean, a real belly laugh that gives one a sense of release and freedom. Laughing, when it is genuine, is purifying. It is part of your success mechanism, jet-propelling you to victories in life. If you haven't laughed since the age of 10 or 14, go back into the school of your mind and re-learn something you should never have forgotten.

5. *Dig out your buried treasures.* Don't let your talents and resources just die inside you; give them a chance to meet the test of life!

6. *Help others.* Giving to your fellows can be the most rewarding experience of your life. Don't be cynical; understand that many people who seem unpleasant or hostile are wearing facades that they think will protect them from others. If you give to others, you might be amazed at their grateful, appreciative

response. Some people who seem the hardest are really soft and vulnerable. You'll feel great when you can give without thought of profit.

7. *Seek activities that will make you happy.* Golf, tennis, water skiing? Painting, singing, sewing? I can't tell you. You'll have to tell yourself. But an active life is a happy life if you're doing what's right for you.

# 8

## CAST OFF YOUR EMOTIONAL SCARS

I HAVE BEEN A PLASTIC SURGEON FOR OVER 25 YEARS, AND I KNOW JUST ABOUT all there is to know about physical scars. They intensely affect some people, bringing them embarrassment, making them afraid to examine themselves in the mirror, causing them to retreat from social functions and encase themselves, hermit-like, in a shell of pain.

Luckily, physical scars can often be removed. I am grateful that my hands have had the power to undo the cruel effects of automobile crashes and other destructive accidents and, in so doing, to restore people's peace of mind. I feel I'm fortunate to render a service to others—it makes me feel good. I feel happy when a patient leaves my office, all smiles after my operation has corrected a facial scar that was responsible for inner sorrow.

About 10 or 15 years ago, a young actress came to see me. She was a gorgeous girl and very sweet, but she was in tears over a scar near her nose, the aftermath of one of the holiday weekend statistics you read about in the newspapers every year.

"Don't worry!" I said. "I've seen much worse than that. You'll be fine." My reassurance did no good. She continued to sob; she was a free spirit, and her whole body heaved with the enormity of her grief. "Here," I said, handing her a mirror. "It's not so bad, is it?

"And, next time you see me, you'll be as good as new."

She just hung her head and said nothing. Her face to her was her fortune; it meant stage career, meeting a man, marriage.

I operated on her that day. When she returned to my office later that week, I removed the bandages, and when she saw her face, she rushed over to me and kissed me on the cheek. Her face was bright, and she clicked her heels excitedly as she left to go out into the street to face life with renewed hope.

Yes, physical scars can be removed.

## EMOTIONAL SCARS ARE PAINFUL

But what about emotional scars?

You can't see them; emotional scars can be infinitely painful. You can't feel them—but they can make the stomach rumble and the heart palpitate. There is no outward evidence of them, but they can cause dizziness, nausea, insomnia, heart attacks, and indigestion.

They are deeper than physical scars and harder to remove. They bring on a vicious cycle of negative feelings, which never ends until you resolve to heal the wound. *When you are determined to do this, you can set about removing the emotional scar.*

Suppose you're a young man in your late twenties. You've had three or four jobs, but you didn't like them, and, after a year or so, you gave notice and started looking for greener pastures. Your hunt, however, turned up mostly muddy fields until, one day, you found the job. A large publishing concern hired you as an assistant personnel director. The director, who hired you, was skeptical of your experience but felt that you might produce what was needed in this job. The salary was good, and the prospects of advancement were promising.

There was one catch, however. Most of your experience had been with banks in a clerical capacity. You needed three or four months to adjust to your new duties. If your boss would be lenient with you for that period, you felt confident that you could make the grade, and then your future would be rosy.

The director, an impatient man, afraid of your inexperience, kept an eye on you from the moment you started on the job. You made mistakes; he was critical, and soon you became nervous and committed several blunders. One day the director called you in and said he was sorry, but you just weren't suitable for the job.

Since then, you have felt a failure; an emotional scar has taken root within you. You feel resentful. You hate the director, thinking that if he'd only been patient, you would have adjusted to this fine opportunity. You vow that if anyone asks you for a favor—it doesn't matter if it's the loan of fifty cents or help in pushing a car—you will turn him down. You will get even, you tell yourself. If you can't get even with the director, you will take it out on your sister, or the postman, or maybe the cat. Bristling with hostility, you flaunt your emotional scar at the world, and the world reacting with resentment sets up a nightmarish crosscurrent that seems unending.

How do you heal this emotional scar? You have been treated unfairly, haven't you? What is the answer?

I would say this: You have been treated shabbily and, since this job was important to you, a certain amount of resentment is natural. If you were bitter and short-tempered for a few days after you got the notice, this would be understandable, maybe even desirable, for it is often better to cleanse your system than to let inner hate eat away at you.

But you should not let the scar of resentment take hold of you and permanently dominate your thoughts! There are good things in life; there are other avenues down which you can drive, there are other jobs, other fields. There is a place for you in society if you will meet life halfway.

Forgive the director. You don't know what problems are making him insecure so that he couldn't give you a fair chance. It took courage for him to hire someone inexperienced in this area. When you made mistakes, he might have been fearful of his responsibility for them.

Forgive because you are a human being too, and you're not always fair yourself. Remove the emotional scar and apply yourself to positive goals once again. Get your old perspective back; oil up the old machine, and get back on the ball.

## TO OTHERS, YOUR SCAR MIGHT SEEM A SCRATCH

Your troubles can often seem overwhelming—worse than other people's—to you. But this can work in two ways. To others, your scar might seem like a scratch.

One man might sulk for years after losing a particular job, but another might shrug it off in 24 hours and go on to a life of success. One girl might resent a lover who married someone else all her life; another girl might buy a new dress, go places with a girlfriend and meet another man better for her.

If you feel you have the right to be happy, you will not let misfortunes defeat you. You will fight your way through defeats until your life is brighter. You will readjust your aims, realign your compass, set the ship once again on course, and sight future victories.

In *The Power of Your Subconscious Mind*, Dr. Joseph Murphy writes: "If you really want peace of mind and inner calm, you will get it. Regardless of how unjustly you have been treated, or how unfair the boss has been, or what a mean scoundrel someone has proved to be, all this makes no difference to you when you awaken to your mental and spiritual powers. You know what you want, and you will definitely refuse to let the thieves (thoughts) of hatred, anger, hostility, and ill will rob you of peace, harmony, health, and happiness. You cease to become upset by people, conditions, news, and events by identifying your thoughts immediately with your aim in life."

In short, you will recognize that your scar is a scratch. You will wash it with soap, apply iodine or a Band-Aid and go about your job of living zestfully.

## YOU'RE TOUGHER THAN YOU THINK

Some people feel that they've taken too many "hard knocks" during their lifetime and that these struggles will inevitably take their toll.

This perception is not so. The human body is a marvelous mechanism, and so is the human mind. As a human being, you are truly resilient. You have the bounce of a rubber ball, the drive of a jet engine. You're tough; you can take it—unless you choose to destroy these qualities in yourself.

Polio struck down Franklin D. Roosevelt, but he did not let it stop him. Being partially paralyzed for most of his adult life, he could not walk. Still, he carried out the President of the United States' extraordinary responsibilities without the full use of his limbs.

Helen Keller was deaf and blind, but she was a strong-minded person and contributed much to the world—as a writer and lecturer and as a cheerful, giving human being who did not waste her time moping over handicaps that would make most people just sit down and cry.

This amazing woman graduated cum laude from Radcliffe College and spent her life helping other blind and deaf people like herself. She wrote articles and books and traveled worldwide doing work for organizations such as The American Foundation for the Blind.

Walt Disney had his rough times too. In 1931 he had a nervous breakdown. The consummate artist that he was, he could not fully accept his genius at this time in his life. His perfectionism led him to expect too much of himself, and he had trouble sleeping. He could not tolerate the imperfections in his productions.

Advised by the studio doctor to leave his work for a while, Disney refused to let his temporary setback crush him. He learned a lesson from it, learned to relax more, and went on to his great career as a cartoon creator and movie maker.

Comedienne Fanny Bryce also had to take it on the chin and bounce back. In *Fabulous Fanny* (Alfred A. Knopf Inc. 1952–53), Norman Katkov tells how crushed "Baby Snooks" was by her divorce in 1927.

"I watched him leave that room," Fanny wrote long years later, "and I didn't believe what was happening. I didn't think we were through, and I didn't believe I'd never see Nick again as my husband. The lawyer went away to arrange the hotel-room thing, and I knew I was just as much in love with Nick that day as the day I first saw him.

"I waited for Nick to stop the divorce. Even when the lawyer came to take me to court, I thought Nick would be downstairs to call it off. I thought he would be outside the court to stop it. I thought he would be in the court to tell the judge, 'Forget it, judge, my wife and I made a mistake. We're in love. Why, we don't want a divorce.'

"But he never showed up. All I remember is that it was a beautiful day. I was like in another world. It was like watching me standing there in that court-room. I didn't hear my lawyer. I didn't hear what the judge said. All I know is they gave me a bunch of papers to sign, and I signed, and they gave me a copy."

Fanny recovered from her hurt to be a great radio and movie comedienne for many years.

These people were tough—and so are you! You have to realize the positive forces in you and put them to use, developing faith in yourself as a growing human being who does not knuckle down to a few "bad breaks."

## HOW I HELPED A SALESMAN CONQUER HIS FEARS

An insurance salesman came to see me about a year ago. He had read *Psycho-Cybernetics,* and he came from Dallas, Texas, for several reasons, one being that he wanted to discuss a problem with me.

He sat opposite me in my living room and, staring unhappily at the carpeting as he talked, told me of his fear of addressing insurance sales meetings in Texas. He was a successful salesman, one of his company's top producers. But when he stood up to address his fellow salesmen, he would panic, mutter a few words and sit down, ashamed of himself. His terror was so great that he would be afraid of fainting.

Sometimes he would take his wife to these meetings, and he would be distressed that she should witness his degradation. He would imagine that people in the audience were talking about him, ridiculing him.

I saw before me this middle-aged, good-looking, intelligent man. There was something clean-cut and decent about him, and I smoked my cigar and tried to figure out what I could say that would bring him comfort.

"It's strange," I said, "that you, a salesman, who has to make an impression on others, should be afflicted with an imaginary illness."

"It's not imaginary," he answered. "I feel scared."

"*It is* imaginary. You're a good speaker. You're articulate. Yet something happens when you step up to address a group of salesmen in your field.

"Let me tell you a story about myself, and then I'll tell you what's wrong with you.

"The whole business of fear can translate itself into many ridiculous patterns that make you much less than what you are.

"I remember when I was a medical student, and in a course on pathology, as the oral examination, the professor would call on me to answer questions. Invariably, I was like you. When I saw the faces of 80 other students staring at me, fear overcame me. I panicked and couldn't think. I would sit down without answering the questions, feeling defeated, because I could immediately put my thoughts together and figure out the answer to the questions I had flubbed.

"On written exams, I didn't have to face all the students. Looking through the microscope, I wrote down what I saw. Calm, I got an A on the written exams, but I was afraid I would flunk the course because of the orals and not become a doctor. I was like a poor swimmer who had to make it to shore or drown. I had to master my problem to survive.

"I said to myself that, when called on, I would imagine I was looking through a microscope at slides, and this would give me more confidence. Also, I would tell myself that I had a right to make some mistakes and that they shouldn't make me ashamed of myself.

"The next time, I stood up and answered the questions. Once, when I hesitated, I told myself that I was only human, and I recovered my composure. I passed the course with honors.

"I went through the same pains as you in a different way, but for the same reason. I was afraid to make a mistake, and this fear caused me to lose control of my rational thinking for a moment, so I lost the answer.

"My friend, this should be a lesson for you because your trouble is that you're afraid to make a mistake in the presence of your fellow salesmen. You're emotionally scarred because this fear obsesses you.

"But remember, your colleagues have made mistakes too. And also remember, you've had successes. When you get up to speak next time, think of how you felt last time you sold a big insurance policy. This memory will give you confidence in yourself and remove the scar.

"The beginning of living is not so much fear, but overcoming the fear of making a mistake. Living begins when we rise above our failures."

The salesman went back to his home in Texas. Since his return, he has been able to address insurance sales groups effectively. His aims remain high, but he is no longer ashamed when he is not perfect. His emotional scar has gone.

You can remove your emotional scars; these two suggestions will help you:

1. Do not try to be someone else.
2. Do not be fearful of making a mistake.

## HOW TO FIGHT YOUR WAY OUT OF A DEPRESSION

Sometimes you will feel depressed. I don't care who you are; now and then, your mood will be heavy, and you'll think dark thoughts. You'll hate yourself for all the sins of commission and omission that you've ever committed. You will be hard to please and, when you look in the mirror, you won't be fond of what you see.

Many areas of depression stem from maladjustment within the self. If you accept yourself, your depressed mood will not last long. Your depressions will be chronic only if you cannot make peace with yourself.

Here's how to fight your way out of depression:

1. Accept your mood. Don't blame yourself for it.
2. Drop your grudges against others; remember that they have problems too.
3. See your past successes and recapture your good feelings about yourself.

Feeling depressed once in a while is not hard to take if you know you can quickly find your way back into the sunshine.

## BELIEVE IN YOURSELF AND YOU WON'T BE HURT

Life is like a game of football. You're the quarterback, but sometimes you'll call the wrong plays. You'll send your fullback—also you—straight ahead, one yard to a touchdown, and he'll bump into a wall of tacklers and go nowhere with only bruises to show for it. Just don't let these bruises become permanent scars that sour you on life and blind you to its moments of beauty.

Psychologists tell us there are "accident-prone people." When they get tackled hard, they are good bets to get seriously injured.

Others can carry the ball and, when jolted to the ground, get up crisply and run back to the huddle, ready to try again. They believe in themselves, and therefore they're not easy to hurt.

Some days will go wrong. The alarm clock won't go off, and you'll be late to work, you'll get caught in a rainstorm without an umbrella, your wife will be cranky, and the baby will be howling. Your car will need a new repair, and you'll wonder how to fit that in the budget; someone will make a mildly sarcastic remark, and you'll bark at him as if he had set your house on fire.

You have something to sustain you when irritations pop up—if you believe in yourself. You must be kind to yourself; see yourself as someone worthwhile. Instead of harping on your weaknesses, you must see your strengths and picture yourself at your best. You must visualize the you that you like and believe in your positive impulses. If you do, you'll score touchdowns every day. You'll kick extra points too, and you won't get carried off the field on a stretcher.

## YOU CAN SHAKE OFF OLD EMOTIONAL SCARS

"But," you may say, "I'm not a youngster in his twenties. I'm 60, and life hasn't been easy. How can I possibly shake off old emotional scars when they've hardened over the years?"

It's not easy. We all wish for a paradise on earth, living on a Polynesian island watching the blue ocean glitter, with coconuts falling off the trees to give us succor. Often we refuse to renounce this dream and, disillusioned, encase ourselves in shells of resentment, thinking of our life full of disappointments and compromises.

But you can get rid of your emotional scars.

Are you a married woman, bitter at your husband because he never could earn enough money to provide you with the material possessions you wanted?

Or a lonely bachelor, still angry at a girl who turned down your marriage proposal almost 30 years ago?

Or a divorced woman, still resentful of your former mate, blaming him for all your troubles?

Or a middle-aged man, a clerk, who feels ashamed that you never climbed higher up the ladder of vocational success? If you are—or if different emotional ailments plague you—it is time to remove these scars and face life fresh. You can do it if you will surrender your resentment and, like a newborn chicken breaking through its shell, look at a new world, which is the only one you've got.

The key to your surgical kit is forgiveness.

## FORGIVE OTHERS—THEY ARE ONLY HUMAN

Forgive others. Do it not only for their sake but for your own. If you don't, you will feel nauseating resentment within you, destroying you from within.

Physical scars are not always negative. In some societies, physical scars are signs of prestige. Some natives of Africa disfigure their noses and put rings in them; they then consider themselves beautiful. Creoles in this country used to show off facial scars as symbols of bravery.

But emotional scars always hurt. When you hold a grudge against someone, you may hurt his feelings, but you will harm yourself more.

When someone has done you a real or imagined wrong, an initial angry reaction is natural. Perhaps you should tell the other person how you feel about his action. You might then take measures to correct the situation.

If the wrong can't be undone, seething about it for weeks, months, years will not help. The anger will just hurt your stomach, and you may end up with ulcers.

Remember that the other person is a human being, the same as you, and few of us can say that we have never stepped on another's toes.

So forgive—and forget. The chances are strong that you have nothing to forgive anyway.

## DON'T HOLD A GRUDGE AGAINST YOURSELF!

Most importantly, forgive yourself. You cannot be happy and successful if you hold a grudge against yourself.

Remove your emotional scars with the ointment of kindness. Apply it gently in the areas which hurt. If your lifelong fear of romantic entanglements has kept you from marriage, be your own gentle doctor and accept this limitation. If your inability to channelize aggressive forces has kept you from vocational achievements, apply the soothing salve of kind thinking to this wound and rub gently till it no longer hurts. If something you blurted out once greatly hurt a dear friend, be good to yourself and forgive yourself for being human.

Here are four "Miracle drugs" for your emotional scars; they've helped others, and they'll help you:

1. *Accept your limitations.* No one is perfect; we all have our faults. If you stretch even a rubber band beyond its limits, it will break.
2. *Forget your mistakes.* We've all done things we'd like to undo, but it can't be done. Stop torturing yourself with self-blame!
3. *Forgive others.* They're just as fallible as you are. They're not gods, and they're not machines; they're just human beings.
4. *See yourself at your best.* Picture yourself in the situations you've relished when things seemed to fit into place, and your world was as you like it. Remember how you felt, recapture the good feeling, visualize it in glowing technicolor, and don't be afraid to hold on

to this glorious feeling if its impact shocks you. Keep these pleasant images alive in your mind; reject your "failure" images and the sinking feeling in your stomach that goes along with them. Feed your success mechanism!

You can heal your emotional scars with these concepts, enhancing your self-image. Once you begin to like yourself better, undoing the past damage, you will be ready to move toward achieving successes that are realistic for you and toward the cultivation of constructive habits that lead to happiness.

# 9

# WHEN THE CURTAIN GOES UP,
# YOU DON'T NEED A MASK

I INVITE YOU TO RELAX IN THE PLAYHOUSE OF YOUR MIND AND SEE A DRAMA IN which you take part. It's a masquerade ball at the home of a friend of yours. There's laughter and excited conversation. Everyone wears a mask; you can't even recognize the host, even though you know his face well.

A blonde woman wearing a pink mask says "hello," and you answer her greeting. She's tall and slim, you know her from somewhere, but who is she? A man with cowboy clothes and a black mask takes her arm and leads her over to an improvised dance floor, a space made by pushing back the sofa and the TV set. He's not Tom Mix or the Lone Ranger, but who is he?

It's all very confusing, but it's a game, and you're having fun. You drink some punch—"what's in this bowl anyhow?"—and join a laughing group of people. No one takes life seriously for the moment.

Symbolically, this scene is true to life, for most people wear masks almost every day of their lives. You can't see them, but they're there. Our real-life masks are tragic, where the masquerade disguises are amusing. They serve an insidious purpose: to hide your real self, which you feel is unacceptable, from a threatening world.

Many people live their little masquerades till the day they die, putting on the faces they feel will shield them from others' censure. They keep their real selves locked up inside, like some dark secret that terrifies them.

Some people live to ripe old ages without anyone ever really knowing what they're like. Their masks keep them from the imperfect, chaotic give-and-take that is living.

## THE MASKS WE ALL WEAR

Are masks necessary?

Our primordial ancestors, many centuries ago, were animalistic. When two of them, searching the earth for food, came face to face in an open field, they would both grit their teeth, jut out their lips in defiance and stare at each other menacingly until they finally came to blows. After the fight, the loser would feel fear and might weep unrestrainedly, while the worry on the victor's face would be gone, replaced by the laughter of success. When they met in the future, the beaten man would look fearful, maybe terrified, while the winner would wear the face of confidence.

We, in this civilized society, are also winners and losers, but the picture is grayer. Most of us know the taste of both success and failure, and our days may be up and down.

As young children, we are primitive, like our ancestors. If a boy of three takes a bad fall and severely skins his knee, he may howl with pain. If a girl of five receives a pretty birthday present, she may squeal with satisfaction and clap her hands. Most young children openly express what they feel.

In later childhood, adolescence, and as adults, we learn to wear masks to hide our clear-cut feelings or modify them. This conscious control is part of the civilizing process; if we live in a society that can endure, we cannot physically attack each other. We must sometimes put reins on our emotions and the actions which flow from them. We must think of more than our well-being; our neighbors count too.

In certain situations, we must mask our feelings. If you don't like your boss, for example, and you need the money your job brings you to support yourself, a wife, and children, you might have to conceal your dislike to survive.

The trouble is, however, that many people wear masks *when they don't have to.* These masks lead to over-civilization, inhibition, confusion, and weakening of the person's self-image.

We wear too many masks.

The weak man wears a mask of stoicism that covers up his oversensitiveness to injury.

The vain woman wears a mask of indifference that covers up her desire to be liked.

The man who feels he has failed as a breadwinner may wear the mask of the braggart, boring people with his tall tales of success.

The woman who wants to get married pretends that's the last thing that would ever enter her head.

THE MAGIC POWER OF SELF-IMAGE PSYCHOLOGY                    537

These are just a few of the many masks we wear. Sometimes they protect you from a snide remark or two, but they also isolate you from contact with the millions of people who appreciate fundamental honesty, a trait that is becoming rarer and rarer.

## DON'T LET "PERFECTION" FRIGHTEN YOU!

Some people retreat into a defensive shell because of their superficial evaluations of other people. Heavily masked people fool them.

Most people who seem perfect frighten others. Their poise is so complete, their appearance so impeccable, and they hide their emotions so flawlessly. Since they appear to be almost inhumanly perfect, they produce inferiority feelings in others, who feel worthless by comparison.

Don't let such pretense frighten you. Recognize it for what it is: another person's defensive attempt to camouflage his human frailty.

When you see constant perfection in another person, never feel that you must imitate it.

If you can be yourself, with all your human weakness, you're far better off than someone who has to mask himself to stand the strains of modern life.

## YOU CAN BE GENUINE

It's not always easy to be yourself because your weaknesses would then be open to attack, and, realistically, there are always bullies around looking to lift their egos at someone else's expense.

There are some situations in which being yourself, totally unmasked, is unwise. If you're an unconventional person, uninhibited conduct could cost you a job; you also undergo a great deal of embarrassment in situations in which societal control governs rigidly. You certainly would have the common sense to suppress a whoop of happy laughter during the solemn part of a marriage ceremony, even if your emotion was only a friendly one.

Too many people, however, hide their true selves when such suppression is not necessary. This hiding is something like putting yourself in jail for an offense you haven't even committed.

Some people are afraid that if they're genuine, they'll be criticized for being "different." This seems to be an odd criticism since we are all different, and we should be grateful we are individuals. Being genuine gives our lives importance we wouldn't have if we were just robots. Yet some of us prefer to play it safe, living like robots and avoiding potential criticism.

This suppression of self is a terrible sacrifice. Criticism can sting, but if you have any belief in yourself, you can take it, and if a bully picks on you, you will be able to put him in his place. You can, and should, be yourself; life offers you many opportunities without punishment or social ostracism. Sometimes you may even be rewarded for your honesty and uniqueness.

In many fields—entertainment is one—there is a great demand for people whose performance is of high caliber and therefore different. The most attractive person at a party is often one whose comments are interesting because they are all his own. Many business executives climb the ladder of success not through just conforming but because they have been willing to gamble on the original-ity of their creative ideas.

Take a good, long look at your fear of being different, and you'll find that much of your fear is groundless.

Over-conformity can take a heavy toll; it can produce unhappiness. Amy Selwyn's article in the April 1957 *Parents' Magazine,* "Must Your Child Con-form," analyzes the effects of over masking on children:

"Lately, psychologists and sociologists have been taking a close look at chil-dren's social relationships. Their research shows that children who fit smoothly into the group and pattern their activities to match their friends are generally more popular and admired. Some of these children are happy and secure, and their compatibility with the other children is for them a sign of sound develop-ment. But some children who seem outwardly the same are tortured by anx-iety and deep emotional problems. For example, ten-year-old Joe is the most popular boy in his class. The other children always pick Joe first for a team, a committee, or the lead in a class play.

"You might wish that your child were as popular as Joe and fitted as smoothly into his group. But a series of psychological tests showed Joe to be a gravely troubled boy, full of anxiety and fear of failure. He sees himself as unable to cope successfully with life. He doesn't know why he feels this way but thinks that somehow it is all his fault. He has strong feelings of aggression and hos-tility that he doesn't dare express. It is primarily to cover up his inner anger and guilt that he is friendly and conforms to the other children's expectations."

Popularity often cannot compensate for the self-injury involved in over masking. Furthermore, in acting out a part, you may end up losing track of who you are.

## A GOOD FRIEND WILL LIKE YOU FOR YOURSELF

Did you ever hear the story about the fellow who, when describing a friend of his, said, "He's always smiling, always helpful, I've known him 15 years, and he's never once lost his temper or even been irritable"?

At which point, his companion sagely remarked, "He sounds like a saint, but is he a *friend?*"

A good friend will like you for yourself, not for the disguises of who you are.

On Halloween, young friends band together, don masks, and prepare for a day of doorbell-ringing and fun. Masks and Halloween spell gaiety.

For adults, however, forgetting such festive occasions, built-in masks generally spell tragedy. They point to friendships built out of paper, not granite. They mean hiding, not giving. If you feel that you must conceal your real personality from a friend, then one of you is not a good friend. A real friend will accept you as you are, with your strengths and weaknesses, mistakes, and victories. The marriage vow, made "for better or for worse," binds two friends who, ideally, get to know each other in all moods and situations, with disguise impossible, and accept each other, ignoring imperfections.

A good friendship will be like this. You and your friend will know each other, unmasked, and will be loyal to each other's interests.

## HOW A SCHOOLTEACHER MOVED TOWARD FREEDOM

Five or ten years ago, a schoolteacher came to my office. She was unhappy with her face. No feature pleased her. Her nose was too long, her chin too weak, her ears stood out—or so she thought.

I looked at her. I had never seen her before and felt that my appraisal was entirely objective. I saw that she was not a bad-looking woman, that her trouble was her poor estimate of herself.

I improved her appearance with some minor plastic surgery, less than she thought she needed; as I got to know her, I observed that her manner was extremely guarded. She rarely showed even the mildest emotion on her face.

"That's all I can do for you as a plastic surgeon," I said.

She seemed annoyed, but her voice was perfectly modulated as she studied herself in the mirror. "You didn't change my face very much," she accused.

I decided to be completely frank. "Only a little work was needed. I did it, and there's now nothing at all wrong with your face. It's the way you use it, as a mask to cover your feelings."

She looked hurt; her head drooped. "I do my best."

"I'm sure you do," I said. "But, tell me, do you over-control yourself as a teacher?"

Sensing that I was sincere in my desire to help her, she slowly let her defenses down and told me about the miseries in her life. She hated teaching, feeling that she had to be a perfect example for her pupils. Every day she would go to school wearing her imprisoning mask, a model of propriety, hiding all feelings except what she felt to be the "correct" ones. She had always been reserved; now, after three years of teaching, she felt unbearably tense. Not knowing what the trouble was, she misplaced it onto her facial features.

She concluded her story, then burst out weeping. "The kids laugh at me," she sobbed. She stopped suddenly, blew her nose, and sat erect in her chair, looking at me guardedly as if she'd let a horrible secret out.

I smiled. "That's better," I said. "Crying shows that you're human, that you have feelings."

Slowly she relaxed and smiled back.

"The kids laugh at you," I said, "because they can feel that you're always acting, always put on. As a teacher, of course, you have to have self-control. You have to appear competent and mature. But, you don't have to be perfect. A good teacher can look foolish once in a while, and her pupils will still respect her if she's basically sound. They'll like her for being human. Get rid of your mask! You'll feel better with yourself, and you might even enjoy teaching."

She felt better when she left my office, resolving to be a freer person. A few months later, she wrote to me that she no longer worried about her face and felt more relaxed. She felt that she was a more human teacher and, while she still had anxieties in her job, she was confident that in time her classroom would cease to be her jail.

## UNLOCKING THE DOOR TO YOUR REAL SELF-IMAGE

Learn a lesson from this story; let it help you. Your self-image will be strong only when you unlock the door to your human feelings and failings. Otherwise, you will be masked, like a criminal, about to break into a bank.

Assuming that you are not a bank robber, you do not need a mask, not basically, anyway. Your feelings are not so dreadful that you need to inhibit them continually. If you think they are, it is your thinking that needs revision, not your feelings.

If you bury your feelings deep inside you, you cannot have an accurate self-image because you cannot possibly know what you're really like. You can only know what you are pretending to be.

If you're at a party, explaining a heartfelt idea to some people and they frown, do you stop talking or change the subject? You must develop the power of your convictions and stop looking to others for approval or recognition. Otherwise, you will choke off your self-expression and hide behind a mask, crushing your creative self.

Many people were squelched as children and have come to feel that they are unimportant. They continuously take a back seat to others, feeling they are failures and suffer from a deep sense of inferiority.

If this describes you, bury the past and throw off your wraps! Assert your right to be an individual! Be a good parent to yourself; throw off the chains of over-caution and unlock the door to a self-image that has room to expand!

## THE SECRET OF PERSONALITY

Much has been written about "personality," which *Webster's Dictionary* defines as the "quality or state of being personal, or of being a person."

Some writers tell you that to have "personality," you should be dynamic, learn some social skills, or talk about interesting experiences you've had.

I'm against none of these things, but their approach to the subject is superficial. To have "personality," to have "the quality of being a person," you must be able to shed your mask and be yourself, not someone acting out a part in a play that he hasn't written or even helped create.

The great secret of personality is that you must *learn to throw away* your mask and *be yourself.* These concepts can help you:

1. *Do not be afraid to be different.* The people who will scoff at you for your uniqueness are beneath your attention; our most extraordinary creative minds and practical leaders are not afraid to be different; if they were, they wouldn't have reached their levels of success.
2. *Lose your fear of "perfect people."* They are not perfect; they are only acting a part. Don't compare yourself unfavorably to such "paragons of perfection!"
3. *Try to be more spontaneous.* Learn to let go a little. When you're about to talk, don't prepare beforehand what you will say; let the words come out! Most people hate to listen to "canned" conversation; they don't trust it. Remember this: if you say something that sounds silly, nobody's going to shoot you for it. You'll still be alive, and it won't be the last time that you'll be imperfect—at least, I hope not.

4. *Rely on yourself.* A mature person accepts himself, does not look to others for approval. A storyteller who looks from face to face for a smile as he tells a joke will probably end up with no audience. People like to be entertained, dislike being forced to respond. If you look at your actions with kindness, you will be able to express yourself freely.

5. *Squelch your self-critical thoughts.* If you keep criticizing yourself, you will crush your courageous impulses. When you tell yourself, "Maybe I'm foolish," or "Perhaps I'm too assertive" or "I shouldn't have talked so fast," you destroy your real personality, and you're liable to hurriedly get a mask on your face, feeling almost hysterical. Declare war on your self-critical thoughts. Stop tormenting yourself!

6. *Shed your mantle of dignity.* Too many people feel they must be dignified, that it is not proper to express enthusiasm. This idea is ridiculous. A full person should be able to express indignation and, even more, to express positive feelings such as love and enthusiasm. If a friend does you a good turn, don't feel it's shameful to say, "Joe, that was wonderful of you" And, if your wife looks beautiful, don't just nod your head quietly. Put your arms around her and tell her she looks gorgeous. You'll enjoy the wonderful feeling that you can make others happy, and they will like to be with you.

A word of caution, once again: In some situations, you must realistically inhibit yourself. If you have a new job or a new boss, and you're working in a very conventional setting, it might be wise to be cautious. But don't overdo the restraint And, in even such a situation, there may be more freedom for you than you might think.

## PRACTICE EXERCISE: BE YOURSELF

Let's get back to one of the wonderful tools you have at your command—your imagination. Sit in a quiet place where you can concentrate on the job of unmasking yourself and being yourself without camouflage and pretense. Quiet down your thoughts, wrestle away your worries, and just relax. Now call on your imagination to project you into the future. Set a goal for yourself, the achievement of which would make you happy, and picture the steps you will take. Mentally imagine the situations in which you will be involved; see them in concrete detail.

As you move toward your goal, you will make clever moves, and yet sometimes, you will stumble and fall flat on your face. Here's the main point of this exercise: As your mental pictures weave in your mind, *accept your mistakes as well as your winning ways.* To be realistic about yourself and have the ability to be yourself without a mask, you *must be willing to examine and accept your failings.*

Your aim is self-improvement, not the encouragement of error. But you must always have a bottom under you to give you support when things go wrong. If you have no such support, then you'll have to wear a mask.

Let's take an example. You're trying something new. You're a widow, your husband having died two years before. Since his death, you've kept to yourself, feeling sad and lonely. Now you feel a desire to have some people over to your house; you invite them over.

It's a new experience. Your husband used to help you as co-host, and you feel anxious. You're afraid you might appear ridiculous as you try to push people to talk. Or maybe you'll tell a story and forget the punchline. Well, you might. Here's the main point: If *you do, and you still accept yourself, you have the floor under you, and you have nothing to fear.* You do not need to wear a mask!

This story is just an example of what I mean. Naturally, each of you will have your dreams, your specific situations, your problems.

In the sanctuary of your mind, picture your goal and move toward it step by step. Then, as you imagine your erring, see and feel the embarrassment of it, but also see yourself accepting your lack of perfection, living with it, giving yourself understanding when you need it.

This exercise will help you be yourself; if you can live with your mistakes, you will never hide behind a mask.

# 10

## SEX AND THE SELF-IMAGE

SEX IS MUCH TALKED ABOUT IN PUBLIC AND IN PRIVATE. IT USED TO BE A TABOO subject when I was a boy, but today almost everybody talks about it. In pre-Freudian days, people would blush at the mention of this "sinful" word; today, it is a fashionable word. In a way, this is healthy, for it is harmful to hide anything important in darkness.

And yet, with all the fuss, many *people talk about sex with* such *ignorance*.

You've all stopped at a newsstand and glanced around you at endless magazine covers of bosomy blondes trying to entice you. Then there are paperback book covers of muscular "he-men" attacking half-naked, curvy girls and newspaper headlines screaming of sexual attack in large, black type.

Is this what sex is all about? Is sex a woman with a 38-size bosom and perfect legs? Is sex a man six-foot-tall with bulging muscles?

Remember the old proverb: *You can't judge a book by its cover?* Well, it's that way with sex! And men who are five foot two can take comfort. So can women who are somewhat tall or overweight by current beauty standards. Sex is not just something physical. You can't order it at your department store, and you can't buy it, all packaged, at your supermarket.

*Sex is spiritual; sex is something that is in your heart and soul.*

### THE HOLLYWOOD SEX IMAGE

Where did all the trouble start? When did sex become a commodity? I'm not a sociologist or a sexologist, so I can't give you a definite answer.

But probably the development of the film industry had something to do with it. As the popularity of movies became a national institution, people began to hero-worship beautiful (or handsome) Hollywood stars, and these stars became symbols of desirability. In film, being a visual communications medium, the emphasis on the image and physical appearance became of paramount importance. Adolescent boys and girls, forming their self-images, tried to model themselves after reigning movie queens and kings. Still, this imitation was often superficial and as hollow as many of the unrealistic movies that have come off the production lines. And so, too often today, grownups, who were once adolescents, model their sexual self-image after the concepts they have learned watching Hollywood movies. But sexual appeal is much more than a physical thing. Good looks are nice, but they are secondary to spiritual substance and emotional maturity.

## THE HOMELY BOY WHO GOT THE DANCE WITH THE PRETTY GIRL

Believe me; I am telling you the truth. But do more than this: *visualize it!* Go back into the theater of your mind. Sit down in your chair, munch some popcorn if you wish, and enjoy the drama I will unfold for you. The plot is real; this is not an unrealistic soap opera.

There's a school dance in this large gymnasium. The 14-piece orchestra is playing, and the dance floor is crowded. The boys are wearing suits, ties and white shirts. The girls are wearing pretty red and blue and black dresses, their hair is pretty, and they wear high heels. There's laughter and conversation as people enjoy themselves or try to pretend they're having fun. On the sidelines, many teenagers stand in groups. Three girls stand together, giggling, and nearby are six boys, trying to look sophisticated and confident. A tall, handsome young man leaves his group, walks smoothly up to one of the girls, an attractive redhead in a green dress, and asks her for the next dance.

"Sorry, Jim, but all my dances are booked up."

The boy's chin drops, and he mutters something and goes back to his group. "I'm a jerk," he snarls. "Why did I even ask her? Who does she think she is?"

The other guys kid him. Then one fellow, not so good-looking, a head shorter, too skinny, says, "Well, I'd like to ask her."

The tall, good-looking fellow says, "Come on. She wouldn't dance with you—not in a million years."

The shorter fellow smiles agreeably, walks over to the girl, she nods at him, and they walk over to the dance floor and begin foxtrotting.

Later, there's an intermission and, while the orchestra takes a break, Harriet and her girlfriend Geraldine drink punch at the refreshment table. Harriet says, "You know, Jeri, I couldn't help hearing the boys talking to Jim a few minutes ago. He's sore because you turned him down."

"Jim? Who does he think he is? What a conceited nothing! He has looks, sure, but he's too aggressive and overbearing. He thinks he's God's gift to women. He can fool some girls, but not me.

"Now Steve, he's short, but I like him. He has a wonderful sense of humor, and he's just himself—he doesn't try to impress me or to be someone else. He's friendly and considerate, and he doesn't think he's doing me a favor by asking me to dance."

All right, you have seen this drama. Learn from it!

## IS SEX SKIN-DEEP?

Learn that sex appeal is not good looks. It is not "glamorous" clothes. It is not a smooth manner.

If your success mechanism works for you, if you feel that men are your brothers and women are your sisters, if you feel part of humanity, if you're willing to bend if you make a mistake, if you're not afraid to love somebody, then you're on first base sexually.

If you care about people, if you are capable of feeling compassion, these qualities contribute to your sexual attraction. If you have a sense of direction and are capable of understanding another's needs, if you have self-confidence and accept yourself as you are, these qualities also enhance your sexual appeal. These qualities are essential to the appeal of a woman as well as that of a man. In my drama, Jeri chose Steve over Jim because he was a well-rounded person whom she liked. Jim's negative character traits took away from his physical attractiveness. Steve, on the other hand, was a charitable person.

By "charitable," I don't mean that one gives large financial contributions to the Community Chest or the Red Cross. A charitable person is sympathetic to people, and understands his role in the world, knows that he will get what he gives. Steve's attraction was his outgoing personality, which he gave to others. Jim was narcissistic, felt only for himself, and thought that was enough.

Whether she's 18 or 60, a woman looks for this consideration in a man without knowing it. The newspapers are full of stories about Hollywood stars leaving young musclemen because so often she discovers that's all the guy has—muscles. The more mature a girl is, the more she will go toward men with strong emotional qualities.

If a woman has an average appearance, a sensible man will also go toward her if she is emotionally mature. As a young man, he may be attracted mostly to physical qualities, but when he wants to get married and settle down he will, if he's wise, look for a woman with a heart. Famous men often choose to marry normal, average women who are considerate and comfortable to live with.

This doesn't mean that beautiful women are just nothings. More and more, they realize that they need more than beauty. But some beautiful women are spoiled. Like the muscle men, some women are used to taking, not giving; some expect the world to be handed to them on a platter. They are heading for heartache, and when they get older and their physical beauty fades, they feel that they have lost everything.

The physical aspect does exist, though, in sex, and an ugly deformity brings suffering. Literature is full of deformed people who come to tragic ends. There's the classic case of the "Hunchback of Notre Dame" and the pitiful story of Toulouse-Lautrec, who felt that only a prostitute could tolerate him. In these cases, personal appearance has a deep meaning.

The millions and millions of dollars that women spend each year on cosmetics and hairdressing—this too has meaning. They are not just throwing their money away. Such care for one's physical appearance is healthy. However, a woman is unhealthy when her looks become primary to her, and she overlooks the existence of deeper qualities. Hiding behind a wig, a woman may hide her self-image.

Still, a woman likes to see a good-looking man, and a man likes to see a pretty woman. Real ugliness can be a deterrent to sexual appeal. The *"Ugliest Girl in America"* reminds me of a story.

About 20 years ago, a magazine decided that, instead of looking for the most beautiful girl in America, it would run a contest to choose the ugliest girl in the country. Its motives were not cruel; perhaps, it was felt, they could transform this girl into someone physically desirable. The magazine would be doing something positive in staging this contest. They would give this girl a chance to improve herself.

The magazine was flooded with photos from all over the country, and the editors picked the "winner," a girl with poor features, terrible grooming, and appalling clothes.

Her fare was paid to New York, and specialists went to work on her. I was called in to fix her nose and build up her chin, a hairdresser improved her hairdo, clothes experts fitted her out with new dresses and hats, and a few other technicians did their part. And she became stunning almost overnight. To cap this amazing Cinderella story, a few months later, she was married. I heard about her a few years ago. She has five or six children, if I remember correctly, and I believe she's now a grandmother. Her change in physical appearance brought meaning to her life.

This makes me wonder, Suppose she had never been selected? What would have happened to her? Would she have gotten married? I don't know, but I doubt it. Indeed her improved looks helped her chances.

But it was not just because of the improved appearance. Before the change, she was inhibited. After she was able to give of herself to others and she met her husband. This is–It is a success story, and it should be a lesson to anyone whose physical appearance is holding her (or him) back. She indeed received an extraordinary amount of help but, without this aid, you too can better your appearance if it's poor, if you are willing to drive yourself into action. It is a way to take care of yourself. She had some surgical touch-ups that are not always necessary, but the care for her appearance boosted her confidence. Anyone can work with what they have.

And good physical appearance, along with other aspects of the success mechanism—understanding, compassion, sense of direction, charity, self-esteem, and self-acceptance—will improve your self-image and your chances to achieve a good sexual adjustment.

## THE TRUTH ABOUT SEX

Still, today's people are very conscious of appearance; almost everyone makes the most of their natural equipment—physically. Most women especially are neat and trim, well dressed, and well-groomed.

So that if there is trouble with sex today despite all the boastful talk—and I certainly feel there is–It is that many people think it is a purely *physical* thing. The real truth about sex is a glorious one experienced by only a lucky few.

Studies reveal that many of the students in U.S. colleges have inferiority feelings. Indeed, their concepts of themselves are mainly concerned with sex, these being young people in their late teens and early twenties.

These are also times of troubled marriages and frequent divorces. Moreover, many people fear marriage too much to undertake such a "traumatic" enterprise and spend their lives in constant, superficial dating, going from summer resort to summer resort and from dancehall to dancehall. This social treadmill is great for a young man of 25 but is not nearly as appropriate when he's 45 and is still afraid of a deep, basic relationship.

Studies on sexual adjustment in marriage have revealed the existing difficulties. In one study, only slightly more than half of the people interviewed believed there had been a good sexual adjustment from the beginning of the marriage and 12 percent believed they had never succeeded, even after being married for two decades.

A survey of 1000 marriages found that two out of every five people were sexually maladjusted.

In another study, almost half the married people interviewed cited sexual maladjustment as the chief trouble in their union.

The case of Marilyn Monroe, one of this century's great "sex symbols," was an especially tragic one. With all her beauty, she thought she lacked something and was lonely in her heart. Gorgeous as she was, her concept of herself was a negative one. To my knowledge, it has not been conclusively proved that she killed herself, but if she did, it is because she thought she was of little value as a person.

I met Marilyn Monroe once on the west coast when she was married to Arthur Miller. I also met her at Sardi's in New York when we were dining with the same group. I thought to myself that she was an interesting, alive, intelligent woman. Her opinions were sincere and serious. She seemed charming to me.

But her self-image was apparently weak, and the opinions of others could not change this.

Ironically, movie publicity developed the great image of Marilyn Monroe for millions to see—one of the celebrated sex images of our time—and yet her own self-image was neglected. Today she is dead, a tragic heroine, so people throw bouquets, as they sometimes did when she was living and seemed burdened with personal guilt stemming from an unhappy childhood. When one's self-image is poor, it is not easy to live with oneself.

And so others gave her a stature which she apparently could not give herself!

This reminds me of something that happened to me a few months ago. My nurse told me that a woman wanted to see me. She had read my books and knew a friend of mine, and she wanted to tell me about her troubles. I'm not a psychiatrist, but I said I'd be happy to listen to her if it would help ease her mind.

She had been raped by a soldier in a small town when she was just four years old, and later, at ten, her father had made sexual advances. She seemed relieved to tell me about these sordid childhood experiences and to feel that I still accepted her.

I saw before me a good-looking middle-aged woman, intelligent and sensitive, but I could also sense that she did not feel her own worth. This blot from the past still infected her soul, and she had no proper focus on the fine qualities she possessed. I doubt that she emotionally felt worthy of enjoying a full sexual experience with her husband.

Sex appeal, real sex appeal, is accentuating the positive and eliminating the negative. It is overcoming your failure instincts and relying on your success mechanism.

Fear, anger, uncertainty are feelings that make people withdraw from other people into a world of emptiness. To attain real sex appeal, you must lick these negative feelings and live dynamically and positively.

The sex act itself is more than a physical act. It involves genuine participation and unreserved giving between two people.

## MASCULINITY AND FEMININITY

There is much talk these days about "masculinity" and "femininity." What should a man be like, and what should a woman be like?

I feel that this is another little-understood subject. There are men, and there are men; there are women, and there are women. All are unique. God created all to be themselves, not to be governed by rigidly prescribed rules.

This is another area of illusion in these troubled times. Suppose you see a tall, hairy, handsome young man in a television commercial, and he looks vigorous and athletic. Is he more "masculine" than, say, Albert Schweitzer, who has dedicated himself to humanity?

Curiously, some people would say he is. They would fall once again for the physical image and forget about the heart that gives and the mind that makes us what we are.

The Schweitzers of this world who give of themselves to other people, *I believe* are real men. I don't know how tall he is or how muscular; perhaps he is physically strong, and maybe he is not, but this is a man.

Dorothy Dohen, in *Women in Wonderland* (Sheed & Ward, 1960), describes sociologist Margaret Mead's research on males and females in primitive tribes. She studied the customs of the Arapesh, Mundugumor and Tchambuli tribes. "Among the Arapesh she found both sexes gentle, responsive, unaggressive and 'maternal,' both men and women participating in child care; among the Mundugumor, both men and women are aggressive, harsh and violent; among the Tchambuli, sharply divergent roles are prescribed for the sexes and are accompanied by marked temperamental differences, but the roles reverse Western notions about what is naturally male and female; economic life is supervised by the women, and the men devote themselves to art and ceremony.

"Margaret Mead's research seemed to prove once and for all that biology is not determining and that it is culture which accounts for the different personalities of men and women," the author concludes.

So you see that different societies have different standards for men and women. In our society, dominated by advertising media and movies, the masculine ideal is the strong, young muscleman with flashing teeth. The feminine ideal is the shapely, bosomy blonde with the perfect legs and the come-on manner.

I cannot fall for this nonsense. To me, a man is biologically a man, and a woman is biologically a woman, and the physical characteristics take care of themselves. I look for the person. I look for such qualities as compassion and relatedness and self-respect. If a man treats other human beings with the compassion he would have for a loved brother, I say that he is a good man. If he relates to other people simply and sincerely, I say that he is a good man. If he has self-respect, if his self-image is an asset, he is truly complete.

I would judge a woman by the same standards.

Let me say to you reading this book: Do not worry about being "masculine" or "feminine." Just insist upon your right to be yourself, to live as creatively and happily as you can, and to enjoy dynamic give-and-take with your fellow human brothers and sisters.

## YOU DON'T HAVE TO BE A SUPERMAN

Many of you have doubtless seen the movie *Period of Adjustment,* adapted from Tennessee Williams' play. One of the main characters in this comedy is a young man who feels he must be a "superman." As a result, he develops the "shakes," is hospitalized, and, when married, gets into all kinds of fights with his wife because he must keep proving what a great, big man he is.

He is all around you. So many men today feel that they must be all-powerful, immune to hurt, stoical. They imprison their soft feelings, crush other people to prove they're men, and make life—which, God knows, is difficult enough— just a little harder for other people. And, they torture themselves if they're not just as brave as a private eye they've seen on TV or a cowboy they've seen in a Hollywood movie.

If you, reading this book, feel like this, let me help you relax and enjoy yourself, please. It's so simple! Just remember that you were once a little boy who cried when he skinned his knee. Just remember that you're a man, and you don't have to prove it all the time, sexually or any other way. Just stop trying to be a superman. You'll feel so much better.

## YOU'RE AS BEAUTIFUL AS YOU FEEL

And you women, be yourselves! You don't have to look like Lana Turner or Sophia Loren, you don't have to have a perfect figure, and you don't have to act sophisticated or phony.

If you're neat and make the most of your physical traits, if you're genuine, you'll get along if you do your best to fulfill your responsibilities. And, if you feel sisterly compassion for others, people will love you for it.

Remember this absolute truth: if you feel beautiful, you are beautiful, and no one can take it away from you unless you renounce the power of your own happy feelings.

## SEX AND MARRIAGE

Sex is a simple animal function, yet it can be given on the deepest level between two people. In marriage, it helps to unite two people who have chosen to merge their destinies.

If two people can give to each other, they can reinforce each other's strengths and encourage each other's talents and resources in the partnership of marriage. Through the God-given sexual function, they can produce children who are the fruit of their joy.

If these married people accept each other as they are, without fault-finding, and if they want to be happy and successful, sex will be no problem. It will need no effort, no advice, no learned study.

Marriages are in trouble when people cannot give to each other. A marriage is a complicated social relationship, with endless functions and responsibilities involved, especially when there are children. When there's dissension, it can go downhill fast. A house divided against itself will have a hard time surviving.

If two people care for each other and are willing to forget their grudges after a fight, their marriage can bring them closer to each other and the rest of the human race. Love is the essential ingredient of a good marriage.

When the children grow up and leave, happily married people will not be desolate, for they still have an affectionate feeling for each other.

## IF YOU LOVE, YOU ARE SOMEONE

Everyone wants to be important; I guess it's a universal desire to want to be "someone." But you don't have to be a millionaire; you don't have to be elected to public office; you don't have to be glamorous or muscular; you don't have to be a war hero! If you love, you are someone!

If you care for other people and do your best to be a contributing member of society, if your liking shines through other people's mistakes and weaknesses, even their occasional hypocrisy—you are someone. People will give you recognition for something that is increasingly becoming all too rare in this world. As the great English poet Spenser wrote many years ago: *Love is lord of truth and loyalty.* Some day people will stop talking about sex and go back to talking about love.

## GIVING WILL ENHANCE YOUR SELF-IMAGE

It is love that involves giving, practicing the qualities that lead to success, and inhibiting those that breed failure. Giving to others without idealizing them helps you to accept yourself for what you are. It provides a true dimension to your self-image. It involves reaching out to other people and living more fully. Psychologist Erich Fromm has expressed this beautifully in *The Art of Loving* (Harper & Row, 1956):

"The most fundamental kind of love, which underlies all types of love, is *brotherly love.* By this, I mean the sense of responsibility, care, respect, knowledge of any other human being, the wish to further his life. This is the kind of love the Bible speaks of when it says: love thy neighbor as thyself. Brotherly love is love for all human beings; it is characterized by its very lack of exclusiveness. If I have developed the capacity for love, then I cannot help loving my brothers. In brotherly love, there is the experience of union with all men, of human solidarity. Brotherly love is based on the experience that we all are one. The differences in talents, intelligence, knowledge are negligible in comparison with the identity of the human core common to all men. In order to experience this identity, it is necessary to penetrate from the periphery to the core. If I perceive in another person mainly the surface, I perceive mainly the differences, that which separates us. If I penetrate to the core, I perceive our identity, the fact of our brotherhood."

This quality of brotherly love can enable you to communicate fully with the people in your world. Without this ability, you would be separate and fearful, and you would be forced to withdraw from life or distort its true value. Your self-image can thrive on identification with other people and compassion for their needs since this helps you to accept your problems better and appreciate your virtues.

We are our brother's keepers. God meant it so. Too often, we forget this, being embroiled in the dog-eat-dog competitiveness of modern civilization. But, when we love others, we are closer to ourselves and a healthy self-image.

Sex in marriage should represent the height of spiritual and physical giving. Two people ideally give to each other as Nature intended, ensuring the propagation of the species—the continuation of life.

Too few people relate this way. A good percentage of the population does not get married, and many marriages end in difficulty or divorce. Deep friendship is not common.

If you have not achieved a feeling of closeness with the opposite sex, do not feel that it is beyond you. You can, with effort, if you'll change your self-image.

If you feel worthless, you have to see new truths about yourself. Otherwise, you'll never go out toward others. You'll figure it's safer to hide behind a shell of inhibitions, as did the "ugliest girl in America" before her physical change.

There are beautiful truths about each of us—if we dehypnotize ourselves from ingrained, negative concepts. Give yourself a break. See yourself at your best, work at developing your most constructive abilities, imagine the triumphs that lie ahead, and work to make these mental pictures a reality.

Relax with a self-image that you're proud of and take a crack at success and happiness. Go back to the practice exercises at the end of many chapters in this book and work on these exercises. Do more than that, think about these ideas and understand how you can make a happy, successful little world for a self that you like.

If you're at peace with your self-image, you'll be able to give to others and will have an excellent chance to consummate a deep sexual relationship, which will have real meaning.

# 11

## ACCEPT YOUR WEAKNESS AND YOU'LL BE STRONG

CHARITY BEGINS AT HOME. YOU CAN'T BE COMPASSIONATE TO OTHERS AT THE same time that you're cruel to yourself.

If you are cruel to yourself, your compassion will not be entirely genuine; you will feel envious when you give something you cannot give yourself. It's something like a poor, struggling man finding ten dollars in the gutter and giving it all to a hardpressed friend of his. How can he help but begrudge his generous gift?

Yet many of you are cruel to yourself. You are critical and condemning of yourself. When you take part in a discussion, you don't like your contribution.

When you look at yourself in the mirror, you don't like what you see. When you survive your life, you are dissatisfied with your achievements. You tell yourself that you are weak, and you hate yourself for it. *The truth is that you are weak, and so am* I. And it's not such a terrible thing!

"Stronger by weakness wiser men become," wrote Edmund Waller, 17th century English poet, and his words ring true today.

We are not supermen, and we are not automatons; we are not gods, and we are not machines. We are all human beings and the offspring of parents who were human beings. We are products of error and creatures of error. Living in troubled times, we all have moments of despair.

In the words of Erich Fromm *(The Art of Loving),* "Man is gifted with reason; he is *life being aware of itself;* he has awareness of himself, of his fellow man, of his past, and of the possibilities of his future. This awareness of himself as a separate entity, the awareness of his own short life span, of the fact that without his will he is born and against his will he dies, that he will die before those whom he loves, or they before him, the awareness of his aloneness and separateness, of his helplessness before the forces of nature and of society, all this makes his separate, disunited existence an unbearable prison. He would become insane could he not liberate himself from this prison and reach out, unite himself in some form or other with men, with the world outside."

Yes, man has needs and terrors. But weakness is not a horrible thing; it is not a curse at all if you accept it.

## WHAT DO YOU EXPECT OF YOURSELF?

The trouble starts when you hate yourself for your weakness. This self-hate destroys you from the inside, defeating you before you can get off the ground. Your expectations of yourself are unfair.

If you own an automobile, are you satisfied if it drives smoothly at 50 miles an hour for 350 miles—or do you expect it to rise off the ground and fly?

If you have a dog, are you happy if it's affectionate and comfortable? Or do you resent it because it doesn't speak English?

Of course, these questions are ridiculous, but they point to the absurdity of your expectations of yourself.

Remember this: *The more you accept yourself as you are, with your weaknesses, the better you will be able to function despite the stresses and strains of civilized living.*

You've all heard the "funny" stories of patients in mental institutions who thought they were Napoleon. Poor, suffering souls. They could not accept the mistakes and failures that were part of their lives and, miserable with loathing for themselves, had to live in a make-believe world where they were all-powerful—like Napoleon. They expected so much of themselves that they destroyed their sense of reality and their connection with the world around them.

If you're a baseball fan, you'll recognize these illustrations of this inherent truth.

How many times have major league teams signed bonus players for huge sums of money only to see them fail, probably crushed by the pressure of others' great expectations of their performance. Then unsung players quietly move up through the minor leagues, learning their trade, to major league stardom!

To feel secure, you must raise the ceiling to rise to the heights and keep a floor below you so you don't fall too far.

## THE "TOUGH GUY"

Most American men expect themselves to be tough and stoical. If they fall below specific superficial standards of toughness, they condemn themselves and crawl into shells of fear and resentment. This can be carried to fantastic extremes. I know men, talented and decent human beings, who have achieved extraordinary things in their lives, who are afraid of the slightest suggestion that they are not "tough guys," too.

Isn't this silly? Yet this "tough guy" fabric has taken root among men in our culture.

I wouldn't be surprised if some men who have committed suicide have done this dreadful act out of self-hatred, arising from their inability to accept weaknesses in themselves, normal weaknesses which most human beings share.

I know men who thought of armed combat during World War II not as an unavoidable duty but as an enjoyable opportunity to prove their courage. They were not sadists, nor were they blind to the genuine dangers of death or crippling. Their desire to prove to themselves and the world that they were "tough" was so strong that no other considerations ever existed.

The August 3, 1963, *TV Guide* issue contains an interesting article about Skitch Henderson, the talented musical conductor of TV's *Tonight Show*. ("Skitch Henderson," by Maurice Zolotow.)

". . . . His mother and father had one of those unbearable marriages, which resulted in divorce when he was very young. Then his mother died.

"He was abnormally underweight and oversensitive as a boy. He was a physical coward.

"He was always being beaten up and ridiculed. His male identity was so threatened that when he grew up, he was continually risking his life to prove he was not afraid to die—racing on the official team of the Mercedes-Benz company, slaloming down the steepest slopes of Sugarbush, Vermont, volunteering for the Army Air Force during World War II.

"He flew the P-38 Lightning with the 15th, 9th, and 4th divisions of the U.S. Air Force in the Pacific. He still holds the rank of major in the aviation reserve. Whenever reporting for his annual service, he flew a jet. He has the kind of raw guts that one does not normally associate with a musician.

"He didn't want to be a musician, really, but it was the one way he had of establishing anything real about himself."

This story is instructive. Here is Skitch Henderson, a charming, talented, and extremely successful man in his field, a man of outstanding sensitivity—

and yet he, too, seemed to fall for the American "tough guy" myth, risking his life to prove himself.

Millions of you American men are in this boat, with a Captain Bly-like, slave-driving master egging you on. You may think the pursuit is worthwhile, but it will lead you only to high blood pressure and a shattered self-image.

A noted psychologist recently blamed the "suicidal cult of manliness" for the fact that, in American society, men seem to lack women's longevity. Many would rather switch the old saying around and be a "dead hero" rather than a "live coward."

Though it's not a question of either heroism or cowardice, we're talking about a common-sense approach to a man's simple self-acceptance, as opposed to the artificial ideal of the "tough guy." We're trying to recognize that every man is not 100% "he-man," nor should anyone expect him to be like this. [Editor's note: Today this might be referred to as a "toxic male."]

One of the most intelligent analyses of the subject is in Dr. David Abrahamsen's *The Road to Emotional Maturity*:

"In reality, we are all a mixture of masculine and feminine traits. Although this mixture is at the root of many of your personality upsets, *it can also be one of your most valuable allies in* helping *you to cope with* many *of your daily problems*. On your road to achieving emotional maturity, you can utilize your knowledge about your male and female characteristics in a way that is beneficial to your emotional development.

"Generally, as we grow up, we are taught to consider certain personality traits as either masculine or feminine. For instance, a man is *supposed* to be hard and unemotional; and a woman *should* be tender and sympathetic. When he is little, a boy is expected to want to run out to play ball with the boys all the time; a girl is expected to want to sit home and play with her dolls. If, as happens in many cases, the boy prefers to sit home and read, listen to music, or do something by himself, he is called a 'sissy,' meaning that he has feminine traits. If the girl prefers to play ball, she is considered a tomboy.

"In a like manner, the man is *expected* to be independent. The woman is *expected* to be dependent. She should not *want* a career; a man should be domineering. A woman should *be* submissive; he serious, she flirtatious; he logical, she intuitive. We can see how a conflict begins to arise because men and women just don't fall into a pattern of either all masculine or all feminine traits—but they feel that they are expected to.

"'What really is femininity and masculinity?' you may wonder at this point, for we have described the traits which are generally considered feminine or masculine. *Femininity, we may say, means that a person prefers a passive goal* to an active goal—*Masculinity, we may say, means that a person prefers an active goal to a passive one.*"

A man does not have to be "tough" all the time. Does it make you more of a man if you talk out of the side of your mouth, like a Prohibition Era gangster? Does it make you less of a man if you cry when a tragedy hits you? Of course not. Use your common sense, and accept your weaknesses as well as your strengths.

## THE "PERFECT WOMAN"

American women wrestle with a different kind of obsessive problem. Too many feel they must achieve a kind of physical perfection, or they are unworthy. This is the other side of the same coin and is equally ridiculous.

As a plastic surgeon, I've met so many beautiful women who thought they were ugly because the slightest blemish was unacceptable to them. Dozens have asked me to operate on deformities that were nonexistent, and I've refused to do this because it would be unethical to take money for doing nothing.

Women do not dread feeling fear or expressing it in their actions. They see nothing wrong in crying now and then. Many are openly nervous and accept it without difficulty.

"Weakness" to them is physical imperfection.

In *The Challenge of Being a Woman* (Harper & Row, 1955), Helen Sherman and Marjorie Coe emphasize the social pressures on modern American women: ". . . In a recent issue of a popular women's magazine, more than half the pictures of women showed them as decorative only, with not even a suggestion that they ever did any work. Only five were women seemingly over forty, while the 20 percent ostensibly working were impractically glamorized."

The authors feel that this goal of physical perfection goes beyond herself to that of her entire environment. ". . . The typical American home no longer resembles a Currier and Ives lithograph crowded with adults and children having a good time together. It looks instead like a composite advertisement for the latest in furniture, home appliances, wallpaper, and broadloom carpeting, with the family seldom all together because one or another of them is elsewhere on achievement bent."

Let's face it: Every woman cannot look like Elizabeth Taylor, and the fact that she doesn't is no cause for inferiority feelings. If she feels she must, she is courting defeat, encouraging the destruction of her self-image.

Women should try to get a fuller perspective of life, developing their spiritual and creative resources, setting goals for their days. Most important, stop blaming yourself if you're not the "Perfect woman" that doesn't even exist.

## WE ALL MAKE MISTAKES

Any formula for happy living that prescribes 100 percent this-or-that is doomed to failure before it is applied because, as human beings, we cannot measure up to such rigid yardsticks without excess tension. We all make mistakes, and we must face up to this realization without bombarding ourselves with self-hatred.

In a Detroit automobile assembly line, perfection is required. One lapse in the mechanics could produce a car that is not safe to drive.

Human beings cannot live up to such perfection, and it is not necessary. We can function quite well despite our shortcomings.

According to the Bible, "My strength is made perfect in weakness."

Please note the phrasing: "made perfect." Nothing about tolerating weakness, but an acknowledgment of the role weakness plays in promoting one's strength.

We all have made mistakes in the past, and we will blunder in the future also. We will fall into negative thinking now and then; we will feel hatred and envy when things look black.

If you're a salesman, you'll sometimes use the wrong approach in trying to close a sale.

If you're a mother, you will not always dress the baby appropriately for the temperature, and she will get a cold.

If you're a student, you'll pass English and history but do poorly in physics.

If you're an investment counselor, you'll occasionally give a customer unwise counsel.

Mistakes are part of living; you can't always avoid them.

## IF YOU PUNISH YOURSELF FOR YOUR MISTAKES, WHAT DO YOU GAIN?

The tragedy is that many people berate themselves for their mistakes for days, weeks, even for their whole lifetime.

"If I had only not put that money in that property . . ." they say. Or "If I'd only been a little more alert, the accident wouldn't have happened."

Re-enacting their failures over and over in their minds, they remind themselves what fools they were, what incompetents.

They punish themselves remorselessly in a never-ending castigation that serves no positive purpose.

This self-criticism not only makes them feel miserable but also afflicts them with nervous tensions that will bring on more mistakes in a vicious cycle that knows no end.

Some women never stop thinking about physical imperfection. They dwell on it as if it's the only thing in the world that is real.

If their bosom is not the specified size or their nose hooks slightly, their resentment knows no bounds. They punish themselves as if they were to blame for this pseudo-calamity.

What do they gain from this? Nothing. What do they lose? The serene power of a healthy self-image.

Stop punishing yourself!

## BE KIND TO YOURSELF

Even the most successful men have their limitations.

Former Vice President Richard Nixon played football for unsung Whittier College. He was a tackle but too light for the position; he was only a second-stringer.

He rarely played in a game, but he still missed few practice sessions and cheered his teammates from the bench for most of the four football seasons. Nixon's acceptance of his limitations won his football coach's admiration and helped lift his team's morale.

All men have difficult moments.

Carl Sandburg, the great American poet-author, tells of his in *Always the Young Strangers* (Harcourt, Brace & World, Inc., 1952–1953): "I had my bitter and lonely hours moving out of boy years into a grown young man. I can remember a winter where the thought often came that it might be best to step out of it all.

"After that winter, the bitter and lonely hours still kept coming at times, but I had been moving in a slow way to see that to all the best men and women I had known in my life and especially all the great ones that I had read about, life wasn't easy, life had often its bitter and lonely hours, and when you grow with a new strength of body and mind, it is by struggle."

Life is a bitter struggle indeed, and you can happily survive only if you are kind to yourself. Success is a process of overcoming one's defects and plunging through desert land to an oasis of greenery.

A biographer wrote of Thomas Edison that "Shy or retiring he might be, but once he began to talk about an idea or an invention that was close to his heart, he could become surprisingly lucid and even eloquent." (*Edison*, by Matthew Josephson, McGraw Hill Co, 1959.)

A classic case of a man who was kind to his shortcoming and rose through them to great heights is that of our great President, Abraham Lincoln. In *Living Lincoln* (Rutgers University Press, 1955), editors Paul M. Angle and Earl Schenck Miers tell the story of the Lincoln-Douglas debates. "Voters saw two men as different as men could be. Although Douglas was little more than five feet in height, his broad shoulders, massive chest, and deep musical voice conveyed an impression of strength and sturdiness. Lincoln—thin, bony, awkward—stood a foot above his rival. As he began to speak, his voice would be high-pitched and nasal, but as he warmed to his work, the pitch would drop, and his words would carry to the outer limits of a crowd of thousands.

"On January 5, 1859, the General Assembly of Illinois confirmed the fall election result by returning Stephen A. Douglas to the United States Senate. By this time, Lincoln had put the defeat behind him and plunged into his law practice—partly to make up for the time he had lost and the money spent in the preceding six months and partly to push the memory of failure from his mind.

"But Lincoln could no longer devote himself wholly to law. His debates with Douglas had been reported all over the country.

"A short six months earlier, the name of Abraham Lincoln had hardly been mentioned outside the state of Illinois, now millions knew it. Letters came from strangers asking for Lincoln's views on political questions; others begged for speeches. Despite the defeat, he had become a man of national prominence."

Here is a wonderful man whose inner strength shone through his defects because he accepted his weaknesses and concentrated on the job at hand—because he believed in himself, and because he could be kind to himself.

He was a human being, just like you and me. His deification as a political figure was in the future. What he could do, in terms of his concept of himself, you can do in terms of your self-evaluation. Maybe you can't be President, but you can be a successful human being.

## ACCEPTING YOUR WEAKNESS WILL FORTIFY YOUR SELF-IMAGE

If you make peace with your weaknesses, you will fortify your self-image. In ceasing to criticize yourself, you will emphasize the "plus" factors in your personality. You will look for things to like in yourself, and you will find them.

These hints will help you:

1. *Learn your limitations.* We all have our breaking points, physical and mental. They vary with the individual; some people can stand up under some forms of pressure but will buckle under other stresses. Stop criticizing yourself for being "weak," and instead, get in the habit of recognizing your limitations.

2. *Honor your limitations.* Once you are aware of your breaking points, use this knowledge to help yourself. Don't push yourself beyond your limits just to prove to other people that you are courageous! It takes courage to make decisions for yourself, even if some insensitive people may sneer at you.

3. *"Toughness."* Men should not feel that they have to be super-masculine heroes! Most characters of this type are fictional creations, products of writers' lively imaginations. Real-life men have failings as well as strengths. Sometimes troubles will pile up, and, in despair, you'll feel like crying. It is nonsense that a man shouldn't cry; liberate yourself from such a foolish belief!

4. *"Perfection."* Women have other attributes more valuable than the physical image one can see in a mirror. Shake free from the superficial thinking that leaves scars on your self-image! You can't afford these scars.

5. *Always be true to yourself.* None of us likes the friend who smiles at us when we're rich and disappears when we've lost our money. It's the same way with yourself. If you admire your strength and hate your weakness, you're not true to yourself. Your self-image will never be steady; you'll never be happy. Accept yourself when you hit rock-bottom, and you have a foundation for growth.

## LOOK AHEAD TO A BRIGHT FUTURE

One word of caution here: Do not resign yourself to weakness.

Your strength lies in accepting your weaknesses and then trying to rise above failure to succeed. When I talk about accepting your weaknesses, I don't mean that you resign yourself to permanent, self-induced inadequacies.

Since most people downgrade themselves and are afraid to go forward, there is a danger that some of you will misunderstand my meaning. I don't admire the Calamity Joes and Calamity Janes in life, always crying in their soup about what terrible things life has done to them.

This book's purpose is positive, helping you improve your self-image, so I must point out that in accepting your weaknesses, you accept yourself as a total human being with the assets and liabilities to which you are heir. With full awareness of your limitations, you plan your days optimistically, accepting your limitations and yet rising above them to your full potential strength. You should make peace with your failings, forget about them, and move on to your daily goals—all in the process of living.

Forget the failures of yesterday and the fears of tomorrow—they don't exist! Think of today and achieve something worthwhile—and you'll be strong!

# 12

# HOW TO BE AN INDIVIDUAL
# IN AN AGE OF CONFORMITY

IN VAST NUMBERS, SOCIAL CRITICS HAVE LABELED THIS "THE AGE OF CONFOR-mity," postulating that modern man, terrified by technological and other forces beyond his control, tries to gain security by imitating the other fellow. He sacrifices his individual identity but achieves a sense of comfort in his feeling of oneness with other human beings.

*In America as a Civilization* (Simon & Schuster, 1957), columnist-educator Max Lerner writes that "Cultural stereotypes are an inherent part of all group living, and they become sharper with mass living. There have always been unthinking people leading formless, atomized lives. What has happened in America is that the economics of mass production has put a premium on uniformity. America produces more units of more commodities (although sometimes of fewer models) than other cultures." The real dangers of the American mode of life are not in the machine or even in standardization as much as they are in conformism. Is "rugged individualism" a thing of the past? Are we today puppets which Fate pulls this way and that, controlling our destiny? The answer to both questions is *no, if*—if your self-image allows you the freedom that makes a human being God's proudest creation.

If you enslave yourself to others' opinions, inhibiting your thoughts and actions, it is because you have no genuine regard for yourself. Other people must shower approval on you because you do not trust yourself; you must continually act the way you feel others expect you to act because you have no faith in your own standards.

## THE PIONEER SPIRIT

Some social scientists approach the subject of "conformity" from a historical standpoint.

They see a relationship between the expansive, optimistic, outgoing American of the nineteenth century and the existence of unclaimed lands in the West, which gave the restless spirit somewhere to go.

In those days, they say, a man felt a sense of freedom in living his life. If pressures hemmed him in or if his fellows labeled him a failure, he could always pack up and travel to some less-populated region where he might make a fortune almost overnight.

The pioneers, living in an atmosphere of sudden death and sudden wealth, were individualists.

Theodore Roosevelt wrote about the early range men, "Yet there was not only much that was attractive in their wild, free, reckless lives but there was also very much good about the men themselves. They were frank, bold, and self-reliant to a degree. They feared neither man, brute, nor element."

The wild life had negative aspects, too: when unrestrained self-interest flared up, and people shunned civilized codes, violence snuffed out lives swiftly.

Still, the pioneers were cheerful people who lived dynamic, though numbered, days. If the newly evolving society's rules were too strict, the open spaces of unsettled lands offered them refuge.

Lerner believed that "Self-reliance, courage, alertness, obstinate endurance, friendliness, a democratic informality are traits that emerged from the continuous cycles of land settlement."

"Home on the Range," once reputedly President Franklin Delano Roosevelt's favorite song, admirably captured this spirit.

## END OF THE FRONTIER

With the end of the nineteenth century, the frontier, geographically speaking, came to an end, but many areas were sparsely populated. During this century, people have emigrated to these pockets of opportunity, filling them up. Texas, which in 1900 had a population of slightly less than three million, in 1960 boasted over nine million. California, whose population was about one and a half million in 1900, reported a 1960 population of around fifteen and a half million. The open spaces have been occupied more and more, and dissatisfied people have not had a land of opportunity as barren as they used to have.

Railroads have long since joined together big cities and out-of-the-way spots.

Airplanes have further narrowed the gap, timewise, and radio and television have invaded small-town outposts with big-city values.

If civilized pressures plague you today, there is no longer an easy way out—at least not in this heavily populated country. But do not let this cause you the slightest despair.

*This populated world need not be the end of your frontier; you need not pull in your horizons.* Inside you, you have powers that dwarf any of the phenomena just described. Perhaps they have been lying dormant within you, waiting for proper cultivation.

This understanding of your inner horizons is essential to remember when you feel depressed: Thinking, mental picturing, *about yourself, and your world, here is your great secret weapon.* Read this chapter thoroughly, and you will begin stockpiling ammunition that will fortify you to be your own person in this mechanical age.

If this is what you want, you can do it.

## "KEEPING UP WITH THE JONESES"

Living in modern society is simple if we know how. In certain areas, we must conform to the rules of the group. There is no alternative if we are to be accepted as members of our civilization. Simultaneously, there are other areas in which we are free to express the fundamental individuality that separates us from others. One of the significant errors in modern life is people's overestimation and overapplication of the first area. Too many people buy the latest model car because their neighbors did or move into a specific style house for the same reason, a phenomenon popularly known as "keeping up with the Joneses."

There's an illuminating passage in Vance Packard's big-seller, *The Status Seekers* (David McKay Co., 1959): "While observing the 1958 convention of the nation's home builders in Chicago, I heard one of the featured speakers, a home-marketing consultant, report that he and his aides had conducted 411 'depth interviews' in eight cities to find what people are seeking when they buy a home. In many cases, he reported, mid-century home buyers are buying themselves a symbol of success, and he discussed at length strategies for giving a house being offered for sale 'snob appeal.' Many other experts in home selling have recently cited snob appeal as one of the great secret weapons. One strategy, he said, is to drop some French phrases in your advertisement. French, he explained, is the language of the snob. Later in the year, we began seeing newspaper advertisements of housing developers drenched in French."

If you over-conform like this, you cannot be happy because you are not living your own life. *You are living someone else's, and thus you're only partly yourself.*

Conformity, however, need not be a negative word; it can be a positive one. Civilizations endure because there is a certain amount of positive conformity from their citizenry.

"We are members one of another," we find in the Bible.

By conformity, in its practical sense, I don't mean being like someone else but agreeing to share with others the wonders of the world—if we agree that there are limits to this process. This understanding of the word is fruitful conformity, a vitamin pill that gives us all sustenance.

Conformity, in the true sense, means helping each other without stepping on each other's toes or stepping on your own toes. It is an active concept, rooted in the life-giving feeling of liking your neighbor and experiencing compassion for others. It is a token of brotherly love, in which one gives of himself instead of sitting around waiting for someone to give to him.

## WE MUST CONFORM TO CERTAIN RULES

Living among people and compartmentalized in living space, we must follow specific rules for the common good. We must honor others' property and drive an automobile safely; we must not set fire to our neighbors' houses if we are angry at them. On the job, a man must often watch his step. If your boss is an envious man and he drives a five-year-old Ford, it might be dangerous for you to show up for work driving a brand-new Cadillac. By the same line of reasoning, your wife might cost you your job at your office Christmas party if she comes in a gorgeous $85 dress when your boss' wife is dressed more simply.

"Making a living" means just that: the man of the family, the "breadwinner," is earning the money that ensures his family's very existence, and in this area, a person must sometimes be very cautious. If you work for a large corporation, conforming to specific rules may be essential if you are not to lose your job. Working women also may encounter similar pressures, as many mothers engaged in community activities. Many of you, however, have vast areas of freedom that you do nothing to exploit. You give about eight hours a day to your job, but that leaves you eight to relax and eight in which you can sleep. There is nothing in the contract that says you have to sleep on the same kind of pillow the boss uses or smoke the same kind of cigars he likes. There is nothing in the contract that says you can't buy an air conditioner because his wife hates air conditioning. Your conforming ends when you leave your job to go home, and you can balance this conforming by developing your individual thoughts and resources when you are away from the job.

You can plan the future for your wife and children your way. You can relate to your friends your way. You can think your thoughts and work on your hobbies and, in your own home, you are a king, and your wife is the queen.

In your community, your active conformity in projects that you believe in, the spirit of brotherly love you give to such enterprises is the positive type of conformity. I mentioned earlier; this conformity can develop your personality in healthful channels if you have the courage of your convictions. In these activities, too, you can express your uniqueness as you participate in group causes.

## YOU CAN BE YOURSELF

So, you do have vast areas in which to express your unique personality and to be yourself. Too many adults fail to take advantage of these growth opportunities, preferring to submerge themselves in the herd.

Allen Funt, the originator of "Candid Camera," said recently *(TV Guide,* "Allen Funt's Candid Kids," June 22, 1963), "Children are beautiful. . . . They're so original, so independent.

"They're everything you wish adults were.

"But adults are consistently herd-minded, conformant, subject to group pressure. They're moving in the wrong direction. They're moving away from individualism toward the herd."

Funt contrasts two film clips for "Candid Camera." One shows a man walking up a "down" escalator. Another adult shortly follows him until, unquestioningly, a group of adults tramps up the "down" escalator.

The second film clip illustrates the greater individuality of children. A child walks up to a large, empty box. He inspects it carefully, decides it's a fortress.

He gets into it and shoots away at the enemy. Another child strolls up to the box. He decides it's a house, gets into it, and plays grownup. A third child sees the box, decides it's a roller coaster, and gleefully slides it down an incline.

Why not recapture your individuality, which is your birthright? After you have fulfilled your community's responsibilities, how about treating yourself fairly, exploring your avenues of personal self-development?

A few years ago, I spent a day at the seashore. It was a sunny day, with blue skies, and I was enjoying the beach, talking to friends, watching people leaping the waves. Nearby a young married couple with a young baby were putting down a blanket. The mother put the baby down, and off the little one went, staggering on her unsteady little baby legs.

Her face dead serious, she wobbled up to a family sitting in deck chairs and, to my surprise, picked up a child's chair and carried it over to her amused parents.

She then turned around and, with startling accuracy, carried it back to where she'd picked it up. She then climbed up on it (with difficulty), sat down regally, and surveyed the world with serious calm.

I found myself laughing delightedly at her spontaneous, individual purposefulness.

She was herself, so unlike adults who spend their lives trying to do what they think people expect of them.

As adults, we must respect personal property more than does this baby, but we also can learn from her a lesson in the art of cultivating our *personalities,* which should spring fresh from our inner being.


## YOU OWE IT TO YOURSELF TO BE AN INDIVIDUAL

Deep down, no two people are exactly alike, and you owe it to yourself to develop your individuality. There are too many "carbon-copy" people these days; be an original. This does not mean you should be eccentric unless that is who you are. I certainly do not mean that you must grow a beard or get up on a soapbox and deliver lectures.

Dwight Eisenhower is very much himself, and people love him for it. He is a simple man, above pretentiousness. As a military leader, his humility was remarkable. In *My Friend Ike* (Frederick Fell Inc, 1956), his Army subordinate Marty Snyder tells of Eisenhower's visit to his restaurant after World War II:

"When General Eisenhower returned from Europe, he came to the restaurant for dinner.

"As we sat together, I told him how much I wanted to see him become President, and I admitted that I was talking to many people about it.

"He laughed.

"He said, 'Look, Marty, I'm a soldier, and that's all I want to be.'

"'General,' I said, 'I never wanted to be a soldier, but they drafted me. I guess you can be drafted to run for President if it comes to that.'"

"'I'm sure it won't,' he said."

Ike was just being himself.

## HAVE A MIND OF YOUR OWN!

Your mind is one of your most precious possessions; don't give it up by default! Think your own thoughts, not what you believe others want you to think.

According to John Stuart Mill, renowned nineteenth-century English essayist-philosopher, "If all mankind minus one, were of one opinion and only one person were of the contrary opinion, mankind would be no more justified in silencing that one person than he, if he had the power, would be justified in silencing mankind."

Your inner thoughts especially, are yours to own. Living in a civilized society, rules, customs, and laws may sometimes pose restraints on your actions, but never on your inner thoughts.

"My mind to me a kingdom is," wrote Sir Edward Dyer, the 16th century English poet. Make your mind a kingdom, not a jail! Let your thoughts be free as birds that fly in the sky; don't censure them and criticize them and hate yourself if they don't always fall in with the pocket of the majority opinion, as you know it.

## LEARN TO KEEP YOUR IDENTITY IN A CROWD

Some people have the inner strength to feel their individuality when alone but give up their identity in a crowd of people.

Is this you? When you express an opinion at a social gathering, and someone else laughs at it, do you keep silent and slink off into a shell? If you do, digest these ideas as if they were a good meal. They will give you a different kind of energy, the power to keep your identity in a crowd of people.

1. *Recognize your right to differ.* This country is a democracy, and we all have this right, but many people do not exercise it. Stop playing follow the leader! When you disagree with the majority, some people may criticize you, but a mature person will not inhibit himself when others frown or sell himself for a few approving smiles.

2. *Give yourself approval.* You've got to be your best friend. You can't always count on the other person, even if he's a good fellow, because he's got his own interests to look after, and internal problems may be eating at him.

   Only you can entirely give yourself the acceptance you need and fortify yourself with the "heart" one must have to maintain identity in a crowd.

3. *Don't fear the* bully! Almost all people are decent if you give them a fair chance.

Still, fearful people sometimes discover unscrupulous tactics that win their status. Some exploit people's tendency to feel inferior, dominating crowds of people with verbal brilliance and a threat of ridiculing potential competitors. Learn to withstand verbal taunts and stand up for your right to express your beliefs and your feelings. Remember that deep down, the bully is afraid, and his attacks are defensive cover-ups.

4. *Visualize your successes!* Some days you won't be feeling so good, or you just won't get along so well with a specific crowd of people. You might feel like an outsider.

Don't be depressed! This happens to everybody once in a while. You can restore your confidence if you picture happier moments when you felt freer and more alive. If the mind pictures don't come at first, keep trying. It's worth the effort.

## PEOPLE WHO STUCK TO THEIR GUNS—AND WON

Life has no rose-strewn lanes leading to a door-marked SUCCESS. It's more an up-and-down struggle with grayish graduations of accomplishments.

Former heavyweight champion Joe Louis knew days of bleak poverty as a child in the South.

The great politician Al Smith fought his way out of the slums to power and honor.

Satchell Paige, the remarkable black pitcher, had his greatness obscured for many years when baseball was still a segregated affair.

The very talented Jackie Gleason knew poverty as a child and another bright TV star, Dick Van Dyke, once knew near penniless days.

Others have fought their way up to successful positions in life and maintained their individuality in the process.

A man courageous enough to stand alone is the hero of the movie "High Noon." The small-town sheriff, deserted by his friends, has to stand alone against the band of killers returning to town. Scared, he conquers his fears and subdues the outlaws. This case is fictional but true to life nevertheless.

Has ever a man sustained himself better in the face of criticism than Harry Truman? I doubt it. He refused to be typed, stuck to his convictions, and ignored the attacks of his critics. Newspapers insulted his ability, and even politicians doubted him, but *he kept faith in* himself.

In *The Man From Missouri* (G. P. Putnam's Sons, 1962), Alfred Steinberg reports on a meeting between Truman and Winston Churchill:

(Churchill): "The last time you and I sat across the conference table was at Potsdam, Mr. President."

Truman nodded in agreement.

Churchill's tone changed.

"I must confess, sir, I held you in very low regard then. I loathed your taking the place of Franklin Roosevelt." Truman's wide grin vanished.

"I misjudged you badly." Churchill went on after a long pause:

"Since that time, you, more than any other man, have saved western civilization."

Churchill's initial estimate of Truman was the popular one. According to Steinberg, "No matter how influential his actions or how unswerving his dedication to basic principles, many politicians failed to take Truman seriously. Some could not accept the fact that he was President.

"And when the nation was stunned by Franklin Roosevelt's death on April 12, 1945, part of this emotional shock was attributed to the realization of who had succeeded him. Yet within Harry Truman's lifetime, historians agree that he must be ranked with the strongest of American Presidents."

Truman's "rugged individualism" never passed a stiffer test than in his Presidential victory over Thomas Dewey. Counted out by pollsters and the nation's press, he kept insisting that he would win the country's mandate. He trailed Dewey in early returns, and newspaper headlines even announced a Dewey win, but Truman calmly went to sleep and was not even surprised when he woke up to find he had won.

## OVER-CONFORMING DISTORTS YOUR SELF-IMAGE

In the Bible, we find the assertions that "We are members one of another" and "if a House be divided against itself, that house cannot stand."

These sage comments tell us why a primary measure of conformity is a prerequisite for the continuance of civilized life as we know it.

Over-conformity, too much a part of modern life, is something entirely different. It is a sacrifice of individual identity when this surrender accomplishes no worthwhile purpose.

When you over-conform, you distort your self-image. You no longer know who you are at all because you are always trying to please others. Looking for constant approval when you don't need it, bowing and scraping to relieve your anxiety, you twist out of shape the unique qualities that make you an individual.

To be happy, you must have areas where you can express your uniqueness without fear of real danger. These areas exist if you don't take them away from yourself. When you find them, you will see a part of yourself that will make you feel more whole. Your self-image will be on more solid ground, and you will be happier.

# 13

## HOW TO FUNCTION SUCCESSFULLY UNDER PRESSURE

LIKELY, THE WORLD HAS NEVER SEEN SUCH DAYS OF PRESSURE. THE POSSIBIL-ity of mass destruction is always with us; we must learn to live with the real dangers of the twentieth century.

We used to consider the Balkans the "powder keg of Europe," and an incident in this area set off the explosion that ignited World War I.

Today the whole world is a "Powder keg," and one awesome explosion could kill millions of people in minutes.

The specter of the atomic and hydrogen bombs hang over us. Each day the awareness of the bomb brings diplomatic challenges. Besides technological terrors, this is an era of turmoil, with changes in morality, breakdown of the family, and movements of social unrest, as oppressed peoples increasingly assert their rights all over the world.

A noted nuclear physicist recently stated that we are today in a period of extremely rapid change, technological and social, almost unprecedented in the annals of history.

The September 24, 1963, issue of *Look Magazine* featured an article outlining today's stresses. "Each of us must make difficult moral decisions.

"We are witnessing the death of the old morality. In our world of masses of people, jet-age travel, nuclear power, and fragmented families, conditions are changing so fast that the established, moral guidelines have been yanked from our hands." ("Morality, U.S.A.," by J. Robert Moskin.)

Some contemporary developments have positive possibilities, too. We can use nuclear energy constructively as a source of power, bringing increasing comfort to people. The fight to end racial and color discrimination is a noble one when executed without violence, and the August 28, 1963, civil rights demonstration in Washington was a dignified, forward-looking action. We can optimistically regard the terrifying weapons we have today as deterrents to future world wars because such holocausts would be unthinkable.

Still, the pressures do exist. To deny this would be to stick one's head in the sand, ostrich-like, in defense against fear.

## LIFE IS A SERIES OF CRISES

Aside from global problems, life is a series of minor and major crises.

If you're a mother with young children, one moment, you may be relaxing with a healthy family, only to find that an hour later, the baby may have an alarming temperature of 104 degrees.

If you're the family breadwinner, if your prosperous corporation agrees to merge with another concern, with job cuts in the offing to reduce operating expenses, this may endanger your secure job.

If you're retired, living on a small pension, your purchasing power may dwindle as the cost of living rises. Having a fixed income, you may worry about money almost constantly.

No matter who you are, each week usually brings problems. To live happily, you must accept them as part of reality and bend your energies to cope with them. You cannot shut them out or refuse to see them. If you do, you are pulling away from life into a living death. You cannot expect to solve them permanently and "live happily ever after." This denial of reality is childishly omnipotent thinking, a carryover of baby-carriage days.

You must face up to life. Each day you must get up out of bed, recharge your batteries with a nourishing breakfast, and set out on a day full of pitfalls as well as promises, pain, as well as plenty.

You must plan your daily goals with fresh courage and keep on plugging until you attain their maximum realization.

## WHAT IS YOUR PRESSURE-TOLERATION QUOTIENT?

A basic question here is: How much pressure can you tolerate? What is your breaking point?

This question of your tolerance is subtle, and there is no absolute answer to it. One's ability to function is not as measurable as time. It varies with inner conditions, physical and mental.

One thing is certain, however. Many people do break down under the stresses of modern life. Our crowded mental institutions bear witness to this statement.

Many other people stagger along, functioning marginally, feeling vaguely upset about what is going on around them and inside them, addicted to poor habits of eating, drinking, and smoking.

How about successful people? How do they handle stressful situations?

Simply put, they can rise above crises by relaxing no matter what the external situation.

Their belief in themselves, the strength of their self-image, is impenetrable armor, which protects them against shattering events.

## THE SECRET OF WINNING

This ability to remain calm when others feel harassed and confused is their big secret. They can feel secure regardless of pressures; their self-image holds up.

In *Your Thoughts Can Change Your Life* (Prentice-Hall, 1961), Donald Curtis writes about Bing Crosby's calm in an emergency:

"Many years ago, when I was beginning as a radio actor in Hollywood, I was called for a small part on a show on which Bing Crosby was the guest star. He was his usual relaxed self right up to air time.

"However, the rest of us all felt the mounting tension as we waited for the producer to give the signal that we were on the air.

"The producer raised his arm for the signal. Then with only ten seconds to go, Bing dropped the script. Panic broke loose in everyone but Bing. While actors, agency men, stage hands, and musicians scrambled to pick up the fluttering pages of the script, Bing nonchalantly bent down, picked up the elusive first page, cocked his hat on the back of his head, and came in exactly on cue. That night he gave a tremendous performance without any fuss whatsoever."

You must also be able to adapt yourself to changing conditions. Sometimes, to succeed, you must change your plans.

In *The Road to Successful Living,* Louis Binstock tells an amusing story about the famous American artist James McNeill Whistler:

In 1854 be was a cadet at West Point on his way to a career of soldiering. In Chemistry class one afternoon, he was asked to discuss silicon. He rose and began, "Silicon is a gas."

"That will do, Mr. Whistler," said his instructor.

A few weeks later, Cadet Whistler was discharged from the Academy.

Years later, when he was quite famous as a painter, he liked to say, "If silicon had been a gas, I would have been a general."

## THE STORY OF MY FIRST PATIENT

During my sixty-odd years of living, I've had my share of crises. One was the turning point of my life.

When I came back from my postgraduate studies in Berlin, Vienna, Paris, Rome, and London, I opened up an office on lower Fifth Avenue in New York City. At the time, very few people, even physicians, knew about plastic surgery, so I took a chance to enter this embryo profession. I furnished five large rooms as best I could with my limited funds. I then put up a shingle outside my door and waited for my first patient.

I had operated successfully on many patients in Europe during my training and, despite the newness of my field, I figured that I would be an overnight success. I thought that my services would be in immediate demand.

I waited.

There were no telephone calls during the morning—none at all. As the afternoon wore on, I ate a leisurely lunch but felt impatient. I began staring at the telephone, hoping to mobilize it into action, but I couldn't force it to ring. Then, toward the end of the day, the phone rang, and I dived for it.

"How are you doing?" It was my mother.

"Okay," I said, my spirits falling.

During my first week, there was not a single phone call, except toward the end of the day when my mother called to ask how I was making out. As much as I liked my mother, her voice became more and more an omen of doom.

This went on for three weeks. My office was as quiet as a morgue, and my telephone seemed an unnecessary extravagance, an object that I resented. Slowly, my confidence began to fade, and I felt nervous and worried. For the first time in my life, I knew panic.

What was my fear? To make ends meet, I'd have to make at least $500 the first month, including a small check I wanted to send my mother to show her how successful I was.

I had no cash reserve to tide me over more than this one month.

As the fourth week began, I became obsessed with the fear that I would be a failure, that all my years of training would prove a waste of time, energy, and money. In another week, I would have to close my office unless I got a patient. In my mind's eye, I visualized the taunts and reprimands of my mother, relatives, and friends, all of whom had advised me to become a general practitioner or train in a better-known specialty where the future would be more sure.

It was my first great crisis. I didn't know what to do. Slumping in my chair,

I looked out the window. A new building was going up across the street, and I watched a laborer going up to the fourth or fifth floor on an elevator, carrying bricks. His job looked dangerous, and in those pre-union days, his salary probably was slim, but for a moment, I wished I could junk all my medical training and change places with him, just so that I could feel the security of an assured wage. Grimly, I sat and waited and waited.

Shrilly, the phone rang out. As I picked it up, I glumly said to myself, "It's mother!"

But it wasn't.

It was a doctor, a childhood friend.

He had heard of my work from my family, and he had a patient for me. He asked when he could bring him over. Although I felt desperately dependent on this case, I summoned up my courage and adopted a professional manner. "Just a moment," I said. "Let me look at my appointment book!"

I looked at the empty pages for thirty seconds, then said, "I have time for you right now.

"Come right over!"

Shaving quickly, I put on a white coat and waited for my first patient. I forced myself to be calm, forgetting my urgent need, and remembering my surgical skill, seeing what I could do for a patient.

I thought he'd never come and was beginning to fidget in my armchair when the doorbell finally rang. There were the Doctor and a young man with a severely bashed-in nose, a lifelong reminder of a childhood accident. He was a shoe salesman in his twenties, and he felt depressed about his appearance and concerned about the difficulty he had breathing properly.

My panic was entirely gone. All I felt was a professional interest in helping the man. I looked at his nose in my examining chair, quickly saw that I could perform a successful operation, and then we agreed on a fee. My crisis was over.

Somehow I had lived through the toughest month in my life and survived my anxiety. My second case was not long coming, and soon I was an established plastic surgeon.

## HOW I HELPED AN ACTRESS OVERCOME STAGE FRIGHT

A few years ago, I was in California, ready to fly to Europe over the North Pole. I went backstage to see the star of a musical comedy about to open in Los Angeles, a well-known actress. She was feeling the pressure of opening night. She was panicky, felt she couldn't perform, was certain she would lose her voice. She told me she could barely move her feet; she felt so paralyzed.

"What's wrong?" I asked.

"I suddenly get this panicky feeling. I usually get nervous before going on, but this is different."

"What's so different?"

"Doctor, I don't know. I'm afraid I'm losing my voice."

"Do you know your lines?"

"Of course."

"Do you know your songs?"

"Of course."

"Then what's the matter?"

"I don't know. A fear came over me that I won't reach my high notes in the songs."

We were in her dressing room, filled with beautiful costumes, a huge dressing table, and a mirror at the side, flowers in vases from admirers. An assistant flitted back and forth, arranging her costume changes.

She looked at herself in the mirror, began singing, and stopped.

"Go on," I said.

"I can't; I just can't." She began to cry.

What could I do to help her? I wondered. I had no drugs to calm her, and there was no time to send out for anything.

"Well, don't worry," I said. "You're a real pro, and you'll get over your attack of nerves. I have just the right thing for you in my bag. It's a new drug and will work quickly."

Telling myself that this white lie was necessary, I took a sterilized syringe from my black bag, broke a small glass vial of distilled water, and sucked it up into the syringe.

I gave the actress an injection and promised her it would take immediate effect. "Sit down," I said, "and relax."

When a stage assistant poked his head in a few minutes later to prepare her to go on stage, she was calm.

"What wonderful medicine this is, I could kiss you for it."

She did. "I feel wonderful, Doctor, and I'm so grateful!" She went on stage and gave a marvelous performance.

Later, at a dinner party to celebrate the opening, I went over to her table.

"Do you know, that was one of your best performances!"

"Thanks to you," she said.

"No, thanks to you. You did it, not me. Do you know that the medicine I gave you was only distilled water?"

She turned pale, then she laughed. Ever since, she has felt nervous at times, but never hysterical, for she would remember that night when, with only imaginary help, she pulled herself out of a crisis and won the audience and critics' applause.

Today she is still one of the big talents in show business.

## SET YOUR GOALS

To function successfully under trying conditions, you must concentrate on realizable goals for which you have enthusiasm.

These serve as propellants to keep you going when things get tough and eliminate conflicting thoughts that destroy your calm.

For example, in a football game, suppose a team has the ball on its opponents' three-yard line, first down, and goal to go. They try to score three times, but the other team is muscular and determined, and they don't gain a foot. The offensive team needs a touchdown to win the game; a field goal won't do. In the face of such fierce resistance in this pressure situation, they could feel like giving up. If they didn't care, they would. It is only the intensity with which they seek their goal, a touchdown, that gives them a chance to realize it. With this goal set firmly in eleven minds, they will figure every possible avenue to getting across the goal line. Even if they don't succeed, they will have the satisfaction of knowing they did their best.

Life is like football: you must set your goals. You must set in motion your success mechanism.

When I was sweating it out, waiting for my first patient, this one factor helped me—*I knew what I wanted.*

The actress, paralyzed with fright on opening night, shared this spur to successful functioning. Since her objective was clear, she needed just a little support to get her over the top.

In *10 Days to a Great New Life* (Prentice-Hall, 1963), William Edwards emphasizes the importance of goal setting: He relates: "One of the most enterprising companies in America—the leader in its field—requires all 50 of its vice-presidents to write down their specific goals—short-range, medium-range, and long-range. It keeps things stirred up, gets everyone thinking ahead. It spurs the imagination to picture an effective future. It plants the 'image seed' of things to come. It's made the company explosively successful."

Once you know what you want, you have reached first base, and you feel the security that goes with this accomplishment. The next question is, how intense is your desire to achieve these goals?

## BELIEVE IN YOUR GOALS

The firmer your belief in your goals, the better you will do. When you sharply channel your determination, you can move aggressively and act with calmness at the same time.

General Douglas MacArthur had this belief. "From the day of his confident parting message to the Filipinos, (I shall return) no deviation from MacArthur's singleminded plan is discernible. Every battle action in New Guinea, every air raid on Rabaul or PT-boat attack on Japanese barges in the Bismarck Sea were a mere preliminary for the reconquest of the Philippines." *(MacArthur 1941–1951*, by Charles A. Willoughby and John Chamberlain, McGraw Hill, 1954.)

You may never be a general or even a PFC (God willing!)—but you can believe just as fervently in your aims, and they are no less noble. An automobile mechanic who cares when a stranger brings in a malfunctioning car and tries to do a clean, complete job is a good man. His belief in what he's doing will help him keep calm and weather crises.

## BRING BACK YOUR TRIUMPHS

You've read this earlier in this book, but I can't emphasize it often enough: You'll help yourself if you'll bring back into your mind your better moments, picturing the details of situations that were happy and successful for you. Focusing on these images will bring you peace during tense times; it will help build up your self-image.

While I was waiting for my first patient, and it seemed that no one knew my phone number, I had to battle to keep my confidence in myself. My best weapon was an image of myself operating flawlessly during my training days, and I saturated my mind with this mental picture until I reached my objective.

I can't say what was in the actress's mind, but once I had given her support, I'm sure that her recollection of previous stardom moments helped her go on stage and give a great performance.

You might be thinking, "But I've never been a dramatic success—nothing like that at all."

Yes, but you're not going to perform on the stage in front of thousands of people. You will perform just on the stage of your mind—again, and again until you can bring your most successful picture into reality.

You don't have to be an actress or a doctor. You have to be only yourself, operating realistically in your own potential areas of competence, withdrawing wealth from your bank of experience, the bank that pays off with interest.

## DON'T BE AFRAID TO BE NERVOUS!

Sometimes you'll be nervous, no matter who you are. What do you do then? You simply accept it and keep going until you regain your self-assurance.

Nervousness is not a terrible thing at all unless you think it is. When you feel nervous, remember that you're not alone in this respect.

According to Dr. Peter P. Steincrohn *(How to Master Your Fears,* Wilfred Funk, 1952), "The world is sick with fear.

"The best way to combat fear is to recognize it and then face up to it. The first step is for each and every one of us to admit that we are frightened. That in itself will bring some measure of relief."

Comedian Paul Lynde has even made a career out of nervousness. *TV Guide* reports: "Certainly he is the only performer ever to pay a press agent good money to write of him: 'Paul [was known] as one of the worst nervous shambles in show business, both while performing and in private life. Even now, after two years of psychotherapy, he says, "if I ever completely lost my nervousness, I would be frightened half to death." ("Paul Lynde's Traumatic Success," July 13, 1963.)

I'm not telling you that if you get the shakes, Perry Como will hire you for his TV show, as he did Paul Lynde, and I'm certainly not advising you to induce nervousness in yourself. But if your nerves should be on edge and you can't help showing it, so what? That's my main point; don't blame yourself!

## YOUR POWER IN A CRISIS

Once you have set goals that you believe in, brought into your mind success pictures of the past, and prepared yourself to accept your human weaknesses, you will feel the power in a crisis. You will feel capable of dealing with situations as they arise.

You have powers inside you that will help you deal with emergencies. Once you are wholehearted in your determination to succeed, and once you have pinpointed your goals, you are in a position to mobilize these powers.

Your success mechanism is now ready to help you carry the ball. Having given it clearly defined objectives, basically in the form of mental pictures, you have set in motion this automatic servomechanism.

It will work for your welfare—and difficult situations will not destroy the efficiency of this marvelous power, which resides within all of you.

You need not let crises floor you; you can overcome your fears and deal realistically with your world.

## PRACTICE EXERCISE NO. 6: LIVING WITH CRISES

This exercise will help you pull through many crises with steadily decreasing anxiety if you work at it.

You know the procedure by now; you're in as quiet a place as you can find, and you're as relaxed as you can make yourself.

Once more, enter the playhouse of your mind and rummage around in your backlog of motion pictures, real-life films made from the events of your life. Dig out a "horror" story, a Frankenstein story in terms of your alarm, and examine it. It's a crisis scene, one of the many little crises in your life. Still, you over-reacted out of all proportion to the reality, inflating irritation into a Frankenstein monster of terror.

Perhaps your husband has said he'd be home before midnight, and you were still waiting up at two in the morning, your imagination full of dread fantasies.

Or maybe you'd argued with your wife over coffee and, just before you left for the office, she shouted that she was going home to her mother and that she never wanted to see you again. You drove to work, your mind full of dire possibilities, though you knew she just had a bad temper.

Or your boss had looked at you searchingly one time after you had made a mistake and set a severe deadline for your next assignment. Your mind became obsessed with the fear that he was preparing to fire you.

Bring the mental picture of this minor crisis back into your mind and feel your terror.

Feel it. Recall your morbid thoughts, and fear now as you did then.

Remember the frightening possibilities that took over your mind as you conjured up all the nasty things that could happen to you. React to your mental pictures as you did then, with such deep feeling that your physical symptoms of that period return; the palpitating of your heart, the sudden flow of perspiration, turning pale, nausea, whatever your symptoms were—if there were any.

It is not pleasant to re-experience your over-reaction to this small crisis, but it will help you.

Why? Because nine times out of ten, one's fears—even in a problem moment—are not remotely justified. Your negative mental imaging was your worst enemy.

Now, bring back what really happened. Feel once again your relief that the worst had not happened, that your imagination had been your enemy. *Feel* it. As in waking up from a bad dream, relax, realizing it wasn't real, that you're safe.

Understand that this life-or-death feeling had little basis in reality, that we all face problems and crises, that your negative imaging is the chief culprit.

Practice along these lines over and over, and you'll produce inner changes in yourself that will amaze you. Picture a different situation each day, feel the over-reactive panic, then the relief when reality discloses the negative workings of your imagination.

The more you work on this exercise, the more you will understand that the real crisis is in your mind, part of your inadequate self-image. When you meet situations that currently unnerve you, question your anxious response's validity and picture events in the past to which you overreacted. This will help you put the present in better focus, calming you and increasing your ability to function effectively.

As you mature, replacing negative picturing with successful imaging, setting worthwhile goals for yourself, and strengthening your self-image, you will handle difficult situations more competently.

Call on these two old friends to help you pull through major and minor crises:

1. *Truth.*

    The truth is that we are rarely involved in "life-or-death" emergencies; realizing this may keep you calm when you would otherwise be undermining your positive side with anxiety.

2. *Imagination.*

    Man is blessed with this faculty but so often uses it negatively. Be a king in your mind, and you'll be all right.

# 14

## WINNING FRIENDS CAN BE EASY FOR YOU

ABOUT FOUR CENTURIES AGO, THE GREAT ENGLISH SCHOLAR FRANCIS BACON, writing about Friendship, commented, "It redoubleth joys and cutteth griefs in halfs."

Hundreds of years later, English poet S. T. Coleridge wrote that "Friendship is a sheltering tree."

Friendship is just as important today—maybe it's even more vital because of the strain under which we live. I'm not talking about "fair-weather" comradeship, but about the loyal, "through-thick-and-thin" mutual supportiveness that is the meat of good human relatedness.

The man who has sincere friendships is richer than the millionaire or the billionaire—no amount of money can alter this. This may sound like a cliché but it is an unquestionable truth. You can lose your money. Of course, you can lose good friends too—they can die, but if you have the capacity for Friendship, you can always make new ones. Moreover, you can lose a good friend only physically; if you loved him, he would always remain in your heart.

Will Rogers is supposed to have once remarked, "I've never met a man I didn't like."

This sentimental statement comes from a man whose simple, generous nature won him the love of a nation. It touches one's heart because it is friendly.

## LIFE IS PEOPLE

Life is more than a heartbeat or the ability to breathe, eat, see, and feel. An individual's life rotates around the quality of his relationships with other people.

Life is people, and it is not so much what they do for you as what you do for them and what you give each other.

In assessing the traits that make for a well-adjusted human being, psychologists place a high value on his ability to reach out and relate to other people. The person who can't get along with others is at a grave disadvantage vocationally; many avenues are closed to him. Living in a prison of his own making, he walls off his feelings and cremates his resources. His soul cannot soar: when his moods change, he moves from Alcatraz to Sing Sing.

He cannot live with people, yet he is unable to live happily without them. If he shuts himself off in an "ivory tower," he feels a sense of deprivation that he cannot long deny. If he mingles with the crowd, he feels inhibited, and his relationships lack satisfaction. Some people feel loneliest when people surround them. This is understandable; a person feels more contact in the company of one trusted friend with whom he can be himself than at a large gathering where he feels he must wear a mask.

An individual who is capable of building real friendships is a happy man. Even if he doesn't make much money, he is content, reaping the rewards of sweet human relationships. The word "friendship" is one of the warmest words in the English language.

## THE ART OF WINNING FRIENDS

Books on the art of Friendship crowd our library shelves. They contain fairly helpful suggestions, concepts that could induce you to become a more accepting, considerate person.

In the best-selling *How to Win Friends and Influence People* (Simon & Schuster 1936), Dale Carnegie quotes, with approval, a statement of Henry Ford's.

"If there is any one secret of success, it lies in the ability to get the other person's point of view and see things from his angle as well as your own."

Carnegie himself states: "*You can* make more friends in *two* months by becoming *interested in other people* than you can in *two years* by trying *to get other people interested* in you." In *Personality and Successful Living* (Bruce Publishing Co. 1945), James A. Magner's approach is similar. "We come to tolerate, to understand, and to love people not by waiting for them to serve us, much less by allowing them to display their defects, but by assuming the active role ourselves and giving others positive reasons for tolerating and loving us. Nothing wins friends so much as an unselfish concern on our part. Nothing makes us so worthy of Friendship as developing ourselves, our resources, our personality by a program of friendliness and usefulness to others." These are positive ideas. The writers know people, and their suggestions are worthwhile.

*But, basically, your ability to form sincere, enduring friendships depends on the strength of your self-image.*

## IF YOU LIKE YOURSELF, OTHERS WILL

You can learn to be more considerate; this is a fine quality.

You can go out of your way to be useful to other people; this will help. There are other constructive moves you can make to win friendships. You can master a variety of social skills; you can volunteer to share your material possessions.

But the core of your capacity for Friendship is in your thinking about yourself. If you like yourself, others will usually share your feeling. If you despise yourself, so will other people. By liking yourself, I don't mean the narcissistic form of infantile self-admiration, in which the individual's love centers on himself, to the exclusion of others. You can't really like yourself unless you like others.

If you short-change yourself, however, chances are you'll do the same thing to other people.

"Without confidence, there is no friendship," wrote the ancient Greek philosopher Epicurus.

True, and confidence has its beginning in one's attitude toward himself!

## WHY BE SHY?

The shy person finds it difficult to make friends generally. Inhibiting his free expression, out of fear, he limits his contact with other people.

Martin Tolchin's description is poignant in "The Roots of Shyness." (*New York Times* Magazine, June 19, 1960.)

He is a quiet child—too quiet and too well-behaved. He lacks the "bellyful of fire" that the late William Bryon Mowery thought all small boys had or should have. Instead, he stands wistfully on the sidelines, unable to wade into the rough and tumble savored by a boy among boys.

Left to his own devices, he may outgrow his shyness or learn to live with it. Or he may abandon the effort to establish contact with the rest of the world.

The experience can be humbling. Shyness can come between a man and the woman he needs. It can undermine his usefulness to society by preventing him from getting the job for which he qualifies. It can place an intelligent, accomplished person in the position of a social beggar who is thrown conversational crumbs at functions he cannot evade.

Unfortunately, there are many shy people in this world. Life can teach, but it can also frighten people, driving them into shells.

If you are shy, you can learn to be more outgoing. Once again, it is mainly a question of changing your false truth about yourself—because shyness is a technique for hiding from people.

## YOU CAN COME OUT OF YOUR SHELL

Feel sorry for turtles! Some of them live to ripe old ages but spend their whole lives in a shell. There's just nothing they can do about it! If you're shy, you're luckier because you can do something about it. You can come to a better appreciation of your good qualities; you can recall moments when you were proud of yourself and see them once again. You can learn to live with your weaknesses. You can readjust your image of yourself, truthfully, positively.

Once you feel better about yourself, you won't be too frightened to come out of your shell. Did you ever see the birth of a chicken? The cracking of the shell, and then the little chick coming out into the world for the first time?

If you're timid, you can be like the little baby chick and burst through the shell into the daylight—into a brighter world than you ever knew existed, the world of Friendship, the best world there is.

Before you're ready for real Friendship, however, you must have the courage to burst through your shell.

## THE MEANING OF FRIENDSHIP

A word of warning: There is much Friendship these days that is political and insincere. Some people use "friendship" for vocational advantage, selecting and shedding friends with rapidity and without real feeling.

They shop for friends as they would for an automobile, looking for a bargain, figuring out in advance which friend will help them advance their career. As they achieve promotions and rise into a new social status, they then discard their old pals without feeling and begin hunting out new alliances, which are more likely to pay off in terms of cold cash, present, or future.

These people do not basically differentiate between one person and another but make their choices after a careful survey of the economic advantages involved.

Other people select friends and make efforts to cement these "friendships" in an attempt to make others think them popular.

Their reasoning is that if people see them always in the company of this person or that, on apparently friendly terms, they will be considered socially acceptable. They think of this as a success, though it really isn't.

They don't really care, in a compassionate way, about the people they use for their social prestige. Indeed, they use them with the same degree of concern that one would feel in washing dishes or polishing the family car. Their only concern is that their ally is a superficially acceptable commodity, a person with enough status in the community to enhance their own social prestige.

Obviously, no genuine value inheres in these forms of "friendship." There is nothing beautiful or ennobling about these selfish alliances, and I am writing about an entirely different type of relationship, one in which the main ingredient is not expediency but brotherly love. This honest, giving kind of Friendship is one of the most precious things in life, and it is this warm brotherly-sisterly relatedness that I hope I can help you achieve.

## MAKING PEOPLE SEEK YOUR COMPANY

If people really like you, you won't have to go out and look for friends; not only will they seek your company, they will come clamoring after you.

Let's try out our mental picturing apparatus again. Sit down, make yourself comfortable in a quiet place, and relax in the playhouse of your mind.

*Scene* 1: This man goes to a party. He knocks timidly on the door, feeling uneasy because he won't know many of the people.

Ted was invited by Cora, whom he knows casually, from the library where he works. He's 35, has worked as a librarian for almost ten years, is lonely. The hostess greets him, and he shuffles into the living room, which is crowded with talking, laughing people.

"Hello." A girl comes over to him and smiles.

He returns her greeting, nervously wondering what he should talk about.

"What's your name?"

Ted introduces himself, forcing himself to ask hers and feeling all fingers and thumbs as he wonders what to do with his hands.

"What do you do?"

"Oh, oh, here comes that question again," he thinks, groaning inwardly.

"I'll have to tell her I'm nothing but a librarian." His shoulders slump, and he avoids her gaze as he answers her.

(Here is a sure blueprint for failure. This man's basic quality is a self-hatred that tramples all his intelligence and his potential for creative expression. He must strengthen his self-image before he is ready for the warm givingness that constitutes Friendship.)

*Scene* 2: It is the same party, half an hour later. John arrives and greets his hostess. He's also a librarian; it's a clannish gathering. He's also in his thirties, unmarried, but he's looking forward to the evening.

He's eager to meet Cora socially and see her in a pretty dress. Perhaps they'll dance and talk and flirt, and perhaps he could take her home later.

"How nice you look!" he says to the hostess, meaning every word.

He laughs as she blushes and shakes hands with Peter and Frank, both of whom he knows at work.

They're glad to see him and bring him over to other people.

"What do you do?" one fellow asks, glass tinkling ice in his hand.

"I'm a librarian," John says, looking curiously, yet with a friendly smile, at the other man. "I've always loved good books. What do you do?"

He finds some of the people at the party interesting to talk to and enjoys the exchange of ideas, food, and drink. People come over to chat with him, enjoying his easy friendliness and his lack of pretension and arrogance. At midnight, he takes Cora home. (People seek out this man because his self-image is healthy. He sees himself as a nice guy and therefore does not have to feel self-conscious or apologetic. Liking himself without being narcissistic, he is able to appreciate others. They sense this and cluster around him, as bees around honey.)

## YOUR SELF-IMAGE CAN MAKE YOU LIKABLE

You can learn a lesson from these dramas: a healthy self-image can make you likable to other people.

People crave good company. They may mask this desire because they're afraid of rejection, but they feel this need very deeply. It is a basic need, almost as essential as the need to appease one's hunger with food.

Next time there's a fire in your neighborhood, observe the people in the street. Go with them as they rush to the scene to watch the fire engines come clanging up the street, and the firemen go rushing out with hoses. Notice how they cluster together, talking animatedly to each other as they watch the firemen put out the blaze.

Chances are, if you're observant that you'll sense that, more than the fire, they're interested in taking advantage of this opportunity to talk to other people, even complete strangers. Any emergency situation gives people this chance to group together with many people, feeling somehow more full, more whole.

If your self-image gives you the strength to be a considerate person, you will never feel starved for companionship.

## YOU CAN PUT OTHERS AT EASE

*Friendship! mysterious cement of the soul!*
*Sweetener of life and solder of society!*

—*Robert Blair*

If you give yourself peace of mind, you can tranquilize other people, sweetening their lives and cementing the potential good-heartedness in their souls. You can help them live restful yet animated lives. If they feel that you accept them as they are, without the need for pretense, they will come out of their shells and reveal genuine, wonderful qualities that they usually hide from other people, who they fear are hostile to them.

Francis Bacon once wrote, "A principal fruit of Friendship is the ease and discharge of the fullness and swellings of the heart. . . ."

If people trust you, they will confide to you their most terrible fears and guilts, easing their burdens, giving them more energy to direct into positive channels.

If you are an accepting person, you can bring them a sense of relaxation that few others can bring them.

If you can help make life sweet for just two or three friends whom you cherish, how fortunate you will feel!

## FRIENDS CAN MAKE YOU A BIGGER PERSON

Many people spend their lives hunting around in what they see as a jungle. Occasionally they cut through the underbrush to some buried treasure and rush it to the bank before other beasts of prey can sink their claws into it. But their lives mainly consist of "dog-eat-dog" adventures.

Competitors surround them, and they choose their "friends" for strategic purposes.

In *Understanding Fear In Ourselves and Others* (Harper & Row, 1951), Bonaro W. Overstreet writes: "Sometimes we know people who live to be old without achieving any identification that takes them far beyond themselves. They may form any number of overt relationships, may hold jobs, marry, rear children, join clubs. Yet they never actually identify with anyone. They can only use people, cling to people, dominate people. They may profess love in the proper setting, even love of mankind. But people remain for them means to ends. They never affirm anyone as real in his own right."

This is pathetic because real friends can make your life so rich. In the warmth of your life-giving interaction, you can discover qualities in yourself that you never knew existed. You can become a bigger person through friendships that are giving.

A friendship makes demands on you; you must give consideration to your friend's needs as well as your own.

In the words of Emerson, "Friendship should be surrounded with ceremonies and respects and not crushed into corners. Friendship requires more time than poor busy men can usually command."

Do not concentrate so much on your materialistic needs that you crush your friendships into corners! What material goods are more valuable than a good friend? Give time to your friendships, and you will receive wonderful dividends!

If you are an open-minded person capable of appreciating all kinds of people, you can receive many rewards from broadening your friendships.

In the Feb. 1960 *Reader's Digest* ("Have You Made Any New Friends Lately?"), Vance Packard writes: "Some people contend that we are happiest when we stick to 'our own kind' in developing friendships. The person who wears blinders of this sort will never experience the enthrallment of having as companions such colorful and often vividly articulate individuals as clam diggers, turkey farmers, house detectives, lumberjacks, seamen, or antique refinishers. He'll never know the exhilaration that comes from the discovery of someone exciting in a seemingly unlikely place.

"Another reward that comes from broadening your friendships is the new insight you gain from people who have a different perspective. One day I had a long ride in a Boston taxicab with a jovial, elderly driver. We had chatted on a variety of subjects when he suddenly exclaimed: 'You know I have achieved supreme happiness. I'm glad I'm doing what I'm doing; I've learned not to fight my background. I'm glad I'm who I am.'"

## FIVE RULES FOR WINNING FRIENDS

Apply these concepts, and you will never lack friends:

1. *Be a friend to yourself.* If you're not, you can't possibly be a friend to others. If you downgrade yourself, you can still admire other people, but your respect will be tainted with envy. Others will sense the impurity of your Friendship and will not respond positively

to it. They may be sympathetic toward your problems, but pity is not a strong foundation for Friendship.

2. *Reach out to people.* This is the next step. When you're with a casual acquaintance, and you feel like talking, express yourself as uninhibitedly as is proper for the situation. Don't tell yourself that you're silly if you crack a joke or unstable if you're nervous and want the other person to like you. Look for the other person's positive qualities and try to bring them out; watch for overcritical thoughts and stamp them out, for they are enemies to Friendship.

3. Imagine you're *the other person.* This mental picturing will help you. If you try to imagine him in his total life situation, as accurately as you can reconstruct it, you can sense his needs and try to meet them as much as is within your ability and within the dimensions of your relationship. You can also understand his responses better. If he is touchy in certain areas, you can try to avoid stepping on his toes. When you feel like being generous, you can attempt to build up his self-image.

   If he is a worthwhile friend, he will be grateful for your kindness and will give to you in return, in his own individual way.

4. *Accept the other fellow's individuality.* People are different, especially when they're genuine. Don't try to alter this fact. The other fellow is not you; accept him as he is, and he'll value you too, as you are if he's worth his salt. It is a serious mistake to try to force another person to conform to your preconceived ideas. If you resort to such domineering tactics, you'll likely have an enemy, not a friend.

5. *Try to meet others' needs.* Too often, this world is a cutthroat place in which people think of their own needs and then stop thinking! Go out of your way to be considerate, and you'll be a valued friend. Many people talk at people; they deliver lectures, and the other fellow is just an ear.

   Never do this to a friend; talk to him! And make sure to listen.

## PRACTICE EXERCISE NO. 7: YOUR SELF-IMAGE WITH PEOPLE

I've offered you some of the wisest advice you'll ever read on winning friends, and if you apply these concepts effectively, your relationships will have a new vivacity that will thrill you.

Your self-image is the prime factor. When you are with people, your feeling about yourself will influence your thinking about them and your conduct in relation to them. This is inevitable.

If you feel you're basically worthless, you may distort your thinking into one of these patterns:

1. You will withdraw into a defensive shell (defending yourself against yourself), inhibiting any spontaneous actions and frowning on spontaneity in others.
2. You will wallow in overcritical thoughts about people, lifting your own weak ego but destroying any chance of friendly relating.
3. You will become gushingly talkative, making a frantic effort to prove you're not worthless (an accusation you've made against yourself).
4. You will be constantly competitive, always trying to knock the other fellow down and pull yourself up over him in status.

I'm sure that you recognize people who relate in these ways, making friendly relating difficult. You yourself may rely on one or more of these defensive mechanisms. If you do, it's time that you strengthen your self-image when you're with people so that you can relate more naturally, without taking something away from others.

As you sit quietly, work on this practice exercise.

*Tell yourself* that you were made in God's image and that He fashioned you to love your fellow man and to live at peace with him. You were made to be warm and human, and these qualities are in you somewhere, even if it is not superficially apparent.

Remember the simplicity of your childhood friendships. Picture in vivid detail, as best you can, things you did with your childhood friends, possessions, and feelings you shared. Recapture your favorite moments of early Friendship, imaging the events. Regain the feeling that you can be spontaneous and alive, that you can throw off the burdens of over-civilization.

*Concentrate* on the loving feelings you have felt for people during your life. Forget the hate and the disillusion! Start off afresh and bring back into your memory your feelings of gratitude for something nice your mother did for you or a considerate gesture made by your father.

Bask in the warm glow of bygone birthdays when people indulged you and in the shared confidences with trusted friends.

If your life has been hard, concentrate on the isolated cases in which you felt genuine gratitude to other people.

Keep your loving feelings alive as you would a fire to keep you warm, for they are the whipped cream, the champagne, of your self-image. Without the active feeling of love in your heart, life is incomplete.

*Reject* from your mind emotional scars. We all have them, but if you dwell on them, you will undermine your chance to grow in the world of people. If you are a person who spends his time nursing grudges, you can't think very well of yourself without being unrealistic.

*Accept* your imperfections. If you expect too much of yourself, your self-image with people will be weak.

You'll always be looking over your shoulder to see if someone has noticed this fault of yours or that mistake.

In addition, you'll expect others to measure up to your impossible standards, and they will feel that you are unaccepting. Once you accept yourself as you are, you will find it easy to give quiet Friendship to others, and one of life's most wonderful experiences will be yours.

Some of you may have had few friends during your lifetime and feel you're unlovable. This is not so; your trouble is that you've not been fair to yourself. There is something lovable in every one of us—it just has to be brought out.

Your pride in yourself and your friendliness to others is something that you have to bring out for yourself. No matter if it's difficult, only you can do it. Go over and over the material in this practice exercise and help yourself to grow in stature in the world of people.

# 15

# FINDING PEACE OF MIND
# IN A TROUBLED WORLD

WHEN YOU WAKE UP IN THE MORNING, PERHAPS YOU OPEN YOUR FRONT DOOR and reach down for the bottled milk and the daily newspaper.

Perhaps you carry the milk to your refrigerator, shut the door, sit down in the kitchen chair, and unfold the newspaper.

The headlines shriek out at you in large black type—of nuclear weapons, diplomatic threats, individual crimes, government abuses.

"There," you may say, "there's proof positive. You can't relax in this world. There's too much trouble everywhere, and it's gotten out of hand." *You're wrong. You can relax. You can create peace of mind even when others reel with anxiety.*

Tension is nothing new. The world has seen many troubled days throughout history. Strife has always been part of civilization's fabric, from the Greco-Roman wars of antiquity through the bitter French Revolution to the world wars of the twentieth century. The Industrial Revolution brought about disquieting change. No period in American history was more chaotic and senseless than the mid-nineteenth century when our great Civil War forced fellow Americans to kill each other. Some soldiers even had to kill personal friends of more peaceful days.

No, tension and catastrophe are not unique diseases singling out twentieth-century man. There have always been challenging crises to cloud the sunnier part of life. You can learn to live with these pressures and even to win out in life's boiling pot. Your life is not worthwhile if you cannot attain a feeling of quietness. You must bed down with your soul and breathe in gentle tranquility.

In the words of the great Greek philosopher Plato, "Nothing in the affairs of men is worthy of great anxiety."

Chapter 4 gave you some hints on how to relax, but the subject is so urgently crucial in today's high-pressure world that I'm also devoting this chapter to the vital area.

## YOU CAN LEARN TO BE CALM

First off, you must believe that a state of inner calm is a realizable goal. Calm is not as easy as it sounds; if you're used to having harassed, jumpy, pushing people around you, you may come to think of calm as an unattainable state.

Our leading magazines and newspapers feature articles describing today's teenagers' inner turmoil, the explosiveness of their tensions.

Our most respected social scientists tell us of the abnormal anxiety that pervades modern-day life.

Philosophers, psychiatrists, and religious leaders agree that today's people live without spiritual quiet, full of conflicting emotions, disturbed by resentment.

Millions of people torture themselves with anxiety. Indecisive and fearful, they cannot accept their feelings or their shortcomings. It is difficult for them to make up their minds about anything, and they feel guilty over what they regard as their failures in life. They act too impulsively—or are afraid to act at all.

Anxiety becomes a way of life for them.

Phobias and neurotic obsessions fill their minds instead of feelings of success and confidence. I know people who have never enjoyed a calm week *in years*.

Is this further evidence that serenity is beyond your grasp? It is not. I mention these sordid states to show you once again that if you are anxious, you are not alone. There are conditions today that encourage anxiety. Therefore, in your fight to become calm, start by accepting your worries, not blaming yourself for them. The more secure your self-acceptance is, the more you can come to peace with yourself; with your weaknesses, the more attainable is the goal of calmness.

Believe me; you can be calm. This chapter is full of suggestions that will help you to reach this goal.

## TRANQUILIZERS FOR THE SPIRIT

First, go toward activities that bring you contentment. This is highly individual. Certain hobbies or rituals serve as "spirit tranquilizers" for some people but would only bore others.

An old lady, a friend of my family who passed away several years ago, told me that she used to read her Bible when she felt jittery. That would settle her nerves. She would just rock back and forth in her chair and read.

A friend of mine, a doctor who would come home tense from his practice pressures, would find tranquility in playing the piano. He mostly played Chopin and Gershwin. Sometimes I'd go over to his apartment, light up a cigar, and relax with him as his hands flitted agilely over the keyboard.

"I don't know what it is," he once said to me, "but when I'm playing the piano, I relax and just forget the pressures of life. I just enjoy myself. I stop worrying about patients who are in pain; I forget the ones with incurable diseases. Maybe this is wrong of me."

"No," I said. "You've got to relax and forget even your most unfortunate cases, or you'll be no good as a doctor, and you'll be unable to help the people you can make better.

"The piano gives you peace—accept this gift!"

You all potentially have your spiritual uplifter. Find out what it is, and then take advantage of the good it does you!

## YOU CAN MASTER YOUR WORRIES

Are you a slave to worry? If you are, ask yourself this: Do you believe in slavery?

This is not a joke. If your mind travels from one worried thought to another, it is genuinely enchained. You are not free.

Do you say, "But there is so much to worry about"?

You don't have to itemize your problems: I grant your point. But this is a negative way to use the extraordinary power of your mind.

In *How to Relax in a Busy World* (Prentice-Hall, 1962), Floyd and Eve Corbin write:

> If you have been in the habit of inviting negative thoughts—jealousy, envy, resentment, and self-pity, think of these as intruders in your mind. The old Chinese saying fits here: "You cannot stop the birds of the air from flying over your head, but you need not let them nest in your hair."
>
> Face and define your troubles. Gather knowledge about them from every good source. Confide your worries to God. Do all you can about the situation that is causing them. Don't contaminate your friends and loved ones with them.

This is good advice. Worry is one of the most destructive scourges of mankind; if it takes over your mind, your days will be miserable, and your nights will be intolerable. Even if the worst misfortune should befall you, it is no worse than a worried mind.

The famed philosopher Soren Kierkegaard once wrote, "No grand inquisitor has in readiness such terrible tortures as has anxiety, and no spy knows how to attack more artfully the man he suspects, choosing the instant when he is weakest; nor knows how to lay traps, where he will be caught and ensnared as anxiety, knows how, and no sharp-witted judge knows how to interrogate, to examine the accused, as anxiety does, which never lets him escape . . ."

These ideas will help you master your worry:

1. *Bring your fears into the open.* Talk about them to friends without hiding details, which may be ridiculed. The more you express your concerns, the less severe they will seem to you, and the sooner you will forget them.
2. *Seek solutions to your problems.* When you feel you've done your best to solve a problem, even if you haven't found a clear-cut answer, you'll feel better about yourself and will be more inclined to allow yourself the privilege of relaxation.
3. *Guide your thinking into constructive channels.* Once you've done your best to alleviate some trouble, thinking about it will only make it worse. Use your imagination more positively, picturing happier situations. Or undertake activities that will give you pleasure.

## HOW TO SPOT YOUR OVER-REACTIONS

We all have our Achilles heel, areas in which we feel vulnerable. Some people fear traveling by airplane intensely but are entirely at home behind the steering wheel of the family car. Others feel precisely the opposite. Some people fear neither planes nor cars but hate to cross crowded streets on foot.

Over-reactions, if unchecked, can undermine your peace of mind. They can remove your thinking from channels appropriate to the real circumstances and distort it into patterns that bear no relation to reality.

Dr. Peter J. Steincrohn tells a story of over-reaction *(How to Master Your Fears):* "The year was 1929. Mr. Smith was worth a million dollars just before 'Black Thursday' of the market crash. A month later be had only a hundred thousand dollars. What did he do? Most of us have read of the many such Smiths who jumped from hotel windows. But the average man said: 'Imagine jumping with a hundred thousand dollars in your pocket. I was left without a nickel to my name, and you couldn't have pushed me out of a window.' There you have what we like to call the normal and the abnormal reactions to a difficult situation."

How do you spot your over-reactions, preventing them from upsetting your calm and plunging you into difficult situations? The best way I know is to talk your situation out with two or three trusted friends, explaining your reactions as you go along. They will, in most cases, be able to see the objective reality far better than you will, and they'll be able to help you get back on the ball, planning a new day of full living.

## DELAY YOUR RESPONSE

Sometimes you will not be able to help yourself, and a flood of anger will pour into you, threatening to overwhelm the calmness you've worked so hard to maintain. At such times delay your response, hold it off, and count to 12 (an even dozen).

Suppose, for example, that you live on a tight budget. Any unforeseen expenses that pop up endanger your sense of economic security.

You over-react in this area so that any annoyances of this sort will trouble you even more than is realistic.

You're sitting quietly in your favorite chair, smoking your pipe, digesting a tasty dinner.

Even the newspaper headlines please you, giving promise of income tax savings, and no commercials interrupt the pleasant music from the radio. Your ten-year-old son has just brought home a report card full of excellent grades.

You just sit and let your imagination wander through fields of rich mental pictures.

Then your wife says that the kitchen linoleum is worn out, and the TV picture is blurred.

You feel irritated at the thought of expenses, but you are not thrown. Then your wife reminds you that your $180 dentist bill hasn't been paid. Now the anger starts building, and you know you can no longer check it.

This is the time to start counting slowly, "One . . . two . . . three. . . ." By the time you get to 12, you may still be irritated, but your rage will be more subdued, and you'll be better able to control your actions.

This delay may prevent you from giving vent to explosive destructiveness. You may be able to regain control of your rational faculties and resume channeling your energies in more positive ways. You can go back to enjoying your pipe, visualizing the more pleasant enterprises which will follow the payment of your bills.

## A PLEASANT ROOM IN YOUR MIND

When you were a child, did you have a favorite room to which you went when you were unhappy with the rest of the world? Maybe it was furnished cozily, with soft-cushioned chairs and throw rugs and your most treasured possessions.

This is what each of us needs—a serene room in his mind—a retreat in which to nurse one's wounds when the strains of the world become unbearable. In the seclusion of this peaceful chamber in our mind, we can recuperate from life's fast pace, refresh ourselves for the new day to come. In this little mental compartment, you can make peace with yourself, accepting your insecurities, re-picturing your most cherished memories, setting your present goals, imagining a future full of life, faith, and hope, free of resentment and worry.

As you've done while reading this book, you can build a stage on which you can imagine real-life dramas, the kind that will help you to the creation of a self-image strong enough to allow you to lead the good life.

## TAKE A DAILY VACATION

As a boy, I knew adults who worked 60, 70, 80 hours a week; this was quite common in those days. Today most people work 35 or 40 hours, and Saturday is a day off. They have at least a two-week vacation every year.

Even so, many people feel tense nowadays because of the pressures they feel under. The truth is that the length of the workweek seems to have limited meaning in relation to one's ability to relax.

What is important is that you take a meaningful vacation and that you take it *every day*. Not once in a while, but every day. Every day take a flight into the freedom you can give yourself in the quiet room of your mind.

Birds have long been symbols of freedom, and poets have envied their ability to rise above the confinements of earthly existence as they soared through the skies.

In the serene room of your mind, the soaring range of your imagination can give you this sense of freedom. You can temporarily escape from the shackles of civilization, reaffirm your convictions, and return to the realities with increased vigor.

You can take this wonderful vacation if your imagination is your friend if your self-image is healthy enough to allow you this luxury. Keep sharpening these potent tools as you read this book and as you re-read it. Then you'll be able to take a wonderful vacation every day—all expenses paid.

## DO YOU BELONG TO MAÑANA UNLIMITED?

These relaxation tools are not meant to be excuses for laziness; ideally, they will free you to function more efficiently. Do not become a member of Mañana Unlimited! What is Mañana Unlimited? Mañana in Spanish means "tomorrow," and Mañana Unlimited is an organization that leaves things undone until tomorrow. It is the world's largest organization with more members than any religion, political philosophy, or industrial organization. To join up, you must cling to one glaring fault: the tendency to put things off until tomorrow. Millions slavishly follow this blueprint for failure for a lifetime. Colleges give no courses in it because its learning is instinctive and does not lead to advancement.

This doesn't mean that we shouldn't believe in the art of leisure, which is different from putting things off. Idle people have the least leisure, for leisure is the reward of work and feeds the body and mind to meet tomorrow's demands. As Thoreau said, "He employs true leisure who has time to improve his soul's estate." The man who leaves things for tomorrow hasn't time for improving anything, and this uselessness is emptiness.

Mañana Unlimited espouses a negative philosophy of failure because no one has ever seen tomorrow. We indulge in wishful thinking when we believe that tomorrow will bring a Utopian state of affairs free of trouble. However, we can constructively plan for tomorrow, looking ahead for ways to better ourselves instead of tying ourselves to techniques that will leave us marking time, wallowing in a vacuum.

Therefore, every day we must strive to break away from our membership in Mañana Unlimited.

We must break away from the oppressive hold of fear, hatred, and worry making us charter members who stay lazy and say, "Well, we'll take care of that detail tomorrow." We must send in our letter of resignation.

Say to yourself every day: "I will do something even better than that tomorrow. "I will improve myself tomorrow and will try to be more sincere with others and with myself."

But, more important, forget about tomorrow completely.

Start improving yourself today, now!

## DON'T BE AFRAID OF "ESCAPISM"

Some people frown on the word "escapism." It's as if they're saying, "Face up to it! To escape is cowardly!"

To live a happy life, you must come to grips with reality; anything else is an evasion and a misuse of your productive energies. But it is a fatal mistake to feel that this is a 24-hour-a-day task. If you take yourself this seriously, you will always be tense. You will be able to tackle your problems more forcefully if you can relax and reinvigorate yourself with restful sleep.

Sometimes "escaping from it all" can help the busiest, most successful person. Don't be afraid to "escape," and don't look upon it as a waste of time!

I'm most certainly not discussing harmful, self-destructive escape mechanisms. I recommend to you wholesome, positive escapes from pressure: Into the peaceful room of your mind, to the country's healing calm, into the intoxicating enlightenment of travel, into the soothing caress of music.

These and other escapist devices are refreshing to your soul and, properly used, will not harm you. They will give you the nourishment that will ready you to function more effectively in our swift-moving world.

## THE PEACEFULNESS OF THE COUNTRY

In 1798, the great English poet William Wordsworth wrote these beautiful words:

> ". . . and again, I hear.
> These waters, rolling from their mountain-springs
> With a soft inland murmur.—Once again
> Do I behold these steep and lofty cliffs,
> That on a wild secluded scene impress
> Thoughts of more deep seclusion; and connect
> The landscape with the quiet of the sky."

They celebrate the calming effect of Nature, the solace that it can bring a troubled human being. They sing of the comfort one can find in Nature's vastness.

These days expanding industrialization has cut swathes in our countryside, but our country is still blessed with large areas of natural beauty, which is ours to enjoy.

Something is healing about being close to Nature, and I know many people who drive, tired and tense, to the country on Friday night and come back to the city Sunday night soul-satisfied and bright-eyed, ready for a week of productive work.

While it's true that we can't always rush off to the country when we feel that fenced-in feeling, we can go into the quiet of our minds and picture the glories of Nature that we've seen. These sweet images can help us relax.

## CHANGING YOUR SURROUNDINGS

Sometimes a change of pace can do you good, and this is why many people love to travel.

New images of known or unknown places bring refreshment to your mind, just as eating a delicious new dish brings satisfaction to your palate.

Travel can sometimes help you solve your problems. Suppose you have to make a decision. You keep weighing the pros and cons, but the more you think, the more tired you feel, and you're farther from a definite conclusion than you were when you started thinking. At such a time, forcing your thinking will only harm you. You need to escape from the problem for a while; you need relaxation before your mind is ready to go to work again. A weekend auto trip, a few days in strange surroundings, with interesting sights to see and no pressing responsibilities—this prescription might put you in shape to make a good decision a few days later.

## THE SOOTHING SALVE OF MUSIC

Another tranquilizer of the spirit is music. Good music is readily available, and its effects are beneficial, yet many fail to take full advantage of this lovely art. The word "music" is synonymous with qualities of sweetness such that Shakespeare once wrote critically of "The man that hath no music in his soul."

Psychologists have recently noted the soothing effects of music. Studies of industrial concerns have revealed that music increases the efficiency and contentment of working personnel. Studies of mentally disturbed individuals have credited music with exerting a quieting effect on them.

Today, many restaurants pipe in calming music to make meals more pleasant for their customers. Even some skyscraper elevators have pleasant melodies to soothe the up-and-down journey of bustling city dwellers.

One of the world's greatest composers of all time, Ludwig van Beethoven, was deaf when he wrote some of his masterpieces, but his love of music was so great that he could feel and hear the notes in his mind. All you have to do to hear good music is flick a radio dial and try several stations or put some records on the phonograph. Don't be too lazy to give yourself an hour of softness when you need it!

## HOW TO FIND INNER CALMNESS

"But I want first of all—in fact as an end to these other desires—to be at peace with myself. I want a singleness of eye, a purity of intention, a central core to my life that will enable me to carry out these obligations and activities as well as I can.

"I want, in fact, to borrow from the language of the saints, live 'in grace' as much of the time as possible.

"I am not using this term in a strictly theological sense. By grace, I mean an inner harmony, essentially spiritual, which can be translated into outward harmony."

These beautiful lines come from Anne Morrow Lindbergh's *Gift From the Sea* (Pantheon, 1955). They signify the author's understanding of a fundamental concept in any individual's search for happiness: the "inner harmony" that means so much.

*In Peace of Mind* (Simon & Schuster, 1955), Joshua Loth Liebman expresses similar ideas.

> Slowly, painfully, I have learned that peace of mind may transform a cottage into a spacious manor hall; the want of it can make a regal park an imprisoning nutshell. The quest for this unwearied peace is constant and universal. Probe deeply into the teachings of Buddha, Maimonides, or à Kempis, and you will discover that they base their diverse doctrines on the foundation of a large spiritual serenity. Analyze the prayers of troubled, overborne mankind of all creeds, in every age—and their petitions come down to the irreducible common denominators of daily bread and inward peace. Grown men do not pray for vain trifles. When they lift up their hearts and voices in the valley of tears, they ask for strength and courage and understanding.

In this genuinely compassionate passage, Liebman emphasizes the importance of "inward peace," a life goal worthy of any man. The man who attains this quality has found the key to living.

How do you find this inner calmness? It is all up to you and your self-image.

If you hate yourself, your thoughts will whiz by in your mind with the speed of auto racing cars, and you'll have trouble even knowing what you're thinking. You will have to deceive yourself and run away from yourself, and running and running is not restful.

If you accept yourself as you are, then you are well on the road to calm and happiness with all your human frailties.

If you see yourself in a favorable light, if your image of yourself is pleasant, if temporary defeats cannot shake this visual concept of yourself, then you have reached the goal achieved by only the fortunate.

This image of yourself is powerful, more powerful than any words in the dictionary. When you *see* yourself as a success, as a nice guy, ignoring imperfections yet staying close to reality, your conceptual image has great power—and this brings you calmness.

I've given you other suggestions which will help you achieve peace of mind. They are effective, and I hope you'll try them out with wisdom, but in the final analysis, it is the strength of your self-image, which will bring you real calm.

You may feel like saying to me, "I've always been tense. Life has always seemed tough. I've had my share of bad breaks, and I worry a great deal and don't know how to stop."

If you're implying that relaxing is not easy, I must agree with you. I have no prescription that will take immediate effect and give you "relaxation ever after." The main point is that no matter how high-strung you've been, no matter how long you've felt this way, you can feel peace of mind and in a reasonably short time.

You can learn to see new truths about yourself, erasing old falsehoods you have taken for truths. There's something good in you, all of you, that you do not realize. I cannot write this often enough; so solidly entrenched are so many people's inferiority feelings.

There's a very touching passage I came across recently in Lowell Russell Ditzen's *You Are Never Alone* (Henry Holt & Co., 1956):

"In childhood, we are first introduced to the feeling of 'aloneness.' We come into the world helpless and dependent, and adjustment to new environments and experiences is neverending, as poignant in later years as it is in our youth. And not often can we reach across these years to help those who are just starting out on their journey through life.

"Marguerite Bro tells of a child away from home writing to her mother. 'Mommie, I'm lonesome. Deep down inside, I'm terribly young and afraid. I feel so unsure of myself and so helpless.' These words might be written by an individual at 80 as well as eight."

So many people feel this way—lonely, frightened, helpless. Peace of mind seems far away.

But it's not.

As you read this chapter and re-read it, as you go through this book and work on the practice exercises again and again, as you understand more and more your responsibility to yourself, you will gradually begin seeing yourself more accurately and more kindly.

You will strengthen your self-image and, with it, find calmness.

# 16

## YOU CAN LIVE FULLY AT ANY AGE

AT THE AGE OF 65, OR SHORTLY AFTER THAT, MANY MEN RETIRE FROM THEIR lifework. Some do it voluntarily, looking forward to some hazy, unrealistic dream of living out their years in a land of sunshine reclining under a coconut tree. Others are forced by society's rules to give up their jobs, which often represent their most dynamic contact with life.

"Retiring" is, for many, a negative concept; it is contrary to living. It is one of the worst words in the English language.

After retirement, many men deteriorate rapidly. Feeling that they are no longer productive members of society, they feel they are no longer worthwhile human beings. They feel bored with inactivity and feel that they just don't count. Their self-image is negative, that of useless, unimportant nonentities. Many even die within a few years of their retirement.

### RETIREMENT FROM LIFE

Retirement from their jobs seriously injures the self-esteem of many men; retiring from life and its dynamic pursuits literally kills them. How horrible to spend one's last years sitting on a park bench waiting for death! How negative it is to fear death anyway; the person who has lived zestfully, enjoying each day, accepts death as part of God's plan for life.

The man who retires from his job at about 65 should first substitute other activities which will take its place. He should plan to fill the emptiness in his days so that they are still productive.

If he has creative resources or develops them, his retirement years could be vintage years, devoted to things he always wanted to do but for which he never had the time.

For the man of 65 can still grow up in areas which he never explored. There are always new worlds to conquer, new life to experience, new ways to give yourself to life, and people.

So, if you must retire, plan for it. Not listlessly, pessimistically, but with a gleam in your eye. Resolve to go on living for life is not just for the young in age; it is for the young in heart.

## "RETIRING" IS THE OPPOSITE OF LIVING

If you "retire," period, you are giving up on life instead of embarking upon an era of continued growth. Never give up! Take me. I've been a plastic surgeon all my life, but I know that sooner or later—I'm over 60—I'll have to stop practicing. So 15 years ago, I started taking writing seriously. I may be old as a surgeon, but I'm only 15 years old as a practicing writer. I chose writing as a new life for myself to avoid the unhealthy aspects of retirement.

When I'm working on a book, I feel young and full of enthusiasm, giving the best I have in me, always trying to improve. I feel as young as I did when I was a kid of 15, playing baseball with my friends or learning more about the world.

Each of you is a unique individual endowed with your special interests and talents.

Some of you older people can become stamp collectors or book collectors; some of you might enjoy gardening or nature study; some might join social clubs or paint watercolors. You know your latent resources; dig out the gold, throw away the waste products.

I know one man, a veterinarian working as a meat inspector for the government, who was forced into retirement after almost 40 years on the job. Instead of moping, he joined a discussion group, took an active part in it, won popularity as a contributing member of the group, and now moderates its discussions. Never before a public speaker, he now lives dynamically in an area that was never before a part of his life.

Another man, who started working when he was a poor kid of 14 and has spent his life working in the wholesale food products field amassing a fortune, found himself retired at 65. He had never had the time to get a formal education; a wealthy man, he didn't even know what a paragraph was and had read less than a dozen books in his lifetime.

These last few years, he has spent as a "schoolboy," getting the education he'd previously missed out on.

## DON'T RETIRE FROM YOUR TRUE SELF-IMAGE!

When you 'retire," you retire from your true self-image. You destroy a self-image that has taken a lifetime to build; you put yourself in prison, making an underprivileged inmate of yourself.

Faster than George Washington cutting down the cherry tree, you slash your self-image to ribbons. You surround yourself with barbed wire, make yourself the victim of brutal jailers, snuff out your life force. No police come in the middle of the night and enforce this indignity upon you; you do it to yourself.

How can you be of consequence to yourself and others if you do this? In this book, I hope to help you improve your self-image and free your creative life forces so that you can get more out of life.

What I did, you can do. I'm past 60, but when I write, I'm young. As I sit in the playhouse of my mind and hold the mirror up to look at myself, I feel that my self-image is youthful. Some days I practice as a plastic surgeon, some days, I write. But whatever emotional hardships there are in writing, every day has a goal, something to look forward to. So, at my age, I put a revitalizing cream on the face of my self-image, manufactured by the factory of my desire and will in this field.

And look, a miracle! I have turned back the clock. I'm past 60, but I feel each day the zest of a boy of 15 who has bright days ahead of him. And this is realistic, for my days are bright, and I live them as if I've found the fountain of youth. I have, and I'm happy to share my secret with you.

*And, if I can do it, so can* you.

## YOU'RE AS YOUNG AS YOU FEEL

You're 65 now, so you've arrived at middle age; you are still in the prime of life; new horizons lie before you, and the future is yours.

"What!" you say. "Maybe you didn't hear me right. I said I was 65, not 35!"

I heard you.

You're 65, and you think you're old, and lots of people think you're old, but you're not. I'm in the same boat as you and, as I've told you, I'm young.

I wake up in the morning, and I see the sun shining. The sky is blue in my world, and the birds sing, *and people live.* I eat a hearty breakfast, and I don't gulp it down absently. I *eat* it and enjoy it, and plan a constructive, life-filled day.

*You, too, can be young,* and I don't care what your chronological age is. Some people are old at 21 because their self-image is dried up. And some people are still young in spirit at 80.

Bernard Baruch and Winston Churchill come to mind.

Don't live by the book! Write your own book of life! Often we think ourselves into old age.

Expecting to grow old at a certain age, we prepare ourselves for negative goal images. Tapering off on both physical and mental activities, we lose both the flexibility of our joints and our minds and spirits' life force.

With this type of attitude, one naturally becomes old.

But today, a person of 65 is middle-aged. Advances in medicine are increasing life expectancy, and diseases which are dread killers today will be curable tomorrow. Furthermore, increases in the scope of Social Security coverage are making it possible for older people to live more comfortably for many years.

So, if you're 65, enjoy your middle age and if you're 75, enjoy your old age. Take part in life and feel young, no matter what your age. Give to life, and it will give back to you, and you'll feel that life is good.

Naturally, there are limits. It goes without saying that you don't play basketball like a teenager when you are in your sixties and don't run a mile at top speed. At the same time, proper exercise is good for you all of your life. Do you ever give up walking or swimming? Keep your mind fertile and your body useful, and you'll feel young all your life.

## MORE LIVING: A PRESCRIPTION FOR YOU

If you get the flu, perhaps you'll see a doctor, and he'll prescribe some medicine to help speed your recovery.

I'd like to repeat my prescription for people of retirement age who suffer from the disease of apathy and lethargy: More life!

The whole business of living is to remember that every day is a composite lifetime for the person who is happy. A day must have a beginning, a middle, and an end, and the whole must be harmonious.

Those who are happy look forward each day with faith and hope to realize the goals that they set for themselves. Each day there must be goals related to life and the society in which we live, no matter how simple they are basic. For some, the goal might be baking a cake, while for another, it is to bicycle through the park.

Don't laugh at these goals, for if these people have their hearts in what they're doing, the activities are important. To one, a bike is a symbol of living, enjoying movement through the park.

Standing still, you may fall down.

It is in doing nothing, in being bored, that people die inside. Did you see the motion picture "Marty"? This is a fine, realistic film showing young people who are old because they sit around with time on their hands.

Retirement from life is criminal because it's self-inflicted. You become a traitor to yourself when you walk away from your daily goals, denying the life force that God has given you. Age is no excuse at all.

When you retire from life, you walk away from reality and self-respect, write off your self-image and voluntarily isolate yourself in an inner prison and your soul in jail.

Some of you probably think that money represents the solution, but experiments on the problems of living longer have indicated otherwise. Researchers interviewing over 1,000 people 50 and over have found that money was not a key factor in the happiness of older people. A retired industrialist earning a six-figure income and a man who retired on Social Security checks were found to have identical problems. Preparation, vitality, interest in the contemporary world, work, and ability to take pleasure in others—the researchers found that these were the things that made these people happy.

In short, these trained observers found that people were happy who went toward life.

## THE EDITOR WHO RETIRED FROM LIFE

A few months ago, I had lunch with the editor of a men's magazine, and he told me about another magazine editor he knew who had been forced to retire from his job because of his age.

They threw a retirement party for him, and all the higher echelon folks showed up. There was plenty to eat, even champagne; everyone showered praise on him and then—retirement.

For years his colleagues had admired his dynamic dedication to detail and the intelligent flexibility of his mind. His productive ability grew with the years and was still growing when, because of his age, he was forced to retire.

One day after the party, he was like an old shoe, thrown away after years of service.

Today he is a sick man, mentally sick because his productive powers are dying inside him, denied creative expression. After 35 years of dedicated work for his company, this was his reward.

How much better to have allowed him to continue on the job he loved instead of compelling him to retire! Some more understanding firms make retirement optional, and I take my hat off to them.

## THE DOCTOR WHO FOUND YOUTH

Another man, a surgeon, worked at a New York hospital till he was 65 and was then asked to retire. I know him well, and for a while, he was depressed and moody. This was not like him at all; he was the kind of person people liked, and I was used to seeing a smile on his face. But, for the first time in many years, his self-image had taken a setback. He felt that he was no longer useful.

A resourceful man, he got a new job lecturing at a college. Today he is a professor on the medical faculty and delivers stimulating lectures on the background and history of medicine and on methods of surgery.

He has regained his feeling of youth and is alive with his students.

## LIVING FULLY ALL YOUR LIFE

Today more thought is being given to the problem of compulsory job retirement as enlightened people realize the trouble it can create. Some firms make retirement optional.

In *Live Better After Fifty* (McGraw Hill, 1953), Ray Giles states that "public health authorities, leading geriatricians and others especially interested in the problems of aging, are putting themselves on record as against compulsory retirement at 65.

> At national conferences on problems of aging, outspoken criticism is being voiced against hard and fast retirement policies. The economic waste to the nation is being pointed out.
>
> Statistics prove that in many occupations, older people commonly outproduce younger employees. Older employees, statistics show, are more reliable, have fewer accidents, and are less often absent from work.

Don't let your age keep you from remaining on the job if you are allowed your free choice! On the other hand, if job retirement is voluntary and you feel that you can live more fully without employment, then retire and do all the things for which you've never had the time. The thing to remember is that only you, in the final analysis, can decide what's best for you.

But whether you must retire or *choose* to retire from your job, remember, once again: *First, prepare yourself in new areas of living.*

In *Ways and Means to Successful Retirement*, Colby Forrest outlines many helpful suggestions for activities after retirement.

Your librarian can recommend other books that may give you ideas for enriching your retirement years.

There are organizations in almost all communities that offer activities designed for older people: community centers, YMCAS, settlement houses. They have much to offer you; why not take advantage of their facilities?

Private social work agencies will help the older person with his individual problems, no matter what their nature. So will the religious leaders in your neighborhood church or synagogue.

These people can help you fashion a new, refreshing life for yourself after you've retired. But your main tool is your own self-image and your determination to keep it bright and shining. If you have pride in yourself, and if you feel that you're young and still attractive, you will create from deep inside ideas with spirit and goals that move you.

When you wake up in the morning, you will feel like tasting more life, and you *will feel youthful as long as you live*. You will be a living example of what God meant when He created the human race.

There's a funny story in *Live Better After Fifty:* "In January 1953 Henry Bailey Little looked back over his 55 years as president of the Institution for Savings in Newburyport and vicinity and came to an important conclusion. When his board of directors asked him to serve another term, he declined. He said the time had come for a younger man to take his place. So William Black was made the institution's new head.

"So far, this doesn't sound very exciting. Actually, it was interesting news because the retiring Mr. Little was 102 years old and the 'younger man' chosen to take his place was 83."

Perhaps the moral of this story is: *Life begins at 83*. It can, you know!

Don't be taken in by movies whose heroes and heroines are physically young and handsome or by TV commercials featuring young people without a wrinkle on their foreheads! They are not the only important people around. You—if you're older—count as much as they do, and God created each of you in His goodness.

Wine is not good until it is aged; it mellows with the passing of the years. It can be like this for human beings. Young people may be able to race effortlessly around tennis courts and may be capable of dancing around a ballroom all night without tiring. They may climb mountains and swim oceans. But they often lack understanding, which comes only through the experience of many years of living. They make tragic mistakes, products of their inexperience. And they often lack compassion and wisdom.

If you're older, you've had many successes and many failures. It must be this way—no life is perfect. Don't dwell on the failures; picture your proud moments.

See yourself at your best and admire your self-image! If you do, you will never shrink from life; it will hold no terrors for you. You will live all your life fully, living each day the best you know, going to sleep peacefully when the day is done, dreaming pleasant dreams.

You will live fully after 65 and as long as you live with goals, with friends, without self-pity, without resentment, without regret. Loving life, you will never retire from it—as long as you live!

# 17

## YOUR DAILY DOZEN

### 12 WAYS TO A NEW SELF-IMAGE

YOU'VE READ MOST OF MY BOOK, AND I HOPE YOU'VE ENJOYED IT AND IMPROVED yourself through reading it and applying the principles I've set forth for you. If you make use of these concepts faithfully, you will be able to change your self-image and your ability to enjoy a full life.

In this chapter, I am summing up the all-important weapons which you have at your command, your "daily dozen."

They are just words outlining concepts, but they pack the kick of an artillery cannon.

With one exception: They will not destroy fortresses but will simply guide you toward the good life.

1. *Truth.*

The Greeks had a proverb, "From the gods come the saying 'Know thyself,'" but your "truth" about yourself is so often *false*. Most people tend to downgrade their abilities, their value as human beings, their assets. Dwelling on failures and overlooking successes, they whip themselves emotionally with an almost sadistic intensity. Is your truth about yourself real, or is it an alien concept divorced from reality and destroying you from within? Learn to see yourself as you really are in your best moments.

2. *Imagination.*

What a wonderful tool this can be—but most people do not cultivate it. "The great instrument of moral good is the imagination," wrote Percy Bysshe

Shelley, England's great romantic poet. Shelley claimed, "Imagination is the eye of the soul."

Neglected fields will not produce prolific crops; a neglected imagination will not lead you into the green pastures of abundant life. Learn to use mental picturing to plot for you the way to a better future.

Visualize yourself in the roles and situations you have relished; keep imaging yourself in these successes, over and over, till your "success pictures" blot out your "failure pictures." Make your imagination a friend to be treasured instead of a storehouse of fears.

### 3. Relaxation.

Life is short, and the individual who wastes it worrying throws away this precious gift that God gives you. Benjamin Franklin said, "He that can take rest is greater than he that can take cities." This is true; taking cities involves superior firepower while taking rest involves a deep spiritual capacity.

Forgive others, for forgiveness soothes the feelings and brings peace of mind. Forgive also because no one is perfect; when you hold a grudge against someone for years, you may be blaming him for an inconsiderate act that you, in your own imperfection, might have committed.

Accept others with their human faults and relax with yourself, fallible as you are. Relax with your failures and aim at the achievement of worthwhile goals.

And forgive yourself!

### 4. That Winning Feeling.

This feeling can move mountains for you if you feel you are a good fellow who deserves success and happiness. I'm not a soothsayer, I have no crystal ball, and I don't believe in palmistry, but I can foresee victories for the person who gets that winning feeling, that image of himself in successful roles. In the words of Emerson, "Self-trust is the first secret of success," and when this self-trust is crystallized into an image of winning, it carries a big punch.

The spirit with which you tackle projects, your feeling about the self which performs in the world of reality, almost predetermines the results of your efforts.

Once it is a part of your basic personality, this belief in yourself will pull you through crises and, though it may be temporarily shaken, will revive you if catastrophes befall you.

As long as you keep stoking the fires of this feeling, you are rich. You feed your automatic success mechanism, and it produces for you.

5. *Good habits.*

"Men acquire a particular quality by constantly acting in a particular way," wrote Aristotle. Your habits added up and consolidated into a whole, are you? If they are positively oriented, you are a person who goes toward success. If they are pernicious, you are stalking failure. The great Roman poet Ovid believed that "Habits change into character."

Many people believe that you cannot change your habits; this is not so. You can discard bad habits and develop good ones if you're willing to work hard at change. Re-read chapter 6 for a thorough analysis of this vital subject and learn to question habits that seem almost a part of you and yet are harmful to you.

6. *The Aim of Happiness.*

People have different goals. Some are basic, some minor. For example, you may have a basic goal of being a good schoolteacher and a minor one of putting your photo album in order when you get a few hours to spare. As total individuals, people's basic aims vary. Some dedicate their lives to worry or to holding grudges, or obsessive cleanliness. Why don't you dedicate yours to happiness? Think of the feelings that will make you happy, the skills, the successes, the relationships with people, the concepts about yourself, the material accomplishments. Then aim at their realization, keeping this in mind: You must feel that you have a right to be happy; otherwise, consciously or unconsciously, you will put roadblocks in your way. Insist on giving yourself this right: it is your natural heritage.

Don't take it away from yourself.

People achieve happiness in different ways. The great Roman orator Cicero thought that "A happy life consists in tranquility of mind," while the Roman satirical poet Juvenal wrote that "We deem those happy who, from the experience of life, have learned to bear its ills, without being overcome by them." Find your happiness; don't follow someone else's prescription.

7. *Unmasking*

When you are driving a car 55 miles an hour on one of our thruways, do you wear a blindfold? Of course not.

Still, you may go through life wearing a mask to hide your true feelings. This is a blindfold because, in hiding from others, you blind yourself to your potential qualities as a person. This degree of concealment is so unnecessary;

it shows that you think of yourself as an undesirable person: a weakling, or a monster, or God knows what.

Your truth about yourself is false.

When you learn to see yourself with kind eyes, you will have no need for a mask.

8. *Compassion.*

This is one of the qualities that separates human beings from beasts—or it should. When you feel for others, deep in your heart, you are soaring to your most wonderful moments as a human being. Others' gratitude may come in return for your brotherly concern, but your real reward is the warm feeling you will experience toward others and toward yourself. "Thou shalt love thy neighbor as thyself" St. Matthew.

This love for your neighbor will make you feel good about yourself, about your capacity as a worthy human being.

Your meals will taste better, you will sleep better, and you will work better if you can feel genuinely compassionate.

In the words of Beecher, "Compassion will cure more sins than condemnation."

9. *Accepting Your Weakness.*

How would you feel if you occupied a sixth-floor room in an office building, and there was no floor? Insecure, naturally. It is like this with people. You may be strong, healthy, and successful, but there are no guarantees in life, and sometimes everything will go wrong for a while. Your strong self-image will befriend you, but as your troubles mount, you will eventually feel tired and weak. Now the question is, Do you accept your temporary weakness in a human way, or do you blame yourself for it, feeling that you're a total failure? This is a key question. If you reject yourself when you're weak, then you have no floor under you, and you can never feel secure. Your strength is not real. You are only a "fair-weather" friend to yourself, and your self-image is made of paper. Only when you accept your weakness and your strength can you reach your full stature.

10. *Living with Your Mistakes.*

"The man who makes no mistakes does not usually make anything." These are the words of Bishop W. C. Magee and truer words I know not. If you want happiness, you must overcome the perfectionistic streak in you that decrees you must never err. You cannot live with this kind of attitude; you can only cower in a shell of your own making, afraid to try anything. If Babe Ruth had condemned himself every time he struck out, he would have destroyed his confidence in his ability to hit home runs.

Stop destroying yourself with criticism and learn to laugh gently at yourself when you blunder.

If striking out in the game of life doesn't bother you, then you can learn to hit home runs!

11. *Being Yourself.*

John Stuart Mill once wrote that "all good things which exist are the fruits of originality." This is a sentence to remember when you feel that you must live your life according to others' prescriptions. Only when you are yourself does your life have real meaning.

Stop basing your personality on the smiles or frowns of other people and give yourself the smile of approval that you need. Strengthen your self-image, and others' criticism will just bounce off you without ever getting beneath your skin. Ignore people who try to bully you into submission to their will, understanding that they do this out of weakness. You are truly successful only when you live your life the way you wish.

12. *Never Retiring.*

Ancient civilizations devised a means of measuring time.

Centuries, decades, years, months, weeks, days, hours, minutes, seconds. These statistical devices, some people think, tell us whether we are "old or young," but they don't. If you fill your days with activities that excite you, you are young—even if you're 100 years old. If everything bores you, you are old, even if you're 18.

When you approach 65, which society has long labeled a "retirement age," you may be compelled to retire from your lifework. Whether you are or not, continue to lead a useful, interesting life! Prepare some interest before retiring—whether you have children or not—in case you are forced to retire. The time to grow up in one field is when you are retiring from another.

Never go into an artificial state of hibernation that is unnecessary; it will only weaken your self-image.

These are your "daily dozen." Don't be skeptical about them; they will help you to live a better life. When things are going wrong, and you feel depressed, read this chapter. Read it again and again, and you will fortify your self-image. Once you feel better about yourself, you will see the world through different colored glasses.

It will look better to you, and you will look better to it.

# 18

## RAVE NOTICES FOR YOU

AT THE BEGINNING OF THIS BOOK, WE TALKED ABOUT GOING INTO THE PLAYHOUSE of your mind to create the kind of images that will, with effort and intelligence, positivize your concept of yourself and of the world around you.

You can change—but you must be willing to work at change.

As Theodore Roosevelt wrote, "There never has been devised, and there never will be devised, any law which will enable a man to succeed save by the exercise of those qualities which have always been the prerequisites of success— the qualities of hard work, of keen intelligence, of unflinching will."

So work hard in the powerful world of mental pictures, and improve yourself in the world of reality. Make a new, better world for yourself!

Now, go back into the playhouse of your mind once more and relax while I unfold a fascinating story—about you!

### THE SPOTLIGHT'S ON YOU

Did you ever read in the Bible, "Physician, heal thyself"? You are the only one who can improve yourself, you are your physician, and that's why you are the central character in this drama. You are the producer, the director, the chief actor, the prop man.

You are going to be in the spotlight.

This is a new role for you because you've always hidden your talents in a closet of fear, buried your resources in a mass of shame. You've always thought so little of yourself that you wore a mask of indifference everywhere you went so that people couldn't see your "dreadful" feelings. You've always imagined the worst catastrophes befalling you, and you've been overcautious about taking chances in life. You've buried yourself in negative habits and have resented those who seemed to be enjoying life.

But you've changed. You're a new person now. Working faithfully on the practice exercises in this book, you've changed one all-important mechanism—your mental picturing. You *see* yourself differently.

The pictures in your imagination have become more pleasant; at times, they glow. They are not unrealistic; as you have altered your image of yourself in your mind, emphasizing your successful qualities, you have gradually brought the impact of this new self into real-life situations. Yes, you have changed!

## RING THE CURTAIN UP

The curtain rises, and you are on the stage, the center of attention. There was a time when you would have been terrified by this, would have run for cover. Sure, you're a little nervous, but you accept it humanly and don't criticize yourself for it.

You don't inhibit your actions because people are watching you. You remain yourself and do not look to the audience for reassurance. You approve of yourself, and that's enough!

Horace, the great Roman poet, once wrote, "Adversity has the effect of eliciting talents which, in prosperous circumstances would have lain dormant."

Of course, you have known days of adversity during your life, but these hard times have contributed to your full development as a person. For one thing, you feel compassion for the next fellow, understanding troubles as you do. Your ability to feel compassion makes you a full human being. If life had spoiled you if you'd always been wealthy and sheltered, your sense of identification with other people might have been blunted.

The audience sees a growing human being in front of them, whose healthy self-image will enable him to enjoy life.

## YOU'RE A HIT!

Confucius, the famous Chinese philosopher, once said, "In all things, success depends upon previous preparation, and without such preparation, there is sure to be a failure."

But you needn't concern yourself with failure—you're a hit! You have prepared your thinking for the tasks that will face it. You see new truths about yourself, truths that give you star billing as an individual, that provide you the courage to stand out on the stage and be yourself. For this drama is not fictional; you are playing yourself, and you're going to have a long run! You'll get happiness from your new role and, if you want it, you'll get money too. You'll make lasting friendships because you are a good friend to yourself, in a wholesome way, and can give to others.

## YOU'VE RE-WRITTEN THE SCRIPT

The script of this drama is mastery. There's no other word for it. Your heroics equal any Horatio Alger story as you climb from failure to success.

You will not travel in an absolutely straight line—no one does. There is bound to be some failure even in the happiest of lives.

No one is omnipotent; life is not a fairy tale. Success is not a one-way road.

You understand this realistically, and this will help you. Being prepared for occasional failures, they will not destroy your morale.

Disappointments may depress you now and then, but you will never again be buried in depression because you have the weapons with which to: fight your way out and the insight to know when to use them.

This is a creative script. You are creating the most valuable state of mind in the world—happiness.

## A LIFETIME OF LIVING

Your days are now adventures in self-exploration and the exploration of the world around you.

Your world is a bright, happy place: you like yourself, and you have good friends. You work about eight hours a day and enjoy it, relax about eight hours a day and relish it, sleep about eight hours a day, and it's not "tossing-and-turning" sleep. When you go to sleep, you're out.

You don't have every little thing you want; such an expectation would be ridiculous.

You're not a child who must have every toy he sees; you're an adult with a mature understanding of the imperfections of life.

The important thing is this: *What you need, you now have.* You like yourself; you can relax with your thoughts and with your friends, you have goals, your goals, you are moving toward your successes—and you are happy.

Your whole attitude toward life has changed; you no longer are defensive, looking for ways to hide from potential enemies. You have taken the offensive. You go toward life with assurance, prepared for success, and ready to accept failure.

You feel indestructible because you will not destroy yourself.

## EACH DAY CAN BE JOYFUL

Each day has meaning. You don't just sit around wondering how to pass the time. If anything does bother you, it's that each day has only 24 hours and you have so much living to do.

You're young, like a happy child who fights sleep because he doesn't want to miss out on all the fun he might have had if he was awake.

Every activity has enjoyment. Each meal brings satisfaction; each personal encounter is dynamic; each tree is beautiful; each goal inspires you.

You want to share your joy with others, and you feel wonderful when you brighten the life of a human brother. He appreciates your compassion, and when you are down, he will try to give you a helping hand.

This is an uplifting drama—and *it is realistic*. Cynics may criticize it, calling it overly optimistic, but a strong self-image can do all this for you. Why see reality as shabby and poverty-stricken? Reality can be beautiful too.

Your belief can make it so.

## LIFE IS YOURS TO LIVE

You don't always feel strong, but it's no crime to feel weak. There are several forms of weakness, one of which bends. The other, unfortunately, breaks. When you feel weak, you "bend," and then you go on to a reaffirmation of your strength.

Feeling strong, you live dynamically. You need friends more than ever *so that you can give to them*. You need this feeling of giving to others as an extension of your feeling of overflowing happiness. If you could not find people to give to, you would feel frustrated in the expression of your full sense of happiness.

"Let there be no strife I pray thee, between thee and me . . . for we be brethren" (Genesis). Your very presence is a reward to your friends, an affirmation of the brotherly feeling of this biblical quote. Your company is a tonic to them because you don't look to tear them down or compete with them but accept them and make them feel better about themselves. You talk to them as individuals, not at them as if you were a lecturer, and they were your disciples. You feel compassion for their troubles and enthusiasm for their good qualities.

## YOU ARE THE MASTER OF YOUR FATE

The world has not changed much. There is still talk about atomic wars, and false gods still drive many people.

But you are changed, and you have changed your world.

You no longer feel helpless. You feel that you are the master of your fate. When you read the morning newspaper and the headlines are disturbing, your agitation does not overwhelm you. If there is anything you can do to better the situation: a letter you can write, a community meeting you can attend, you sometimes may choose to do this.

But once you have done everything within your power in the way of constructive action, you forget about it.

You do not waste your time worrying; you no longer believe in self-torture.

You go back to living a happy life, setting your goals, achieving your successes.

Your successes become easier as you get that winning feeling.

It's like a major-league pinch-hitter who has come off the bench to win game after game.

His confidence rides with him as he pictures his past successes, and when the manager looks down his bench for someone whom pressure will not upset, he knows whom to pick.

You're not a pinch-hitter, though. You're in the game all the time—you're not a part-time performer. Your talents are well-balanced, and your life story could be an inspiration to anyone.

Your drama is a smashing success, and as the curtain comes down, the audience breaks into wild applause. You go backstage, but the audience keeps applauding, waiting for you to come out and take a curtain call.

## TAKE A BOW!

Now, you step back out on the stage and take a bow.

You're the main actor in this drama, the writer and director too, for it is you who have reconstructed your life.

I've just been a helper behind the scenes, a production assistant, a prop man.

You've done the real work. You've worked hard on the practice exercises, you've read and re-read chapters that have special meaning for you, you've dedicated your energies to your self-improvement. You deserve all the credit in the world.

The audience applauds again. Most audiences are appreciative and will re-

THE MAGIC POWER OF SELF-IMAGE PSYCHOLOGY

turn good for good. They applaud excitedly, sending waves of love through to you in response to your fine, winning effort.

Change is not easy. It takes work. You've worked, and you've changed. You've overcome the skepticism of acquaintances and your own tendency to belittle yourself. You're a bigger person, and this is quite a production. Recognizing this, they continue to applaud until you come out and take another curtain call.

This has been the biggest victory of your life. You are happy with your self-image and need not hide behind defenses. I congratulate you on it!

I leave you with one final wish: that, in the years to come, you continue to *see yourself* as the worthwhile person you are.

If you do, you will always be happy!

# BOOK FIVE

# THOUGHTS TO
# LIVE BY

# CONTENTS

# SUMMARY: BE EVERYTHING YOU WANT TO BE!

Dr. Maltz said to people of all ages: "You are embarking on the greatest adventure of your life . . . to improve your self-image, to create more meaning in your life and the lives of others. This is your responsibility. Accept it, NOW!"

If you accept this challenge and his advice you will become a more alert, alive human being. You'll never regret it.

With the help of his wise and sympathetic words, this book, based on the principles of Psycho-Cybernetics, will help you gain new courage and self-confidence, overcome tension and stress, and give your life more meaning. You will greet each day with enthusiasm and hope, and learn to turn a crisis into an opportunity and make every minute count. In addition, you will gain tools to help you learn to relax, build a better self-image, throw off fear and frustration, and rise above failure.

*Thoughts to Live By* is the tonic you've been looking for to put more living into your life.

Dr. Maltz believes everyone was born to succeed. Everyone has a marvelous creative potential that can be discovered and used for a happier, more productive life.

Out of a rich and useful life, he offers you the wisdom gained through many years of study, observation, and medical practice. Here is a practical, reassuring book that will help you discover your self-image, expand it, and thereby expand your potential for living. Here are the simple principles that have helped millions toward self-fulfillment, even in a confusing and troubled world.

This classic reprint is as relevant today as when it was first published in 1975.

# INTRODUCTION

Descartes said, "I think, therefore I am." How important are these five words to you? They should be the most important five words in your life, every minute, every hour, every day, every week, every month, every year. These words are your passport to happiness. You can travel wherever you choose, and you will never be alone. With these words, you create a worthwhile foundation in the world within your mind and heart, a world of light and calm and order. These five words separate you from the animal; they are the keys to the greatness within you that is awaiting recognition.

What a terrible world this would be if we didn't think. Of course, Descartes meant constructive, not destructive, thinking, using your thoughts not to hurt others, or to aggressively step on others, or to destroy yourself with negative thoughts. Descartes didn't mean thinking uncertainty, despair, fear, insecurity, loneliness, resentment, and emptiness, all corroding factors in negative thinking.

If you can grasp the true meaning of these five words, you will have the keys to achievement and happiness. You will be able to live constructively in a creative world, having the power to do your thing productively, understanding your own needs and the needs of others. You can learn to use your courage, self-respect, self-acceptance, and self-confidence to make these five words mean what they really do. We, in the present day, go a little further. We say, "I think, therefore I am . . . and I *do!*" You reach fulfillment when you not only think creatively but act creatively to reach worthwhile goals. This is what Psycho-Cybernetics means: clear, constructive thinking, steering your mind to a productive, useful goal.

You will find in the pages of this book something that will help you on your way to self-fulfillment.

By self-fulfillment, I mean more than the financial security you deserve. I mean finding more meaning to your life, whatever your age, getting more living out of life—something you must achieve for yourself.

You are embarking on the greatest adventure of your life, to improve your self-image, to create more meaning in your life and in the lives of others. This is your responsibility. Accept it now!

# THOUGHTS TO LIVE BY

## COURAGE

These are the words on courage by Cervantes:

*He that loses wealth loses much:*
*But he that loses courage loses all.*

Courage, like compassion, is one of the great ingredients of the success instinct in man. I cannot imagine anyone being a successful human being without courage, without the capacity to overcome obstacles and reach a constructive goal, without the fortitude to cling to ideals that encompass good for him and for his brothers and sisters the world over.

Courage is the outward expression of the three worlds in which man lives—his physical world, his mental world, and his spiritual world.

Courage—I mean creative courage—of necessity implies the search for freedom on these three levels, which in turn means the search for truth for good.

Courage that demands that you stand up for your rights and the rights of others, the kind of glorious courage that built our nation; courage to live with compassion, not aggression; courage to live in belief, not doubt; courage to live in hope, not despair; courage to surmount crises instead of being overwhelmed by them; courage to build self-reliance; courage to accept a mistake instead of rebuking yourself for not being perfect—these are true aspects of courage! Remember, although you are an island within yourself, you belong to the mainland with others and are destined to share your courage with others.

## KEEP GOING

Columbus, as he sailed across the uncharted routes of the Atlantic, not knowing where he was going, wrote in his private log, "This day we sailed on course

WSW." Surely, he must have been filled with hope and faith that he was headed right, that he would reach his destination. Surely, too, he must have had thoughts of despair that he would never reach his goal, that he might flounder endlessly on angry waters, perhaps lost forever to the world. Things couldn't have been worse. His ships were damaged, and the men were threatening mutiny. Did he at times lose his hope and faith and confidence? Of course he did!

But in moments of despair, frustration, and crisis, Columbus called upon his courage. He knew he had to be right, and he kept on going. Why? Because he had inner integrity. Have you integrity during a period of distress? Have you self-respect during crises? Do you call upon your confidence in desperate moments of despair and futility, in panic, when you are lost in the rough seas of frustration? Unable to reach port? Threatening mutiny on yourself? Greatness exists when you are trying to be great. When? At a time of crisis. At a time of doubt, distress, and despair, are you willing to write on a slip of paper the words of Columbus, "This day we sailed on," and then live by them? It is your moral responsibility to do so.

## THE GREAT BALANCE

Here is a couplet written in 1591 by John Florio:

> *When you are an anvil, hold you still;*
> *When you are a hammer, strike your fill*

Life is the great balance between the anvil and the hammer. The eternal struggle between failure and success, between hope and despair, between joy and sorrow. We all have our terrifying feelings of loneliness and despair, and they can strike at any hour, at any moment. Creative living teaches us that under these circumstances, we brace ourselves against the stress, against the shock. These are our anvil moments.

But then we have our hammer moments. With hope and faith within us, there comes a time when we can perform, when we can reach goals and contribute to life, when we can prove by action that we are willing to put our integrity on the line for minorities who are abused. We can really prove that we understand our own needs and the needs of others. We can utilize our confidence creatively to find success and share it with others. We can live in the sunny present instead of the foggy past. Then we are the spiritual hammer. With resolution and determination, we can strike hard at the right place. We can strive for the right goal within our capabilities and forge the big self that we can be, that we are, remembering always to share this bigness of self with other people.

## PRAISE

What is praise? It is a varied expression of love and friendship, and we should use it more often to compliment someone for a deed well done, for a word well spoken. Why be effusive in our praise of someone when he is put to rest in a cemetery and can't hear a word of it?

What is praise? Something we all need now and then. Every human being, whether he is a beggar or a tycoon, a peasant or a philosopher, a student or a teacher, whether he is alone or married, searches desperately for recognition. One of the greatest goals for every human being is to feel needed, wanted for something somewhere. We deserve this praise not when we demand it or search for it, but when we receive it naturally in the process of doing something for others, while we are doing something for ourselves.

Since my book *Psycho-Cybernetics* was published in 1959, 1 have received thousands of letters from people all over the world thanking me for helping them to be themselves, for making them feel they are needed. We all need each other, and we should make it our business to praise when necessary. Remember, love and friendship are priceless at any age. Consider the words of Berton Braley:

*If you think that praise is due him,*
*Now's the time to slip it to him,*
*For he cannot read his tombstone when he's dead.*

## ON PETTINESS

Disraeli said, "Life is too short to be little." Seven words! We should remember these words every moment of every day. "Life is too short to be little." Think about the horrors of war that man has not been able to stop since the beginning of time. Think what has happened in the last fifty years! The advances in medicine and other sciences, landings on the moon, progress toward the cure of cancer, our youth evolving, despite their mistakes, to a greatness that will make this place a better world. We are coming closer and closer to the brotherhood of man.

Every human being has a divine instinct within him to contribute to this new world of greatness through the assets within him: understanding, self-respect, courage, forgiveness, self-acceptance, and self-confidence. Nor should we overlook compassion, which eventually will bring about the peace we so fervently desire.

Under these circumstances, how can one be petty? Suppose we are all that way now and then because we are very fragile and easily hurt. But why not use our inner strength to rise above petty hurts, the pettiness of rancor, jealousy, and envy when the world is asking us, pleading with us to be big with understanding, friendship, and love? Let us devote our lives to worthwhile goals, to creative achievement, to happiness and we won't have to be told to share this happiness with others. We will! We know that life is too short to be petty.

## ON IMAGINATION

The poet William Blake wrote these lines:

> To see a world in a grain of sand,
> And heaven in a wildflower,
> Hold infinity in the palm of your hand,
> And eternity in an hour.

These words describe so clearly the power of the imagination. Do you think that only musicians, poets, artists, and dramatists, those who work through experience to create beauty, have imagination? If you do, you are wrong.

We are all blessed with the power of a creative imagination. A boy of six, with other young students, was studying words ending in "ll" in a school in St. Louis. When they came to the word "kill," he said, "We shouldn't study this word in school. Why don't we put the letter 's' in front of it?" At six, he turned the word "kill" into "skill!" He showed that he could use his imagination creatively, not only for himself but for the whole world.

In these times of violence, when a human being sometimes feels he is worth nothing, the beauty of imagination is lost, hidden, suppressed. The rapid pace in which we live tends to warp the free play of the imagination. But you, all of us, have imagination just as you have self-respect. You cannot ignore your imagination any more than your self-respect if you are to survive in creative terms. It is our human responsibility every day to reclaim our imagination and to see the beauty within us and around us.

## THE HAPPINESS PRINCIPLE

The happiness principle, in simple terms, means this: The more you share your happiness with others, the more you have yourself. It also means that the happier you are, the wiser you are. And, finally, happiness is good, just as unhappiness is evil. When you are happy, the glorious things in nature are more visible: the flowers smell better, the sound of a rippling brook is more distinct, food tastes better, the hand of friendship is firmer, and your voice has more life to it. On the other hand, when you are unhappy, you cannot see the beauty without and within: you don't hear as well as you could, nothing smells right, the food doesn't taste good, your touch is benumbed, and your voice is lost in loneliness. Happiness is internal. It means clear perception within you, where you see the possibilities of becoming bigger and better than you are for yourself and for others. It means sharing your good fortune with others who need your good will desperately. In unhappiness, your spiritual vision is clouded by a mental cataract so that you cannot see the good in yourself; you cannot be kind to yourself or wise enough to realize that loneliness and fear are your blind spots. Remember the words of John Masefield, the famous poet laureate of England: "The days that make us happy make us wise."

## ARRIVAL

Cervantes, the great author of *Don Quixote,* said, "The road is always better than the inn." If you think about these words for a moment, you will discover that they represent a glorious and productive way of living.

In my younger days, when, like anyone else, I was after my goal, I believed that when I reached it, I would find satisfaction and a reward for my achievement. But soon, I realized that we are all goal strivers; and when we reach one goal, we must start for another goal the next day. In other words, each goal achieved is like an inn. It is merely a temporary resting place along the road, the endless road of self-fulfillment. Creative living means motion, movement, turning away from dead ends as you move along the highway to achievement. The great fun and pleasure are the journey, because it is your area of creative effort. The joy of a great painter is more in the creation of a painting than in the final display of it in a gallery. I have always kept moving on various highways toward the operating room, toward the writing of a book, toward medical research in wound healing, toward the lecture platform. Only then could I look back to the joys of accomplishment and look forward with hope, desire, belief, and determination to a new tomorrow.

Each inn of today is a stopping point for a moment; but in reality, it is a starting point for a new adventure. And this road that we travel is all the more beautiful if, at the same time, we travel within the world of mind and spirit, making sure that the dead ends of negative feelings are not there. The great expectation of self-fulfillment improves the prospect of your greatest achievement.

## AN INSIDE JOB

When we speak of an inside job, we usually mean a carefully contrived crime executed by "people in the know." If a bank is robbed and there are no clues, it might be an inside job. If a home is rifled, with valuable jewelry missing, and the theft was executed with neat dispatch, no complications, we ask ourselves if this crime was not an inside job. The most pernicious kind of inside job is the crime we inflict upon ourselves when, through fear or hatred, we rob ourselves of peace of mind by persisting in endless self-criticism. Indeed, we create prison walls around ourselves, preventing achievement of happiness. Are you an "inside jobber" who walks away from reality into the gloomy tunnels of a disturbed mind? Do you hurl yourself into a dungeon of futility?

If you do, do not despair, because Psycho-Cybernetics is an inside job, a creative inside job. You can change. Psycho-Cybernetics will do an inside job that will "unprove" your self-image and help you to grow in stature as a professional human being. This creative inside job will bolster your belief in yourself as you rise above mistakes to self-respect and compassion. You must refuse to make a mountain out of a mole hill, performing daily tasks without pressure. What is your inside job? To use your creative mechanism for success, not failure, achieving your position as a professional human being.

## ON ENTHUSIASM

Enthusiasm is one of our most important traits and assets that keeps us young whether we are three, thirty, six, sixty, nine, or ninety. This means that people of all ages can find eternal youth within or without if they have an eagerness to fulfill themselves. Everyone has enthusiasm, whether they are aware of it or not, simply because enthusiasm is within each of us, waiting to be utilized for creative performance and reaching a productive goal.

You must find your enthusiasm. Like confidence and like opportunity, you must create it for yourself without waiting for someone to thrust it upon you.

In other words, no one can make you enthusiastic without your consent. No one can make you eager to achieve goals without your consent.

Enthusiasm is a thought turned into a performance; it is the kinetic energy that propels you to your destination. But first, you must have a goal you want to achieve. Enthusiasm implies that you believe in yourself, that you concentrate with courage, that you return to your big self to complete a job, that you practice self-discipline, that you have a dream, that you see victory in the distance. You will reach your goal if you use your imagination, grow daily in stature, and adjust to realities while you yearn for improvement.

Can you find enthusiasm with doubt, despair, fear, frustration, worry, or distrust? Of course not. These negative feelings tell you that you are getting old before your time, just as enthusiasm tells you that you can be young and successful as long as you want.

In the words of Ralph Waldo Emerson, "Nothing great was ever achieved without enthusiasm."

## THE STRANGER WITHIN

You meet strangers every day of your life wherever you go. But did it ever occur to you that you, yourself, do not go alone, that there is a stranger who keeps you company all the time. This stranger is close to you, closer than a wife, or a child, or a parent, or a friend. It is the stranger within you. The reason it is a stranger is that you don't know him. You are unaware of his presence, unaware of what his function is. It is important that you get to know him better, because if you do, he can become your best friend. To be truly happy, you must be sincere with this stranger. If you ignore him or don't understand him, he may become your worst enemy.

Do you know that you have a self-image behind your face? This self-image symbolically has a face of its own; it is the face of your mind that dominates your life. It is your inner twin from which you can't escape. This twin controls your life because, whether you realize it or not, you do what it tells you.

This self-image, then, is the stranger within you. It is the heartbeat of your mind, the built-in clock that ticks away the hours of happiness or sorrow, depending on your understanding of him. Your self-image is your emotional thermostat that regulates your behavior to others and to yourself. This stranger, your self-image, is the opinion you have of yourself and is made up of your successes and failures in life. If you are overcome by failures of the past as you try to cope with your daily goal in the present, you are filled with unbelief that distorts and disfigures your self-image. You are then ashamed of this self-image, and you limit yourself in your capabilities through worry and fear.

If you take advantage of your successes of the past, you use belief, courage, and self-confidence for present undertakings. This enhances your self-image. The stranger within you then becomes your best friend, who now encourages you to reach your true stature of dignity and fulfillment.

The most important point to remember is that this stranger within doesn't rule you. You rule him. Rule him creatively, with compassion, and you will get more living out of life. Here is a thought to live by: Napoleon said, "None but myself did me any harm."

## YOUR BEST FACE

The story is told of an adviser of President Lincoln who recommended a candidate for the Lincoln cabinet. Lincoln declined, and when asked why, he said, "I don't like the man's face."

"But the poor man is not responsible for his face," his adviser insisted.

"Every man over forty is responsible for his face," Lincoln replied, and the subject was dropped.

Are you responsible for your face? I believe so; but as a plastic surgeon, I feel we must exclude persons whose faces are scarred as a result of accidents at home, on the highway, and in industry, and children born with disfigurements. These people are responsible for their faces once they are brought back to normal.

What Lincoln really meant was this. Every human being is responsible for his face after forty because forty years of living should put a great deal into a face—the joys, the sorrows, the struggles for survival, the mistakes, the heartaches, the feeling of loneliness and despair, and the determination to surmount problems. As a result of these emotional and spiritual upheavals, people become wiser, gentler, more compassionate. They are able to understand their own needs and the needs of others. They are able to show kindness and sympathy, a willingness to erase resentment, hatred, bigotry, and to stand up to uncertainty and loneliness. Under these circumstances, when you find the big you, it doesn't matter if there is a wrinkle on your face. It is not on the face of your mind. Shakespeare said, "To thine own self be true." We say, "To thine own self-image be true," and you will show the world your best face at all times.

## WHAT ARE YOU BECOMING?

Recently someone asked me "What is hope?" I said hope is our guide to the future. In these violent times, any of us wonder what will become of the human race. That depends on what becomes of each human being. And that, in the final analysis, depends on what each person wants out of life.

Socrates said, "Know thyself." Marcus Aurelius said, "Be thyself." Shakespeare said, "To thine own self be true." I believe it goes further. Every day you must rethink who you are. Every day you must adjust your self-image to the changing conditions of the day. Your image, your opinion of yourself, and the road map of where you are going in life are never static. You are in motion, moving toward a goal, even while you are asleep; because even while you sleep, your success mechanism is at work subconsciously. You think in creative terms of reaching your true stature of self-respect.

It is not so much what your image is but what you are doing with it creatively this very minute. It is not so much who you are as what you are becoming each day: growing, doing, rethinking, redoing, regrowing. The hope of mankind lies in what you are becoming by doing, giving, sharing, growing, by honoring your own integrity and the self-respect of others. This is the only way to remove hate and evil, the only way to become a successful human being.

What are you becoming this very minute? You are becoming the creative you, adding more years to your life and more life to your years. Say to yourself every day as long as you live, "This is the first day of the best of my life," and prove it by living it.

## SIMPLICITY

Ralph Waldo Emerson said, "Nothing is more simple than greatness; indeed, to be simple is to be great."

Yes, I believe that every human being is great when he lives a life of simplicity, refusing to be tied down by the countless weight of details and nit-picking.

Simplicity should be a goal for every human being, because through it, one can move toward his destination without being sidetracked by dead ends that prevent us from becoming our big selves.

You live the rules of simplicity when you get rid of the pollution within your mind today, now, when you get rid of the resentments that inevitably complicate your existence. Simplicity also means one goal at a time. It means that you must stop criticizing yourself and others. It means doing what you can, not trying to imitate or to be someone else.

It means seeing life every day as it is, not dreaming what it should be. Simplicity means peace of mind, and where do you find it? Within you, not thousands of miles away on a sunny island in the Pacific. What do you want out of life? Do you want ostentation that winds up making your image ten inches small, or do you want simplicity that gives you inner security and makes your image ten feet tall?

Remember the words of Henry Thoreau, "Our life is frittered away by detail. Simplify, simplify."

## FAILURE

We all, now and then, fail in some undertaking. This gives us feelings of uncertainty, feelings of insecurity. Some of us are ashamed of failure and let past failures rule our lives. We do so at a time when we are trying to reach a worthwhile goal in the present; but we deter ourselves from this goal by worrying about past failures that make us fearful we will fail again in our present undertaking.

I remember, when I was a premedical student at Columbia University, I failed organic chemistry and feared that I would never become a doctor. But my desire to be a doctor was so great that I took the chemistry course during the summer, studied hard, and passed with an "A." I rose above failure because I had a goal, a goal important to me.

Success in life means not only to succeed but to rise above failures. We have a Failure Mechanism within us made up of past defeats, and the elements of this Failure Mechanism are:

1. Fear
2. Anger
3. Inferiority
4. Loneliness
5. Uncertainty
6. Resentment
7. Emptiness

If we are overcome by these elements of the Failure Mechanism, we walk away from life because we neglect our assets, our built-in Success Mechanism. Failure leads to tension, corrosion, a lack of belief.

We must learn to accept ourselves for what we are. We are never perfect.

We will likely make mistakes that distort our self-image, but we must learn to have courage to profit by these mistakes and not to be sidetracked by them in our present undertakings. Rising above failure results in confidence, and failure has tremendous value; it stimulates us to rise above it.

The greatest failure of all is to be afraid to make a mistake, to be afraid to take the calculated risk of living and improving ourselves. If we rise above this fear, we automatically enhance our self-image, and this is bound to bring the happiness we seek.

Remember the words of Thomas Bailey Aldrich, "They fail, and they alone, who have not striven."

## THIS IS YOUR LIFE

This is your life, and you've got to find somebody. You've got to find somebody very important—your big self. This is your life, and it's far too short to waste any moment of it making yourself less than what you are. This is your life, and it urges you to live in the present, to do one thing at a time. Stop criticizing others and yourself. See the sun around you and within you. Find the good in you and in others. Have compassion for yourself and for others. Refuse to be petty and resentful; refuse to hurt others and yourself.

This is your life. Live it to the fullest without stepping on other people's toes, without stepping on your own toes through negative feelings. This is your life. Refuse to merely exist; live creatively. You do when you redeem yourself, when you come back to your true worth, when you give yourself another chance and another chance.

You will give yourself another chance when you concentrate with courage on what you have to do, when you retrieve the good in you, when you listen to others, trying to help them, when you aspire for yourself and for others, when you try and keep trying, when you encourage others, thereby encouraging yourself, when you adjust to the realities of every day, taking the good with the bad, when you yearn for improvement, making that your daily goal in life.

This is your life, and you must find your big self. Believe me, you can!

## HOW TO JUMP A HURDLE

I know a hurdle champion who won many medals at college. Very few could beat him. He was the epitome of grace, agility, and fast footwork. He had numerous friends who admired him for his athletic prowess, and one of them gave the champ a job as a salesman in his insurance company. Years passed. He got married, and now he has a five-year-old son. But somehow, he never went far in his field as a salesman. He was likable, made friends easily, but could sell only a small amount of insurance during a year. He didn't seem to have the drive, the courage, the perseverance, or the great desire to achieve the perfection he achieved in hurdle jumping. Fear that he would not be a perfect salesman overcame him, distorted his self-image. He was easily frustrated when he was turned down by a potential customer. He forgot that he overcame mistakes in hurdling when he was at college by practice and perseverance.

One day at a class reunion at college, he met his classmates. They spent some time on the field. Some students were practicing jumping the hurdles. His friends coaxed him to see how good he remained. He had a drink or two in him. He borrowed a pair of sneakers and rushed to jump the hurdles, remembering how good he was in the past. He slipped and broke his leg. He was in a cast for a month, and this gave him time to think, to take stock of himself.

He recalled that he became a champ through constant practice, by overcoming failures. He realized that he was much too old for hurdle jumping; but he remembered that when he was a student, he had self-confidence and understanding of his skill. He also remembered courage, self-respect, self-acceptance. He recalled that he had a sense of direction when he jumped the hurdles toward his goal. He suddenly realized that there was no reason on earth he couldn't be a champion salesman. Why couldn't he jump the hurdles of life, why couldn't he jump the hurdles of his job, why couldn't he do better? He knew that fear and lack of confidence kept him from being a champion.

When he got well, he approached selling insurance with the same understanding, the same tenacity that he had applied to hurdle jumping. He practiced in his mind how to approach his customer and how to overcome possible obstacles. In less than a year, he became a top-flight salesman, increased his earning capacity, and was very happy.

We, too, can jump the hurdles of tension and stress by preventing our failures of the past from stopping us, from inhibiting us. We must approach the present goal of today with confidence, with self-assurance that we can rise above failures, knowing we can hurdle the problem of living. Remember always the old proverb, "Failure teaches success."

## THIS VERY MINUTE

It is appalling that, in these hectic and violent times, there are countless numbers of mental and psychoneurotic patients crowding our hospitals and institutions, and countless numbers waiting to be admitted. What is the reason? Tension! Too many of us suffer ills from tension by holding onto the burdens of yesterday and the fears of tomorrow. When we look in the mirror, what do we see? Sixty percent of what we see deals with yesterday. Twenty percent of what we see deals with tomorrow. But where is today? Lost in the panic of yesterday and tomorrow. Too many of us suffer from a disease that I call Yesterday Tomorrow Complex. There are 1,440 minutes to a day, and we live very few of them in the present. We must not live in the past any more than we should try to live in the future.

You must live today. Not just to exist or survive, but to live creatively, every day, searching for goals within your capabilities. You must realize that tomorrow is an extension of today. You must live in the present, every day, this very minute, live creatively, not destructively, live with belief, not unbelief. Here is what Pablo Casals, the great cellist, said when he reached his ninety-third birthday, "Every day I am reborn, every day is a new lifetime for me." Live today, this very minute!

## SUCCESS

Don't measure your success by counting prestige symbols and imitating other people, but by living the aspects of the Success Mechanism:

S: Sense of direction. You must have a goal, a goal within your capabilities.

U: Understanding. You must understand your needs and the needs of others. You may be an island within yourself, but you belong on the mainland with others. You must remember the words of Anatole France, "It is better to understand a little than to misunderstand a lot."

C: Courage. You must have courage to take your chances in life, to get your feet wet. If you make a mistake, try again. Try. Try. Try! Think of the words of Alfieri, "Often the test of courage is not to die but to live."

C: Compassion. You must have compassion for yourself as well as for others. You must see yourself and others with kind eyes if you want to be happy and discard the terrifying feeling of loneliness. Schopenhauer said, "Compassion is the basis of all morality."

E: Esteem. If you have no respect for yourself, no one will give it to you. Epictetus, a Greek philosopher, said, "What I made I lost; what I gave

I have." When you contribute to life, you enlarge your sense of worth, your self-respect.

S: Self-Acceptance. You must accept yourself for what you are. Never try to be someone else. George Bernard Shaw said, "Better keep yourself clean and bright. You are the window through which you see the world." We say, "Better keep your Self-Image clean and bright. It is the window through which you see the world."

S: Self-Confidence. You must remember the confidence of past successes in your present undertaking. You must concentrate on success like professional players in sports. They forget the times they lost in the past. They are out to win Now. You must use that technique to be a champion in the art of living, remembering that you cannot be a champion 100 percent of the time.

## LOOK INSIDE THE HUSK

*"And what is a weed? A plant whose virtues have not been discovered."*
                                        *—Ralph Waldo Emerson*

When did these splendid words occur to Emerson? Perhaps one day when the harvest was ready to be gathered and the bright fields rippled in the wind with wheat for the winter's bread. For, ages ago, wheat was thought to be a weed, quite useless to mankind.

Perhaps on that day, looking at the ripe, bronze fields, Emerson thought of his friend and teacher Bronson Alcott, a tireless, undefeatable, unquenchable man. Perhaps he paused to reflect on Alcott's stubborn insistence that it was never the "bad boy" or the dullard who was erring, but those who lacked patience to probe beneath the surface, however unpromising or unfriendly, to discover what was there. There were no "weeds" in Bronson Alcott's schoolroom.

So many times, in clinics and in hospital wards, I have seen the apparently hopeless misfit transformed into a hopeful and helpful person—into a giver, not a taker—by the simplest display of interest and belief in him. It makes me wonder how many good citizens, creators and builders, contributors to our health as a nation, have been lost because someone, somewhere, was misled by the husk and did not see the golden grain within.

I suppose it comes down to this: our first must for every day should be to pause before passing judgment, remembering that the apparently useless weed may, with care and cultivation, provide tomorrow's bread.

## ON SELFISHNESS

William Gladstone said, "Selfishness is the greatest curse of the human race." It is evil and immoral in that it prevents the person afflicted with this dread disease from growing into maturity. He does not set worthwhile goals and keeps others from reaching theirs. It is painful that selfishness finally adds up to unhappiness and loneliness. Selfishness is cancerous. It robs you of emotional and spiritual security, leaving you an empty human being. If you are a taker and live only for yourself, you wind up by yourself, and what kind of *self* is that when you cannot communicate with yourself or with others in a creative way.

It is natural in life to look for security by taking from life through some useful goal where you do not step on other people's toes and where you do not step on your own toes. If you receive, learn to give in return to others who are in desperate need of good will and compassion. The cure for selfishness is setting goals, creative goals for others and for yourself, for people, ideas, and for causes. The person with only self-interest is nearly always doomed, since self-interest makes him less than what he really can be and leads to atrophy of the mind, spirit, and body. If your self is used for you alone, you stay alone. If your self is used to understand your needs and the needs of others, you have friends. Which shall it be, selfishness or self-fulfillment? Remember the words of Sir William Osler, "We are here not to get all we can out of life for ourselves, but to try to make the lives of others happier."

## ON HUMOR

Mencius said, "The great man is he who does not lose his child's heart." And a child's heart is full of humor, full of laughter—the child on a swing, the child on a pony, the child making sand worlds on the beach, the child dancing, the child running with cheerful playmates. The world of children is a serious world, but it is also a world characterized by laughter and joy.

We are more apt to display a sense of humor when we are ourselves. We become devoid of humor when we are pompous, pretentious, obviously hiding an unmistakable feeling of inferiority. We cannot enjoy a true sense of humor when we feel inferior. What is the value of humor anyway? It is an important value, since this trait belongs to the family of well-being, to the family of wholesomeness, and to the art of relaxation so desperately needed in our times. Humor is there for the asking for anyone who refuses to take himself too seriously, who is willing to let go of tensions even for a moment, to laugh and break the circuit of distress to which we are all heir. Of course, laughter should never be an unkind corrective or a form of ridicule. That's not laughter, that is envy or revenge. Then it is not relaxation, but an invitation to tension.

If you say you have never had a sense of humor, I don't believe you. You merely didn't permit humor to grow in your life. Here is a little exercise to practice if you are frowning. Go to the mirror and try to frown with your mouth wide open. You'll suddenly find yourself laughing, and the greatest expression of humor is laughing at yourself before you laugh at others.

## ON MAKING MISTAKES

One of the tragedies in life for many of us is that we want to be perfect. We dread making a mistake, and when we do, we reprimand ourselves, can't live with ourselves. We're full of tension, unable to concentrate, unable to sleep, unable to find peace of mind. For that reason, the fear of making a mistake is the worst mistake of all, because it creates fear, uncertainty, inferiority. It makes our image shrink to the size of a small potato without ever testing true worth. After all, a mistake can be corrected, so why must we suffer endless torture? Why must we give away hope and belief in ourselves before we try to find out who we are and what our potential may be? And very often, mind, spirit, and body suffer enormously through an error, a blunder, a mistake.

The greatness in man consists of trying to be great, and you cannot be great if you demand of yourself to be faultless. Such a ridiculous demand results in isolation and emptiness. The true greatness in any human being lies not so much in making a mistake as in rising above it. We are all mistake makers, but thank God we have the power to be mistake breakers. The capacity to rise above a mistake is the beginning of success in the three worlds in which we live, in the body, in the mind, and in the spirit.

Thank God for a mistake, a blunder, a misfortune, an error. They give us an opportunity to make something of ourselves, to find our true worth, our big self. That is what success is all about. Remember the Words of Wang Yang-Ming, a Chinese philosopher, "The sages do not consider that making no mistakes is a blessing; they believe, rather, that the great virtue of man lies in his ability to correct his mistakes and continually to make a new man of himself."

## WINNING

I'd like to tell you about a memorable Kentucky Derby. Over 100,000 spectators stood and sang in the rain as the band played "My Old Kentucky Home."

Excitement mounted as the horses reached the starting gate, and the crowd tensed as the starter shouted, "They're off!" The Kentucky Derby is an exceptionally exciting event; and for the countless thousands who watch the Derby on TV or hear it reported on radio, it is in a class by itself.

The contest, a grueling test, was over quickly in two minutes—and to the jockey who won the "Run for the Roses" it was a marvelous prize.

Yes, two minutes and it is over, and one man becomes a champion. Can you be a winner, a champion in your own Derby? I believe you can; I believe all of us can.

Our "Kentucky Derby" is a special kind that we can win every day of our lives. How? Every day we allot two minutes to ourselves. We sit in a quiet room, and we become a racing contender. We see ourselves running for our self-respect. We imagine we are running toward our goal—without holding ourselves back with negative feelings. Every day is a new day, a new lifetime for us, when we can become winners and can use the confidence of past successes in our present undertaking. When we do this, when we keep our mind on our self-respect, we never lose. We are always the winner in the run for self-fulfillment, the greatest "Run for the Roses" of mankind.

And do you know something? When you run your own Kentucky Derby, it is always sunny. You can always find the sun within yourself if you will only search.

## BLUFFING

Does bluffing help achieve success? No. Absolutely not. In the end, you wind up fooling yourself. Shakespeare said, "To thine own self be true." What he said long ago is valid today, even though we live in frantic times in which too many people are takers in life, caring little for others. This can never lead to happiness or tranquility. I know millionaires who are just as miserable in the south of France as they are in New York or Dallas or Los Angeles, simply because they were merely takers and never thought of giving to others.

Bluffing is pretense; and when you pretend, you play games with yourself and with others, false games that leave you empty as a human being and lead to despair and self-destruction. You are part of life and a part of others. You belong to others whether you like it or not, and you can't live creatively and successfully if you fool others and fool yourself. Pretending uses up too much valuable energy on a negative, worthless purpose.

We all wear colored glasses when it is sunny to protect our eyes. You must not wear symbolic glasses to color your entire life, to make believe what you are not. If you do, you put yourself behind the eight ball. It never works. See things as they are; live life as it is. See yourself with kindly eyes, and you will suddenly become important. Rise above your errors with truth. Help others. You can, and it will bring you a great feeling of satisfaction to share your happiness with others.

## DAILY REQUIREMENTS

What are the daily requirements of man? There are many, but the following are the most important. I call these the daily dozen.

1. Love. Without it, we cannot survive. This incorporates love between man and woman and the psychological and spiritual love of mankind, which is the foundation upon which we build the Brotherhood of Man.
2. Security. There is a need for financial security, but there is also a very great need for emotional and spiritual security within oneself that will provide peace of mind.
3. Self-expression. We need to do something creative in this world instead of being just idle bystanders.
4. Recognition. We must feel acceptance by others, but first, we must find acceptance within ourselves and recognize our own worth.
5. New creative experiences. These determine our growth and maturity. We must continually remain alert for new opportunities to express ourselves creatively.
6. Self-respect. More than anything else, we should value self-respect and the respect of others and for others.
7. Getting more living out of life. Instead of being passive vegetables, we must create a richer life, each on his own terms, by his own standards.
8. Sharing happiness with others. Man should value his capacity to give. Young people must be taught this value. It is one of the most valuable assets in a happy life.
9. Involvement. One of the essential requirements for people of all

ages. Seek to help others who need your courage, your under-standing, your good will

10. The art of relaxation. We need to get rid of our tensions and re-charge our creative energies for peace.

11. Reaching goals. It is through reaching daily goals that we reach personal success and maturity.

12. Rising above a mistake. We must learn to see the errors in daily life, and we must learn to forgive ourselves so that we can approach new goals with clarity of mind and conscience.

## THE REAL YOU

Finding the real you is not a job that takes a moment, or a day, or a month, or a year. It's a job of a lifetime; and finding the real you should be a great, joyous adventure in self-fulfillment. How can you find the real you? You must remember that the real you is composed of many assets and many liabilities. When you look in the mirror, you see a composite of assets: self-respect, confidence, self-acceptance, and courage. These are your liabilities: frustration, loneliness, resentment, and inferiority feelings. Now the business of finding the real you lies in knowing what the liabilities do to your self-image. They create your little self. The positive aspects, your assets, create your big self. You are a combination of the big-self mechanism, which works to make you grow tall, and the little-self mechanism, which can make you become small. The negative feelings of the little-self mechanism are usually there. They are like warning lights. They tell you to take stock of your assets and do something with them. Your big-self mechanism is your green light, telling you to go forward, to reach goals within your capabilities, and to refuse to let your negative feelings shrink you to the size of a microbe.

How can you find the real you? By realizing that you can never reach total perfection; but you can get a tremendous amount of joy out of life by doing your best every day. And what is doing your best? Finding the real you by rising above personal problems, by rising above daily difficulties, rising above agitation, frustration, and feelings of loneliness and emptiness. As long as you think in creative terms, as long as you try to achieve goals in the present within your capabilities, you are on the road to finding the real you. Every day is a new day, a new opportunity; and as long as you persist in finding yourself, you will achieve fulfillment and be able to express the godlike quality within you.

## OUR WORLD

Where do we belong? First of all, we belong to ourselves. We are an island within ourselves. That island can be as barren as rocks on the moon or as fruitful as an orchard or a beautiful countryside. It is within us to make of ourselves what we want to be—creatively, not destructively. You train for your goals, but they must be realistic, not dreams beyond your reach.

Man is a beautiful island within himself. During moments of stress and tension, he can take a vacation. He can take this vacation every day for a few moments, and its costs him nothing. The daily vacation is within you, in the room of your mind. For five minutes or so, you should vacation every day, making a habit of it like brushing your teeth, until it becomes second nature with you. Go on this vacation when pressures are great. Relax for a few minutes, let go of the tensions, renew your energies for the problems before you.

Yes, it is wonderful to be an island within yourself briefly, but you must not stay that way. You belong to yourself, but you also belong to the world. Happiness lies within the world, not totally within yourself. Prepare yourself to be a big self, but realize that the big self belongs to other people, too, who need your help. Man reaches his true big self when he shares his success and his big self with others. He shares his courage with others when times are tough when there is pressure. He stands up for himself and for others, turning a crisis into an opportunity. The world is always full of crises, and we are here to help each other rise above them, to reach fulfillment and, sooner or later, the Brotherhood of Man.

## BEING SOMEBODY

The first thing to remember is that no person—absolutely no one—has final authority over your destiny but you. You may honor or respect a parent or a close friend, but the closest friend you will ever have is yourself. You must be a friend to yourself first. You must respect yourself first, you must be a success with Yourself before you can be a success with others. The greatest treasure you will ever have is Your self-image, a good opinion of yourself, and You must never let anyone take this away from you, no matter who it may be. If anyone does, he is opinionated and wants you to live his life, not your own.

Of course, you might listen to words of advice from a parent or friend; but in the final analysis, you must make the decision of what you want to be, if what you want to be is within your capabilities and your training, if what you want to be doesn't mean stepping on other people's toes. Go toward your goals aggressively, refusing to let anyone steer you from your course, because you must believe in your goals, and you must drive to reach them.

Your goals, your parents' goals, your friends' goals are different. You must do the thing you feel you have to do; and you must apply the power. It is another way of saying that you must let your belief in yourself work for you, not against you. You must choose your career because you believe in it. Never choose a career to suit someone else. It is the beginning of failure and unhappiness. Respect the integrity of others, but respect your own integrity as well. You are the master of your own destiny.

## BEAUTY

Ponce de Leon once searched for the Fountain of Youth and Beauty in Florida. But you will never find true beauty anywhere in the world as easily as you will find it in your own backyard; or, more specifically, inside yourself.

If you are resentful, full of hatred, envy, jealousy, and conceit, chances are you will look ugly to others and to yourself even if you are physically attractive. External beauty is important, and we should try to be physically attractive as long as possible. Still, young people must learn to realize that inner beauty is far more important than external beauty, because we get older whether we like it or not, but inner beauty can stay with us even at an advanced age.

What is inner beauty? Sharing your happiness and good fortune with others; accepting yourself for what you are, not trying to be someone else; forgiving others and yourself for errors that happened yesterday; seeing the good in yourself and in others and adjusting yourself to realities; longing for the better you inside yourself and inside others and searching every day for self-respect and the respect of others. These are qualities that will give you everlasting inner beauty, that will make you feel more beautiful and look more beautiful. This is the kind of beauty anyone can achieve at any age, even if they don't come up to the rigorous standards of classical beauty advertised on TV. Wouldn't it be just wonderful if inner beauty were emphasized on TV?

## BIGOTRY

A bigot is a person who holds blindly to his own creeds and opinions and finds no room in his heart or mind for anyone else's. The word "bigotry" comes from the Spanish expression "man with a mustaches." However, in modern usage, it implies a hostile and biased attitude. People who practice bigotry don't realize that it means inner hostility and the destruction of one's self.

What is the anatomy of bigotry? It consists of the following:

> *Belligerent.* You are belligerent to yourself before you can be belligerent to others.
> *Intolerant.* You're intolerant of yourself before you can be intolerant of others.
> *Grotesque.* You appear grotesque to yourself before you appear that way to others.
> *Opinionated.* Your opinion counts—no one else's—and you thrust your viewpoint on others.
> *Terror.* You terrorize yourself, and you foist your terror on others.
> *Revenge.* There is a feeling of self-destruction within you, and you want to destroy others.

The "Y" in bigotry is *You*. *You* are irrational with yourself, so you are irrational with others. You lacerate yourself, so you want to lacerate others. You're uncooperative with yourself, and you are uncooperative with others. You endure the torture of tension, and you live to create tensions for others. You have gout of the mind, and you want to inflict your agony on others. You resent yourself, and you get false pleasure resenting others. You have eliminated yourself from happiness, so you curse others.

Bigotry is self-inflicted intolerance of self, leading to the wounding of others. Bigotry is self-denial. Only when you realize how terrible and destructive bigotry is to you will you, for your own peace of mind, turn your back on this evil force.

## FAITH AND BELIEF

Often at the beginning of my career as a public speaker, I would be overcome with the panic of doubt, a lack of belief in myself, just before I got to the platform to deliver my talk. How would I begin? What would I say? What mistakes would I make? How could I stand there for an hour and face hundreds of people? How could I get through? But when the time came, I was there. I carried on because I had something to say. I did the best I could, and I came through with flying colors. And I learned that many of our best actors and actresses are especially nervous just before the curtain goes up.

All of us have self-doubts at the beginning of some undertakings whether we are doctors, lawyers, engineers, teachers, students, poets, or salesmen.

Where does faith and belief come from? From within ourselves. We are faith. We are belief. We are also doubt and unbelief. We as individuals must make the decision where we want to go in life, to be the big self or the little self. We must think of our faith and our belief as wings that can make us soar to our destination, to achieve our goals and reach self-fulfillment no matter how critical our times may be.

With doubt and unbelief our creative wings are clipped for the moment, and we can't get off the ground to rise above our self-imposed dungeon. We must thank God for doubt and unbelief. It is our moral responsibility to rise above them to make something of ourselves through faith and belief. These characteristics are eternally within us, waiting to be recognized, waiting for action. Remember the words of William Blake:

*If the sun and moon should doubt,*
*They'd immediately go out.*

## ON KNOWLEDGE

Aristotle said, "All men desire by nature to know." He wrote this over two thousand years ago, but it is still true today. Of course, when he said, "all men," he meant everybody: men and women, rich and poor, black and white, young and old. I suppose there are about 10 percent of people who never want to learn, 10 percent who know it all; but look at the potentiality of the Brotherhood of Man when 80 percent of all people want to learn to improve, to get more living out of life, and to share this good fortune with others.

Man lives in three worlds: the body, the mind, and the spirit. If he stops eating, something happens to him physically. If he stops wanting to learn, something happens to him mentally and spiritually. No food, anemia of the body. No learning, anemia of the mind and spirit. In neither instance can you move in the world creatively and amount to your big self, because you will be working under severe handicaps.

Aristotle tells us what we already know, that every American—every human being—needs, deserves, and should have education. It is as natural for people to learn as it is for them to breathe. Learning is their nucleus of growth and accomplishment. It is also well to remember that the greatest adventure in learning is in getting to know yourself better, and that envy, hatred, stubbornness, indecision, indolence, and fear prevent such an experience. We must resolve to educate our minds to search for and find our big self.

## ON VANITY

Thomas á Kempis said, "He is truly great that is little in himself and that maketh no account of any height of honor." These words are the quintessence of humility, when one is not arrogant of his successes, nor does he complain about his misfortunes. He insists on living creatively every day, every minute, to give happiness to himself and to share it with others. The reverse of this characteristic is vanity, a common trait that infects the mind and spirit of humanity. It's a matter of fact; no one can escape it entirely in a lifetime.

When you have vanity, you have conceit; and in both instances you falsely believe you are more than what you are when, as a matter of fact, you know the truth—that you are less, much less, than what you can be. Then, in your secret embarrassment, you scratch for attention, but it leads to naught. It's like scratching on marble. If the truth be known, you wind up disliking yourself, lost to yourself, neglecting opportunities to find your big self and worthwhile goals. There is nothing in vanity but defeat. Perhaps you would think twice before being vain if you realized that you are playing a depression game, a losing game that automatically makes you a member of the opinionated club; that you become a little dictator who cannot win, who cannot relax, who cannot sleep.

The cure: Think kindly of yourself, but don't gloat over successes. Be a good friend to yourself and you will be a good friend to others. Like Thomas á Kempis said, you will be truly great if you don't make too great an account of your honors.

## BEING YOURSELF

Most people who have failed in an undertaking don't like what they see when they look in the mirror. Young people particularly are affected by this kind of emotional reaction to a problem that seems to defy solution. Just remember that as long as you live, you'll be making mistakes now and then; and when you do, it is only natural for you not to like yourself, not to like the image you see of yourself in the mirror, not to like your little self. The point to remember in being yourself is that you must rise above your little self. You must rise above the mistakes and misfortunes of yesterday. You must try to reach your big self.

People are mistake makers, but they are also mistake breakers. The business of being yourself—your big self—is to accept yourself for what you are when you make mistakes. Look at yourself in the mirror with kind eyes and realize that you are much bigger than any error, any blunder, any misfortune, any heartache. You must live beyond your mistakes instead of with them. You must accept your weaknesses, stand on your feet in moments of crisis, and rely on the confidence from past successes to turn crises into creative opportunities.

If you don't like what you are, get off your own back. Stop living with this hang-up, because you and you alone can either like or dislike what you are. Realize now that you can be your better self, your big self, by rising above your mistakes. That's what successful living is all about. That's what being yourself is all about.

## EMBARKING ON A NEW CAREER

A new career? You're not even entrenched in your selected career, you say? But this is a different kind of career. It doesn't just make you money; it makes one a fuller human being.

That is your goal as you embark on your new career: to make yourself a fuller human being, to make yourself a more professional human being. Your goal is victory for you. You will climb Mount Everest.

Resharpen your focus. What if you can't remember X's batting average, or Y's RBI'S, or Z's earned-run average or won-lost record. So what?

Resharpen your focus. If you wash your car only once or twice a week, it will survive. A few specks of dirt on your precious car, unwashed, unnoticed, unregistered, isn't life or death. So what!

You will find yourself with more time. You must create more time for yourself. You must bypass trivia so you will have time. What can you do with it?

Embark on your new career. Your goal: the evolution of you. Accepting your imperfections. Tolerating your weaknesses. Appreciating and developing your strengths.

How?

1. You must accept yourself for what you are and yearn to grow daily by moving away from negativism.
2. You must think and do creatively as you reach for productive goals within your capabilities and training.
3. You must learn to control the emotional riot within you that distorts and scars your self-image, leading to disaster.

4. You must give to yourself as a friend first, then offer friendship to others.
5. You must learn to love life now, not yesterday or tomorrow. Your real love is for today. You must embark on your new career TODAY!

## OVERCOMING A HANDICAP

High upon a hill in a Central American country sits a house near a cliff, with the beautiful blue-green waters far below. A chair is on the lawn near the cliff, and now and then, a man of forty-five sits in it. This man is a baby specialist, and his chair is a special chair: a wheelchair. He cannot walk—he has no legs—they had to be amputated to save his life.

There was a time when the shock of this disaster almost drove him out of his mind. There was a time when he was tempted to wheel himself over the cliff; but that was more than a year ago. Today, you can see him early in the morning, with his artificial legs, seated in a car specially made for him to drive himself to the children's clinic. You can see him seated in his wheelchair in the clinic with his stethoscope as anxious parents come to him with their children. You can see him at work, bringing back health to bodies and smiles to faces. You can see contentment in his own face for work achieved every day.

He knows that though he has no legs, he is always running in the hearts of children and parents, running for them, winning a race for them as he once won races for himself.

All of us are somewhat handicapped. All of us are somewhat crippled in another sense. The frustrations of the day, the extra tensions of the day may be too much for us. And if I may stretch the metaphor, the legs of our mind are crippled, rendered useless through fear. We feel helpless. But we must learn to live with such handicaps. We must learn to rise above them. We must learn how we can get out of the wheelchair of fear, indecision, of hatred and resentment. We can throw away our crutch by overcoming emotional handicaps and by adjusting ourselves to the extra tensions of the day so that they won't cripple us, so that we can rise to our full stature of fulfillment.

To do so, we must not brood over misfortunes. We must direct our energies to some useful goal every day, including others like the doctor did. We can all help ourselves when we help others. Remember the doctor sitting in his wheelchair, high upon a hill, smoking his cigar contentedly after a fulfilling day's work. The doctor rose above despair. We all must try to rise above despair and failure. This is what success is all about. Remember the words of Virgil, "They can conquer who believe they can."

# DISCIPLINE

A hundred years ago in Vienna, countless pregnant women died in the General Hospital after giving birth. A Professor Klein said it was pollution from the atmosphere. A young doctor by the name of Phillip Semmelweis didn't believe it. Finally, he discovered that childbed fever was blood poisoning brought about by the contamination from the hands of medical students who examined the mothers. Professor Klein represented authority, the established order of things. Semmelweis represented freedom of thought.

Authority kicked Semmelweis out of the hospital, and for the rest of his days, he fought for his principles, fought for the truth, but authority wouldn't listen. Finally, Semmelweis examined a tissue specimen of a mother dead from childbed fever, cut his fingers accidentally, and soon developed fever and died. He contracted childbed fever even though he was a man, proving completely that freedom of thought finally triumphed over authority even in tragedy.

There always will be a battle between authority and freedom of thought. Its variation in the household is the authority of the parents versus freedom of expression by their children. Children have hope and the future on their side; adults have maturity and wisdom on theirs. But parental authority is wrong when it results in punishment brought on by a lack of open-mindedness and understanding. Discipline properly executed on the child, who secretly craves guidance, must have creative characteristics rather than the destructive trait exemplified in Dr. Klein's punishment of Dr. Semmelweis. Discipline is more a test of the adult who uses it than of the child who receives it.

Understanding and self-respect are the guiding keys to creative discipline. These values will reach a child's heart, letting him know that the effort is to guide creatively without rancor. Creative discipline creates a partnership between parent and child. It establishes meeting between the self-respect of the adult, who has already made mistakes, and the self-respect of the youngster, who will make mistakes. In creating this atmosphere of friendship and companionship, discipline reaches its goal, its objective. The adult is able to hold on to his self-respect, and so is the child. The important thing to remember is that discipline imposed on others can only be creative and effective if it reveals self-discipline first. We must control the emotions that make us fail—fear and anger—and use the emotions that make us successful—understanding and self-respect. You must not impose your self-image on your child. The child has its own self-image, and you must help the child realize that he can improve his self-image and be happy with it. Remember the words of Seneca, "No one can rule except one that can be ruled."

## DEHYPNOSIS

Let me tell you of an experience my friend Alfred Adler, one of the great pupils of Sigmund Freud, had that illustrates how powerful belief can be upon behavior and ability. In my book *Psycho-Cybernetics,* I mentioned how Adler, as a boy, got off to a bad start in arithmetic because he couldn't answer a few questions. His teacher became convinced that he was poor in mathematics. One day, however, he saw how to work a problem the teacher had put on the board, which none of the other pupils could work. He announced as much to the teacher. She and the whole class laughed. Whereupon Adler became indignant, strode to the blackboard, and worked the problem, much to their amazement. In doing so, he realized he could understand arithmetic. He felt a new confidence in his ability to become a good math student. Adler had been hypnotized by a false belief about himself. Not figuratively, but literally; he was actually hypnotized.

If we have accepted an idea from ourselves, our teachers, parents, friends, advertisements, or from any other source, and if we are firmly convinced that the idea is true, it has the same power over us as the hypnotist's words have over the hypnotized subject. We are all hypnotized by our fears and frustrations because they become a vicious habit. They create a pattern we can't break, just as a hypnotized person can't break the pattern the hypnotist makes him follow. We carry negative feelings from our job to our home, to our bed, and then back to the job. We burden ourselves unnecessarily with extra tensions that make us less than what we are. These negative ideas have exactly the same effect upon our behavior as the negative ideas implanted into the mind of a hypnotized subject by a professional hypnotist.

The point is that we can dehypnotize ourselves from these extra tensions as Adler did. Regardless of how big a failure we think ourselves to be, there is the ability and the power within us to change in order to be happy and successful. This ability or power becomes available to us just as soon as we change our beliefs, just as soon as we can dehypnotize ourselves from the ideas of "I can't," "I'm not worthy," "I don't deserve it," or other self-limiting thoughts. As Bacon said, "Man prefers to believe what he prefers to be true." Think about it! Dehypnotize yourself from false beliefs!

## MEMORIES

In living, we all create memories, and we store these memories in a mental tape recorder. We can use these memories constructively or destructively. What should we do with memories? Keep them in proper perspective.

I remember on one occasion, I was asked to attend a reunion of my medical class. I couldn't accept at that particular time, but fortunately, twenty-five years after graduation, I attended a class reunion. I put on my tuxedo and went to the hotel to meet my colleagues, but I couldn't find them; I couldn't recognize them. When the guests finally seated themselves at their respective tables— those who graduated before me and those who graduated after me—I looked for my table—the Class of 1923—and there, I saw nine people seated around the table and one empty seat, mine.

I sat down, and the man to my right, a short, fat, bald-headed man, suddenly said to me, "Maltz, what happened to you? Your hair is gray; it used to be black!"

I looked at his bald head and remembered that he had had beautiful blond hair, and I said to myself, "I wonder what happened to him?" Both of us abused our memories.

We must learn to use memories only to remember happy moments, so that we can utilize them for the present undertaking. In doing that successfully, we build memories—happy memories—for tomorrow. The misfortunes of yesterday must be forgotten, lost in the tomb of time. Every day is a new lifetime that must be lived to the full, creatively.

Remember the words of Macedonius (sixth century):

*Memory and Oblivion, all hail!*
*Memory for goodness, Oblivion for evil!*

## CHARACTER

In my book, *New Faces, New Futures*, written many years ago, I mentioned this incident in the first chapter. Three men who believed they could judge character by facial appearance were gathered in my office: a playwright, a lawyer, and a doctor. They were looking at masks of patients made before surgery. The playwright said, "This person with a receding chin is a weakling."

"Wrong," I answered. "He's an aggressive stockbroker."

The lawyer said, "This man with the ugly gash on his cheek must be a gangster. It's a typical squealer's cut."

"No," I said. "He's a sedate businessman who was in an auto accident."

The doctor examined the cast with the broken nose and said, "This fellow looks as if he's been in a number of fights. Is he a pugilist or racketeer?"

"No," I answered. "He's a schoolteacher who fell on his nose when he was a child." I then showed them the casts of these patients after surgery. They were astounded. They could not believe that these normal faces had once been horribly distorted.

To this day, many people persist in believing that the face is an index to character. Many businessmen ascribe a good measure of their success to their supposed ability to read character from facial features. These are hasty, reckless judgments. Even Aristotle, that great Greek philosopher, made the same mistake when he said, "Noses with thick bulbous ends belong to persons who are swinish." We cannot say that a man has big ears because he is stupid any more than we can say that he is stupid because he has big ears.

As Professor Jastrow said, "Judging by behavior, expression, gesture, manner, conversation has far greater value than judging by looks."

I venture to say that the self-image is the only accurate guide to character. The self-image is the result of our successes and failures in life. Using past successes in the present gives us confidence and enhances our character. Being ashamed of our self-image because we are overcome by past failures in a current undertaking diminishes our usefulness, diminishes our character, and makes us less than what we really are and can be.

There is an old Latin proverb that says, "A man's character is the arbiter of his fortune."

## THE TUFTED PUFFIN

There is a little island off the coast of British Columbia whose stony crags are inhabited by a species of bird called the "puffin." It is a small tufted bird, a tufted puffin. The most amazing characteristic of this bird is its habit of living in that spot only. Take it away from that area, and it cannot survive. It has no resistance. This tufted puffin is so fragile that it cannot endure or overcome stress. It dies if you take it away from its normal habitat.

What kind of bird are *you*? Are you a tufted puffin with sawdust stuffin'? Or are you a goal-striver, a stress-survivor? That is what success is all about, rising above a problem, a stress.

There is a poem by Victor Hugo called "Wings":

*Be like the bird that,*
*Pausing in its flight awhile*
*On boughs too light,*
*Feels them give way,*
*Yet sings!*
*Knowing she hath wings.*

Do you have wings? Of course you have. Your wings are your faith and belief in yourself. And you can soar to your destination if you'll only give yourself a chance. Through frustration and despair, you tie your wings, and you cannot get off the ground.

What kind of bird are you? A tufted puffin? Or can you, with wings of faith and belief, reach your destination? I believe you can; you have to believe it too. You have to believe that you came into this world to succeed, to rise above fear, to rise above a stress, turning your life into a continuous creative opportunity.

## THE CLEFT PALATE

In my practice as a plastic surgeon, I have operated on many cleft palates. This is a hole in the upper lip. One out of every 2,500 children is born with this defect, which can be corrected soon after birth. After World War II, I taught surgeons in a number of Latin American countries how to perform cleft palate surgery.

In one country, a boy of seventeen came to the capital from a village in the interior. When he was about to be put under anesthesia, he shouted, "I'm going to die! I'm going to die!"

I assured him that I was his friend and that he would be all right.

He tried to be calm, but I saw terror in his eyes. Finally, the anesthetist put him to sleep, and I repaired the hole in his lip.

Two weeks later, the final dressing was removed, and I said to him, "Take a look at yourself in the mirror."

He hesitated. I urged him, "Don't be afraid."

That minute, before he slowly walked to the mirror, must have been a lifetime to him. Finally, he looked—and stared at himself in disbelief. I knew what was running through his mind. He saw someone he had never seen before. He turned his head in different directions as he kept looking at his new face. Finally, he turned to me with tears of joy in his eyes and cried, "I'm going to live! I'm going to live!"

Are you going to live? Have you an emotional cleft palate? Have you a cleft palate in your mind and soul because of some hang-up where there is a gap between you and your integrity, where there is a hole between you and your dignity? Many of us have. You must remove the gap. Be your own plastic surgeon and bridge the gap between you and your self-respect with threads of compassion and self-understanding.

## DAILY PLEASURE

Do not set conditions for your pleasure.

Do not say, "I'll have fun when I make $10,000."

Or "My happiness will begin when I get on that plane for Paris and Rome and Vienna."

Or "When I'm sixty-five, and I retire, I'll just lie in a deck chair in the sunshine."

There should be no *ifs* about the pleasure in your life.

Every day, one basic goal must be an inner feeling that you deserve to enjoy yourself, whether you're a millionaire or a pauper. A millionaire with a weak self-image can say to himself, "Someone will steal my money, and then nobody will talk to me." A poor man with a strong self-image can say to himself, "While my creditors are chasing me around the block, I can enjoy the exercise."

Don't fool yourself; if you really want happiness in your life, you'll find it, but only if you can live with good fortune.

Let me repeat, *if you can live with good fortune.*

Believe me; I have known many people who could not live with happiness. After a great success, instead of relaxing, their anxieties would intensify. Everything and everyone seemed to be chasing the diseases, lawsuits, accidents, Internal Revenue, even relatives—in their minds. They could not relax until they once again tasted what they were really looking for—failure. Learn to court pleasure, not pain. Pay homage to its virtues; feel that you are worthy.

Find pleasure in little things: food that tastes delicious, friendship that is sincere, a sun that is warming, a smile that is meant to cheer.

In *Othello,* the sophisticated, worldly-wise William Shakespeare wrote, "Pleasure and action make the hours seem short." Short or long, make your hours ring and bubble with pleasure. Laugh at people who say that pleasure is not part of life, because they are ignorant; but forgive them, because they are not as wise as you.

Know that happiness is real, that it is internal, that no one can make you unhappy without your consent.

You must remember every day that happiness is a gift you give to yourself, not just during Christmas but all year round.

# HUMILITY

Recently, I was riding a jet on my way from New York to London, and I overheard a man and his wife talking in front of me. She said, "What a beautiful sight. How insignificant it makes us feel." He said, "You mean how grateful we are to be alive in this universe." This exchange made me realize what humility gives us. The purpose of humility is not to make us feel insignificant but in our own right to get to know who we are and to contribute to the universe. Great men like Einstein and Gandhi were humble. They certainly were not self-disparaging. They were self-confident about their knowledge, about their goals for humanity, their desires to make the world a better place for people.

Humility is not self-denial, it is self-affirmation, belief in our integrity and dignity as human beings. It is a blending of success and failure, where we keep failure in proper perspective in the past and success in proper perspective in the present. We let neither dominate us. It is the balance between trying to be no more than we are and no less than we are, not trying to be superior or inferior. It is poise, in that we do not inhibit ourselves by past failures, nor do we brag about present successes. It is an emotional thermostat that keeps us being ourselves, that keeps us young.

I remember many years ago I was visiting with an editor friend of mine and he noticed I was unhappy. A story of mine had been turned down by a magazine. He said, "Maxwell, what gave you the idea that you could be successful as a writer overnight? You'll get many rejection slips before you succeed." That editor taught me humility. I did succeed in time by overcoming errors instead of letting errors overcome me.

Humility has these eight ingredients:

1. Sincerity. Being sincere with ourselves and with others.
2. Understanding. Understanding our needs and the needs of others.
3. Knowledge. Learning that we are what we are and that we don't have to keep up with the Joneses.
4. Capacity. Extending our ability to listen and learn.
5. Integrity. Constantly building an inner sense of values and adhering to them.
6. Contentment. Building a state of peacefulness through understanding and not making mountains of molehills.
7. Yearning. Looking for new horizons, new goals, new successes and reaching out for them.

8. Maturity. The pot of gold at the end of the rainbow. With maturity you will understand humility, and with humility you will be a successful human being.

There is no humiliation in humility. It takes time to acquire humility, but it is worth it since it brings happiness. Or, as James S. Barrie said, "Life is a long lesson in humility."

## ARE YOU CREATIVE?

Many of us are firmly convinced that people are born creative or noncreative, that only a limited number of people can create in different generations. Leonardo da Vinci, Shakespeare, Beethoven, Alexander Graham Bell, and Einstein all used their creative gifts wisely. Each one had the power to use his imagination properly, productively.

What are the characteristics of a creative mind? First, a sense of direction, a goal. Then, a problem, clearly defined, and all the possible solutions. After that, the selection of the best solution and acting on it. You must have the ability to forget a problem, temporarily, if it defies solution and the capacity to rise above failures.

I believe that all of us are creative. We have a creative mechanism working for us that steers us toward success. For example, the simple exercise of picking up a pencil. We forget that, as children, we picked it up clumsily, zigzagging in the direction of the pencil until we learned to do it successfully. This successful performance was registered in the mental tape recorder for future use. This, in a mild sense, is a creative effort.

We all can create because we all have imagination. We use it daily without realizing it. For example, when we worry, we use imagination in a negative way to create something that doesn't exist. We project on the screen of the mind scenes that haven't happened as yet because we fear we will fail. On the other hand, when we are happy, we use the imagination constructively. We picture a worthwhile achievement of the goal we seek by remembering past successes to achieve pleasure in the present.

We are all made up of failures and successes, and to think creatively, we must rise above the mistakes of the past and use the self-confidence from past successes in our present undertaking.

We can think creatively when:

1. We think clearly about a problem.
2. We think of all possible solutions.

3. We accept the best and act upon it.
4. We forget the problem, temporarily, if it defies solution. The servo-mechanism within us will do the job for us subconsciously by utilizing the ingredients of our past successes.

The greatest creative effort for all of us, great or small, is to create the habit of happiness. This we can all do by making a habit of it every day, by recalling the happiness of past successes and using this good feeling in our present undertaking. Remember Elbert Hubbard's words, "Happiness is a habit—cultivate it!"

## ON BEING OPINIONATED

One of the great problems throughout the ages has been that too many of us try to force our opinions on others, implying that we cannot be wrong. This leaves little room for self-improvement and throws a roadblock in the path of success. Imagine ten of the greatest living painters seated at a round table painting an apple in the center of the table. Each will paint the apple differently because each sees the apple differently.

It is the same with opinion. Beliefs are different depending on many factors of birth and environment, and we color opinion by these factors. The tragedy of being opinionated is that it prevents growth, progress, and self-fulfillment. It implies perfection; and since no one can be perfect at all times, it is a foregone conclusion that the opinionated person—in defending his weakness—will be unhappy and isolated.

What can you do to prevent being opinionated? You can make it your business to listen, to hear the thoughts of others. You might be wrong in your opinion, and then you must have the capacity to make a worthwhile change.

Being opinionated is a negative trait; open-mindedness is a constructive trait. The first leads to failure and isolation, the second to success and friendship.

You can stop being opinionated by stretching out your hand of friendship to others, by learning from others, by reading that others have the same rights as you, that all of us came into this world to succeed and not to fail. You can thus reactivate the success mechanism within you instead of holding on to a failure trait.

Remember the words of James Russell Lowell, "The foolish and dead alone never change their opinion."

## ON STUBBORNNESS

Life means change. Your image changes every day simply because you are different every day and the situations of each day are different; and that is the way it should be. Man progresses by change. Nature progresses by change—spring, summer, winter, fall. Can you imagine if a tree in the spring were stubborn and refused to bud and bear leaves, if a flower were stubborn and refused to bloom, if a vegetable or fruit were stubborn and refused to grow and ripen?

Are you stubborn? Do you refuse to change and grow in stature? Are you resistant to creative living, to a smile, to friendship, to forgiveness, to the Brotherhood of Man?

Michel de Montaigne said, "Obstinacy and heat of opinion are the surest proof of stupidity."

To get more living out of life, you must start getting rid of negative feelings that create stubbornness and obstinacy, envy, indolence; they all give rise to resistance that makes you shrink to the size of a microbe.

Are you a microbe or a whole human being? You have the answer within you if you overcome stubbornness through forgiveness and friendship to yourself.

There *is* one kind of stubbornness that is creative. If, after sharp analysis, you find your beliefs worthy of humanity, fight for these beliefs. That is not pigheadedness; that is constructive determination, growth for yourself and for others.

## PATIENCE

John Dewey, who was my teacher of philosophy when I was a freshman at Columbia University, said, "The most useful virtue is patience."

Patience gives us hope as we wait and wait for an end to the wrangling in the UN, when we wait for the dawn of a new world—one world, a people's world.

Life becomes more complex every day, and technocracy threatens to strip man of his individuality. But it is during this time of pressure that you can learn to relax. This is a time for creative concentration and clear thinking. Don't make haste or make waste, but sit in a quiet room in your mind and use your imagination creatively to relax, to control your fears, anxieties, and uncertainties, to find tranquility through patience.

Sit in the quiet room of your mind and use your imagination. You can see a motion picture of yourself on the screen—your assets and liabilities, your smiles and your frowns. And, since you are the writer of the script, the actor, the director, and the audience all in one, you can change the script. You can use your assets of self-respect and self-confidence to find the patience that is within you, ready to be utilized for a constructive effort. It is through this technique that you encounter fewer failures, fewer frustrations. You find the inner you, the better you, which is the beginning of patience because it implies forgiveness. Patience is almost synonymous with forgiveness, almost synonymous with peace of mind, *almost synonymous* with finding your big self.

## FLOWERS

The other day, I overheard two men talking over drinks in the dining room of their club. One said, "Don't send me flowers when I'm dead. I can't smell them then." The other nodded glumly.

These two sentences tell us briefly that we in this world live by three essential emotions: love, hatred, and aspiration. One of our daily quests is love which, in itself, signifies that we strive desperately not to be alone. Hatred is more difficult to explain. We resort to it too frequently without considering that this emotion degrades us and robs us of our dignity. The third emotion is aspiration, a dream to rise to the very heights of our true self-image to achieve happiness.

We are always accepting a challenge to move forward, to turn the unknown of tomorrow into success and security. The man who said, "Don't send me flowers when I'm dead," is successful in every sense of the word. He has financial security, has two children who adore him, is compassionate toward the needs of others. He is a giver in life, not a taker. And he started as a poor boy. What he meant by his remark was that man gets along best in life by utilizing the worthwhile traits within him: belief, hope, self-respect, and self-acceptance. He said, in other words, that what we give we never lose and that we do not need bouquets from anyone if we live our lives creatively without stepping on other people's toes.

The man who listened has resorted to shady practices in order to be successful in business. In one stock transaction, he told friends to buy stock as he unloaded his own shares. This man has a lot of money, but he is not happy. He has few friends. He always says that money talks, and he buys his way in life. He knows little about relaxation or peace of mind. He knows he has enemies, and he pretends to thrive on it, but he needs pills to fall asleep.

Remember, we are our own plastic reconstructive surgeons. Every day we shape our future happiness or despair, depending on whether we understand or refuse to understand that we do not live alone. We must live in relationship to others; we cannot ignore the needs of others. When we cultivate self-respect and compassion, we automatically cultivate our own garden of flowers. We bring growth and beauty to our surroundings. Remember the words of Dorothy Gurney, "One is nearer God's heart in a garden than anywhere else in the world."

## YOUR UNTAPPED WEALTH

It is a tragedy that throughout history, so few people have fully exploited their potentialities. Yes, almost all people have rich, untapped areas of talent.

Don't be a "doubting Thomas." Follow the example of another "Thomas," Thomas Jefferson, America's third president. Thomas Jefferson's accomplishments are almost beyond belief. His confidence in his powers must have been extraordinary. In the process of serving out two full terms in our nation's highest office, he negotiated the famed Louisiana Purchase, which some historians have called the outstanding bargain in American history. This was preceded, of course, by his famed drafting of our great Declaration of Independence.

Jefferson's other achievements as a statesman are too numerous to mention. Few American statesmen in our history have done so much; it is doubtful if any have done more.

The astonishing quality about Jefferson was his full use of his creative powers in other fields as well. A married man with two daughters, he was the president of the American Philosophical Society, established the University of Virginia, and supported the first American scientific expeditions. He was also a topflight architect, who designed not only his own home but those of friends.

I am not suggesting that you are in any way a failure if you cannot measure up to such monumental achievements as those of Thomas Jefferson. My message is simply that you should reach out to the world with your full capabilities, whatever they may be, that you should emulate Jefferson in utilizing your resources instead of blocking them.

Here are the words of William Hazlitt, "He who undervalues himself is justly undervalued by others."

## ON GIVING UP

We all suffer from crises in our time—some of us more than others—but what is creative living but standing up to a crisis, turning a crisis into an opportunity to find your big self, succeeding despite a blunder, a mistake, a handicap. And when does the real action begin? When we stand up to despair and use our compassion and our self-respect, remembering we are greater than an error, a blunder, or a heartache. It is during a moment of crisis that we must call upon our own sense of worth, call upon our courage to use our mental and spiritual muscles to move into the world of people where we belong, not to be alone in a world of loneliness.

Edmund Burke said, "Never despair, but if you do, work on in despair." Burke knew, as all of us know, that despair does not comprise a day or even a week of unhappiness, but that it is one dreary day dragging on endlessly to another as if there were no hope in sight. And that is why he said, "work on in despair," because at a time of crisis, we can call upon our courage and compassion to move us into the world with others searching for the peace of mind we crave.

Each day is a new lifetime, and we cannot give up a day that has not come as yet; we cannot give up a new day without even trying to find the promise of peace that can come at the least expected moment.

Despair is a kind of suffering we all know. It means, for the moment, retiring from life; and we must not retire from life at any age as long as we live. Life will not allow us to give up. Which shall it be, giving up or giving the best that is in us in a crisis?

## RELAXATION

Every generation speaks about uncertain times. Born in uncertainty, living in uncertainty, we pass on in uncertainty. By living creatively, we bend uncertainty to our will so we can reach goals and a sense of fulfillment. We live successfully by rising above our tensions. We can do this effectively if we practice the art of mental and spiritual relaxation by remembering these four points:

1. *Forgive others, with no sense of condemnation.* A clean, clear slate—not forgiveness on the installment plan. I love you today but can't stand the sight of you tomorrow—that is not forgiveness. A difficult habit to learn, but worth fighting for.
2. *Forgive yourself for your errors or blunders.* Another difficult task, but you can do it. Forget the blunders of yesterday and make it a habit to live fully today. To err may be a human failing, but to forgive is a human achievement. Shakespeare said, "To forgive is divine." Still, who is asking you to be divine? Be human and achieve your fulfillment as a human being.
3. *Keep up with yourself, not with someone else.* Trying to imitate others merely forces you to play second fiddle. Remember, you can't be someone else without tension. Every day you must try to make your self-image grow; this you can do.

4. *See yourself at your best.* Stop concentrating on your worst. You are your most wicked enemy when you torture yourself with feelings of frustration every day. You are at your best when you practice confidence every day. You have a choice; select wisely. Remember, you must forget yesterday, and you can forget yesterday through substitution: thinking and working toward your present goal. The more you think of reaching your present goal, the less time you will have for the worries and heartaches of yesterday.

## ON FAULTS

Thomas á Kempis wrote, "How seldom we weigh our neighbor in the same balance with ourselves." I have spoken and lectured to groups of people all over the world for the past fifteen years, to people in industry, religion, and education. Now and then, I would ask those in the audience: "How many of you have expressed resentment at least once in the last thirty days?" And all the people in the audience would raise their hands, and there was always laughter.

Yet, with all that, it is a very strange thing indeed that our own offenses seem nothing compared to the offenses of others. When we have done something for which we are ashamed, something destructive that makes our image shrink to the size of a small potato, we have a scapegoat—we blame our conscience. We say, "My conscience bothers me." And then we quickly condone ourselves.

But when it comes to a fault, a blunder, a mistake, or resentment in someone else, how quickly we discredit the individual. How derisive we are at catching someone in a lie, forgetting the countless lies we ourselves have told. To grow in stature as human beings, we must remember that we all have faults, that we are a mixture of good and evil, success and failure, belief and despair, friendship and loneliness, fear and courage. Men are alike in that they can be their big selves or their little selves at various moments in their lives; and it is only through forgiveness that we can find our better selves a greater share of the time.

## NO LIMITATIONS

In the Bible, we are told that when a prophet was in the desert and hungry, God lowered a sheet from the heavens containing food. To the prophet, it didn't look much like good food. It was "unclean" and contained all sorts of "crawling things." God rebuked him, admonishing him not to call "unclean" that which God had offered.

Some doctors and scientists today turn up their noses at whatever smacks of faith or religion. Some religionists have the same attitude of suspicion and revulsion concerning anything "scientific." Everyone's real goal is for more life, more living. Whatever your definition of happiness may be, you will experience more happiness as you experience more life. More living means, among other things, more accomplishment or the attainment of worthwhile goals, more love experienced and given, more health and enjoyment, more happiness for yourself and others.

I believe that there is ONE LIFE, one ultimate source, but that this ONE LIFE has many channels of expression and manifests itself in many forms. If we are to "Get More Living Out of Life," we should not limit the channels through which life may come to us. We must accept it whether it comes in the form of science, religion, psychology, or through other channels.

One of the most important channels is through other people. Let us not refuse the help, happiness, and joy that others may bring us, nor should we deny what we can give to them. Let us not be too proud to accept help from others, nor too callous to give it. Let us not say "unclean" just because the form of the gift may not agree with our prejudices or our ideas of self-importance.

Refuse to place limitations on your life.

Here are the words of Samuel Johnson, "The business of life is to go forward."

## ON FAIR PLAY

The title of one of Charles Reade's novels is "Put Yourself in His Place."

You will be a happy human being if you make a habit of living with these five words until the practice becomes second nature to you. These five words, lived, not read, will put you on the road to maturity and self-fulfillment, because you will think twice before passing judgment on someone else who has a point of view different from yours and who wants to stand for his rights as you do for yours.

At a moment of stress when you are overcome with doubt and unbelief, when you are overcome with aggressiveness and fear, at that moment when you are ready to denounce someone, say to yourself, "What would I do if I were in his place?" Fight for your rights if you must, but don't fight for something wrong out of hatred or revenge.

Friendship is desperately needed in these chaotic times, and the first light and glow of friendship with others starts when, at a moment of irrationality, you ask yourself, "What would I do if I were in his place?"

Most important, you must have a sense of fair play with yourself. Never denounce yourself because of an error; never become a displaced person because of it. At such a time, ask yourself as you look in the mirror, "Would I do this to my best friend?"

## DESIRE

"Desire accomplished is sweet to the soul" (Proverbs xiii:19). Build an unquenchable desire for emotional control. To live creatively. To understand yourself. To master the inner destructive forces that could, out of control, lead to disaster.

No matter how great your positive forces, you cannot grow emotionally if your fears and resentments overwhelm you. Not even your enormous desire to live will always help you here.

How can you hold your negative feelings in check?

First, you must keep yourself alert. Your ears are supersensitive: when the alarm system inside you goes off, they hear.

Second, when the alarm goes off, you must refuse to panic. You must keep your fingers off the panic button, off the trigger. Instead, you delay action a while, you reason with yourself, you accept yourself.

Then you solve your crisis, whether it is internal or external. You work to snuff out the fire inside you, or to stop the burglarizing of yourself by yourself. You use your understanding of yourself, developed through your long efforts, to improve yourself, to regain your good feelings, your peace of body, mind, and spirit.

In defeating your internal negative forces, you keep alive your unquenchable desire to get the most out of life.

## ON UPS AND DOWNS

The following words come from the sacred book of the Hindus, "Bear shame and glory with an equal peace and an ever-tranquil heart."

You are a combination of happiness and unhappiness, success and failure, joy and grief, compassion and resentment, belief and unbelief.

In other words, you are a combination of the creative forces within you that will make you ten feet tall and the destructive forces within you that will make you ten inches small. And creative living proves that every day counts. Every day is a complete lifetime that must be lived to the full. Can you live life to the full every day if disappointments make you walk away from yourself, make you walk into a dungeon of your own choosing?

Does a mistake, an error, or a blunder do that to you? Do these things make you a shadow, a ghost of yourself, losing your identity in a fog of uncertainty and despair?

The business of creative living is to keep calm in times of adversity, and doubly calm when good fortune smiles upon you. Of course, love and hate defy the rules of philosophy, but neither one should make you less than what you are. You are small if you succumb to hate, and you are just as small if you succumb to love of self. You stand on the foundation of your true worth if you are able to stand up under stress as well as success.

## YOU CAN DO THE IMPOSSIBLE

Carlyle said, "Alas! The fearful unbelief is unbelief in yourself." Of all the traps and pitfalls in life, lack of self-esteem is the deadliest and hardest to overcome, for it is a pit designed and dug by our own hands, summed up in the phrase, "It's no use—I can't do it!" The penalty of succumbing to it is heavy both for the individual in terms of material rewards lost and for society in gains and progress unachieved.

As a doctor, I should also point out that defeatism has still another aspect, a curious one, which is seldom recognized. It is more than possible that the words of Carlyle represent a confession of the secret that lay behind his own craggy assertiveness, his thunderous temper and waspish voice, and his appalling domestic tyranny.

Carlyle, of course, was an extreme case. But isn't it on those days when we are most subject to the "fearful unbelief," when we most doubt ourselves and feel inadequate to our task—isn't it precisely then that we are most difficult to get along with? Aren't we taking out our feeling of inadequacy on our family, our friends, our fellow employees?

The reflection almost automatically follows that, rather than to make ourselves and everyone else miserable, it might be a good idea to take another look at the root of the trouble, the private Demon of Unbelief, who proclaims in his cold, sad voice, "No, no, it's impossible." It is that good hard second look—taken not just for one's own sake but everyone else's too—that very often reveals that the "impossible task is quite possible after all.

The Demon of Unbelief is the result of past failure, which inhibits us from being our true selves in our present undertaking. This distorts our self-image. We must leave past failures and the Demon of Unbelief in the past where they belong, remembering that we can reach our true stature of dignity only when we rise above failures and mistakes of the past. We must recall the successes of the past in an effort to reach success in our present goal. This gives us the self-confidence, the self-respect we had in the past, and we can utilize these assets for the present undertaken. This will make us proud of our self-image instead of ashamed of it. In that way, what seems "impossible" is possible after all.

Remember the words of Edward Young, "What we ardently wish, we soon believe."

## DO YOU FEEL SUPERIOR?

The other day I watched a motion-picture producer on TV being interviewed about his latest picture, and it seemed to me he made a very poor impression. He was bored and talked down to people, revealing that he felt superior to the man who interviewed him and to the audience.

Was he actually superior? I'm sure he wasn't. He was condescending, barely tolerant, arrogant, all of which indicated not superiority but inferiority, since these traits are distorted variations of hatred that demean people.

I recently attended a christening at a Franciscan church, and the priest— young, of Italian extraction, with a kind smile on his face—mentioned how poor and humble his little church was. Of course it wasn't said in any form of complaint, but indicated rather that he knew the blessings of humility.

One of our greatest gifts is humility, because only through this trait can we reach full maturity and be in God's image. By being humble, I don't mean weak and inadequate. I mean strong, but with ability to understand ourselves and others, to keep our successes in proper perspective in the present without feeling superior, without displaying condescension, superiority, or arrogance. People who look down on others think they are playing God, when actually they are playing the role of the devil.

The great tragedy of feeling superior is that it leaves no room for improve- ment, no room for making a mistake, which is the basis for improvement. Only with humility can we rise above failure and reach our goal of maturity and happiness. Only then do we really become superior, not over others but over ourselves, showing that we have refused to deny ourselves the right to improve. Remember the words of William Hazlitt, "No really great man ever thought himself so."

## WHAT DO YOUR HANDS REVEAL?

There are no two people alike, no two faces, no two hands, no two fingerprints. Yet hands, like the face, reveal our emotions within. I don't mean that one can tell the character of people by reading their palms. At best, this is a pseudo-science, as inaccurate as telling the character of people by the bumps on their heads or the size of their nose, chin, or ears. What I do mean is that our hands can be the extension of our emotions, representing without what is going on within. A closed fist can indicate stress as an open hand reveals relaxation. Fingers also represent a language to the deaf-mute, to the men at work in the stock exchange, and to engineers signaling to each other as the steel framework of a skyscraper slowly rises into the air. Fingers also represent a symbol. The winner in a civic election will raise his right hand and separate the index and middle fingers to form a V for victory.

I remember when I was operating on patients in a hospital in Panama many years ago, I saw a boy of eight in the clinic who held his right hand in his pocket, ashamed of his condition. The index and middle fingers had been joined since birth, a not too uncommon condition. He watched some children who poked fun at him playing baseball, and he envied their good fortune. And when I asked him why he wanted his fingers corrected, he answered that he wanted to play baseball. It was his way of saying that he wanted to be part of youth, not alone.

A week after the operation, before leaving for Costa Rica for another clinic, I removed the final bandages from the boy's hand. As he looked at his fingers, I said, "Separate them." At first, he was afraid, and then slowly he did separate them into a V—something he could never do before—and said, "V for victory!"

And this brings me to my point. Fingers and hands can be of different sizes and shapes, but they all reveal the successful or unsuccessful part of our nature. Does our hand reveal the clenched fist of anger or the open hand of goodwill? The clenched hand of tension or the open hand of relaxation? Does it reveal fear, resentment, emptiness, or does it reveal love, self-respect, self-confidence?

Let's keep our hand open as a symbol of friendship, offering to others the best that is in us. Let us, every day, for a moment, separate our fingers to make a V as a symbol of daily victory over failures. Remember the words of Montaigne, "Man is capable of all things."

## THE MINUTES

How many minutes are there in an hour? As many as we want to put into it. We are responsible for the continual, unceasing flow of minutes that make the hour. That makes us what we are. When we have a goal every day, every minute counts. When we have no goal, when we are lazy, every minute flies away uselessly.

I know a doctor who wanted to be a plastic surgeon. He watched me do surgery one morning at 8 a.m., was fascinated, and wanted to be my pupil. I agreed to teach him. He came once, twice, and suddenly didn't appear. A few days later, he came to my office and explained that he had overslept. He asked if I operated in the afternoon. I told him that I always operate in the morning at the hospital because it is best for the patient psychologically. He never took the course. He couldn't get up early enough. He was lazy.

We are all made of assets and liabilities. When we have a goal, we make time. When we are indolent, when we procrastinate, we lose precious time with fear, unbelief, uncertainty, and loneliness, because these thieves take us away from creative living and happiness.

There are twenty-four hours or fourteen hundred and forty minutes in a day. When we have a goal each day, every hour means a day of adventure; we make every minute count. When we are lazy, we can't find enough time in an hour. It's like a day wasted. There are fourteen hundred and forty useful or useless minutes in a day. If we use these minutes to advantage, we are on the road to successful living and happiness.

Here are the words of Thomas á Kempis, "Remember that lost time does not return."

## SLEEP

There are three eight-hour periods in a day. Eight hours for work, eight hours for diversion, and eight hours for sleep. These eight hours for sleep are nature's way of keeping the mind, body, and spirit in proper tone and condition, so that problems can be faced the following day.

Shakespeare said, "Sleep that knits up the ravelled sleave of care." Yet sleep is one of our great concerns in these frenetic times. Fortunes have been made by pharmaceutical companies who manufacture pills that are supposed to induce sleep.

I remember a time after I had lectured on Psycho-Cybernetics and Creative

Living at the First Church of Religious Science in San Francisco, I boarded a plane to New York. On the plane was a friend of mine, a producer of film. He took a sleeping pill, then asked me if I wanted one. I told him I never had occasion to use them because I fall asleep naturally. In the early morning, when we reached New York, my friend woke me up. He hadn't slept at all despite the pill. He told me he had been worrying about his next film.

We all have worries and problems; but I've learned not to let them intrude upon my eight hours set aside for sleep. By far, the greatest reasons for insomnia are tension, anxiety, or negative feelings that make us restless and prevent us from falling asleep.

Relaxation is the best preparation for sleep, because sleep is deep relaxation in itself. To relax is not easy these days, but we still can make a habit of it when, during the eight hours of diversion, we take five minutes off and walk into the room of our mind. Of course, this is an imaginary room. But since we live with our imagination every day, whether we realize it or not, we should take advantage of this imaginary room where we relax, look out the window, and see a geyser letting off steam. This is a symbol for us to release a geyser, to let go of tensions for the moment, to break the electric circuit of distress even for a second. Making a habit of this is making a habit of sleep. Whenever we think of troubles, we are not prepared for sleep. When we prepare ourselves for sleep, we must not let troubles interfere. Try my prescription. It may take time; but sooner or later, it will work, and you won't need a pill.

Remember the words of Publius Syrus, "He sleeps well who knows not that he sleeps ill."

## HOW TO DIG FOR TREASURES

Archeologists, proud plunderers of time, have found hidden treasures in ancient Greece.

Digging near a vegetable-growing village on the east coast of Attica, Dr. John Papadimitriou, Director of Antiquities in Greece's Ministry of Education, uncovered fifteen wooden vases carved in geometrical designs, the first such find in history. Knowing that fresh air would decompose the wood, which had been preserved in fertile mud since the fifth and sixth centuries B.C., the archeologist rushed them twenty-three miles to Athens for a thorough preservation bath.

Professor John L. Casky, of the University of Cincinnati, found in Greece a Mycenean settlement dating back 3,500 years, complete with temple, palace, private homes with inside plumbing, and a municipal sewer system.

And so, from time to time, we hear of new excavations that bring old civilizations to light.

How useful it would be if, as creative archeologists, we dug a little inside ourselves. We don't need an axe or a shovel, or any instrument for that matter. All we need is five minutes when we are resting after a day's work. We should use these five minutes to concentrate on ourselves. Concentration is thought in action. A thought has a beginning, a middle, and an ending. We must reflect logically, one thing at a time, with a beginning, a middle, and an ending. Then we will come to the realization that we are not our mistakes or failures, that we have assets too, and that we must not allow our assets to be buried under our mistakes. If we understand ourselves a little better, we can remove the debris of failure, and we are certain to find treasures more important to us than those treasures from a bygone civilization.

Personal treasures are self-respect, understanding, self-confidence, and courage. We must discover these within ourselves to help us tackle life's problems, to help us reach our daily goal, to give us our true self-image, which, in turn, brings happiness. Here are the words of Appius Claudius, "Every man is the architect of his own fortune."

## YOUR INVISIBLE PILL

Modern science has created experts in the manufacture of billions of pills. It is impossible to count the incredible number taken during the year.

I know an industrialist who travels constantly but never without a pillbox. Here is his daily intake of pills: a pill for indigestion, a pill containing all vitamins, a tranquilizer, a stimulant, and a pill to put him to sleep at night.

I believe people take more pills than they require, and I suppose it is merely an expression of the turbulent times in which we live. Besides medical pills, we take other pills during the day without realizing it; they are invisible and affect our emotions and peace of mind.

Some time ago, I was sitting in the restroom in a health club on the French Riviera, and I couldn't help but overhear two men talking. One said, "You know, Harry is a crooked manipulator. He takes sick organizations and makes them well after freezing out the original owner. Then he hides some of the cash in a vault. You know, one of these days, the government will get wise to him, and he'll find himself in jail. It's a terrible thing to rob a man of his business."

The other man nodded.

Actually, the first man, Sam, had taken an ugly pill without knowing it. He was spitting out venom against another member of the club. If the truth were told, Harry would have been depicted as an honest man who merely was a little faster than Sam in making the deals. When we use hatred or revenge, we are merely swallowing an invisible pill that makes us ugly and repulsive. It takes us away from truth, away from ourselves into a maze of uselessness. We waste a lot of energy in the process, energy that ought to go toward constructive purposes to reach a worthwhile goal.

Hatred or revenge abuses most the one who uses it. How much better it is to use our courage, our self-respect, and our self-confidence to achieve a goal no matter how small—without stepping on other people's toes. If we make a habit of that, without realizing it, we use a happiness pill for our mental well-being instead of an ugly pill.

Did you have your ugly pill or your happiness pill today? Remember the words of Hosea Ballou, "Hatred is self-punishment."

## FORGIVENESS

The "wrong"—particularly our own feeling of condemnation of wrong—must be seen as an undesirable thing rather than a desirable thing. Before a person can agree within himself to have his arm amputated, he must cease to see his arm as a desirable thing to be retained but as an undesirable, damaging, and threatening thing to be given up.

In facial surgery, there can be no partial, tentative, or halfway measures. The scar tissue is cut out completely and entirely. The wound is allowed to heal cleanly. Special care is taken to make certain the face will be restored in every particular, just as it was before injury.

Therapeutic forgiveness is not difficult. The only difficulty is to secure your own willingness to cast aside a feeling of condemnation—your willingness to cancel out the debt with no reservations.

We find it difficult to forgive only because we take comfort in a sense of condemnation. We get a perverse and morbid enjoyment out of nursing our wounds. As long as we condemn another, we can feel superior to him.

No one can deny that there is a perverse sense of satisfaction in feeling sorry for yourself.

In therapeutic forgiveness, we cancel out the debt of the other person, not because we have decided to be generous or to do him a favor, or because we are morally superior. We cancel the debt because we come to recognize that the debt itself is not valid. True forgiveness comes only when we are able to see, and instantly accept, that there is and was *nothing for us to forgive.* We should not have condemned or hated the other person in the first place. Therapeutic forgiveness is active forgiveness, turning your good thoughts into creative performance. Here are six points to remember:

1. Use foresight and clear thinking. Live in the present, but look toward your goal.
2. Seize opportunities to improve yourself now.
3. Develop insight into yourself to check negative feelings and rise above them.
4. Concentrate on compassion for yourself and for others.
5. Forget yesterday's trials; remember the good things.
6. Try to relax. You can if you live the principles mentioned in this book. If you see yourself at your best, not at your worst, and if you keep up with yourself, you will relax.

Here are the words of Robert Browning:

*Good to forgive;*
*Best to forget.*

## RECEIVING GIFTS

Long ago, I was invited by the government of Nicaragua to operate on a number of people with facial disfigurements. When I got to the capital, Managua, I went to the Hospital of God and there examined the patients I had been asked to help. In the line were two children, a boy of eight and a girl of seven. They were sister and brother, and they were both born with a deformity of the upper lip known as a cleft lip. A rumor had spread that I would operate on just one cleft lip, and the boy tried to get in front of the girl. Then there was a scuffle. Immediately, I explained that I would operate on both children, whereupon the mother, who was the cook at the hospital, stood erect and sang "The Star-Spangled Banner" to show her appreciation. Then she rushed into the hospital.

Ten days later, while I waited at the airport, the father of these children—a huge man of about three hundred pounds—came to me with a little bag in his hand. He opened the bag, took out an old rusty pirate's pistol and an old stuffed lizard, and said, "These are my best possessions. I'd like you to take them as an expression of my gratitude for helping my children." I took them, and in the plane on the way to Tegucigalpa, the capital of Honduras, I felt happy that through my gift of surgery, those children became normal. The best gift in life is the gift of understanding. When the person receives it, he is happy, and his image is improved. The same thing happens to the person who offers it because, in that process, he too grows in stature, in human dignity.

Here are the words of Ralph Waldo Emerson, "The only gift is a portion of thyself."

## WHAT DID YOU FORGET TODAY?

I know a man who hates his boss because he hasn't given him a raise. He comes home from his office resentful of the boss. And, unable to control his irritation now and then, he casts his resentment on his wife and daughter. Then he is miserable. He gets to bed and cannot sleep as he plans ways to do away with his boss. He gets up in the morning, deciding to tell his boss off; then, he sits at his desk and buries his resentment temporarily.

There comes a time when you get to bed and hit the pillow. You are utterly alone with your thoughts. And you take inventory of yourself, your assets and your liabilities. Then you ask yourself what you forgot to do during the day that has gone forever. Did you forget to smile at least once a day? Did you forget to compliment someone for a deed well done, for a word well spoken? Did you forget that you can be happy, that you can make a habit of happiness? Did you forget resentment, violence, these negative feelings that take you away from yourself and make you the small person you actually aren't? Did you forget that you were born to succeed in life? Did you forget you have assets within you that God gave you? Did you forget that you have dignity because you were made in God's image? Did you forget to be sincere? Did you forget to understand the needs of others? Did you forget to be compassionate? Did you forget to be self-confident? Did you forget to accept yourself for what you are and not try to be someone else? What did you forget today? Think of one thing you don't want to forget tomorrow. It will make you relax. Take stock of yourself. It will improve your self-image and give you peace of mind for tomorrow's goal.

## ARE YOU A DISPLACED PERSON?

During the time of the Nazi insanity in Germany and elsewhere, countless thousands of innocent victims were displaced in their effort to escape Nazi terror. Many found themselves in different countries of Latin America, even in the far-off reaches of the Orient. Many landed in various areas of Europe after the Allies conquered Germany.

I remember, many years ago, a middle-aged woman consulted me. She raised the long sleeve of her dress and asked me if plastic surgery could eradicate the tattoo on her arm. The numbers were: 138756. She had lost her husband and son in a concentration camp. Displaced to America, she met a man who fell in love with her and was going to marry her. She wanted the numbers removed, the past forgotten. She wanted to forget yesterday and start a new life today. I operated on her. She married the man, a machinist, and they now live in upstate New York.

Many of us who were never in Germany and who know little of concentration camps or displaced persons often become displaced persons without realizing it. Instead of being displaced by some outside force, we displace ourselves from our true selves when we give vent to negative feelings, emotions which throw us off balance and make us less than what we are. I mean the emotions of hate and violence, of envy, despair, and frustration. These destructive emotions make us walk away from life, from others, make us walk from ourselves into a concentration camp that we build with the branches of our minds, where we move in a circle of loneliness and emptiness.

It is well to remember then that making a habit of negative emotions destroys our self-respect. These disfiguring emotions are symbolically the tattoo numbers we ourselves place on our arms, isolating ourselves from reality.

We must resort to the courage and self-respect within us and use these qualities for the present to prevent ourselves from displacing ourselves from the goal we seek. We must not permit ourselves to be displaced persons if we are to live creatively. When we rise above failure, we move toward the goal of happiness. Remember the words of John Dryden:

*Of all the tyrannies of humankind,*
*the worst is that which persecutes the mind.*

## OUR EARS

Like fingerprints, no two pairs of ears are alike. Their remarkable variation in size, shape, and appearance is regarded as proof that they are shriveled organs inherited from some remote semi-human ancestor to whom they were of more use. For instance, the dog and horse have pointed ears, as does the monkey. The human ear has two distinct peculiarities: the folded upper margin and the lobe.

Conceptions of beautiful ears differ greatly with time and geography. Lubbock wrote of the East Islanders who punctured and enlarged their ears until they hung down to the shoulders. To them, monstrously distorted ears were envied as beautiful. Our concept of beauty is different.

Disfigurements of the ear are many. One of the most dramatic ear tragedies of all time occurred in the life of Vincent van Gogh, the artist. Terrified, Paul Gauguin contacted Van Gogh's brother to tell him that Vincent, in a state of terrible excitement and high fever, had cut off a piece of his own ear and brought it as a gift to a woman in a brothel.

From the beginning of time, efforts have been made to find some relationship between the size and shape of the ear and man's mental and emotional capabilities; but there is no truth to such correlation, even though children with protruding ears are often ridiculed and nicknamed "jackass."

I remember years ago in Rio, Brazil, where I was operating on many patients who needed plastic surgery, a man of seventy consulted me about his protruding ears. I asked him why he wanted his ears made normal in appearance at his age. He said, "Doctor, ever since childhood when I worked on a farm in Sweden, I was teased by others with the word 'donkey.' I grew up, left the farm, came to Brazil, married a Brazilian woman, had two children, a boy and a girl. I became successful. Now my children are gone on their own. My wife is gone. But I can't forget the taunts of my youth. I never looked normal. I wondered if you could fix my ears now so that when I leave this world, God will see me with normal ears, the way they should be."

PS.: I did the operation.

The shape of the ear is less important than the sound it carries to the hearing organ within. And this leads me to the point. It is more important for us to learn to shut our ears to evil gossip and hatred and to open them to compassion and understanding. We are all children of God, and we are entitled to each other's respect. Remember the words of Epictetus, "Nature has given to men one tongue, but two ears, that we may hear from others twice as much as we speak."

## IMPERSONATION

"Impersonation" is a word with a negative effect. As used generally, "impersonation" implies that you are trying to be someone else—an athletic hero, a movie star, an idol. In that process, you devalue yourself, depreciate your worth, and fail as a human being.

What you must do—if you will allow me a little artistic license in my use of the word—is "impersonate" yourself. Be yourself . . . whenever you can. If circumstances force you to adopt a protective facade, know what you are doing, and return to yourself as soon as you can.

Recently I was on a ship, the *Michelangelo*. We sailed across the Atlantic Ocean, from New York to Cannes, France. I noticed a stocky woman in her late forties. She was eating with some friends near my table, and she kept explaining to them how she stays thin by walking and walking and walking around the deck of the ship. She claimed that it took pounds off her.

But by the end of the voyage, she looked much heavier; her face was extremely full, and every time I looked at her, she was eating.

She was playing a game of make-believe, pretending that her walking lost weight for her while she gorged herself every meal and gained perhaps fifteen pounds during that short trip. It was a physical distortion, and an emotional one too. Most of us distort ourselves emotionally by pretending we are what we are not.

Accept yourself for what you are. This is your personal responsibility to yourself.

Remember the words of Miguel de Cervantes, "All affectation is bad."

## "I JUST WANTED TO HELP"

I recall a time I went to Lake Orion, near Detroit, Michigan, to talk to a group of priests who had succumbed to alcoholism. They came from all over the world and were treated for four months, then returned to their flocks cured. During the stage of sobriety, they used my book *Psycho-Cybernetics* as a bridge to walk back to themselves.

After lecturing, I went to sleep for a few hours. I was awakened at 1:45 a.m. Lake Orion is about forty-five miles from Detroit, and I had to catch the 4:35 plane back to New York so that I could operate on a child who had been seriously injured in an automobile accident.

The night man, after waking me, took me to the house of the priests' sanitarium and made me scrambled eggs and coffee. This simple action touched me because it was not his job, and I had not asked him to make a meal for me.

He stood there, bushy hair, rosy cheeks, and asked me if the eggs were okay.

"Fine," I said, and thanked him for putting himself out for me at 2:00 a.m.

"I just wanted to help," he said, and gave me a shy, friendly smile.

After some small talk, he told me about himself. He had a bad heart. Under his shirt, he wore a pacemaker, an electrical instrument attached to the chest wall. The instrument helped him keep his heart beating normally, enabled him to live and work as a night man at the sanitarium.

"Another cup of coffee?" he asked.

I nodded.

"I like to help," he said. "I really do. Since I had my heart trouble, especially, I live a good life. I like to help people, and I take other people's help. I've got no complaints."

On the plane from Detroit to New York, I thought about this man who lived a simple life and enjoyed it. I said to myself, "If a man who can't live without an electrical instrument will not give in, we can all learn the lesson that, despite our problems, we can stand up to the stresses of the day and refuse to withdraw from our strength. By activating our success mechanism, every day, we can live each day to the full."

Here is a quote from Pliny the Elder (A.D. 23–79), "For a man to help another is to be a god."

## A SPIRITUAL FACE LIFT

To live creatively, we must be willing to be somewhat vulnerable. We must be willing to be hurt a little, if necessary, in creative living. A lot of people need a thicker and tougher emotional skin than they have. But they need only a tough emotional hide, not a shell. To trust, to love, to open ourselves to emotional communication with other people is to run the risk of being hurt. If we are hurt once, we can do one of two things. We can build a thick protective shell, or scar tissue, to prevent being hurt again, or we can "turn the other cheek," remain vulnerable and go on living creatively.

An oyster is never "hurt." He has a thick shell that protects him from everything. He is isolated. An oyster is secure but not creative. He cannot "go after" what he wants; he must wait for it to come to him. An oyster knows none of the "hurts" of emotional communication with his environment, but neither can an oyster know the joys.

Try giving yourself a "Spiritual Face Lift." It is more than a play on words. It opens you up to more life, more vitality, the "stuff" that youth is made of. You'll feel younger. You'll actually look younger. Many times, I have seen a man or woman look five or ten years younger in appearance after removing old emotional scars. Look around you. Who are the youthful-looking people you know over the age of forty? The grumpy? Resentful? The pessimistic? The ones who are soured on the world? Or are they the cheerful, optimistic, good-natured people?

Carrying a grudge against someone or against life can bring on the old-age stoop just as much as carrying a heavy weight around on your shoulders would. People with emotional scars, grudges, and the like are living in the past, which is characteristic of old people. The youthful attitude and youthful spirit, which erases wrinkles from the soul and the face and puts a sparkle in the eye, looks to the future with expectation.

So, why not give yourself a face lift? Your do-it-yourself kit consists of relaxation and positive thinking to prevent scars, therapeutic forgiveness to remove old scars, providing yourself with a tough (but not a hard) epidermis instead of a shell of creative living, a willingness to be a little vulnerable, and a longing for the future instead of the past. Remember, your future happiness depends on living creatively today, every day.

## ARE YOU EASILY HURT?

Many people are "hurt" terribly by tiny pinpricks or what we call social "slights." I'm sure you know someone in your family, your office, your circle of friends who is so thin-skinned and "sensitive" that others must be continually on guard lest offense be taken at some innocent word or act.

It is a well-known psychological fact that people who become offended the easiest have the lowest self-esteem. They are "hurt" by things they conceive as threats to their ego or self-esteem. Fancied emotional thrusts that pass unnoticed by a person with wholesome self-esteem slice these people up terribly. Even real "digs" and "cuts" that inflict painful injury to the ego of the person with low self-esteem do not make a dent in the ego of the person who thinks well of himself. It is the person who feels undeserving, who doubts his own capabilities, and has a poor opinion of himself who becomes jealous at the drop of a hat. It is the person who secretly doubts his own worth and feels insecure within himself who sees threats to his ego where there are none, who exaggerates and overestimates the damage from real threats.

We all need a certain amount of emotional toughness and ego security to protect us from real and fancied ego threats. It wouldn't be comfortable for the physical body to be covered over completely with a hard shell like a turtle's. We would be denied the pleasure of all sensual feeling. But the human body does have a layer of outer skin for the purpose of protecting us from the invasion of bacteria, small bumps and bruises, and pinpricks. That skin is thick enough and tough enough to offer protection against small wounds, but not so thick or hard that it interferes with all feeling. Many people have no covering over their ego. They have only the thin, sensitive inner skin. They need to become thicker-skinned, emotionally tougher, so that they will simply ignore petty cuts and minor ego threats.

They need to build their self-esteem, get a better and more adequate self-image so that they will not feel threatened by every chance remark or innocent act. A big strong man does not feel threatened by a small danger; a little man does. In the same way, a healthy strong ego, with plenty of self-esteem, does not feel itself threatened by every innocent remark.

## POKER FACE

I know four women who meet every Friday night in one of their homes. For many years, this has been a ritual. They are quite unusual. When they get together, they don't smoke, they don't drink, they don't gossip. They are so fascinated with what they are doing, they don't talk about children, husbands, relatives, the weather, politics, or world affairs.

Sitting around the table, they conduct their business as if it were the only thing that mattered on Friday evening. Their business is cards: poker, dealer's choice. None of them plays it cagey; all are liberal players and sometimes reckless. Over the years, they have learned to know each other's game. Each has her special secret weapon, the knowledge of the others' facial expressions when they hold a winning hand. One coughs, the second smiles, the third frowns, the last tries to look astonished.

The game has been going on every Friday, year after year. Now it is at Harriet's house regularly because she has arthritis and has to sit in a special chair. They play, they enjoy themselves, and at the end of the year, they break even.

They play poker, but they do not wear poker faces. They know each other's game just as they know each other.

In life, people too often wear poker faces and watch other people doing the same; the idea is to fool each other. They corrugate the skin of their faces into all sorts of poses and affectations. This does not work. The trick is to do what these four women do every Friday night. The trick is not to trick. Be yourself. Be true to yourself. Like yourself and let others like what you really are. Don't be affected, don't wear a poker face. Just be natural and show that you like people, that you are willing to help. Let this true face be your poker face, and you will always have an ace in the hole. That way, you will never lose.

## CONFRONTATION

We hear a great deal of talk these days about "confrontation." What is the greatest confrontation of this generation? Is it the confrontation between young people and the "Establishment"?

Is it the confrontation between young people and the powers that be in education and religions?

Neither of these, well-advertised though they may be, is the greatest confrontation of today.

The greatest confrontation of today may not even show sufficiently to be observed by the people with whom we have everyday contact, because it takes place within each one of us; it is the confrontation inside us, and it involves the different sides of our nature. It involves our success and our failure instincts; it involves the meaning that we will or will not give to our lives.

Who will win in this eternal battle?

The abrasive side of you, hating every imperfection in yourself, afraid to take chances because you may fail or stumble, blaming yourself for everything you do wrong? Or the kind, accepting side of you, supporting yourself when you are weak or inadequate or unthinking or offensive?

The winner must be willing to live richly with support and acceptance. That is how you will come out the winner.

## THE GOAL OF "ETERNAL" YOUTH

A human attitude, a compassionate attitude toward yourself, will be decisive in the success with which you are able to achieve your goals.

You must live with yourself and your image of yourself; there is no escape from this. You can travel to Paris or Calcutta, to London or Rome, to Buenos Aires or New Delhi—but you cannot escape. No matter where you are, you take yourself with you.

You are either your lifelong partner or your lifelong enemy.

A wonderful goal I hope you will achieve is the goal of feeling youthful always—regardless of your chronological age. I define youth as fresh, vigorous, alive; it is something that bubbles, that does not stagnate.

Champagne is youthful when it pours from the bottle, full of sparkle and zing. It has lost its youth when it sits untouched and unwanted; it is then inert, flat, dead.

Youth is song, it is enthusiasm, it is fire. It comes from the spirit, fills the mind, comingles with the success instincts, tingles in the bloodstream.

Here is a goal to pursue every day—if only for a few minutes—the goal of feeling youthful for as long as you live. Think of what you can do to make your days more fun. Use your sense of direction to point the way.

Remember your goal—more zest, more fun.

Youth—as long as you live.

Look for the youth in you. It will enrich your days and years of creative living. This is one of the best goals of all.

## HUMANITY—TOWARD YOURSELF

You must learn to accept your human weaknesses. This is of tremendous importance to you.

Most people, if they stop to think, understand the plight of underprivileged groups.

Most people, if they pause in the midst of a hectic day, are sympathetic to the problems of their neighbors.

Many people feel for the frailties and blunders of people they have never met.

And yet, these same people, confronted with their own human failings, are inhuman.

During the Spanish Inquisition of the fifteenth century, Torquemada earned historical infamy for his relentless cruelty. If you are familiar with this part of history, you likely feel revulsion on seeing his name in print. Yet you could be treating yourself with comparative cruelty.

When you stammer during a conversation because of reacting to tension or confusion—do you forgive yourself?

When you burn the toast, and the three-minute eggs become thirteen-minute eggs, do you forgive yourself?

When you misplace a five-dollar bill or lose it, do you forgive yourself?

When you forget an appointment, do you forgive yourself?

When your day goes wrong, and you lose your temper and shout and scream, do you forgive yourself?

You must learn to be human toward yourself, to forgive your shortcomings; otherwise, your success mechanism will not function, and you will not attain goals that will be really satisfying. Success and self-hate cannot live together. They are enemies, not partners.

When you rub the sleep out of your eyes and sit up in bed, tell yourself first thing, "Today, I will be human toward myself."

## ON ENVY

In this day of prestige symbols, you are often more tempted to imitate others than to build your own self-respect. And when you imitate someone, you are playing second fiddle, and consequently, you can never find your true worth. You renounce your self-image and live in the self-image of someone else, and this means unhappiness.

It is the same with envy, a destructive trait that takes you away from your true self and prevents you from your "big self." Instead you prefer to become petty and small. You are filled with wrath and lose your reason and sense of fair play. You think in destructive terms and seethe with resentment at another person's good fortune, hurting yourself in the process. The chances are that the person you envy doesn't know that you are alive. And alive you are not when you live in envy; you are merely existing, a small dark shadow of your true self.

Envy is high blood pressure of the mind that paralyzes you preventing you from becoming your big self.

Is there a cure for envy? I think so. If you were to face the mirror to take stock of yourself, and realize that this trait is hurting you, you would think quickly about making a constructive change. How? By using compassion on yourself first, it is the beginning of wisdom and humility. It is the beginning of forgiving yourself for an error and rising above it. Perhaps you can start a new day for yourself by remembering the words of Ovid, "Envy, the meanest of vices, creeps on the ground like a serpent."

## YOUR WORST ENEMY

Many of us do not realize what we believe when we look in the mirror. Many of us do not see our own image but someone else's image that we feel we must please, thinking it might be of value. But there is no value or glory playing second fiddle to someone else. You cannot live your life with someone else's image. It means self-destruction; you become your worst enemy.

You are your worst enemy when you want to be perfect. You become fearful of making a mistake, so you don't assert yourself; therefore, you cannot achieve happiness in life. You cannot gain friendship that way or in any negative way where you symbolically walk around on your knees trying to get attention by trying to please everybody.

Friendship begins with you; you can't be a friend to others unless you are a friend to yourself. What is equally important is that you can't be a friend to everybody. We all see things differently. That is the way it should be; and because of that, it is inevitable that we will make enemies with people who violently disagree with us. If we firmly and honestly feel that our cause is right, we should not be afraid of making enemies but should try to maintain harmony.

There is an old Chinese proverb that says, "Just as tall trees are known by their shadows, so are good men known by their enemies." By far, you are your worst enemy either when through fear and indecision you live to please someone else, or when you refuse to live at all because you are fearful of making a mistake.

## NEGOTIATION WITH YOURSELF

You must negotiate with yourself. Insist on your human rights. You must try to narrow the gap between your big self and your little self. You must work to create a proper climate within yourself for the development of your total personality. You can do this by eliminating past grievances about yourself, by forgiving yourself, and by setting a limit to the inhumanity in yourself toward yourself.

The troubles in the Mideast and in Southeast Asia seem interminable. Don't let this happen to you. You must negotiate an end to the riot and violence within you, so that you can make yourself whole and healthy and move toward a spirit of brotherliness and full participation in living.

You have empathy for other people only when you have empathy for yourself first. Don't downgrade yourself, and then try to extend a helping hand to others. That's absurd! Empathy starts at home. It's a daily enterprise in a daily climate. You can pick up your telephone and dial the weather forecast. Then, daily, tune in to yourself to see how you feel, what you need. Does a mother, without really listening, hear her baby crying in another room? Yes, and you, without special effort, can listen for your emotional heartbeat, screening out the hectic hustle bustle of the world to give attention to your prime personal responsibility—yourself.

## SINCERITY

I remember a time when a mother brought two daughters to my office. The older girl was beautiful, the younger was ugly. She had a receding chin that needed correction. The older daughter suddenly said, "I don't see why she has to have any work done. God made her that way, and that's the way she should be."

Do you think this beautiful girl was religious? I don't. I think she was insincere. She wanted to be the only beautiful child in the family and resented the fact that something could be done for her younger sister.

On another occasion, I remember a humorist pretending he was a candidate running for election. He said, "Friends, I want you to vote for me for mayor for the simple reason that the symbiosis of the calcium makes it evident that I'm the right man. Besides, you must understand that the *res ipse loquitor* of my dignity makes it imperative that I'm the man for the job." Now, these words and others that followed formed a lot of sentences that meant nothing—double talk. This, done seriously, is insincerity. Insincerity leads to exhaustion.

To be sincere, we must do three things: We must look behind us, within ourselves and, finally, in front of us. When we look behind us, we must remember the mistakes we made in the past in order to correct them and improve the future. When we look within ourselves, we must remember that we are made of assets as well as liabilities. We must try to enhance our assets as much as we can. Finally, we must have the capacity to look forward, to realize that the day—a full day—is a lifetime in itself and that we must have a goal for this day, a goal within our capabilities and training. When we reach this goal with integrity and with sincerity, we become useful not only to ourselves but to others. We are then on the road to happiness for the simple reason that we are improving our self-image, striving—always striving—for self-fulfillment.

Remember the words of Confucius, "Sincerity and truth are the basis of every virtue."

## THE COMMON BOND

Terence, who was born a slave and made something of himself in Rome twenty-one centuries ago, said this, "I am a man; nothing that concerns mankind is alien to me." He was a comedian and was the first to proclaim the principle of common kinship in man.

Whether he is black, red, brown, or white, whether his language is different from yours, whether he is rich or poor, whether he is a slave or free, whether his appearance is different from yours, whether his thoughts about life are different from yours, you have one common bond with any other person in the universe.

The suffering, the sorrows, the grief, the despair, the loneliness and emptiness, the insecurity and uncertainty, the doubt and fear are the same. We all suffer the same. But there is a far greater bond that can hold us together. The faith and hope, fortitude and persistency, smiles and laughter, understanding and courage, self-respect and self-acceptance, confidence and encouragement we can give each other in times of crises and in times of peace, seeking peace of mind. This is the greatest bond of all to hold us together as we struggle in the slow evolution from hatred, to tolerance, to love.

At no time in history has the call for unity of all people been greater than now. In this time of agonizing wars, in this time of the atom bomb that threatens man's very existence, I believe that human understanding and sympathy, I believe that human encouragement and dignity will hold us together for a better world.

## ON FALSE PRIDE

Listen to the words of Carl Sandburg:

*"Look out how you use proud words.*
*When you let proud words go, it is not easy to call them back.*
*They wear long boots, hard boots . . .*
*Look out how you use proud words."*

Pride sometimes is a destructive trait—when it carries with it anger, prejudice, and resentment, when it knows nothing of compassion, love, or friendship. False pride means intolerance, arrogance, and ignorance—ignorance of the great fundamental truths of creative living, simplicity, humility, encouragement.

Man's great goal to improve and to make something of himself and of others less fortunate lies in his imagination, the power of his imagination to find his true worth. False pride means only that you use your imagination destructively to hurt others and, equally important, to hurt yourself without knowing it. False pride takes you away from reality, from the beauty of living, and you are then unable to find happiness for yourself.

The tragedy of false pride is that it is immoral and sinful in that it prevents a person from rising to his full stature of integrity. Can you have false pride and self-respect? Never! Can you have understanding and false pride at one time? Never! Can you have forgiveness and false pride at the same time? Never!

True pride comes from compassion for yourself—a happy combination of achievement and humility.

Proud words (undeserved) are not easy to call back. But you can call yourself back from the illness of false pride and find the big you through compassion for yourself.

## UP TILL NOW

I had dinner one evening with a friend who is a successful businessman, married then divorced. He has two children, a boy and a girl, who are at college. After many years of living alone, he married again. I asked him, "Joe, how does it feel to be married again?"

He replied, "Okay, up till now."

"What do you mean?" I went on, "You've been married only six weeks."

He said, "Well, everything is fine. I don't have to run around, make all sorts of dates. I have a home now. I have companionship and peace of mind. I'm just hoping it stays that way. That's what I mean by 'Okay, up till now.'"

What Joe was thinking is exactly what most of us think, but in different circumstances. He was thinking about the future. We all live in hope for a happy future. This keeps us young, because the main characteristic of youth is hope for the future. The reason is that youth has no real past and looks to build a future as it moves toward the threshold of adult life. However, hope and the future are certainly not passive words. Passive words take us away from ourselves and lead us to nowhere. Thus, when we passively hope that when tomorrow comes, things will be all right, or when we dream of the happy past when we are failing in the present and hope that by some magic happiness will return tomorrow, we are not hoping for the future creatively. We are just using words, expecting the words to open the door to happiness when tomorrow comes. No one ever sees happiness when tomorrow comes; it is today.

To use the symbols of hope and tomorrow creatively, we must live for today. Every day must be a complete lifetime, and we must live it to the full. We must strive to reach a useful goal, even if we are momentarily sidetracked by failure. We cannot use the phrase "up till now"—it implies doubt, fear, and a lack of belief.

All of us must actively create in the new day when it comes. We must use courage and self-respect to keep love and companionship in true perspective. This is active hope, which builds a happy future by living the present day to the brim. This is the true hope for tomorrow that will keep us young. We should remember the words of Samuel Johnson, "Learn that the present hour alone is man's."

## ON BEING COMPLACENT

Being satisfied and pleased with oneself is one thing. Having respect for oneself is another.

If you have a goal and you reach your goal, it gives you confidence. You use this confidence to achieve new goals. That is what creative living is all about.

When you develop confidence on your own initiative, there is no shame in being proud of your achievement. You don't have to brag about it; but you can look at yourself with kind eyes and, with approval, you can accept yourself for what you are and what you can be. This does not mean complacency, being satisfied with your lot, and staying that way. Psycho-Cybernetics teaches that when you reach one goal, you start after another goal the very next day, never being fully satisfied with yourself or your achievements.

Complacency is a variation of conceit, because you like yourself and go on liking yourself for what you have achieved, feeling you need not achieve any more.

Complacency and humility do not go together, but confidence and humility do. The danger in being complacent is that you become passive and rest on your laurels, whatever they may be. To become passive is to become inactive; and, when you become inactive, you retire from the realities of life. Creative living means that you must always keep moving in the stream of things. You can still enjoy a vacation now and relax in the room of your mind to renew your energies and your courage to tackle life's problems. Complacency signals that you are resting too long. All rest and no work makes you dull, uninteresting, lifeless.

No one can make you complacent without your consent. If you are self-satisfied, it is a symptom of fear—fear of what is real.

Remember that complacency is God's gift to little men.

## OUR IMPULSES

Should we obey an impulse? We should if the impulse is constructive. Impulses can also be destructive. When we hate, we often, through imagination, dispose of the individual. This creates negative impulses that have no value because they distort the self-image.

We live every day with imagination. Worry is a form of imagination. Here we throw on the screen of the mind past failures, which inhibit us in our daily tasks of the present. When we are happy, we throw on the screen of the mind past successes, which give us the confidence we exercise in the daily tasks for the present. A good impulse is nothing more than imagination that seeks action to improve the self-image.

When I was a young man, I had the impulse, the desire, to be a plastic surgeon. This was during a time when the specialty was practically unknown. Despite tremendous objections from family, I obeyed my impulse.

I know a doctor who, twenty years ago, had the impulse to be a baby spe-
cialist. He loved children and would have been excellent in this specialty. But
he was undecided. He said he'd wait until he had saved enough money, until
he could properly provide for his wife and child. One indecision followed an-
other, and he never became a baby specialist.

Indecision is unbelief. Unbelief is fear. And this constant fear prolongs
tension and, finally, puts us in a state of paralysis. This scars and distorts the
self-image, making us less than what we are, preventing us from reaching our
true stature of fulfillment.

I know a married woman who has two children. She suddenly had the
impulse to do abstract painting. She followed her impulse despite objections
from her family. Now she sells her paintings. She has made her family happy
and herself happy. The point to remember is to obey your impulse, the good
impulse. It is a challenge to be happy. It is a chance to put the imagination to
work, to reach a worthwhile goal, to fulfill ourselves.

Remember the words of George Herbert, "He begins to die who quits his
desires."

## IDEAS

What are ideas? They are the product of the imagination, of thinking and
concentrating on a specific subject. An idea is a brainchild, but what kind
of a child is it? Is it a child born of resentment or hatred? Is it a deformed
child born out of deception and trickery? Or is it a beautiful child born out
of love and encouragement, out of hope and belief? These latter children of
the mind and spirit are so desperately needed in these chaotic times when
it seems that a cannon is more important than a human life, that money is
more important than goodwill, that the destructive thought of taking ex-
ceeds the creative thought of giving.

It is now, this very minute, that we have to search for self-respect, for the
assurance that peace of mind can be ours in this lifetime. It is at this very mo-
ment, when reason and patience are undergoing an eclipse, when wars are in-
tended to destroy the world forever, that we must live in the hope given us by
creative ideas. We should strive to build ideas on compassion and humility, on
love and friendship, on taking less and giving more while we are alive, if life
on this planet is to be sustained for the future.

It is at this very moment that mass fulfillment demands that we see the good
in others, not the evil; see the hope in others, not the frustration; see the joy in
others, not the sorrow; see the faith in others, not the despair.

Great ideas are truths waiting to be fulfilled, and no idea is worth anything unless and until we turn it into a worthwhile performance for the benefit of all humanity.

Oliver Wendell Holmes said, "The ultimate good is better achieved by the free trade in ideas."

## GRIEF AND LONELINESS

Grief brings loneliness. There is an ancient Greek saying that, of all ills common to all men, the greatest is grief. None of us can escape it. It makes some men tender and compassionate, and others—not as strong perhaps—it makes hard, encased in protective armor.

I remember after I graduated from medical school and became an intern, I put on my white uniform for the first time and was quite happy about it. I telephoned my father and told him about it. He was overjoyed and said he would take the subway and come up to the hospital in an hour or two to see me.

An hour passed and then another, and he didn't come. Later on, I received a telephone call. I rushed to another hospital downtown, and there, my father lay dead. He had been killed by an automobile.

I was overcome with grief, and I wondered if I would ever survive it. I couldn't get out of my mind the fact that my father was dead and that he would never see me as a doctor. Finally, I terminated my self-imposed isolation from others and returned to the world of people.

We can suffer up to a point. The body can endure so much torment; then no more. It is fitting; it is a need of the soul to grieve for a loved one lost; but the time comes when we must stop grieving and return to the joyful business of living. Endless grief becomes a self-destructive force that must be stopped, like a leak in a roof; otherwise, there will be a flood and enormous loss in its wake. Endless obsession over pain means separation from other people; it means loneliness.

Shakespeare believed that everyone could master grief, except the one who feels it; nevertheless, we must learn to master sorrow. Time will help us if we help time. The thing to remember is that we must eventually shake off grief and return to everyday realities—before the inner scar becomes permanent. When this happens, we have an illness—worse than an ulcer—which we contract deep inside ourselves, bathing in a form of selfishness that is unpleasant and leads to a feeling of loneliness. Then one may find false pleasure indulging in grief, proving Samuel Johnson's contention that grief can be a species of idleness.

The cure for grief is movement toward people, reaching out toward people with the richest qualities you have in you to give. You must learn to break down the wall of separateness that is the fence behind which the lonely person hides.

It may be helpful to remember the words of the British statesman Benjamin Disraeli, "Grief is the agony of an instant; the indulgence of grief the blunder of a lifetime."

## ON MORALS

Is happiness a moral issue? I think so. I believe that every human being has a moral responsibility to be happy, and to share happiness with others. I believe it is completely immoral to be unhappy. I believe it is immoral for people who think they are moral and want to change people to be like them, to act, think, and live like them.

The prophets of happiness see life as it is, a far healthier view than the dreary moralists of gloom who want to make people good rather than happy. The point is you can't be good unless you are happy. And since happiness is internal, it means you are happiness. You have a responsibility to live it and to share it with others; and the more you give, the more you have. The dreary moralists don't give; they take away from the pure joy of living, and in that context, they are immoral.

These are the words of Robert Louis Stevenson, "If your morals make you dreary, depend upon it they are wrong." He didn't mean that if your life seems dull that you must abandon moral standards and seek happiness by stepping on other people's toes or on your own toes with indulgence and indolence. To live by fear, intimidation, frustration, and indecision is immoral to the extent that it makes you your little self, living in a dungeon you create for yourself. To live with the joy of life every twenty-four hours is another way of expressing love for others and for yourself, respect for others and for yourself. To me, this is creative morality.

Here is a thought to live by, written by George Bernard Shaw, "What is morality? Gentility."

## THE BARBERSHOP QUARTET

In San Diego, I went to a barbershop to have my shoes shined. I sat down and listened to the talk around me. A quartet of men were singing the praises of their cars.

"I have a Chevy, a beauty. It's done close to 30,000 miles and no trouble."

"Mine's done over 40,000."

"How often do you get the oil changed?"

"Oh, I don't know, maybe every 2,000 miles. How about you?"

"I don't think that's enough, pal. I get mine changed every 1,000 miles. Filter every 3,000 to 5,000. That's the way to keep your car in good shape."

"I don't know. My car's done over 60,000, and I change the oil every 1,200 to 1,300 miles."

"You take care of your car; it'll take care of you."

The four men kept talking, two getting haircuts, two cutting hair. The shoeshine fellow and I just listened.

I thought to myself, "These fellows seem to know cars—and there's nothing wrong with that—but do they know anything at all about self-image? They look to be about thirty-five to forty-five, all of them, but do they practice creative living? They apparently like to be good citizens; they are all shaved, they keep their hair cut neatly, they oil their cars, they probably spend Sunday mornings washing their cars down so that the metal sparkles. Their cars will certainly get them where they want to go, but do they believe in other positive goals each day? Do they see a glistening self-image, or have they lost it in their fight for money and status and in their exclusive absorption in cars and such?" George Bernard Shaw said, "Better keep yourself clean and bright; you are the window through which you see the world." I say, "Better keep your self-image clean and bright. It is the window through which you see the world."

Most of us, regrettably, take better care of our cars than we do of the image of ourselves, which disappears somewhere—and with it goes our drive for happiness. What is your daily goal? Do you strive for creative living and self-fulfillment, steering your mind to productive, useful goals? If you try, try, try, you'll never have an energy crisis. You will have all the mental and spiritual fuel necessary to reach your destination.

## THE SMALL POTATO

Carlyle said, "Society is founded on hero worship." We see it expressed dramatically in our lives. We cheer the winner in a prizefight, the actress for a memorable performance. We cheer our favorite football or baseball team and shout for joy when they are the winners of the season.

We love a winner because we love ourselves; and vicariously, we put ourselves in the place of the successful man, dreaming and hoping that someday, it will be our turn to be cheered and applauded for outstanding achievement.

We all have our hearts set on success, naturally. We persevere, believing that the day will come when we will reach our goal. Yet by the very nature of things, man is a paradox. He performs various acts daily that are inconsistent with achieving importance. He persists in doing the very things that will make him unimportant—the very things that will make him a small potato—and he takes all the time in the world to become insignificant.

All of us, more or less, receive little wounds from people in the daily struggle for contentment, and we exaggerate their significance by brooding over them. These wounds become so great to us, though unimportant, that they make us insignificant for the time we spend coddling them, thereby wounding ourselves more in the process.

Many of us are so concerned with the business of being a small potato, I thought it would be of value to jot down what to do and what not to do about it. With practice, you can become a small potato indeed.

Coddle your regrets. Let your mind continue to long for what has passed. Complain and be discontented when things go wrong at the time you expected the reverse. Forget that contentment should be your first step to progress. Be petty about your neighbor's good fortune. Stay hurt and disappointed about small matters.

Don't stop brooding over a grievance. Don't devote your time to worthwhile actions and feelings. Don't dare to think of a great thought, of wonderful affection, or of a lasting undertaking. Don't remember that every scrap of time is worth saving. Don't remember that you are here for a few decades at best and that life is too short to be a small potato.

Follow these precepts carefully, and I can assure you that you will become the smallest of the small potatoes.

## YOU CAN'T RETIRE FROM LIFE

When I was in medical school, more than fifty years ago, a fellow student named Mickey was hospitalized with a severe case of influenza. He almost died from the disease, which was a much more serious problem then than it is today.

He recovered partially, and his condition was no longer critical, but his recovery was not complete. My fellow students and I would visit him at the hospital; it was extremely depressing. Formerly husky and energetic, with bristling blond hair, Mickey was pale, had lost much weight, and he still looked sick. His skin was colorless, his eyes were somber. You felt when you saw him that he envied you your health. My friends and I felt uncomfortable talking to him at his bedside, but we took turns visiting him.

Then one day, there was a sign on his closed door: NO VISITORS. We were alarmed, but there was no cause. Mickey's life was not in danger.

Mickey had asked the doctor to put up the sign. The visits of his friends and relatives had not cheered him. Instead, they had made him feel more glum. He wanted nothing to do with us. Later, Mickey told us how he felt during these days when he wanted nothing to do with the world of people. He felt scornful toward everybody and everything. He felt that each of us was worthless or ridiculous as a person. He told us that, in the prison of his mind, no one escaped the lash of his criticism. He just wanted to be left alone with the misery of his thoughts. There was no pleasure in him. Depressed by his physical deterioration, he felt a rejection of life growing in him until he renounced the world.

These were truly days of no-pleasure for Mickey. His resentment was too great for him to tolerate.

But he was lucky.

The day nurse, understanding his state of mind, decided to help him.

One day, after some tricky preludes, she told him that there was a girl patient who was suffering emotionally; Mickey could lift her spirits if he would write her love letters. Mickey wrote her one letter, then two. He pretended that he had seen her briefly one day and that he had thought about her ever since. After they were both well, he suggested, in a note, perhaps they could take walks in the park together.

Mickey felt pleasure in writing these letters—for the first time in many days—and his health began to improve. He wrote many letters and was soon walking spiritedly around the room. Soon, he was to be discharged from the hospital.

This knowledge saddened him because he had never seen the girl. So much pleasure had been derived from writing of his adoration, and a glow of love would come to his face at the thought of her. But he had never seen her—not even once!

Mickey asked the nurse if he could visit the girl in her room. The nurse approved and gave him the room number—414.

But there was no such room. There was no such girl.

And Mickey learned the truth—that the nurse had done her best to make him well. Seeing his gloom, sensing his critical, hating thoughts toward everyone, she felt that to recover from his illness, he needed pleasure in his life. She sensed that what Mickey needed to give him pleasure was the opportunity to give to a fellow patient, a fellow sufferer. She told him about the imaginary girl, and that turned the tide of his emotions.

So, Mickey left the hospital wiser, knowing in his heart the futility of resentment—and the happiness one gets from giving. He told us the story, for we were once again his friends. Mickey told it to us contentedly. His eyes gleamed, his cheeks were aglow, because he knew how it felt to escape from the dark world of self-inflicted gloom into the sunny world where one can live with pleasure.

Remember the words of John Donne:

*Despair is the damp of hell, as*
*joy is the serenity of heaven.*

## OUR GOOD EARTH

Paul B. Sears, the distinguished naturalist, said, "This is our world."

In these four short words, he expressed man's responsibility throughout the ages to do something to really mean this is our world. Man evolves as a better human being when he realizes his responsibility to come to terms with nature, with his fellow men, and with himself. However, he must come to happy terms with himself before he can accomplish anything constructive with others and with the outside world. The three worlds in which he lives—the world of his body, his mind, and his spirit—are his good earth. He cannot come to terms with nature if he doesn't come to terms with himself. He cannot be a friend to others or nature unless he is a friend to himself. He must save his own existence from destructive forces before he can talk about preserving the life of being in the forest. He must control the violence within him before he can control the violence around him. He must control the pollution in his mind and spirit, control the garbage of hurt feelings before he can control the pollution of air and water. Wars and the hydrogen bomb have taught us that we can die together. Even though no workable formula has been devised to show us how to live together, we can each make a start right now by doing something about the dignity crisis, respecting our personal dignity and the dignity of others, understanding our personal needs and the personal needs of others.

## ON WISHFUL THINKING

Wishful thinking is a form of daydreaming. When we cannot stand up to the tensions of reality, when we make a temporary compromise by walking away from truth, we think we are sustaining ourselves through passive inaction, and we hope that things will turn out the way we want. Of course, this never happens, because daydreaming or wishful thinking accomplishes nothing. Sooner or later, we have to return to reality, adjust to it in a creative way, and accept daily living as a challenge, not as a compromise. Wishful thinking is a compromise that doesn't work satisfactorily for anyone.

You cannot compromise with creative thinking. You cannot compromise even with destructive thinking. Which shall it be? Constructive or destructive? You can make the choice, but you can't use daydreaming in the process.

There is nothing wrong with daydreaming now and then for a few moments or hours if it is used as relaxation from tension. Then you recall happy moments, successful moments in the past to renew your energies for the present.

Miguel de Unamuno said, "To think is to converse with oneself." But will this conversation be productive or unproductive? When you converse with yourself, you must play ball with yourself to find the big you. Only then will you be able to converse with others. When you are a friend to yourself, you will be a friend to others. And you cannot be a friend to yourself by inadequate thinking, by wishful thinking, or by daydreaming. As we say, think creatively, then do creatively. When? Now! Is this our world or isn't it?

## FISHING

Many years ago, I had a yacht that I used for fishing; but I must confess I never caught a fish on any weekend during any season.

If the truth were known, I got rid of the yacht because I found a simple way of catching fish—and I don't mean by buying them in a fish store. I was sitting on my terrace one sunny afternoon. I held a string in my right hand about a foot long. It was dangling in the air when I conjured up the idea I was fishing. I will pass this idea on to you because you do not need a yacht, a smaller craft, or a boat at all to go fishing. Moreover, you do not need a rod and reel, a hook, or bait. All you need is a string, any string, a foot or less in length.

You sit in a chair anywhere, and you suspend the string from your hand as if you are angling for symbolic fish. As you wait to catch the fish, you will have time to reflect, which you can seldom do during the hectic activity of the day. Reflection means relaxation, when you have the opportunity to take stock of yourself, to see if it is possible to do something for yourself and be a better person for tomorrow. And this you can do.

Just think of a moment when your mind was distorted by a destructive emotion like anger. Perhaps you are going through the throes of it now. Notice how it makes you see red. You forget how useless such waste of energy really is. You forget that in hurting someone else, you have accomplished nothing except to hurt yourself. If such a wasteful emotion is devouring you, hold on to that string in your hand. Wait patiently. If you do, you may not actually grab a fish, but you will be able to do something far more important; you will be able to grab hold of yourself. Try it!

## NUMBER "65"

The book *Life Begins at Forty* helped lift the ceiling on worrying about age, like a moratorium on debts, but the number sixty-five remains a deadly number. This is partly a socioeconomic factor. Many business corporations, feeling sixty-five symbolizes the end of a person's value as a producer, have established this age as one of compulsory retirement. At any rate, sixty-five is not a number to ring out in musical chimes; it may soon threaten the status of thirteen as the unmentionable numeral. Many people, at sixty-five, tell themselves that life is over. They think constantly about death and dwell on physical symptoms that could cause death. Each day becomes a delaying action against the forces of death instead of a dedication to enjoying life. Their thoughts brim over with fear, and their conversation is a recital of the deaths and illnesses of friends and relatives.

Worry sweeps around in their minds like pigeons descending upon breadcrumbs, and they spend the rest of their years living with death.

Others reach sixty-five and collapse in a kind of rosy inertia. They have, they feel, reached the sunshine years and are entitled to complete retirement. They want to sleep at night and take catnaps during the day; they want to lie in their beds at night and occupy deck chairs in the daytime. Their attitude toward everything is horizontal, never vertical. They will not walk, they will ride in cars; they will not do, they will rest. They will not even think; TV or the newspapers will do their thinking for them! Surely after the years of struggle, making money to pay the bills, raising children, the retirement years must be glorious. The number sixty-five is deadly to these people They—is it you?—waste their time fearing death, since death is a natural process that they can do nothing about. They—is it you?—will not enjoy retirement from life; it is a premature death.

Some younger people—is it you?—dissipate their productive energies with worry over what will happen to them when they come face to face with age sixty-five.

While you have the privilege of life on this earth, and it is a privilege, in spite of unceasing problems you should live. You should live, whether you are sixteen or sixty-five. Be like Ezio Pinza, an inspiration to millions when he starred in *South Pacific,* reaching the peak of his career at an age when some people retire. Pinza was young when others his age force themselves to decay; he was far younger in spirit than some less fortunate people in their early twenties. Naturally, older age requires a person to place sensible limits on his physical capabilities. When you are older, you can't run around like a young kid and, if you have a heart condition, you must further restrict your activities. Yet, the older person has qualities that the child or adolescent hasn't even begun to develop.

The main point is: IN OLDER AGE, EACH DAY CAN BE THRILLING. It's really up to the individual. It's up to you. Still, if you are over sixty-five and have already wasted time moping, stop blaming yourself. You're not perfect, no one is, and self-blame will not help you. You must have self-respect as long as you live. So live creatively every day of your life.

When Pablo Casals reached ninety-five, a young reporter threw him a question, "Mr. Casals, you are ninety-five and the greatest cellist that ever lived. Why do you still practice six hours a day?" And Mr. Casals answered, "Because I think I'm making progress."

Your goal is to make progress every day of your life.

## FRUSTRATION

How can you overcome frustration?

Everyone experiences one kind of frustration or another every day. Frustration should stimulate us, help us solve a problem, not yield to it. When we are crushed under it, it becomes a chronic type of negative feeling.

We become creative artists when we let our servomechanism create ideas and solve problems. But too many of us jam our creative mechanism with worry, anxiety, and fear, trying to force a solution with the forebrain, the seat of our thinking but not the seat of doing. This jamming of the creative servomechanism doesn't serve us at all. It inhibits us from our goals, putting a roadblock of negation in front of us, creating frustration.

There are five roadblocks of frustration:

1. *We worry not only before making a decision but after.* We carry this extra fifty pounds of worry on our minds all day.

The cure? Express anxiety before we make a decision—not after. There are, let us say, five solutions to a problem. Anxiety is creative while we choose which road to take. Once we choose, however, we must stop worrying and call upon the confidence of past successes to guide us in the present. If we call upon the failures of the past to guide us in the present, we create immediate frustration.

2. *We not only worry and fret about today, we worry about yesterday and tomorrow.* This sets up a pattern of instant frustration because we call upon past failures and future apprehensions to guides us in the present. We can't think positively with negative feelings.

The cure? Think only of today. Every day is a complete lifetime. Forget yesterday; lose it in the vacuum of time. Tomorrow doesn't exist; when it comes it is another day. Let your servomechanism do what it can do well; respond to the present. Try, try, try—now, now, now.

3. *We try to do too many things at one time.* This creates tension of tone, spasm instead of comfort. When we try to do too many things at one time, we try to do the impossible.

The cure? Don't fight relaxation. Join it. Learn to do one thing at a time. This brings relaxation. This frees you from the burden of hurry and failure.

4. *We wrestle with our problems twenty-four hours a day without letup.* We carry our problems from the job, to the home, to our bed. This creates tension that produces frustration.

The cure? Sleep on your problem if you are unable to solve it. Sleep on it, not with it. Let your success mechanism work for you when you hit the pillow as you recall past successes.

5. *We refuse to relax.* We don't know what it is. We just know the word, that's all. The spasm of repeated worry produces the spasm of frustration. You can't have someone relax for you. You've got to do it on your own.

The cure? You sit in a room of your mind, and you relax there to cut the electric circuit of distress.
Relaxation overcomes frustration. Don't think it. Work for it. Do it—now!
Remember these words of Plato, "Nothing in the affairs of men is worth worrying about."

## COURTESY

Laurence Sterne said, "Hail the small sweet courtesies of life, for smooth do they make the road of it."

What is courtesy? It is the beginning of friendship. It is the beginning of an open mind, when you realize that all people are children of God and that they deserve the same consideration and treatment that you expect yourself. It is the will to succeed through a gesture, a little thing. Life is full of little things that make it big and worthwhile, when we overcome small pains and petty grievances that little remedies like courtesy can cure.

Courtesy is thoughtfulness and consideration for the feelings of others as well as your own. It is caring put to use. Courtesy is a smile turned into a creative performance. When expressed, it increases the well-being of all concerned.

The small blows to our respect and integrity, the small jolts to our sense of worth, cause an incredible number of heartaches in the world.

What is courtesy? It is the goodwill you offer another human being. And more. It is goodwill that you offer to yourself, better health to yourself. Could you express courtesy and at the same time feel angry, inferior, uncertain, frustrated, or empty? No, of course not. When you express courtesy, you see the big self in others and feel it in yourself.

Think of courtesy as an important goal that automatically creates empathy for others and for yourself.

## GARBAGE DISPOSAL

A secretary who works in an advertising agency comes home from work every evening, feeds her poodle, then herself. After dinner, she looks at herself in the mirror for a while, pulls out a straying hair from her eyebrow, makes up her lashes, then gives her lips a dab of lipstick. She runs a comb through her short, cropped hair and sweeps a few of the graying strands along to their proper place. After eyeing herself with a final critical gaze, she moves toward the door. The poodle is accustomed to this routine because it happens the same way at the same time every day. He watches her open and close the door behind her.

She walks down the steps, through the door down below, down the stone stairs to the street, where she stops beside a garbage can to deposit the paper bag full of garbage she has carried with her. Then, she looks around toward the end of the street, facing the park as though she were expecting to see someone. With finality, she walks up the steps to her apartment where the poodle is waiting near the door.

Her neighbors don't know why she grooms herself just to dispose of the garbage. The fact is she hopes that one of these days, her husband, an army chaplain, will return. He had been reported missing in action years ago. She sometimes thinks there is no hope, yet she clings to hope. Therefore, she clings to tidiness, orderliness, attractiveness.

Recently, a writer on her return from Europe criticized New York as being the filthiest city in the world, with garbage all over the place. However, travel should have shown her that all cities, particularly the large ones, have problems with garbage disposal, and they all make efforts to meet these problems. Human beings should make an effort to dispose of personal garbage, too. I don't mean the garbage in the house; I mean the garbage in the mind. We all have it to a lesser or greater degree. Mental garbage is the waste that piles up from indolence and indecision, from fear and resentment. These destructive traits clog up the mind, with refuse and easily infect and fatigue the spirit.

It is very easy to groom yourself like the lady in this story; it is just as easy now and then to clean the house of your mind by symbolically taking hold of the garbage of hurt feelings, throwing it into a receptacle—the past—and walking away from it forever.

## MAÑANA INCORPORATED

Are you a member of Mañana Incorporated? "Mañana" in Spanish means "tomorrow," and Mañana Incorporated is an organization that leaves things undone until tomorrow. It is the world's largest organization, with more members than any religious, political, philosophical, or industrial organization. To join, you must cling to one glaring fault: the tendency to put things off until "tomorrow." Millions slavishly follow this blueprint for failure for a lifetime.

Colleges give no courses in it because it's too easy and does not lead to advancement.

This doesn't mean that we should not learn the art of leisure, which is totally different. Idle people have the least leisure, because leisure is the reward of work. It feeds the body and mind to meet the demands of tomorrow. As Thoreau said, "He employs true leisure who has time to improve his soul's estate." The man who leaves things for tomorrow hasn't time to improve anything, and uselessness is emptiness.

Mañana Incorporated espouses a philosophy of failure, because no one has ever seen tomorrow. We indulge in wishful thinking when we dream that tomorrow will be free of trouble. However, we can constructively plan for tomorrow, looking for ways to better ourselves instead of tying ourselves to techniques that will leave us marking time, wallowing in a vacuum.

Every day we must strive to break away from our membership in Mañana

Incorporated. We must break away from the oppressive hold of fear and worry that makes us lazy and say, "Well, we'll take care of that detail tomorrow." We must send in our letter of resignation.

Say to yourself every day, "I will do something better tomorrow. I will improve myself tomorrow, and I will try to be more sincere with others and with myself." But more important, forget about tomorrow until it gets here. Start improving yourself *today, now, this very minute!*

Listen to the words of Horace (65–8 B.C.), "Cease to inquire what the future has in store, and take as a gift Whatever the day brings forth."

## HOW TO SHADOWBOX

Shadowboxing is one of the arts necessary in the career of the boxer. It teaches him poise, agility, and grace: how to shift quickly with his feet as he dances away from his opponent. In a way, shadowboxing is a modified form of dancing.

I always think of the ballet dancer as a person who, avoiding an enemy, pirouettes and flies through the air, then disappears. I have one concrete example to prove my point. Many years ago, I operated on a patient for an injured nose. He was known as the Coca-Cola kid, who with amazing fancy footwork considered to be a form of shadowboxing—danced right out of Hungary, away from the enemy behind the Iron Curtain, and into an American audience.

We should all train ourselves in a form of shadowboxing for the battles we have to fight every day. The kind of shadowboxing I mean will give agility, grace, and quick movement to *your mind* so that it can avoid or overpower its greatest enemy—*laziness.* Laziness can destroy us faster than a Firpo, faster than a Johnson, a Sharkey, a Fitzsimmons, a Tunney, a Dempsey, a Marciano, or a Mohammed Ali.

All you have to do to become a champion is to shadowbox for a few minutes every morning when you get up. You stand in front of the mirror and you shadowbox. You are fighting laziness; you can outsmart him, you can tire him out, he can't keep up with your creative thinking. You outmaneuver him. Laziness is not going to stand in the way of your victory. Give him the old one, two. Make laziness a has-been. Don't be defeated by a worthless opponent.

Remember the words from the Bible (Proverbs, xxiii:21), "Drowsiness [laziness] shall clothe a man with rags."

## BLACKOUT

I was one of millions inconvenienced by the power failure years ago that crippled a huge area on the eastern coast of the United States. My lights were out; my phone was dead. I lit a candle and located my transistor radio, learning that nine states were hit; thirty million people in darkness.

The blackout occurred about 5:30 p.m. I had to catch a 9 a.m. plane for California the following morning; I was scheduled to lecture.

The lightless night passed, hour upon dark hour. I went to bed early, but I could not sleep. I argued with myself.

"Why worry? No one can blame you for not going. Go next week."

"No, I was looking forward to lecturing, and I'm going."

It was like a tennis match. I batted the ball back and forth. At 3:30 a.m. the lights were still out; the elevator was still dead. Living on the eighteenth floor was no advantage in this situation.

Finally, I decided that I was going toward my goal. I dressed, grabbed a hat, coat, my two grips, and a candle. I opened the door to the stairway. In candlelight, I dimly saw stairs, stairs, and more stairs below me.

Then I dropped the candle and saw nothing at all.

What to do? In a wave of negativism, I told myself to go back to my apartment and give up on what I wanted. But my big self overcame these negative thoughts, and I proceeded toward my goal. Step by step, I inched my way down to the seventeenth floor, walking slowly, carefully, then down to the sixteenth, the fifteenth, the fourteenth . . . down to the street. When I stood on New York's still dark sidewalks, I dropped my luggage with a thud. I felt as if I had just released a couple of five-hundred-pound weights. I was partway to my goal; I still had to get a taxi to take me to the airport. I stumbled around, waving my hands. Getting a taxi seemed impossible.

I figured a cab would need an hour to get to the airport. At 7:55, a taxi stopped for me—just in time. Departure time for the plane was 9 a.m.

I turned my back to pick up my luggage, and then saw the taxi moving off without me.

After my first reaction of anger, I felt despair. "I did my best," I told myself. "I'll go back to sleep."

"No," my big self urged, "you can still make it." And I did. A responsible cab driver picked me up. He took a few seasoned shortcuts and drove swiftly and safely. I made the plane. Hours later, I was in San Francisco, then Monterey. I enjoyed speaking, enjoyed my trip—more so because I had not blacked out with the city.

I felt good because, in the battle in my mind between success and failure instincts, my success instincts had won, and I had not let adverse circumstances keep me from my goal.

My story is illustrative, not an exercise in self-praise. Truthfully, I have failed myself many, many times in my life. Still, even as I grow older, I feel happy that I am not falling into the nonliving blackout that crushes so many people. In harnessing my active, goal-oriented success instincts, I strengthen my enjoyment of life all the time. The blackout affected thirty million people for a short time—blackout beyond human control. Emotional blackouts crush millions more every day—and often for a lifetime—a blackout we can control if we remember we came into this world to succeed, not to fail.

You must resist the emotional blackout of negative feelings that keep you from living creatively. You can move out of an emotional blackout into brightness and hope.

Here is a thought to live by, by Thomas Fuller (1608–1681), "It is always darkest just before the day dawneth."

## THE STOCK MARKET

Many of us play the stock market because we live in hope that we'll strike it rich sooner or later and profit enough to hoard for a rainy day when we can take it easy, travel, live a leisurely life. So we listen to tips on the market whenever they come, from wherever they come. We want to believe that what we hear is true, hopeful that we will make money to fulfill a dream.

I am acquainted with one professional who knows the market thoroughly. He can sense oncoming fluctuations in the stocks with uncanny accuracy. When I go to meet him on a Sunday at noon at a restaurant for lunch, I prepare myself. By that, I mean I sit to his right or to his left, but never on the other side of the table. He was never convincing when I sat opposite him. Before, during, and after lunch, he would glare at me as if possessed. The veins in his bald head would bulge, and he would tell me about the eccentricities of the stock market. To convince me thoroughly, he would tug violently on my sleeve to punctuate his remarks. Strange as it may seem, most of the time, he is right, though I must confess he occasionally pulls a real loser.

I pride myself as an expert also; but I am an expert in another kind of stock. I am an expert in mental and spiritual stock. Happily, the tips I can give you are always good. I never make a mistake like my friend, and I don't have to pull at your coat sleeve. The stocks I speak about are blue-chip; they never go down; they always go up, and the dividends are regular and more than gratifying. The stocks of which I speak are charity, understanding, courage, and self-respect. They are the success stocks. Invest in them, and you'll never go wrong. This is a sure tip. You are bound to make a handsome profit.

## TAKE A BOW

The custom of bowing has existed since the beginning of civilization, and many schools of thought have existed in different countries on how to bow. Every country, depending on custom and tradition, has its own method and preference. History tells us about the French musketeer bowing low and gracefully before his lady, sweeping his multicolored plumed hat to the ground. It tells us of the Italian courtier of the Renaissance who bowed more carefully with studied precision as he paid his respects to Lorenzo de Medici. History points out a romantic variation when Sir Walter Raleigh lowered his cape to the wet earth and, bowing, helped Queen Elizabeth I across the path. History gives a variety of methods, including the Siamese courtiers who knelt and bowed their heads to the ground before their emperor.

As many ways as there are of bowing, there are that many reasons for doing so. A slave long ago bowed low out of fear. And those of us who pray today bow not out of fear but out of reverence, out of faith. Once, we bowed out of loyalty to a king; but times have changed, and in our democratic way of life, it would be a rare occurrence for a laborer to bow before the President of the United States. Both would be embarrassed. People from all walks of life shake hands. We have dispensed with fear, with feathers, with frills, and with finery when we bow; and that maneuver or act is essentially relegated to receiving praise.

Praise is a useful ingredient in our daily routine. It indicates accomplishment in one form or another. Praise is what an actress, a violinist, a singer needs at the end of the performance.

Even though self-praise is no recommendation, there is a time now and then when you can indulge in it. Then you should take a bow, not for the great things you did but for the many things you did *not do*.

You should take a bow because you did not worship such a false god as greed. You did not strangle your enemy even though an inclination was there. You did not steal. You did not speak ill of your neighbor. You were not envious of your friend's success; or, if you were, you concealed your envy until you yourself were no longer aware of it.

Take a bow, good person. You deserve it.

## FIVE MINUTES CAN CHANGE YOUR LIFE

I have asked you before, and I ask you again to give yourself five minutes of the day to walk into a room in your mind. Of course, this is an imaginary room. You should imagine you are sitting in a chair, and as you look outside the window, you see a geyser letting off steam. This is a symbol for you to let go of the tensions that have oppressed you during the day.

You must take stock of yourself. You have assets and liabilities. Your liabilities are fear, loneliness, resentment, and uncertainty. Your assets are faith, understanding, compassion, self-respect.

Your liabilities, the destructive emotions, are the deadly poisons that infect you within. They disfigure your self-image. Your never-ending doubt or fear is a never-ending spasm, corrosion, a never-ending paralysis. Your resentment may abuse someone else but will abuse you most of all.

On the other hand, the assets of your built-in success mechanism enhance not only someone else's image but also your own.

As Tolstoy put it, "Faith is the force of life." Spend five minutes a day finding out who you are. Discover that your assets are there for you to use, that you have a moral responsibility to do so. Let the improvement of your self-image five minutes a day be your personal faith in your worth, urging you to rise to your full stature of dignity to become the big you—the you that you really are. Make this your daily goal for as long as you live: to change your life for the better.

## THE ITCH

The itch, no matter where it occurs, is a cutaneous irritation usually followed by uncontrollable scratching, and the performance of the fingers has all sorts of variations depending on the severeness of the itch and the physical and mental condition of the individual. For example, a vigorous truck driver will tackle the itch quite differently from a fragile schoolteacher. He will apply force to relieve it while she will approach it as if she were slowly turning a page of a book.

There are various gradations between the rough and the delicate approach— the staccato peck or the lingering, procrastinating stroke, the fastidious scrape or the tender, indulgent pat, the angry scratch or the exhilarating tickle. And, depending on personal preference, there may or may not be a vocal accompaniment.

An itchy area of skin can erupt with a rash caused by a severer form of irritation from the outside world or from within; but the usual itch is not accompanied by such manifestation. All itches are destructive, even if only in a minor way and even if the itch is purely a mental one. We all now and then get the itch to run away from trouble; but the itch I should like to speak of is constructive, and it is worthwhile getting it now and then. To travel away from trouble is futile. It leads nowhere, for you must have a point of departure and return before you go.

The best itch to get is the itch that reaches the mind and the soul—the constructive itch; the itch to improve yourself. Don't be stagnant and lethargic; don't be smug and satisfied with yourself. Sit down and take stock of your assets and liabilities now and then. Build your assets, lessen your liabilities. You surely have learned that it is good to get a physical checkup once a year. Get the itch to check yourself mentally and spiritually at least once a year. You don't need a physician for it; you can do it yourself.

Remember the words of Plautus, "To mean well is nothing without to do well."

## EXPECT A MIRACLE

One Sunday, I drove from Salinas, California, to San Jose—approximately sixty miles away—to speak at a church. Time was running short, and we didn't know the road too well. *"Only a miracle will get me there on time,"* I said to myself.

One minute before the services started, I walked into the pastor's office, and we both sighed in relief. Behind his chair, I saw a sign. It read, EXPECT A MIRACLE.

All of us suffer occasionally from the feeling of frustration and despair and feel that we are unlucky, that we just cannot get a break in life. I do not believe that there is anyone who doesn't, once in a while, feel that way. At such times all of us can use a miracle, or the expectation of a miracle.

You have every right to expect a miracle—every right to feel that a miracle is forthcoming—not in a literal sense, of course, because no one should expect miraculous intervention on his behalf.

Your miracle must come from inside yourself. It must come from your faith in yourself no matter how trying the pressures. It must come from your attitude of determination in crises, as you turn crises into creative opportunities. It must come from the support you give yourself in all circumstances.

The miracle you should and must welcome is your self-acceptance.

Your acceptance of your weaknesses.

Your acceptance of your strengths.

Your acceptance of your imperfections.

Once you accept yourself, you can give yourself help that is little short of miraculous.

## PERSONALITY

Can personality be changed? Of course!

Remember, you are made up of liabilities and assets. You have within you the desire to be happy and unhappy, the will to succeed and the will to fail, the desire for self-fulfillment, and the desire for self-destruction. When you look in the mirror, you will find two different people at two different times. Sometimes, you will have a frown on your face and feel frustrated; sometimes, you will have a smile on your face because you feel successful. When you like the better you, you are at that moment enlarging the scope of your personality. If you choose frustration as a way of life, you undermine your personality and make your image shrink. In other words, you and you alone can add to your assets or accumulate more liabilities. No one else can do this for you. Here are some points you can utilize to be the better one, the big you, with a better personality.

1. Do one thing at a time, shoot for one goal at a time.
2. Live in the present. Live today.
3. Forget the mistakes of yesterday. Yesterday has gone forever.
4. Stop criticizing yourself and stop criticizing others.
5. Yearn for self-improvement.
6. Hold on to your self-respect by appraising yourself honestly.
7. Learn to listen to others. It helps remove bias from your opinions.
8. If you have a goal, reach for it. If you make a mistake, try again.
9. Don't be timid in conversation. Talk even if you make a mistake.
10. Exercise your imagination creatively to achieve success.

Remember the words of Charles Schwab, "Personality is to a man what perfume is to a flower."

## IMPORTANT YOU

Recognize your importance to yourself. You must realize that it is not egotism when you come to understand that you are the most important person in the world to yourself. It is not conceit or vanity or selfishness when you brush aside life's trivialities and irrelevancies to give your inner self the attention it deserves.

Important you! You must not interpret this narcissistically—that is, being in love with your image, absorbed in yourself to the exclusion of other people in this world. You should merely attune yourself to your possibilities, work patiently with yourself to grow and accept your growth—because you are important—and then you should go out to meet life, share with other people, try to make the world a warmer place. Daily practice will make you the important you that you really are; creating, when you need it, instant confidence.

When you spend your days building and building, trying and trying, emphasizing your emotional capacities over and over, increasing your confidence in yourself, accepting yourself, getting closer to yourself, what do you have? Important you.

Now and then, face the mirror and say to yourself, "No matter how tough things are, I'm with me! I shall spend time to make the most of each day, use it to give the greatest possible meaning to my life. This is what creative Psycho-Cybernetics is all about: becoming a professional human being, creating a new dimension in personal freedom, on my own terms."

Recognize the big you, the important you.

Remember the words of Epicterus, "He is a wise man who does not grieve for the things which he has not, but rejoices for those which he has."

## SET YOUR GOAL

Many of us feel that we have no goals, but that is far from the truth. The truth is that all of us have goals of various kinds; but one goal common to all is the desire to live and to be happy.

Millions of men and women waste much of their lives on small details that get them nowhere. We live fast, but to what purpose, to what end? We get nowhere, and we do it on the double. We are not able to simplify our lives by remembering our generic goal—to be happy. And you can't rush after happiness, not because happiness is elusive but because when you run after it, you are running away from it. Why? You must remember that happiness is internal. You are happiness, and you can't run after it when it is already within you.

You must be realistic and live creatively instead of running around a vicious cycle of nothingness. If people who run around as if they don't know what they want would stop to think a moment, they would know what they want. Then slowly, without rushing, they would work for it and live for it. Remember, *live creatively instead of quickly.*

You don't have to take to the woods and forget it all. Take to yourself, resolve within yourself what goal you want to achieve, cut out the useless details that take you away from yourself. Then go after your goal with thought, determination, and belief, a goal within your capabilities and training.

You go forward toward your goals when:

1. You reach for today's opportunities.
2. You exercise your right to succeed.
3. You use your courage to stand up under stress.
4. You jump the hurdles of doubt and indecision.
5. You are aware of your real potential.
6. You see yourself as successful.
7. You seek improvement.
8. You nourish your self-image with faith and belief.

Here is a thought to live by: "Be ashamed to die until you have won some goal for yourself and for others."

## JOY IN AN ACTIVE LIFE

THERE IS JOY IN THE ACTIVE LIFE FOR ALL OF ONE'S LIFE. A goal every day is important, something to move toward in this pulsating world. It is terrible to throw away your years sitting around moping, feeling sorry for yourself. The idea of escaping into your mind now and then to relax a bit when you need it and I believe most people do—is not at all inconsistent with this active philosophy of doing and moving.

The person who lives creatively will stay in the swim of things, will be busy and interested and involved—and will be able to clear an hour or two relaxing, escaping to a room of his mind to let go of tension. He will be able to rebound from life's hard knocks.

Baseball player Larry Brown of the Cleveland Indians came back from a fractured skull that he suffered in a collision with another player to play ball again less than seven weeks later.

Entertainer Sammy Davis, Jr., was in the headlines a number of years ago after his crippling accident, but since then, he has come back stronger than ever as one of America's most versatile performers.

Poet Robert Frost, honored on his seventy-fifth birthday years ago by the U.S. Senate, was at first ignored in his own country. It was in England that he had his first poems published, then he came home and started on the road to renown.

You, too, may have to rebound—many times—from many troubles. To live creatively, you will have to keep pace with life and stay young.

An occasional retreat may help you.

Then back to living—not only when times are easy, but when times are tough.

The greatest joy in an active life is standing up to stress, rising above a problem, a misfortune, a blunder.

Here is what Jonathan Swift said, "May you live all the days of your life."